Excel 2019 Business Basics & Beyond Table of Contents

Excel 2019 Business Basics & Beyond

Printed in USA by Hess Print Solutions

First Printing: September 2019

Authors: Smitty Smith

Copy Editor: Kitty Wilson

Technical Editor: Bill Jelen

Indexer: Nellie Jay

Compositor: Jill Cabot

Cover Design: Alexander Philip

Published by: Holy Macro! Books, PO Box 541731, Merritt Island FL 32954

Distributed by Independent Publishers Group, Chicago, IL

ISBN 978-1-61547-061-7 Print, 978-1-61547-144-7 Digital

Library of Congress Control Number: 2019930680

Introduction

Microsoft Excel is one of the most powerful tools any business has at its disposal. It can help you automate your business finances rather than track them manually. It can streamline the process of preparing staffing schedules. It can help you get much more information from your business data. In this book, you'll learn how to harness your business data and put it to use. Some of the many topics covered in this book include preparing financial statements; displaying data for maximum impact by using formatting tools, tables, charts, and PivotTables; using customer information to create customized letters with Mail Merge; importing data from the web or applications like Microsoft Access or Salesforce; calculating the costs of doing business with financial formulas; and finding prepackaged business templates such as calendars, planners, financial forms, and more.

Features of the Book

Throughout the book you'll find interesting tips and tricks to make your Excel use more efficient, along with real-world business examples. Most chapters include one or more companion files that you can download and use to follow along with the chapter. Using the companion files isn't required, but it will make it easier to absorb each step. You can find them at https://1drv.ms/f/s!ABPoJ87A3v-MgocX.

You'll notice that instructions for navigating in the Excel Ribbon menu are listed as follows: ***Primary Ribbon tab* > *Menu item* > *Selection*** (e.g., **Home > Format as Table > Select Table Style**). Note that these instructions don't specifically call out an item's Ribbon group unless necessary. Keyboard shortcuts are listed as follows: ***Key1+Key2***. For example, the keyboard shortcut for the Copy command is **Ctrl+C**, and the shortcut for the Paste command is **Ctrl+V**.

> **Note:** Occasionally you'll see notes, hints, and cautions that give you extra information that's related to the nearby text.

Structure of the Book

This book is presented as a dozen chapters that introduce you to Excel and how it works and go through certain tasks that are common in everyday business use. Each chapter stands on its own, so you can skip around if you want. For instance, if you're already familiar with the Ribbon in Excel and other Office apps, then feel free to skip ahead. The following sections describe the book's chapters.

Chapter 1:Excel Basics

Simply put, Excel is the number-one spreadsheet application on the planet, and this book gives you a fantastic opportunity to learn about what Excel is and how it can help you manage your business. In Chapter 1 you'll explore the fundamentals of what you can do with Excel, see firsthand what makes this powerful application tick, get used to how it works, and see how to begin using it to simplify your business needs. You'll learn the ins and outs of the Ribbon user interface, which brings a consistent experience to all of the Office applications. You'll also discover the key elements of intelligent spreadsheet design and the steps to take when starting a new project.

Chapter 2: Understanding Basic File Operations and Setting Up Excel the Way You Want It

In this chapter, you'll learn how to set up Excel so that it's just right for you. In this chapter you'll learn about Excel's multiple user interface options and how to customize certain elements that you want to see all the time. You'll also learn to modify the Quick Access Toolbar, where you can place your favorite Ribbon controls.

Chapter 3: The Home Tab in Depth

This chapter fully exposes all the functionality behind the Home tab, which is the default Ribbon tab and contains all of the most commonly used menu commands.

Chapter 4: The Ribbon in Depth: The Insert, Page Layout, Formulas, Data, Review, and View Tabs

This chapter moves on to the rest of the Ribbon elements, which are much more specific in nature than those on the Home tab. You'll discover how to insert charts, set up page formatting for printing and distribution, expose the hundreds of functions that are available, and much more.

Chapter 5: Entering and Manipulating Data

In this chapter you'll learn the elements of good spreadsheet design and the phases involved, such as planning, designing and building, adding data, formatting, and distributing to others. You'll see how to save your work and the various options available. You'll learn the difference between entering text and numeric values, and you'll learn when you can use them together. You'll also see how to have Excel automatically enter data for you with lists and AutoFill.

This chapter describes the differences between formulas and functions and shows how to enter them. It also talks about data validation, which allows you to control what information users can enter and how. Finally, you'll learn how to insert and delete ranges, rows and columns, and worksheets.

Chapter 6: Using Functions and Formulas

In this chapter, you'll learn what functions are and discover the power they bring to your spreadsheet applications; this is where Excel really starts to shine. You'll learn about different methods for entering functions and how to make them flexible and dynamic. You'll also discover how to calculate the differences between dates and times and how to retrieve information from other worksheets.

This chapter reviews the most common functions from each of the primary function type groups:

- Financial
- Logical
- Text
- Date and Time
- Lookup and Reference
- Math and Trig

- Specialized functions, such as those in the Statistical, Engineering, and Compatibility groups

There are also a number of new dynamic array functions that allow you to do things in Excel that only an Excel expert could accomplish in the past:

- FILTER function
- RANDARRAY function
- SEQUENCE function
- SORTBY function
- UNIQUE function

Chapter 7: Formatting, Printing, and Sharing

This chapter shows you how to spice up your worksheets so they're easier to read and present. You'll learn how to choose from predefined styles or apply your own formats. You'll also learn to format cells for data types (for example, Currency, Date, Percentage) and how to apply custom formats (for example, for phone numbers, zip codes, Social Security numbers) and even create your own. You'll see how to quickly sort and filter data without having to rearrange things by hand.

When printing from Excel—whether to paper or to an electronic format—proper page setup can be challenging. In addition, there are a lot of printing options available. This chapter discusses the most common print formats, how to add custom header and footer details, scaling (so you can, for example, stretch a worksheet to fit 11" x 17" paper for printing detailed information such as shift schedules), collating, and more.

Chapter 8: Graphics

Excel 2007 introduced an entirely revamped set of graphics and tools called SmartArt, and Microsoft continues to update them. This chapter discusses how to add them to your worksheets and what you can do to customize them to meet your needs. You'll also see how to insert your own graphics, such as company logos, shapes, and drawing objects. While Excel isn't a graphics application per se, there are many graphical elements that you can add to a workbook to help make certain key data stand out or to fulfill specific needs for graphics (e.g., product brochures, fantasy sports league brochures that includes player pictures and profiles).

Chapter 9: Charts

Charts are some of the most powerful tools you can use to display data for at-a-glance snapshots of what's going on behind your numbers. In this chapter, you'll learn how to quickly transform business data into informative charts, including bar, stacked, column, line, and scatter charts. This chapter also discusses resources and methods for using multiple charts to create business dashboards, so you can compare multiple business elements in one spot.

Chapter 10: Excel Tables and Subtotals

Excel tables enable you to easily tell Excel that a particular group of data is all related. As you add more data to a table, Excel automatically expands the table to include the new information; Excel also automatically updates any PivotTables or charts that are based on the table data. Tables are really handy because they can be formatted using multiple style options, they allow you to quickly apply intuitive formulas, and they make it easy to filter and sort data. Furthermore, Excel tables are structured so that they work well with PivotTables, which you can use to analyze your data.

While Excel tables are handy for structuring your data, and PivotTables are fantastic summary tools, sometimes you just want to have a quick summary of your data without. Subtotals allow you to quickly manipulate your data and subtotal data by almost any data category, but they don't work with Excel tables.

Chapter 11: PivotTables, Power Pivot, and the Data Model

PivotTables are one of the most powerful features in Excel, yet most people either aren't familiar with them or are afraid to use them. PivotTables give you the ability to manipulate your data in ways that were previously available only in database applications; they allow you to switch rows and columns, apply different functions, subtotal data, and perform many other functions, just by dragging and dropping data fields from one place to another or toggling simple options. PivotTables also include powerful charting capabilities.

Power Pivot takes PivotTable data analysis to the next level, letting you work with millions of rows of data in Excel, even though Excel itself supports only around 1 million rows. Power Pivot lets you analyze lots of data in Excel with PivotTables.

The Data Model allows you to create database-type relationships between tables, which you can then use in your PivotTables. Think of the Data Model as a behind-the-scenes data storage and manipulation tool. The Data Model exposes your data to PivotTables and Power Pivot at the same time.

Chapter 12: External Data and Mail Merge

Sometimes it is incredibly time-consuming to get information that exists in one digital environment (for example, an internal database, SAP, Oracle, Salesforce, Facebook) into Excel so you can use it. This chapter discusses ways to get data from a few of those sources and introduces you to some powerful data cleansing tools available with the Power Query Editor.

For a small business owner, there are few things more important than being able to efficiently utilize data to communicate with customers. If you've ever been frustrated by having to send marketing letters, special offers, billing, and so on, then you'll love Excel's Mail Merge feature. In this chapter you'll learn to set up a customer list and automatically mail merge it with a Word document.

Excel Version Notes

This book focuses on Excel 2019 for Office 365, the subscription version of Excel, for which you can choose to pay monthly or annually. There is also a one-time purchase version of Excel 2019, which is referred to as the *perpetual version* since you own it forever. The notable difference between versions is that Office 365 is constantly being updated, whereas the perpetual version is not. Because of version differences and updates, some of the screenshots and functionality you see here might differ from what you see and have available. This book points out any features that aren't supported in the perpetual version.

Microsoft constantly updates Office, and how soon you see updates depends on which release channel you're in. Most people are in the general release channel, meaning you get updates along with just about everyone else. You'll know when Office has been updated when you get a What's New notification when you open your Office applications. If you're a corporate Office user, then you likely have no control over your update channel. But if you're not, you can go to https://insider.office.com and join the Office Insider program, which gives you access to updates before everyone else. If you like being on the cutting edge and testing new features, the Insider Program is for you. It also gives you the opportunity to give Microsoft feedback on your experience, which helps shape feature development.

About the Author

Chris "Smitty" Smith is a content developer on the Excel team at Microsoft. Before joining Microsoft, he was a trainer/lecturer for a wide variety of corporate clients, including the U.S. Department of Treasury, CalTrans, Apple, Verizon, General Electric, and many others.

Smitty has over 25 years of business experience using Excel. Prior to corporate life, he worked as a Ranch Manager in Texas, Colorado, Wyoming and Australia after graduating from the Ranch Management program at TCU. He fondly remembers convincing ranch owners to move from paper ledgers to spreadsheets. When he is not busy at work, he is an avid Rock & Ice climber and occasional mountaineer. He lives in Seattle Washington with his wife, daughter and their mediocre Pyrenees dog, Ellie.

Chapter 1: Excel Basics

Excel is one of several spreadsheet applications available today, but it's the one you're most likely to be familiar with—and for good reason: It's the best. Microsoft first introduced Excel for the Mac in 1985, and it made its way to the PC 2 years later, so it's been around for over 30 years. Excel is, without a doubt, one of the most powerful tools in the Microsoft Office suite. An estimated 800 million plus people use Excel, making it the most used single piece of software in the world.

Whether you want to use Excel as an integral part of managing your business—such as for accounting, employee scheduling, maintaining customer lists, or sales reporting—or are just get started with it, this book will prepare you to tackle Excel on your own. In addition to learning about the basic elements of Excel, you'll be privy to a number of tips and tricks that will make your everyday use more efficient. This helpful guide to Excel walks through everything from how to set up Excel's default settings the way you want them, to how to enter formulas, to how to create PivotTables.

Understanding Spreadsheets and Spreadsheet Terminology

A *spreadsheet* is basically a big piece of digital graph paper that can perform calculations. It's a two-dimensional grid of *rows* and *columns* that converge to create individual *cells* capable of housing data and performing calculations. Columns, which are ordered from left to right, have *column headers* labeled alphabetically from A to XFD. Rows, which are ordered from top to bottom, have *row headers* labeled numerically from 1 to 1,048,576. Since 2007, Excel has allowed more than 16,000 columns and more than 1 million rows, which means there are more than 16 billion individual cells on a single spreadsheet in which you can enter data or formulas!

The *active cell* is the cell where you have your cursor at any given moment. The intersection of the column and row headers at the active cell makes up the *cell address*. For instance, D3 refers to the cell at column D, row 3. The *active workbook* is the workbook you are working in at the moment; you can have multiple workbooks open at any time, but you can work in only one at a time.

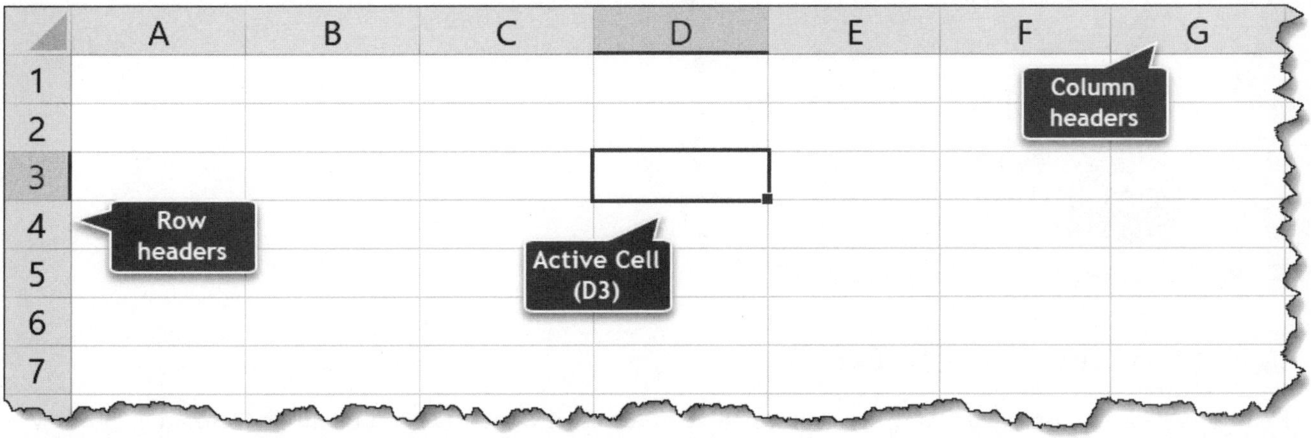

In Excel, an individual spreadsheet page is referred to as a *worksheet*. Some people tend to use the terms *spreadsheet* and *worksheet* interchangeably; while this wording is acceptable, technically it isn't accurate. *Spreadsheet* refers to the broader scope of any digital spreadsheet application. A worksheet can also be called a *sheet* or a *tab*. A *workbook* is a collection of worksheets, and while a workbook can contain only one worksheet, it must contain at least one. Think of a workbook as a book on your desk and worksheets as the individual pages that are between the covers.

> **Note:** Excel doesn't limit the number of worksheets a workbook can hold. The only limitation is imposed by your available system memory.

There are two distinct layers to any worksheet: The worksheet layer holds those billions of cells, and an invisible layer above the worksheet layer holds any objects that you insert, such as graphics, charts, and SmartArt. When you insert an object into an Excel worksheet, it doesn't become part of the cells but instead floats above them, where it won't interfere with any values that have been inserted into them. Microsoft includes some special in-cell features that include graphical objects, such as sparklines and conditional formatting graphics, such as data bars and icon sets. These tools are built into the application and should not be confused with objects that reside above the worksheet layer. For instance, you can't copy an image from a website and place it in a cell; rather, when you paste it in, it resides above the worksheet.

A *range* is a group of cells. For example, B3:C7 refers to the range of cells starting at cell B3 and moving down and over to cell C7. To refer to areas of a worksheet in formulas, you use ranges.

When you manually *select* a range of cells, the selected cells are highlighted. In the example below, the range B2:C6 has been selected. Note that cell B2 isn't highlighted here; this indicates where the selection started. You can select a range by clicking on a cell and dragging or by holding down the **Shift** key and then using the arrow keys. You can also select noncontiguous cells by holding down the **Ctrl** key while clicking the left button on your mouse on each cell you want to select (represented as **Ctrl+click**).

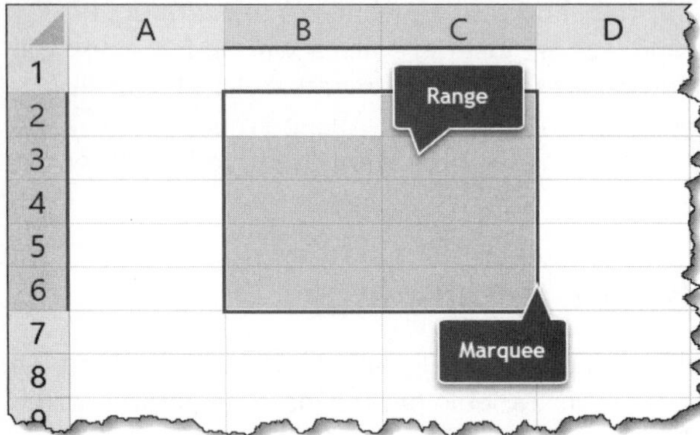

The *marquee* is the box around the active cell or selected range. The row and column headers are also highlighted to show you where you are. If you have only one cell selected, these headers are still highlighted, and the highlighting will automatically adjust as you move around.

As shown below, when you've copied a cell or range of cells, you see *dancing ants*, a dotted moving marquee that indicates the copied material.

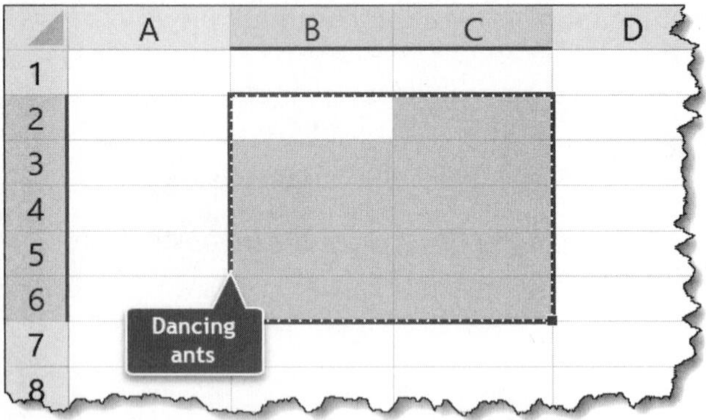

What Can You Do with Excel?

Excel is not just incredibly powerful, it is also diverse in terms of what you can do with it. Here are just a few examples of how you can use Excel:

- To build an electronic check register
- To keep track of household budgeting
- To create calculators (home, mortgage, etc.)
- To create a financial portfolio tracker
- To manage a fantasy sports league
- To create calendars
- To make to-do lists
- To keep vehicle maintenance logs
- To track fitness and weight loss
- For medical record keeping (blood pressure, weight, etc.)
- For tax planning
- For wedding planning
- For school projects
- To create class gradebooks and schedules

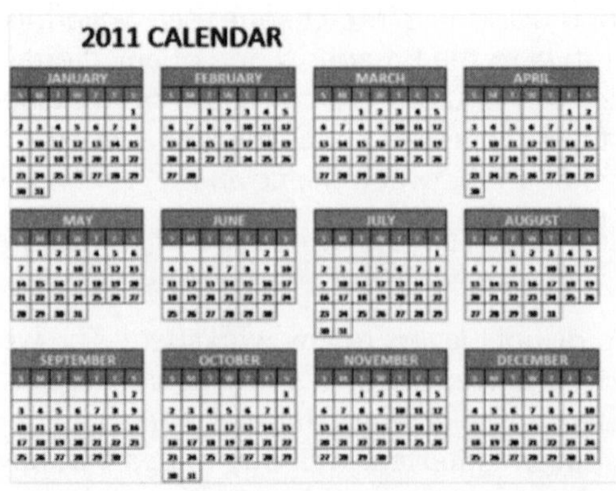

- For surveys and tests
- To create invoices
- For employee scheduling
- To build expense reports
- For product pricing
- For commission and compensation planning
- To do complex financial analysis
- To create balance sheets
- To make profit-and-loss statements
- For sales analysis
- For budget tracking
- For forecasting
- To track profitability
- For breakeven analysis
- For marketing planning
- For project planning/tracking
- For business valuation
- To create charts
- To create complex diagrams

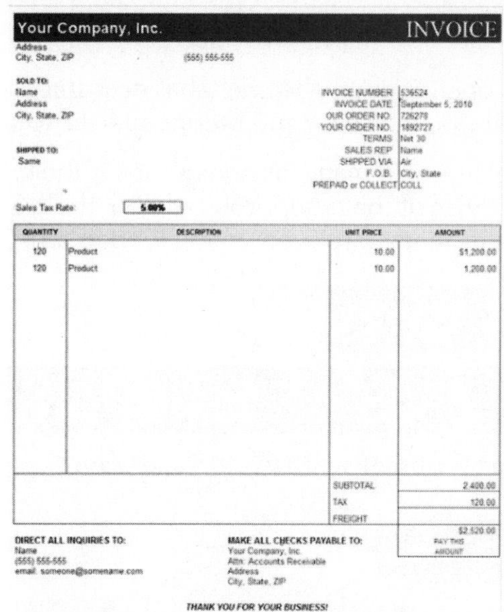
Your Company, Inc. INVOICE
Address
City, State, ZIP (555) 555-555

SOLD TO:
Name
Address
City, State, ZIP

SHIPPED TO:
Same

INVOICE NUMBER	536524
INVOICE DATE	September 5, 2010
OUR ORDER NO.	726278
YOUR ORDER NO.	1892727
TERMS	Net 30
SALES REP	Name
SHIPPED VIA	Air
F.O.B.	City, State
PREPAID or COLLECT	COLL

Sales Tax Rate: 5.00%

QUANTITY	DESCRIPTION	UNIT PRICE	AMOUNT
120	Product	10.00	$1,200.00
120	Product	10.00	1,200.00
		SUBTOTAL	2,400.00
		TAX	120.00
		FREIGHT	
			$2,520.00 PAY THIS AMOUNT

DIRECT ALL INQUIRIES TO:
Name
(555) 555-555
email: someone@somename.com

MAKE ALL CHECKS PAYABLE TO:
Your Company, Inc.
Attn: Accounts Receivable
Address
City, State, ZIP

THANK YOU FOR YOUR BUSINESS!

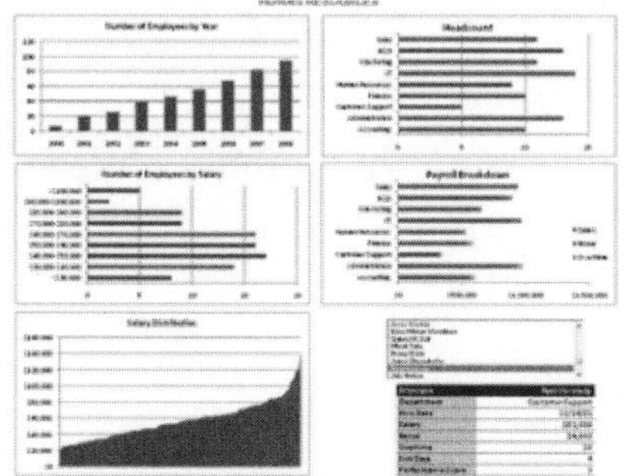

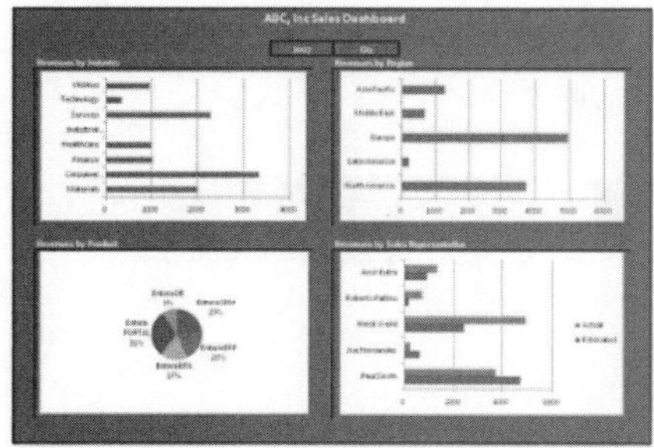

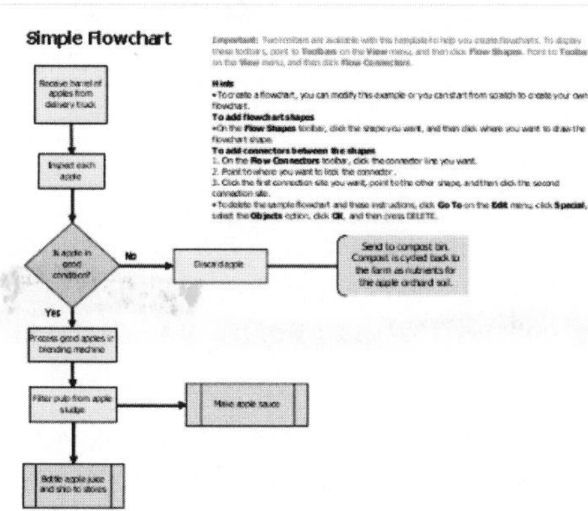

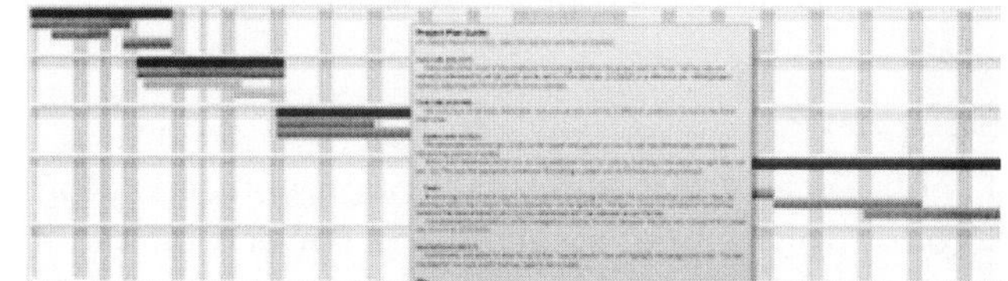

The Excel Environment: Understanding the Ribbon Interface

In all the Office applications, the *Ribbon* is a collection of all the command and menu elements that are available. While each Office application has different features and options, they all share the same Ribbon design for consistency.

The Excel Ribbon is a collection of *tabs*, each of which houses groups of commands that are similar in nature. The Ribbon consists of the following tabs:

- File
- Home
- Insert
- Draw (on touchscreen-enabled devices only)
- Page Layout
- Formulas
- Data
- Review
- View
- Developer (if enabled)
- Power Pivot (if enabled)
- Help

Note: The Office Ribbon also has a number of contextual tabs that appear when you select certain items. For instance, Charts, PivotTables, and shapes all have dedicated contextual Ribbon tabs.

When you first open Excel, the Home tab is activated, and you can see its related command *groups*. When you activate another tab, the command groups specific to that tab are displayed.

An important element in many Ribbon groups is the *dialog launcher*, which is the small button located at the bottom-right corner of the group. You can click the dialog launcher to expand any group that has too many controls to be efficiently displayed on the Ribbon tab.

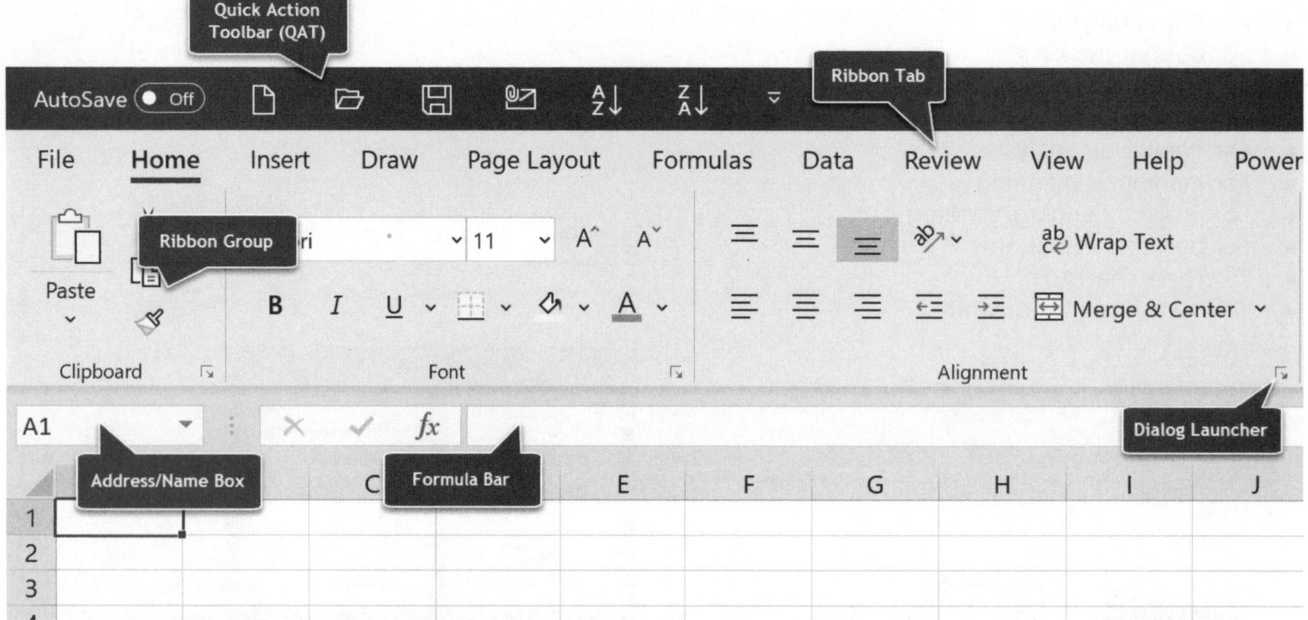

Note: The Office Ribbon intuitively resizes depending on the device you're using, so the images in the book might look different from what you see.

AutoSave

If you have an Office 365 subscription, you can automatically save your Office files to a Microsoft OneDrive account. This is great for Word and PowerPoint, but it's generally not applicable to Excel; with Excel, it's common to open workbooks, make some changes to test a scenario (for example, How much car payment can I afford?), and close without saving. Fortunately, to prevent such changes from being committed, you can disable the AutoSave feature: Just go to **File > Options > Save** and, in the dialog box shown below, make sure the checkbox at the very top is not checked.

AutoSave can be useful in some situations, though, as it causes Excel to automatically save your work as you go. AutoSave also lets you collaborate with other users in real time, and it keeps a collection log indicating each time a workbook is changed, so you can roll back to another version if you need to reject someone else's changes.

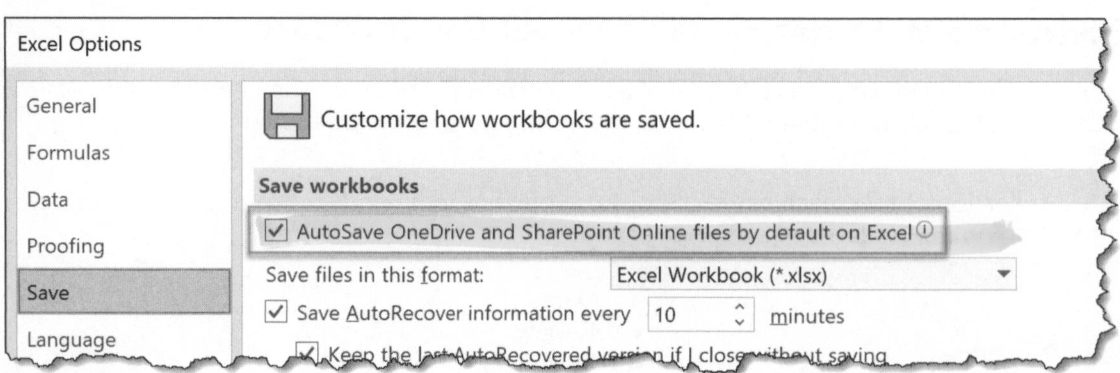

The Quick Access Toolbar (QAT)

As shown in an earlier figure, the Quick Access Toolbar (QAT) appears in the upper-left corner of the Excel window. This is a toolbar where you can put your favorite menu items so you can quickly access them. By default, it's preloaded with options, but you can change them by checking or unchecking them from the Customize Quick Access Toolbar down arrow on the right, as shown at right.

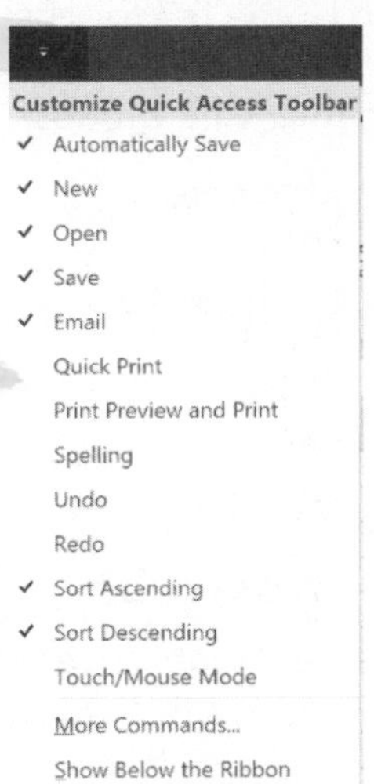

Note the two options at the bottom of this example. You can use the More Commands option to further customize the QAT, and you can use the Show Below the Ribbon option to move the QAT closer to the worksheet.

> **Note:** Options are added to the Quick Access Toolbar in order, so if you want something to be first in the list, but Excel shows it last, use the More Commands option. Select the item that you want to move from the list box on the right side and then click the Move Up (or Move Down) button located to the right of the list box.

Ribbon Tabs

The following sections take an in-depth look at each of the Excel Ribbon tabs. To really get a feel for the tabs, open Excel and play around with the various tabs as you read about them.

The File Tab

The File tab, shown below and discussed further in Chapter 2, is where application-level commands are located, such as Home, New, Open, Info, and, most importantly, Options, which allows you to change Excel's default behavior to suit your tastes. You can also select a new blank workbook or one of several customized learning templates. If you go to **File > New**, you can see a large selection of searchable templates, such as calendars, cash flow and balance sheets, student class schedules, and home loan amortization workbooks.

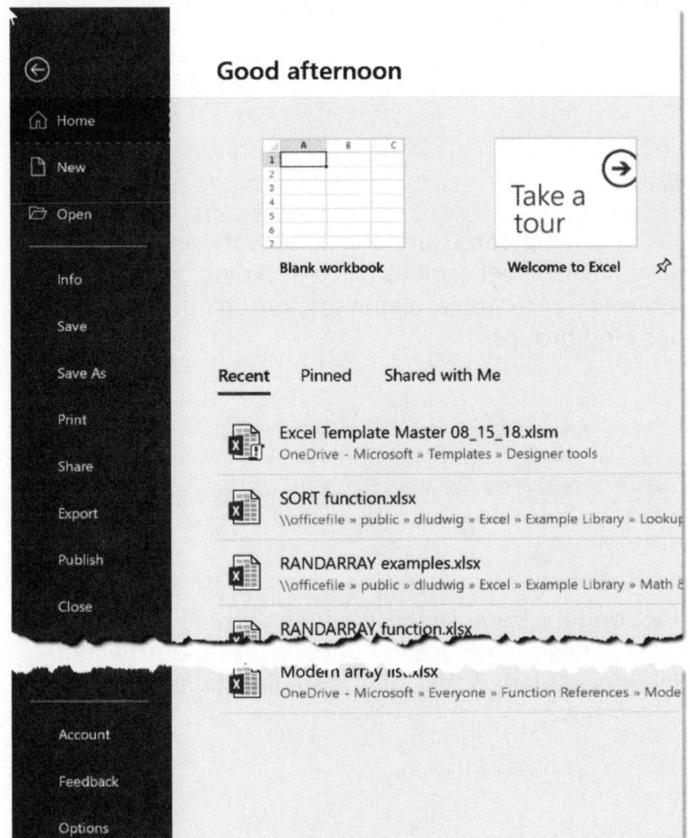

The Home Tab

The Home tab (discussed in detail in Chapter 3) holds the most commonly used menu items, such as those for text formatting and alignment, number formatting, cell styles, formatting, and editing. This tab is divided into the following groups:

- Clipboard
- Font
- Alignment
- Number
- Styles
- Cells
- Editing

The Insert Tab

The Insert tab, covered in Chapter 4, allows you to insert objects—such as PivotTables, charts, SmartArt, and pictures—into a worksheet. It consists of the following groups:

- Tables
- Illustrations
- Add-ins
- Charts
- Tours
- Sparklines
- Filters
- Links
- Comments
- Text
- Symbols

The Draw Tab

The Draw tab appears if you have a touch-enabled device. It has options for drawing on the screen with a finger or stylus (pen). The Draw tab consists of the following groups:

- Tools
- Pens
- Convert
- Replay

The Page Layout Tab

You can use the Page Layout tab to apply themes (predefined styles consisting of colors, fonts, and effects) to an entire workbook, set page setup options for printing, select sheet options (such as hiding gridlines or column and row headings), and use tools for ordering objects (for example, alignment, grouping, rotation). The Page Layout tab, discussed in Chapter 4, has the following groups:

- Themes
- Page Setup
- Scale to Fit
- Sheet Options
- Arrange

The Formulas Tab

The Formulas tab is perhaps the most powerful of the Ribbon tabs because this is where you can unleash the calculation power of Excel. It groups functions into categories such as Insert Function, AutoSum, Recently Used, Financial, Logical, Text, Date & Time, Lookup & Reference, Math & Trig, and More Functions. It's composed of the following groups:

- Function Library
- Defined Names
- Formula Auditing
- Calculation

Chapter 4 discussed the Formulas tab in detail, and Chapter 6 digs in to the formulas you can build by using this tab.

The Data Tab

The Data tab, covered in Chapter 4, is your gateway to accessing data from external sources, such as databases, other Excel workbooks, text files, and online sources such as Salesforce and Facebook. It also allows you to validate data, remove duplicates, consolidate worksheets, and do subtotaling and outlining. It has the following groups:

- Get & Transform Data
- Queries & Connections
- Data Types (Office 365 subscription only)
- Sort & Filter
- Data Tools
- Forecast
- Outline

The Review Tab

When you're ready to publish a workbook, you use the Review tab (discussed in Chapter 4). The Review tab has all the editing tools you need to make sure your work is free of grammatical and spelling errors. You can use it to add comments as visual aids for those receiving your workbook. In addition, the Review tab allows you to protect worksheets and workbooks to safeguard both your information and any formulas you don't want people to change. The Review tab has the following groups:

- Proofing
- Accessibility
- Insights
- Language
- Comments
- Notes
- Protect
- Ink

The View Tab

The View tab, discussed in detail in Chapter 4, gives you the flexibility to set all your viewing options, such as how the worksheet will be printed, whether to display gridlines or headings, and whether to view multiple worksheets or view workbooks side-by-side. The View tab consists of the following groups:

- Workbook Views
- Show
- Zoom
- Window
- Macros

The Developer Tab

When you first open Excel, the Developer tab is disabled because the majority of Excel users never need it. To enable the Developer tab, you can go to **File > Options**. Then, in the Excel Options dialog, select the Customize Ribbon tab and check the Developer checkbox in the Main Tabs section on the right. This book doesn't delve into programming, but the Developer tab is worth introducing so that you're aware of it.

Within each Office application resides a powerful application-specific programming language called *Visual Basic for Applications* (*VBA*). VBA, which is a subset of the Visual Basic program language that many professional programmers use to write applications, allows you to harness the power of programming code to automate tasks in Excel. Any repetitive task you perform in Excel (and other Office applications) can be automated so that the program does the work for you. A common example is automatically customizing a report for different people and then sending those various versions of the report through Outlook with the click of a button. To ensure that you don't have to be a computer programmer to work with VBA, Microsoft has included a tool called the *Macro Recorder* on the Developer tab. All you need to do is record a macro in Excel, and when you play it back, the actions recorded in the macro are repeated exactly as you performed them.

The Developer tab consists of the following groups:

- Code
- Add-ins
- Controls
- XML

The Help Tab

The Help tab puts multiple help options right at your fingertips. In addition, the Search box on the Ribbon allows you to search for help. To get help by using the Search box, you type in the search terms you want, and Excel offers several possibilities for you to choose from. You can also click **Help > Help** (the question mark button), and Excel launches a dedicated Help pane that has several sections, as shown below.

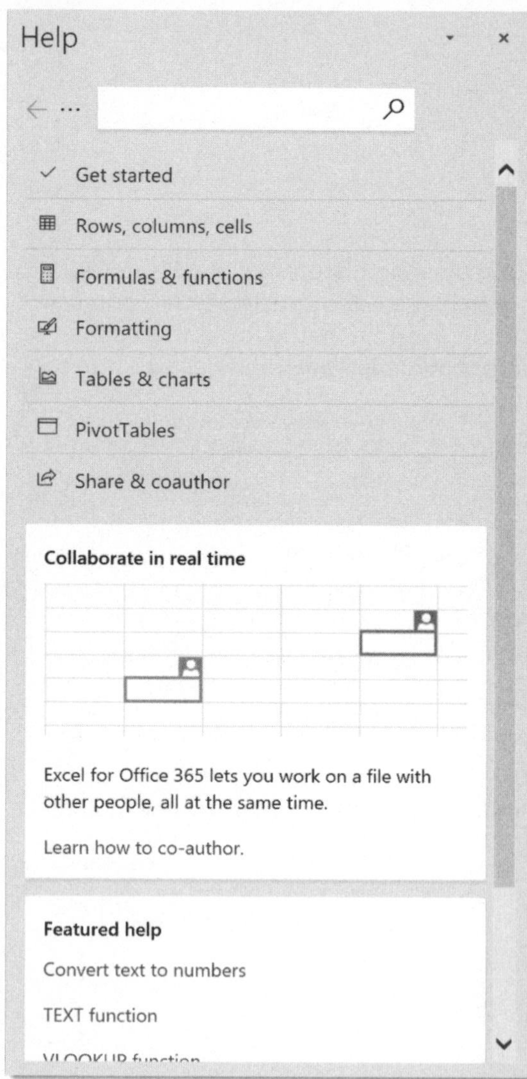

If you type in the Search box at the top of the Help pane, the results you see are the top-rated topics from www.support.office.com, as shown below.

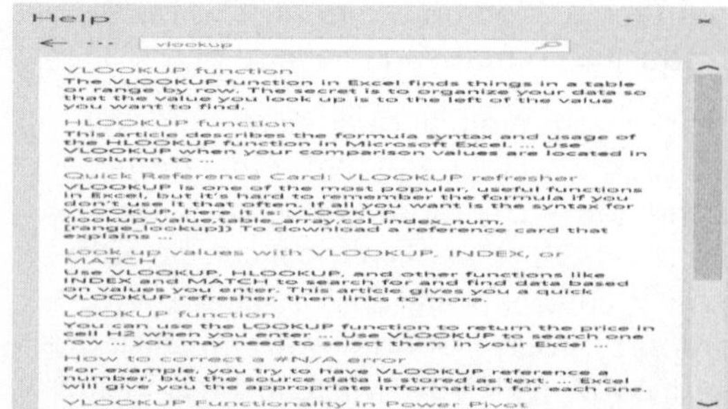

The Help pane provides a series of interactive help options that represent some of the questions most frequently asked at www.support.office.com.

If you can't get the answers you need by using the Help tab and Help pane, you can go to the Excel Tech community (https://techcommunity.microsoft.com/t5/Excel/ct-p/Excel_Cat) and ask a question there. Microsoft hosts this volunteer community (made up of Excel professionals and enthusiasts from all over the world), where you can ask Excel questions and get answers from other users. Microsoft employees and members of the Excel team also participate in the forums.

There are many other help options available online. I am personally partial to www.MrExcel.com/forum, as I believe it's the best Excel question-and-answer forum.

The Power Pivot Tab

Power Pivot is a fantastic tool that allows you to deal with massive datasets in Excel. It makes it possible for you to easily work with far more data than Excel can manage on its own. Power Pivot is based on SQL Server database technology, and it brings that power to you in Excel. As with the Developer tab, you need to enable Power Pivot in order to see the Power Pivot tab. You'll learn more about it in Chapter 11.

The Add-Ins Tab

Add-ins are tools—some written by third parties and many written by Microsoft—that allow you to access additional functionality that isn't natively a part of Excel. Add-ins are generally created with VBA. As a beginner in Excel, you might not have any need to use add-ins, but many add-ins are created with certain businesses in mind. For instance, there is an add-in for carpenters and home builders that can convert cell entries into inch/foot measurements. Similarly, there are enhanced finance add-ins for stock market traders, statistical add-ins for scientists, metric system converters, and many more. The Add-ins tab has only one group, Menu Commands. As you add and activate add-ins, they are listed in this group. If you don't have any add-ins activated, then you won't see the Add-Ins tab.

Additional Ribbon Options

At the very bottom of the Ribbon you can see the Name box and the formula bar, both shown in the following figure.

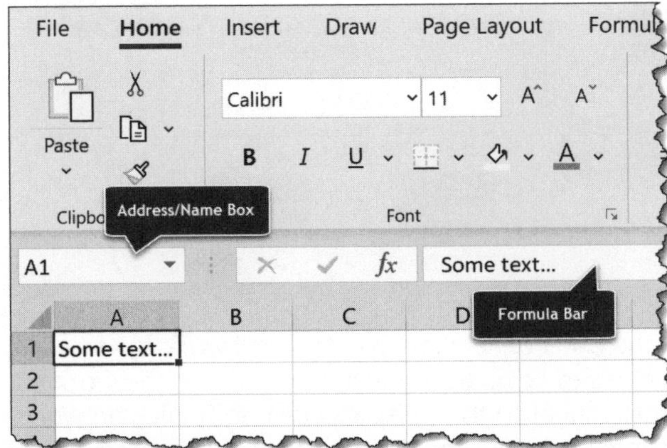

The leftmost box, called the *Address box* or *Name box*, displays the address of the cell that is active at the moment (called the *active cell*). If you happen to have an object like a chart selected, the chart name is displayed. You can also enter a cell address here to automatically jump to it. For example, entering **Z100** would take you right to cell Z100.

The *formula bar*, which is the box to the right of the Name box, displays the active cell's value. When you begin working with formulas, you'll see that you can work with them either in the cell itself or in the formula bar. In addition, when a formula is entered and calculated, the active cell displays the formula's result, while the formula bar displays the formula itself.

As shown below, on the right-hand side of the Ribbon are several more controls that are common to all Office applications.

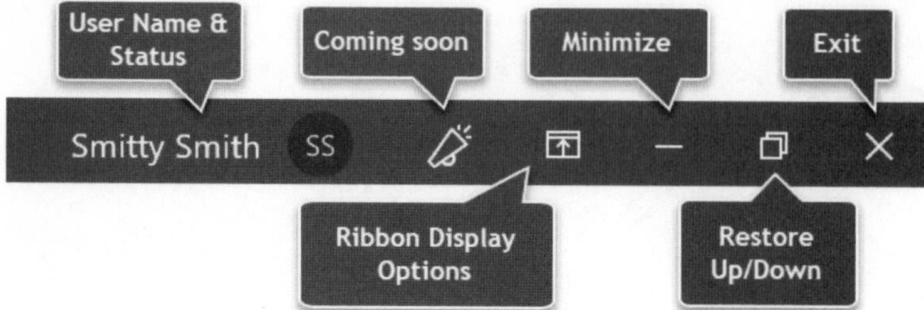

The user name field shows your user name, and if you're an Office 365 subscriber, it also shows your online status. You can click it to log in with a different account or see your account details. The Coming Soon button shows you upcoming features that are due to be released soon. The up-arrow button is the Ribbon Display Options button, and it gives you the following options: Auto-hide Ribbon, Show Tabs, and Show Tabs and Commands.

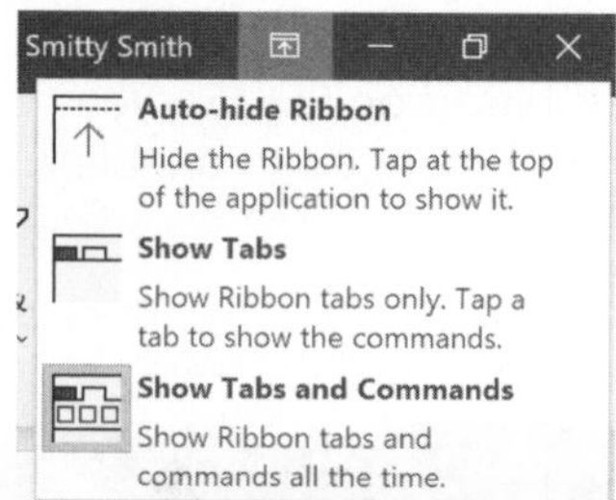

The Minimize button is the small bar that you can click to minimize the application. The button that looks like a stack of paper reduces your screen (Restore Down) or restores it to full size (Restore Up), and the X (Exit) button closes the workbook. If you only had one workbook open, it also exits Excel.

> **Note:** If you haven't saved your work, when you click the **Exit** button, you'll be prompted to do so.

Worksheet Tabs, the Status Bar, and View Buttons

As shown in the following example, the bottom of the Excel screen provides an additional set of tools. The following sections discuss these options in detail.

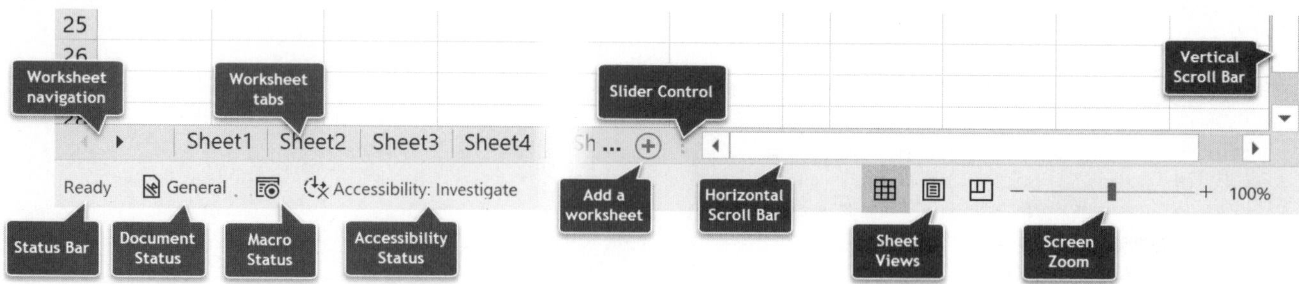

Worksheet Navigation

The two worksheet navigation buttons at the bottom left of the Excel pane allow you to scroll worksheets backward and forward. The left-pointing arrow button allows you to scroll to the first worksheet in the workbook, and the right-pointing arrow button takes you to the next sheet to the right. You can right-click between these two arrows to see a snapshot list of all the worksheets in your workbook, as shown below. You can click on a worksheet name in this window and click OK to activate that sheet.

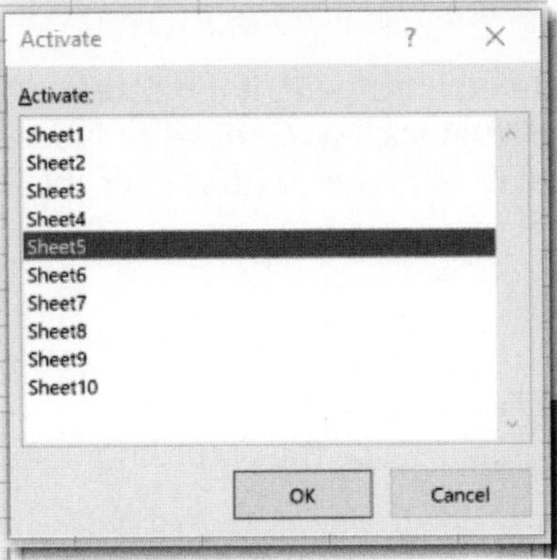

Worksheet Tabs

At the bottom of the Excel window you can see all your worksheets tabs. Clicking one of these tabs activates the corresponding worksheet.

Horizontal Scroll Bar

By dragging the horizontal scroll bar to the right, you can scroll to the end of your data within a worksheet. You can also scroll left to go to earlier data.

Vertical Scroll Bar

The vertical scroll bar has the same functionality as the horizontal scroll bar, but you use it to scroll up and down rather than side-to-side.

Status Bar

The status bar displays messages regarding Excel's state (Ready, Calculate, etc.). If you right-click it, you're presented with a list of options you can choose to display, as shown below.

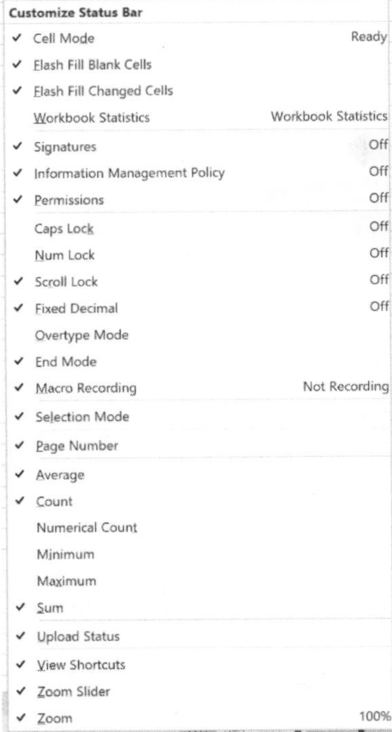

The status bar also has some neat functionality that you'll discover if you select a range of numerical data: You see summary details at the bottom of the sheet, such as the sum and count of your selected items.

Document Status

The Document Status feature is also called Sensitivity, and if you're in a corporate environment, it indicates whether your workbook is open for public or private consumption by showing a level such as General or Non-Business or Highly Confidential. Depending on your configuration, you may or may not have control over this feature.

Macro Recorder

You can record a new macro by clicking the Macro Recorder button. When you click it once, the symbol changes to a square, and you can begin recording a macro. Clicking this button again stops the recording.

Accessibility Status

Office's Accessibility Checker is on by default and constantly monitoring your workbook for potential accessibility issues. Clicking it launches the Accessibility pane, where you can review the results and address them. You can also turn off the Accessibility Checker from here if you want.

Add a Worksheet

You can add a new worksheet by clicking the + button.

> **Note:** You can also add a new worksheet by using the keyboard shortcut **Alt+I+W**.

Slider Control

You can drag the slider control to the left and right to minimize and expand the horizontal scroll bar. This is useful when you have a lot of worksheets and you want to see as many of them as possible.

Sheet Views

There are three sheet view options:

- Normal (default)
- Page Layout
- Page Break Preview

Screen Zoom

You can use the zoom controls to increase or decrease the amount of worksheet you see:

- **- and + buttons**—Clicking on either of these buttons incrementally resizes the screen.
- **Zoom slider**—You can drag this slider left or right to incrementally resize the screen.
- **Zoom %**—You can click on this and manually enter the zoom percentage, as shown below.

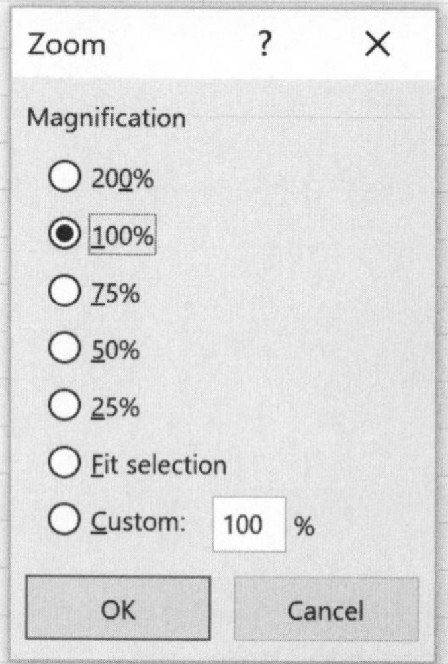

Navigating the Excel Environment

All the Ribbon's tab controls are mouse activated. However, they can also be activated and by using the keyboard. Pressing either of the **Alt** keys (to the left and right of the **Spacebar**), or the forward slash key (**/**), which is the same key as the **?** key, causes the Ribbon to appear with letters beneath each tab group, as shown below. Pressing the corresponding key activates that tab. (For example, if you press **Alt** and then press **P**, you see the Page Layout tab.) When that tab group is activated, a second set of letters appears beneath each menu control. Pressing the corresponding letter then activates the corresponding menu command.

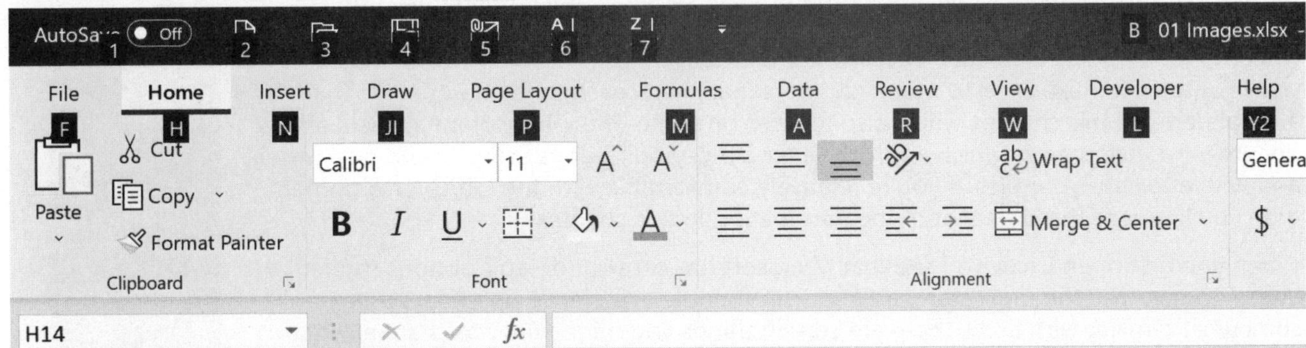

There are many ways to navigate within Excel, including using the options listed in the previous section and clicking on any cell to activate it. However, these actions all require using the mouse. It's generally much more efficient to get around in Excel by using the keyboard. The following table lists some of the most commonly used Excel keyboard shortcuts.

Commonly Used Keyboard Shortcuts for Navigation

Key Combination	Action
→ or Tab	Move one cell to the right
← or Shift+Tab	Move one cell to the left
Up and down arrows	Move one cell up/down
Ctrl+→	Jump to the right-hand side of the current region
Ctrl+←	Jump to the left-hand side of the current region
Ctrl+↓	Jump to the bottom of the current region
Ctrl+↑	Jump to the top of the current region
Home	Jump to the first cell in the row (column A)
Ctrl+Home	Jump to cell A1 (the home cell)
Ctrl+End	Jump to the bottom cell containing data on the right-hand side of the sheet
Page Down	Move one page down
Page Up	Move one page up
Alt+Page Up	Move one page to the left
Alt+Page Down	Move one page to the right
Ctrl+Page Up	Jump to the next worksheet on the left
Ctrl+Page Down	Jump to the next worksheet on the right

Note: If you're entering data and use the **Tab** key to move to subsequent cells, when you're done, you can press **Enter**, and you are returned to one row below where you started.

Chapter Summary

- In this chapter you learned what a spreadsheet is, what Excel is to spreadsheets, and some common spreadsheet terminology.
- You were introduced to the Ribbon interface, which debuted with Microsoft Office 2007.
- You learned how to get help in Excel.
- You saw some of the many ways to get around in Excel.

Chapter 2: Understanding File Operations and Setting Up Excel

In Chapter 1 you were introduced to several key elements of spreadsheets in general and Excel in particular. This chapter dives more deeply into Excel and shows you how to get around the Ribbon by exploring its various elements. This chapter doesn't teach you how to use each element in depth (though the following chapters do). Rather, it provides an introduction so that when you start to get more comfortable with Excel, you'll know where to look for key elements. This chapter primarily focuses on the File tab and shows you how to customize Excel to meet your personal needs each time you open it. There is a lot of detail in this chapter, which also focuses on some of the important aspects of file/document management (which apply to other Office applications as well), and how, when, and where to save your files. If you're relatively comfortable with the Office environment, then you'll breeze through a lot of the information in this chapter.

When you first open Excel, you see that Microsoft has set your default options (preferences) to give you the most standard and user-friendly experience possible. When you're somewhat familiar with Excel, there are certain things you might want to change; what works best for the "default" user may not work best for you. And even if you're not all that familiar with Excel, there will probably be some things you'll want to change. Fortunately, Microsoft understands this and lets you make changes. Before we discuss how to change the default options, we'll go over all the options on the File tab, most of which are relatively straightforward.

The File Tab

If you click on the **File** tab, you see the options shown at right: Home, New, Open, Info, Save, Save As, Print, Share, Export, Publish, Close, Account, Feedback, and Options.. All these options are discussed in the following sections.

The Home Pane

If you select **File > Home**, you see an opening pane on the right that offers several options: a blank workbook option you can select if you want to start fresh and several learning templates you can select if you're not sure where to start and want to take a tour or discover how to do things with interactive learning guides. Beneath that, under Recent, is a list of the files you've used recently. If you don't see much there at this point, don't worry; you'll learn how to change the defaults in a little bit. There's also a Pinned tab, which you can use to select any workbooks that you've pinned to the menu by clicking the pushpin icon to the right of a file name. You may also see a third tab, Shared with Me, that displays any workbooks that others have shared with you. This is most common in a company environment.

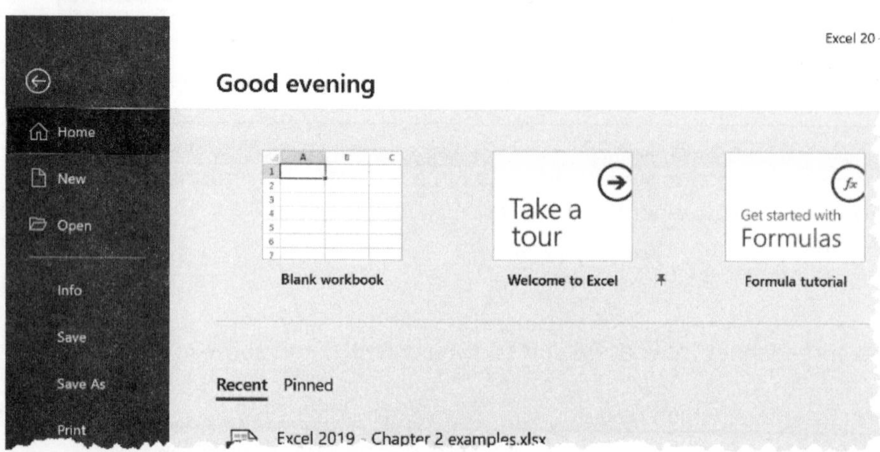

The New Pane

If you select **File > New**, Excel launches a dialog that gives you options for the kind of workbook to create. You can choose from a blank workbook, learning templates (interactive guides that help you learn to do things in Excel, such as using formulas), and some general templates, such as calendars, or you can browse through Microsoft's excellent selection of templates online. You can also create a new blank workbook by pressing **Ctrl+N**. If you choose the blank workbook option, by default Excel gives you a workbook with three worksheets. (However, you can change the default number of sheets by selecting **File > Options > Advanced**, as you'll see later in this chapter.)

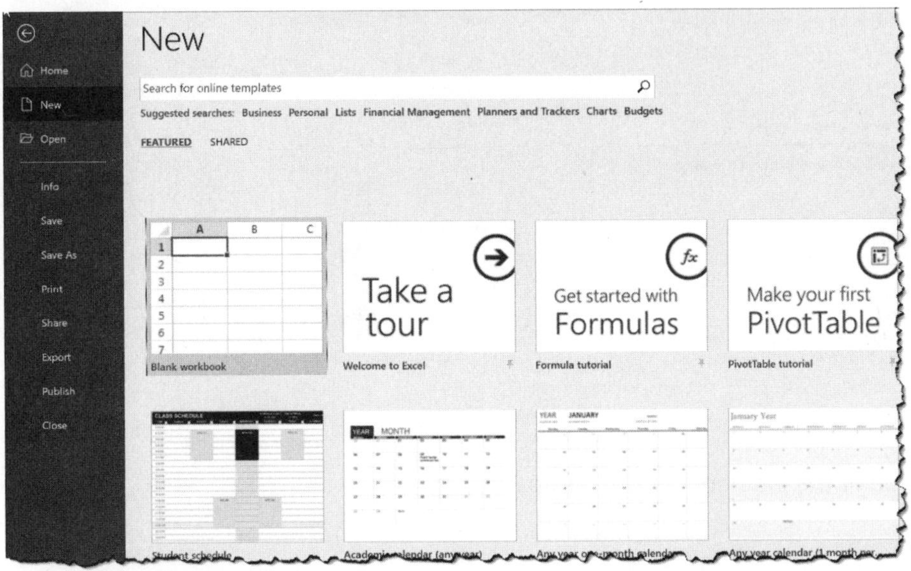

Note: A template is a preformatted document you can reuse to create multiple workbooks that all have the same formatting.

The Open Pane

If you click **File > Open**, you see a pane that lets you browse to the file you want to open. You can also use Windows Explorer (or press **Windows+E**) to find the file you want and then just double-click it to open it.

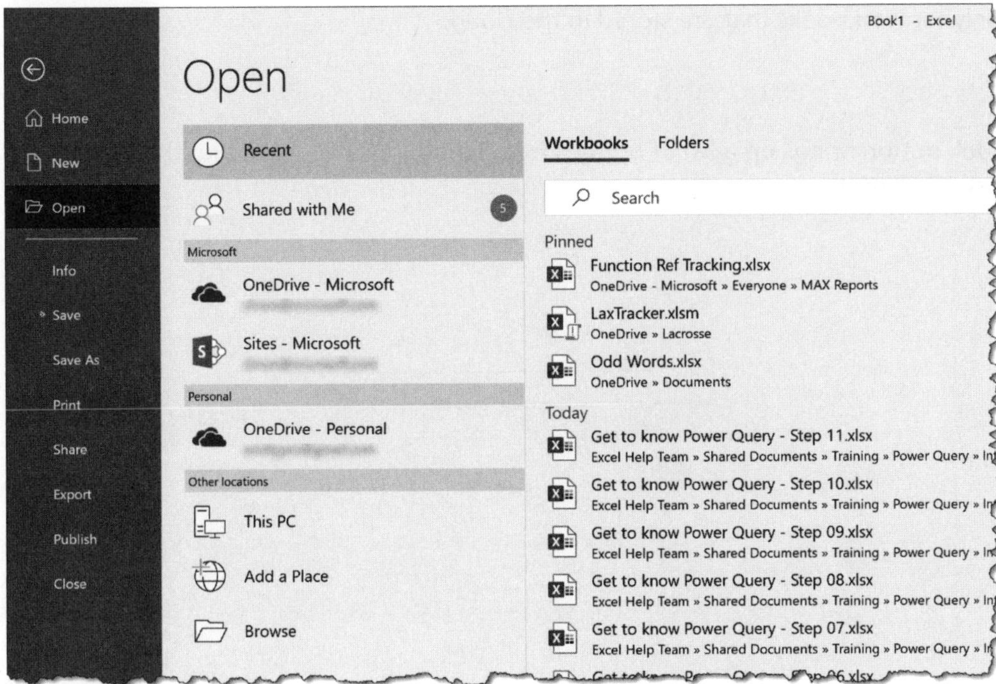

The Info Pane

If you click **File > Info**, you see a new pane that displays relevant workbook information. Your particular setup—such as whether you're an individual user or part of a company domain—will determine some of the fields that you see. As with many other parts of Excel, if you're an Office 365 subscriber, this pane is constantly evolving. You'll notice that the information for a new workbook that hasn't been saved yet will have fewer details than one that has been saved.

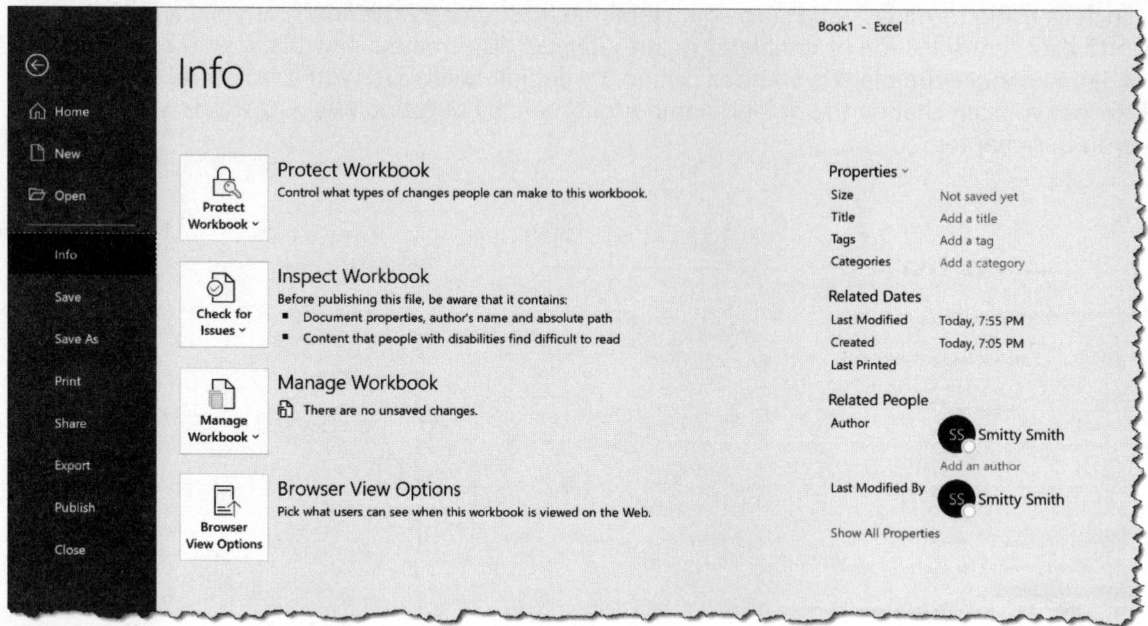

The following sections describe some of the elements of the Info pane.

File Path

At the top of the Info pane is a detailed file path view showing where the workbook is located. If you click on it, you have the option to copy the file path to the Clipboard or to open the file location in Windows Explorer. The workbook in the example above hasn't been saved, so there's no file name to display.

Document Views

The Document Views section provides an at-a-glance view of how many people have opened the workbook over time. This is relevant only for workbooks that are stored in the cloud.

Protect Workbook

Clicking the Protect Workbook button brings up a list of options for distributing and protecting the current worksheet, as well as the workbook itself.

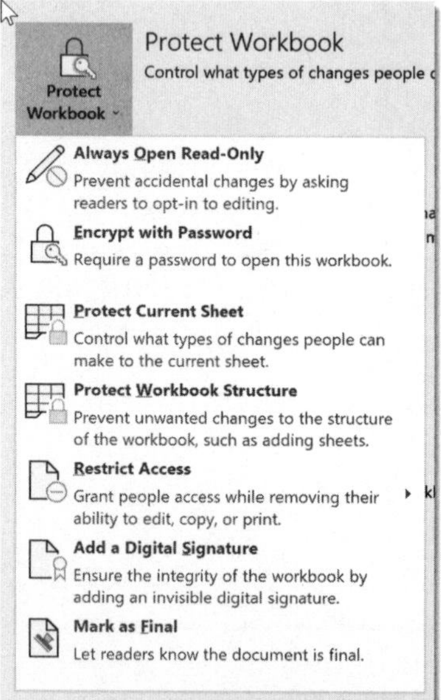

Check for Issues

The Check for Issues button allows you to evaluate the workbook for any potential problems before you share it. You'll probably rarely need to use this feature; it is most useful when you're publicly distributing workbooks and need to remove personal information or get accessibility recommendations.

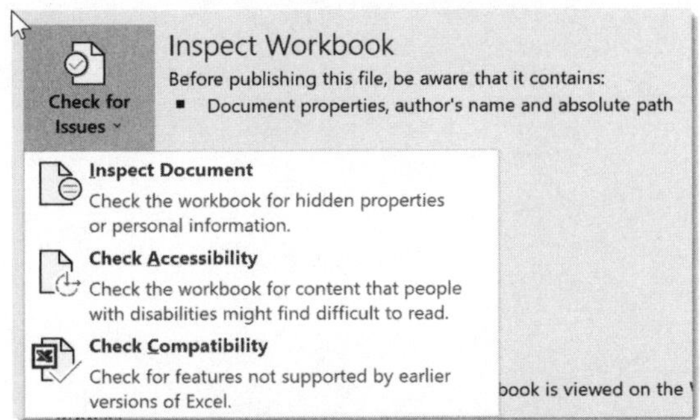

Note: *Accessibility* refers to ensuring that your workbooks can be used by those with limited vision or other physical challenges.

Manage Workbook

The Manage Workbook button lets you know if there are any preexisting versions of the workbook. You can click the View and Restore Previous Versions link to open a new task pane that lets you see all versions of a workbook that you've been working on. If you're using the AutoSave option, this list can be pretty long.

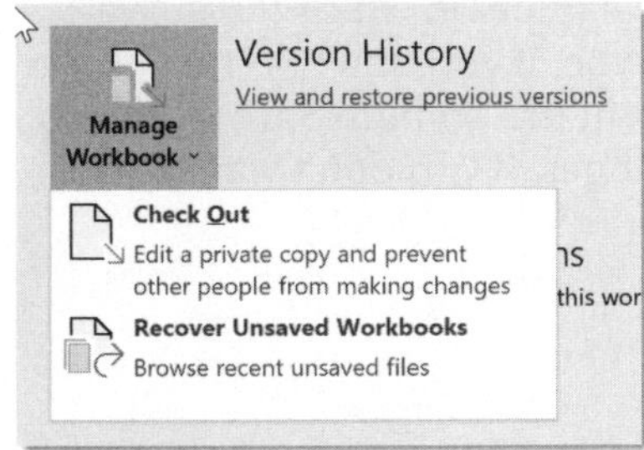

Properties

On the right-hand side of the Info pane is a Properties list. You can manually edit any of the editable workbook properties simply by clicking them, making changes, and pressing Enter. You can't change intrinsic document properties such as the size, modified/created dates, and so on. At the bottom of this list is a link that says either Show All Properties or Show Fewer Properties.

The Save Command

The Save command allows you to save the active workbook. It's fairly simple but often forgotten until it's too late. Regularly saving your work is paramount. It is also important to ensure that if you open a workbook and make changes to it, you're absolutely sure you want to keep those changes *before* you save the workbook. Otherwise, your previous workbook will be overwritten by the new one, and your chances of recovery are slim (unless you have a backup version you can recover). In Excel and other applications, a lot of work around the world gets lost because of this issue every day. The AutoSave option can be very useful if you're forgetful about saving (as I am), but it can also cause problems by automatically saving changes you might not want to save. It also requires you to have a Microsoft OneDrive account to sync to the cloud.

The Save As Pane

The Save As pane lets you save the active workbook with another name and/or as another type of file. Let's say you make some changes to a workbook, and you want to keep them, but you don't want to alter the original workbook. In this case, you would use the Save As option.

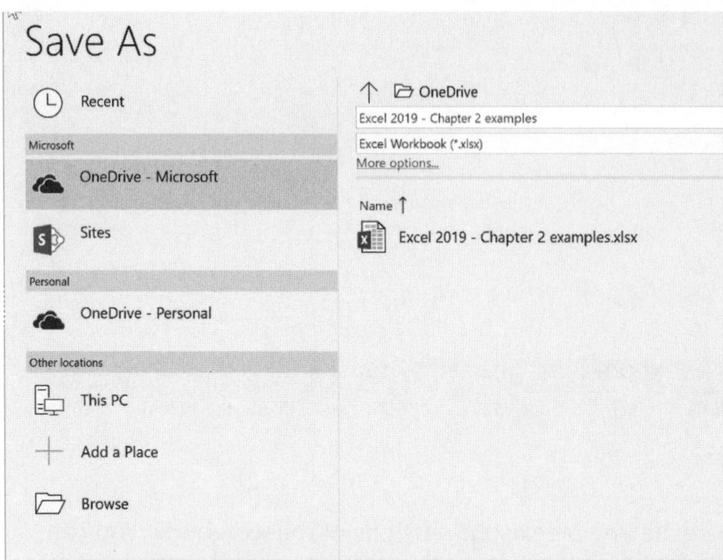

Note: If you have AutoSave turned on, you see Save a Copy instead of Save As.

The Save As pane (or Save a Copy pane when AutoSave is turned on) starts in the folder in which the active workbook was opened. You need to select the file name and enter a different name. If you don't do that and try to save, Excel asks you about it, as shown in the dialog below. If you click Yes in the Confirm Save As dialog, you save the file over whatever was in your workbook before you made any changes. If you don't want to do this, then just click No, and you have a chance to enter a new workbook name.

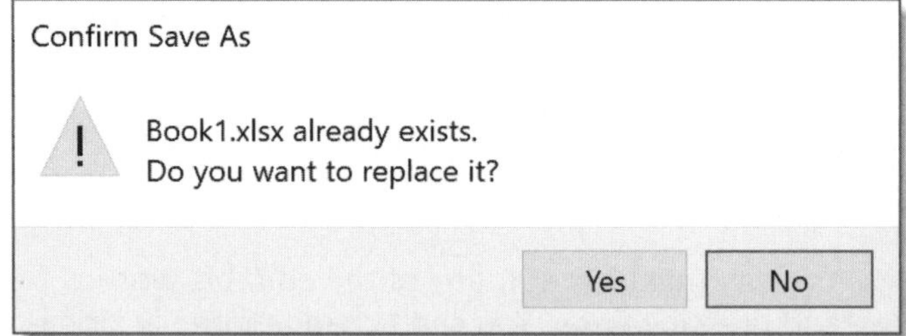

From here you can choose a different workbook name and browse to the location of your choice. Again, one of the first things you should do when making changes to an existing workbook is perform a Save As if you want to keep the original work; otherwise, you stand a very good chance of losing it. This becomes especially important when you start working on complex models that you want to keep intact. (They don't even have to be complex actually; lose an hour's worth of work, and you'll be upset.)

Hint: To reiterate: Be sure to use Save As right after you open a file to avoid losing work that you would then have to re-create.

The Save As dialog gives you some important additional options related to who you might be sharing your workbooks with later, but you first need to be aware of some naming conventions when you try to save a workbook. Microsoft has done a great job of expanding the rules for file names, but there are still some limitations on characters you can and can't use, as shown below. If you try to use any of the following characters in an Excel file name (or any other Windows file name for that matter), you'll get an error message: * | \ ? : " < >

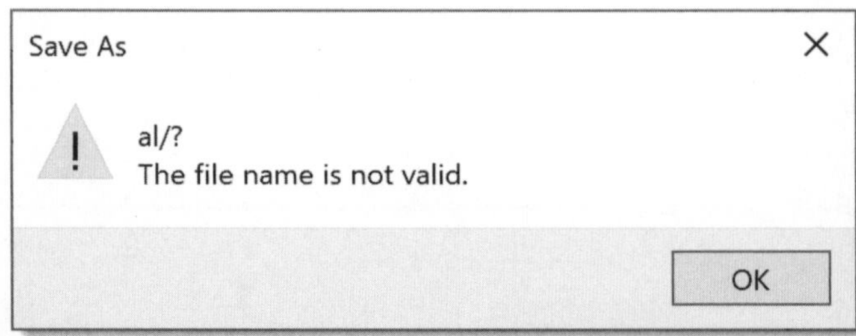

In the Save As dialog, you can also select the file type. You see the following drop-down selections if you click the arrow at the right end of the Save as Type box. This drop-down lets you save your workbook in a number of ways.

In general, the default option is fine, but you do need to know about the differences between the various options, especially if you want to share a workbook with users who have earlier Excel versions or if you recorded some macros and want to keep them. For every software application, a particular *file extension* is appended to the end of the file name (e.g., xlsx in MyFile.xlsx), which identifies it and helps separate different applications from each other. Whereas earlier versions of Excel had only two file extensions, Excel 2007/2010 introduced some new ones. Microsoft also now gives you a lot of new ways to save your workbook with the new versions, but for now you shouldn't need to worry about anything except the default, which is Excel Workbook (.xlsx). The following table lists the Excel file extensions.

Excel File Extensions

Extension	Description
.xls	A pre-Excel 2007 workbook
.xlt	A pre-Excel 2007 template workbook
.xlsx	A post-Excel 2003 workbook
.xlsm	A post-Excel 2003 workbook that has macros
.xlsb	A post-Excel 2003 workbook in binary format
.xltx	A post-Excel 2003 template workbook

If at some point you decide to start recording macros, be aware that when you try to save a workbook with macros, Excel prompts you to change the file to a macro-enabled workbook. If you choose not to do so, Excel deletes the macros in that workbook, and you lose your macro work. (This can be okay if you don't want to share your macros with anyone, though.)

If you click the More Options link in the Save As dialog, you see more options, as shown below. The following sections describe the various options available in this window.

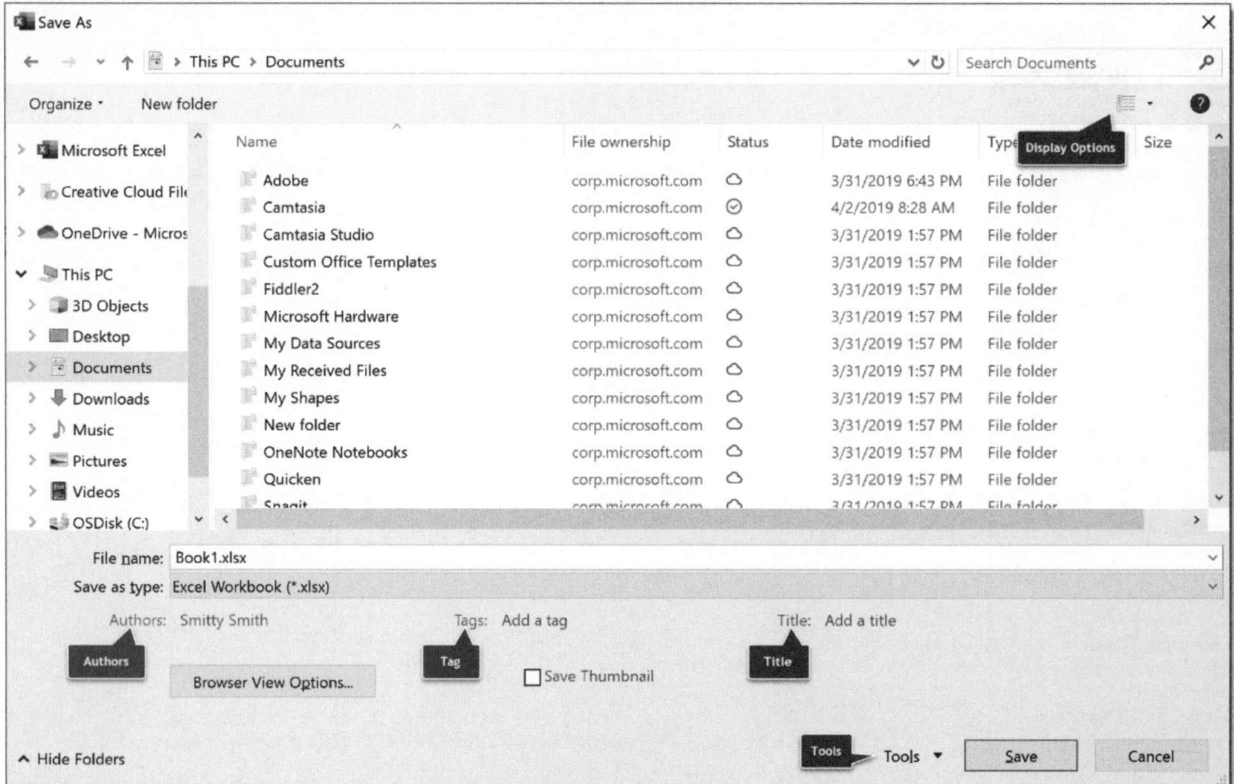

Display Options

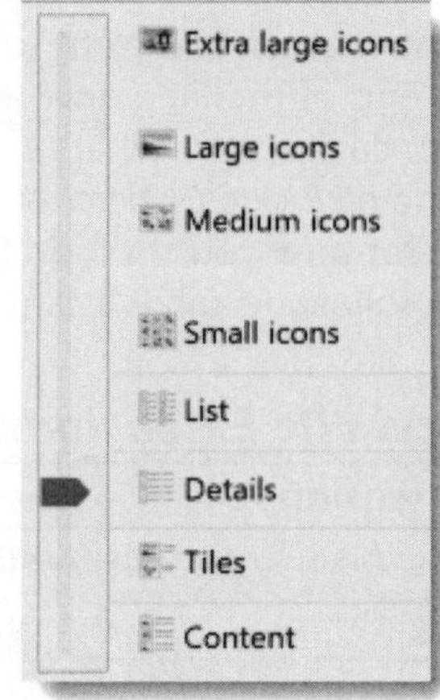

You can click the Display Options button to set the way in which documents display in the Open, Save, and Search dialogs. Some people prefer icons, especially if they deal with a lot of graphic images, while others prefer just a plain list of files. If you choose to see details, as shown at right and in all the examples in this chapter, you see the file name, date modified, type, and document size. This option gives you the most information about the files you want to open or save.

Authors

The name in blue text next to Authors is the name that you entered into Office when you installed it. But you can click on the blue text to change this name right here. The change is then applied throughout Office.

Tags

The Tags option allows you to give a short description of what's in the workbook (payroll, schedule, etc.). This can help speed up indexed searching when you use Windows Explorer to find files on your PC or network.

Title

Title, which is very similar to Tags, allows for an extended description of your workbook's function beyond the file name. Frankly, unless you're dealing with thousands of documents or saving and sharing files on a large corporate network, neither Tags nor Titles will be useful to you.

Save Thumbnail

If you click the Save Thumbnail checkbox, Excel adds a graphic image of your workbook that you can see when you search and open files. This is generally a waste of resources, since Excel has to save that image along with other file properties.

Tools

The Tools drop-down makes available some advanced settings that can come in handy if you need documents to be secure. There are four options here.

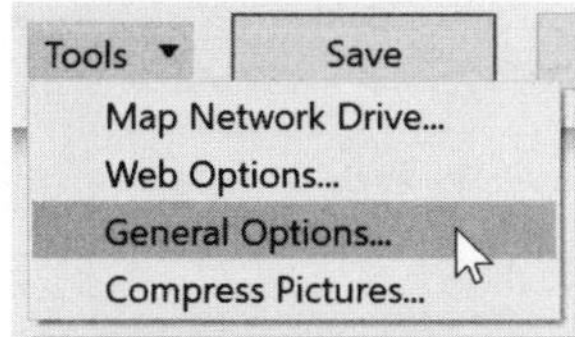

Most of them are broad Windows options and not really relevant to daily Excel use, but if you select General Options, as shown above, you get the following options:

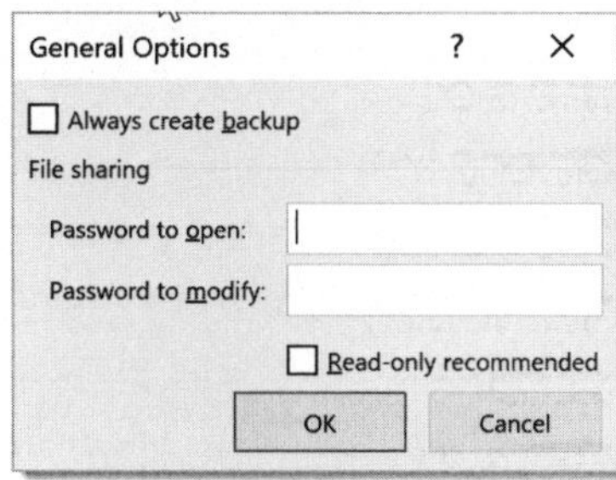

- **Always Create Backup**—If you select this checkbox, Excel will create a backup copy of your workbook whenever you close it. This is a good idea if you don't consistently back up files to an external source, but bear in mind that the backup copy will be created in the same folder as your workbook. Unfortunately, this means that if you lose access to the workbook's location for any reason (hard drive failure, folder deletion, etc.), you'll also lose the backup. Also note that a backup copy will be created as soon as you save your workbook, so if you accidentally save over a file, the backup will be a copy of what you saved over, too.
  Hint: AutoSave might be a better option than Always Create Backup, as it automatically saves your data directly to the cloud, so you don't need to worry about hard drive failures.
- **Password to Open**—This option is handy if you keep workbooks on a shared drive and you don't want other people to access them.
- **Password to Modify**—This option allows people to open your workbook but allows them to make changes only after they enter the correct password. This is handy if you want to share your workbook but don't want others to make changes.
- **Read-Only Recommended**—You can select this checkbox on its own or in conjunction with the Password to Open and Password to Modify options. It enables you to save a workbook as a read-only document. This means that others can access the workbook, but any changes they make can't be saved unless they save the workbook with another name. Again, this option is handy if you want to distribute your workbook but don't want people changing your original.

Close

You can click the Close command (or the X in the upper-right corner of the window) to close the workbook. If you haven't made any changes to the workbook since you opened it, then clicking the Close button will close the workbook without any prompts. If you have made changes to the workbook, Excel asks if you want to save the workbook before closing it. Sometimes you might want to open a workbook to make some quick assumptions and then close without saving them; in such a case, you need to be sure *not* to save the workbook. If you have AutoSave turned on, Excel does not prompt you to save when you close, and any changes you made will be final.

> **Note:** Some functions, like those that deal with dates and times, cause a workbook to recalculate when it's opened. With such a workbook, you'll be prompted to save when you close the workbook, even though you might not have manually made any changes to it. AutoSave ignores such automatically made recalculations.

The Print Pane

If you select **File > Print**, Excel brings up the Print pane. Your options for printing both the active worksheet and the entire workbook are on the left side of the pane, and a preview of the active worksheet is shown on the right. Chapter 7 discusses the many details of this pane.

The Share Pane

If you select **File > Share**, Excel enables you to email a link to a workbook. You see this option only if the workbook is saved to a shareable location, such as a OneDrive or SharePoint folder. You can choose to share directly from the dialog shown below, or you can use the Copy Link option to create a link that you can then paste into an email.

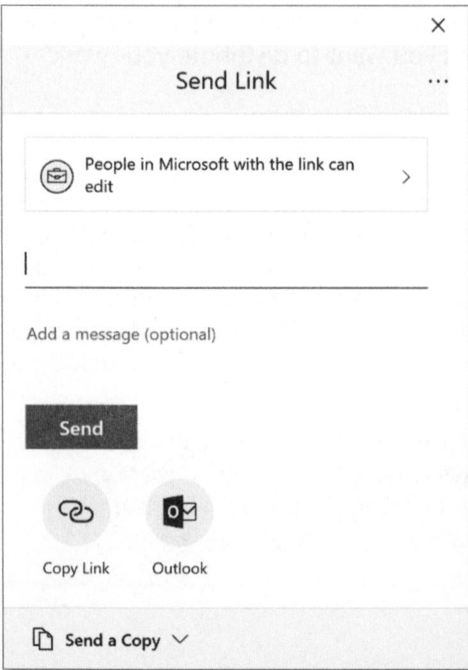

The Export Pane

If you select **File > Export**, you see the Export pane, which lets you convert a workbook to a PDF or XPS file. PDF is a very secure format for distributing workbooks, especially if you want to share information but not the formulas or structure behind your workbook. The XPS file format allows documents to be viewed online and retain their source formatting. Unless you plan on putting a lot of workbooks on the Internet, the odds that you will ever use this option are slim.

The Publish Pane

If you select **File > Publish**, you see the Publish pane, which lets you send a workbook to Microsoft's Power BI reporting tool. This is a free desktop application for building powerful, dynamic dashboard-type reports with fantastic data visualizations. You can download it at PowerBI.Microsoft.com. MrExcel also has several books on Power BI; see https://www.mrexcel.com/store/index.php.

Changing Excel's Default Settings So They're Right for You

In general, Excel is set up very well from the start. However, you can tweak the defaults to make it even easier to get Excel to do what you want.

> **Hint:** It's a good idea to get acquainted with Excel before you decide to change any of the options.

Some of the options you won't bother changing from Microsoft's default settings, some of them you'll only change one time, and some you'll change between workbooks, depending on what you're doing. When you change certain options, you must exit and restart Excel in order for the changes to take effect, but Excel lets you know if you need to do this.

When you select **File > Options**, the Excel Options dialog appears. This dialog has multiple tabs, discussed in the following sections.

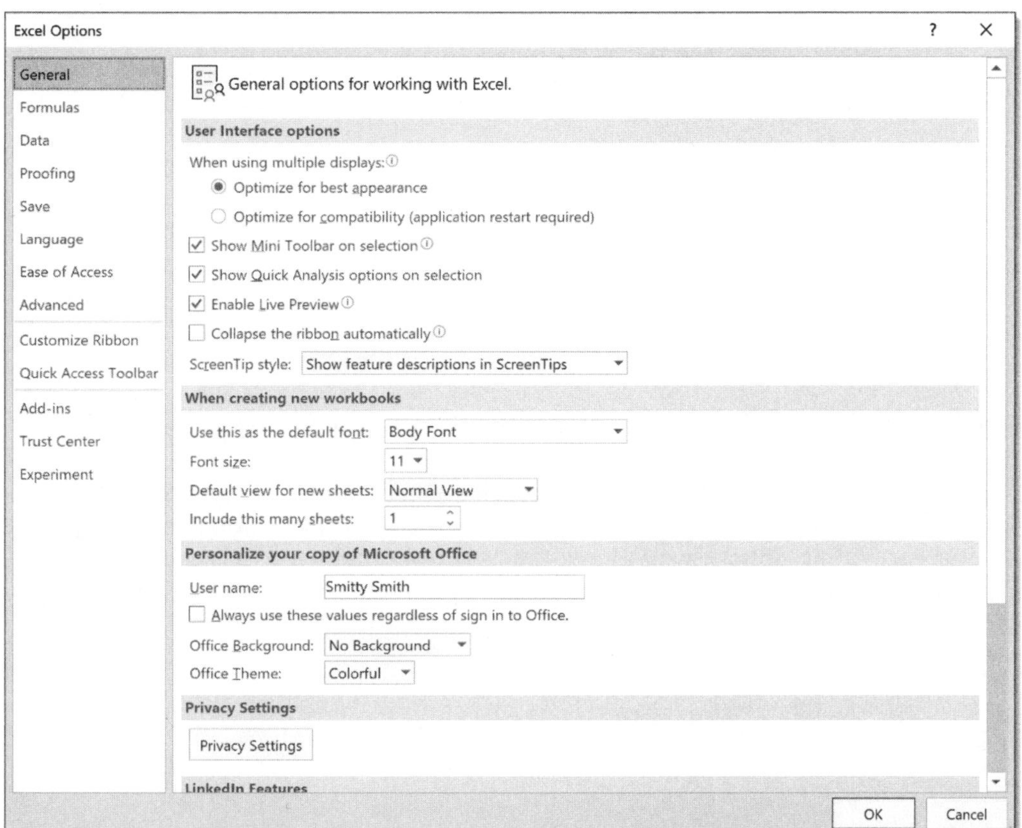

The General Tab

Most of the sections of the General tab are self-explanatory, but let's examine a few that are especially good to understand.

The User Interface Options Section

The User Interface Options section of the General tab includes the following options:

- **Show Quick Analysis Options on Selection**—When Excel senses that you're working with data that can be analyzed, it offers you a preview gallery of options you can apply to the selected data. The best way to learn about this feature is to actually work with some sample data to see how powerful this tool is. You can open the Chapter 2 companion workbook to play around with some sample data. After you select a data range, press **Ctrl+Q** to launch the Quick Analysis dialog.
- **Enable Live Preview**—Live Preview is something Microsoft has been working on for a while, and it's pretty slick. Essentially, it allows you to preview the effects of a change to an object (cell, chart, etc.) and decide whether that's the change you want to make before you commit to it. Previously, you would apply a change, decide if you liked it or not, and then go back and do it again until you got what you wanted. Imagine how time-consuming it could be to try to get a font right when you have a long list of fonts from which to choose. Live Preview has been such a big hit that Microsoft has a crew of people devoted to expanding it—and not just for Excel but for all the Office applications. Following is an example of changing the font selection for a cell. As you scroll through the list of available fonts, the text in the cell automatically updates to the font you selected (and it can go as fast as you can scroll!).

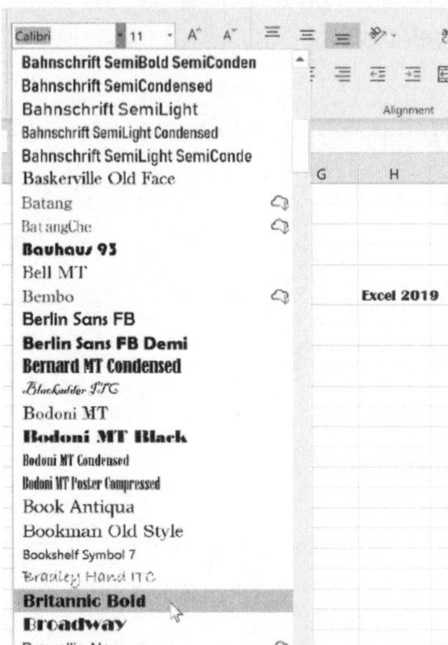

- **Collapse the Microsoft Search box by Default**—If you think the large Search box takes up too much space, select this option to collapse it to a magnifying glass.
- **ScreenTip Style**—If you choose Show Feature Descriptions in ScreenTips, a long description appears if you hover over a Ribbon control. The following example shows the ScreenTip that appears when you hover over the Conditional Formatting option in the Home tab. When you get used to Excel, you might want to change this to Don't Show Feature Descriptions in ScreenTips.

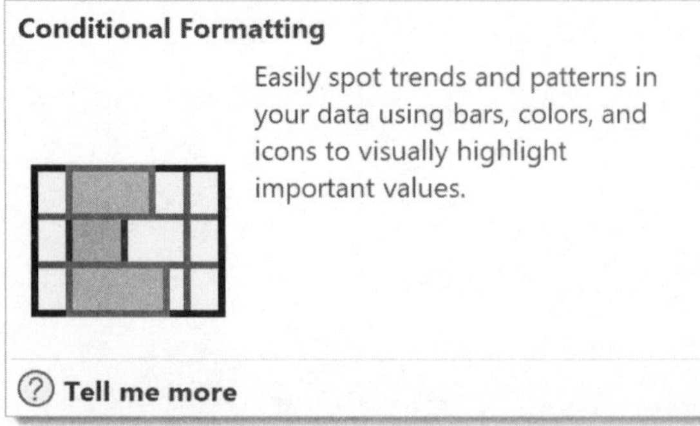

Note: If you click the Tell Me More link when a ScreenTip is visible, Excel takes you to a Help file for that topic.

The When Creating New Workbooks Section

The When Creating New Workbooks section of the General tab includes the following options:

- **Use This as the Default Font**—The default font is something that's often overlooked by finance and accounting types, who tend to stick with boring fonts like Arial or Helvetica. In Excel 2007, Microsoft changed the default to something called Calibri, which is a substantial improvement. But you might want to use something different (Times New Roman is tried and true), and with the Use This as the Default Font option, you can change the default font to whatever you want.
- **Font Size**—The default font size is another element that you can change. The default is 11 point. Most people generally don't use a size under 10 or over 12, but you can change it until you get it where you want it.
- **Default View for New Sheets**—You have three options here. Normal View is the default. The other two, Page Break Preview and Page Layout View, are primarily for page setup before printing, but some people prefer them to Normal view.
- **Include This Many Sheets**—The default is to open a workbook with 3 worksheets. If you create a lot of 1-worksheet workbooks, you might want to cut that to 1 instead of sending out workbooks with 2 extra sheets or having to delete them before you send them out. The number of new worksheets you can have in new workbooks is limited purely by your sanity; most people will never need more than 3 on a normal basis, but if you deal with a lot of monthly scenarios, you might want to set this option to 12 (1 for each month) or 13 (1 for each month and 1 for a summary worksheet).

The Personalize Your Copy of Microsoft Office Section

The Personalize Your Copy of Microsoft Office section of the General tab includes the following options:

- **User Name**—The default user name is whatever name you entered when you installed Office, but you can change it here to be whatever you want. A lot of corporate installations simply use the company name, or a login name, and this is where you can personalize things a bit. The User Name field accepts punctuation, so you can have a proper name like "John "Doc" Holliday IV, Esq." if you want. This is one of the areas where Microsoft has gone to great lengths to allow you to personalize Excel the way you want it.
- **Office Background**—I've never found a use for this option, but if you want a bit of flair at the top right of your screen, give it a shot.
- **Office Theme**—The Office theme options are limited to Colorful (default), Dark Gray, Black, and White. I generally leave the Colorful option selected, although Black is very popular.

The Formulas Tab

Many of the options on the Formulas tab won't yet make sense to you if you're new to Excel, so it's best to leave the defaults in place for now. The following sections walk through the various options on this tab so you can come back to this part of the book when you're ready to customize the Formulas options.

The Calculation Options Section

The Calculation Options section of the Formulas tab includes the following options:

- **Workbook Calculation**—The primary options to consider here are Automatic and Manual. Normally a worksheet automatically calculates whenever you complete a formula and then press **Enter**; this is referred to as *confirming* a formula. However, you can control when a worksheet calculates by setting Workbook Calculation to Manual. This can be important if you ever build a workbook with a lot of formulas, and you don't want Excel to slow you down by continuously updating.
- **Recalculate Workbook Before Saving**—This option is especially useful if you have a workbook that takes a long time to recalculate, and you don't want to wait for it to do its thing while it closes. You'd think that with today's computers, this wouldn't be an issue, but keep in mind that Excel has an expanded working area with more than 1 billion cells (compared to just over 1 million in earlier versions). It's easy to overwhelm your computer when you start building workbooks that have hundreds, thousands, and even hundreds of thousands of formulas.
- **Enable Iterative Calculation**—This option is related to certain data analysis tools and complex formula methodology, so it won't be a concern to you at this point—and it may never be. In all my years of using Excel, I don't think I've needed to change this option more than a handful of times.

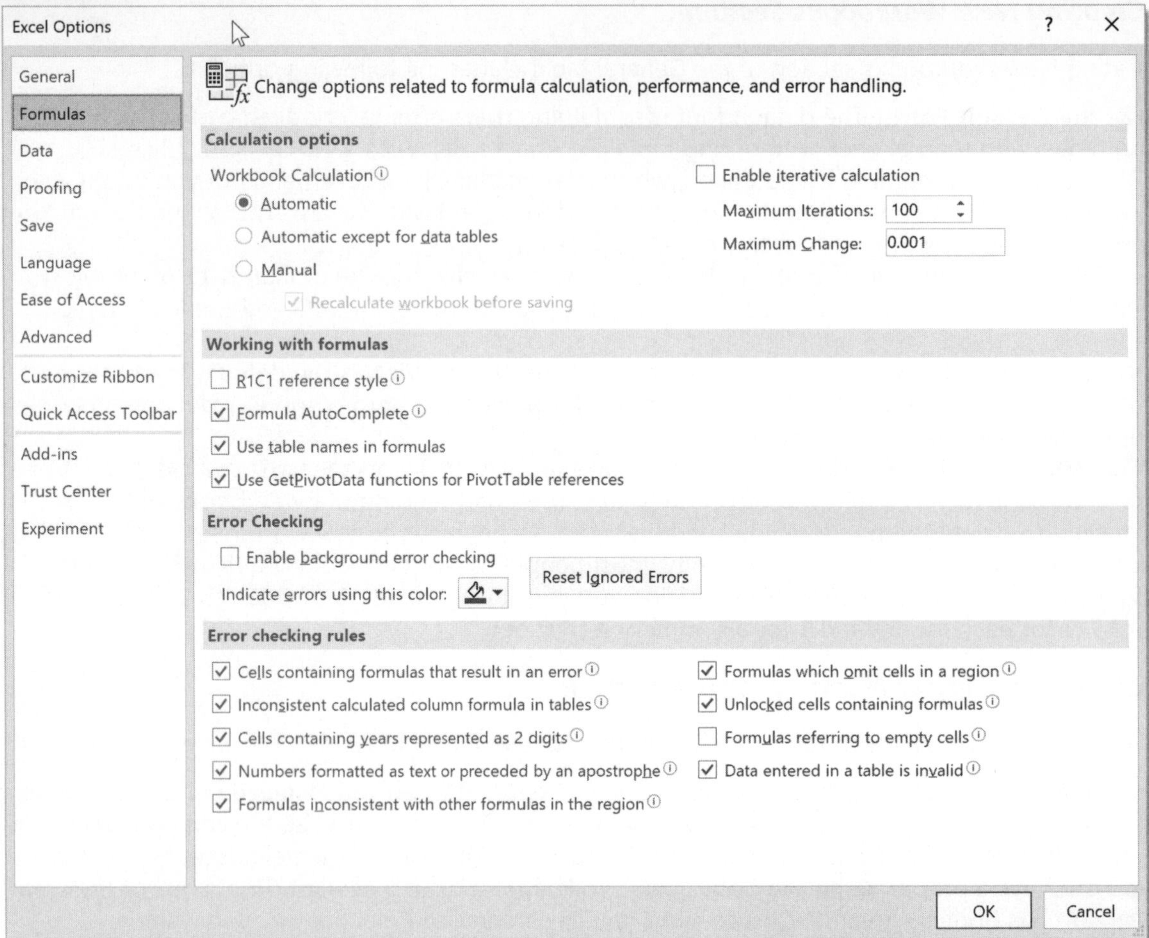

The Working with Formulas Section

The Working with Formulas section of the Formulas tab includes the following options:

- **R1C1 Reference Style**—This option changes your formula references from the A1 style, where a cell or range location uses the column and header address to name the address (e.g., A1:C7) to R1C1 style, which uses the much harder-to-read R[1]C[1] notation (e.g., R3C2 for row 3, column 2). This isn't something to worry about now, but it can come into play when you start working with macros.
- **Formula AutoComplete**—This feature is one you should leave on! It allows Excel to finish a formula for you, and while Excel doesn't always get it right, it does a pretty good job and helps you complete formulas much more quickly and accurately than you could do on your own.
- **Use Table Names in Formulas**—Again, you should leave this option as it is. Chapter 10 discusses tables, which have their own syntax called structured referencing; this syntax can be easier to understand than non-table formulas.
- **Use GetPivotData Functions for PivotTable References**—GetPivotData functions are powerful tools for referencing information from PivotTables, which are discussed in Chapter 11. Leave this option set at its default.

The Error Checking Section

If you leave Enable Background Error Checking selected, when you have errors in formulas or inconsistencies between certain ranges, Excel points them out for you by putting a small green triangle in the upper-right corner of a cell. For now, you'll probably want to leave this feature enabled and also leave all of the related default error checking rules checked as well. It is a valuable learning tool. When you're comfortable working with functions, you can start disabling these options. And, in case you're not fond of green, you have the option to change the error color.

The Data Tab

The Data tab deals primarily with data analysis and import tools. For now, it's best to just leave the default settings where they are. The most important option here is the Edit Default Layout button. You'll find this option to be invaluable when you start using PivotTables (discussed in Chapter 11); it's a huge timesaver.

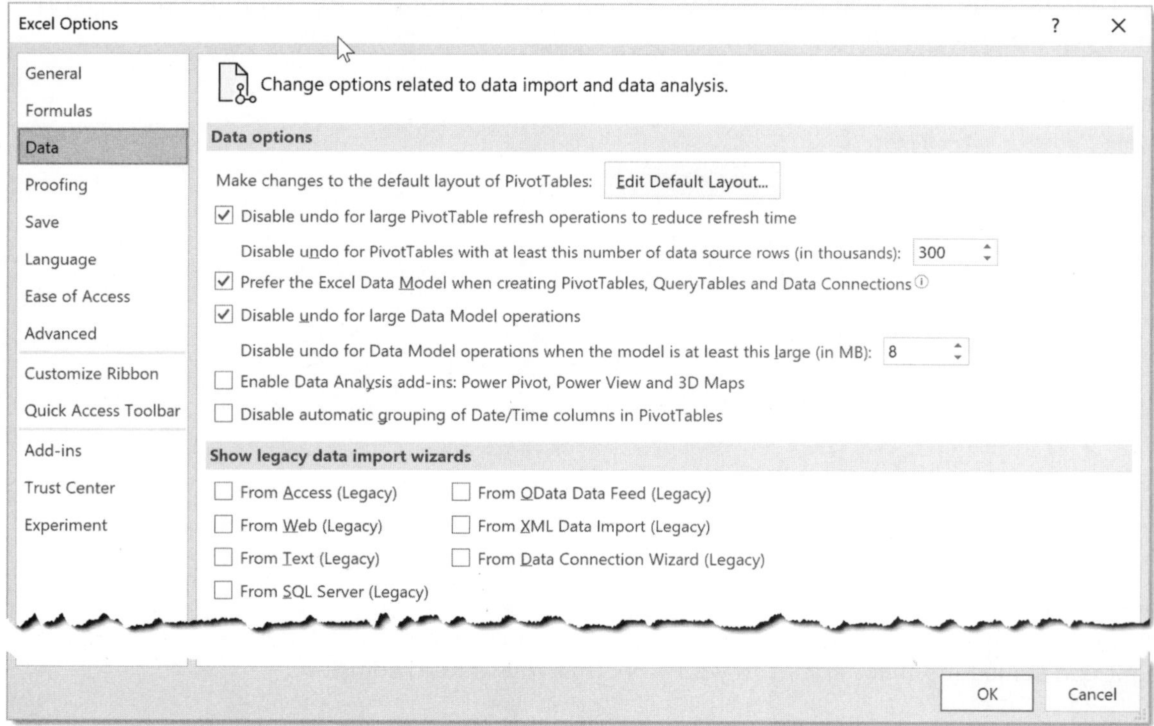

The Proofing Tab

The Proofing tab is a fairly minimal group of options, and the only things to really discuss in detail here are Excel's AutoCorrect and custom dictionary options. The rest should be self-explanatory, and how you have them set will largely depend on how you enter data. For instance, some people choose to enter customer details in UPPERCASE and want Excel to ignore this type of entry. If Ignore Words in UPPERCASE is not selected, then every customer name you enter in uppercase will show up as an error that Excel wants to fix.

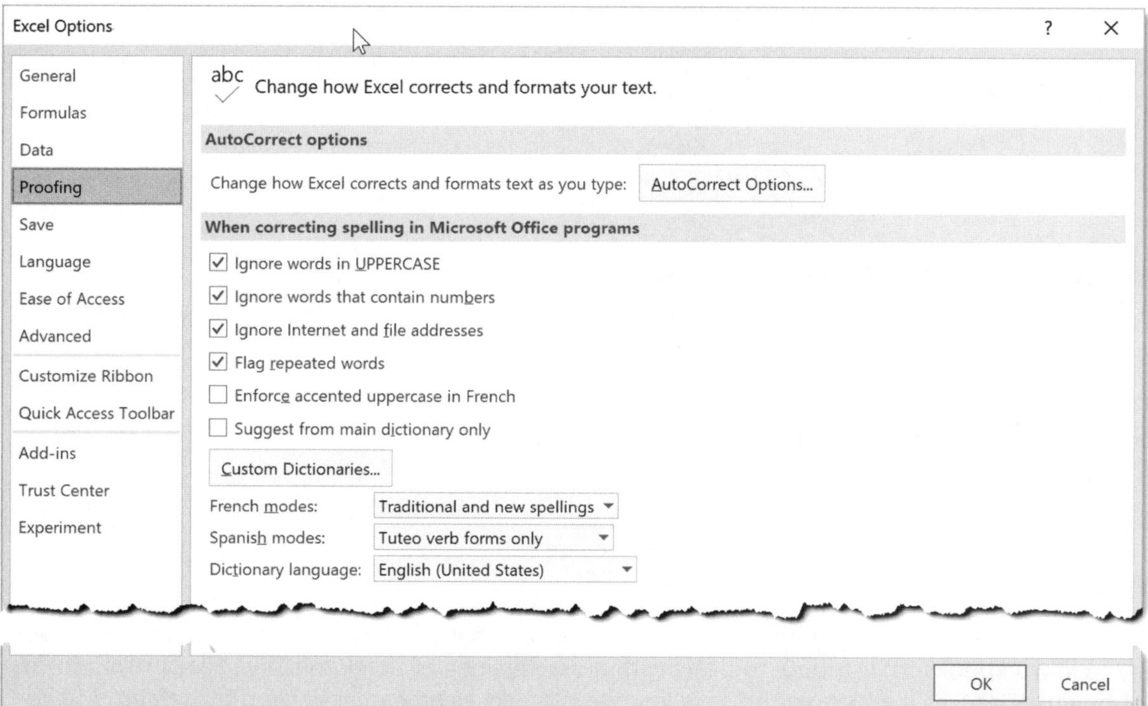

The AutoCorrect Options Button

AutoCorrect automatically corrects your misspellings for you. While Microsoft has done a great job of adding the most commonly misspelled words, it doesn't get them all. If you find yourself consistently misspelling certain words, you can add them to the AutoCorrect list. Just enter your commonly misspelled word in the Replace box and enter the correct spelling in the With box. For instance, if you're like me, you might want to have AutoCorrect replace "Thnaks" with "Thanks".

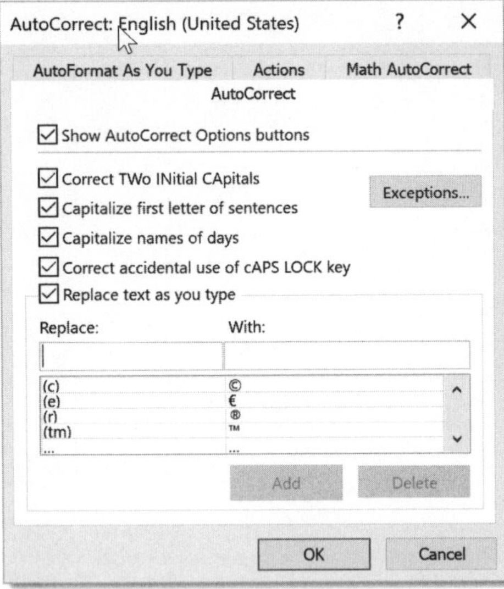

The AutoFormat As You Type, Actions, and Math AutoCorrect options are rarely used, but feel free to explore them. You might find something that pertains to your work that you want to adjust.

The Custom Dictionaries Button

If you work in a business that has specialized names for parts (like a "Fetzer" valve) or its own unique lexicon, you might find yourself using the Custom Dictionaries button quite a bit. This option gives you the ability to add your own words to the Office dictionary. You don't have to come here to add words to the dictionary, though; if you run spell check on a sheet (**Review > Spelling**), you have the option to add any words that Excel doesn't like just by clicking the Add to Dictionary button, shown below.

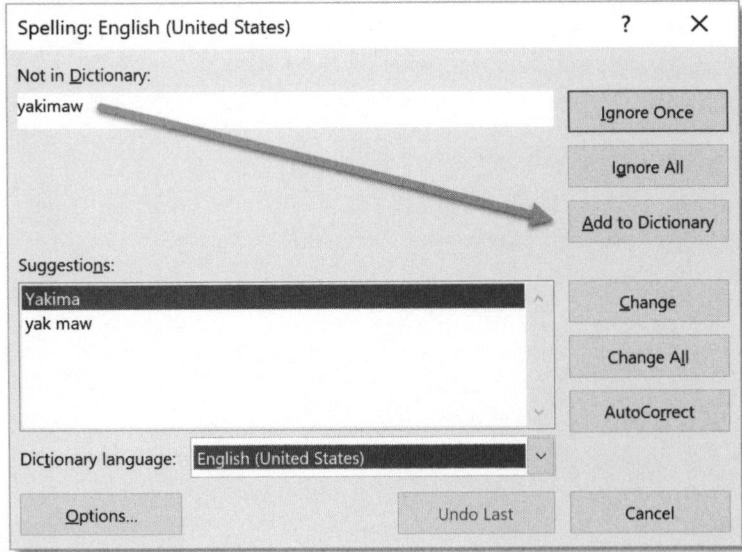

The Save Tab

Your Save tab options are relatively straightforward, and it's unlikely that you'll change much of anything here. If you regularly save workbooks to distribute to users with older versions of Excel, the Save Files in This Format text box might be important, as it allows you to save your workbooks as an earlier version by default. Just realize that if you do this, any elements you might have added that aren't supported by earlier versions will be disabled.

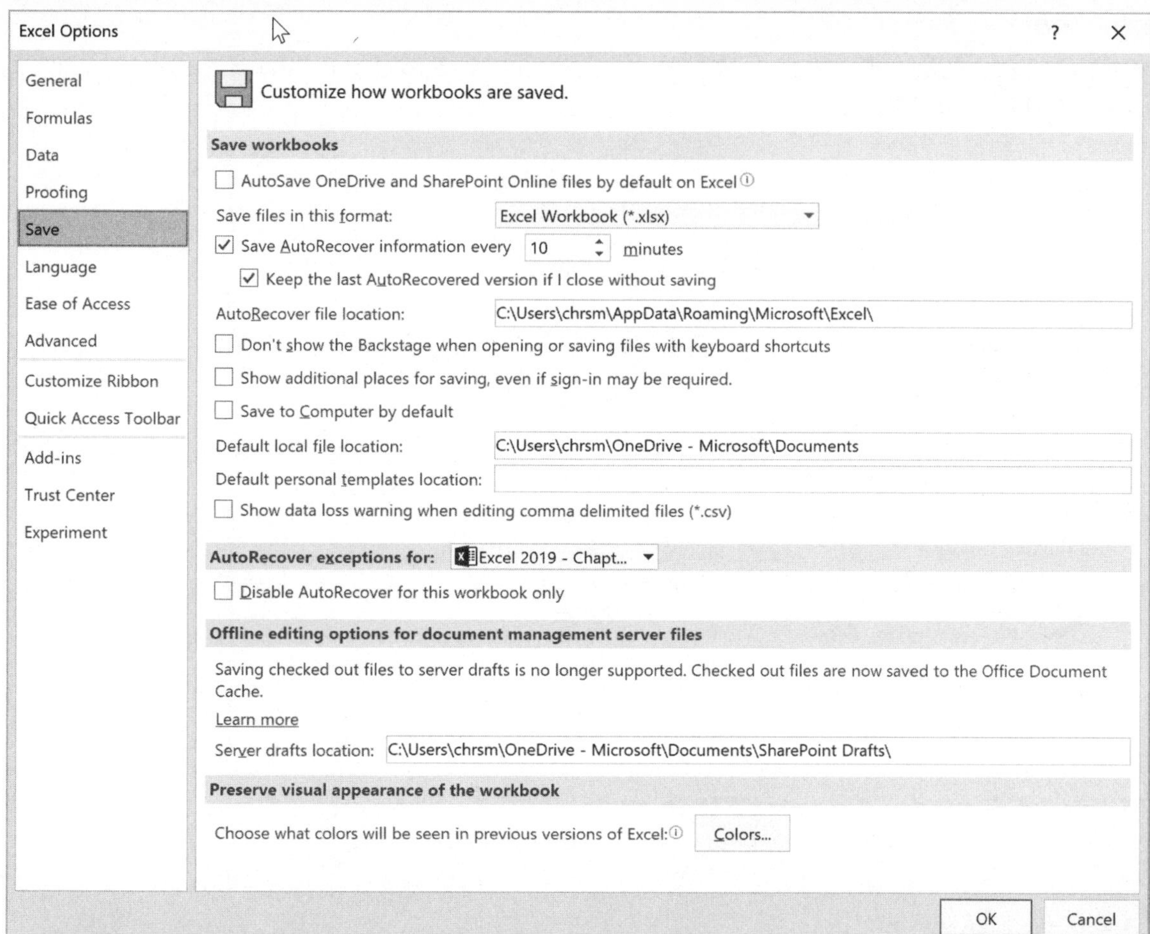

Note: By now maybe you're starting to see that the folks at Microsoft have done their best to link all of these elements together, and it is often possible to access a particular feature or option from multiple places. As you start to get more comfortable with Excel, you'll discover which ways you most like to do the things that you commonly do.

AutoRecover is an important feature, and it's recommended that you leave it on. When you have AutoRecover turned on, if Excel crashes, it uses the latest version of your work to recover. If you don't have AutoRecover turned on, Excel does its best to recover your workbook, but it's likely that you will lose anything you entered between the time of your last save and the crash. Fortunately, Excel doesn't crash very often, but it's still good to know AutoRecover is there. Microsoft sets your AutoRecover location for you, but you can change it to anyplace you want. If you're using AutoSave, then AutoRecover is less important.

The Default Local File Location text box is important if you don't want to have to browse to a particular location each time you save a workbook. When you set the default location here, Excel automatically jumps there when you save a workbook.

Finally, this tab allows you to preserve the visual appearance of the workbook. For example, if you're going to be saving as earlier versions of Excel that don't support as many colors as Excel 2007 and later, you can access the previous Excel color palette. Otherwise, Excel will make a good effort to convert colors to be compatible with earlier versions. It's unlikely that you'll ever find a need for this option.

Note: Microsoft stopped supporting Excel 2003 quite some time ago, so I wouldn't necessarily be too worried about the Preserve Visual Appearance of the *workbook* or any other backward compatibility options.

The Language Tab

If you're based in the United States, the odds are slim that you'll ever need to change any of the options on the Language tab, which is shown here.

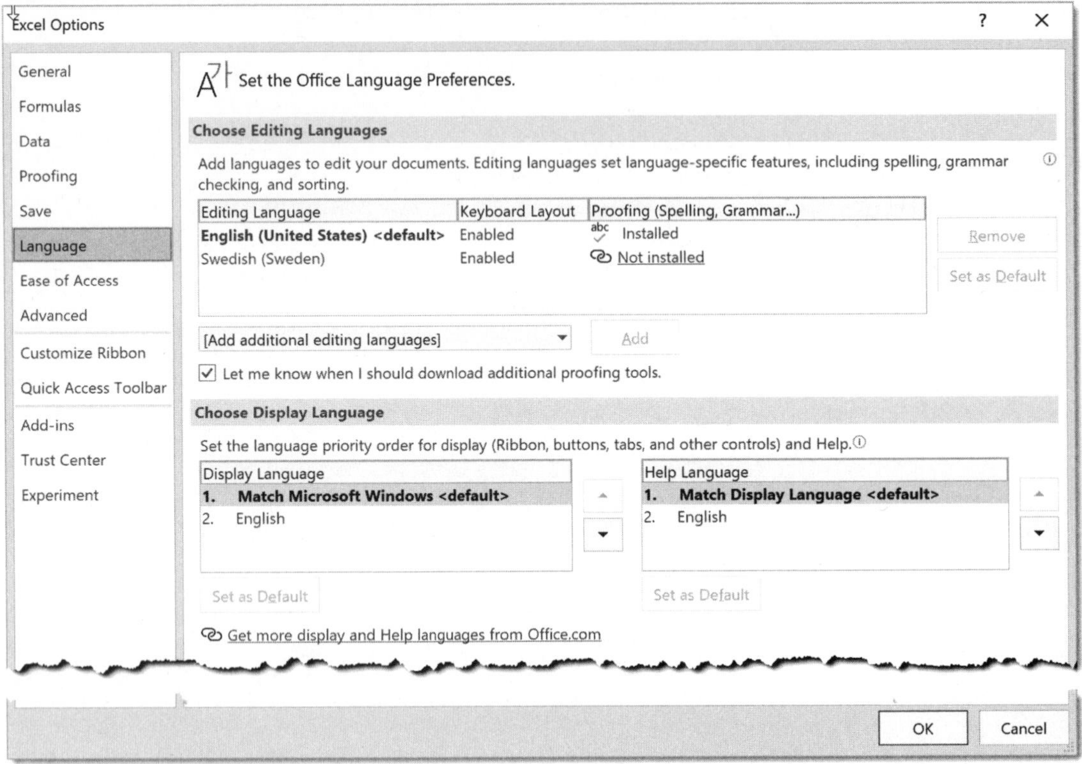

The Ease of Access Tab

The Ease of Access tab provides accessibility options for those with limited vision and other physical challenges. Unless you find yourself creating or distributing workbooks to people with accessibility issues, you can just leave these settings alone.

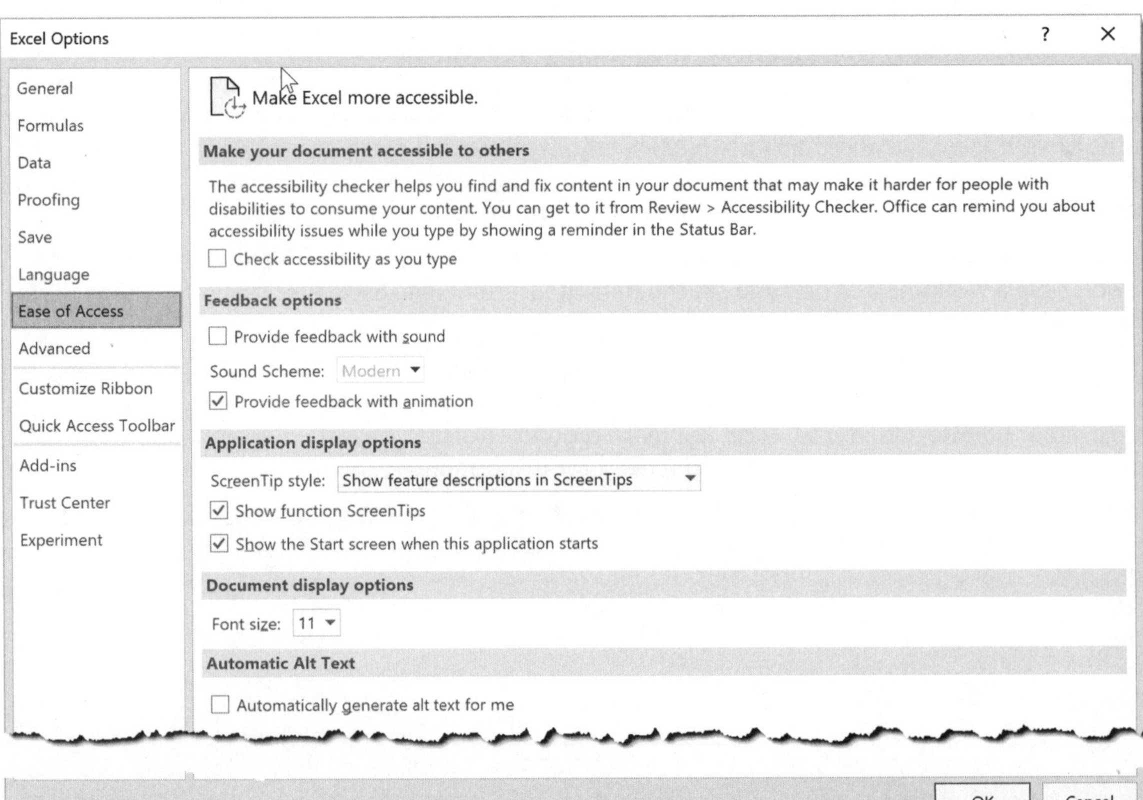

The Advanced Tab

The Advanced tab, where you will do the bulk of your customization, consists of multiple options that affect both worksheets and a workbook in general. You probably won't change any of these settings for now, but you might want to explore them as you get more comfortable with Excel. The following sections discuss some of the ones you're likely to want to play around with.

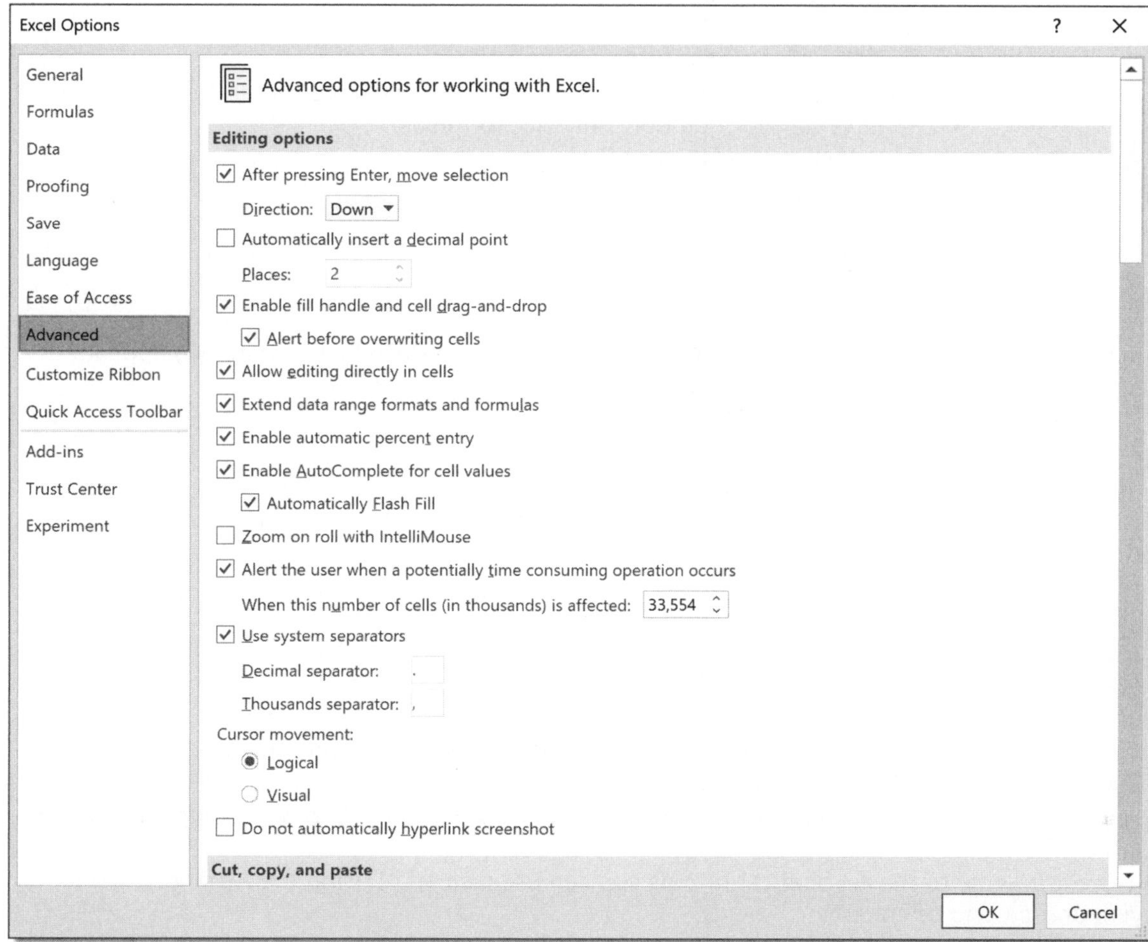

The Editing Options Section

In general, you can leave the options in the Editing Options section as they are. These options apply to the entire workbook, and they can be changed at any time:

- **After Pressing Enter, Move Selection**—The default is Down, but in some cases you might want to change it (specifically if you have to do a lot of data entry and are going from left-to-right or right-to-left).
- **Automatically Insert a Decimal Point**—If you turn this on, it is like the old adding machines. You type 12345 and Excel inserts 123.45 using the default places of 2.
- **Alert Before Overwriting Cells**—If this checkbox is selected and you drag the contents of one cell onto another, Excel ask if you really want to do that.
- **Automatically Flash Fill**—With this intelligent service, Excel helps you split or join text. All you need to do is give Excel a discernable pattern that it can learn from.
- **Zoom on Roll with IntelliMouse**—Go ahead, try it.
- **Alert the User When a Potentially Time Consuming Operation Occurs**—For this option, you set the number of cells to evaluate for potential changes.
- **Use System Separators**—If you're in the United States, you can leave this alone. Some other countries use commas in place of decimal points and vice versa, and you can set such options here.

The Cut, Copy, and Paste Section

The Cut, Copy, and Paste section of the Advanced tab includes the following options:

- **Show Paste Options Button When Content Is Pasted**—Checking this checkbox gives you some expanded pasting options that appear to the right of the pasted cell and when you select **Home > Paste**

drop-down. To try out the paste options, enter something in a cell and click Copy and then click in another cell and click the Paste drop-down. You see the following options, as shown below:

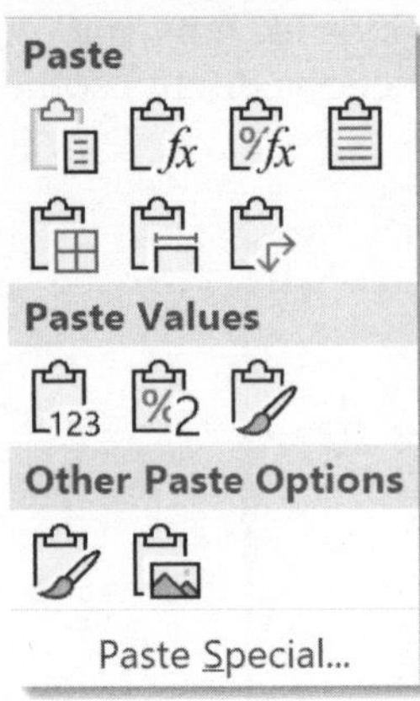

- Paste
- Paste Formulas
- Paste Formulas and Number Formatting
- Keep Source Formatting
- No Borders
- Keep Source Column Widths
- Transpose (which switches columns to rows and vice versa)
- Paste Values (for numbers only, not formulas)
- Paste Values and Number Formatting
- Paste Values and Source Formatting
- Paste Formatting
- Paste a Picture
- Paste Special

- **Show Insert Options Buttons**—If this checkbox is selected, the Insert dialog (shown below) appears when you use a Ribbon command to insert rows or columns.

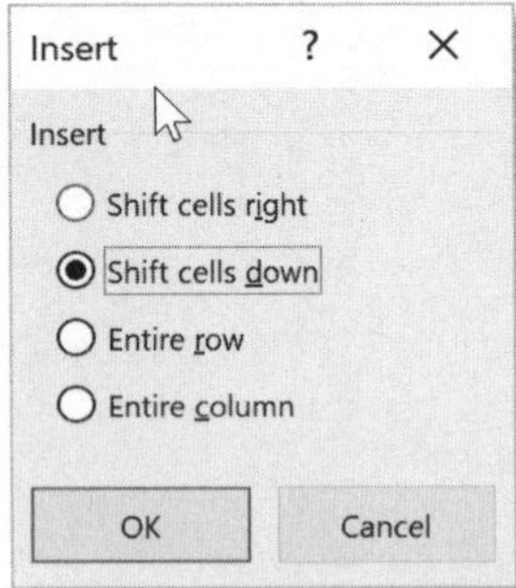

- **Cut, Copy, and Sort Inserted Objects with Their Parent Cells**—If you select this checkbox, Excel makes sure that if you resize rows and columns, any objects (images, controls, etc.) you've added retain their position relative to where you originally placed them. You can also change this for each object in its individual properties by right-clicking it.

The following table lists some of the keyboard shortcuts you can use instead of using the Advanced tab for a variety of copying and pasting operations.

Keyboard Shortcuts for Copying and Pasting

Shortcut	Description
Ctrl+C	Copy
Ctrl+V	Paste
Alt+E+S+V	Paste values
Alt+I+R	Insert row
Alt+I+C	Insert column
Alt+E+D+R	Insert row
Alt+E+D+C	Insert column

The Pen Section

The Use Pen to Select and Interact with Content by Default option works only if you're using a touchscreen-enabled device and have a pen.

The Image Size and Quality Section

The Image Size and Quality section of the Advanced tab includes the following options:

- **Discard Editing Data**—If you select this checkbox, you tell Excel to delete data that it saves when you edit images so they can be returned to their original state if you don't like the changes.

- **Do Not Compress Images in File**—Checking this checkbox can result in very large image sizes (and therefore large file sizes). By default Excel compresses images so they take up less space.
- **Default Resolution**—You can set this option to High Fidelity, 330 ppi, 220 ppi, 150 ppi, or 96 ppi.

The Print Section

The only option in this section is High Quality Mode for Graphics. You should leave this option unselected unless you need to print a detailed parts list or a brochure. Otherwise, Excel will take up a lot of resources printing details you might not need.

The Chart Section

The Chart section of the Advanced tab includes the following options:

- **Show Chart Element Names on Hover**—When you select this option, Excel gives you a tooltips effect.
- **Show Data Point Values on Hover**—If you select this checkbox, Excel shows the value behind a data point on a chart.
- **Properties Follow Chart Data Point for All New Workbooks**—If you select this checkbox, custom formatting and data labels will follow data points in charts as you add new data. This can get irritating if you're creating multiple charts from a single template-style chart since your charts might not update consistently if they have different data sources.

The Display Section

The Display section of the Advanced tab includes the following options:

- **Show This Number of Recent Workbooks**—This is the number of recent file names that will show up in the Recent list in Backstage view (which you reach by selecting **File > Open > Recent**.
- **Quickly Access This Number of Recent Workbooks**—Choose this option and a few recent workbooks will appear in the left panel of the File menu..
- **Ruler Units**—The default is based on your Windows Regional Settings. In the United States it is inches.
- **Show Formula Bar**—You might want to turn off this option if you need to distribute a workbook and don't want people easily seeing your formulas.
- **Default Direction**—In the United States, leave this set to Left-to-Right.

The Display Options for This Workbook Section

The drop-down on the right of the Display Options for This Workbook section title allows you to choose any open workbook. The first three options can be handy when you distribute workbooks and want to minimize what the user sees:

- Show Horizontal Scroll Bar
- Show Vertical Scroll Bar
- Show Sheet Tabs

The Display Options for This Worksheet Section

The drop-down on the right of the Display Options for This Worksheet section title lets you select any worksheet. This section includes the following options:

- **Show Row and Column Headers**—This is an option you might turn off for a distributed workbook where you don't want the headers to be distracting. You can also toggle it on the View tab.
- **Show Formulas in Cells Instead of Their Calculated Results**—Instead of coming to this tab to change this setting, you can toggle it in a worksheet with **Ctrl+`** (which is above the Tab key).
- **Show Sheet Right-to-Left**—Selecting this option reverses the columns in your worksheet and puts the last column on the left and column A on the right. This is for languages that read right-to-left, such as Hebrew and Arabic. It can be fun to change this on unsuspecting co-workers.
- **Show Page Breaks**—Many people find this option very irritating. If you need to see page breaks, you're better off using the Page Break view.
- **Show a Zero in Cells That Have Zero Values**—This is important for worksheets that have formulas that return zeros. With a lot of information on a sheet, you might not want to see a lot of zeros from formulas that haven't populated yet. This is one option you will probably change quite a bit.

- **Show Outline Symbols if an Outline Is Applied**—Outlining is a way of compressing information into groups. The outline symbols let you expand or contract those groups, so you don't typically want to turn off this option.
- **Show Gridlines**—Gridlines are the natural dividers between cells and columns. Most times you will apply your own custom gridlines, so while it's often good to start a worksheet with this option on, you may find yourself coming here to turn it off as you get your worksheet completed. This is easier to toggle on the View tab.
- **Gridline Color**—You can change the default gridline color if the default gray isn't spicy enough for you. Note that your choices here are limited to the Excel 2003 color palette.

The Formulas Section

The Formulas section of the Advanced tab includes the following options:

- **Enable Multi-Threaded Calculation**—If you select this option, you can take advantages of multicore processors to help Excel calculate faster. This is especially important if you have the 64-bit version of Office.
- **Number of Calculation Threads**—For this option, you can select either of the following:
  - **Use all Processors on This Computer**—Select this option to use the number of processors Windows has identified on your system.
  - **Manual**—Use this spinner control to change the number of processors to use.

The When Calculating This Workbook Section

The drop-down on the right of the When Calculating This Workbook section title allows you to choose any open workbook. This section includes the following options:

- **Update Links to Other Documents**—If you have linked to other workbooks with formulas, you can choose to have Excel automatically update them when you open the workbook. Otherwise, Excel will ask you to manually update them.
- **Set Precision as Displayed**—This has to do with rounding and how to calculate values. Unchecking this option can cause problems over time as it can affect your data and formula output with regard to multiple-value rounding, which can lead to unanticipated results.
- **Use 1904 Date System**—This is relevant only if you're using a Mac, which uses a different date system than Windows. Excel for Windows uses dates that begin on January 1, 1900. For some odd reason, Macs start in 1904. Excel won't allow negative times unless you switch to the 1904 date system.
- **Save External Link Values**—Select this option to save values from formulas that are linked to other workbooks, as well as the formulas. It can come in handy if you send workbooks to other people who might not have the linked workbooks: When they open your workbook, they see the formula results instead of errors.

The General Section

The General section of the Advanced tab includes the following options:

- **Ask to Update Automatic Links**—When you open a workbook that has links to another workbook, you are prompted about whether you want to update those links. If you do this a lot, you probably want to turn off this option.
- **Show Add-in User Interface Errors**—Unless you deal with a lot of add-ins or at some point want to create your own, you can leave this alone. By default if there is an error when an add-in tries to load, there's no error message; the add-in just doesn't load. If you select this option, Excel will let you know if there are any errors.
- **Scale Content for A4 or 8.5" x 11" Paper Sizes**—If you select this option, Excel will automatically try to fit your workbook in an 8.5" x 11" format, which is the U.S. standard (A4 is European).
- **At Startup Open All Files In**—If you have a folder that contains workbooks you use daily, you can set the path to that folder, and all the workbooks in that folder will open each time you open Excel. This isn't recommended unless you have a workbook that you keep open all day.
- **Web Options**—By clicking this button, you can set options related to saving Excel workbooks as web pages or posting documents to a website.
- **Enable Multi-threaded Processing**—If you have a multi-core processor, you'll probably want to leave this on. If you don't know what kind of processor you have, don't worry about it.
- **Create Lists for Use in Sorts and Fill Sequences**—This option deals with custom lists, and of all the general options, this is one that you might actually change, especially if you have a business with some fairly

repetitive information you need to enter regularly, such as department names. Clicking the Edit Custom Lists button brings up the following dialog, where you can add your own lists.

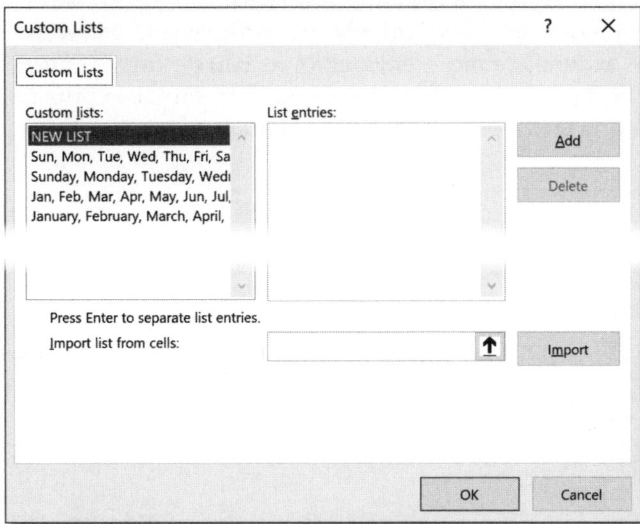

- Custom lists work with AutoFill, which you use by grabbing the fill handle, the little icon that appears at the bottom of an Excel cell when you activate it (as shown below). If you have a defined list, you only need to enter one of the list values and then grab the fill handle and drag it down or across, and Excel completes the list entries for you for as long as you keep dragging—and it repeats the list when it gets to the end of it.

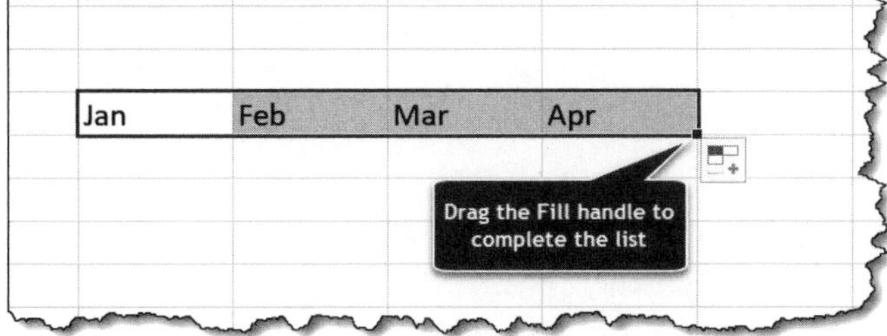

The Lotus Compatibility Section

You can ignore the options in the Lotus Compatibility section. Lotus 1-2-3 hasn't been a viable spreadsheet option for quite some time, and these options are going away soon to make room for new functionality.

The Customize Ribbon Tab

The Customize Ribbon tab allows you to add menu commands to the Ribbon and display only the commands that you want. For now the defaults should suffice, but feel free to play around with the options and see what kind of combinations you can come up with to make your experience more enjoyable. As you get more comfortable with Excel and its Ribbon commands, you might find yourself creating your own Ribbon tabs containing just the commands you use the most. If you don't like any changes that you make, you can just click the Reset button toward the bottom of this tab.

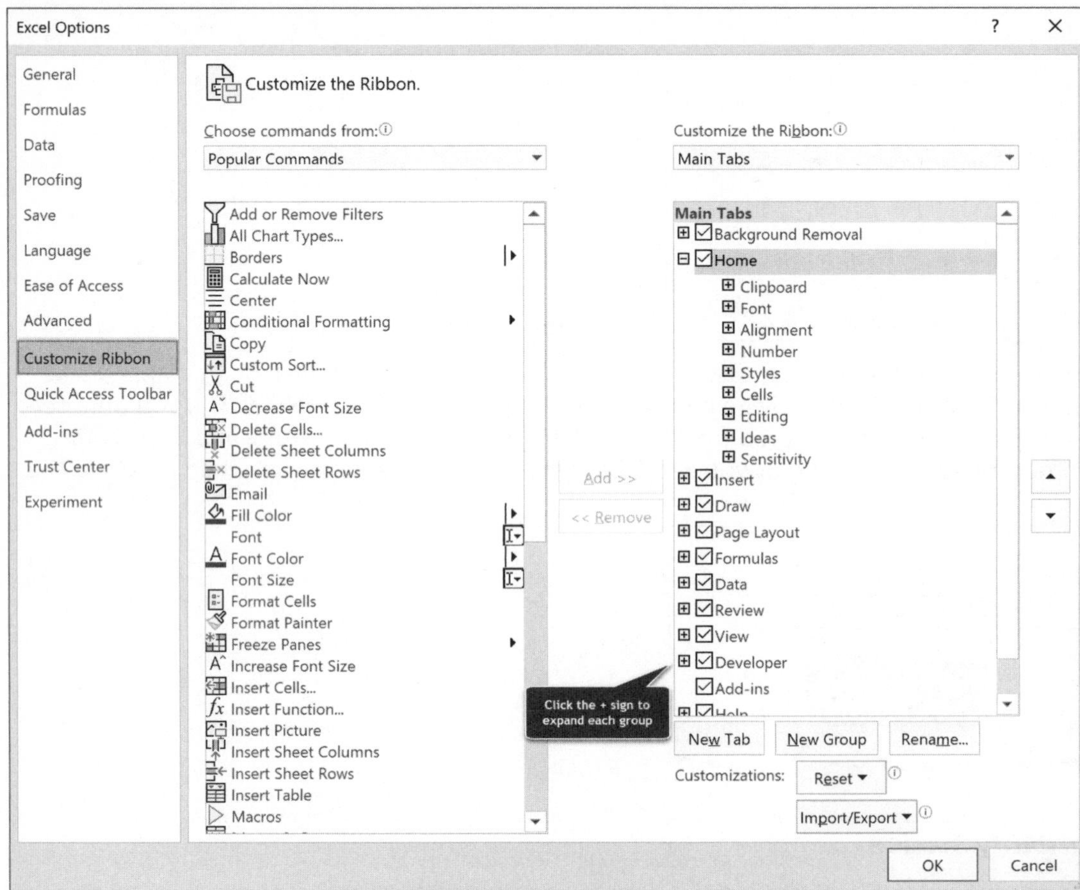

The Choose Commands From option on the left side of this tab (shown in more detail below) allows you to filter the list of available commands. If you don't see something in the current list of options, you should look here.

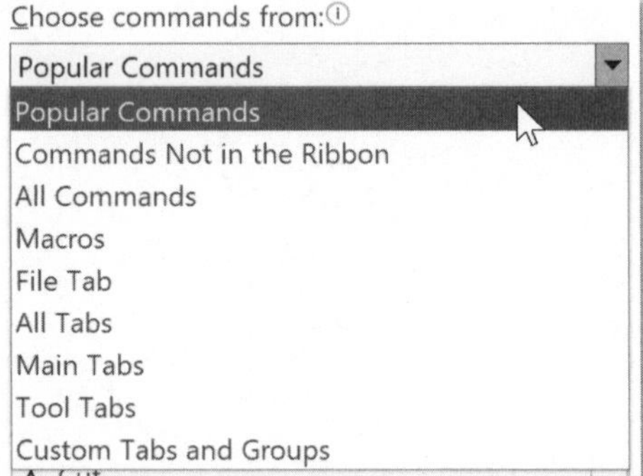

The Customize the Ribbon option on the right side of this tab lets you choose which Ribbon tab you want to customize, as shown below.

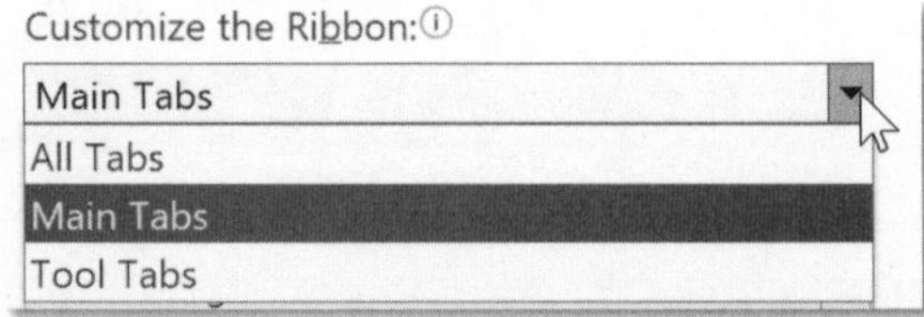

The Quick Access Toolbar Tab

As mentioned previously, the Quick Access Toolbar (QAT) is a toolbar of frequently used commands that sits above the Ribbon. If you're a heavy mouse user, then the QAT will probably come in very handy, as it puts everything right up front for you, so you don't have to go through different ribbon tabs/groups. If you're a keyboard user, you may never even adjust the default QAT settings. The Quick Access Toolbar tab is very similar to the Customize Ribbon tab, but it's a bit simpler. The default setting for the Choose Commands From drop-down is Popular Commands (as shown below), so if you can't find something in the list, just change the selection to All Commands or Commands Not in the Ribbon.

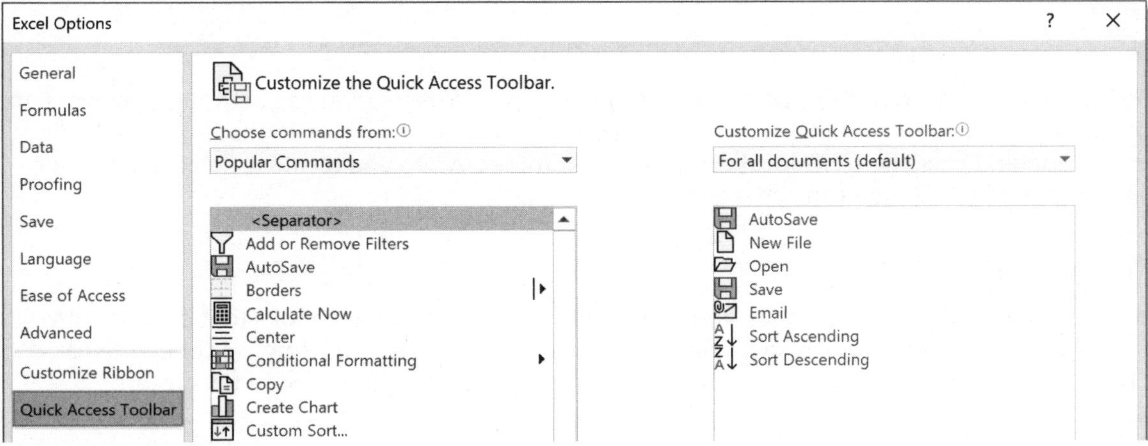

The Add-ins Tab

As mentioned previously, add-ins are additions to what is included natively with Excel. There are add-ins that Microsoft creates, and there are also add-ins created by third parties. The Add-ins tab allows you to manage add-ins, and the Add-Ins tab on the Ribbon exposes the functionality of those add-ins.

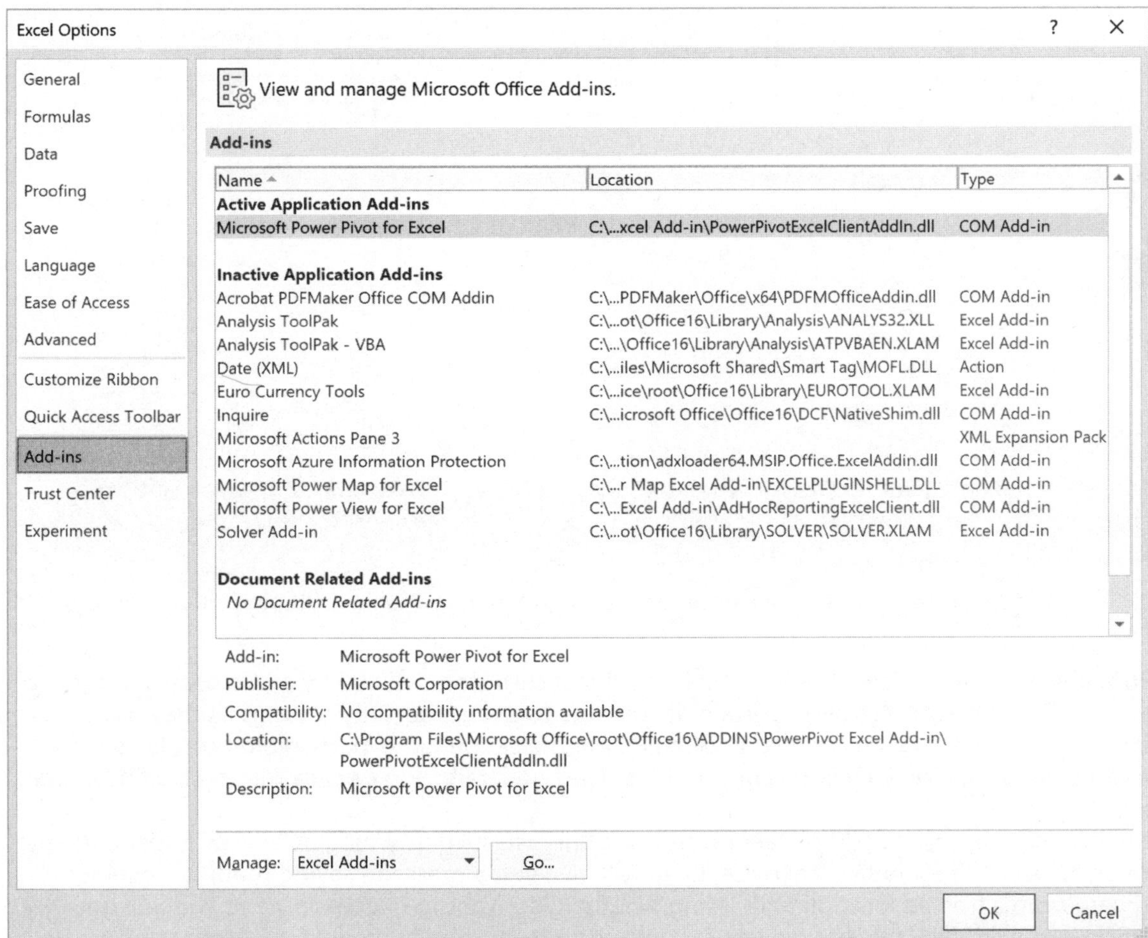

At the top of this tab is the Active Application Add-ins list, and below that is the Inactive Application Add-ins list. If you click on any of the add-ins, Excel shows a description of it at the bottom of the tab.

At the bottom of the Add-ins tab is a Manage drop-down, which lets you select the type of add-in you want to work with, as shown below.

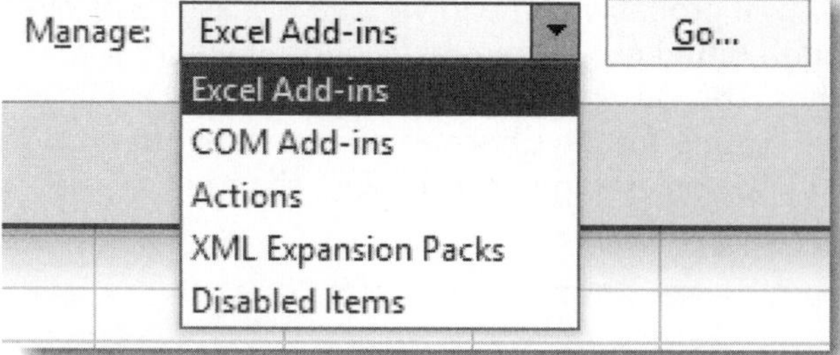

Clicking the Go button brings up a dialog that shows you the available add-ins. You can activate/deactivate an add-in by clicking the checkbox to the left of its name. If you want to activate an add-in that is not in the list, click the Browse button and navigate to its location on your computer. When you locate it, select it and click OK; it then appears in the list, and you can activate it.

The Trust Center Tab

The Trust Center primarily deals with how to tell your computer to respond to workbooks that contain VBA (Visual Basic for Applications) code—which could be code you recorded, code you wrote, or code in third-party add-ins. What you're interested with on the Trust Center tab is the Trust Center Settings button.

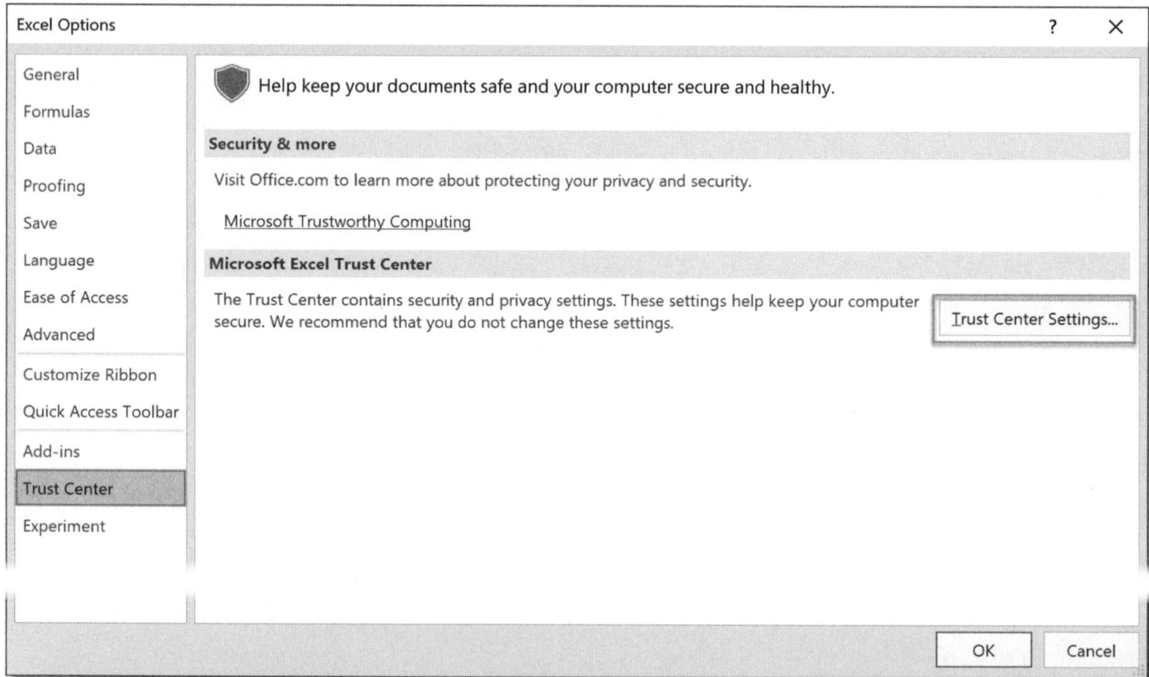

Note: Before you change any of the Trust Center settings, you should make sure to have an antivirus program installed. Microsoft provides Windows Defender for free with Windows, but you need to make sure it's enabled.

When you click Trust Center Settings, the Trust Center appears, and in it you have multiple options, as shown below:

- **Trusted Publishers**—This is relevant only if you have digital certificates issued by a Microsoft third-party certificate issuer. These certificates allow certain documents to bypass security settings as they have been deemed trustworthy. As with Microsoft's SharePoint application, third-party digital certificates are expensive and usually used only by large corporations. They generally don't play a role in small business applications.
- **Trusted Locations**—You should add certain locations to this list, such as your Documents folder and any other folders you access frequently; otherwise, Excel will give you a message saying that the document didn't originate from a trusted location and asking whether you want to enable content. This will get very old very quickly. You can click the Add New Location button to browse to the folder of your choice.

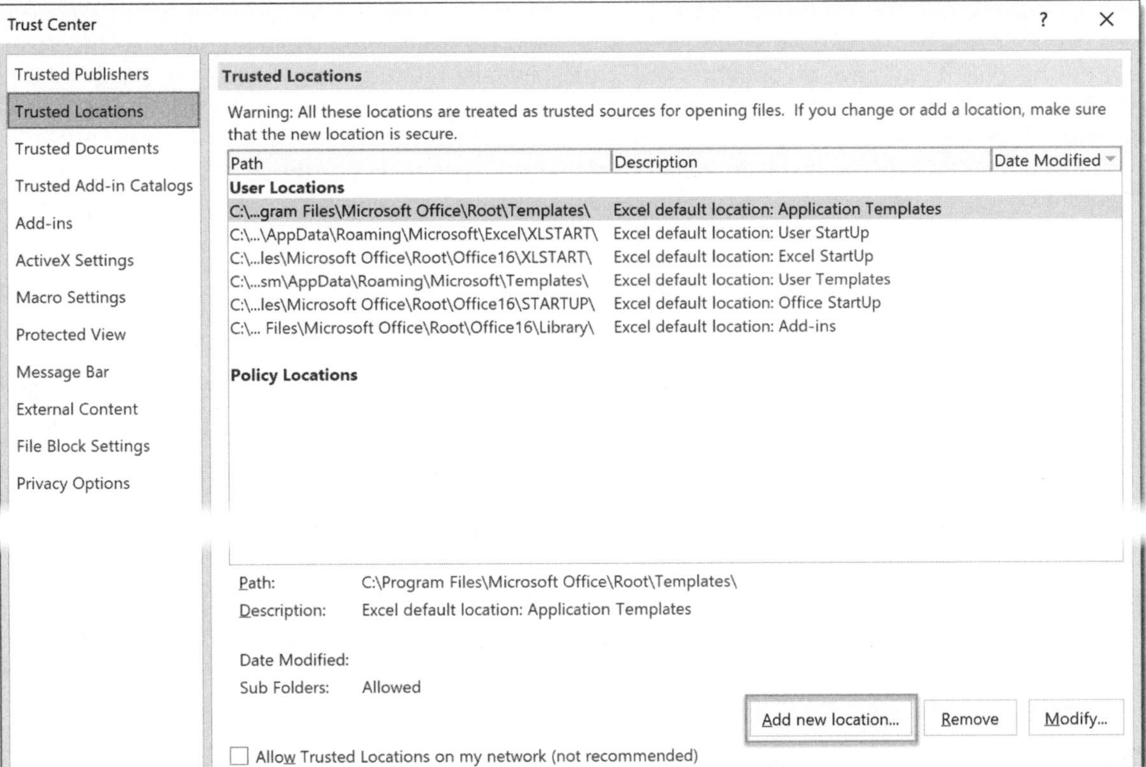

- **Trusted Documents**—When you open a document from an untrusted source, such as a file sharing site, Excel gives you the option to permanently trust it.

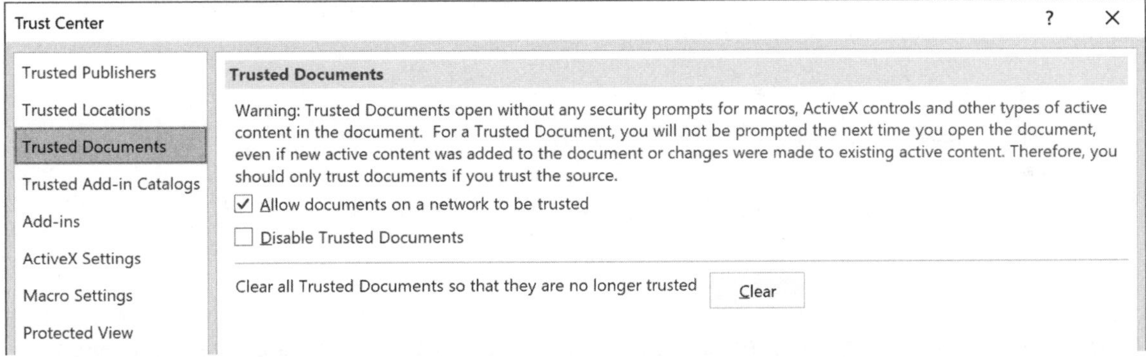

- **Add-ins**—The Add-ins area of the Trust Center simply gives you the option to require that add-ins be signed by a trusted publisher, which requires that they have a Microsoft third-party approved digital signature. If you already know who provided an add-in and have installed it, it's unlikely that you'll need to go to this length. This should, however, show how serious Microsoft is about protecting you and your information.
- **ActiveX Settings**—ActiveX controls are interactive objects such as checkboxes and radio buttons that you can add to your workbooks. They are all controlled via VBA code, so here's another instance where Microsoft is trying to protect you from potentially malicious content. As you can see below, this section gives you several options.

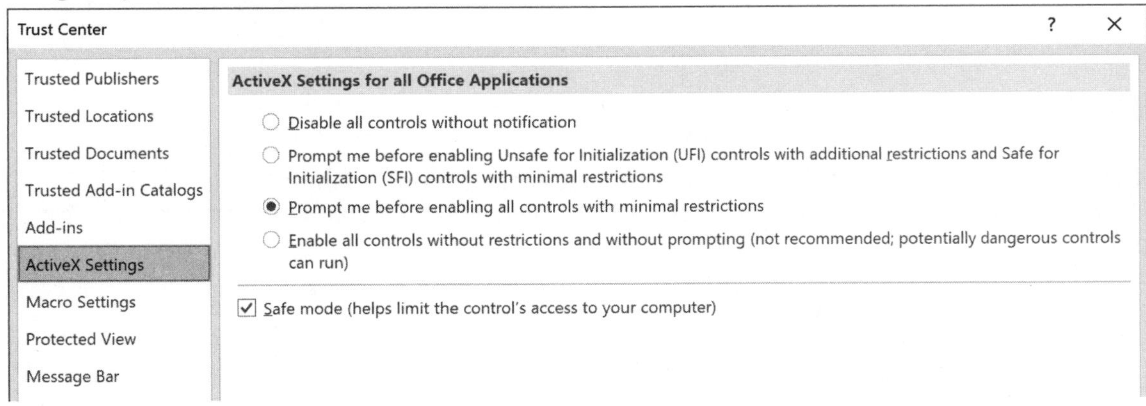

- **Macro Settings**—These options are designed to give you control over what VBA code can run in Excel (including your own). Generally, if you have an antivirus application installed, you use the Enable All Macros option—but do this *only* if you have an antivirus application installed! Otherwise, choose the Disable All Macros with Notification option so that Excel will give you the option to allow macros to run or not.
- **Developer Macro Settings**—This section includes the checkbox Trust Access to the VBA Project Object Model. If you have any VBA add-ins installed, make sure that this is checked, or those add-ins might not work.

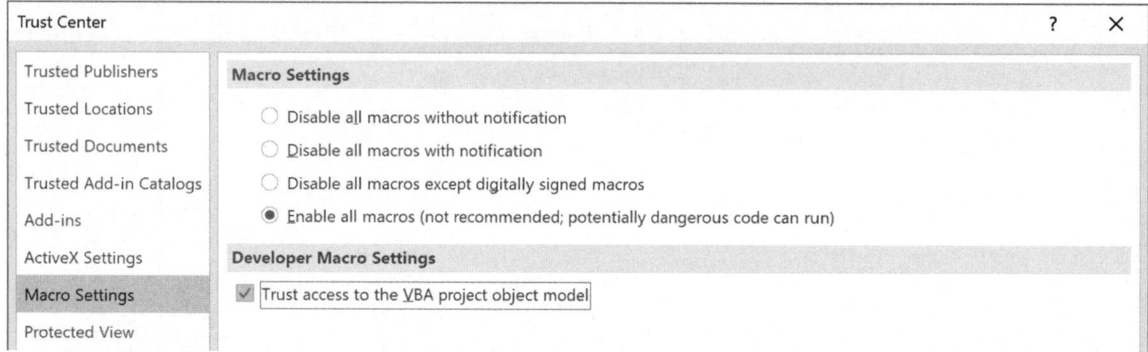

- **Protected View**—This section gives you the option of allowing content from workbooks that originate from the Internet or email attachments. You should leave these options enabled, as you never know what might be in such files. If you have an antivirus application installed, it should scan those workbooks first as well. I've been very happy with Windows Defender, which comes with Windows.

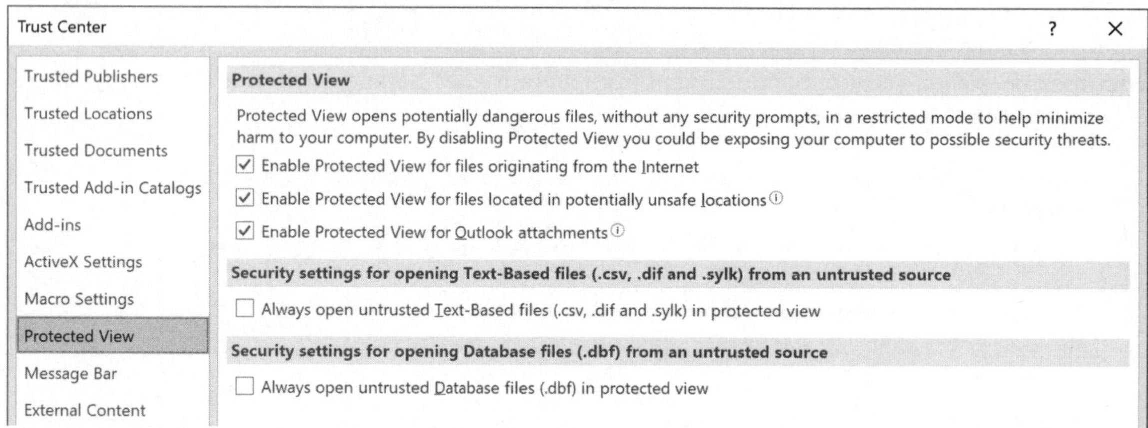

- **Message Bar**—This section enables you to have Excel show a notification when you open a workbook if it has blocked content. It's a good idea to leave this option enabled. You can always choose to ignore the notifications.

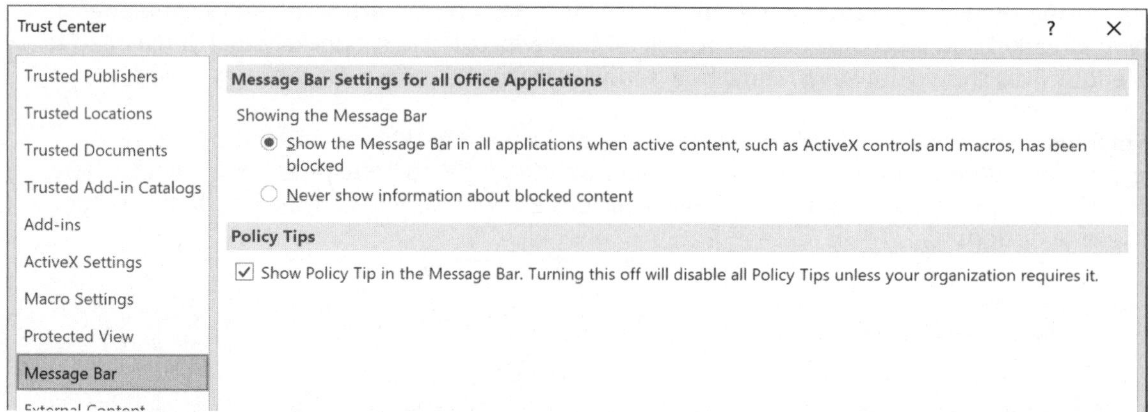

- **External Content**—You'll probably have no need to change these options, as the defaults should be suitable. However, if you deal with a lot of external data or linked workbooks, you might want to disable notifications.

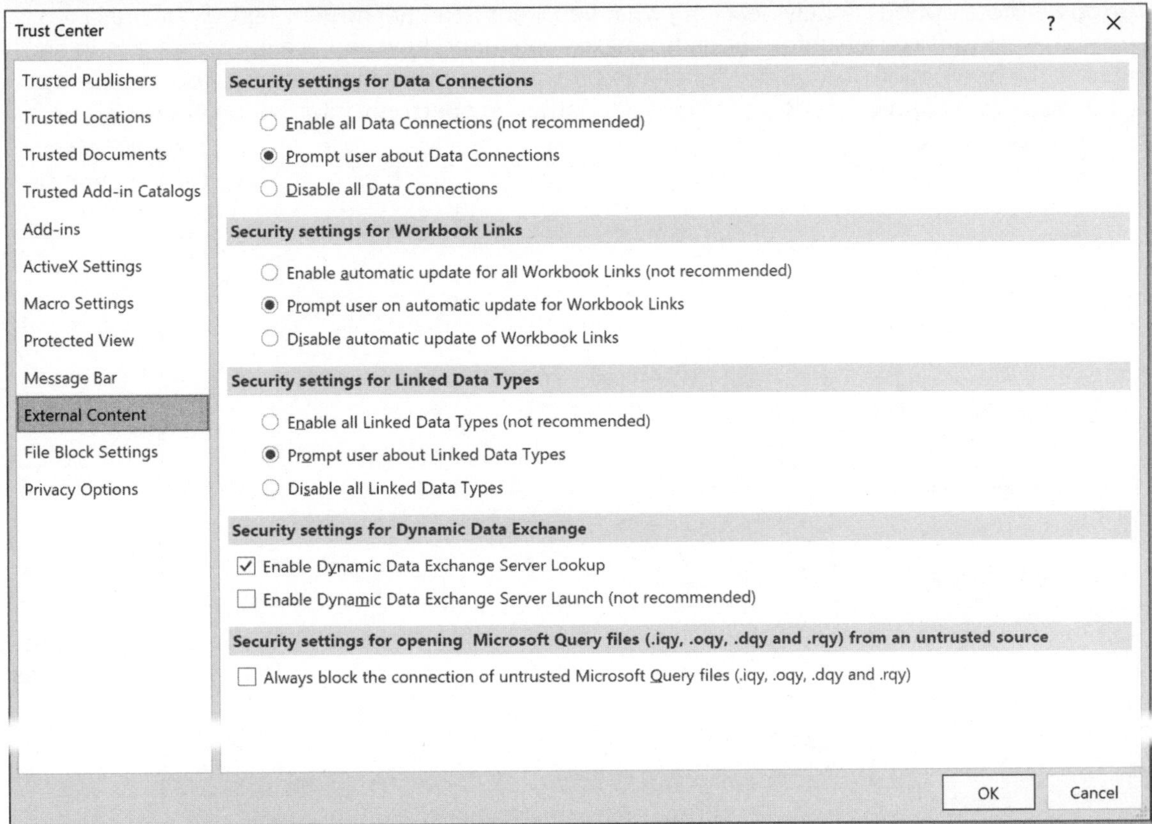

- **File Block Settings**—This section gives you the ability to automatically flag certain workbook types and open them in protected view. Again, the default settings should suffice, unless you find yourself frequently opening files of a certain type and want to make sure their content is disabled.

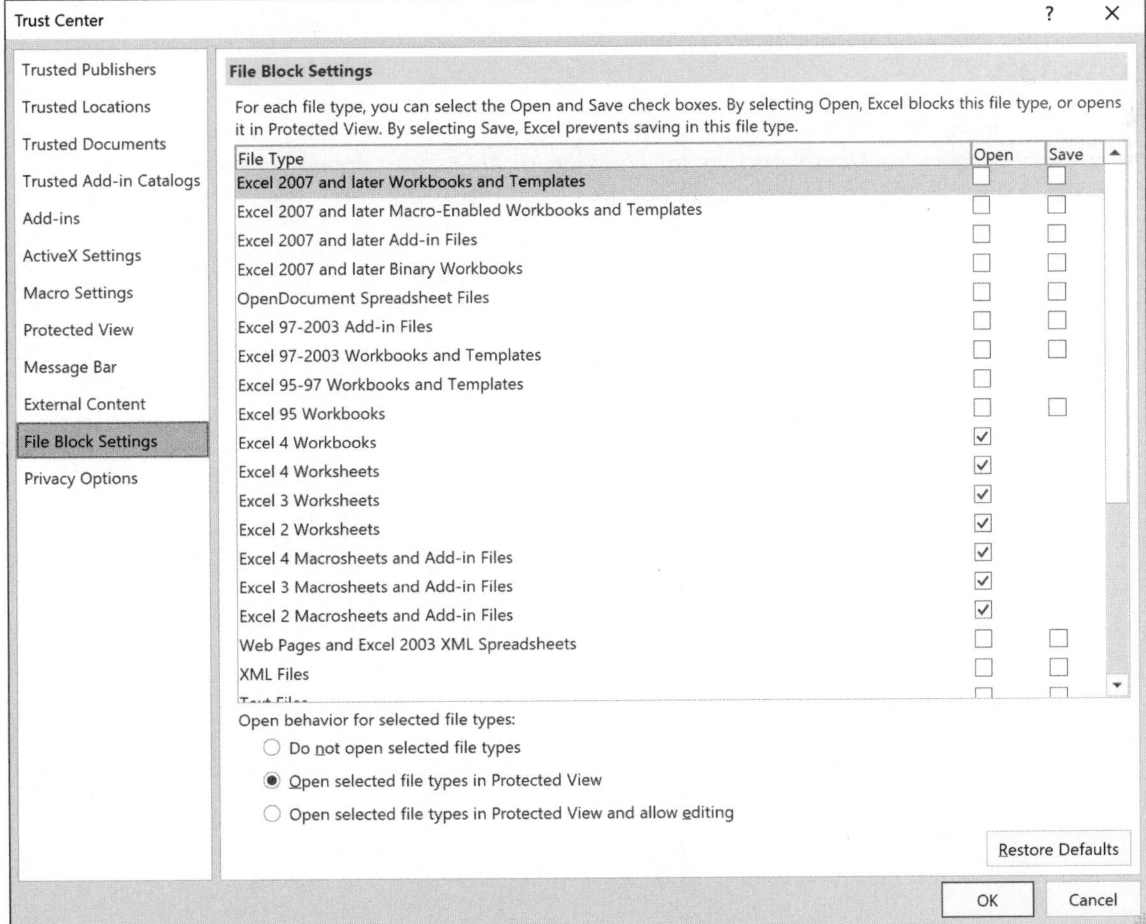

- **Privacy Options**—These options largely deal with what you want Excel to check or report back to Microsoft for you. Microsoft collects information from Excel regarding how you use it, crashes, etc. in an effort to improve the application; it does this for all the other Office applications as well. You can opt out of any of it, but you should know that Microsoft doesn't gather any personal information about you or your data; it's all anonymous.

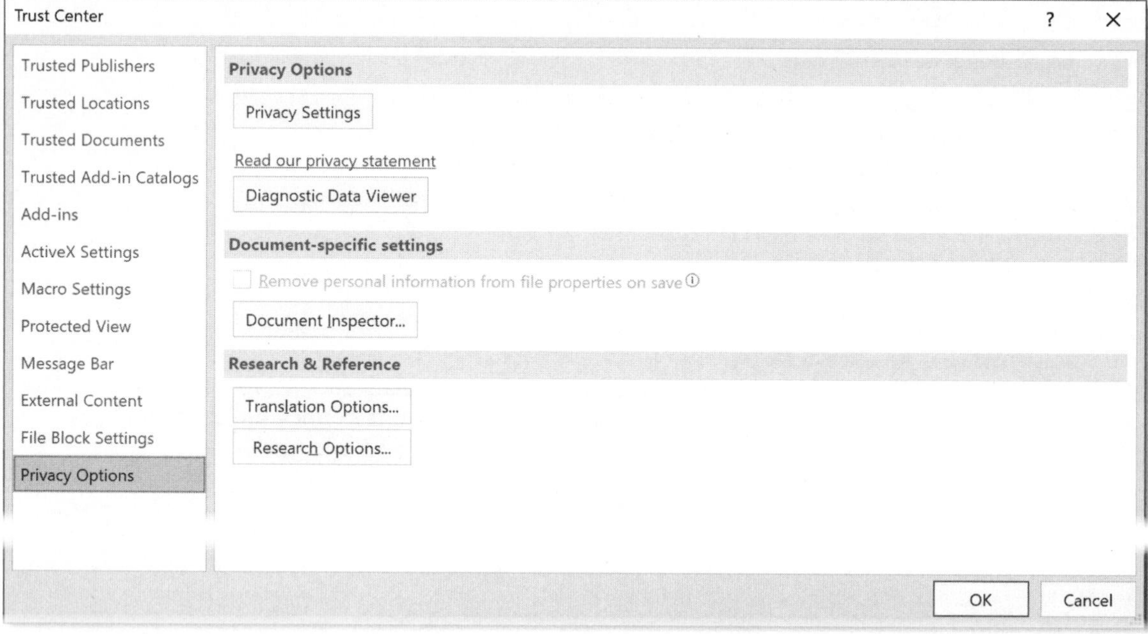

- The Document Inspector button allows you to inspect a workbook for any personal information prior to distribution and allows you to remove it if needed. The Translation Options and Research Options buttons allow you to set your language preferences for translation and research tools when you're proofing a workbook prior to distribution. These options can be useful if you need to provide workbooks in other languages.

Chapter Summary

- In this chapter you learned about basic file operations, such as saving and opening workbooks.
- This chapter walks through all of Excel's options for enabling/disabling certain workbook and worksheet features, both those you can use for every instance of Excel and those you can toggle off for specific instances.

Chapter 3: The Home Tab in Depth

In Chapter 2 you got an introduction to basic Windows file operations, such as saving, and looked at how to set up Excel the way you want it by using the setup options available through **File > Options**. It is likely that you will set most of those options only once and never worry about them again. In Chapter 1 you learned a bit about each of the Excel Ribbon tabs. This chapter looks more closely at the Ribbon's Home tab and its elements. The Home tab is the default tab for the Ribbon, and a great deal of what you do in Excel you do in this tab. Before we get to the Home tab, though, you should understand a bit of the history behind the Ribbon.

The original Excel graphical user interface (GUI) was designed in 1992. Like most other products, Excel has gone through some significant changes since then, each one giving users more capabilities than the last. The engineers at Microsoft had done a great job of keeping this product the number-one spreadsheet application in the world for a long time, but then a new generation of engineers came on board and had some great new ideas, based on their experiences with computers. Just as computer games have evolved since the days of the Commodore and Atari, the Ribbon is nothing less than an evolutionary step in the Excel product lifecycle, and it's something that had to happen if Excel was to remain the most-used application on the market. Oddly, Bill Gates was against the Ribbon, as he feared that its introduction would alienate a large group of experienced users who had grown comfortable enough to memorize all of Excel's keystrokes and, more importantly, knew where everything was. But he was outvoted, and development on the Ribbon for Office applications really took off. Was Bill Gates right? To a certain degree perhaps, but most experienced users have now adopted the Ribbon; those who haven't have been left behind because their customers have moved on.

Probably the most important element of the Ribbon is that it puts everything right out in the open for you, in a great graphical display, which earlier versions lacked. For newer generations of users who are as comfortable with a mouse as with a keyboard, the Ribbon is a natural step, and Microsoft has done a great job with it. There have been some hiccups along the way, which is why you'll find certain things in the Excel 2019 Ribbon that weren't available in Excel 2007, like the options for customizing the Ribbon, but these are just more evolutionary steps. Microsoft continues to do a good job listening to customers and making all of Office more user friendly.

To get an idea of the difference between a Ribbon version of Excel and a non-Ribbon version of Excel, here's a screenshot of Excel 2003, which was the last version of Excel without the Ribbon:

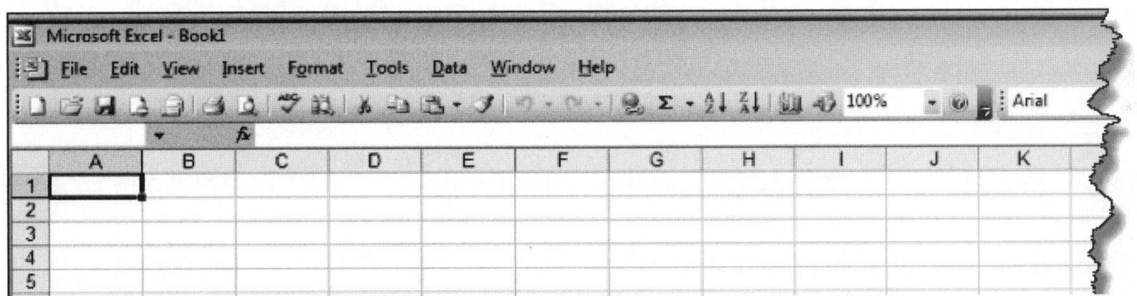

Compare this to the following screenshot of Excel 2019, showing the Ribbon:

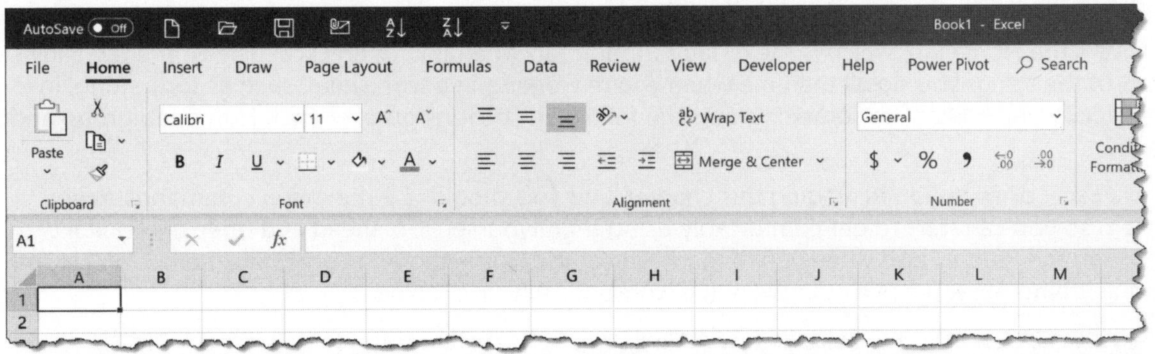

With Excel 2003 and earlier versions, the individual options were displayed as a list beneath the various menus (File, Edit, View, etc.), as shown below.

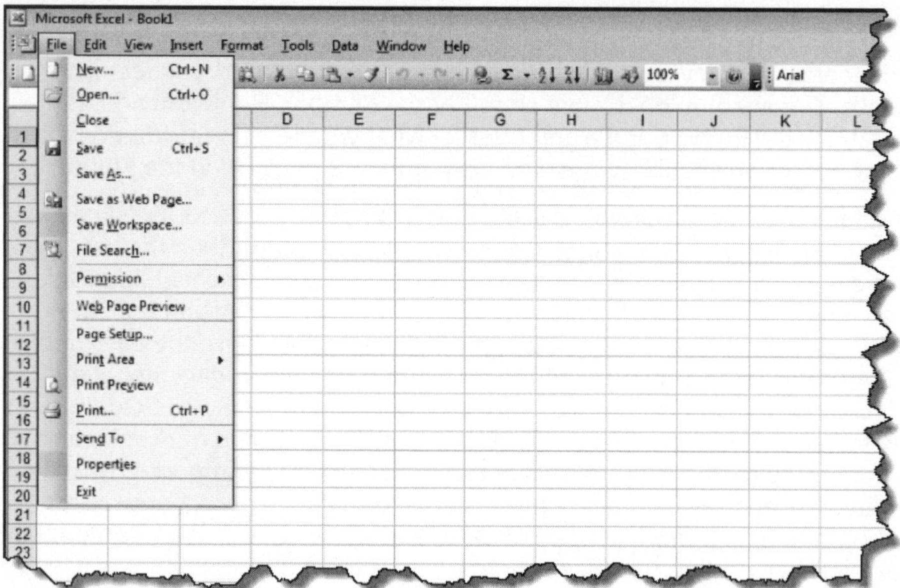

With the Ribbon, however, each tab has its own set of graphical menu commands, as shown in the following image.

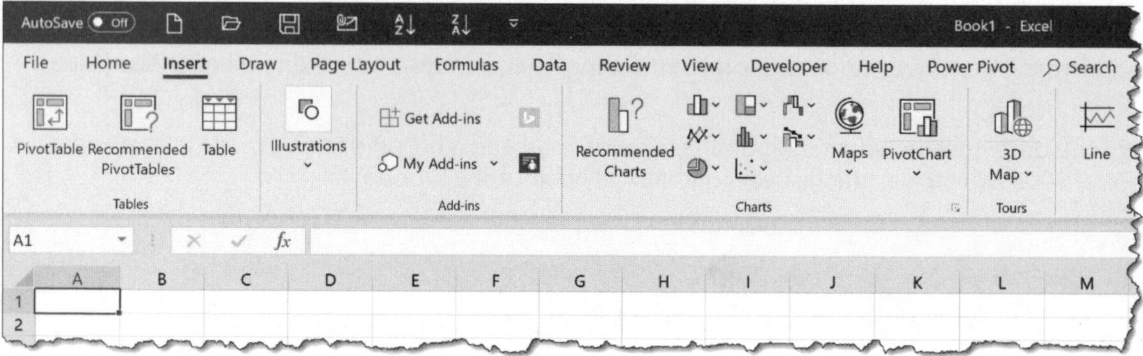

This switch from list-based text options to graphical menu commands has made it a lot easier for new Excel users to get a grasp of where everything is located.

> **Note:** See the underscores in the menu names in the Excel 2003 examples? Those are called *accelerators*, and they told you how to activate those menu items by using the **Alt** or **/** keyboard shortcuts. Ribbon versions of Excel also allow you to easily use shortcuts, but instead of seeing underlined accelerators, you get mini-dialogs that show you which key to press next.

This chapter covers the Home tab, which is the default Ribbon tab when you open Excel. The Home tab allows you to do most of the things you do all the time when you're working in a worksheet, such as formatting, inserting/deleting cells, and editing (to some degree). The following sections go over each Home tab group and what it does.

You should have Excel open as you're reading this chapter, and you should use the menu commands as you learn about them so you can start to get comfortable using them yourself. Go ahead and open a new workbook, look through the Ribbon, and when you're ready, select the Home tab and come back here. Don't worry about messing anything up; you can always close the workbook without saving it.

> **Note:** As you get better at using Excel, you might find yourself wanting to open a workbook to test something and then close it without saving your changes (for example, if you want to test various assumptions in a pricing model). If you do this, make sure that AutoSave is turned off; otherwise, your changes might be inadvertently saved.

The Clipboard Group

The Clipboard group, shown below, allows you to control copying and pasting, as well as the myriad things you can do with pasted data. In Chapter 2 you learned about some of the options for pasting in a worksheet, and in this chapter you'll get to try some of them on your own. In a blank workbook, enter any old sample data (it doesn't matter what it is). For example, you can enter **=1+1** in any cell and then press **Enter** when you're done to confirm the formula. Excel automatically moves you down to the next cell.

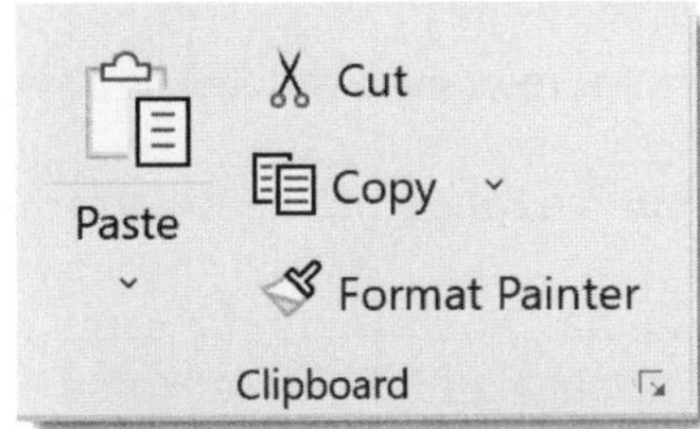

Note: Because this chapter is all about the Ribbon, which is mostly mouse oriented, you should follow along with the mouse, but if you want to try some of the keyboard shortcuts you've already learned, feel free to experiment.

Now, click **Home > Copy**, select the destination cell, and paste by clicking **Home > Paste**. If you just click on the Copy and Paste icons, you will perform a simple copy/paste, but if you select the drop-down arrow that appears with either of these icons, you get expanded functionality. (The same is true for any other Ribbon command that has a drop-down beneath it.)

When you paste, you see a paste options drop-down to the right of the cell—labeled (Ctrl)—and you can open this menu by clicking the paste options drop-down or pressing the **Ctrl** key. If you hover the mouse pointer over any of the commands on this drop-down, a tooltip appears, followed by a key, such as (W). This is an accelerator key, and you can press the corresponding key on the keyboard to activate the paste action associated with that accelerator. The following options are available on the paste options drop-down:

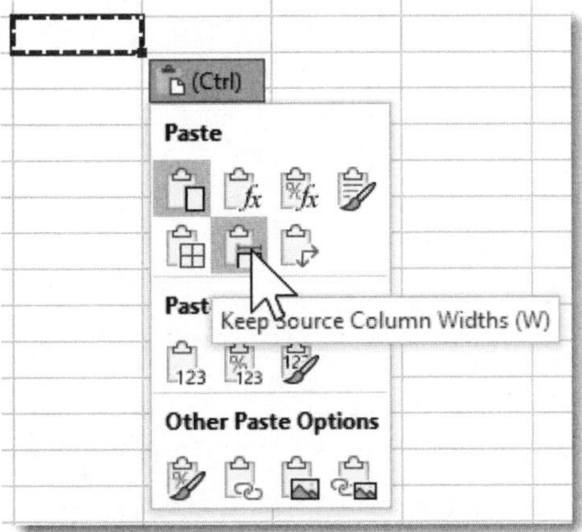

- **Paste (P)**—Pastes formulas, cell formatting, font style, etc. This is the same as a straight copy/paste using either the Ribbon commands or keyboard shortcuts.
- **Formulas (F)**—Pastes only the source range's formula, not any formatting.
- **Formulas & Number Formatting (O)**—Pastes formatted data in unformatted cells.
- **Keep Source Formatting (K)**—Pastes the formatting from the source cell/range, regardless of the formatting in the destination cell/range. You aren't likely to use this option, as you usually want to keep the destination formatting intact.
- **No Borders (B)**—Pastes the source range's contents, including formats, but not any applied borders. This can be handy if you're copying a cell/range that has existing borders but you don't want them in the destination.
- **Keep Source Column Widths (W)**—Pastes only the source range's column widths. This can be handy if you have column sizes that are greater than or less than the default column sizes, and you don't want to have to manually adjust them to match the source.
- **Transpose (T)**—Pastes rows to columns and columns to rows, effectively flipping your data in another direction. There's an example of this in the Paste Special dialog explanation below.
- **Values (V)**—Pastes only the source range's values and eliminates any existing formulas. This option comes in handy when you want to create a snapshot of a range, and you don't want anything to alter

your formulas. It's also very good for distributing workbooks—for several reasons: It can greatly reduce workbook size, no one can alter your data by changing your formulas, and if you have complicated formulas, no one can delete them. If you send out a workbook and get it back with formulas changed, the workbook may be compromised. This can be especially problematic if you don't realize that someone has changed the formulas!

Note: If you need to distribute a workbook/report and are concerned about people changing your formulas, use the **File > Export > PDF** option. This way, Excel creates a static snapshot of your workbook, and your formulas will be safe.

- **Values & Number Formatting (A)**—Eliminates any formulas that were in the source range but keeps any associated number formats.
- **Values & Source Formatting (E)**—Eliminates any formulas that were in the source range but keeps any associated formats, including number formats.
- **Formatting (R)**—Pastes only the source range's formats and no values or formulas. You can do the same thing by using the Format Painter tool, which is the paintbrush icon in the Clipboard group on the Home tab. Just select the cell from which you want to copy formatting, click the paintbrush icon, and click the cell where you want the formatting applied. If you want to apply it to multiple cells, double-click the paintbrush, and it will stay active until you press **Esc**.
- **Paste Link (N)**—Pastes a link to the source cell, such as =A1. Then, any time the source cell changes, the destination cell changes as well.
- **Paste Picture (U)**—Pastes the source cell/range as a picture. This picture, which sits above the grid, is a static screenshot. If you change the source data, the destination image does not change with it. This can be good if you want to give someone a quick snapshot of your worksheet but don't want to send the workbook.
- **Linked Picture (I)**—Pastes the source cell/range as a picture that is linked to the source so that, if you change the source data, the image updates along with it. This can be good if you want to see what's happening in a particular worksheet while you're in a different one.
- **Paste Special**—Offers some additional tools not found in the Paste drop-down in the Clipboard group. You can launch the Paste Special dialog by pressing **Ctrl+Alt+V** or by selecting **Home > Paste drop-down > Paste Special**.

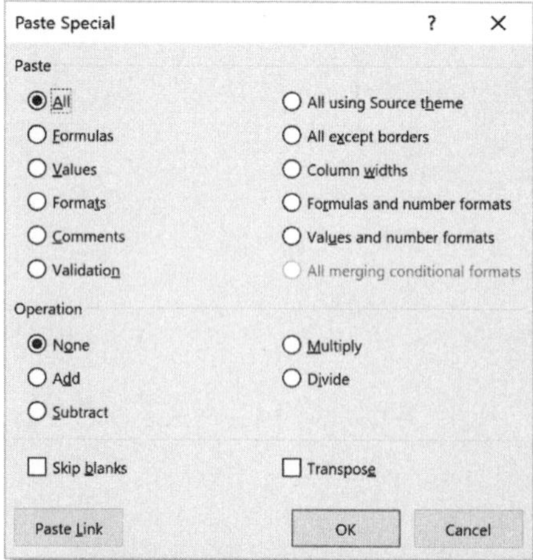

Note: In Office dialogs like Paste Special, when you see a group of round option buttons, you can select only one option from each group. You can, however, select multiple square checkboxes. When pasting, you can only apply one paste option at a time, but you can open the Paste dialog as many times as you want, provided that the copied data is still in the Clipboard. Excel 2016 introduced an enhanced Clipboard that holds on to what was copied and allows you to do other things in between. Pressing **Esc** clears the Clipboard.

- The Paste Special dialog has three sections: Paste, Operation, and Skip Blanks/Transpose. If you compare this dialog and the Paste Special dialog from the Ribbon side-by-side, you see that much of the functionality is shared between the two, although there are some notable exceptions. The following sections discuss some of these options.

The Operation Section of the Paste Special Dialog

The Operation section of the Paste Special dialog is a very neat set of options that lets you copy a source value and apply that value to a range with one of the four major mathematical operators (addition, subtraction, multiplication, or division).

Let's say you have a range of product prices, and you need to apply a 3% increase across the board. In this case, you would enter a set of sample values in a few cells and then put 1.03 in a cell outside that range, as shown below.

Prices	Change by
$66.95	1.03
$44.59	
$88.91	
$66.01	
$64.59	
$53.31	
$42.52	

Then you'd copy that cell and select the range of prices and go to **Paste > Paste Special > Multiply** and see what happens.

Prices	Change by
68.96103	1.03
45.92935	
91.57606	
67.99335	
66.52403	
54.91318	
43.79691	

Unfortunately, as shown above, the destination receives the source range's number format. (You could prevent this by choosing both Values and Multiply in the Paste Special dialog). Or you can quickly reformat the destination range as currency by pressing **Ctrl+Shift+4**. One of my favorite tricks is to change values, see what the result is, and then press **Ctrl+Z** to undo it.

> **Note:** My favorite keyboard shortcut is **Ctrl+Z** (for Undo), and I also like **Ctrl+Y** (for Redo). There are also Undo and Redo options for the Quick Access Toolbar (QAT) for those who would rather use the mouse.

The Skip Blanks Section of the Paste Special Dialog

Skip Blanks is a cool feature that even a lot of seasoned Excel pros don't know about. It lets you paste a range of data that has blank cells in it onto a range of data that doesn't, and only non-blanks cells in the source range are copied; any blank cells in the source range are ignored, and the destination data isn't disturbed. Let's say you have a range of cells like the one shown below.

	A	B	C	D	E	F
1	January	PY	February	PY	March	PY
2	$122.67	$286.31	$830.73	$743.27	$823.67	$86.88
3						
4	Variance	($163.64)		$87.47		$736.79
5						

Now say that you decide that instead of having your monthly variances at the bottom, you want to have them where last year's figures are. You can select the variance range and copy it, as shown below.

	A	B	C	D	E	F
1	January	PY	February	PY	March	PY
2	$122.67	$286.31	$830.73	$743.27	$823.67	$86.88
3						
4	Variance	($163.64)		$87.47		$736.79
5						

Then if you open the Paste Special dialog and select the Skip Blanks checkbox, you see your copied data, as shown below, but your original data remains where there were blanks in the copy range. This is a fairly one-off use, but when you do need it, it's invaluable.

	A	B	C	D	E	F
1	January	PY	February	PY	March	PY
2	$122.67	($163.64)	$830.73	$87.47	$823.67	$736.79
3						
4	Variance	($163.64)		$87.47		$736.79
5						

The Transpose Section of the Paste Special Dialog

The Transpose section of the Paste Special dialog lets you physically flip your data's orientation. Suppose you have a series of data that runs in rows/columns left-to-right, as in the earlier example, but for a certain application, you really need the data to go top-to-bottom. You could come up with all kinds of complicated formulas to transpose the data, or you could use the Transpose feature. Just copy the range A1:F2 from the previous example, find an unused range where you want to put this range, select **Home > Paste drop-down > Paste Special > Transpose** (or press **Alt+E+S+V+E**), and you get the result shown below—with all of your formatting also copied over to the destination.

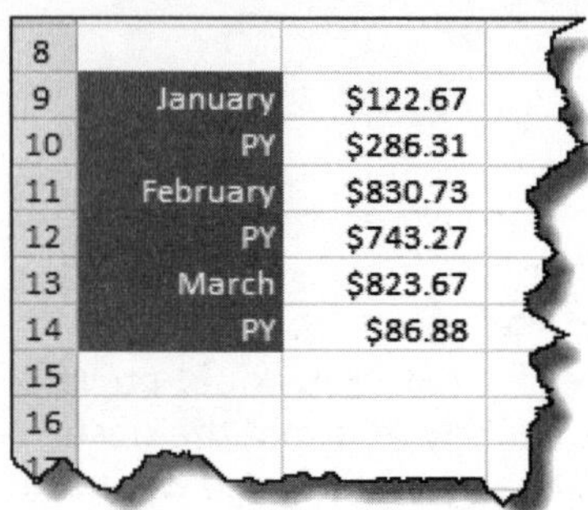

The Paste Link Button on the Paste Special Dialog

By using the Paste Link button, you can paste links to the range you copy. Say that you want to have a copy of the figures in A1:F2 on another sheet, but you don't want to have to update both sets of records. The Paste Link option pastes the source data as formulas that reference the source data. Then, any time you change the source data, the pasted links automatically update. Note that when you paste links, you lose your formatting, so using this option is a good exercise in working with the different pasting options. While your paste range is still active, click the **Paste** button and select the **Keep Source Formatting** option, as shown below (or press **K**).

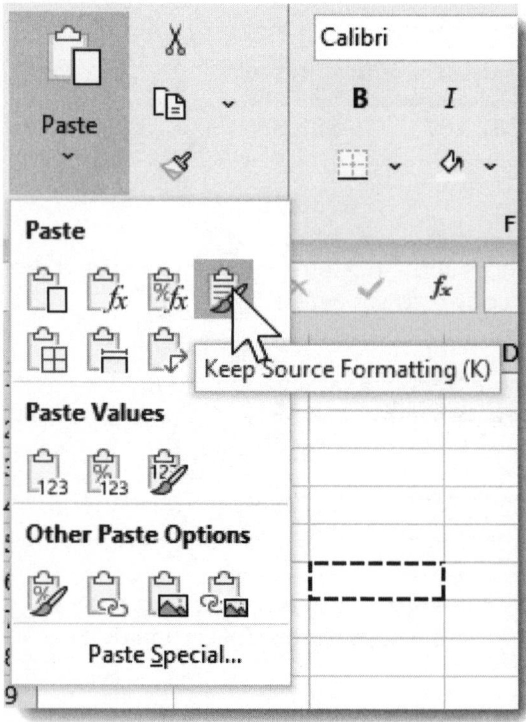

The Clipboard Dialog Launcher

When you click the dialog launcher in the lower-right corner of the Clipboard group, a new pane (shown below) opens on the left of the worksheet window.

The Clipboard stores the 24 most recent items you've copied in Office apps, web browsers, and images. You can come back to any of them and paste them anywhere in your workbook, as long as those items are still in the Clipboard. In the example above, you can see some items I copied between Word and Excel. The Clipboard pane includes the following buttons:

- **Paste All**—Pastes everything that's in the Clipboard.
- **Clear All**—Deletes everything from the Clipboard.

To paste something from the Clipboard, select the cell in which you want to paste the item in question and then click the item from the Clipboard pane that you want to copy. Remember that if you paste an object or an image, it won't paste into the cell but on top of it.

At the bottom of the Clipboard pane, you can click the Options button to see some options for controlling the Clipboard's behavior. I've never found the Clipboard to be very helpful in this respect, but if you need to do a lot of copying between applications, such as copying something from a browser to Excel to Word and then to Power Point, it might be helpful for you.

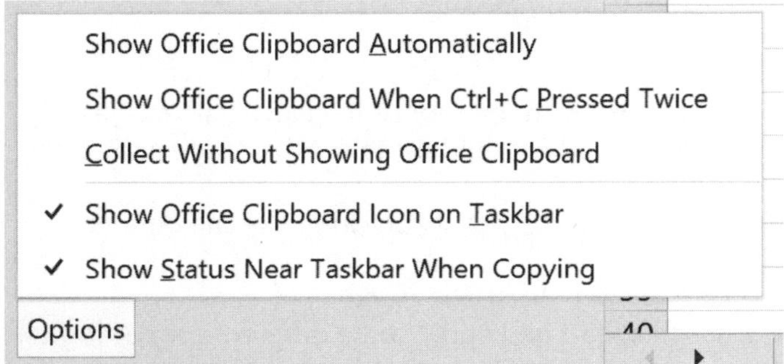

The Font Group

The Font group of the Home tab, shown below, is where you control the font type/style, size, effects (bold, italic, underline), font/cell color, and gridlines. The following are some of the most commonly used options:

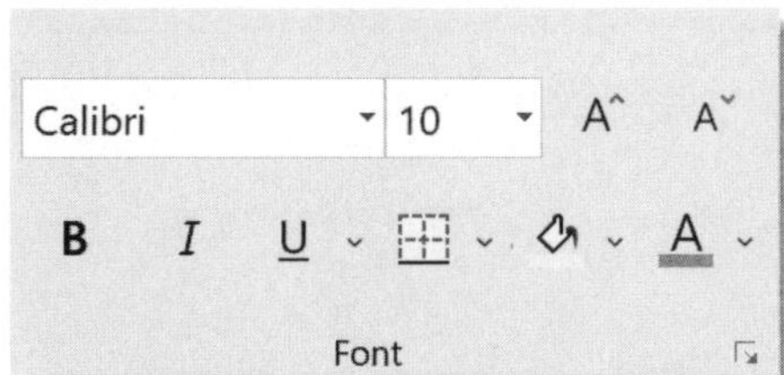

- **Font box**—Click here to browse through the available fonts on your system. Your selection here changes only the font for the active cell or the range you've selected. You should be careful here because it is easy to inadvertently apply different formats to different ranges.
- **Font size box**—This drop-down lets you adjust the font size for the selected cell/range.
- **Toggle font size**—The two A's to the right of the font size box are both clickable; the first one increases the selected range's font size, and the second one decreases it.

- **Bold/Italic/Underline**—Applies bold, italic, or underline to the selected cell(s).
- **Borders**—The icon that looks like an underlined grid (shown below) lets you control the border pattern applied to a range. You'll most likely stick with the border options presented here, and they're pretty simple to grasp. The line color/style options are very handy if you don't like the default black gridline colors or if you want a different line style. Keep in mind, though, that colored gridlines might be hard to see on some monitors, so you're generally better off with a darker color than a light one for gridlines. The following are some of the options available in the Borders drop-down:

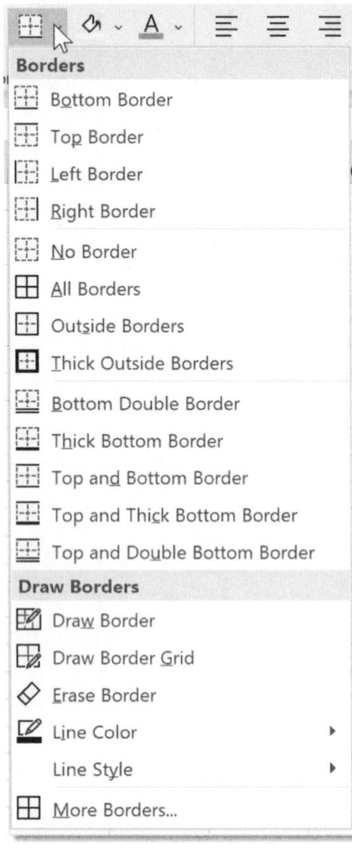

  - **Draw Border**—This option gives you a pen that you control with the mouse to select cells/ranges and actively apply simple borders. If you want complex borders, you should preselect the range and apply the borders from the default options.
  - **Line Color and Line Style**—You can change the line colors and styles if you don't like the default offerings.
  - **More Borders**—This option launches the Format Cells dialog, discussed next.

The Font group options are all relatively straightforward, so go ahead and apply some different formatting to a range of cells to see what you can do. There's no way to cover all the options that Excel gives you, but you can easily try things on your own to get a feel for the possibilities.

The Font group's dialog launcher loads the Format Cells dialog, which has a number of tabs, as discussed in the following sections.

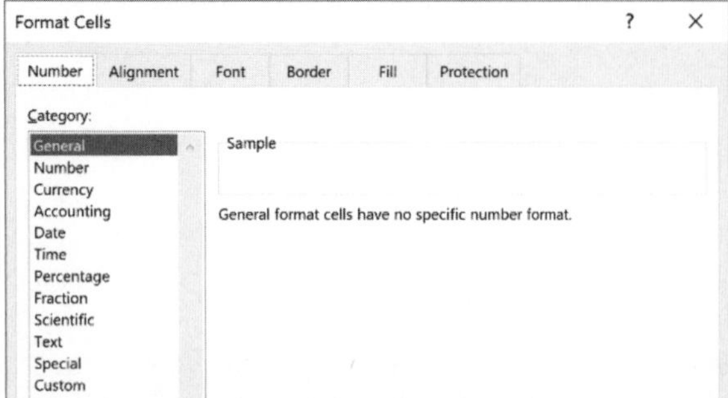

The Number Tab of the Format Cells Dialog

The Number tab of the Format Cells dialog includes the following options:

- **General**—The default number format is General, which means that any numeric value you enter in a cell will appear just as you entered it.
- **Number**—This option gives you a number with comma separator(s) and a variable number of decimal places you select.
- **Currency**—This option gives you a number with a currency symbol, comma separator(s), and a variable number of decimal places you select. You can also change the format for negative values and can choose the currency symbol, as shown below.

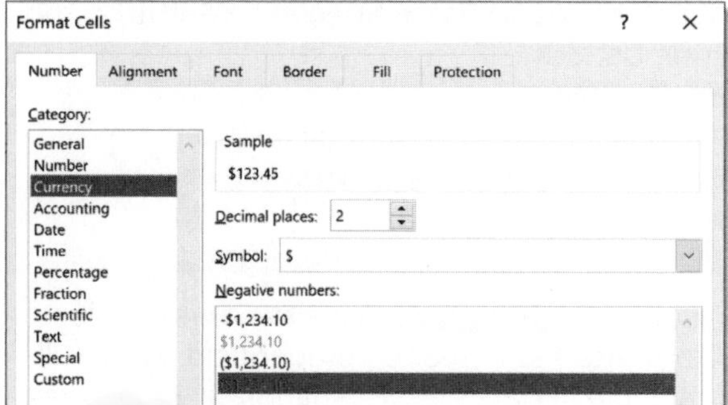

- **Accounting**—This option is the same as Currency but with no color change for negative values, and the currency symbol is automatically placed on the left side of the cell. Unless you're an accountant, you'll probably find this to be a pretty strange way to display currency.
- **Date**—This option allows you to apply different date formats to a range. By default, Excel recognizes any values entered in *mm/dd/yy* format as dates. For instance, Excel would automatically convert 1/1/11 to 1/1/2011. There are multiple date formats available, as shown below.

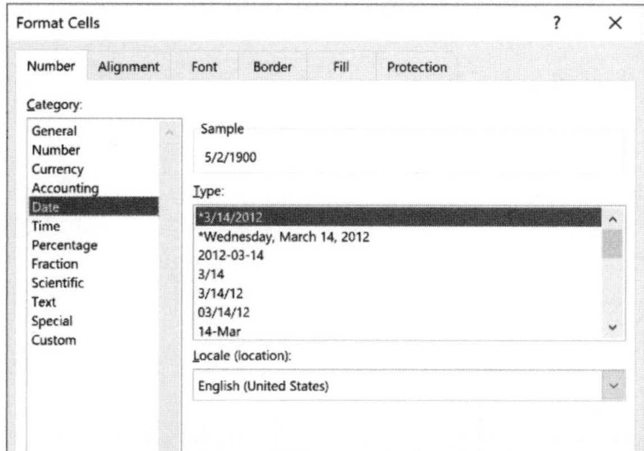

> **Note:** Excel stores dates as what's called serial date/time, which is interpreted as the number of days from January 1, 1900, to the date entered/calculated, with times stored as fractional portions of the 24-hour day. For example, May 26, 2011, 11:47 AM is stored as 40869.49151.

- **Time**—Time entries can be formatted many ways, including in military 24-hour time. The standard time display is *HH*:*MM* AM/PM.
- **Percentage**—This option applies a percentage format to a range with a variable number of decimal places. With percentage format, it's generally advisable to format the range before entering the decimal values (unless they're the result of a calculation) because Excel converts existing values. For example, Excel would convert 125 to 12500% if it weren't formatted first. But if you format the range first and then enter 125, Excel gives you 125%.
- **Fraction**—This option allows you to convert values into their fractional equivalents. If you deal with fractions a lot, you'll find that this format isn't the most dependable and won't always give you the desired results.

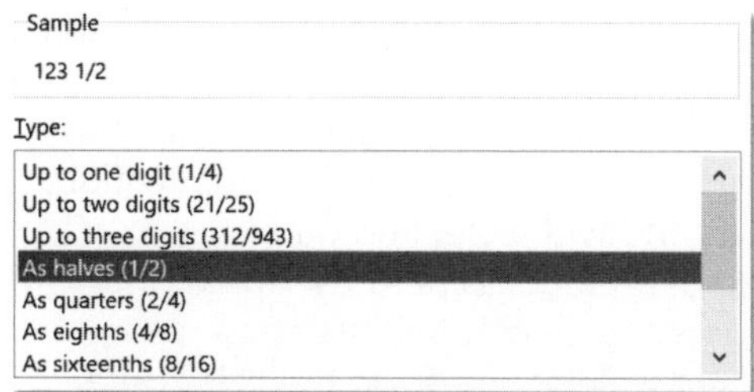

- **Scientific**—This option applies scientific notation to values (e.g., 123456789 is represented as 1.23E+08). This option is generally reserved for very large numbers.

- **Text**—This option converts values into text. Once a value is converted to text, you might find it difficult to perform mathematical calculations on the value without converting it back to a number. This format can be useful for things like part numbers that have leading zeros because if such numbers are formatted as numbers, Excel will strip the leading zeros. You won't likely be performing mathematical calculations on part numbers, so using the Text format is probably the best option. Some data imports can convert values to text, and when you encounter them, you are likely to wonder why you can't work with them as numbers, so keep this issue in mind. When you have numbers that have been stored as text, you can put a 1 in an empty cell, copy it, select the number cell/range in question, and go to **Paste Special > Multiply**. This operation, called *coercion*, forces text values back to being numbers.
  Hint: When entering numeric values that need to be formatted (dollars, percentages, dates, Social Security numbers, phone numbers, etc.), you don't need to add any of the formatting characters as you type. For example, if you format a cell as Currency with two decimal places, when you type 123.45, Excel automatically displays it as $123.45. Just knowing you can do this will save you a lot of time compared to typing all those characters by hand.
- **Special**—This option allows you to apply zip code, phone, and Social Security formats to numeric values you enter. For example, if you enter 2125551212 into a cell formatted as a phone number field, Excel will automatically represent it as (212) 555-1212. This can be invaluable in data entry scenarios, as Excel does that work, and humans don't need to manually type the format.
- **Custom**—This option allows you to define your own custom number formats if the ones available don't work in a particular situation. You can learn a lot about a number format by applying a standard format to a cell with a value it in and selecting the Custom option because Excel shows you the number format that was applied along with all the technical stuff you need to copy it. From there you can select one of the number formats from the Custom list or build your own.

The following table lists some of the keyboard shortcuts you can use for formatting Excel workbooks.

Keyboard Shortcuts for Formatting in Excel

Shortcut	Description
Ctrl+Shift+~	Format using the general format (no decimals)
Ctrl+Shift+1	Format as a number (two decimals)
Ctrl+Shift+2	Format as a time (h:mm AM/PM)
Ctrl+Shift+3	Format as a date (d-mmm-yy)
Ctrl+Shift+4	Format as currency (two decimals)
Ctrl+Shift+5	Format as a percentage (no decimals)
Ctrl+Shift+6	Format using scientific notation
Ctrl+1	Launch the Format Cells dialog
Ctrl+Z	Undo the last operation
Ctrl+Y	Redo the last operation

The Alignment Tab of the Format Cells Dialog

The Alignment tab of the Format Cells dialog allows you to control the way your data is represented in a range. It includes the following options:

- **Text Alignment**—The options in this section give you control over horizontal and vertical alignment and allow you to set an indent if you want.
- **Wrap Text**—This option allows text to continue to a new line within a cell if the text gets too big to display on one line.
- **Shrink to Fit**—Instead of wrapping text to a new line, this option shrinks the text to fit the cell. Note that this works only for alphanumeric entries, not value entries.
- **Merge Cells**—*Never* select this checkbox. Doing so can cause all kinds of problems, especially with sorting. It's here to ostensibly help you do a better job of formatting, but in almost any practical application, it's absolutely useless and can actually cause problems with formulas and with selecting data.
  Hint: Merging cells is commonly done to spread a report header across multiple columns. An alternative is to put header text in the first column of a report and then select the cell and all the columns in that row for the report. Then, on the Alignment tab, select Center Across Selection from the Horizontal drop-down. Although it looks like Excel has merged the cells, it hasn't, and this solution is not going to cause any problems down the road.

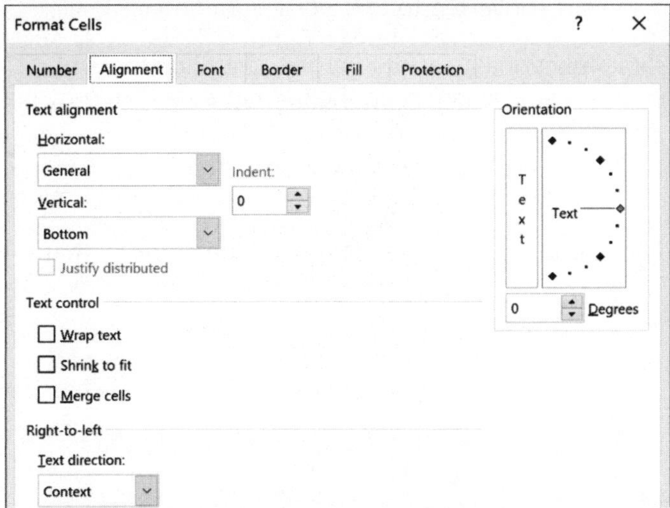

- **Orientation**—This option allows you to change the angle at which your data is displayed in a range. By default, Excel displays data horizontally, or at 0 degrees. You can change that to 90 degrees up or down by dragging the control arm in the Orientation window in either direction, or you can use the spinner control at the bottom of the Orientation window (or enter your own value manually). As shown below, any gridlines you have applied follow the same angle as your text; if you're at 0 or either 90-degree intersection (up or down) you're fine, but if you're in between, as in the 45-degree example here, you'll get some strange behavior.

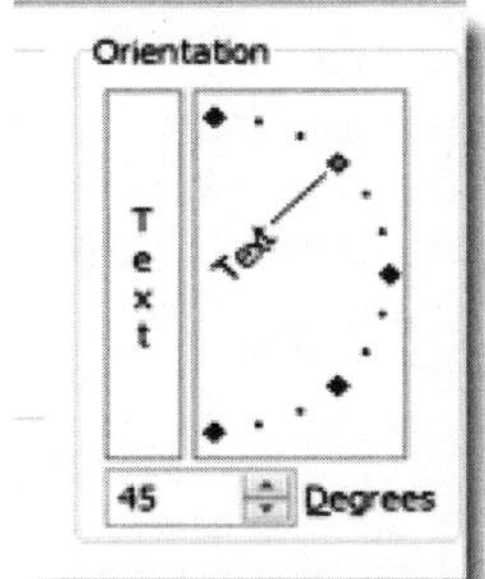

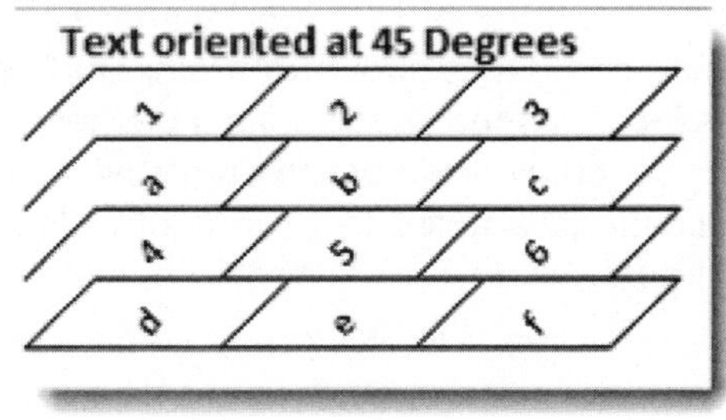

The Font Tab of the Format Cells Dialog

The Font tab in the Format Cells dialog is essentially an expanded version of what you can get on the Ribbon group. However, this tab also allows you to add the following effects to a range:

- **Strikethrough**—Text looks like ~~this~~.
- **Superscript**—Text looks like ^{this}.
- **Subscript**—Text looks like $_{\text{this}}$

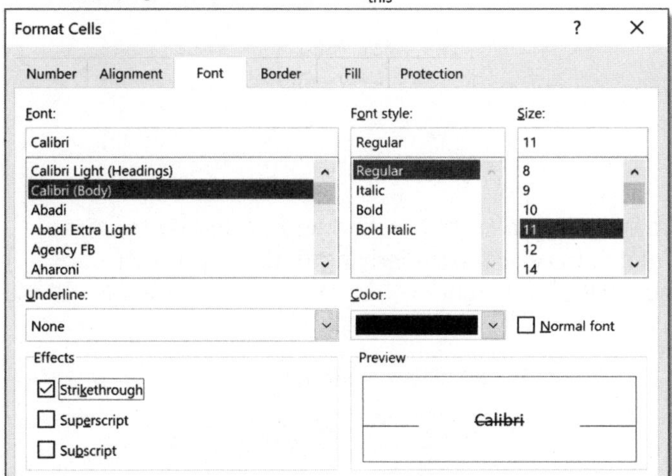

This tab also has a live preview window so you can see what your proposed changes will look like.

The Border Tab of the Format Cells Dialog

The Border tab of the Format Cells dialog exposes the same functionality as the Border control on the Ribbon. Generally, there's not really any reason to use this dialog unless you've launched the Format Cells dialog by using the **Ctrl+1** shortcut.

The Fill Tab of the Format Cells Dialog

The Fill tab of the Format Cells dialog can be very handy because it exposes the following functionality that's not included in the Ribbon:

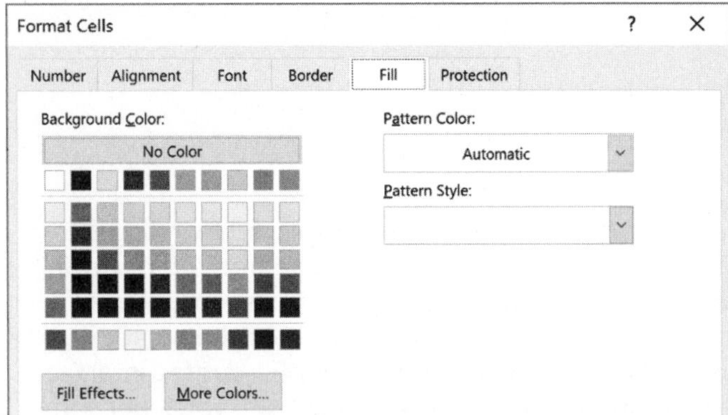

- **Fill Effects**—Clicking the Fill Effects button gives you access to handy tools that allow you to apply gradient shading to a range. You can get very creative with these tools, which can be great for formatting things like dashboards or areas to which you want to attract special attention. Just remember that colors should be used sparingly, and they should not be too loud. Bright pink and yellow might look great to you, but they probably won't be as pleasant to someone else (like a banker or an investor). Excel 2007 and later give you the ability to access a lot more colors than before, but that doesn't mean you need to use them all. The following examples show fill effects applied to a range of cells and then to a range that's been merged in a dashboard type of example.

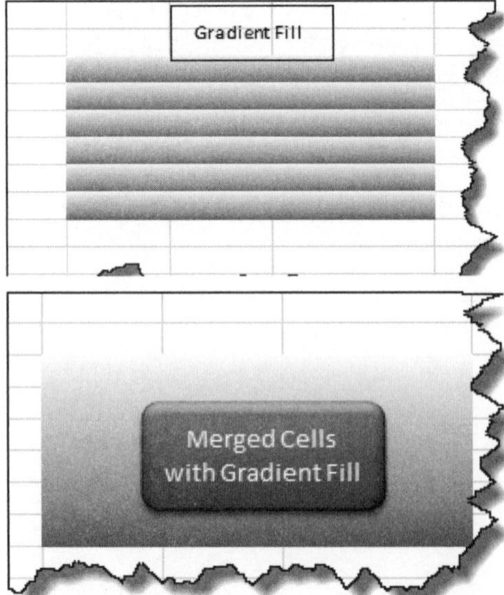

- **Pattern Style**—This drop-down gives you access to very simple cross-hatched and dotted designs you can apply to a range. Note that they can make it difficult to read the underlying data, and some printers that can't achieve the detail necessary to render them will simply render them as black, completely hiding your data.

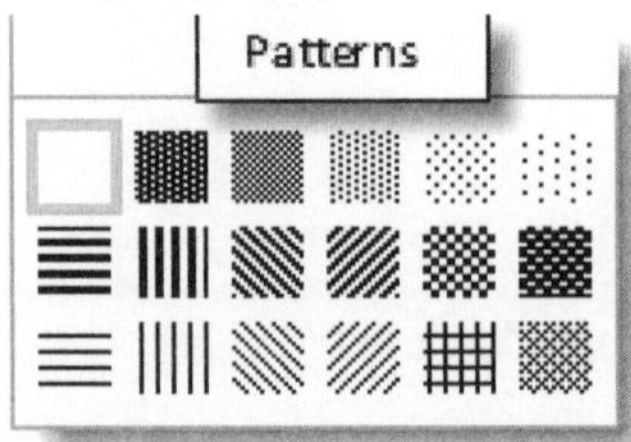

The Protection Tab of the Format Cells Dialog

The ability to protect Excel worksheets is one of its coolest features. You can protect a worksheet so that no one can make any changes, or you can unprotect certain cells so that users can enter information only where you say they can. You can also hide formulas from view so that only their resulting values are visible. By default, all cells on a worksheet are set to Locked. In order to allow entry, you need to select those cells and, on the Protection tab, uncheck the Locked checkbox. You can check Hidden if you don't want formulas to be visible, but you generally should not use both Locked and Hidden, as you normally don't have formulas in data entry cells. After choosing Locked/Hidden, when you protect the worksheet (using the Review tab on the Ribbon), only those cells will accept entries.

Caution: Protected workbooks and worksheets are only as safe as your recipients make them. Excel is not a secure environment, and it has ever been marketed as one. If you need to distribute sensitive material, and there's even a slight chance that someone could alter or otherwise use your data in a manner inconsistent with your expectations, you should save it as a PDF and send it out that way. Think of Excel protection as a lock on a door: All it does is keep honest people honest. Excel security is good enough for 99.9% of the population, but be aware that those who want to break your passwords and access your information can do it.

The Alignment Group

The Alignment group of the Home tab is where you control how your text will behave in a cell/range. This is probably as close as you can get to trying to get Excel to act like Word. Just be aware that it's limited in what it can do, just as Word is limited in the calculations it can perform. (However, the two programs do work brilliantly with each other, as discussed in Chapter 12.)

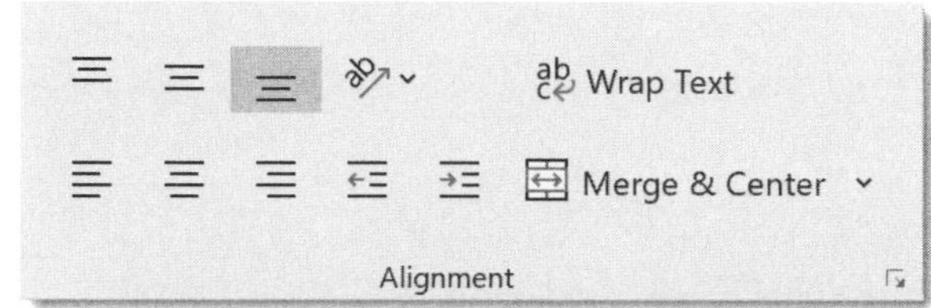

Note: Everything you see in the Alignment group of the Home tab is also contained in the Format Cells dialog discussed earlier in this chapter. Again, Excel gives you multiple ways to expose certain command elements. Most of the time, using **Ctrl+1** to launch the Format Cells dialog is a lot faster than using the mouse to get to the Ribbon commands, but which method you use is really a matter of personal preference.

The following example shows that Excel aligns text to the left of a cell and numbers to the right. This is handy because if you see numbers aligned to the left, you know Excel is seeing them as text, not as numbers.

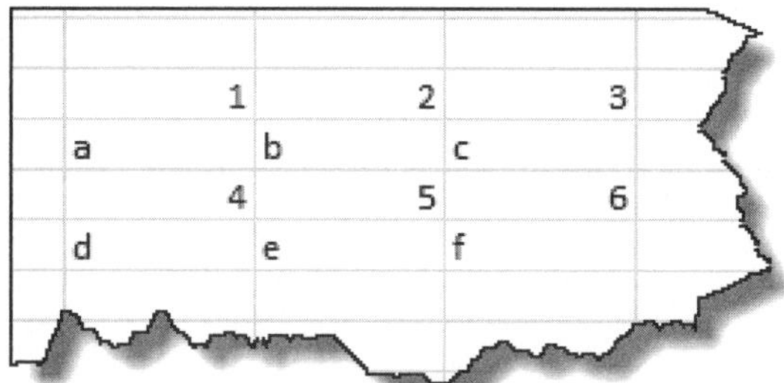

The options in the Alignment group of the Home tab are almost the same as the ones in the Format Cells dialog. On the top are the vertical alignment options (top, center, and bottom), and beneath those are the horizontal options (left, center, right). To justify text, you need to open the Format Cells dialog and use the Alignment tab.

Next are the orientation options and then the decrease/increase indent controls. To the right of those is the Wrap Text option. At the bottom right is the Merge & Center option, which, like Merge Cells, you should avoid at all costs.

The Number Group

Most of the number formatting options are available in the Number group of the Home tab, but if you want something that is not in the default list, you can either click the More Number Formats selection at the bottom of the drop-down or use the dialog launcher, both of which launch the Format Cells dialog.

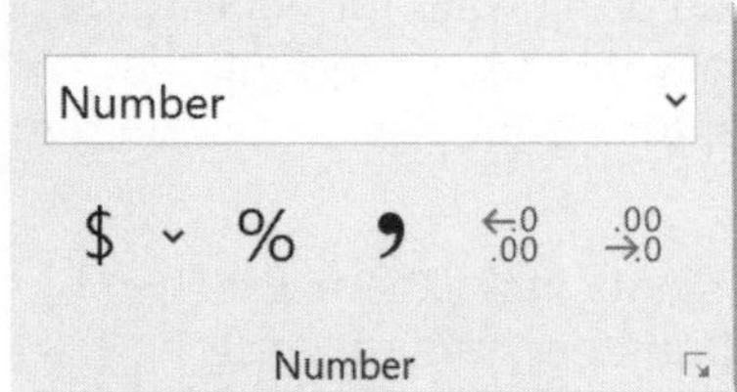

Both the Currency and Comma number formats give you two decimal places by default. If you want more or fewer decimal places, you can use the decimal toggle buttons to the right. The Currency and Accounting selections have an additional option that lets you change the currency symbol (dollar, pound, euro, yen, franc, and, yes, even bitcoin), as shown below. If you need more, you can click More Accounting Formats for a list of expanded options.

The Styles Group

The Styles group on the Home tab allows you to really make your work look good with minimal effort. The following sections show you where everything is, but the only way to really learn to apply the different options is with practice, so start playing around to see what you can do. Remember that you can always get back where you started with **Ctrl+Z** (Undo).

The Conditional Formatting Drop-Down

The Conditional Formatting drop-down allows you to apply rules to cell values and graphically distinguish the cells that meet those rules. Common uses are for dates that fall before or after a certain period or to highlight cells that are above or below a certain value. For instance, you might want to format all cells where customer payments are 30 days overdue. (Chapter 7 discusses conditional formatting in depth.)

There are five major conditional formatting components, as shown below:

- Highlight Cell Rules
- Top/Bottom Rules
- Data Bars
- Color Scales
- Icon Sets

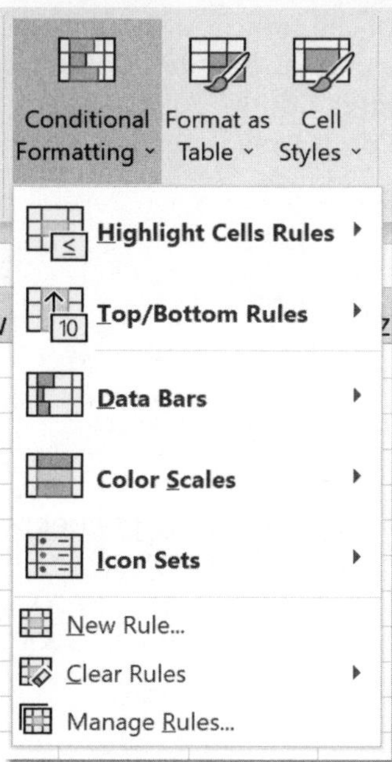

If you select New Rule, you can define formats based on the following:

- Cell values (e.g., high and low ranges)
- Only cells that contain certain values
- Top or bottom-ranked values
- Values above or below average
- Only unique or duplicate values

You can also select Use a Formula to Determine What Cells to Format. This is probably the most powerful option in the New Formatting Rule dialog because you can write your own complex rules, but by no means are any of the other choices lightweights!

Data bars, color scales, and icon sets were new additions to Excel 2007, and they can really help you quickly tell a story with your data, as you can see in the following example.

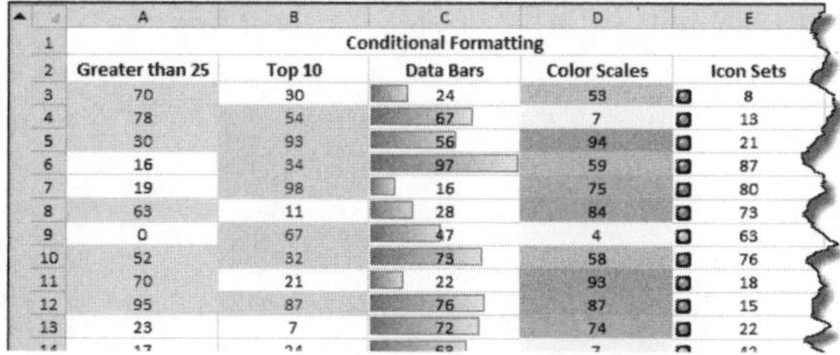

	A	B	C	D	E
1	Conditional Formatting				
2	Greater than 25	Top 10	Data Bars	Color Scales	Icon Sets
3	70	30	24	53	8
4	78	54	67	7	13
5	30	93	56	94	21
6	16	34	97	59	87
7	19	98	16	75	80
8	63	11	28	84	73
9	0	67	47	4	63
10	52	32	73	58	76
11	70	21	22	93	18
12	95	87	76	87	15
13	23	7	72	74	22

The Format as Table Drop-Down

The Format as Table drop-down is a cool feature that lets you quickly apply formatting to your data, provided that it has a contiguous structure, meaning no blank rows or columns in the intended table range because they would be excluded.

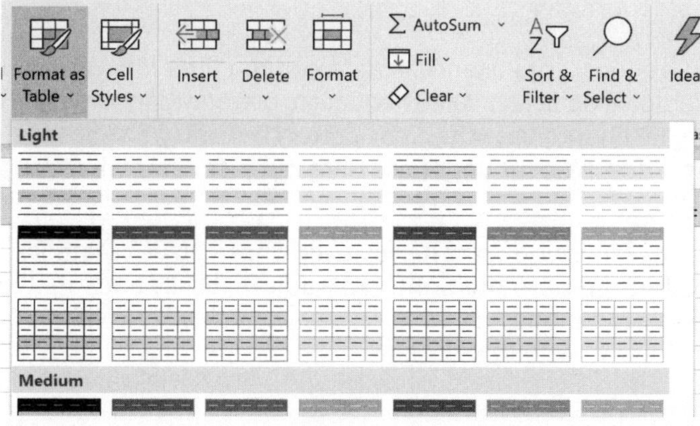

Select any cell in your data area (you don't need to select the whole thing) and then select the table format that you want to apply from the table styles gallery. As soon as you select a table style, you get a dialog asking you if Excel got the range right and whether you have headers for your data. Most of the time you should choose the My Table Has Headers option. If you don't, Excel creates headers for you and labels them Column1, Column2, and so on. If you do have headers but didn't select the My Table Has Headers option, your headers will be in row 1 of the table. You can press **Ctrl+Z** (Undo) and repeat the process to do it over, if needed.

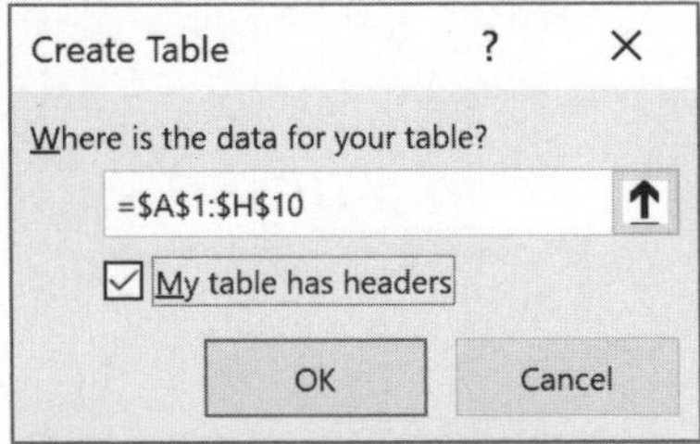

You can use **Ctrl+T** to create a table, and Excel will apply a default blue table style for you. The example below shows unformatted data with this table style applied.

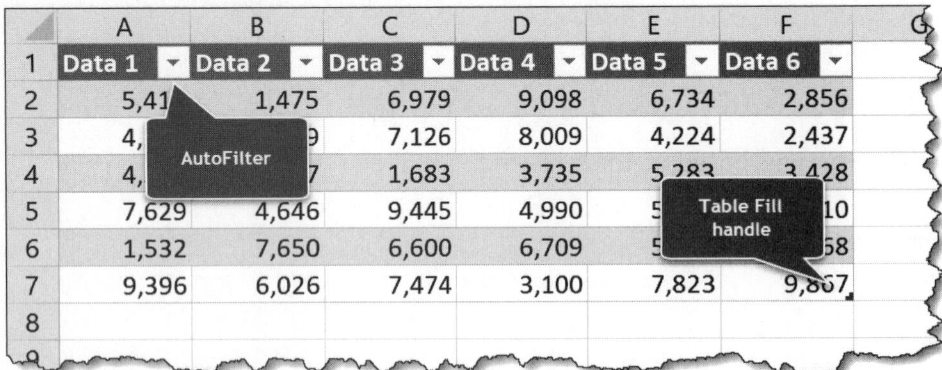

After you select a table format, you can go back to the table styles gallery and switch between various styles. As you do this, Excel gives you a live preview of each selection so you can see it before you commit to it.

The example above shows the AutoFilter drop-downs in the header row and the table fill handle. These are very handy tools that can speed up your work. The AutoFilter drop-downs allow you to quickly filter your data table by the criteria you select. You can click on the drop-downs in any header column to expose the AutoFilter options, shown below.

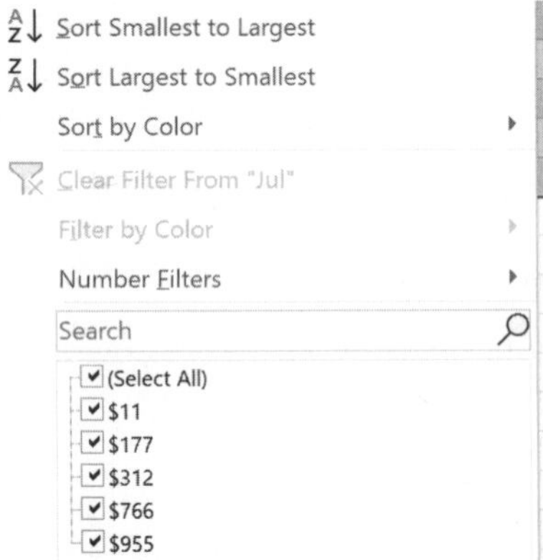

For certain types of data, Excel exposes certain filtering options. For instance, a date column filter lets you filter by week, month, quarter, and so on, and a numeric filter lets you select values equal to, greater than, or less than a certain value, top 10 values, averages, and so on. Filtering gives you great power to display a snapshot of what you want to see at any given moment. And Excel doesn't alter your base data but just hides what you don't want to see until you want to see it again.

The table fill handle lets you drag the table range down as far as you want it. However, once you've created a table, all you need to do to expand it is add data to the bottom or to the right. Excel automatically adds that data to the table and extends the formatting to the new data for you.

The Table Tools Tab

After you've converted data to a table, any time you select the table, Excel displays a contextual Ribbon tab, called Table Design, as shown below. Contextual Ribbon tabs are great because they show up only when they're needed. You see them with tables, PivotTables, and charts. (Chapter 10 is devoted to tables, so I don't go into the Table Design tab properties here.)

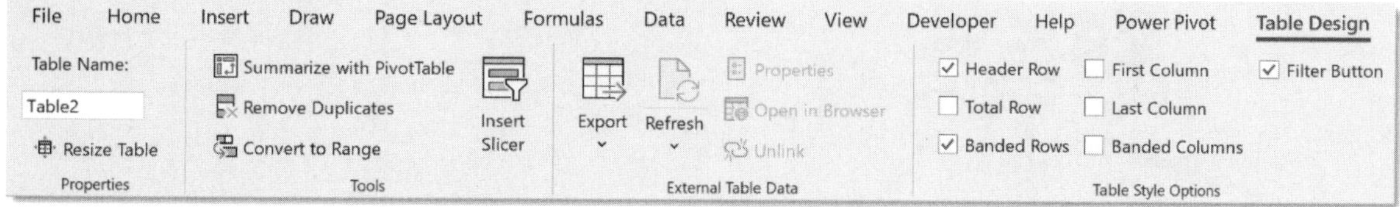

The Cell Styles Drop-Down

The final element of the Styles group is the Cell Styles drop-down, which opens the styles gallery. With this tool, you can select a range of data, such as a header row or individual input cells, and quickly apply a format to give users visual clues about what they should do. This can be very useful for your users, but there are a lot of options here, and it's easy to add so many to a worksheet that it's more confusing than helpful, so be careful to use them judiciously.

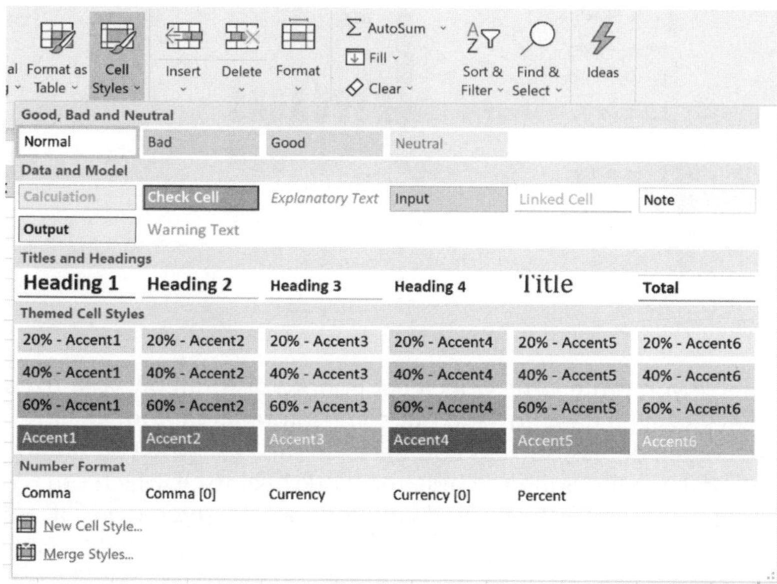

One of the best things about the styles gallery is that it can eliminate an incredible amount of redundant work. Many new (and even seasoned) Excel users make the mistake of manually applying formats such as cell background or font color to cells from the Font dialog. While this certainly works, it can be problematic because if you ever want to change the format, you need to find each and every cell that has the format and change it manually. With styles, you simply right-click on a style and select the Modify option, and you are presented with the Format Cells dialog. The beauty of this method is that you only need to change the format in one place, and every cell in the entire workbook that has that format applied automatically updates. If you don't see a format that suits you, you can click the New Cell Style option to create your own. In addition, styles aren't limited to only cell backgrounds and fonts. For instance, you can use the Input style to set Protection to Unlocked but leave the other properties (background and font) alone. That way, you can protect a worksheet, and all Input style cells will be editable. It's a lot easier to do this than it is to set the background color, font, and protection for a group of cells in multiple steps.

> **Note:** The easier you make it for people to interact with your workbooks and worksheets, the less resistant they will be to using your Excel creations. If you make it difficult for people to give you the information you need, then they'll make getting it difficult as well. You can easily overwhelm users with too many styles, but as you attempt to direct users to enter data in certain areas, styles can help you provide seamless user interaction. You can also unlock certain cells for data entry and direct users to those cells/ranges. Balance is key, and it's up to you to determine what's right for a particular situation.

The Cells Group

The options in the Cells group are very simple. This group allows you to insert and delete rows and columns and change physical elements such as height and width. There are also some more advanced options that deal with not just rows and columns but the worksheet itself. The following sections describe some of the commonly used options in the Format drop-down of the Cells group.

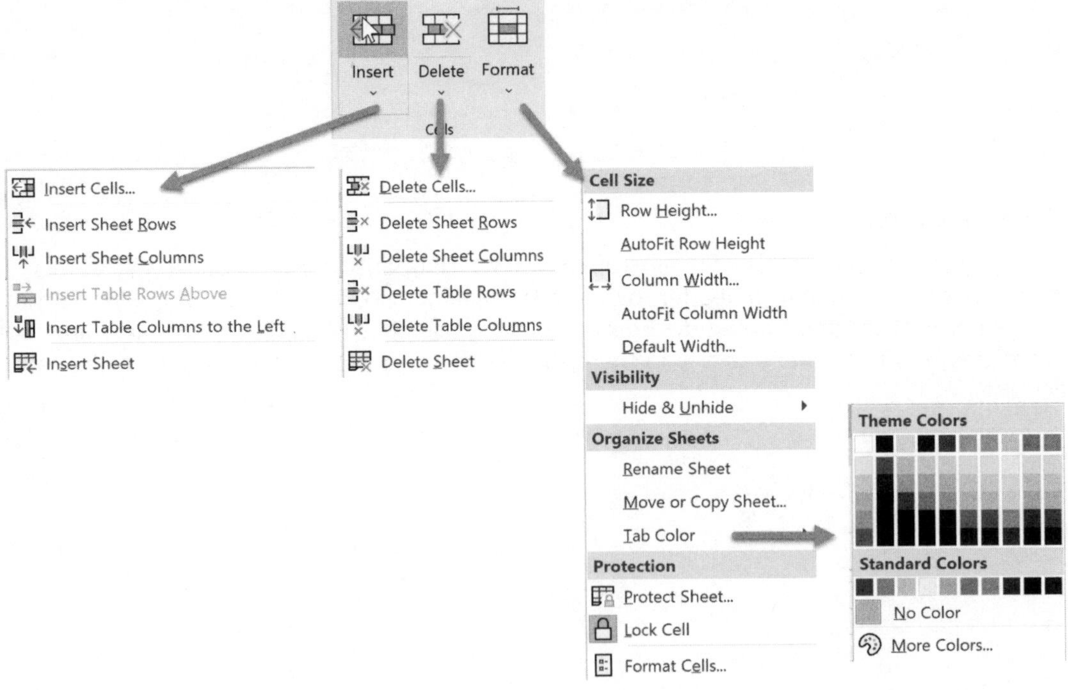

Visibility

You can hide rows and columns in any worksheet. If you protect the worksheet prior to distribution, your users can't unhide those hidden rows and columns. Let's say you need to send out some information from an employee table, but you don't want anyone to see certain details, such as addresses. In this case, you can simply hide that column(s) and protect the sheet. You also have the option to hide the worksheet itself, which can come in very handy if you have sensitive information on some sheets, and you don't want people to see it.

Organize Sheets

The Organize Sheets section offers the following options:

- **Rename Sheet**—You can rename a worksheet by clicking this option to launch a Rename Sheet dialog, as pictured below, or you can double-click on the worksheet tab itself. In either case, you type the new sheet name and press **Enter** (or click OK if you're in the dialog) to confirm it.

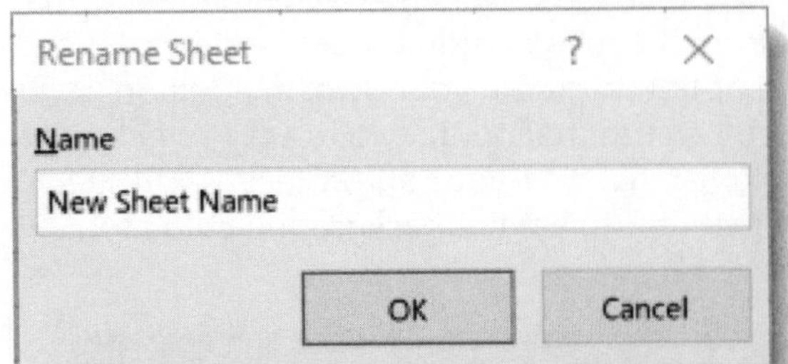

> **Note:** You can't use any invalid characters (: \ / ? * [ ]) or more than 31 valid characters in a sheet name.

- **Move or Copy Sheet**—This neat feature lets you perform some tasks that you would otherwise need to do manually.

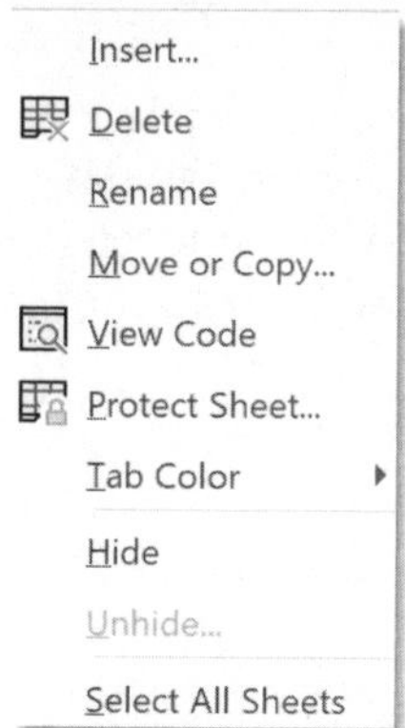

- The following example shows the dialog that appears when you select Move or Copy Sheet.

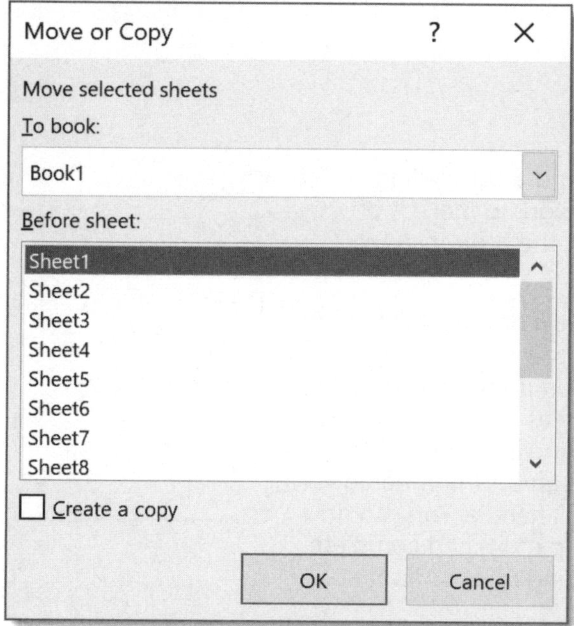

- In the To Book section of the Move of Copy dialog, you can choose any open workbook or even have Excel create a new workbook for you. From there, you can move the sheet to another location. You can also create a copy of an existing worksheet, which can be particularly handy if you don't want someone to see your entire workbook, and you don't want to hide all your worksheets. Let's say you have a workbook with all your prices, by supplier, and each supplier has its own worksheet. You can copy one supplier's worksheet to a new workbook, send it to the supplier for updates, and then replace it when the supplier sends it back.
- **Tab Color**—This is a great feature because it helps you visually identify which worksheets do what. For instance, data entry could be yellow, reports might be green, sensitive data might be red, summaries could be blue, and so on. Again, it is possible to go overboard with your color selections, so don't try to do too much.

Protection

We discussed worksheet protection earlier in this chapter, and this section of the Format drop-down just gives you another location to invoke it. In this section, selecting Format Cells brings up the Format Cells dialog, so this yet another example of Excel giving you access to a tool in multiple places.

The Editing Group

The Editing group at the right end of the Home tab allows you to quickly add functions without writing them yourself. You can, for example, click Fill to find commands that let you add or remove data to/in ranges with just a few clicks, sort and filter your data, and find and select data. The following sections discuss the options in this tab group.

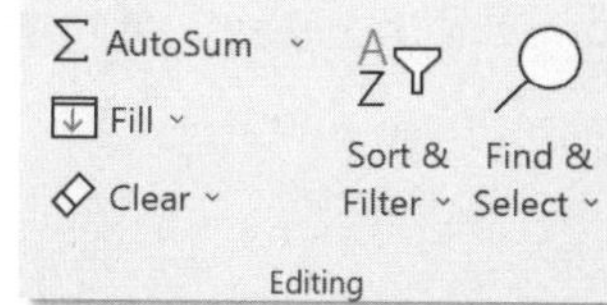

AutoSum

AutoSum can do a lot of work for you, and it's especially handy if you're not very comfortable with Excel's functions. All you need to do is go directly beneath a column of data to the first empty row beneath the data and click the AutoSum tool. You are immediately presented with a list of common functions. When you select an option from the list, Excel automatically creates a formula for you. You just need to press **Enter** to confirm it. The following options are available in the AutoSum drop-down:

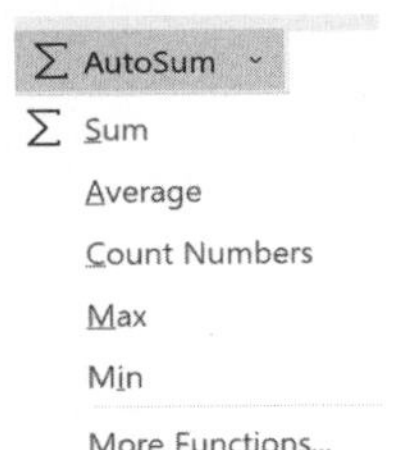

- **Sum**—Returns the sum of the values in the range.
- **Average**—Returns the average of the values in the range.
- **Count Numbers**—Returns the count of the values in the range.
- **Max**—Returns the highest value in the range.
- **Min**—Returns the lowest value in the range.
- **More Functions**—Launches the Insert Function dialog, which is discussed in more detail in the Chapter 6.

Fill

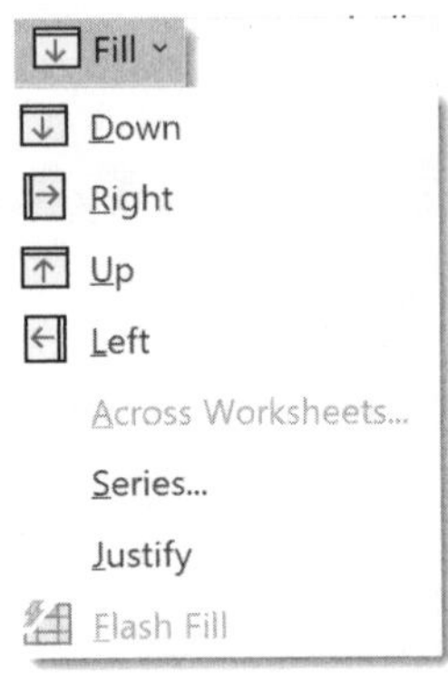

Fill, shown at right, is an interesting feature, but I've never found a compelling reason to use it, as it's not very intuitive and requires a bit of work to make it do what you want. I think it's much easier to use the fill handle at the bottom-right corner of the active cell to fill a range.

The fill handle lets you input the beginning of a series, and Excel does its best to complete the series for you. For example, if you want a list of row numbers, you could type **1** and **2** in adjacent cells, select them both, and then drag the fill handle down or right, and Excel will continue your list (3, 4, 5, etc.) for as long as you drag the fill handle. You can create an even-numbered list by entering **2** and **4** in adjacent cells and then dragging the fill handle, or you can create an odd-numbered list by entering **1** and **3** in adjacent cells and then dragging the fill handle. You can do the same with dates, months, etc. Excel tries to recognize the pattern and complete it for you. This can be a huge timesaver when it comes to setting up a worksheet.

The following sections describe two of the useful items in the Fill drop-down.

Series

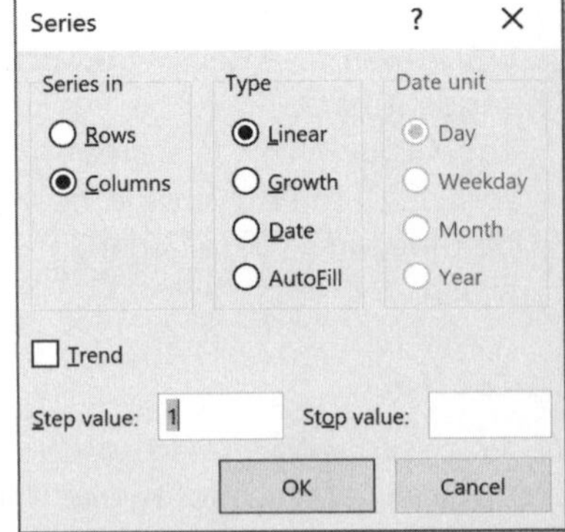

When you select **Home > Fill > Series**, you see the Series dialog. Thanks to this dialog, you don't enter your initial data in one cell and then the increment you want in the next cell. You simply enter your starting value in any cell, select **Home > Fill > Series**, and use the options in the Series dialog.

Let's say you want to start with 1 and fill down the series but increment by 0.5 for each subsequent row. To do this, enter **1** in A1, reselect A1, and select **Home > Fill > Series**. You need to select Columns under Series In to fill down. You can accept the default option Linear, which simply adds the number you enter in the Step Value box (1 in the example at right) to the next entry down or across. In this case, enter 0.**5** in the Step Value box, and in Stop Value enter the maximum number you want to extend this iteration. Then click OK, and you see something like the image at the top of the next page.

This is a lot easier than trying to do the same thing with the fill handle, especially if you're looking at hundreds or even thousands of rows. And you can do the same thing across columns instead of rows.

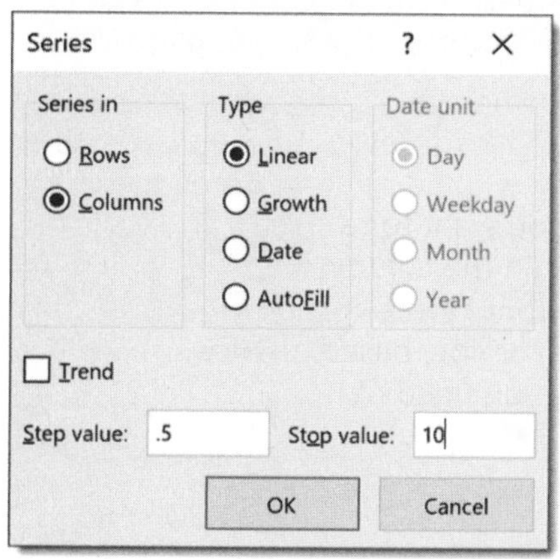

	A
1	1.00
2	1.50
3	2.00
4	2.50
5	3.00
6	3.50
7	4.00
8	4.50
9	5.00

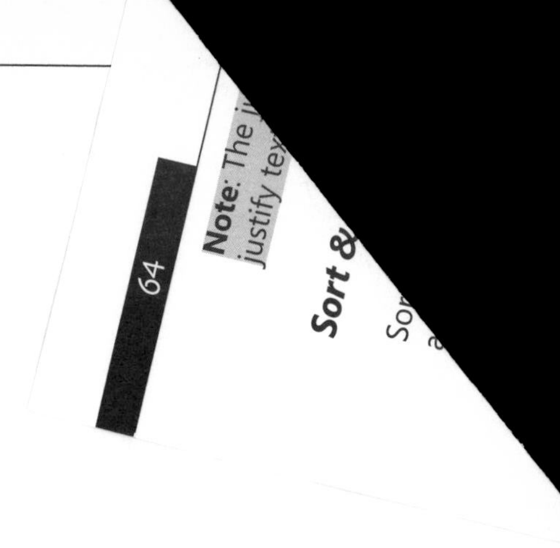

These are the other options in the Series dialog:

- **Growth**—Builds your list by multiplying each subsequent value by whatever you put in the Step Value box.
- **Date**—Allows you to increment dates. When you select Date, the Date Unit options become enabled.
- **AutoFill**—Extends the same AutoFill behavior as dragging the fill handle.

Justify

The Justify option in the Fill drop-down allows you to work with text without having to merge cells or wrap text. This is invaluable for maintaining data integrity if you happen to have text strings in a document.

Although I don't recommend that you use Excel as a text editor, you do have some options for arranging text the way you need it. Let's say you have a long string of text that you've input to be at the bottom of a form, but you want it all to wrap within the confines of your form's width.

> **Note:** Why not use Excel as a text editor? There are three good reasons. First, Excel doesn't often play nicely with text. Second, Excel is a spreadsheet application; Word is meant for working with text. Finally, while you *can* build form letters in Excel, you should instead use Word's Mail Merge feature with your Excel workbook as the data source.

You could try to select the right number of cells that the text might fit into and then experiment with Word Wrap and Merge Cells. Or you could use the **Home > Fill > Justify** command to have Excel do it for you. Just select the cell holding your text, drag it down to the end/side of your form, as shown below, and select **Home >Fill > Justify**.

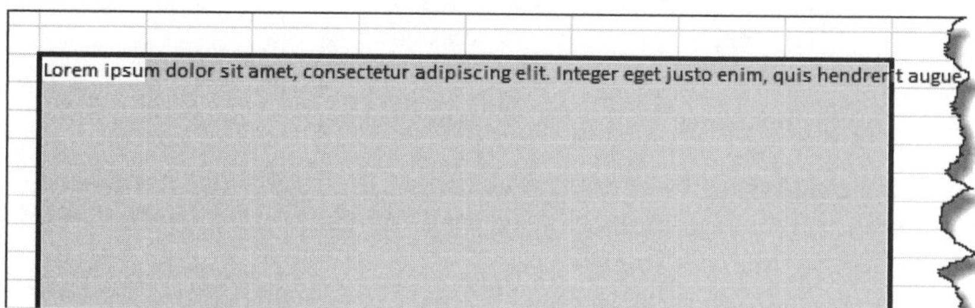

You end up with this:

Lorem ipsum dolor sit amet, consectetur adipiscing elit. Integer eget justo enim, quis
hendrerit augue. Maecenas congue pulvinar ultrices. Nunc varius purus ac erat mollis at
porttitor augue tempor. Nullam eleifend, purus et pulvinar posuere, augue magna

Note that Excel automatically slices your text string into smaller chunks that fit the range you selected. Yes, you can see that it has been physically separated, but don't worry: Excel can put it back the way it was. To revert to your original text string, just select the entire range of justified text and extend it across as many columns as it takes to put it back. From there select **Home > Fill > Justify**, and Excel reverts it for you.

ustify command only works when the original text is less than 256 characters wide. If you t that is longer, the command will truncate each line at 255 characters without warning.

Filter

ting is something you'll probably do quite a bit if you have data that you want to re-rrange. To quickly sort data, just put the cursor in any cell in any dataset (in the column that you want to sort first) and select **Home > Sort & Filter > Sort A to Z** or **Home > Sort & Filter > Sort Z to A**. Excel automatically selects the sorting range for you, based on where the cursor is at the time. If you want to sort by multiple criteria, you need to instead select **Home > Sort & Filter > Custom Sort**.

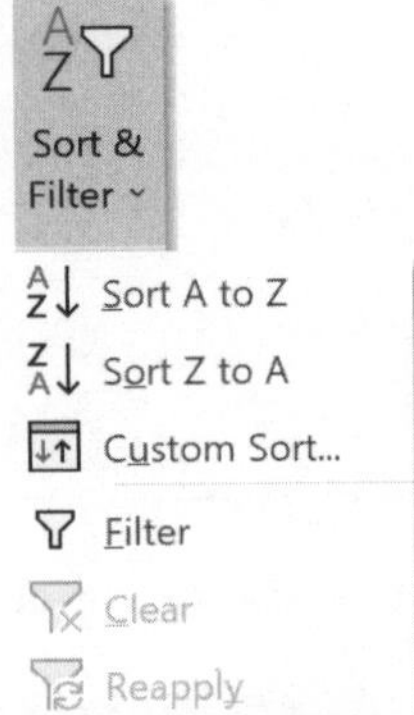

Earlier versions of Excel offered only three Sort By options, but now Excel offers up to 64 of them (although it's not likely you'll ever need that many).

One of the best ways to completely screw up your data when sorting is to have column gaps in it. If you sort, make sure that any data you want to sort is in contiguous ranges and that you don't have any empty columns between vital data. For example, if you insert an empty column in your data to give it a visual spacer (which is commonly done to separate right-justified numbers from left-justified text), Excel doesn't recognize the range past the blank column unless you have manually selected the entire range—and even then you can have problems. The portion of your data where the cursor was when you invoked the sort will be fine. However, the data that was outside the range because of that column separation will no longer be associated with the data that was sorted! If you find yourself in this position, the first thing to do is **Ctrl+Z** (Undo). If you're too late for Undo to work, close the workbook without saving it. You might lose some work, but at least your customer data won't be completely messed up.

Here's an example of some customer data with an empty column (D) as a spacer.

	A	B	C	D	E	F
1	Customer Name	Customer #	Order #		Item	Invoice Amount
2	Tom Jones	35546	A123		Sprocket	$125.00
3	Larry Thompson	A325	B768		Manual	$50.00
4	Bob Smith	1234	456		Fetzer valve	$200.00

Here's what happens if you have the cursor in cell A1 and haven't selected the entire range but then choose **Home > Sort & Filter > Sort A to Z**:

	A	B	C	D	E	F
1	Customer Name	Customer #	Order #		Item	Invoice Amount
2	Bob Smith	1234	456		Sprocket	$125.00
3	Larry Thompson	A325	B768		Manual	$50.00
4	Tom Jones	35546	A123		Fetzer valve	$200.00

Uh-oh, Excel just did exactly what you told it to do: It sorted the contiguous range. But look what happened to the Item and Invoice Amount columns! They didn't change in relation to their rightful orders. Unfortunately, it's not uncommon at all for entire datasets to be corrupted in this way.

The following is an example of the same dataset sorted after the entire range was manually selected:

	A	B	C	D	E	F
1	Customer Name	Customer #	Order #		Item	Invoice Amount
2	Bob Smith	1234	456		Fetzer valve	$200.00
3	Larry Thompson	A325	B768		Manual	$50.00
4	Tom Jones	35546	A123		Sprocket	$125.00

Note: Don't put blank rows or columns in your datasets! If you need to have a gap between left-justified and right-justified data in columns, use the Indent tool rather than using an empty column as a separator. Empty columns in the midst of your data can cause more problems than merged cells (which at least won't destroy your data if you accidentally sort it)!

You can avoid this behavior if you convert your data range to an Excel table. A table recognizes the entire table range, regardless of blank columns. Chapter 10 is devoted to tables.

> **Note:** Excel offers a number of cool sorting features, including Sort by Cell Color, Sort by Font Color, Sort by Conditional Format Icon, and Sort by Custom List.

The Custom Sort Dialog

When you select **Home > Sort & Filter > Custom Sort**, the Sort dialog appears. This dialog gives you Add Level, Delete Level, and Copy Level options, which let you add or delete criteria and copy one level to repeat. This dialog also has an Options button. The most important item in this dialog is the My Data Has Headers checkbox. In most cases, your data will have headers (as in the previous customer example), so you'll generally want to have this checkbox selected. If you don't, Excel will sort your header row along with your data. If that happens, you'll know about it immediately because your header will simply disappear to someplace in your data.

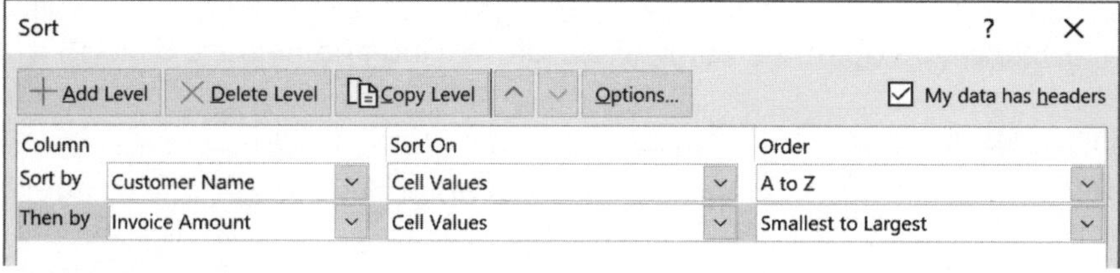

Find & Select

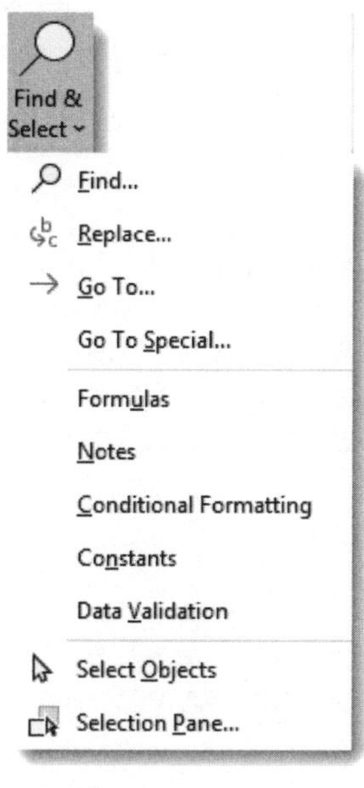

The Find & Select drop-down in the Editing group exposes a lot of functionality that can come in very handy. The following sections discuss some of the options.

Find

The Find option does just what it sounds like: It lets you find items in a worksheet or an entire workbook (text or values), in formulas, and in comments. You can even tell Excel to find certain applied formats. Simply enter your search criteria and tell Excel how you want to search. When you click **Home > Find & Select > Find**, the Find and Replace dialog appears, as shown below.

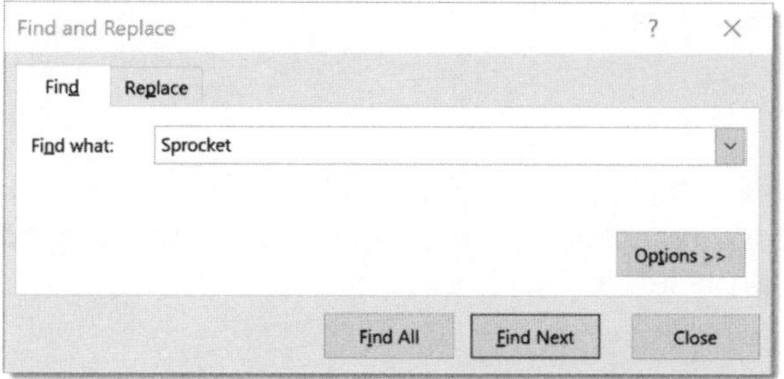

If you click the Options button in this dialog, you get an expanded version of the Find and Replace dialog, as shown below.

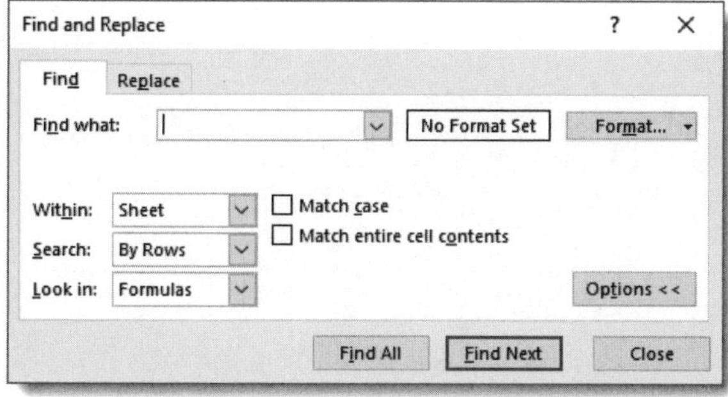

A simple search doesn't always return the results you expect. In such a case, you can expand the Options dialog and narrow your search criteria. These are the options you see on the Find tab of the Find and Replace dialog:

- **Find All**—Finds all matching instances of your search criteria
- **Find Next**—Finds the first instance of your search criteria. Each successive button click moves on to the next match.
- **Options**—Opens the expanded Find and Replace dialog, which includes the following additional options:
  - **Within**—Searches the sheet or the entire workbook.
  - **Search**—Searches by rows or by columns.
  - **Look In**—Searches formulas, values, or comments.
  - **Match Case**—Allows you to specify an uppercase or lowercase search.
  - **Match Entire Cell Contents**—Allows you to search precisely. Use this option only if you know exactly what you're looking for, such as a product or employee name.

Replace

By selecting **Home > Find & Select > Replace**, you open the Replace tab of the Find and Replace dialog.

It is very similar to the Find tab, but the Replace tab allows you to not only find something but replace it with something else. This is incredibly helpful when you need to make mass changes to a worksheet or workbook. It's especially powerful for making changes to a lot of formulas, but note that it will replace whatever you tell it to, so it is possible to inadvertently reduce your formulas to garbage if you're not careful. For example, if you replace **E** with **A** in the formula =Sheet1!E1 but fail to select the Match Case option, you will end up with =ShAAt1!A1, which isn't be exactly what you were after.

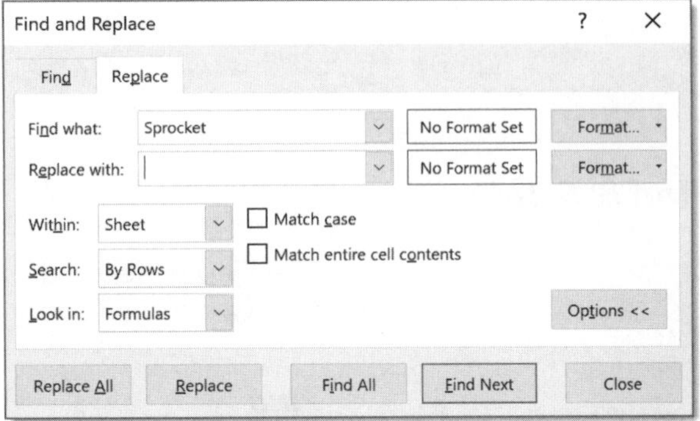

(Excel also pops up an irritating dialog, asking you to locate the workbook where "ShAAt1" is located; changing 500 formulas at once and getting the criteria wrong is a hard way to learn a lesson.) When replacing formula elements, it's best to be as specific as possible. In this case, you could search for **!A** and replace with **!E** to resolve the problem, or, as mentioned before, you could be sure to select Match Case. As you start getting into more functions later in this book (especially Chapter 6), you'll be able to quickly identify which elements you can use as Find/Replace criteria.

Go To

If you select **Home > Find & Select > Go To**, Excel opens the Go To dialog, shown below, which enables you to go to a specific cell or range. You can also open the Go To dialog by pressing **F5** or even just by entering the cell address in the Name box to the left of the formula bar.

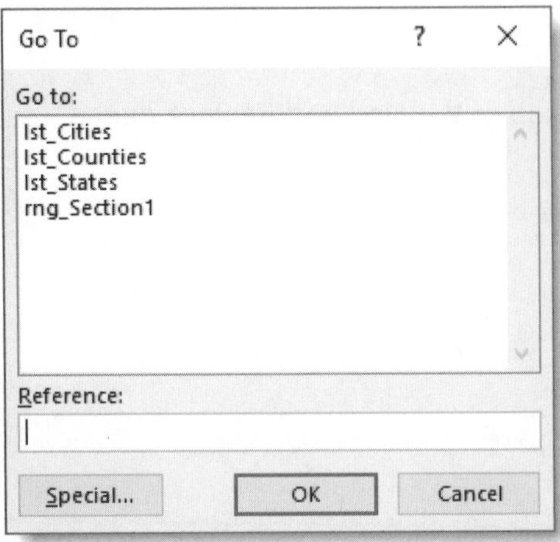

Go To Special

The Go To Special dialog, which you open by clicking the **Special** button in the Go To dialog, gives you a lot of features that you probably won't use until you have a lot more experience, but it does a lot of things you should understand. This dialog gives you the ability to select cells with all kinds of different characteristics, such as all the formulas or blank cells in a region. Think of the Go To Special dialog as an auditing tool that lets you identify areas that you would otherwise need to find manually. It includes the following options:

- **Notes**—Finds all cells with cell Notes. (Notes, which are entered through the Review tab, are addendums you can make to cells that are independent of the cells' values.)
- **Constants**—Finds any non-calculated cells, such as text entries (employee names, city, state, etc.).
- **Formulas**—Finds any calculated cells.
- **Blanks**—Finds any blank cells in a region. This option can be really helpful for identifying or filling in missing data.
- **Current Region**—Selects the current region of contiguous cells. This is helpful if you have disparate datasets on the same worksheet and need to isolate them for sorting, charting, etc. You can accomplish this with the shortcut **Ctrl+*** from the number keypad or **Ctrl+Shift+*** from the regular keypad.
- **Current Array**—Finds an array.
  Note: Arrays give you a way of getting Excel to evaluate a large range and produce multiple results. This book doesn't cover arrays in depth, but if you're interested, you can find lots of documentation on the Internet and in the Help file.

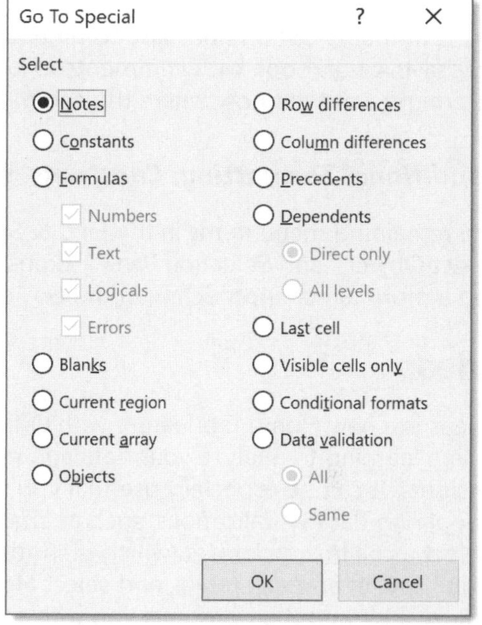

- **Objects**—Selects any objects you may have on a worksheet (buttons, graphics, charts, etc.).
- **Row Differences**—Highlights any rows that are different from the active cell. This option essentially invokes the error checker in case you turned it off. Note that you need to select a range or an entire row to be able to do this; if all you have selected is the active cell, it won't do anything.
- **Column Differences**—Selects column differences the same way Row Differences selects column differences.
- **Precedents**—Finds any cells that lead to the active cell via formulas (i.e., any cells that the active cell references).
- **Dependents**—Finds any cells that are dependent on the active cell for calculations (i.e., any cells that reference the active cell).
  Caution: Excel workbooks can blow up in size if you apply formats or formulas to a large range—even if you don't use all the cells in the range. Let's say you add a formula to A1:A1046000 but use only A1:A110; Excel views the last cell with the formula (or format) applied as the last cell that had data input, even though you are using a cell much lower in the range. The problem with this is that you can delete the formulas/formats you're not using, but Excel will still remember that you had something there and may increase the file size as a result. The only way to get rid of unused ranges is to delete the unused rows and columns. Therefore, you should only add formulas/formatting to the ranges you actually need!
- **Last Cell**—Finds the last cell in a worksheet that contains data. This option can be very useful if you have what should be a relatively small workbook that's blown up in size.
- **Visible Cells Only**—Allows you to safely delete filtered rows without touching any hidden rows.
- **Conditional Formats**—Selects all cells that have conditional formatting applied. If you've applied some formats and forgotten about them, this option will help you find them. This generally isn't a problem, however, because conditional formatting tends to be quite visible.
- **Data Validation**—Selects all cells that have data validation applied. This is similar to the Conditional Format option, but data validation cells can be harder to find than conditional formats, as data validation options don't appear until you actually activate a cell.
  Hint: Both the Conditional Formats and Data Validation options can be handy tools when you're preparing a workbook for distribution and want to make sure the user interface is perfect.

Formulas

The Formulas option identifies all formulas on a worksheet. It's useful when you want to distribute a workbook without formulas and make sure you haven't missed any. It also gives you some useful functionality in that you can edit the first cell (i.e., F2) and then **Tab** between all the selected formula cells to see if you need to edit them.

Comments

The Comments option finds any comments you might have entered. This is usually not very important, but if you have a workbook with comments to aid users with data entry, and now you're at the distribution stage, you might want to know where the comments are in case you need to get rid of them.

Conditional Formatting, Constants, Data Validation, Select Objects, and Selection Pane

The remaining menu items in the Find & Select group—Conditional Formatting, Constants, Data Validation, Select Objects, and Selection Pane—expose the same elements you find in the Go To Special dialog but give you a more direct approach than the Go To Special dialog.

Ideas

Ideas is a new Home tab feature with Office 365 that uses machine learning to analyze your data and return meaningful insights. It can be especially useful if you're not well versed in preparing data visualizations, such as charts and PivotTables. Just select a cell in any dataset (which is another great case for having your data in an Excel table), and select **Home > Ideas** . Excel thinks a bit and then presents you with some relevant options, based on the analysis of its intelligent services. At right is an example using the customer data from earlier in this chapter.

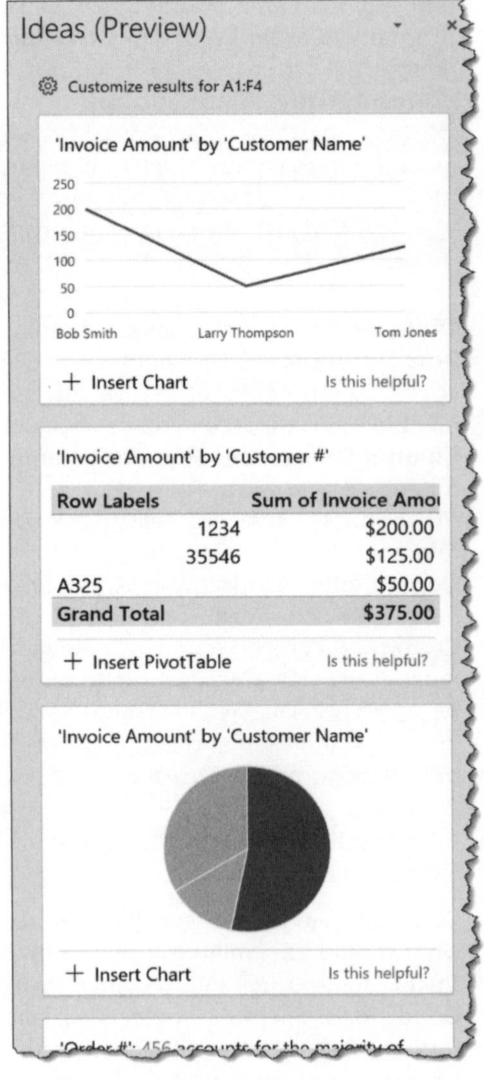

Chapter Summary

- In this chapter you learned the ins and outs of the Home tab on the Excel Ribbon. Since this is where you'll generally spend the most time, it's probably the most important Ribbon element to learn.
- You learned about the Home tab's elements and also saw that there are multiple ways to expose the various elements by using tab options, keyboard shortcuts, and dialog launchers.

Chapter 4: The Ribbon in Depth: The Main Tabs

In Chapters 2 and 3, we explored two of the primary Ribbon elements: the File tab, which you can use to customize the Excel environment so that it's right for you, and the Home tab, which holds the most commonly used Ribbon elements. In this chapter we'll explore the rest of the Ribbon elements, one tab at a time.

The Insert Tab

The Insert tab contains options that primarily deal with objects you insert on, in, and onto worksheets (PivotTables, charts, pictures, SmartArt, etc.). The following sections discuss the various groups on this tab.

The Tables Group

The Tables group on the Insert tab includes the PivotTable, Recommended PivotTables, and Table options, as discussed in the following sections.

PivotTable

PivotTables are incredibly powerful data analysis tools that allow you to quickly get different looks at your data in a manner that would otherwise be available only to those skilled at using databases. PivotTables allow you to turn transactional data (e.g., customer orders) from single entries into complex and dynamic summarizations like this:

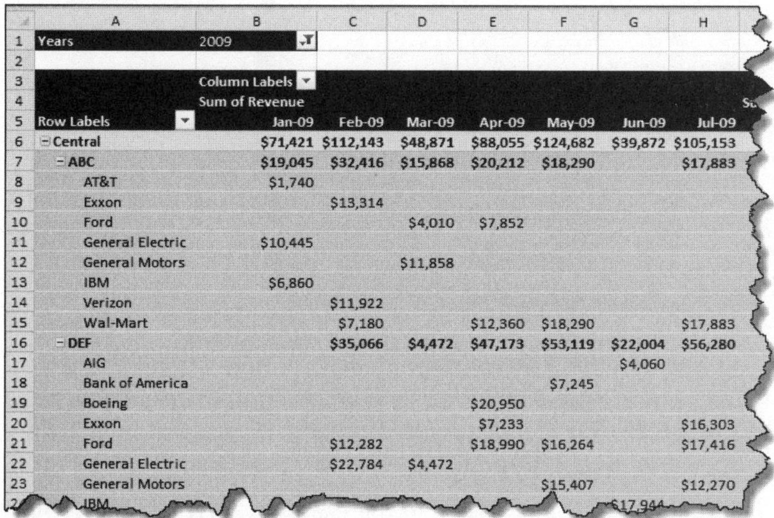

	A	B	C	D	E	F	G	H
1	Years	2009						
2								
3		Column Labels						
4		Sum of Revenue						
5	Row Labels	Jan-09	Feb-09	Mar-09	Apr-09	May-09	Jun-09	Jul-09
6	Central	$71,421	$112,143	$48,871	$88,055	$124,682	$39,872	$105,153
7	ABC	$19,045	$32,416	$15,868	$20,212	$18,290		$17,883
8	AT&T	$1,740						
9	Exxon		$13,314					
10	Ford			$4,010	$7,852			
11	General Electric	$10,445						
12	General Motors			$11,858				
13	IBM	$6,860						
14	Verizon		$11,922					
15	Wal-Mart		$7,180		$12,360	$18,290		$17,883
16	DEF		$35,066	$4,472	$47,173	$53,119	$22,004	$56,280
17	AIG						$4,060	
18	Bank of America					$7,245		
19	Boeing				$20,950			
20	Exxon				$7,233			$16,303
21	Ford		$12,282		$18,990	$16,264		$17,416
22	General Electric		$22,784	$4,472				
23	General Motors					$15,407		$12,270
24	IBM						$17,944	

You can select **Insert > PivotTable** to add a PivotTable to a worksheet, as discussed in Chapter 11.

Recommended PivotTables

If you're not sure what kind of PivotTable you want, you can select **Insert > Recommended PivotTables**, and Excel will take a look at your existing data and make some recommendations for you. This is a great way to let Excel do some of the hard work for you.

Table

Data entered in Excel is often in a structured format, with defined column headers and each row of data representing a unique item. This type of setup is appropriate for things like parts lists, employee rosters, and transactional data, such as sales orders. By itself, this data can be relatively boring, and working with it can require a lot of manual work. Fortunately, Excel tables take a lot of manual effort out of working with data in that they allow you to automatically format and extend data ranges and formulas as you add data. Most importantly, you can work with the data in a table independently of any other data on the worksheet. For example, you can delete a row in a table without deleting the associated row in the Excel grid. Tables also include dynamic formula functionality called *structured references*, which can automatically update themselves as you add new data.

When you use Excel tables, you can start with data that looks like this:

	A	B	C	D	E	F	G	H	I	J
1	Region	Product	Date	Month	Customer	Quantity	Revenue	COGS	Profit	
2	Central	ABC	01/09/08	Jan-08	General Motors	800	$16,416	$6,776	$9,640	
3	Central	ABC	01/12/08	Jan-08	IBM	300	$6,267	$2,541	$3,726	
4	Central	ABC	01/25/08	Jan-08	CitiGroup	1000	$20,770	$8,470	$12,300	
5	Central	ABC	02/08/08	Feb-08	CitiGroup	100	$1,817	$847	$970	
6	Central	ABC	02/09/08	Feb-08	General Motors	300	$5,157	$2,541	$2,616	
7	Central	ABC	02/19/08	Feb-08	Wal-Mart	500	$10,385	$4,235	$6,150	
8	Central	ABC	02/20/08	Feb-08	Exxon	600	$11,124	$5,082	$6,042	
9	Central	ABC	02/27/08	Feb-08	Ford	900	$16,209	$7,623	$8,586	
10	Central	ABC	03/18/08	Mar-08	Wal-Mart	800	$16,696	$6,776	$9,920	
11	Central	ABC	03/22/08	Mar-08	Wal-Mart	300	$5,355	$2,541	$2,814	
12	Central	ABC	03/23/08	Mar-08	Wal-Mart	200	$3,756	$1,694	$2,062	
13	Central	ABC	03/27/08	Mar-08	General Motors	300	$5,358	$2,541	$2,817	
14	Central	ABC	04/06/08	Apr-08	General Electric	300	$5,886	$2,541	$3,345	
15										
16										
17										

And you can change that data to look as follows—in just a few mouse clicks:

	A	B	C	D	E	F	G	H	I	J
1	Region	Product	Date	Montl	Customer	Quant	Reveni	CO(	Pro	
2	Central	ABC	01/09/08	Jan-08	General Motors	800	$16,416	$6,776	$9,640	
3	Central	ABC	01/12/08	Jan-08	IBM	300	$6,267	$2,541	$3,726	
4	Central	ABC	01/25/08	Jan-08	CitiGroup	1000	$20,770	$8,470	$12,300	
5	Central	ABC	02/08/08	Feb-08	CitiGroup	100	$1,817	$847	$970	
6	Central	ABC	02/09/08	Feb-08	General Motors	300	$5,157	$2,541	$2,616	
7	Central	ABC	02/19/08	Feb-08	Wal-Mart	500	$10,385	$4,235	$6,150	
8	Central	ABC	02/20/08	Feb-08	Exxon	600	$11,124	$5,082	$6,042	
9	Central	ABC	02/27/08	Feb-08	Ford	900	$16,209	$7,623	$8,586	
10	Central	ABC	03/18/08	Mar-08	Wal-Mart	800	$16,696	$6,776	$9,920	
11	Central	ABC	03/22/08	Mar-08	Wal-Mart	300	$5,355	$2,541	$2,814	
12	Central	ABC	03/23/08	Mar-08	Wal-Mart	200	$3,756	$1,694	$2,062	
13	Central	ABC	03/27/08	Mar-08	General Motors	300	$5,358	$2,541	$2,817	
14	Central	ABC	04/06/08	Apr-08	General Electric	300	$5,886	$2,541	$3,345	
15	Central	ABC	04/13/08	Apr-08	CitiGroup	400	$8,016	$3,388	$4,628	
16	Central	ABC	04/30/08	Apr-08	Ford	200	$3,802	$1,694	$2,108	
17	Central	ABC	05/10/08	May-08	Exxon	500	$8,785	$4,235	$4,550	
18										
19										

All you need to do is make sure that the active cell is within the data range (it doesn't matter where) and go to **Insert > Table** and select the table style you like from the table styles gallery. Excel automatically converts your data range into a table. Alternatively, if you press **Ctrl+T**, Excel gives you a table in the default blue style shown above. You can later change the table style by selecting a different option from the gallery.

One thing that's neat about tables is that if you were to add data in row 18 in the example above, Excel would automatically extend the table, its formatting, and formulas to the new row. You can add data by copy/pasting or by typing in any cell directly beneath the table. Excel also extends a table if you add data to the first column to the right of the table. What you can't see is that behind the scenes, Excel has defined the entire table area as a specific range, so it knows exactly where it starts and ends. This comes into play when you add functions to a table, as Excel also automatically extends the table range. In the preceding example, if you go to cell J2 and add a SUM function with AutoSum, you see Excel build the function shown below.

Quantity	Revenue	COGS	Profit	
800	$16,416	$6,776	$9,640	=SUM(tbl_Ledger[@[Quantity]:[Profit]])
300	$6,267	$2,541	$3,726	
1,000	$20,770	$8,470	$12,300	
100	$1,817	$847	$970	
300	$5,157	$2,541	$2,616	
500	$10,385	$4,235	$6,150	
600	$11,124	$5,082	$6,042	

As soon as you press **Enter** to confirm AutoSum's solution, the table automatically reformats itself and extends the new SUM function to the entire column range, as shown below.

Quantity	Revenue	COGS	Profit	Column1
800	$16,416	$6,776	$9,640	33,632
300	$6,267	$2,541	$3,726	12,834
1,000	$20,770	$8,470	$12,300	42,540
100	$1,817	$847	$970	3,734
300	$5,157	$2,541	$2,616	10,614
500	$10,385	$4,235	$6,150	21,270
600	$11,124	$5,082	$6,042	22,848
900	$16,209	$7,623	$8,586	33,318
800	[illegible]	$6,776	[illegible]	[illegible]

Unfortunately, AutoSum isn't perfect. In the example above, it includes the entire numeric range in the SUM function, written in the structured reference nomenclature: **=SUM(tbl_Ledger[@[Quantity]:[Profit]])**. Obviously, you wouldn't want the quantity included in the sum, and you would subtract cost of goods sold from profit, so you would want to adjust the formula to be **=[@Revenue]-[@COGS]** (which is equivalent to **=G4-H4**). Here you might see one of the benefits of structured references: They refer to your table headers instead of using range references. Another benefit is that as you select different columns to include in your formulas, Excel automatically adds the structured reference language for you, so you don't need to type **[@ Revenue]** or worry about typos.

The Illustrations Group

The Illustrations group allows you to access all the design objects you can place on a worksheet. The following sections discuss the options available in this group.

Pictures

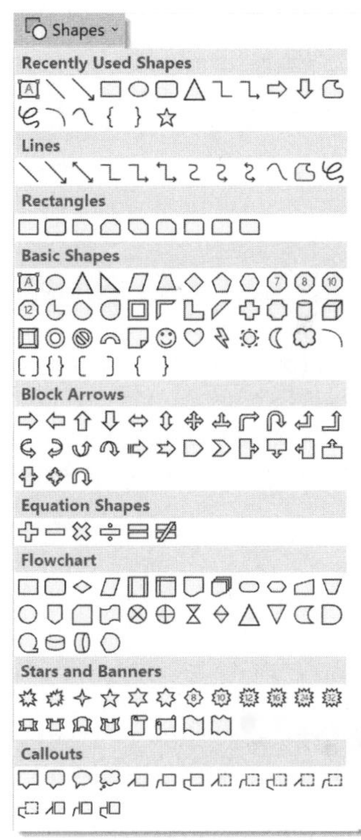

The Pictures option allows you to insert a picture from a location of your choice. It has to be a picture format that Office can read, such as .jpeg, .gif, or .bmp.

Online Pictures

With the Online Pictures option, you can search galleries of stock photos in different categories, such as business, sports, animals, nature, and so on. The images in these galleries are royalty-free images provided by Microsoft.

Shapes

With the Shapes option, you can select from a huge variety of shapes, called *drawing objects*, that you can resize and format; you can even add text to some of them.

If you select a shape that you want to insert, as soon as you hover your cursor over the worksheet, it turns into a cross. After you click on the worksheet wherever you want to place the shape, you can drag it to the vertical/horizontal size that you want and release the mouse button to place the shape. You can adjust the placement and size of a shape at any time. The following examples shows a few different shapes placed on a worksheet.

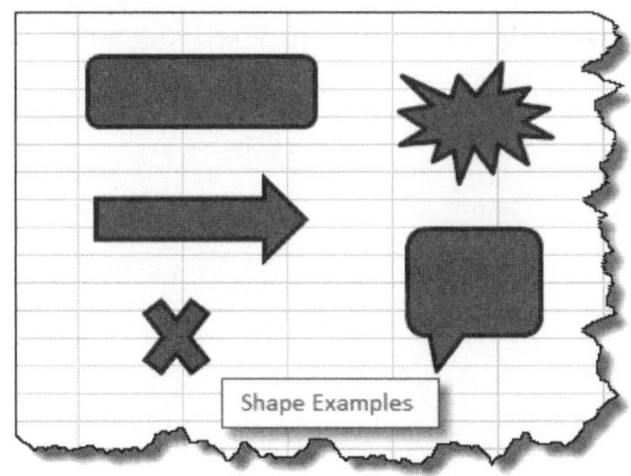

As soon as you insert a shape, you see the Ribbon change to show the Shape Format contextual tab, shown below.

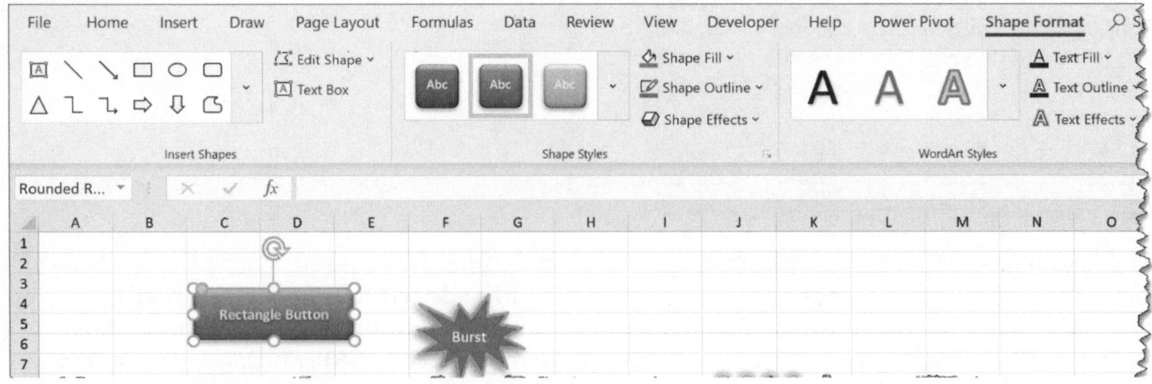

The Shape Format tab contains the following groups:

- **Insert Shapes**—This group is somewhat redundant, since you just inserted a shape.
- **Shape Styles**—Microsoft's design experts have done an outstanding job of giving you some fantastic options in this group. There are too many ways to customize these objects to cover here, but I encourage you to draw some shapes and see what kind of formats you can come up with. If you want to add text to a shape, just right-click it and select the Edit Text option.

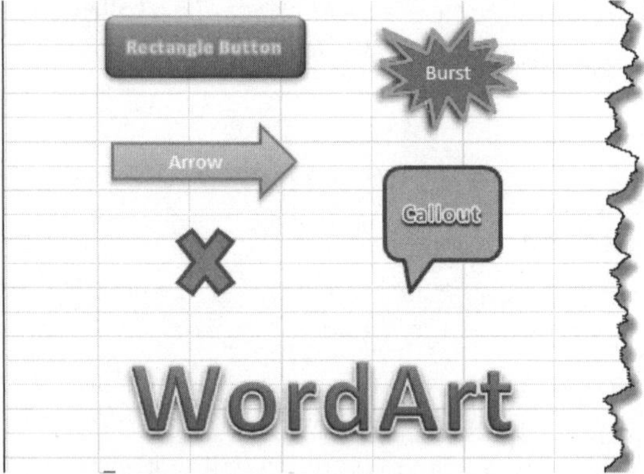

- **WordArt Styles**—These options apply only to text, although you can apply them to text you've embedded in a shape via the Edit Text option. There is also a WordArt command on the Ribbon, which we'll look at momentarily. Again, there are too many potential combinations to possibly cover here, so you're encouraged to work on some of your own.

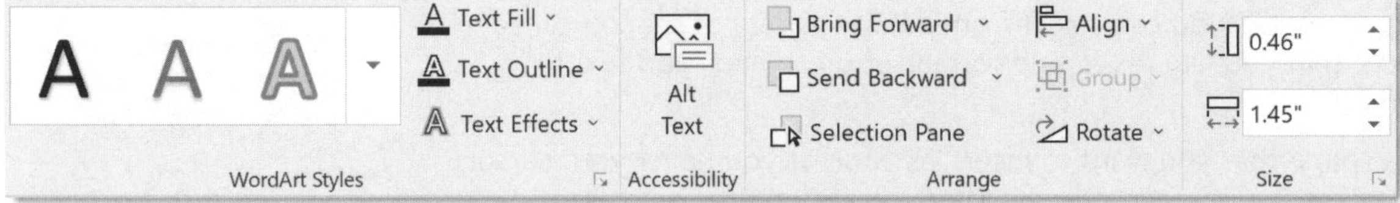

- **Arrange**—The Arrange group options are relatively straightforward:
  - **Bring Forward/Send Backward**—If you place objects on top of each other, you can use these options to specify their order. For instance, say that you draw a callout on a chart, and Excel decides to place it beneath the chart instead of on top. With the callout selected, you would just select **Insert > Bring Forward > Bring to Front**, and Excel would move your callout to the top.
  - **Selection Pane**—This option opens the Selection pane, shown below, which lists all the shapes you have on the worksheet and allows you to order them in the list.

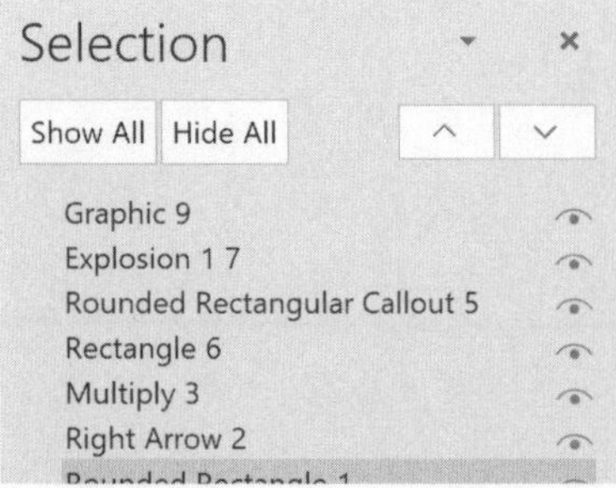

- **Align**—If you have two or more shapes on a worksheet, you are likely to use this option all the time. It allows you to easily position shapes in relation to each other without having to move them around manually. In the previous shape example illustration, the three shapes on the left were set with the Aligned Center and Distributed Horizontally options, which is a lot easier (not to mention faster) than trying to position them by yourself.
- **Group**—Once you've gotten your shapes where you want them in relation to each other, it's a good idea to select all of them (you can use **Shift+click** to select multiple shapes) and then select Group. This keeps the objects together. Unfortunately, Excel doesn't always behave well with shapes, but grouping them ensures that they don't jump all over the place. This is especially useful if you'll be using a workbook on different screens, which might not all treat your shapes the same way.

Note: You can use **Ctrl+click** to select objects, but be aware that if you use **Ctrl+click** and then drag a shape, you end up copying it. This is handy if you want to copy a shape, but you need to be careful not to inadvertently copy all the ones you have selected.

- **Size**—The Size group shows you the height and width of a shape. If you need to make sure that multiple shapes are the same size, it's often easier to adjust them all here than to try to get them the same size by wrangling their handles.

Note: When a shape has a rotate symbol above the shape handles (as shown below left), you can rotate the shape by simply dragging it to the angle you want. The yellow symbol beneath a shape (as shown below right) allows you drag the object's tail wherever you want.

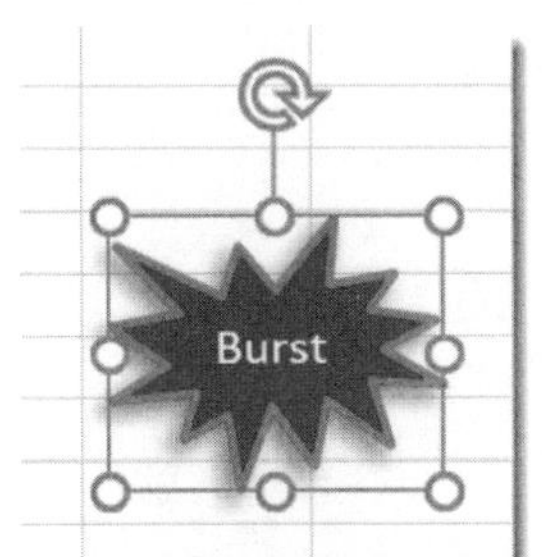

Icons

The Icons option gives you access to a group of categorized SVG (scalable vector graphics) icons that you can add to worksheets. They are customizable, and you can adjust their fills, outlines, and effects.

For example, the following example shows an icon that has had its fill, outline, and effects adjusted.

3D Models

You can use the 3D Models option to import 3D models from applications such as Paint 3D, which you can download for free from the Microsoft Store. Once models are installed, you can select from a gallery of pre-built designs.

SmartArt

The SmartArt option exposes more predesigned graphic elements that Microsoft added with Excel 2007. What you used to have to create in another application, like Adobe Illustrator or Microsoft Visio, you can now draw directly in Excel. If you deal with organization (org) charts, you'll be especially interested in the Hierarchy group. When you select **Insert > SmartArt**, Excel opens the dialog shown below.

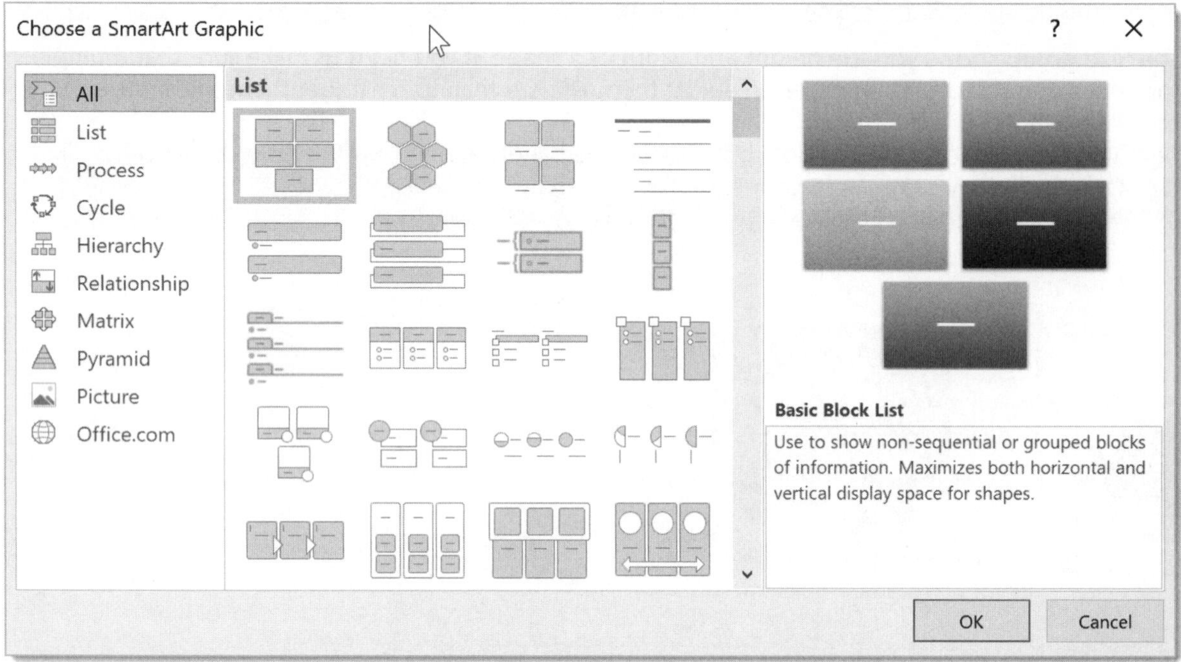

Here is an example of basic cycle SmartArt graphic:

When you first draw a SmartArt graphic, you see the text entry flyout to the left of the graphic. When you're done entering your data and click off of the graphic, the flyout disappears. As with other detailed properties in Excel, SmartArt activates its own Ribbon subgroup, as shown below.

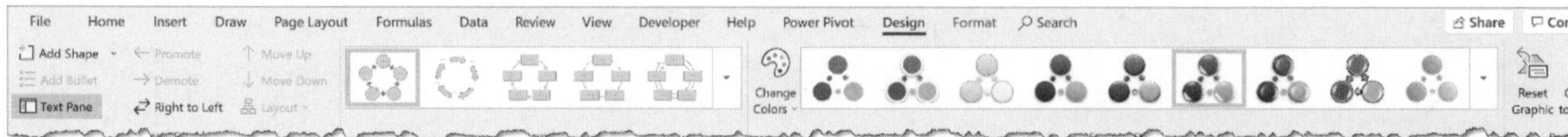

You'll see that you can get pretty fancy with the layout and style options that you have at your fingertips. And another nice thing is that a live preview kicks in as you hover over different layouts and styles, so you can see how a selection is going to look on your worksheet before committing to it. This means you can test different layouts like the ones below before you decide on a final choice.

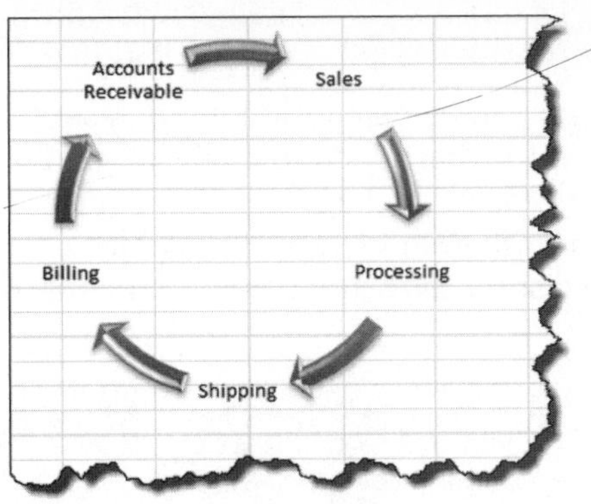

Screenshot

The Screenshot option allows you to insert a screenshot of any open application that has not been minimized to the taskbar. (The example below is a screenshot from this chapter.) This option isn't especially practical in Excel, but it does come in handy in Word, especially if you're trying to document a process flow for a spreadsheet or create a users' guide. If you use the Screen Clipping button at the bottom of the Screenshot window, you can select a portion of the most recently active application window to insert.

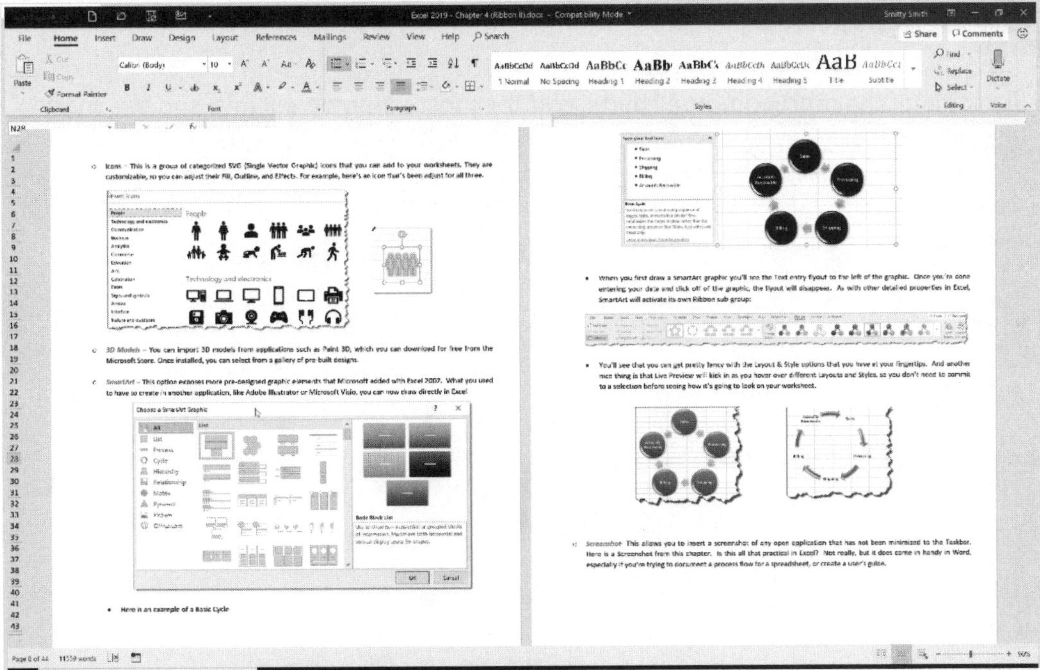

The Charts Group

Charts allow you to convert numeric data into graphical representations that provide at-a-glance information about what the numbers say. There are currently 10 primary chart groups: column and bar, line and area, pie, hierarchy, statistical, scatter, waterfall, combo, map, and Pivot Chart. Within those groups are other chart types, such as radar, stock, funnel, and so on. As with so many other things in Excel, you have thousands of formatting and display options with charts, so you should explore them on your own and see what works best for you.

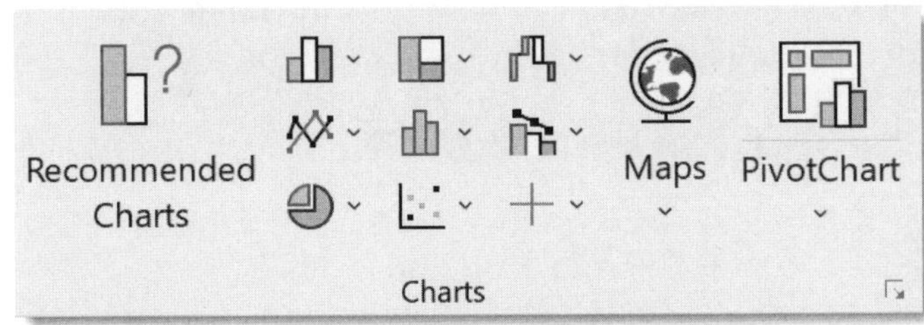

Caution: Keep in mind that charts provide a way of telling a story with images, so if you add too much formatting, you can go overboard and lose your message in the noise.

To draw a chart, just put your cursor somewhere inside the dataset that you want charted and select the chart type you want. If you're not sure which chart to choose, click **Insert > Recommended Charts**. Excel's charting engine analyzes the data and gives you several options. There are entire books devoted to charting, and you should spend some time with your own data to determine which chart best suits your needs. In many cases, you'll use different chart types to display the same data in different ways.

	A	B	C	D	E	G	H	I
1	Region	Product	Date	Month	Customer	Revenue	COGS	Profit
2	Central	ABC	01/09/08	Jan-08	General Motors	16,416	6,776	9,640
3	Central	ABC	01/12/08	Jan-08	IBM	6,267	2,541	3,726
4	Central	ABC	01/25/08	Jan-08	CitiGroup	20,770	8,470	12,300
5	Central	ABC	02/19/08	Feb-08	Wal-Mart	10,385	4,235	6,150
6	Central	ABC	02/20/08	Feb-08	Exxon	11,124	5,082	6,042
7	Central	ABC	02/27/08	Feb-08	Ford	16,209	7,623	8,586
8	Central	ABC	04/06/08	Apr-08	General Electric	5,886	2,541	3,345

In the center of the Charts group are a number of icons that allow you to create a bunch of different types of charts, as described in the following sections.

Column and Bar Charts

Column and bar charts are some of the most common charts, and the most common column and bar charts are 2-D and 3-D.

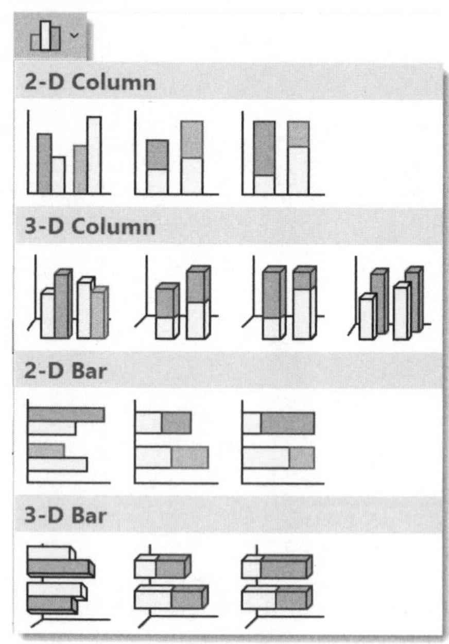

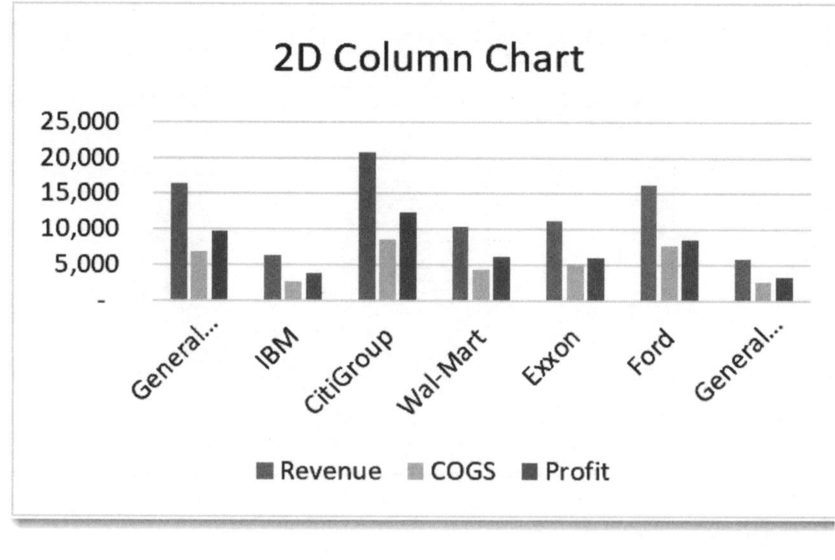

Column charts display your data in vertical columns, as shown above right. They're especially good at displaying multiple data points for several groups, such as revenue and profit by company. A bar chart is simply a column chart turned on its side.

Hint: If a dataset includes information that you don't want charted, you can select just the range you want charted. Or you can select the entire data range and simply hide the rows and columns you don't want charted because hidden rows/columns don't plot on a chart. To quickly create a chart of the default type, place the cursor in any cell in the chart data range and press **Alt+F1**.

Line and Area Charts

Line charts, which are as common as column charts, display data in a series of horizontal lines. Line charts are generally used to show data over a given period, such as weeks or months.

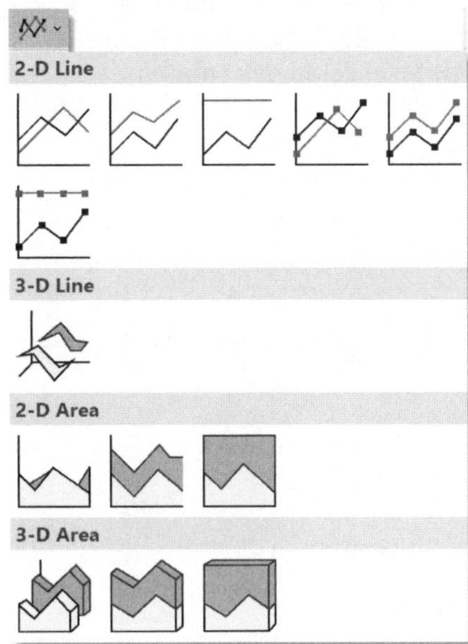

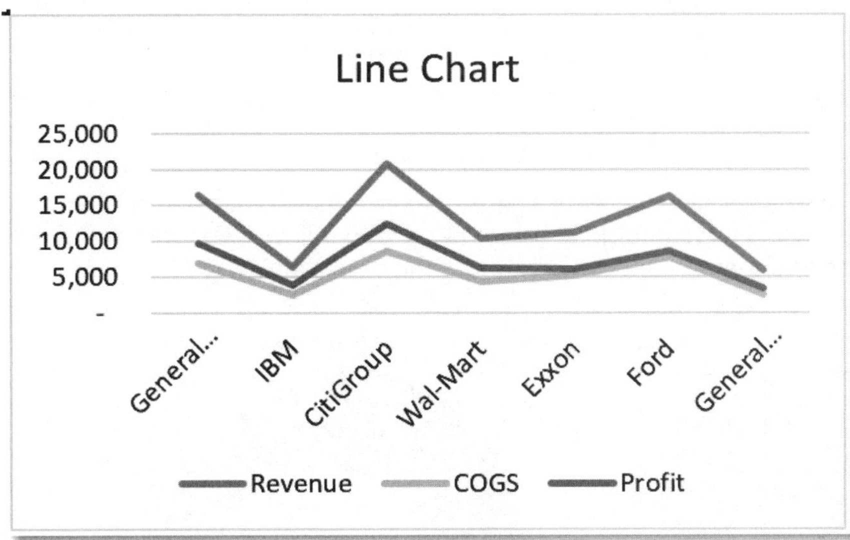

Area charts fill in the lines between line charts. Unfortunately, I've always found them more difficult to understand than they're worth.

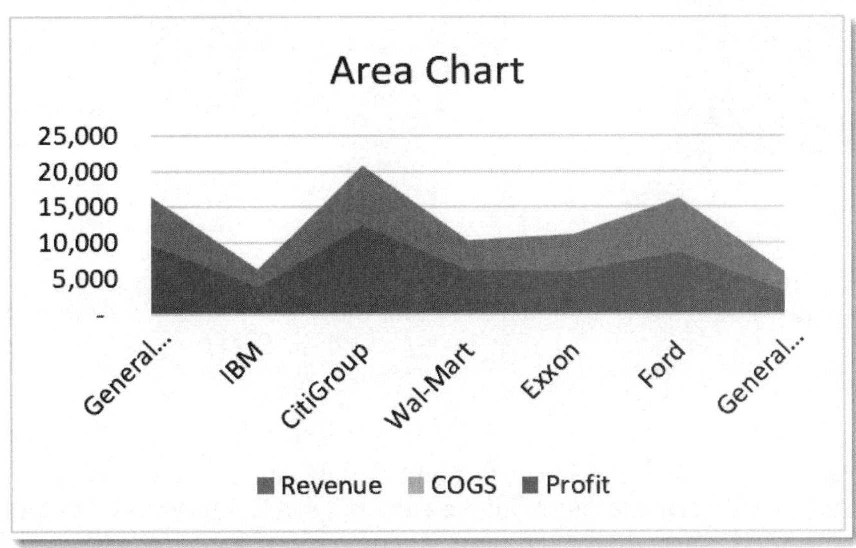

Pie Charts

While pie charts are also relatively common, I don't recommend using them because they're generally good for only small datasets, but people seem determined to fit as much as they can into them. Pie charts may also inaccurately represent data from a visual perspective; this is especially a problem with 3-D pie charts, due to the way that they render when drawn, so that the bottom/front part of the chart looks bigger than it actually is because of pixel density. If you're going to use pie charts, try to keep your dataset relatively small.

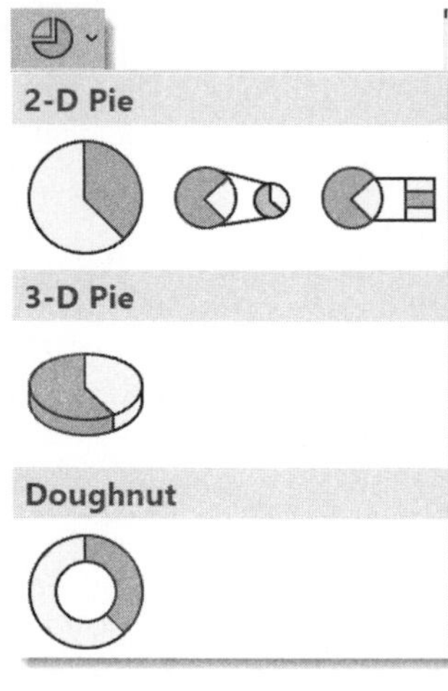

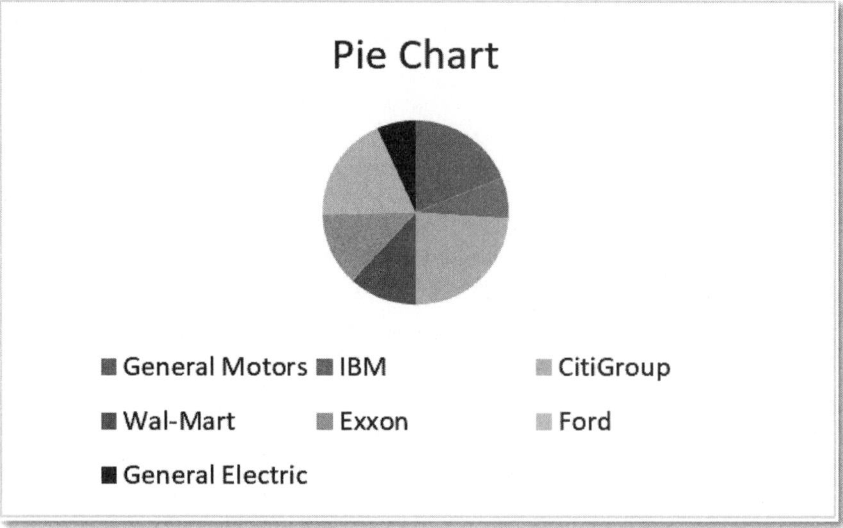

Hierarchy Charts

Excel has added a relatively new group of charts, called hierarchy charts, that include treemap and sunburst charts. These types of charts provide interesting ways to display data. You need to follow the same rules as for pie charts and avoid cramming too much into them, or they'll quickly lose their meaning.

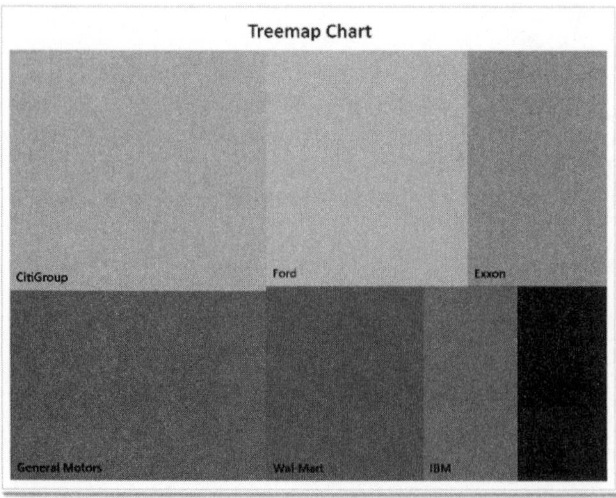

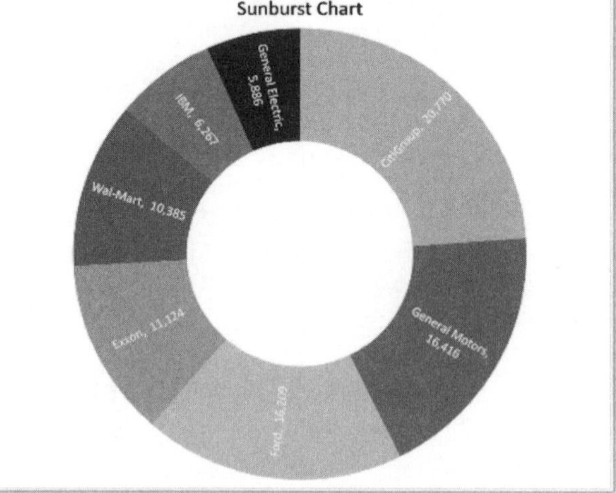

Statistical Charts

Statistical charts include histograms and Pareto charts, both of which are used in statistics, as well as box-and-whisker charts. Because they're relatively specialized, this chapter doesn't cover them, but you can find more specifics at support.office.com.

Scatter Charts

Scatter charts are good for comparing pairs of data, such as temperature and rainfall data, as shown below. Like area charts, scatter charts can be hard to understand, especially if the data isn't suitable for the chart type.

Month	Temperature	Rainfall
January	45	5.2
February	48	3.9
March	52	3.31
April	58	1.97
May	64	1.57
June	69	1.42
July	72	0.63
August	73	0.75
September	67	1.65
October	59	3.27
November	51	5
December	47	5.43

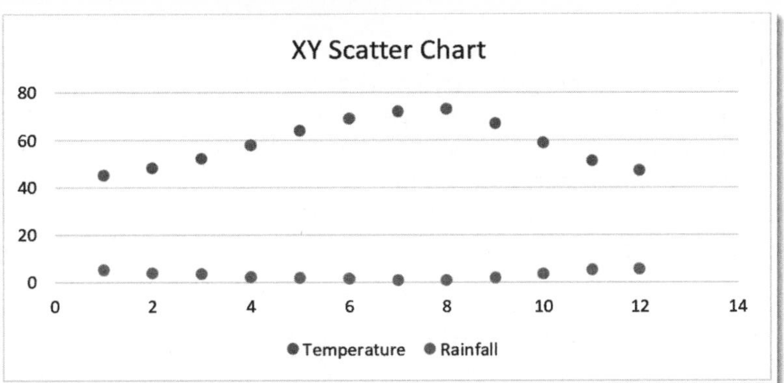

Waterfall, Funnel, Stock, Surface, or Radar Charts

Waterfall, funnel, stock, surface, and radar charts are relatively specialized, so we don't go into them in depth here. However, the following figure shows a funnel chart, which is a new chart type in Excel that shows a top-down funnel of items based on rank or order of importance.

Stage	Amount
Prospects	500
Qualified prospects	425
Needs analysis	200
Price quotes	150
Negotiations	100
Closed Sales	90

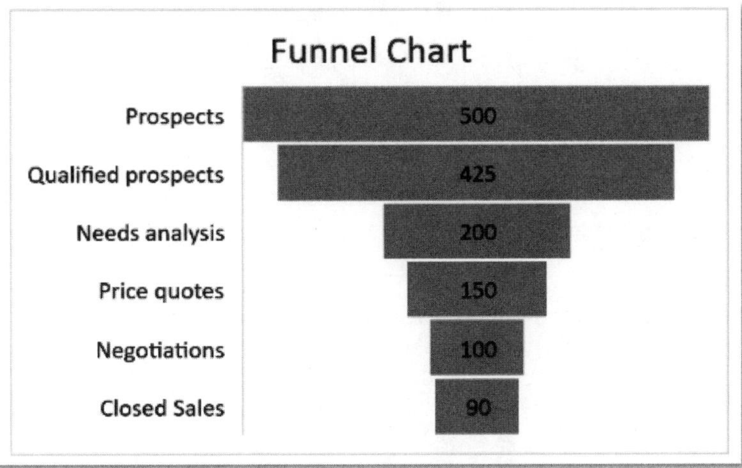

Map Charts

Map charts use the Bing mapping service to compare geographic-based values and map them. You can use a map chart when you have geographic regions in your data, such as countries/regions, states, counties, or postal codes. Note that map charts do not map to specific addresses, but if you want that functionality, you can install the 3D Map add-in for Excel.

Country	GDP
China	11,391,619
India	2,250,990
United States	18,561,930
Brazil	1,769,600
Russia	1,267,750
Mexico	1,063,610
France	2,488,280
Argentina	541,748
Australia	1,256,640
Sweden	517,440
United Arab Emirates	375,022
Namibia	10,183

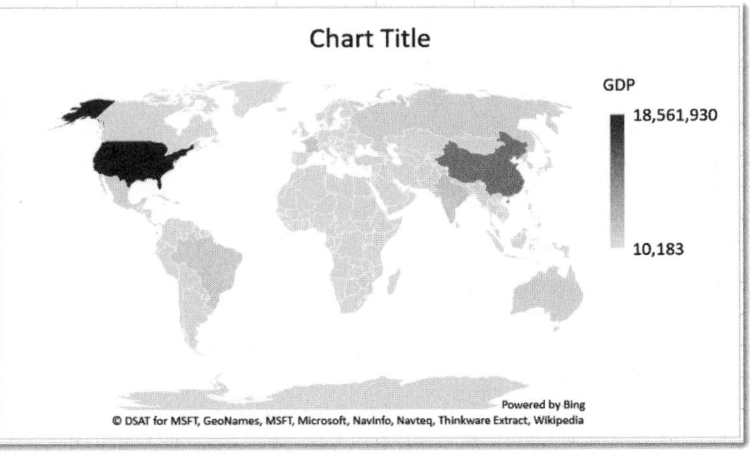

Combo Charts

Combo charts are fantastic when you're trying to display disparate datasets, such as gross revenue and profit percentage or temperature vs. rainfall. Both points will plot on a standard column chart, but since one is so much smaller than the other, the values will technically display but will be too small for you to discern any meaningful pattern. A combo chart lets you plot the smaller value on what's called the secondary axis as a line chart. This way, the smaller figure can be displayed on equal footing with the others. The following charts show monthly average temperature vs. rainfall for Seattle. This one is a column chart:

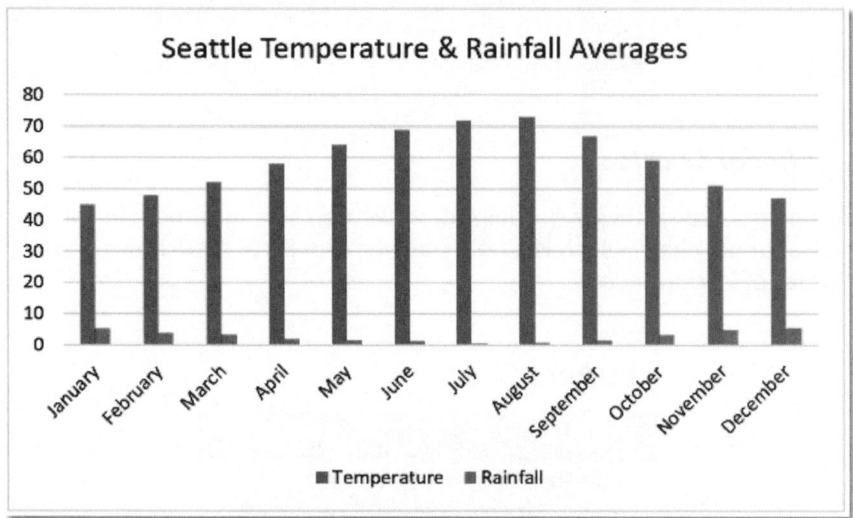

And this one is a combo chart:

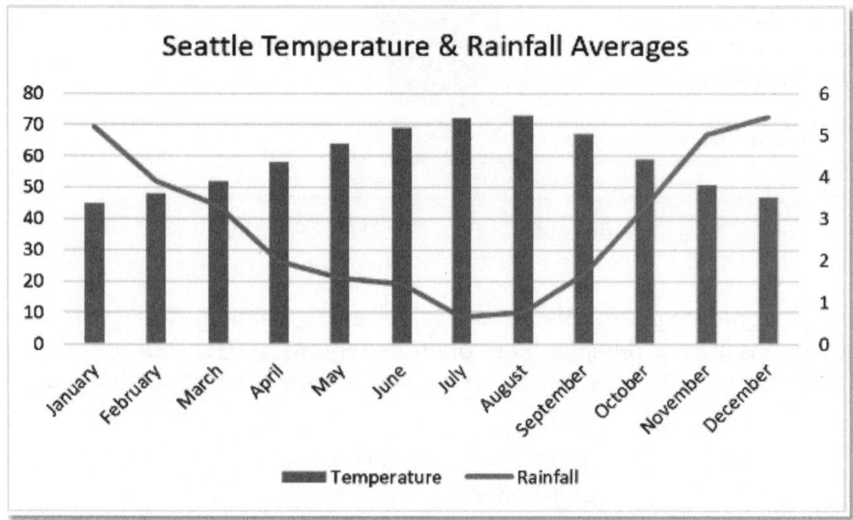

In the column chart, rainfall is plotted, but the values are so small compared to temperature that it's hard to get any real sense of what's going on. In the combo chart, the rainfall amounts really get a chance to stand out. Here it's easy to see the seasonal relationship between temperature gains and decreasing rainfall.

Pivot Charts

The **Insert > PivotChart** option lets you add Pivot Charts without first creating an associated PivotTable. Chapter 11 discusses PivotTables and Pivot Charts further.

The Tours Group

The Tours group opens the 3D Map add-in. You can plot data points on a 3-D map and build tours which allow you to fly through the data. You can find more information about 3D maps at support.office.com.

The Sparklines Group

The Sparklines group allows you to insert mini charts in cells to represent the data you've selected. A sparkline doesn't have to be adjacent to the data, but it's a generally a good idea to have it nearby so that you maintain a visual reference to it. The following example shows some sparklines.

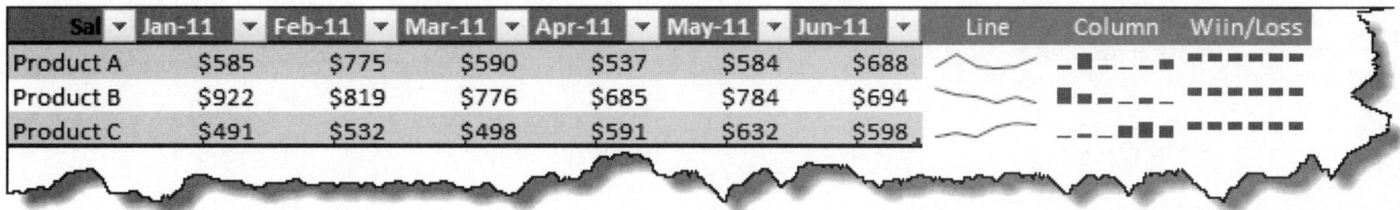

Sal	Jan-11	Feb-11	Mar-11	Apr-11	May-11	Jun-11	Line	Column	Wiin/Loss
Product A	$585	$775	$590	$537	$584	$688			
Product B	$922	$819	$776	$685	$784	$694			
Product C	$491	$532	$498	$591	$632	$598			

Sparklines are great for dashboards and summary reports, where a large chart (or a series of them) might be overwhelming.

To insert a sparkline, just select the data range and then choose the appropriate sparkline type by selecting **Insert > Line**, **Insert > Column**, or **Insert > Win/Loss**. You can place a sparkline in only a single cell per data range, and it can't span multiple rows or columns.

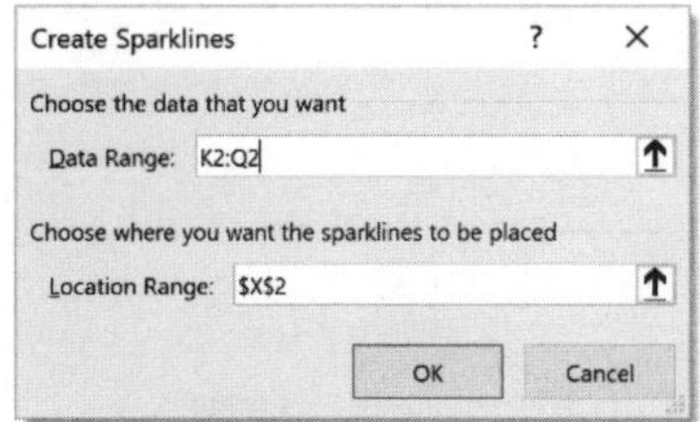

As soon as you place a sparkline on a sheet, the Sparkline Design Tools Ribbon tab is activated. On it, as shown below, you can edit the data points, change the sparkline type, show certain data points, and select a style for the sparkline. Once again, there are too many options to detail here, but feel free to experiment with the examples in the Chapter 4 workbook or create your own.

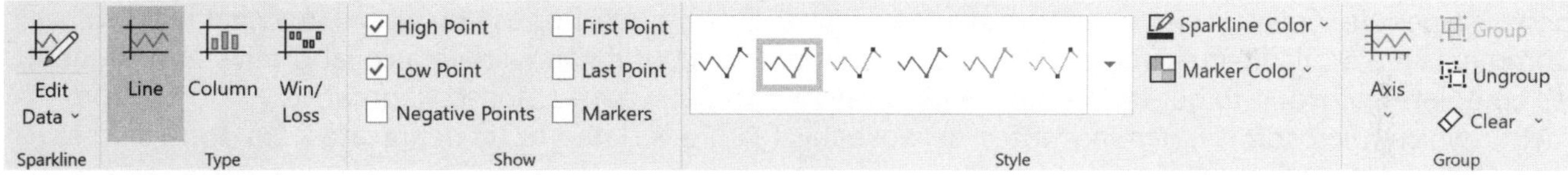

The Filters Group

The Filters group contains only two options: Slicer and Timeline. A slicer is a control that allows you to query certain table and PivotTable elements. A timeline lets you filter a PivotTables based on dates. Chapter 11 discusses these options in more detail.

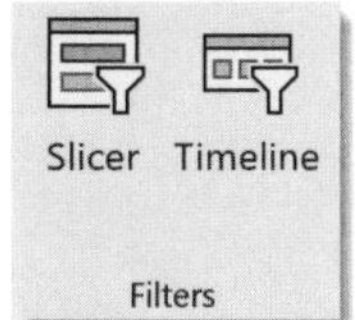

The Links Group

The Links group contains only two options: Recent Items and Insert Link. Recent Items lets you link to recently opened documents. Selecting either **Insert > Link** or **Insert > Link drop-down > Insert Link** causes Excel to open the Insert Hyperlink dialog, which allows you to insert clickable navigation text links that take users to websites or different locations in the workbook/worksheet or that even open another program.

Hyperlinks in a workbook can be somewhat handy. For instance, you can create a table of contents that lists all worksheets and includes links to them. But hyperlinks can also be irritating, especially as Excel's default nature is to insert a hyperlink for any text that includes the @ symbol in the text string. You'll notice this right away if you try to enter an email address in a cell. When adding a hyperlink, you can add an input mask in the Text to Display text box in the Insert Hyperlink dialog (shown below); when you do this, you add a hyperlink without what might be an otherwise confusing or long address. For example, the dialog below shows how you can use the input mask hyperlink Excel Help rather than inserting the hyperlink https://support.office.com/excel.

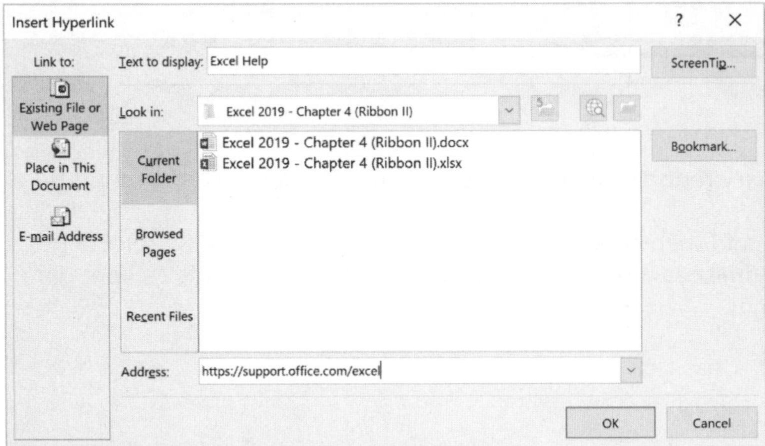

The Comments Group

Threaded comments allow users to collaborate in real time. You can select any cell and then select **Insert > Comment** to start a dialog with others. You can specifically call out someone else with what's called an @ *Mention*. Once you type the @ symbol, the comment displays a list of contacts from your Office address book. Simply select a name, type your comment (see the example below), and click the send button, and that person gets an email with your note. That person can open the workbook and reply to your comment directly or just make changes to the workbook. Note that responses to comments aren't required in order to edit the workbook. As people reply to comments, you see the original dialog grow, just as you would in a chat window. Comments are available only in the Office 365 version of Excel, but if you work in a collaborative environment, it's completely worth it to get this version. Earlier versions of Excel have a non-collaborative version of comments, which Microsoft is renaming Notes. Because this feature is slated to be deprecated, we don't discuss it here.

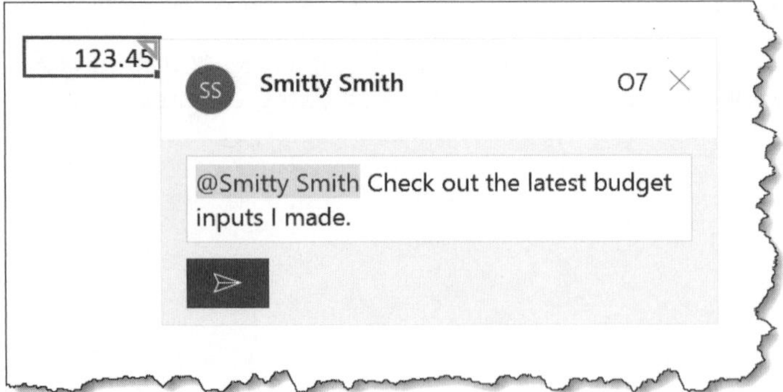

The Text Group

The Text group contains the Text Box, Header & Footer, WordArt, Signature Line, and Object options, as shown below and discussed in the following sections.

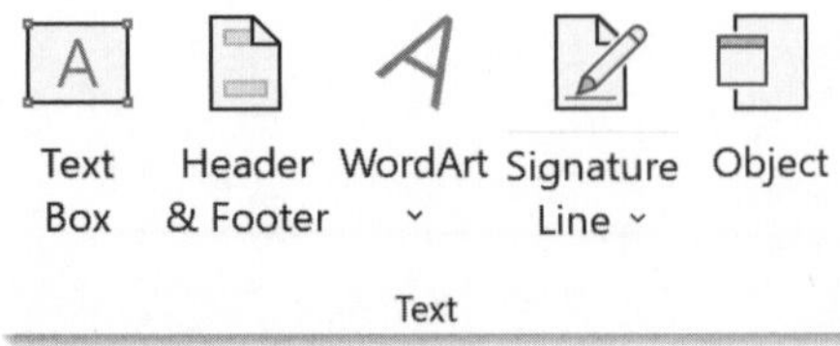

Text Box

The Text Box option gives you a free-form, floating text box that sits above the worksheet, or grid. There's generally very little use for text boxes in Excel unless you're trying to mark a distribution document with a release note, such as "DRAFT" or "CONFIDENTIAL" (see below). As with any other object, text boxes don't interfere with the cells they sit above or their performance.

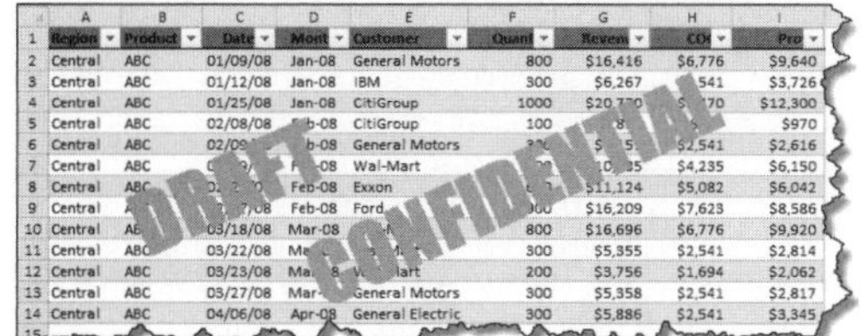

When you select **Insert > Text Box**, the cursor turns into an inverted cross. You can click the cross and drag across the sheet until you have the box the size you want, and then you can insert your text, as shown below. When you're done with that, you can apply any formatting you want to this text.

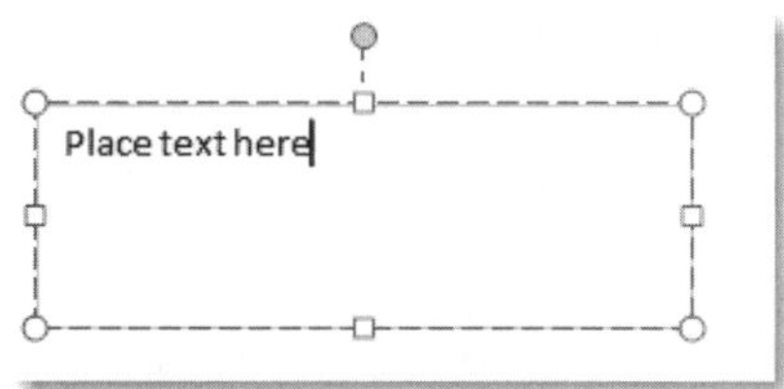

> **Note:** If a text box is in edit mode (as if you're entering text), you need to highlight all of the text before you can format it. Otherwise, you need to click out of the box and select it again so that you're out of edit mode. You can tell you're in edit mode if the cursor is blinking. You can use the Shape Format tab for all other text box elements.

Header & Footer

The Header & Footer option gives you the same choices as the Header/Footer options in the Page Setup group of the Page Layout tab, but it lets you input them directly on the worksheet, so you can see a preview version of what they'll look like. This can save a step or two compared to inputting this data through the Page Setup dialog, where you have to go to **Page Layout > Page Setup > Header/Footer > Print Preview** to see the result. However, using the Header & Footer option really only exposes the header and footer, but not the other Page Setup elements, so what you gain on one side, you lose on the other because you still need to go through the Page Setup group to prepare your worksheet for printing. In addition, what you enter with this method is viewable only through the Page Setup view; you don't see it in Normal view.

WordArt

WordArt can be great for introductory worksheets and on dashboards (if you have ample space), but you won't find it widely used in financial or business applications. When you select the WordArt option, you are presented with a series of styles, as shown below.

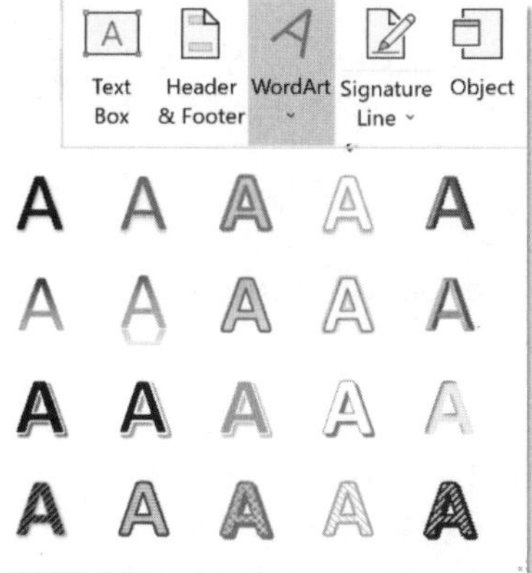

After you make a selection, Excel automatically inserts a WordArt text box for you, as shown below. All you need to do is start typing your own text. As soon as the WordArt text box has been drawn, the Shape Format tab appears, and you can use it to format both the text and the text box itself.

Signature Line

The Signature Line option is Microsoft's attempt at adding digital signature security to documents, but it's very unlikely that you'll ever use this feature to its full capacity, as it requires a third-party authentication service (and these services are not cheap). It does, however, allow you to add a static signature line (as shown below) to a document more quickly than you can draw it yourself, and this can be helpful if you use Excel for printed documents that might need signatures, such as customer estimates/quotes or contracts.

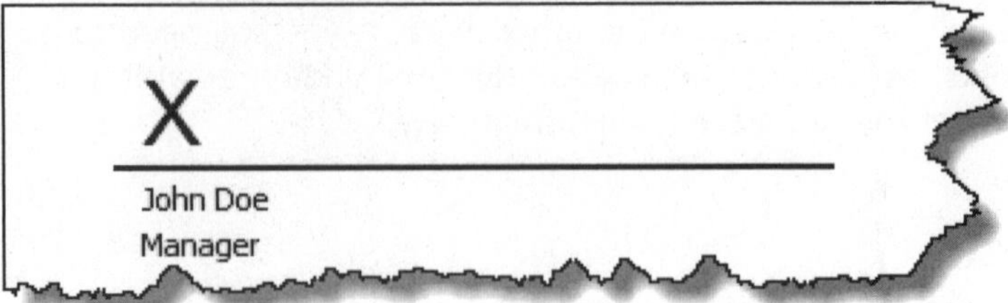

Object

The Object option allows you to insert an embedded object from another application, such as Word. You generally won't use this in Excel, but you will often insert Excel objects into Word or PowerPoint documents.

The Symbols Group

The Symbols group includes the Equation and Symbol options, as discussed in the following sections.

Equation

Equation is a great tool for dealing with mathematics, and it is a far cry from the days when complicated equations really couldn't be done in Excel. When you select **Insert > Symbols > Equation**, you see a list of detailed equation options, as shown below.

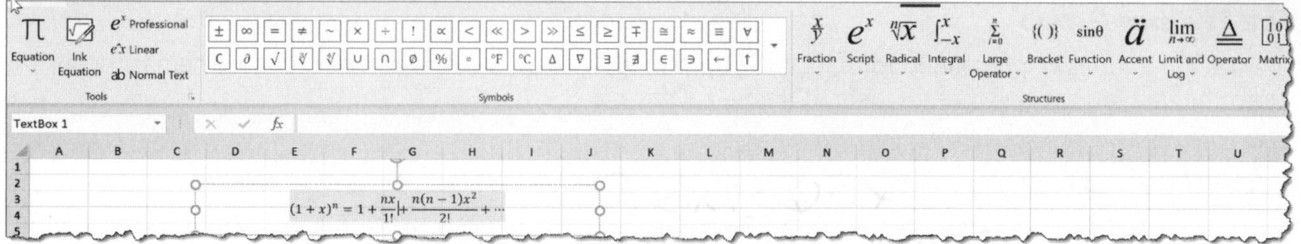

You can select an equation from the drop-down list to place it on the sheet; at the same time, the Equation tab becomes active. The topic of equations could fill a book on its own, but for the purposes of this book, you just need to know that this is where you find the equation options.

Symbols

You are likely to find day-to-day functionality on the Symbols menu, which gives you different symbols for every font you have installed on your system, as well as a series of special characters, such as the trademark symbol (™) and copyright symbol (©). There are too many options to possibly cover them all here, but feel free to explore by selecting **Insert > Symbols > Symbol**. You can select an option from the Subject drop-down or scroll through your options with the vertical scroll bar beneath it, as shown in the dialog box below.

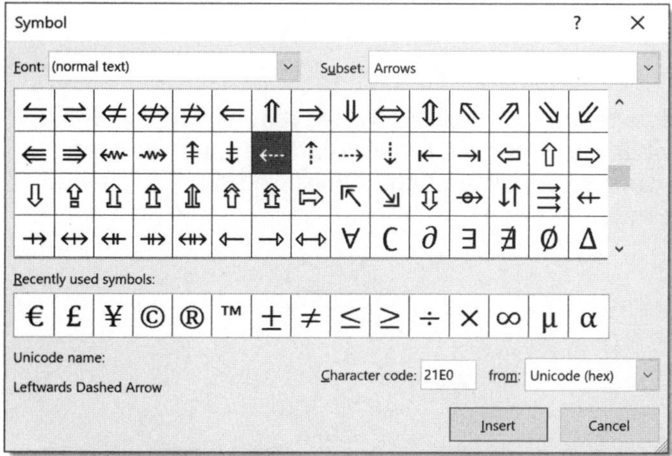

Note: You can quickly insert a bullet point in a cell by entering **Alt+7** using the 7 on the 10-key pad. If you don't have a 10-key pad, you need to use the Symbol dialog.

The Page Layout Tab

The Page Layout tab allows you to apply themes to an entire workbook, and it is also where you prepare a worksheet for printing and distribution. The Page Layout tab consists of the groups discussed in the following sections.

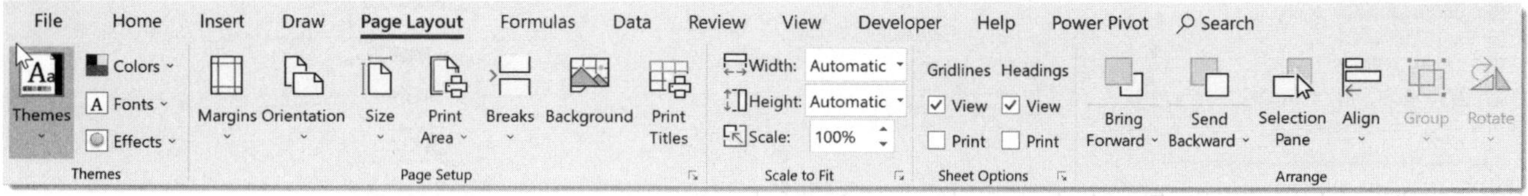

The Themes Group

Themes are a series of predefined formats that you can apply to an entire workbook. In the Themes menu shown below, you can see that the default theme is Office.

If you were to change this default and then format a data range as a table, you'd see that new theme applied to the table. Microsoft can only give you a limited number of themes out of thousands of potential possibilities, but you can create your own themes, and you can also adjust existing themes. You can also change colors, fonts, and effects, as shown in the examples below.

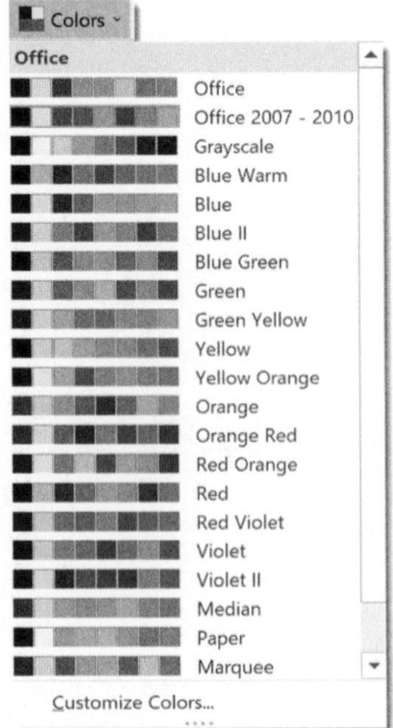

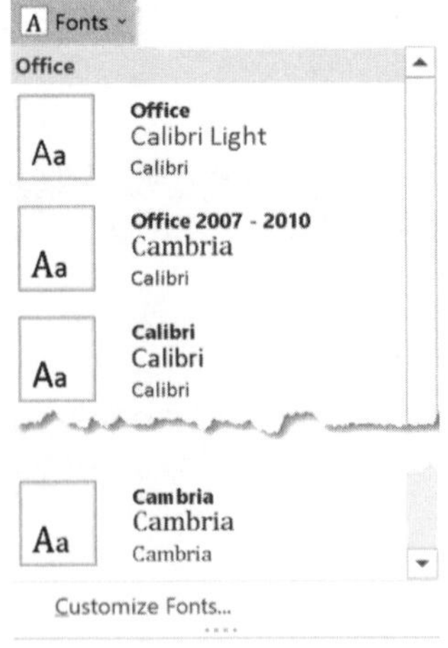

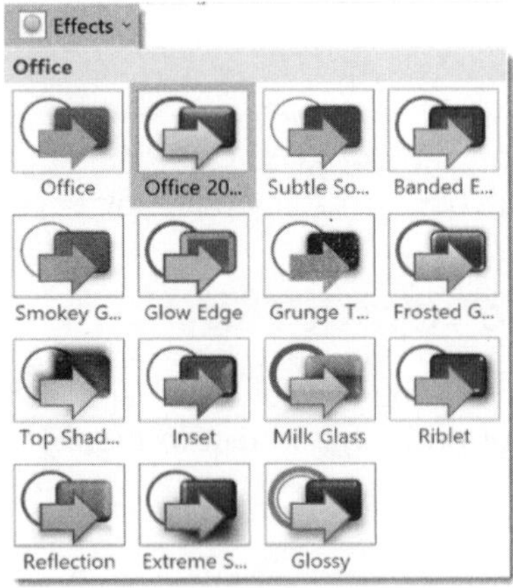

The Page Setup Group

In the Page Setup group, you can set up your worksheets so that they print in the format you want. (These options are covered in detail in Chapter 7.) The Page Setup group consists of the Margins, Orientation, Size, Print Area, Breaks, Delete Background, and Print Titles options, as shown below and described in the following sections.

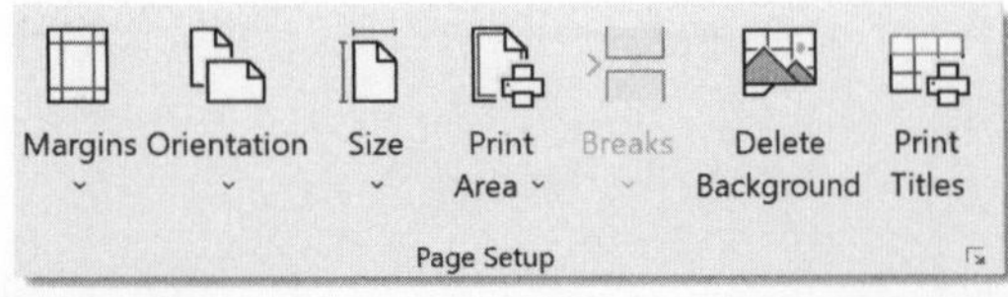

In this group, you can click the dialog launcher to open the Page Setup dialog, which lets you set any of the page setup items you need. Unless you're just quickly changing a setting like margins or orientation, you'll probably find it easier to come to this dialog to set up your worksheet for printing.

Margins

The Margins option displays the most common margins as well as the settings you used most recently, if they're not one of the defaults.

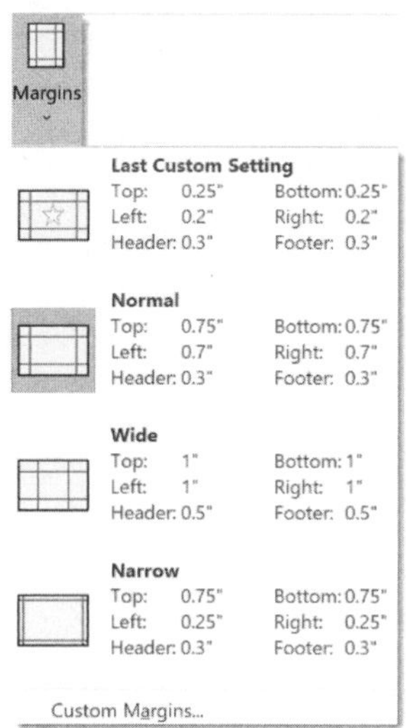

Orientation

The Orientation option allows you to quickly toggle between portrait and landscape orientations. As you can see in the Margins selections shown below, the worksheet in this case is in portrait orientation, which is the default. If the worksheet were in landscape orientation, the margin images would reflect that.

Size

The Size option lets you choose from the most common paper sizes. The default in the United States is 8.5 by 11 inches.

Print Area

The Print Area option often trips up even the most experienced users. Let's say you have a worksheet, but you want to print only part of the worksheet and not reveal certain parts of it. Excel automatically adds the entire used range to the print area, so if you try printing without checking this first, your printer will spit out much more than you wanted. To fix this issue, you need to select Clear the Print Area, select the area you do want to print, and then select the Set Print Area option. Excel then leaves out what you don't want to print.

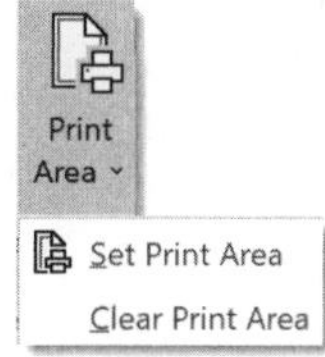

Breaks

The Breaks option allows you to select a row or column and set a page break. Unfortunately, this isn't a very useful feature. **View > Page Break Preview** (see Chapter 7) is a much more useful feature as it allows you to just drag breaks where you want them.

Background

A background image is the only thing you can actually put behind a worksheet, and the Background option allows you to insert an image into the background of your worksheet. This option is very useful if you need to add something like a company logo as a watermark or want to have an intro page; however, you need to be careful with the image you select, as it can get very overwhelming and make your worksheet all but impossible to work with if you're not careful. The image also gets tiled (i.e., repeats) across the entire worksheet, so it's not a display-in-one-spot thing; it's all or none. You also get only one image for the background, not multiple images, so if you want to layer a company logo or photo in the background and add a "DRAFT" or "COMPANY CONFIDENTIAL" label as well, you need to prepare that in a photo-editing program (such as Paint.Net, which is a good one and is free); then you can import the finished image.

The following background examples show the difference between not displaying and displaying gridlines.

Print Titles

The Print Titles option gives you the ability to have columns and rows repeat on each worksheet.

The Scale to Fit Group

The Scale to Fit group lets you choose how much of your sheet to print and on how many pages. You can select **Automatic** and let Excel choose for you, or you can define how many pages wide by how many pages tall the sheet should print. For financial statements, such as balance sheets, you'll often choose to fit to 1 page wide by *blank* pages tall. With these settings, Excel prints all columns of your worksheet on one sheet of paper, regardless of how many rows you have.

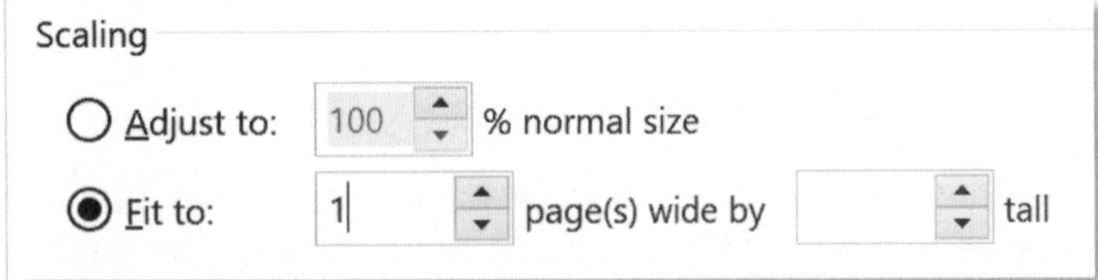

The Sheet Options Group

The Gridlines option in the Sheet Options group lets you view and print gridlines, which are the visible borders around each cell. The Headings option in this group allows you to view and print headings, which are the row (1, 2, 3, etc.) and column (A, B, C, etc.) headers. If you're distributing a workbook that's for viewing only, you'll probably want to make sure both of the Headings options are unselected, but if you're expecting some degree of user interaction, you should leave them selected to make it easier for your users to navigate your worksheet(s).

The Arrange Group

The Page Layout tab is a somewhat illogical place for the Arrange group, which it deals with objects, rather than page layout, as shown at right. This is another case where Excel gives you the option to interact with different menu items in multiple places.

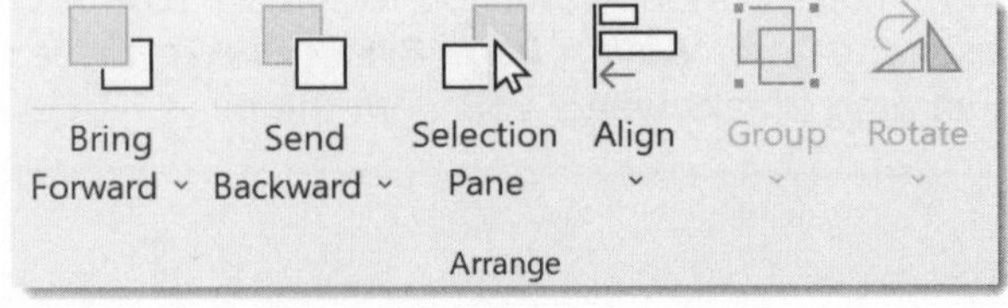

The Formulas Tab

The Formulas tab is where you can access all of Excel's native functions and start building formulas on your own. Formulas allow to you calculate values that you enter into cells. This might not sound like a big deal, but when it comes to data analysis and getting the most from your data, it is where Excel really shines. Even if all you're ever going to do is use Excel to manage lists, such as customer details, you'll still find at least a few of the options on this tab handy. In fact, once you start getting used to formulas, you'll wonder how you ever got things done without Excel. The following sections review the Formula tab functionality, but because there are so many great tools here, we discuss formulas themselves in Chapter 6.

> **Note:** What's the difference between a formula and a function? Not much really. A function is a pre-built formula in Excel that you can use to perform certain calculations, such as **=TODAY()** to return today's date or **=SUM()** to add up values. A formula can use functions, or it can use just mathematical operators, such as **=1+1** to do this simple addition or **=TODAY()+30** to get today's date plus 30 days. Excel functions are always CAPITALIZED.

The Function Library Group

The Function Library group breaks down Excel formulas into the most commonly used options, discussed in the following sections.

Insert Function

If you select **Formulas > Insert Function**, Excel launches the Insert Function dialog (shown below), which exposes the function categories you see on the Ribbon. At the top you can search for a function. For instance, if you search for "Look up a value," Excel gives you a list of LOOKUP formulas. The Insert Function dialog is a useful tool—but only if you know how to define what you're looking for; otherwise, it can be fairly frustrating. If you know roughly what you want to do, you can narrow the list, just as you can on the Ribbon, by selecting from one of the defined categories.

When you select a function, Excel defines its syntax at the bottom of the dialog, and you can also click the **Help on This Function** link at the bottom to open the Help file for that topic.

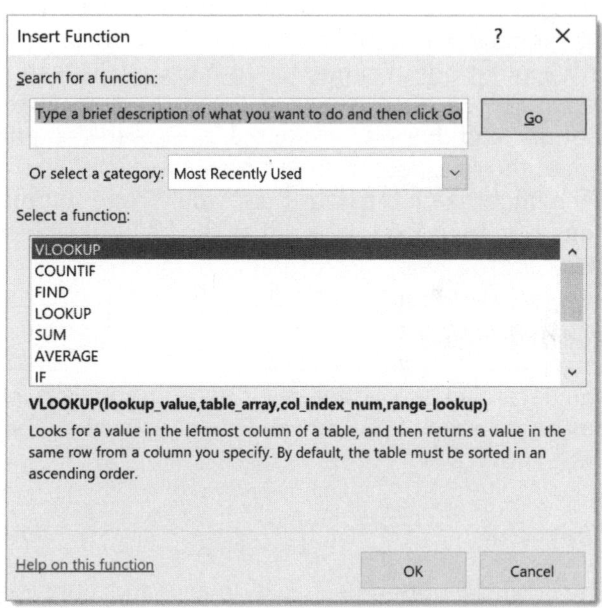

After you select the formula you want, Excel launches the Function Arguments dialog, which details the formula. In the following example you can see the arguments for the VLOOKUP function, which is one of the most widely used functions on the planet. (In fact, if I were a betting kind of person, I'd bet that there are more VLOOKUPs in the world than people.)

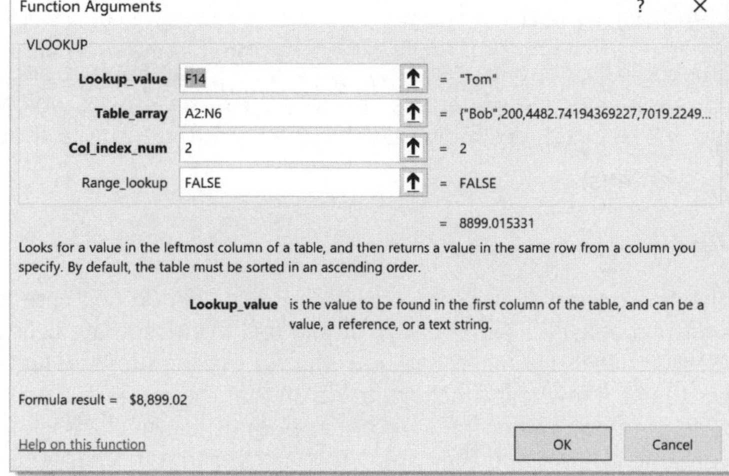

AutoSum

While most power users strictly write their own formulas, sometimes Excel can do the job faster than even those pros, and when you're getting used to formulas, it can be very convenient to let Excel do the work for you. The following example shows the Sum option under AutoSum used to sum revenue for a particular salesperson.

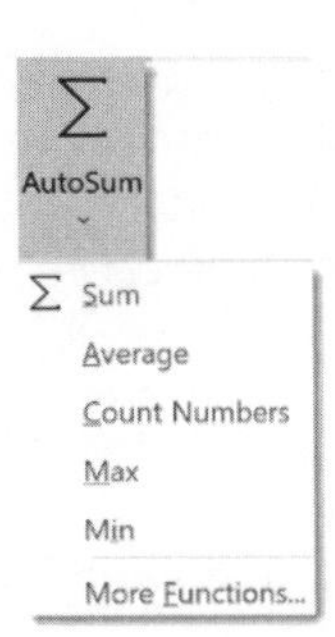

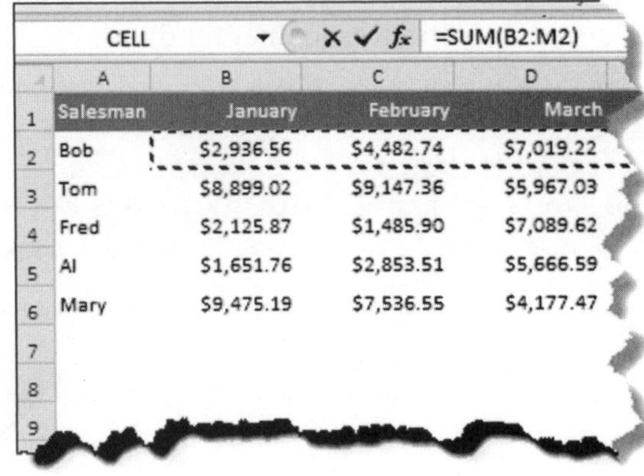

	A	B	C	D
1	Salesman	January	February	March
2	Bob	$2,936.56	$4,482.74	$7,019.22
3	Tom	$8,899.02	$9,147.36	$5,967.03
4	Fred	$2,125.87	$1,485.90	$7,089.62
5	Al	$1,651.76	$2,853.51	$5,666.59
6	Mary	$9,475.19	$7,536.55	$4,177.47
7				
8				
9				

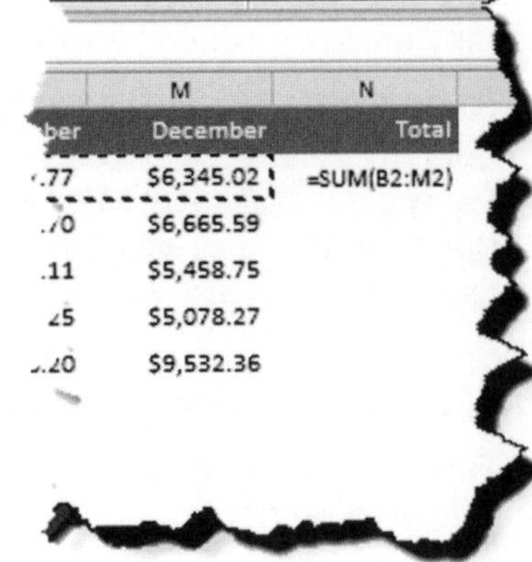

M	N
December	Total
$6,345.02	=SUM(B2:M2)
$6,665.59	
$5,458.75	
$5,078.27	
$9,532.36	

With the cursor in cell N2, you just select Sum from the AutoSum list, and Excel automatically applies the formula for you. You see Excel's proposed formula in the selected cell and also in the formula bar. Excel highlights the range where it thinks you want the formula with a marquee, or a moving border (also called "dancing ants"), but it doesn't enter the formula yet. Instead, Excel wants you to verify that it got it right, so if you're happy with Excel's selection, you can just press **Enter**. Excel then selects only numeric cells to include in the formula (and doesn't include the salesperson's name). Next, you can copy and paste the formula down to the rest of the salespeople. In this case, the cursor was to the right of the data, so Excel knew to go left; had you been underneath the data, Excel would have summed upward. Does AutoSum always get it right? No, but it does a pretty good job, and that can be invaluable when you're starting to explore the vast world of formulas in Excel.

Recently Used

The Recently Used option is supposed to provide a list of the last 10 formulas you've used. This functionality has been broken for decades. The list usually offers SUM, AVERAGE, IF, HYPERLINK, COUNT, MAX, SIN, SUMIF, PMT, and STDEV.

Financial

The Financial option deals with finance functions, such as those for calculating payments on equipment at a given rate.

Logical

The Logical option is used quite frequently to tell Excel to do something if a condition is met. The most common selection under this option is the **IF** statement, which looks for a true vs. false condition. For example, **=IF(A1=1,1,2)** simply says that if A1 = 1, the formula should return a 1, and otherwise it should return a 2.

Text

The Text option allows you to do things like change text case (e.g., the UPPER, LOWER, and PROPER choices), split text apart (called *parsing*), or join text from separate cells (called *concatenating*). Let's say you have "SMITH, JOHN" in a cell, and you want to get the first and last names in separate cells, as shown below. You could use a few text functions to do all that for you instead of retyping the information. You'll learn about this type of thing in Chapter 6. Another option is to use Flash Fill, which uses machine learning to establish a discernable pattern and then apply it. We cover that in Chapter 5.

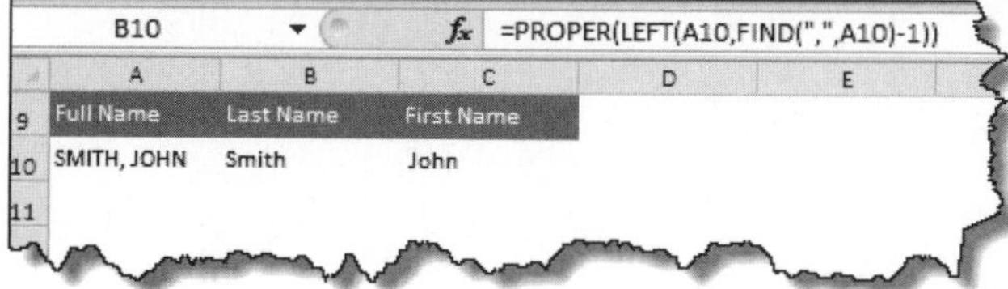

Date & Time

The Date & Time option lets you enter dynamic dates and times into a worksheet. It also allows you to perform calculations on them. For example, you could calculate the number of years between an employee's start date and today's date to determine vacation hours earned. Or, if you have kids, you can calculate the difference between their birthday and today or Christmas and today as a countdown.

Lookup & Reference

The Lookup & Reference option puts perhaps some of the most powerful formulas at your disposal. It lets you store data in one place and retrieve it somewhere else instead of having to re-create it. Let's say you have a customer list in a worksheet, but you need to enter a customer name in another worksheet, and you don't want to have to copy and paste all of their related information. You can use a referential formula on the customer name to return that data for you.

Math & Trig

The Math & Trig option primarily deals with mathematical equations for higher math, but there are some choices here, such as rounding, that can be valuable to a small business.

More Functions

The More Functions option exposes unique functions that are not common in a typical business setting. You're not likely to use these functions unless you're in a relatively specialized business, such as engineering.

The Defined Names Group

The Defined Names group on the Formulas tab is often overlooked. These tools allow you to give a range a name and refer to it by that name instead of by using the range address. For instance, you can put a tax rate in a cell, name it Tax, and then use Tax in any calculation in your workbook. The great thing about this is that you can change the rate in that cell any time you want, and all your formulas automatically update. If you're worried about people changing your inputs, you can also apply a formula or a value to a name, such as **=A1*Tax**, where Tax refers to a value like =0.0975, not a range. Another benefit of named ranges is that many people feel it is easier to read formulas that use named ranges. For example, **=VLOOKUP(A1,SalesData,2,FALSE)** can be easier to read than **=VLOOKUP(A1,Formulas!$A$1:$N$6,2,FALSE)**.

Using defined names is largely a matter of preference, and some people will go their entire Excel careers without ever touching them, while other people rely on them heavily. I cover only the basics here, but you should definitely experiment with them and see which camp you're in.

Name Manager

The Name Manager option is where you add new names, delete old ones, and adjust existing names. When you click this option, the Name Manager dialog opens, and in it you can see any existing names in your workbook. When you select one of these names, you can see at the bottom of the dialog what it refers to, as shown below.

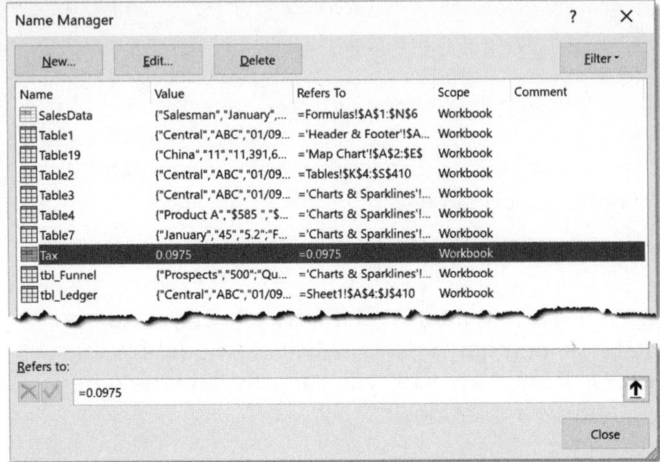

In this case you see that Tax refers to =0.0975. You can also see some that tables that have been defined, but they have not been renamed, so they have the original table names that Excel automatically assigned. When you create a table in Excel by applying a table style to a range, Excel automatically names that range. It's a good idea to name tables as you create them because it can be hard to remember what Excel's names (e.g., Table21) refer to. I use tbl_ and then a descriptive name, such as BalanceSheet, to come up with tbl_BalanceSheet for the table name—but that's just the convention I like. You can figure out your own naming scheme; the important thing is to make sure the names are consistent and provide good descriptions of what's going on.

The following options are available in the Name Manager:

- **New**—Clicking New causes Excel to launch a New Name dialog, where you can add a new named range or value/formula.
- **Edit**—Clicking this button does nothing more than relaunch the New Name dialog and let you change any part of what you have already entered.
- **Delete**—When you click the Delete button, Excel deletes the name you have selected at the time, and as with so many other things, Excel asks if you really want to do it, as shown below left.

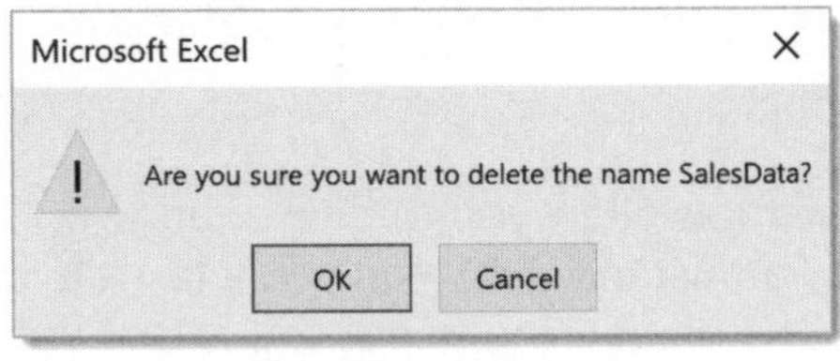

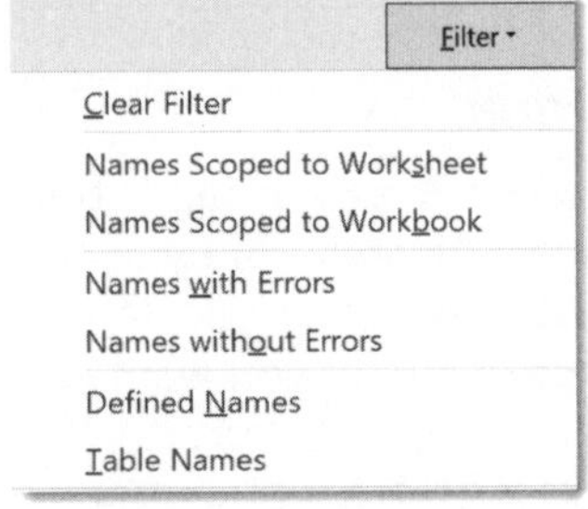

- **Filter**—Filter, as shown above right, is a neat drop-down that it lets you narrow the scope of the names you want to see in the Name Manager, but unless you're dealing with a lot of names, you probably won't use it.
- When you click either New or Edit in the Name Manager dialog, you see the Edit Name dialog, shown below, which includes the following options:

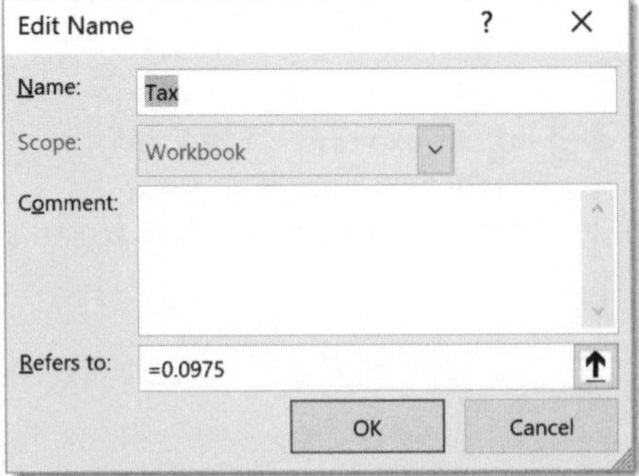

- **Name**—Using this text box, you can change the name Excel creates for you. A name can't have spaces or other illegal characters in it, but underscores are allowed.

- **Scope**—*Scope* refers to whether a name should be used throughout the workbook, as in the Tax example, or whether it should be limited to a particular worksheet. Keep in mind that you can define a name on a specific sheet and reference it somewhere else. For instance, you might define a name for a list and then use that name in another sheet for a drop-down list. The primary difference between the New and Edit dialogs is that scope can only be defined for a new name; it can't be edited after a name has been created.
- **Comment**—Comments can come in really handy when you start having a lot of names in a workbook, and you want a quick reminder of what they are. You probably don't need to create comments if you have only a few names that are obvious.
- **Refers To**—By default, this text box is automatically filled with whatever range you had selected prior to invoking the Name Manager. If that's not what you want, you can use the range launcher at the right end of the Refers To text box to directly select the range you want after calling the Name Manager. This is one of those personal preference things, and there's no one "right" way to do it.

Define Name

There are two options in the Define Name drop-down:

- **Define Name**—Selecting this option just causes Excel to bring up the New Name dialog shown in the preceding section.
- **Apply Names**—Let's say you wrote a few formulas and then decided it might be easier to have some defined names in them. Excel doesn't automatically change your existing formulas to reflect the new names (although it does when you start writing new formulas), so you can click Apply Names to update the named ranges in your formulas. For instance, in the following example, values were placed in A1 and B1, and the formula **=A1+B1** was placed below:

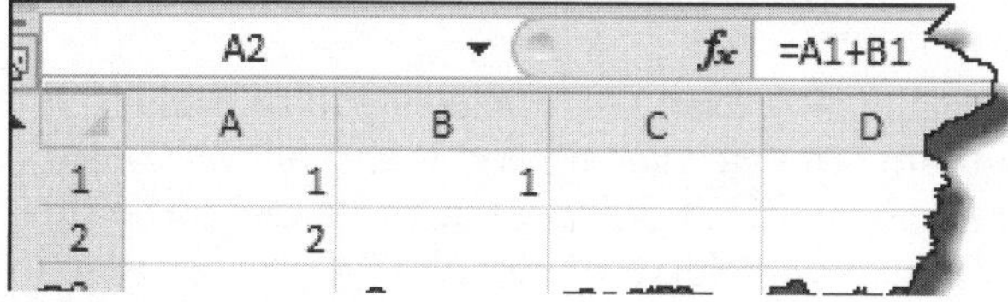

After that, A1 and B1 were named New and Old, respectively, and then the Apply Names tool was invoked, as shown below.

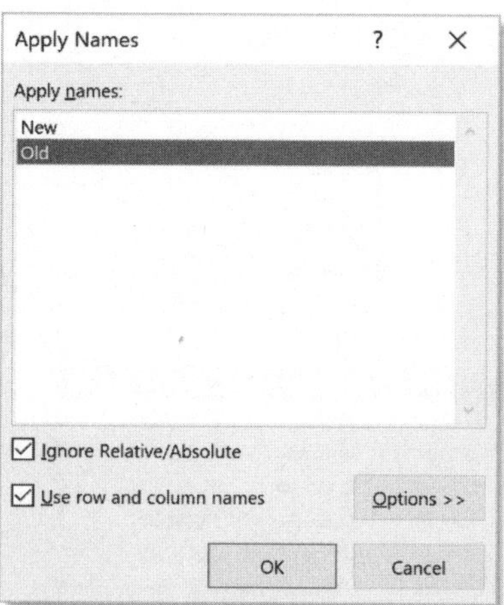

Here is how the spreadsheet looks after naming the ranges using Apply Names:

- The Apply Names option is relatively rarely used, but feel free to try it on your own. If you find yourself to be a fan of named ranges, this option may be very useful to you in the future.

Note: If you use tables for your named ranges, you don't need to worry about them because a table doesn't care how big or small your table is. A table internally knows its dimensions. If you do happen to define a range that's not formatted as a table, you can quickly expand its range by adding a row or column *before* the last row or column of the range. If you don't do that, you need to manually expand the range in the Name Manager.

Use in Formula

The Use in Formula option simply allows you to select from your list of names when you decide to start a new formula or place a name in a formula that you're writing. This is another option that's rarely used.

Create from Selection

As shown at right, when you use the Create from Selection option, Excel tries to read your mind and create a named range for you, based on a range you select. It is not infallible, and unless your table ranges have relatively straightforward structure that you know won't go wrong, you're better off not leaving anything to chance and using the Name Manager. Hunting down an error in a named range can be really difficult.

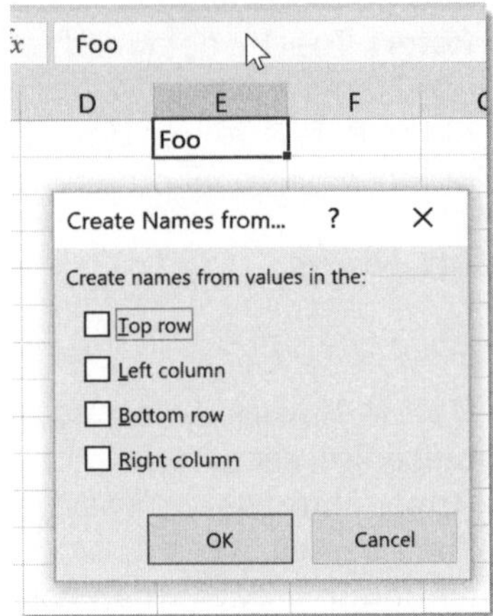

The Formula Auditing Group

The Formula Auditing group offers somewhat advanced functionality. For example, it allows you to evaluate formulas to determine if there are any cells dependent on them (and vice versa), and it also allows you to watch Excel calculate a formula in steps, so you can see if some part of it isn't doing what you expect. The options in this group are used in detailed models, and while they are very useful, the odds that you'll use them in the beginning are slim.

Trace Precedents

The Trace Precedents option shows you what cells a formula depends on.

Trace Dependents

The Trace Dependents option shows you what cells are dependent on a formula, as shown at right.

Note: If a formula trace leads to another worksheet, you see a small image of a worksheet with no information about where it leads, as shown below.

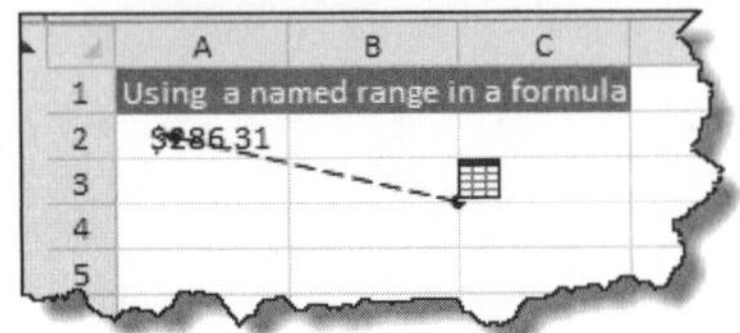

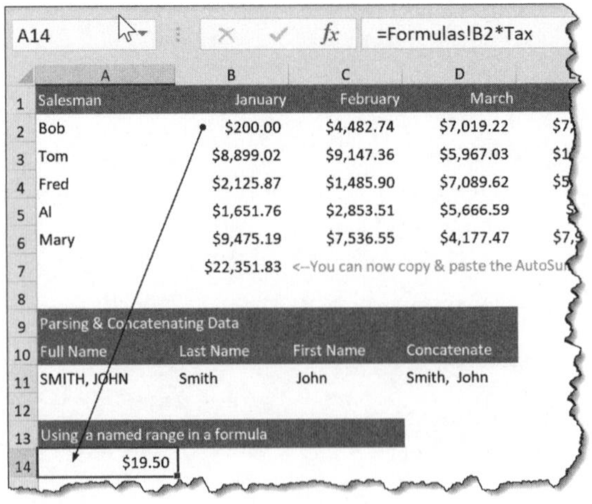

Remove Arrows

The Remove Arrows option resets the formula trace arrows. If you have a lot of formulas, the arrows can get overwhelming, as they can be all over the place.

Show Formulas

The Show Formulas option displays formulas in the cells. It can be very handy if you want to distribute a workbook but have forgotten where all the formulas are.

> **Hint:** You can quickly show/hide formulas with **Crtl+`** (which is the accent key above Tab). Note that this shortcut generally doesn't expand your column widths enough to see most formulas in detail, but it's a good tool for locating formulas.

Error Checking

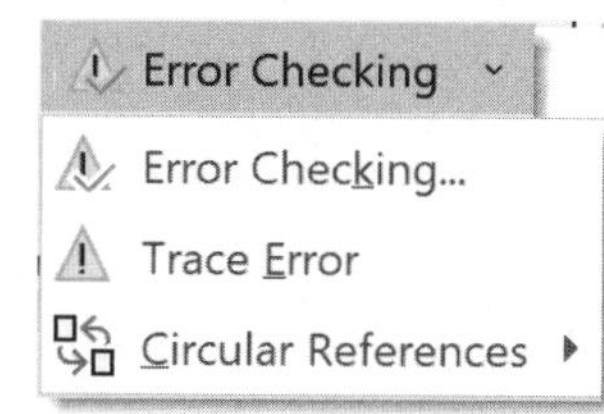

The Error Checking option is a tool for determining why certain formulas might evaluate to errors. Excel has a multitude of error messages to let you know why formulas don't return the results you might expect, and they're very useful (albeit somewhat scary at first). Chapter 6 discusses Excel's error messages in more detail, but for now, we just focus on the Error Checking option, which is a good consolidation tool for newer users, as it exposes several options in one place (see below). Just be warned that the Error Checking tool can only estimate why a formula evaluates to an error; it gives you a good place to start looking but not much more. You might find yourself using Excel's Error Checking option at first, and then, as you get stronger with Excel, you are likely to find that it's often unneeded.

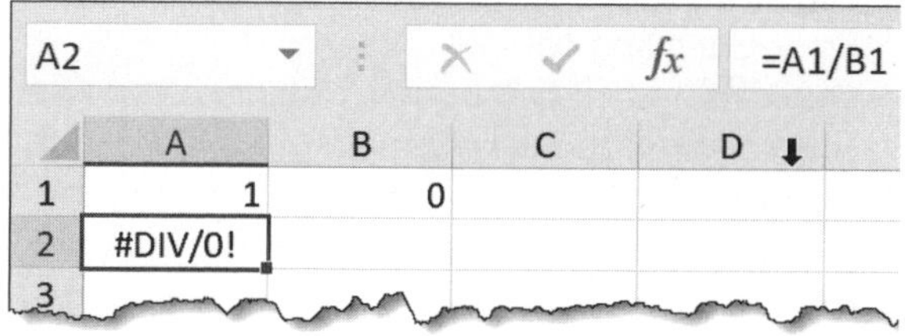

Sometimes it's a good idea to suppress Excel's formula error messages so your users don't think that your spreadsheet is broken when the messages are really just about the users not having entered required data yet. The following example shows how easy it is to get a #DIV/0 error (i.e., a divide-by-zero error). In this case, it's nothing more than =A1/B1, where B1 = 0, so Excel throws an error at you. But what if that 0 in B1 is dependent on user input? You can use an error checking option to catch it and avoid alarming your users by entering **=IF(B1,A1/B1,0)**, which simply says that if a value in B1 exists, return the result of your formula; otherwise, return a 0 instead of an error message.

The following example shows an error created by trying to reference a sales representative who is not in the list of sales reps, so Excel returns an #N/A error. This is one of those cases where Excel is less than useful: It tells you that there's an error in your formula but doesn't tell you how to fix it. Unfortunately, even though the folks at Microsoft have done a pretty good job of trying to make Excel as smart as possible, the software can't read your mind. Excel knows what font, size, color, and even language you're using when you write a formula, but it doesn't know what you intended to do with it, so it can only give you its best shot. As you learn more about using formulas, you'll start to understand what causes errors and how to address them instead of having to rely on the Error Checking tool, but for now using the tool might be a good way to ease into things.

B8 | fx =VLOOKUP(A8,A2:D5,2,FALSE)

	A	B	C	D	E
1	Salesman	January	February	March	
2	Bob	$5,589.00	$4,482.74	$7,019.22	
3	Tom	$8,899.02	$9,147.36	$5,967.03	
4	Fred	$2,125.87	$1,485.90	$7,089.62	
5	Al	$1,651.76	$2,853.51	$5,666.59	
6					
7	Salesman	January			
8	Chris	#N/A			
9					

With the cell in question selected, go to **Formulas > Error Checking** to bring up the Error Checking dialog, shown below, which includes the following options:

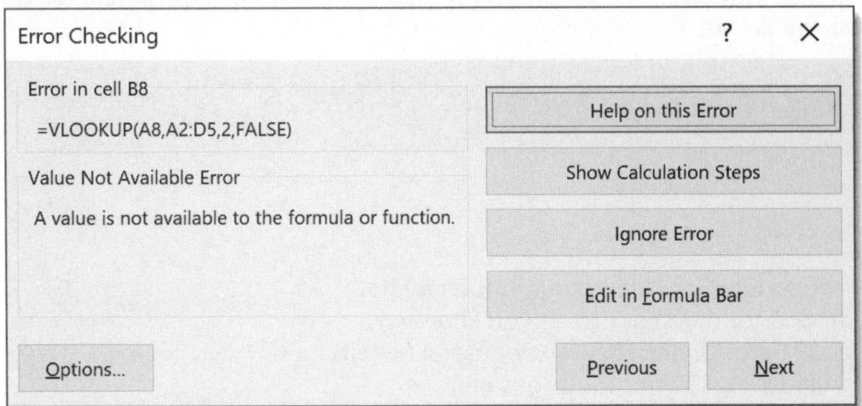

- **Help on This Error/Resume**—Click this button to launch the Office Online Help file and try to find a solution.
- **Show Calculation Steps**—Click this button to bring up the Evaluate Formula tool, which we discuss shortly.
- **Ignore Error**—Click this button to do just what the button says: Ignore the error.
- **Edit in Formula Bar**—Click this button to do your editing in the formula bar. (Keep in mind that you can get there more quickly by just pressing the **F2** key when the active cell houses the formula in question to activate the cell in question or just click on the formula bar instead of taking the extra steps to invoke the Error Checking tool.)
- **Options**—Click this button to launch the **File > Options > Formulas** dialog. It would typically be pretty silly to go all the way here just to invoke that, but sometimes you might find it handy.
- **Previous/Next**—Click these buttons to look for additional errors in your worksheet. Generally, if you're not disabling error messaging in formulas (as discussed in Chapter 6), you know where to look because a cell (or many cells, as is often the case) that should return a value gives you a result like #N/A or #DIV/0, and these errors are pretty hard to miss.

The Error Checking drop-down also offers the following two options:

- **Trace Error**—This simply draws arrows from the formula in question to any dependent cells. It's the same as using Trace Precedents or Trace Dependents. It just provides a visual indication of where your cell dependencies lie.
- **Circular References**—A circular reference generally occurs when you try to get a cell to refer to itself. If you were to enter **=A1** in cell A1, for example, you'd create a circular reference. A circular reference is a problem because a cell can't depend on itself for a value. A real-world example of this would be if you try to calculate employee bonuses based on net profit, which would be Revenue – Expenses. If you were to then try to add that bonus amount back into your expenses, you'd get an error because the bonus calculation is dependent on the difference between Revenue and Expenses, so you can't add that back in because it becomes part of the dependency, causing an error. When a workbook contains a circular reference, Excel lets you know about it, as shown below.

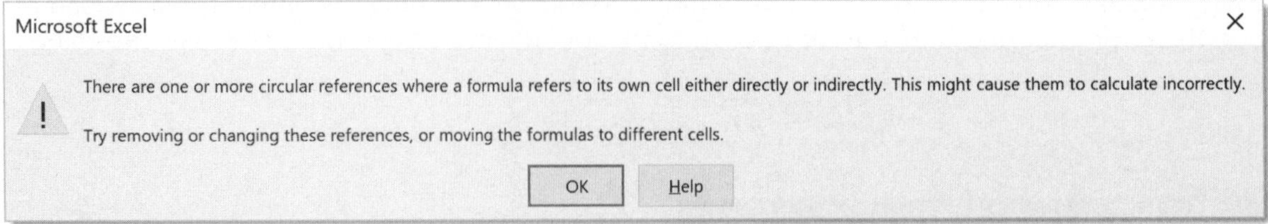

- The Circular References tool simply identifies each cell containing such an errors, and it also displays the address of a circular reference in the status bar at the bottom of the Excel window.

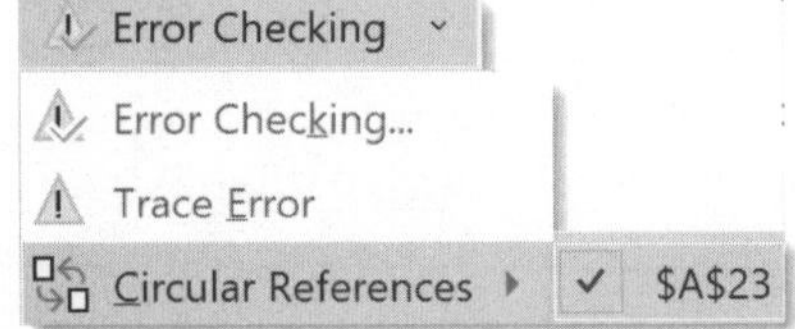

Evaluate Formula

Evaluate Formula is a great tool for checking your formulas if they don't give you the results you expect. For simple formulas, you probably don't need this tool, but for combined formulas (where you use multiple formulas together—sometimes referred to as *mega formulas*), it can be invaluable, as it allows you to evaluate each section of a formula without having to break the formula apart into its different elements. Many people who don't know about this tool break apart a formula into its separate parts and test each one individually until they trace the error. With the Evaluate Formula tool, you don't need to do that but can let Excel do the heavy lifting for you.

Let's look at a simple example, using the formula **=Formulas!B2*Tax**, which is defined as a named range with a value of 9.75%. If you use the Evaluate Formula tool on this formula, you see the first part of the formula underlined, as shown below. If you click the Evaluate button, Excel tells you what that underlined portion of the formula evaluates to. In this case, it's a static number from cell B2, so Excel gives you its value.

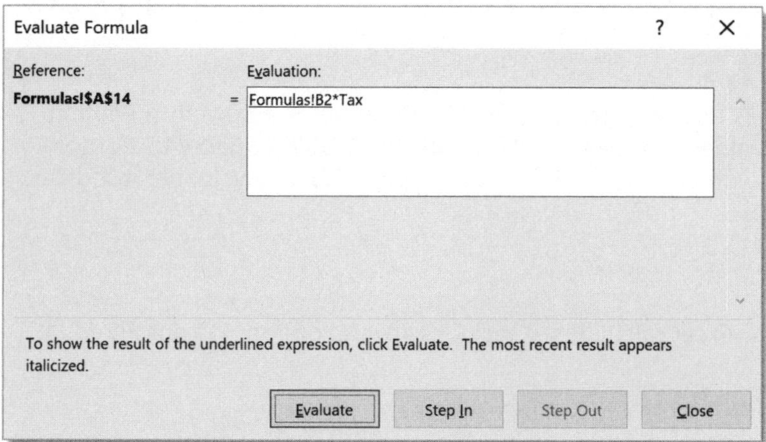

Each click of the Evaluate button moves you to the next portion of the formula. In the following screenshot, you can see that it's evaluated Tax as 9.75%.

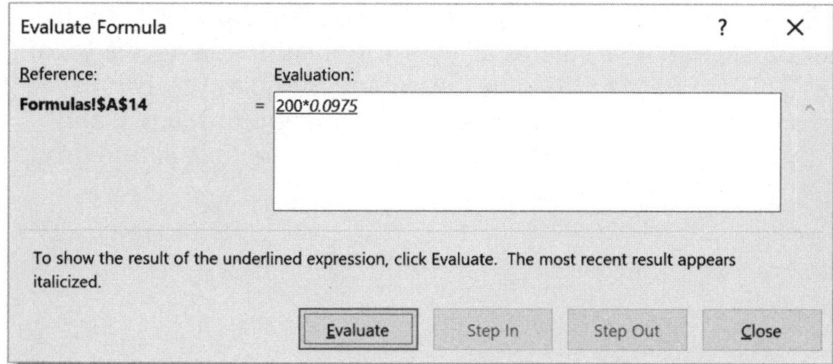

Finally, Excel gives you the result, as shown below, and it's up to you to determine whether it's right.

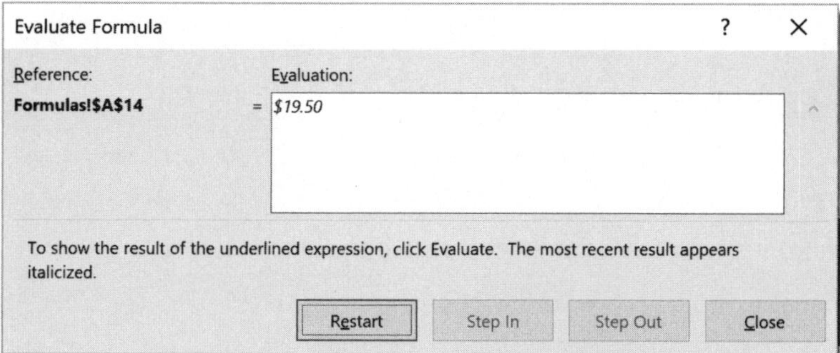

In the Evaluate Formula dialog, the Step In button gives you another way of seeing a different level of detail.

This is a very simple example where you probably wouldn't need to use Evaluate Formula, but imagine how helpful this tool could be for pointing out what might otherwise be very obscure errors. It also provides a very interesting look into how Excel calculates formulas.

Note: You can quickly calculate a sheet at any time just by pressing the **F9** key.

Watch Window

The Watch Window tool is another neat tool for testing or monitoring your formulas. Let's say you have a formula on one sheet that's dependent on the active sheet, but you don't want to have to switch between sheets to see if it's doing what it should be doing. In this case, you can use the Watch Window tool to monitor it right where you are.

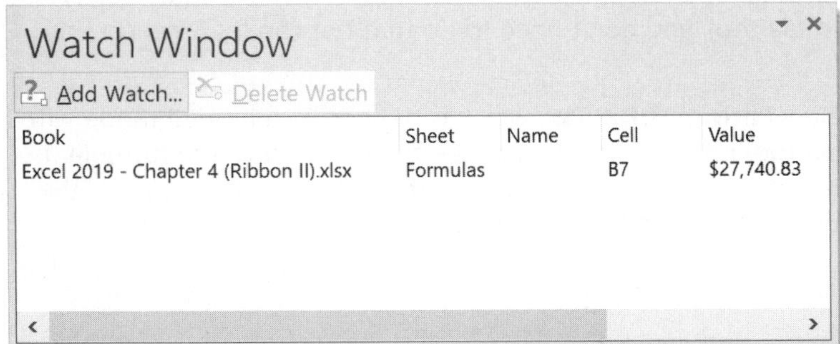

This example shows how you can watch changes in a sales table in cell B7, which holds a SUM formula that adds up the values above. When any of those values changes, Excel updates the Watch Window tool automatically. It's not likely that you'll use this tool a great deal, but when you need it, it's an invaluable resource, just like the Evaluate Formula tool.

The Calculation Group

The Calculation group is where you control how Excel calculates. It includes several options, as described in the following sections.

Calculation Options

Why is the Calculation Options tool important? Let's say you have a complicated model for your business that tracks revenue and expenses and also calculates other things, like profit. It may be dependent on a lot of data entry but may also have a lot of formulas that calculate those figures. If Calculation Options is set to Automatic, as shown below, each time you enter data, Excel recalculates all your formulas. If you have a lot of formulas (and with 16 billion cells on a worksheet, it's not hard to imagine how many formulas you can have), Excel's recalculation can slow your data entry to a crawl. Fortunately, you can set calculation to Manual and have Excel recalculate only when you're done—by using one of the other two options in the Calculation group.

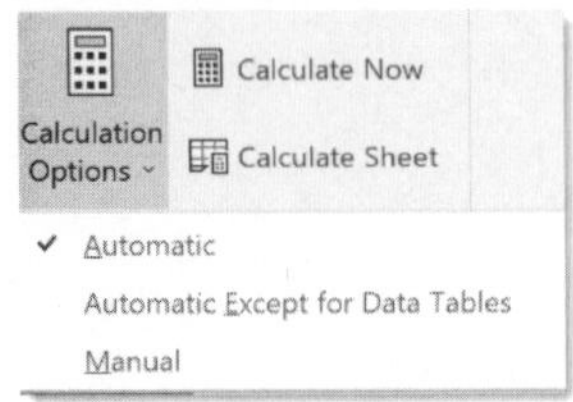

Calculate Now

Clicking the Calculate Now option causes Excel to calculate the entire workbook.

Calculate Sheet

Clicking the Calculate Sheet option causes Excel to just the formulas on the active sheet.

The Data Tab

The Data tab gives you a lot of important functionality for importing, transforming, querying, analyzing, and manipulating your data, such as by sorting, filtering, and doing a lot of other neat tricks. We'll discuss a lot of these operations in Chapter 5, but for now we just cover the basics and look at the various groups on this tab.

The Get & Transform Data Group

The Get & Transform Data group on the Data tab gives you options about the kind of external data you can pull into an Excel workbook, such as a Microsoft Access database, data from the Internet, or even text files.

The Queries & Connections Group

The Queries & Connections group on the Data tab allows you to manage your data connections by refreshing them and even setting intervals for them. For example, you might want to use Excel to keep track of your investment portfolio because you can have Excel update your portfolio data throughout the day. Or maybe you're linked up to a company server that lets you download transactional data specific to your business. Instead of doing it manually, you can use this group on the Data tab to tell Excel to do it for you. (We'll discuss this process in depth in Chapter 12.)

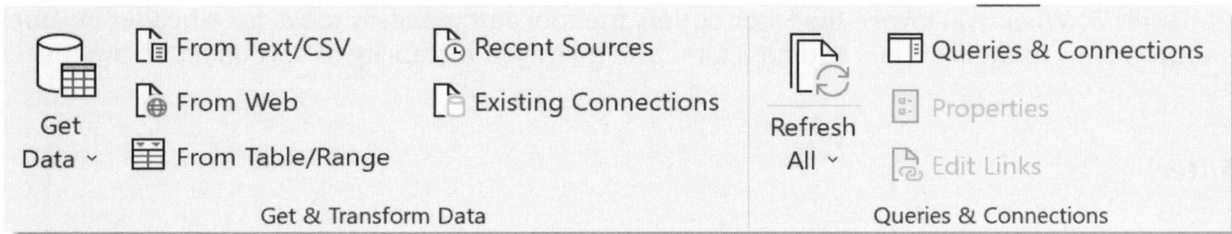

The Data Types Group

The Data Types group, which is available only in Office 365, lets you retrieve data from the web for stocks and geographic data.

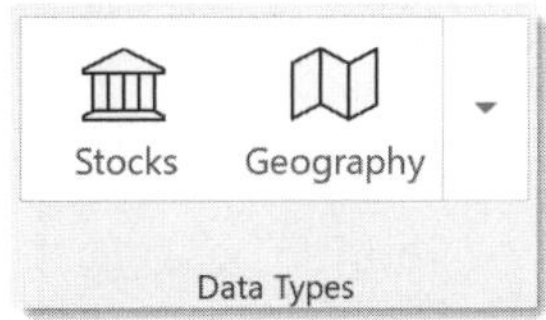

Excel has undergone a fundamental shift in how it stores data: Excel stores multiple data points about each entity listed in a single cell, and that data can be retrieved in adjacent cells. For instance, if you input company names, the Stock data type will return all publicly available information about that company, and you can retrieve information about that stock with a formula such as **=MSFT.Price** to get the current stock price (delayed by 20 minutes) or **=MSFT.Employees** to get the number of employees a company has. The Geography data type returns data based on a geographic location, such as country, county, state, or city. Alternatively, you can use a cell reference to return a country's population with **=E2.Population**.

In the following examples, you see Company Name and Country in the leftmost columns, which have been converted to data types. The columns to the right display data specific to each company/country.

	A	B	C
1	Company Name	Price	Employees
2	Microsoft Corp	$ 111.71	131,000
3	Walmart Inc	$ 95.36	2,300,000
4	Wells Fargo & Co	$ 58.80	264,500
5			

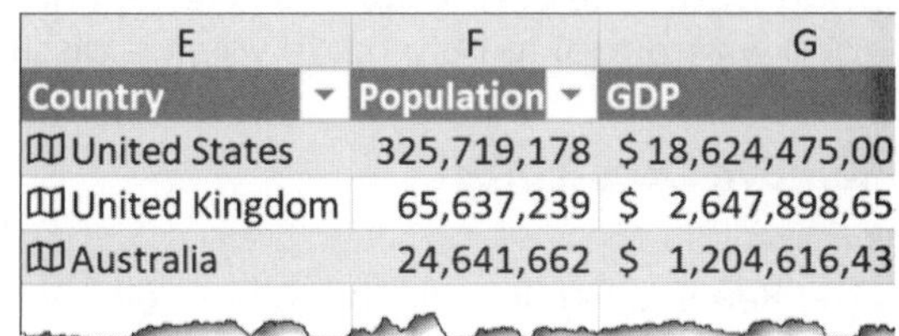

E	F	G
Country	Population	GDP
United States	325,719,178	$ 18,624,475,00
United Kingdom	65,637,239	$ 2,647,898,65
Australia	24,641,662	$ 1,204,616,43

The Sort & Filter Group

The Sort & Filter group includes a number of options, as shown below and described in the following sections, for working with data in a variety of ways.

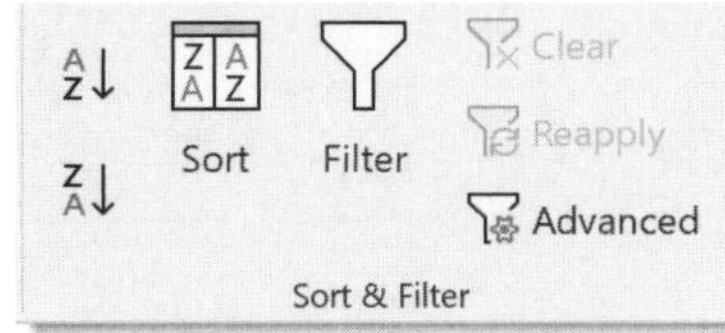

A-Z and Z-A

The A-Z and Z-A options are relatively straightforward: You simply click on the direction you want to sort: A-Z for descending or Z-A for ascending. Even though these sorting options are labeled with letters, they work with numbers, too.

Sort

Clicking the Sort button launches a more detailed Sort dialog.

Filter

Filter is a tool you might have become familiar with if you have worked with Excel tables. (It's discussed in more detail in Chapter 7.) When you invoke the Filter option, the tool automatically looks for a header in your data and adds drop-downs to the first row. Adding a filter also gives you the ability to sort directly from the Filter dialog.

Advanced (Filter)

The Advanced option is a great tool for narrowing down a list. Let's say you have a list of customer transactions, but you want to create a list of just the customer names or items purchased. You can click Advanced to open the Advanced Filter dialog, which you can use to copy the unique records to another place on your sheet. From there, you can move it to another sheet and do what you want with it. Unfortunately, Advanced Filter only copies your data to the same sheet, so you have to cut and paste if you want to move it somewhere else (which you generally do).

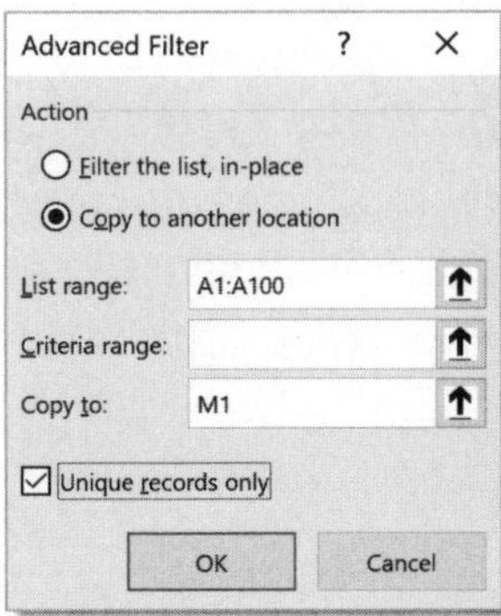

The Data Tools Group

The Data Tools group includes several options that let you physically manipulate your data without having to cut and paste or otherwise do the work manually.

Text to Columns

The Text to Columns option lets you quickly parse data without formulas or manual labor. Remember the example from earlier in this chapter, regarding breaking apart customer names ("Smith, John") using formulas? Using **Data > Text to Columns** is faster and generally a much better way to go with large datasets. Excel has a good wizard tool to help guide you; we discuss it in depth in Chapter 5.

Remove Duplicates

The Remove Duplicates option is a new tool that Microsoft released after years of user begging. Previously, if you wanted to remove duplicate information from your data, you had to either do it manually or write code to do it. Now you can do it in just a few steps. Simply select your data range and click **Data > Remove Duplicates** to open the dialog shown at right.

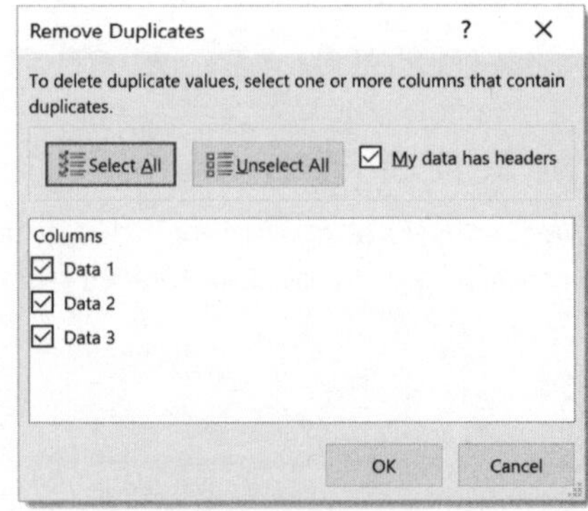

> **Caution:** Excel doesn't mess around when it removes duplicates; it just does it, so make sure to test it on a copy of your data first! If you get unintended results, you can use **Ctrl+Z** to undo.

Data Validation

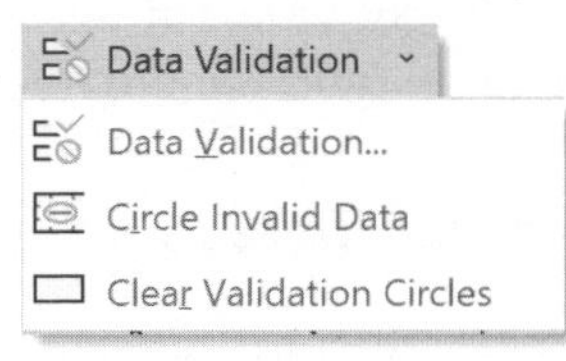

The Data Validation option is one of your most powerful allies when it comes to defining what data users can enter. The most common use is with drop-down lists you create for users. For instance, you can set up a list of cities in which you do business to prevent people from typing in misspelled names. (How many people are going to misspell Mississauga or Onondaga?) If you have formulas that depend on correct spelling, the Data Validation option is invaluable. You can also use it to limit date entries to a certain range, such as making sure that time-off requests only go from the current date forward, or you can define a number range, such as limiting an annual employee increase to 5%. (Chapter 5 covers this tool in more depth.)

Consolidate

The Consolidate option allows you to combine data from multiple ranges in a new consolidated range. It's not likely that you'll use it this early in your Excel work, so this book doesn't discuss it further, but if you are interested, you can take a look at the Help file.

Relationships

The Relationships option lets you define relationships between datasets. It's discussed in more detail in Chapter 11.

Power Pivot

Power Pivot is a data modeling add-in that is discussed in more detail in Chapter 11.

The Forecast Group

The Forecast group contains several data modeling tools, as discussed in the following sections.

What-If Analysis

There are literally entire books devoted to the what-if analysis tools, so this chapter doesn't cover them in detail but just quickly introduces them. Note that these are just the tools that are natively included with Excel's standard installation. You can also find add-in tools from Microsoft and from third parties to perform a multitude of analysis tasks. If you have a relatively unique business model, then odds are you'll find that someone's written a tool to help you analyze it.

The following options are available under What-If Analysis:

- **Scenario Manager**—This tool allows you to define different scenarios based on certain inputs. Let's say you have a best-case scenario for your business, but you also want to be prepared for an economic downturn or a catastrophic event. Scenario Manager lets you build those scenarios without having to build complicated models. You can also combine separate scenarios into a scenario report so you can view them side by side.
- **Goal Seek**—This is a great tool for determining a result based on variable inputs. Let's say you need a new pizza oven, and you know that it's going to cost $30,000. Your credit union will give you a rate of 7% over 60 monthly payments, resulting in a monthly payment of $594.04, but you want to spend only $500 per month. As shown in the following example, with Goal Seek, you can determine that you need to find an oven in the $25,000 range. You can click OK to accept Goal Seek's solution or Cancel to revert to your original values.

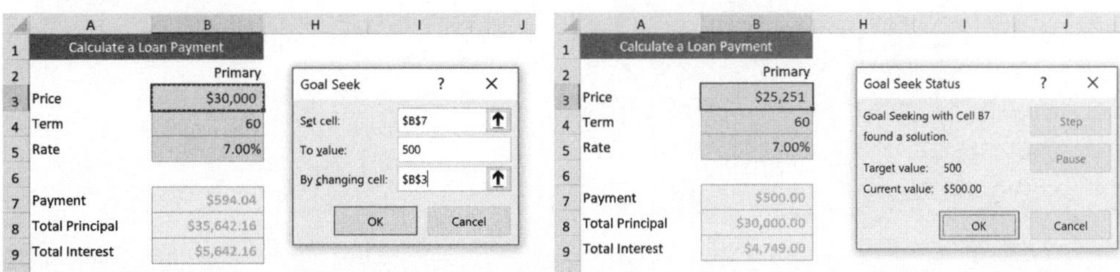

- **Data Table**—Data tables are like scenarios, except that you can build multiple variations in one spot rather than creating individual scenarios that can later be consolidated. For instance, you could analyze the effects of different terms on lease options for a new location.

The Excel Help file provides good documentation on all these tools.

Forecast Sheet

Forecast Sheet is a relatively specialized analysis tool that lets you create a forecast over time. It can get picky about the data that you provide to it. It especially wants a consistent date timeline.

The Outline Group

The Outline group includes the options described in the following sections.

Group and Ungroup

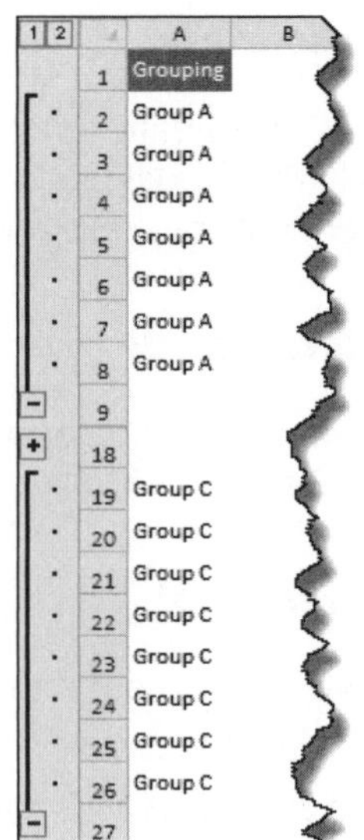

The Group option lets you group rows/columns so that you can easily hide or display them with the click of a button instead of having to do it manually. Simply select the range you want to group and click Data > Group. Excel asks you if you want to group rows or columns, and then it groups the items for you. In order to create groups, you need to have some type of range break between them; otherwise, Excel just adds any additional ranges to the contiguous group. It takes some time to set this up, but doing so can be well worth the effort. You might do this, for example, if you have an employee roster that lists employee names and days of the week. If you want to give each employee his or her own shift schedule, you can group them. Once you apply a group, Excel creates numbered buttons (1 and 2 on the upper-left corner in the figure at right) to the left of the row headings or above the column headings, depending on which grouping style you selected, as well as + and - signs for each group to show you whether they're collapsed or expanded. You can click the 1 or 2 button to expand the entire range of groups, and you can click the + or - to expand or collapse a particular group.

Subtotal

Subtotal is a great tool for analyzing data quickly without having to write formulas. Excel does the work for you! Following is an example of some transactional data for a fictitious company that has several regional sales offices and sells several products, along with the Subtotal dialog.

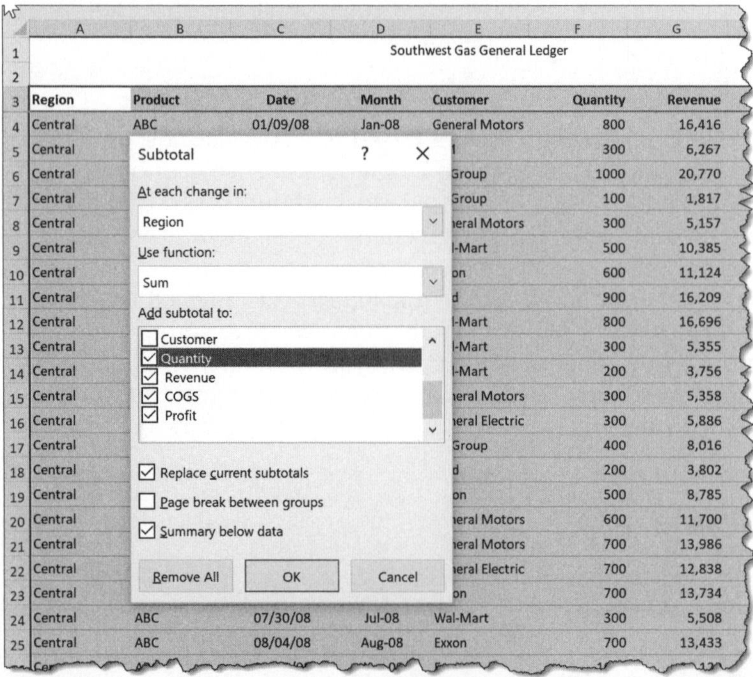

Note: Unfortunately, you can only apply one subtotal function (SUM, AVERAGE, MAX, MIN, etc.) in a single row. In order to use different functions on the same row, you need to manipulate the subtotal formulas by hand.

With the Subtotal dialog, you can select which column you want to subtotal; this example, shows the region selected and then the function (formula) to apply (in this case Sum). Next, you can choose the columns to which you want to apply those formulas. When you click OK, Excel instantly gives you subtotals. Notice below that it also adds grouping layers for you, similar to what we just discussed with grouping.

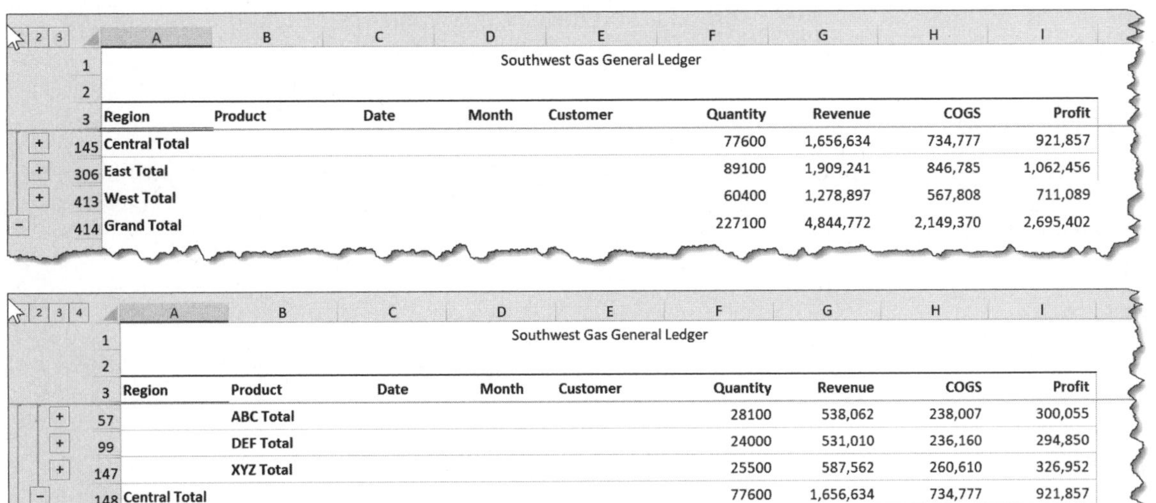

Southwest Gas General Ledger

	Region	Product	Date	Month	Customer	Quantity	Revenue	COGS	Profit
145	Central Total					77600	1,656,634	734,777	921,857
306	East Total					89100	1,909,241	846,785	1,062,456
413	West Total					60400	1,278,897	567,808	711,089
414	Grand Total					227100	4,844,772	2,149,370	2,695,402

Southwest Gas General Ledger

	Region	Product	Date	Month	Customer	Quantity	Revenue	COGS	Profit
57		ABC Total				28100	538,062	238,007	300,055
99		DEF Total				24000	531,010	236,160	294,850
147		XYZ Total				25500	587,562	260,610	326,952
148	Central Total					77600	1,656,634	734,777	921,857
208		ABC Total				30300	584,251	256,641	327,610
263		DEF Total				28400	631,700	279,456	352,244
311		XYZ Total				30400	693,290	310,688	382,602
312	East Total					89100	1,909,241	846,785	1,062,456
357		ABC Total				24800	471,301	210,056	261,245
386		DEF Total				16000	349,082	157,440	191,642
421		XYZ Total				19600	458,514	200,312	258,202
422	West Total					60400	1,278,897	567,808	711,089
423	Grand Total					227100	4,844,772	2,149,370	2,695,402
424									

Hint: You can apply multiple subtotals by first subtotaling on your primary category (e.g., Region) and then invoking the Subtotal dialog again and selecting the second category—but this time unchecking the Replace Current Subtotals checkbox.

The Review Tab

You use the Review tab to get a workbook ready for distribution by checking spelling, adding comments, and protecting workbooks and worksheets from changes. The following sections discuss the groups and options available on this tab.

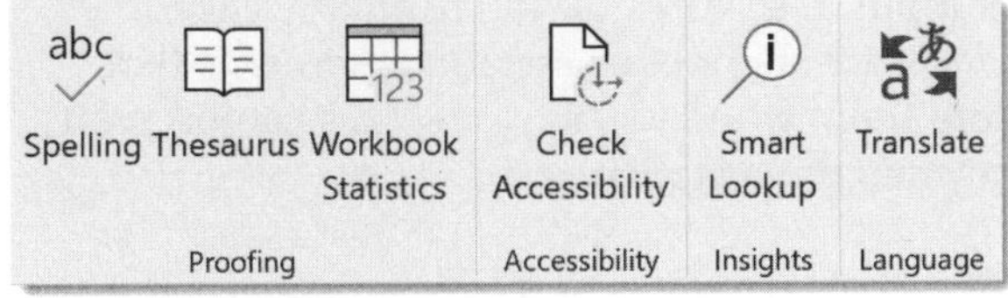

The Proofing Group

The Proofing group includes the options described in the following sections.

Spelling

You can click the Spelling option to spell check your entire worksheet. The spell checking is based on the Office Dictionary and any specific words you might have added.

Thesaurus

You can click the Thesaurus option to bring up Excel's internal Thesaurus tool, which lets you select from different terms for a word you enter.

Workbook Statistics

You can click the Workbook Statistics option to bring up a dialog that gives you a quick snapshot of what's going on in your workbook, such as how many formulas you have in the worksheet/workbook, how many worksheets you have overall, and more. This feature is not in all versions of Excel.

The Accessibility Group

You can click the Check Accessibility option in the Accessibility group to launch a pane on the right-hand side that you can use to analyze your workbook. This pane gives you suggestions about how you can make your workbook more accessible for people with limited vision.

The Insights Group

You can click Smart Lookup in the Insights group to launch an internal search pane on the right and search the Internet for details specific to the active cell.

The Language Group

The Translate option in the Language group can translate words or entire worksheets to another language. Note that Excel can translate only your literal text, but it can't guess your intentions, so use it with caution. Excel does its best to get the translation right, but if you deal with translations a lot, it's best to have a live person proof the document before you send it to anyone. Many a business deal has been lost in translation.

The Comments Group

Comments allow you to insert messages that are specific to individual cells. A cell with a comment has a small, colored callout to indicate that there's a comment attached to the cell. If you choose the Show Comments option, you see all the comments displayed in a new pane on the right.

The Notes Group

Notes are a legacy feature that Microsoft still supports—for now—but does not recommend. Whereas you can use data validation to add comments to a cell to direct user input, the Notes option (formerly called Comments) simply allows you to make note of something. A lot of Excel templates include comments that tell you how to set up a workbook and then instruct you to delete them when you're done. This can be pretty handy, but as with colors, you should use notes sparingly, as they can get irritating fast.

Both notes and comments can be displayed constantly or hidden from view. When a note is hidden, you see a small red triangle in the upper-right corner of the cell. You can just hover over the red triangle, as shown at right, to display the note. As soon as you move the cursor off the cell, the note disappears. You can also choose to selectively hide notes by selecting them and going to **Review > Notes > Show/Hide Note**.

Quantity	Revenue	COGS
800		
300		
1000		
100	1,817	847

Chris "Smitty" Smith:
Go to Data > Subtotal to add subtotals to this table

The Protect Group

You use the Protect group to do a lot of the work required for distributing workbooks to end users. You can, for example, specify that users can only make changes to selected cells or ranges, or you can make it impossible for users to edit a workbook at all. The following sections described the options available in this group.

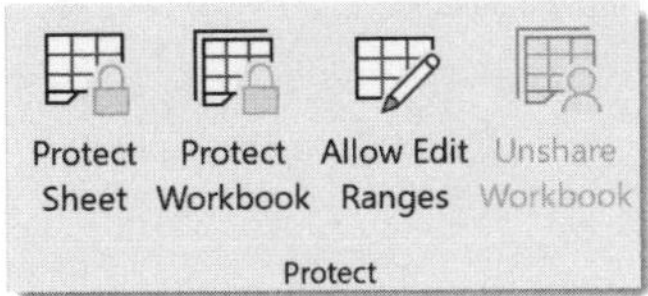

Protect Sheet

By default, all cells on a worksheet are locked, and you need to unlock them prior to protecting the worksheet. First, you need to select the cells you want to allow to be editable; you can select multiple non-contiguous cells/ranges with **Ctrl+click**. When the appropriate cells are selected, press **Ctrl+1** or select **Home > Format > Format Cells** to launch the Format Cells dialog. Go to the Protection tab and uncheck the Locked checkbox to make those cells editable after the worksheet is protected. You can select the Hidden checkbox to hide formulas from view when a worksheet is protected. You often want to hide formulas from people so they don't get distracted by them or try to edit them.

One nice thing about sheet protection is that it introduces a Tab order in the unprotected cells, meaning that the Tab key automatically moves the user from one unprotected cell to the next. However, adding Tab order requires some design considerations, as the Tab order goes from left to right and then down. If you've ever entered data into a website form that had its Tab order out of sequence, like moving from city to zip code, then state, you'll be immediately familiar with this concept.

Prior to Excel 2003, you only had the option to protect a sheet with or without a password. Now, you have a whole slew of additional options at your disposal. For instance, you can allow users to use AutoFilter or sort data, where previously you had to write code or unprotect the sheet to allow this behavior. Unless a worksheet is specifically for you, and you're protecting it to take advantage of the Tab order, you generally want to use a password. When you enter the password, you're prompted to enter it again. You don't need to use a password that's as fancy and secure as the one you use with your online bank accounts. A simple password should suffice. It should also be something that's easy enough to remember.

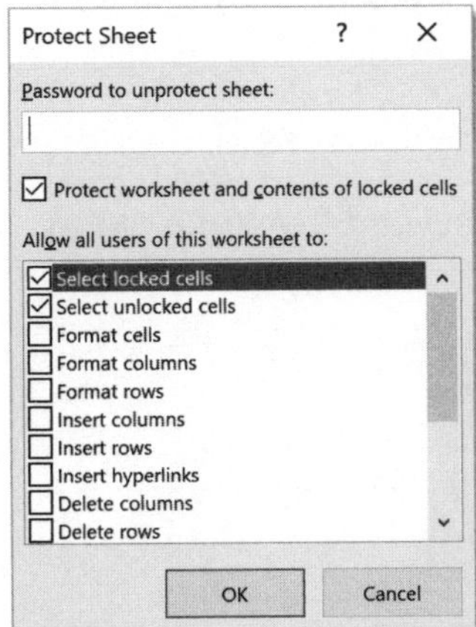

If you try to change a locked cell on a protected sheet, you get a message telling you that the cell you're trying to change is protected.

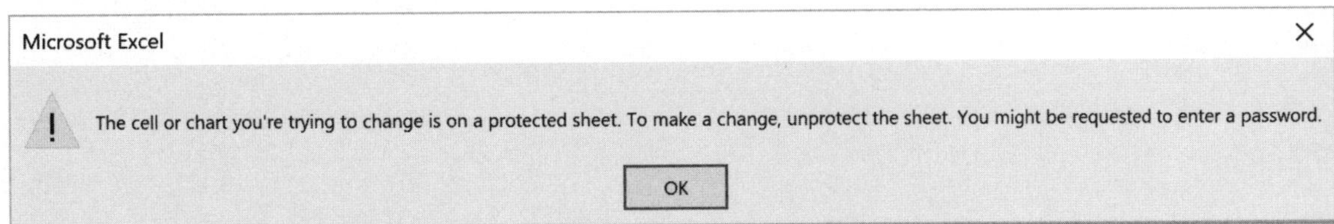

Protect Workbook

The Protect Workbook option prevents users from making changes to the overall structure of a workbook, such as adding or deleting sheets. Here again you have the option of entering a password.

Allow Edit Ranges

The Allow Edit Ranges option allows you to set individual passwords and permissions for individual cells/ranges. This could be handy for something like an online timesheet application, where you don't want people to be able to enter data for anyone except themselves. When you select **Review > Allow Edit Ranges**, the Allow Users to Edit Ranges dialog appears, and in it you can click New to start adding a range.

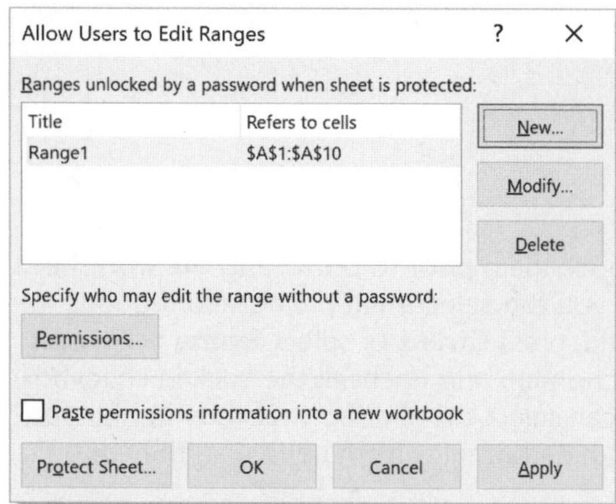

If you add a password, anyone who knows the password can edit the range, or you can define individual user roles by clicking Permissions. If you're not familiar with setting user roles, you might be better off having an IT specialist do this for you.

> **Caution:** Excel is not a secure environment, nor has it ever been marketed as one. Worksheet protection can be broken relatively easily, so think carefully about whether you should share documents that contain sensitive personal information such as Social Security numbers and wage information.

Unshare Workbook

Shared workbooks were a legacy feature that allowed you to let multiple users work on a workbook simultaneously. However, they have been replaced with real-time collaboration so that you can now share workbooks with others and work together in real time when you save files in OneDrive or SharePoint folders. This is an Office 365 feature, but if you need to work with others on workbooks, then it's completely worth it, and it's not limited to Excel; you can also collaborate in real time in Word and PowerPoint.

The Ink Group

The Ink group is dedicated to touchscreen devices that support inking/pen use. It's beyond the scope of this chapter, but for more information, see support.office.com.

The View Tab

The View tab allows you to control the appearance of your worksheets. The following sections describe the groups on this tab.

The Workbook Views Group

The Workbook Views group includes the options shown below and discussed in the following sections.

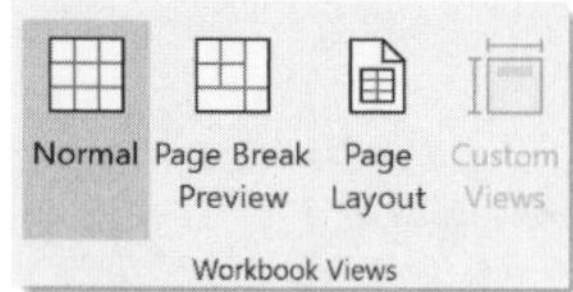

Normal

Normal is the default view for workbooks and is most likely where you'll spend most of your time. You can also toggle views from the status bar.

Page Break Preview

The Page Break Preview option you see where your page break are. The print area is delineate by a solid blue border, as shov below, and everything outsid print area is gray. Horizontal vertical dotted lines indicate Excel has placed page break you can move them manua clicking on them with the and dragging them where want.

Page Layout

The Page Layout optio book has them.

Custom Views

The Custom Views columns. Any existi you can easily add

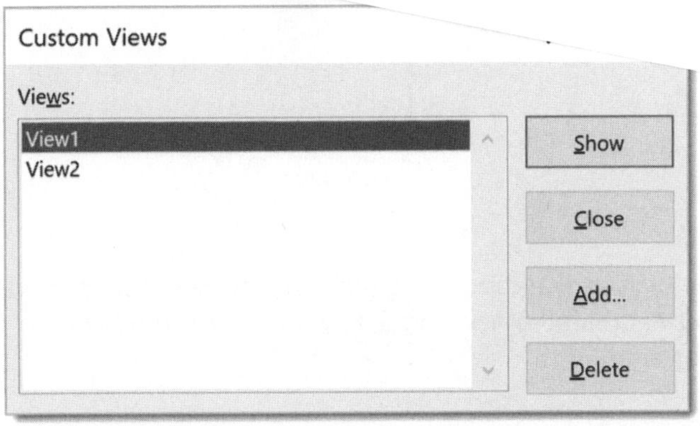

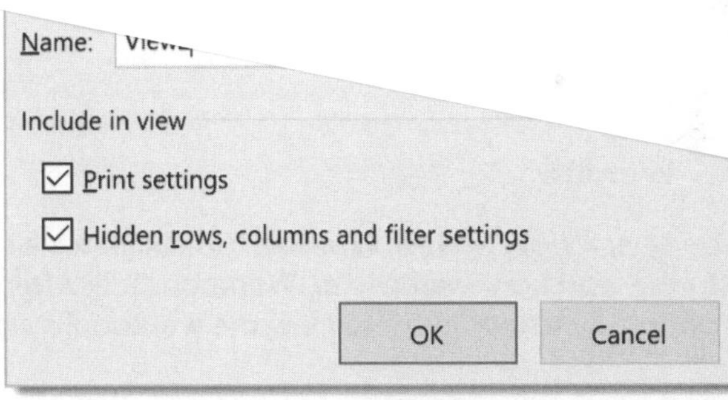

In order to define a new view, you first need to set up your worksheet the way that you want it, hiding rows and columns as necessary. Once you've defined the view, you can unhide everything; after that, invoking that view returns the sheet to the view you set up. It takes some time to set up several views, but if you're in the habit of hiding rows and columns, this can be a huge timesaver.

The Show Group

The Show group allows you to define some of the physical elements you can have on a worksheet, such as the ruler, gridlines, the formula bar, and headings. In many cases, you'll want to turn these off, especially with a report you are distributing for viewing only. For worksheets you are using for yourself, you'll probably want to leave them on as they make it easier to see what's going on.

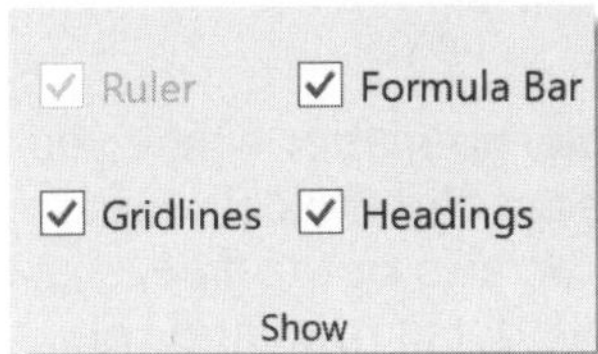

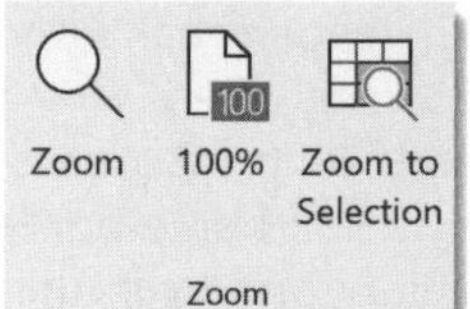

, allow you to zoom in or
ivate the zoom controls on

u choose a preset zoom value or you

heet to 100% zoom.

on allows you to select a range on your worksheet and quickly zoom into it. You
tton or press **Ctrl+Z** to get back to normal.

oup

up allows you to view multiple worksheets/workbooks at once, as well as freeze rows and
at you can always see them, regardless of where you are on a sheet. The following sections de-
ptions in this group.

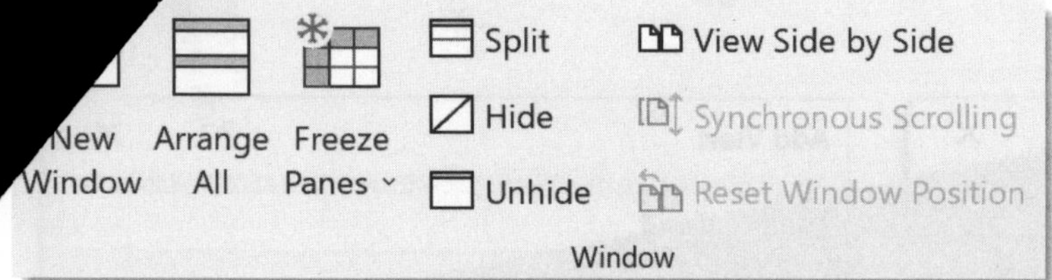

New Window

If you select **View > New Window**, Excel creates a copy of your workbook, with an instance number appended to the workbook name (e.g., Workbook1:2). After you've created a new window, you can use the Arrange All option, described next, to view the workbooks side by side.

Arrange All

The Arrange All option opens an Arrange Windows dialog that lets you choose how you want to compare open workbooks. If you want to view different workbooks, make sure to uncheck the Windows of Active Workbook checkbox.

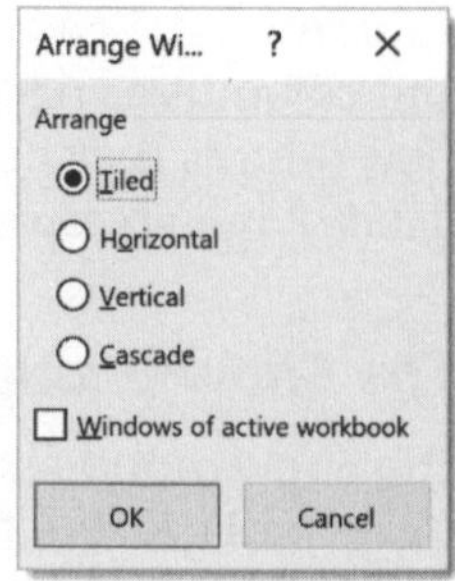

Freeze Panes

The Freeze Panes option lets you freeze columns and rows so that they're always visible, no matter where you scroll on the worksheet. To freeze panes, select the row below the row you want to freeze and the column to the right of the columns you want frozen and then select **View > Freeze Panes**. You can also opt to freeze just the top row and first column; you might do this, for example, if you don't have multiple detail rows and columns you want frozen in place.

Split

The Split option splits your worksheet into multiple panes. (The example below shows a worksheet split into four panes.) This can be useful for large sheets that contain a lot of data because you can view the top of the sheet in one pane and the bottom in another.

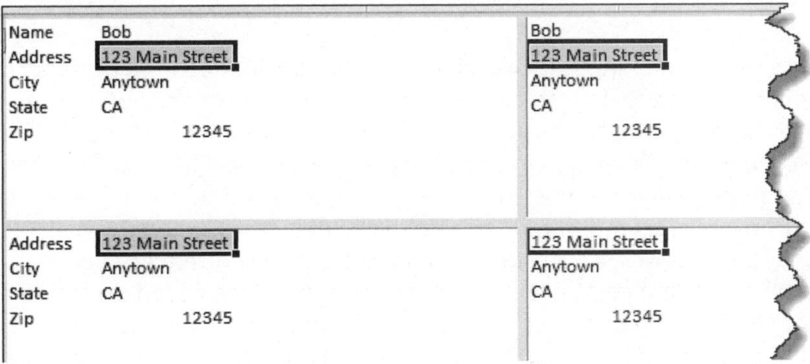

Hide

The Hide option hides the entire workbook.

> **Note:** What if you only want to hide one worksheet? You can quickly hide a worksheet by right-clicking on the worksheet tab and then selecting the Hide option.

Unhide

The Unhide option unhides any hidden workbooks.

View Side by Side

The View Side by Side option allows you to show multiple workbooks in the same pane.

Synchronous Scrolling

The Synchronous Scrolling option is super handy for comparisons between workbooks: As you scroll in one workbook, the one next to it scrolls at the same time and pace.

Reset Window Position

The Reset Window Position option returns your view to its original state.

The Macros Group

You can use the Macros group to view a list of all public macros or record a new macro. The Use Relative References option allows you to tell the Macro Recorder to change its reference style when it deals with cells and ranges. You can also access these options from the Developer tab if you choose to enable it.

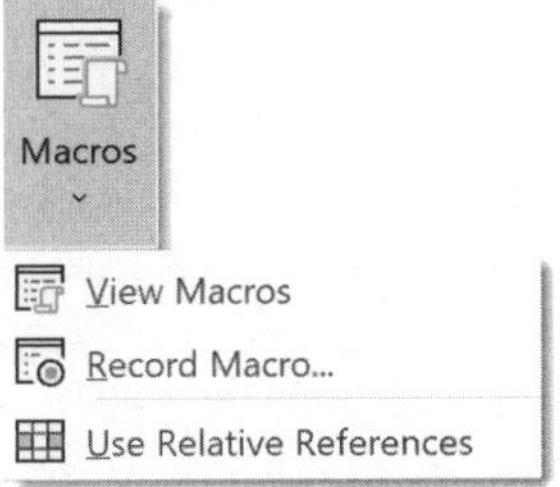

Chapter Summary

- In this chapter you learned the ins and outs of the Insert, Page Layout, Formulas, Data, Review, and View tabs on the Excel Ribbon. You learned about the elements of each of these Ribbon tabs.
- You saw that there are multiple ways to expose most elements, by using keyboard shortcuts, Ribbon options, and dialog launchers.

Chapter 5: Entering and Manipulating Data

In the last few chapters you have learned the ins and outs of the Excel Ribbon interface and the myriad commands that the Ribbon puts at your fingertips. This chapter explores how to use a number of Excel features by showing how to set up some business scenarios, enter and edit data, and format and prepare a workbook for distribution and printing.

Next to using functions to analyze your data, actual data input is one of the most important aspects of using Excel. After all, without data, you have nothing to analyze. In a small business scenario, you might not have a large database or mainframe system for inputting your daily transactions; you might instead rely on manual methods or some type of small business accounting software, like QuickBooks or Peachtree. Often such a system works well, but what if it doesn't adequately measure the aspects of your business that will help you manage it intelligently, such as customer turnover vs. retention rate or employee sales performance? Small business accounting systems are great for telling you where you stand financially, but they often don't give you deeper insights that can really help. While there are certainly merits to making decisions based on gut instinct, when you have a tool like Excel right at your fingertips, you should use it. Similarly, when managing household finances, why do by hand what you can have Excel do for you? Regardless of the need, you have to figure out how to get your information from its source into Excel and then what to do with it.

This chapter explores how to enter and edit data, how to manipulate it once it's in Excel, how to format it so it looks the way that you want, and how to prepare it for printing/distribution. This chapter has a companion workbook that is laid out in steps to help you understand the process.

Before you start putting your information/data into a worksheet, you need to understand some fundamental concepts of good spreadsheet design. These concepts aren't necessarily limited to Excel and can also be used to set up and manage other important business products, such as sales or marketing promotions, employee schedules or expense reports, and customer brochures.

Answering Important Questions

Before you start entering anything in a worksheet, you should look for answers to a few questions to establish your audience and determine what function your worksheet needs to provide:

- Is there another tool that could do this more efficiently?
- Is creating this worksheet necessary? (e.g., Do I really need to create a shopping list in Excel when a pen and paper or my phone will work fine?)
- What do I want to keep track of here?
- What do I want to measure, both broadly and specifically?
- Who are my users? Do I need data input? If so, from whom?
- What is my primary data source? Will I be pulling data from a company server or the Internet, will users manually input data, or will a bit of both happen?
- Will this be an analytical tool (for business planning, for example), is this a flashy daily sales leaderboard I want to post to pump up my team, is it something like an employee schedule or calendar that I'll just post on a wall and let people fill in by hand, or is it more of a data warehouse, like a customer list? All of these options require some degree of data input, but the extent and methods may vary.

If you can answer these questions to your satisfaction, you can move on to the planning stage.

> **Note:** Don't fix what ain't broken! You don't necessarily need to use Excel if there's another tool out there that does what it needs to do, especially if you already use it! Companies around the globe suffer from "report regurgitation," where someone didn't like the format that the company system (or even another department) spit out, and they have someone else reenter the data and make it look the way they want it to look. Once data exists digitally, there's rarely an excuse for reentering it anywhere!

Planning

During the planning stage, you conceptualize your overall design. If it's something simple that you're not going to reuse, you can just go ahead and whip something together. But if this is going to be something sustainable, like a pricing matrix for your products, then you'll be better off putting some time and effort into design before you start tapping away on the keyboard. This may sound counterintuitive, but many of the best spreadsheets and databases are laid out on paper before anyone even turns on a computer. If you can sketch out an overall idea of what you want, it will be easier to set up something that is flexible and can grow with you. It doesn't have to be perfect; you just need a bit of a roadmap to get you going. You certainly don't have to do this type of planning, and many great spreadsheets have been built without it. But keep in mind that a little investment in planning now can help you avoid spending many hours building a spreadsheet only to have to redesign it when you realize it doesn't work the way you need it to.

Hint: If you make it difficult for people to enter data, they will make it difficult for you to get it back. A well-designed spreadsheet can help you get the results you're looking for.

I spent several years working on a large university database project, where the CFO would sketch the forms he wanted on paper, tape them to his wall, and email me screenshots from his phone. Just those seemingly simple steps led to great designs and functionality because I was able to see what he wanted and implement it rather than having to read his mind.

Understanding Design Rules

Excel is an amazingly flexible tool, and while you don't have to follow them, there are some general rules that you should keep in mind when you're designing your spreadsheets.

Rows vs. Columns

When you're dealing with list-based data—for example, a parts catalog or customer list—your detail data should go across, not down. This concept borrows from intelligent database design, which was probably derived from the old accounting ledgers that led to the spreadsheet in the first place. This is commonly referred to as a "flat-file format." If you can just keep this single simple precept in mind any time you start a new spreadsheet, you'll be in pretty good shape right off the bat.

The example on the left is an extreme example of data "gone bad," and the example on the right shows how the same data should instead be laid out:

The format of the example on the right is obviously much easier to use. Notice that it has the data going across, not down.

	A	B
1	Bob Smith	
2	123 Main Street	
3	Anytown, USA	
4	2125551212	
5	Cheryl Smith	
6	345 That Street	
7	Pottstown , PA	
8	9505551212	
9	Bob Thompson	
10	789 Winchester	
11	Murrieta, NV	
12	86532	
13	201555112	
14		
15		
16		

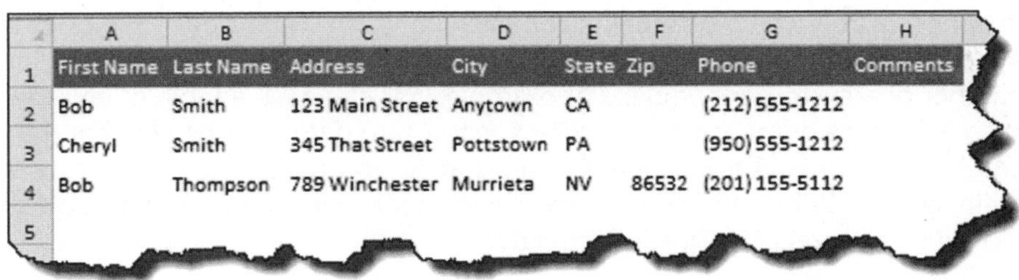

	A	B	C	D	E	F	G	H
1	First Name	Last Name	Address	City	State	Zip	Phone	Comments
2	Bob	Smith	123 Main Street	Anytown	CA		(212) 555-1212	
3	Cheryl	Smith	345 That Street	Pottstown	PA		(950) 555-1212	
4	Bob	Thompson	789 Winchester	Murrieta	NV	86532	(201) 155-5112	
5								

Note: If you have a poorly constructed dataset like the one on the left above, you'll usually find out how bad it is after you've printed out 5,000 flyers with information that's been jumbled because Mail Merge was told to look for five rows, but while some records had five rows, others had six—so Cheryl Smith's flyer went to Bob Thompson and all kinds of other problems cropped up.

The data in the example on the left is largely unusable because there's just no way to discern one record from the next. How do you know when one record ends and another one starts? You might say that you could key on the numeric address (e.g., 123 Main Street), but what if the address doesn't lead with a number (e.g., Evergreen Terrace #3)? Another issue is that there's no normality because the first two customer records don't have zip codes, but the third does. This means you can't standardize any process, such as Mail Merge, without a large degree of failure. Another thing to think about is that even with over a million rows in Excel, you could quickly run out of room by going down because each customer record requires multiple rows. When you're dealing with list-based (or *transactional*) data, you should ideally set up your data on a row-by-row basis, where each row contains data related to a single transaction, or instance (e.g., customer or order details). It is also much easier to read and organize your data when it has column headers that you can consistently follow.

Note: If you have a million or more records, you really should be working with a database, like Access, rather than Excel! Although you can store large quantities of data in Excel, it is not a database application but an analysis tool.

Data Separation

Wherever possible, separate your data as much as possible. For instance, if you store "Bob Smith" in a single cell, the data is much less usable than if you have separate First Name and Last Name columns. It is possible to parse (split apart) a single column by using functions, Flash Fill, or Excel's Text to Columns tool (all discussed later in this book), but such operations are often unwieldy at best and should be avoided if possible. This is especially important when you start dealing with middle names/initials, suffixes/prefixes, and so on. To borrow a math term, the more you can break your data down into its lowest common denominators, the better. Just think of all the Internet sites where you enter first name, last name, address, city, state, and so on separately. The entry forms on those sites are all database driven, and they use that entry style for a reason.

Another thing that can chuck the usability of your data right out the window is to store it all in a single cell, as shown below. In this "really bad data" example, the data has been crammed into one cell, which renders it all but useless. No degree of formulas or VBA code can reliably strip that data out, and you might as well start over. Unfortunately, data entered like this is all too common in Excel. Don't let this type of data into your world!

Note: Power Query has a new command to Split by Delimiter to Rows that can successfully clean some data sets that look like this.

Visible vs. Hidden Data

Oftentimes, you need to have information in a workbook, such as employee or customer details, that you don't want others to see. In many cases, people make the mistake of putting such information out in the open, even though it's easy to hide it and reference it from other sheets.

Excel is like a ream of paper in that it's a series of worksheets stacked on top of each other. You can develop relationships between worksheets and even between workbooks. One of Excel's strongest points is the ability to store data on a worksheet and retrieve only what you need via a unique identifier, such as an employee number or a customer number. For example, you can have a table of employees and information about them (e.g., employee number, name, address, wage, hire date) on one sheet and then a transaction list of sales by employee number. A few simple functions allow you to summarize sales by employee number while leaving their sensitive information on separate worksheets. You can even hide worksheets that contain sensitive employee or customer information from users.

You can also use Excel's internal Data Model to create a relationship between related datasets and then build PivotTable reports to summarize the information. (We'll discuss this further in Chapter 11.)

Designing and Building Spreadsheets

Once you've decided on a function for a spreadsheet, you need to focus on a design. Based on the planning you've already done, you should have an overall concept in mind; for example, you might want to create a balance sheet with expense categories in rows on the left and months as your column headers, or you might be building an employee schedule with employee names in rows and days of the week as column headers. The first few times you set up spreadsheets, you might find the process painful, but after you get a few under your belt, you'll know how to start a new one with relative ease. In addition, as you gain experience building spreadsheets for different scenarios, you'll find yourself reusing your favorites repeatedly.

Note: If you get stuck and need ideas for your initial design, check out the Microsoft Template Gallery, at https://templates.office.com.

The next step is to build the guts of your spreadsheet by defining the row and column headers you want (e.g., Employee 1, Employee 2, Employee 3, etc. and January, February, March, etc.). You still have a lot of options at this point and can easily change your mind and go a different direction, if needed.

It's a good idea to keep things as simple as possible. An overly complex model can be confusing and difficult for users to understand. A spreadsheet with a simple, time-tested design can be very powerful.

Try to reuse elements wherever possible. Why type in *January–December* for each row when you can do it once and refer to the original values throughout the worksheet—or even the entire workbook? That way, if you decide to change to *Jan–Dec*, you can do it in just one place. (You'll see how to do this shortly, when you practice entering dates.)

The following are some tips to keep in mind when editing data (formulas or text):

- After you've entered category labels/titles, you might have to change them at some point in the future. Fortunately, Excel makes it very easy to edit information in cells without having to retype it!
- You can edit a cell's contents directly from the formula bar. Just put the cursor where you want it and make your changes.
- If you're on the keyboard, you can press the **F2** key to enter a cell directly, or you can double-click a cell if using a mouse is handier.
- You can double-click on a word to select it, so you can delete it or change it, and you can press the **Home** and **End** keys to move around.
- You can press the **Shift**, **Ctrl**, and arrows keys to select multiple words, just as you would select multiple cells.
- When you edit a formula, Excel shows a colored border around each cell/range that the formula contains. For example, if you edit **=SUM(A1:A10)**, you see a blue border around the range A1:A10.

Populating a Spreadsheet with Sample Data

Once you've figured out your design (or gotten fairly close), you can start entering sample data. At this point, there's no reason to enter real data unless it just happens to be right there in front of you; instead, you can just make up some numbers that will reasonably represent what you plan on entering later. All you're going to do here is set the stage to evaluate your functionality. You don't want to invest a lot of data entry resources at this point, just in case you decide to completely change your design. I almost always use the following 10-second dataset example to build my models.

B8 | *fx* =RAND()*100

	A	B	C	D	E
1	CASH RECEIPTS	01/03/18	01/10/18	01/17/18	01/24/18
2	Cash Sales	$73.11	$86.49	$94.78	$20.47
3	Collections fm CR accounts	$43.55	$13.18	$72.74	$68.17
4	Loan/ other cash inj.	$62.40	$85.79	$38.78	$11.78
5	TOTAL CASH RECEIPTS	$179.07			
6					
7	PURCHASES	01/03/18	01/10/18	01/17/18	01/24/18
8	Salaries & Wages	$80.94	$61.15	$8.23	$75.81
9	Payroll expenses (taxes, etc.)	$40.64	$28.04	$8.54	$67.74
10	Outside services	$51.55	$18.16	$63.30	$95.15
11	Supplies (office & operating)	$93.18	$34.46	$85.81	$47.00
12	Repairs & maintenance	$29.33	$24.43	$72.77	$62.21
13	Advertising	$69.04	$70.25	$33.86	$11.16

To use your own 10-second sample dataset, select the range where you want some sample data, enter **=INT(RAND()*1000)**, and press **Ctrl+Enter** to fill the entire range. If you want to include decimal places, leave out the INT part. INT converts numbers to integers, or whole numbers, so it strips out any decimal portions.

I've always found it useful to use different number formats to highlight certain values, such as dates vs. currency or percentages. Fortunately, there are some keyboard shortcuts you can use when you're building models to quickly format cells. While you still have the sample data range selected, you can use **Ctrl+Shift+4** to instantly format that range as Currency. You could also go a step further and hold down the **Shift** key and then use the arrow keys to move down and right to pre-format the total row/column.

Refer back to "Keyboard Shortcuts for Formatting in Excel" on page 52 for other formatting shortcuts.

Using Your Sample Data to Determine How to Calculate in a Worksheet

Now you are ready to start taking advantage of Excel's true power as an analytical tool. You can begin developing the methods that you'll use to summarize and evaluate your data, whether by using PivotTables, simple sums or averages, or complex ratios and relational formulas.

Chapter 6 is devoted to using Excel's functions, so this chapter doesn't go too deeply into those waters, but you should try some of the AutoSum features discussed in Chapter 3 to see how they work in a real situation.

The insights you will gain in Chapter 6 about what you can do in Excel will help you expand your design capabilities. One of the limiting factors when people design spreadsheets is that they just don't know that something is possible, so they don't think to add it. But if you look around to see if various operations are possible in Excel, you're likely to have a lot of "Aha!" moments. It's better to ask if something is possible than to not ask and never know.

	A	B	C	D
1	CASH RECEIPTS	01/03/18	01/10/18	01/
2	Cash Sales	$29.77	$14.38	$
3	Collections fm CR accounts	$43.85	$82.00	$
4	Loan/ other cash inj.	$71.39	$2.91	$
5	TOTAL CASH RECEIPTS	=SUM(B2:B4)		
6		SUM(**number1**, [number2], ...)		
7	PURCHASES	01/03/18	01/10/18	01/1
8	Salaries & Wages	$62.95	$19.32	$
9	Payroll expenses (taxes, etc.)	$98.17	$4.79	$

AutoSum in action

Formatting at Just the Right Time

As much as you might be tempted to add formatting elements while you're building a spreadsheet, you should try to wait until it's functional. Otherwise, you will find yourself going back and adjusting the formatting as you adjust your sheet design. (This also holds true in other applications, like Word or PowerPoint, where saving the formatting for last can save you time in the long run.) You can easily get bogged down investing time in formatting a worksheet, just to throw the design away and start over, like crumpling up a piece of paper. It's a shame to have formatting time wasted like that.

Fortunately, formatting is easier than ever with Excel's styles, which we'll discuss in depth in Chapter 7.

Populating Your Spreadsheet with Live Data

When your workbook or worksheet is set up and you have an idea of the calculations you want it to do, it's time to start putting real data into the workbook. If you're going to be relying on users to enter data, I strongly encourage you to take advantage of Excel's protection features so users don't inadvertently overwrite your functions or change your design. In fact, I often protect my own worksheets just to protect myself from myself.

To allow data entry in a worksheet, select the cells/ranges in which you want to allow data entry, enter **Ctrl+1** or select **Home > Format > Format Cells** to launch the Format Cells dialog. Go to the Protection tab and uncheck **Locked**. To protect a worksheet, go to **Review > Protect Sheet**, and in the Protect Sheet dialog, select the options that you want to allow and click **OK**.

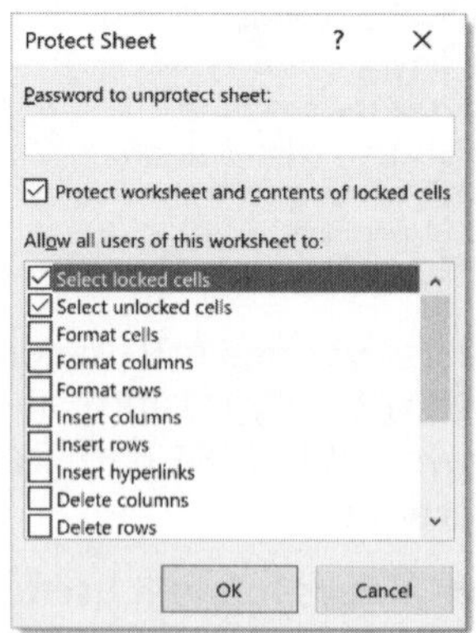

Reporting and Self-Service Reporting

When you have a workbook set up and functioning, what do you do with it? During the design phase, you should have considered the final output you're looking for, based on the workbook's functionality and, most importantly, your audience. Now that you are ready to start using your workbook, you have to think about what story you want to tell with your data and how you want to do it. There is no right or wrong way to do this; it's largely a matter of preference. Some people prefer to let the numbers speak for themselves, others like to tell a story visually with charts and other visual aids, and others want to add "self-service" end-user functionality, with PivotTables, slicers, and timelines. Personally, I like to add a mix of elements and cast the biggest net possible; some people gravitate toward numbers, others like pictures, and some absorb both. You can have your workbook tell a story, so try to get as many people interested as you can. You can get some good ideas by browsing through the Microsoft Template Gallery. In the Northwind Traders Monthly

Performance example, for example, you can see a self-service dashboard, where the underlying data is effectively hidden from view and users are presented with a clean consolidation they can filter to see just what's relevant to them. I've included the workbook shown below in the Chapter 5 companion file Create a Dashboard in Excel, which includes a comprehensive tutorial on how to create a dashboard.

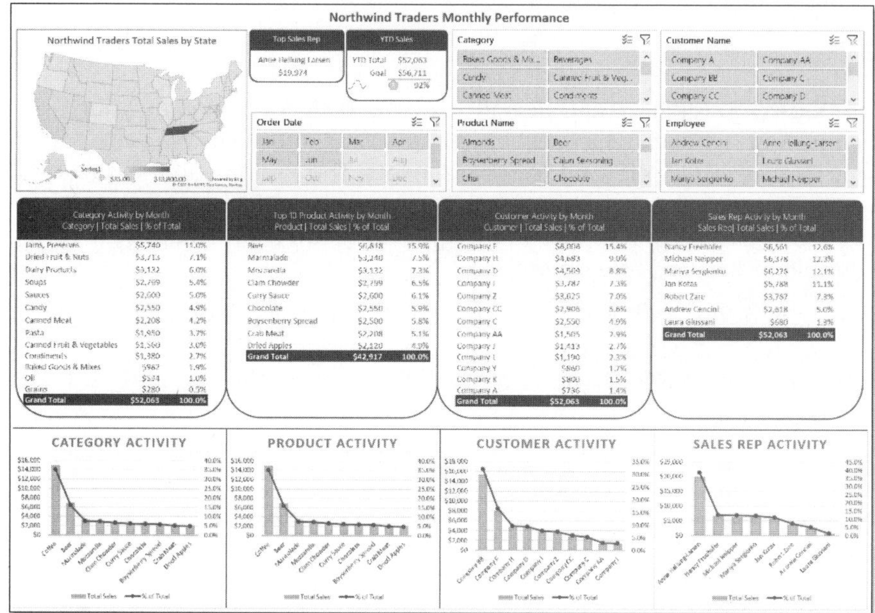

Self-service reporting means users can manipulate what they see without affecting the underlying data. You need to create the workbook only once, but users can manipulate it in a variety of ways to get many different views of the underlying data. I not-so-fondly remember the days when I needed to create individual reports for different departments. What a pain! Each department—Accounting, Finance, Sales, Executive, Manufacturing, Distribution/Trucking, HR, etc.—had to have its own report and, often, its own database queries to get the necessary details. A self-service solution can reshape your week, eliminating hours of redundant work. Thankfully, the folks on the Excel team work incredibly hard to continuously develop solutions that make your life much easier!

Distribution

The last step is distribution. Before you distribute a workbook, you should consider whether any of its worksheets contain sensitive information; if so, you should hide those worksheets. If you hide worksheets, you probably also want to protect the workbook to keep the hidden worksheets from being unhidden. When you've taken the appropriate security measures, you can decide how to distribute the workbook. Again, your audience and use dictate how you're going to send out the information:

- If your workbook is for data entry, you need to take steps to protect sensitive cells or cells containing functions from being overwritten. In this case, you would unlock only the cells that you want to be editable, as discussed earlier in this chapter.
- If the workbook is purely for review purposes, you might want to consider saving it as a PDF or creating a copy:
  - **Saving as a PDF**—Just go to **File > Export > Create PDF/XPS**, and Excel creates a secure copy of your workbook that's easily distributable.
  - **Saving a copy**—If you want to keep the workbook in Excel, you can create a copy of the workbook (by selecting **File > Save As**) and then, on each worksheet, select all cells by pressing **Ctrl+A**, copy with **Ctrl+C**, and finally paste values by selecting **Home > Paste > Paste Special** or pressing **Alt+E+S+V**. This gets rid of all your formulas and also shrinks the size of the workbook. Be warned that if you send out an Excel workbook, even with formulas converted to values only, the data can still be copied, and you might not want that to be possible. This is especially important if you're sending out workbooks containing proprietary or sensitive information.

Note: Excel is not a secure application, nor has it ever been marketed as one. If you have any concerns about distributing workbooks that contain sensitive personal or customer information, it is incumbent upon you to take the steps necessary to protect that information. If the workbook is being used inside your company or department, this can simply involve hiding sensitive worksheets and protecting the workbook. If a workbook is going to customers or other entities outside your company or department, you should probably remove the sensitive information altogether and save the workbook as a secure PDF. Because Excel is not secure, someone who wants to view hidden information badly enough can do so with relative ease; breaking a worksheet password takes just a few seconds for the right person. Think of Excel's protection as being like a lock on your house: It keeps honest people honest, but those who really want to get in can do it.

Entering and Editing Data

Now that you've laid out your plans with regard to function and design, it's time to start developing your workbook. Many people refer to this as *building a model*, so if you hear people say things like "We calculate our pricing using a complex model," they're most likely referring to spreadsheets. The example in this section (which you can follow along in the Chapter 5 companion workbook) is a company's monthly cash flow statement, by week. It's not complicated and is very similar to a report you might download from an application like QuickBooks. It's a very common example of what people do in Excel.

The first step is to determine your primary categories. In this case, the main categories are cash receipts, purchases, and final cash position (i.e., balance). A lot of people put their category headers in ALL CAPS as a way of making them stand out. You could also make them **BOLD** and format the header row. How you present these main categories is entirely up to you.

	A	B	C	D	E	F
1	CASH RECEIPTS	01/03/18	01/10/18	01/17/18	01/24/18	01/31/18
2	Cash Sales	$59.33	$36.82	$77.41	$25.65	$63.03
3	Collections fm CR accounts	$37.35	$28.48	$85.44	$44.13	$76.76
4	Loan/ other cash inj.	$37.16	$67.24	$78.00	$67.43	$76.71
5	TOTAL CASH RECEIPTS	$133.84				
6						
7	PURCHASES	01/03/18	01/10/18	01/17/18	01/24/18	01/31/18
8	Salaries & Wages	$89.78	$5.83	$21.63	$27.57	$92.21
9	Payroll expenses (taxes, etc.)	$21.54	$95.92	$52.08	$69.42	$15.40
10	Outside services	$55.37	$52.96	$4.03	$58.53	$57.96
11	Supplies (office & operating)	$26.88	$42.46	$27.44	$6.74	$58.61
12	Repairs & maintenance	$74.22	$29.36	$48.40	$61.80	$70.31
26	Other startup costs	$1.73	$38.26	$2.98	$46.18	$11.60
27	Reserve and/or Escrow	$98.30	$60.26	$69.42	$36.96	$79.24
28	Owners' Withdrawal	$99.15	$37.65	$91.05	$50.72	$3.14
29	TOTAL CASH PAID OUT	$1,118.42	$175.57			
30						
31	FINAL CASH POSITION	($984.58)				
32						

This example is set up to have weekly entries, so your dates will go across columns B:F. In this case, enter the first week of the month in cell B1 in mm/dd/yy format (e.g., 01/03/18), and then use the formula **=B1+7** in cells C1:F1 to fill the rest of the dates. This formula adds seven days to the original date, and it repeats each time you paste it, always adding seven days to the previous entry.

Note: You can copy the formula across from cell C1 to cell F1, or you can drag the fill handle from cell C1 across to cell F1 and let AutoFill copy the formula for you.

When you have rows and columns defined as above, you need to break down the line items for each primary category and then determine where you want to have subtotals. If you don't already have income/expense categories in mind, you can find plenty of examples in the Microsoft Template Gallery. Cash flow categories are relatively standard, so you probably won't need to make a lot of modifications to whatever list you find. The nice thing about building models like this is that once you have the base model done, you can reuse it any time you want, and you don't have to worry about reentering all that information. With regard to the data entry portion, if any line item lacks detail for a given date, you can just leave it blank. Keep in mind, though, that you should not delete the row. This is incredibly important when it comes to data consolidation with multiple worksheets: If your data doesn't have the same number of category rows each month, it's very difficult to reconcile the months into an annual summary. For example, you might end up with line items in different places between worksheets and could inadvertently add different items together.

Here's an example of a final worksheet that's been formatted and protected. I've included this finished example in the Chapter 5 sample workbook.

	A	B	C	D	E	F	G
1	CASH RECEIPTS	01/03/18	01/10/18	01/17/18	01/24/18	01/31/18	Total
2	Cash Sales	$24.84	$81.84	$19.95	$60.07	$23.70	$210.40
3	Collections fm CR accounts	$64.98	$68.91	$48.96	$95.59	$68.14	$346.58
4	Loan/ other cash inj.	$4.64	$76.12	$64.62	$18.60	$2.59	$166.57
5	TOTAL CASH RECEIPTS	$94.46	$226.87	$133.53	$174.26	$94.43	$723.54
6							
7	PURCHASES	01/03/18	01/10/18	01/17/18	01/24/18	01/31/18	Total
8	Salaries & Wages	$44.85	$85.05	$34.94	$56.28	$64.97	$286.10
9	Payroll expenses (taxes, etc.)	$4.61	$95.26	$85.23	$16.72	$39.58	$241.38
10	Outside services	$17.47	$25.55	$51.69	$70.29	$70.10	$235.09
11	Supplies (office & operating)	$56.01	$29.48	$56.77	$95.50	$16.08	$253.84
12	Repairs & maintenance	$7.30	$99.24	$8.12	$84.57	$87.87	$287.10
24	Loan principal payment	$23.24	$4.07	$6.66	[illegible]	[illegible]	[illegible]
25	Capital purchase (specify)	$40.90	$54.88	$28.34	$20.05	$54.34	$198.52
26	Other startup costs	$36.67	$56.39	$52.89	$75.54	$48.25	$269.73
27	Reserve and/or Escrow	$46.46	$93.45	$4.34	$84.03	$83.11	$311.38
28	Owners' Withdrawal	$8.71	$0.72	$87.31	$93.35	$32.26	$222.35
29	TOTAL CASH PAID OUT	$872.72	$1,060.23	$1,089.82	$1,229.42	$975.73	$5,227.91
30							
31	FINAL CASH POSITION	($778.26)	($833.37)	($956.28)	($1,055.16)	($881.30)	($4,504.37)
32							

Caution: It's time for another reminder on using worksheet protection. If I needed others to fill in the information in the workbook in this example, I'd unlock the data entry cells, such as B2:F4, B8:F28, and so on, and then protect the sheet. I definitely don't want people changing my categories or dates. It would also be possible to use the Input style on those cells to make it obvious where to input data.

Finally, you need to figure out how you want to summarize your data. Certainly, you need to subtotal each primary category (cash receipts, purchases, and final cash position), but you might also want to summarize other details, such as all payroll elements (exempt vs. non-exempt wages, commissions, etc.) as separate line item subtotals beneath the statement. In some cases, such as if you have more than one primary revenue stream or multiple locations, you might also want to break down your cash receipts by those elements. Now is the time to add details because as your model progresses, it becomes a bigger chore to add new elements and also keep track of everything you need to update for those additions throughout your workbook. (Think about what it might take to add a single line item to 12 monthly worksheets as opposed to doing it while you're still building the first one.)

Entering and Editing Formulas and Functions

Once you have your worksheet designed and all the basic elements in place, you have a decent shell. Then it's time to start summarizing some of that data, so let's look at the TOTAL CASH RECEIPTS row in the example workbook. Select cell B5 and then select **Formulas > AutoSum drop-down > Sum**. Remember that when you use AutoSum, Excel inputs the formula for you, and it also gives you a chance to evaluate it and see if it's gotten the range correct. If you agree with Excel's decision, just press **Enter**. Next, copy and paste cell B5 to C5:F5 by selecting B5 and pressing **Ctrl+C** and then pressing **Shift+right arrow** to select the range C5:F5 and finally pressing **Ctrl+V**.

Note that you don't need to move off cell B5 in order to paste. If the source cell and the destination range are contiguous, it's generally faster to copy the source cell and keep it as part of the destination range than it is to move off it. You can go ahead and repeat adding the Sum function for your Purchases category, and then it will be time to calculate the difference (often referred to as the *variance*) between cash receipts and purchases on the FINAL CASH POSITION row.

Up until now, you've been letting AutoSum do the work, and now it's time to look at the steps involved in entering a formula on your own. Select cell B31 in the FINAL CASH POSITION row and enter an equals sign (=) to let Excel know that you're entering a formula. (If you just start typing text, Excel assumes that you want to enter than plain text.) Next, click on cell B5 for TOTAL CASH RECEIPTS and enter a minus sign (-). You now see **=B5-** in the formula bar. Now click on cell B29 for TOTAL CASH PAID OUT and press **Enter**. Excel automatically returns the difference between cash receipts and purchases.

You don't necessarily need to use the mouse-click method to select a formula's cell references. You can also use the keyboard arrow keys to select the cells you want. In fact, just for practice, pick any empty cell, enter =, and start moving around with the arrow keys; as you do, watch the formula reference change itself. See what happens if you enter any operator (e.g., +, -, /, *) and then move to another cell. Each subsequent action locks the previous action into the formula. Therefore, entering the minus sign in your variance formula locks B5 in the formula.

In addition, you don't always have to use mathematical operators. For instance, you can use the formula **=SUM(B10,C13,D20,E24,F28)** to sum cells in a non-contiguous range. To enter this function, you type **=sum(** and then click on the first cell in the range, lock it in place by entering **,** (a comma), and repeat until you have the entire range selected; then you press **Enter** to confirm it. You can actually do this really quickly if you enter the comma with your left hand and click the cells with the mouse in your right (or vice versa if you're a lefty). Also note that you don't need to capitalize the function name; Excel is blind to case and converts it for you. You also generally don't need to enter the final parenthesis to close the formula, since Excel tries to do that for you as well (in most cases...although it can get tripped up on complex formulas that include multiple parentheses).

Once you've entered a few formulas, you need to know how to edit them in case you need to make changes. If you know a formula is just plain wrong and you want to use something else, it's generally fastest to start over by simply typing right over it. As soon as you start typing, the previous values are wiped out, although you can retrieve them by pressing **Esc** before confirming the new formula. If you've already confirmed it, you can press **Ctrl+Z** to restore your original. Editing formulas is a great way to practice using Excel. It's also good practice to examine formulas if you inherit a workbook and want to find out how someone else's formulas work. For instance, you might find a formula you've never seen before and examine it as a way of learning something new. When I first got started with Excel, I took any opportunity I could to look at other people's workbooks just to get an idea of how to do things differently. Remember that there aren't really right and wrong ways to do things in Excel as long as you arrive at a successful endpoint, where you're happy with the results.

At this point, you have your row and column headers defined, you've got your sample data in Excel, and you've checked that your vertical formulas are working, but what about horizontal totals? Right, you need to add those as well, so go to cell G1 and enter **Total**. Then, in cell G2, press **Alt+=** to have AutoSum enter your horizontal total. Notice that AutoSum knows to go across this time instead of up. If you don't confuse it with too much data, AutoSum usually does a pretty good job. But you'll always want to check the highlighted formula border to make sure AutoSum has read your mind correctly. When you're done, you can copy/paste to the other rows where needed.

B	C	D	E	F	G	H	I
01/03/18	01/10/18	01/17/18	01/24/18	01/31/18	Total		
$39.02	$21.31	$78.42	$9.87	$38.54	=SUM(B2:F2)		
$50.08	$21.48	$75.76	$99.83	$24.94	SUM(**number1**, [number2], ...)		
$76.12	$25.70	$80.21	$43.89	$7.97			
$165.23							

Copying Formulas: Absolute and Relative References

So far, you've entered some formulas and copied/pasted them to other cells. This section looks at absolute and relative referencing, which is an essential concept when you start working with formulas and want to make sure they evaluate the correct ranges.

One best practice in spreadsheet design is to make it as simple and efficient as possible. In the Cash Flow sheet of the Chapter 5 companion workbook, the dates in cells C1:F1 consist of a formula that refers to cell B1 (**=B1+7**), where you would initially enter the starting date.

You could copy B1:B7 to the other date header rows and paste as values, but doing so wouldn't be very efficient as you'd need to repeat those steps if your starting date or interval changed. Think about how many potential changes you could make in a big model! To avoid such hassles, you can make all the dates dependent on a single cell, B1. To see how this works, go back to the Cash Flow sheet on the companion workbook and enter **=B1** in cell B7. Then copy that across to cell F7.

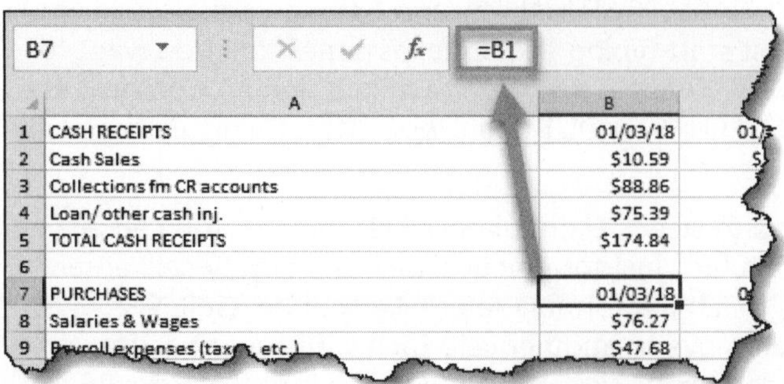

Next, copy cell B7 to the next date header row in cells B33:F33. Unfortunately, you don't get quite the result you expected, do you? You should get something like this, where the dates don't match what you have above:

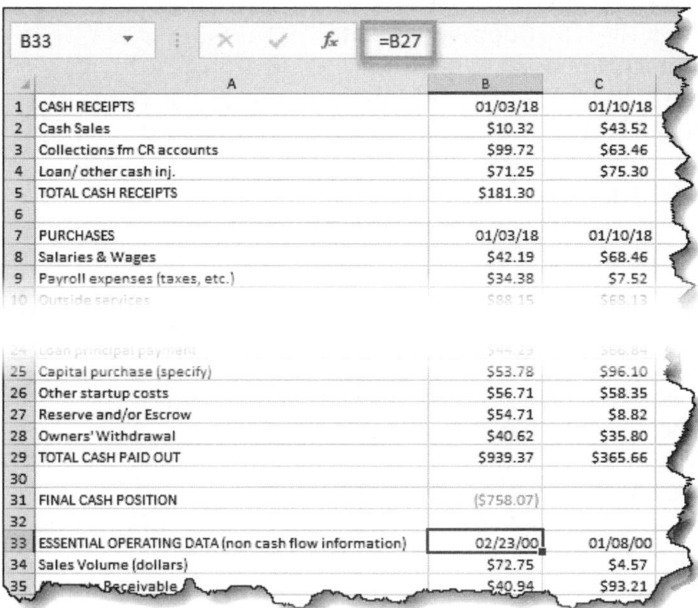

Before you think that Excel's broken, you should understand that Excel did exactly what you told it to do. Look at the formula in cell B33. It's =B27, not =B1, right? Why didn't =B1 remain =B1 when you copied it down? This is called *relative referencing*, and it means that the formula updates relative to its position on the worksheet, not necessarily the cell to which the formula first referred. When you copied cell B7 to cell B33, you moved down 26 rows. Cell B1 plus 26 rows = B27. This means that the formula is referencing a value in the Purchases section instead of a date. This holds true if you're copying a formula up, down, left, or right, so if you were to copy the =B1 formula to the right, it would change to =C1, =D1, and so on.

If you only want to reference cell B1, no matter where you copy it, you need to change the formula to =$B$1. This format is called *absolute referencing*.

But what if you want to use both types of referencing in the same formula, mixing absolute and relative references? Say that you want to refer to the date in column B, but only in row 1. How can you fix the formula to let column B change as the formula is copied across but not change the 1? To do this, you need to use a mixture of relative and absolute referencing, which you do by entering **=B$1**. The $ is the key to absolute referencing, as it fixes whatever it's attached to in place. So, in this case, the B changes as it's copied across, but the 1 always remains a 1 as it's copied down. (You'll see more examples of this in Chapter 6.)

A quick way to update absolute/relative references is to enter Edit mode on a cell by pressing **F2**, selecting the range reference you want to change, and pressing the **F4** key. Each time you press **F4**, you toggle to another reference state (e.g., $B1, $B$1, B$1). In big formulas, this can be much faster than trying to add the $ manually. When you have the formula edited, you can recopy it, and this time the dates correctly reference the master date. You should be aware that not all formulas use referencing the same way; certain formulas use a mixture of the two types of referencing.

If you just want to move formulas around, you can use Cut (**Ctrl+X**) and Paste (**Ctrl+V**) to move formulas from one location to the next without modifying any range references.

> **Hint:** Let's say you need to reorder a list, but sorting won't do what you want. You can select an entire row or column (by clicking the header), hold down the **Shift** key while clicking on the column border, and move the row or column to its new position. If the row or column moved includes formula dependencies, they remain in place if you move the row or column within the current formula range (although this is not the case if you move the row or column outside the current formula range).

Using Lists and AutoFill

Using lists and AutoFill in conjunction with one another can save you untold amounts of time. Unfortunately, these features are often overlooked by even seasoned users. As you may remember from earlier chapters that Excel maintains a set of internal standard lists for days, months, and dates, and you can use those lists anywhere in a workbooks. Let's say you are building a summary worksheet for your 12 monthly cash flow statements, and you have January through December as the column headers in the summary.

The logical assumption for populating those months in the workbook would be to manually enter them. That assumption is partially correct: You need to enter only one month, and AutoFill can do the rest for you. In the Lists & AutoFill sheet in the companion workbook, you can see January entered in A2, as shown below. Select A2, and in the lower-right corner of the cell, hover over the fill handle until your cursor turns into a dark cross, click, and drag down. Watch the tooltip text as you drag down, and you see each subsequent month as you drag. When you release the fill handle, those months are filled in for you. This method is much faster than entering each month manually.

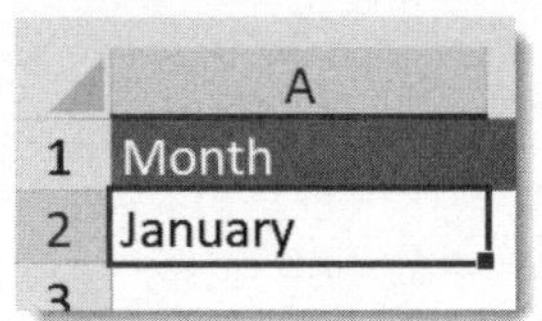

You can also drag across instead of down. To see how this works, enter a month/day/year combination, such as 1/1/18, and then try dragging that down to see what happens. Now you're going to see one of the neat things that AutoFill can do with dates: Right-click on the AutoFill Options button at the bottom-right corner of the range you just filled, and you see the following submenu. That's right: Excel can fill just certain incremental date elements for you. Can you imagine how handy it would be to fill weekdays only in business reporting?

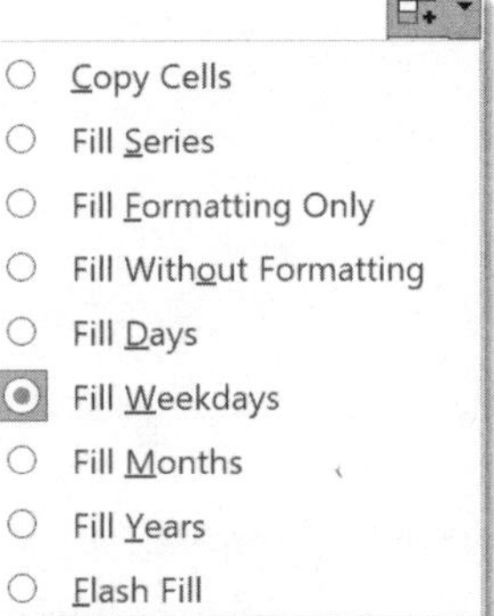

As discussed earlier, another handy feature in Excel is the ability to fill a series without having to use the AutoFill handle; this is great for an extended series. For instance, let's say you are building a pricing model, and you want to see what will happen at certain volume levels, but you don't want to enter them all manually. In cell E5 on the Lists & AutoFill sheet of the companion workbook, go to **Home > Fill > Series**, and you see an expanded Series dialog. In this case, enter **250** for Step Value and **50000** for Stop Value. When you click OK, you see that the 15000 entry in E5 has incremented by 250 in each cell all the way to the right until it hits 50,000.

The list feature is one of the things that drives AutoFill, but it doesn't have to be limited to Excel's built-in values; you can enter your own. Here's an all-too-common scenario: A company has a dedicated workbook that has a lot of relatively static company information, such as operating units (Sales, Production, Accounting), regions (East, West, North, South), offices (New York, Dallas, Los Angeles), and a list of cash flow or general ledger accounts. Whenever a new workbook is created that needs one of those lists, someone opens some other workbook with the list, copies the list in question, returns to the new workbook and pastes it in, and then goes back and closes the list workbook or, worse, copies more data. Users who do this are actually taking quite a few steps when they could get the same results much more easily with AutoFill. The key to being able to use AutoFill in such situations is to build your lists into Excel, which is easy. On the Lists & AutoFill worksheet in the companion workbook, you can see a list of countries beginning in cell A20. Go ahead and select that range and then go to **File > Options** to open the Excel Options dialog. On the Advanced tab, scroll down to the General section and click Edit Custom Lists. Excel opens the dialog shown below.

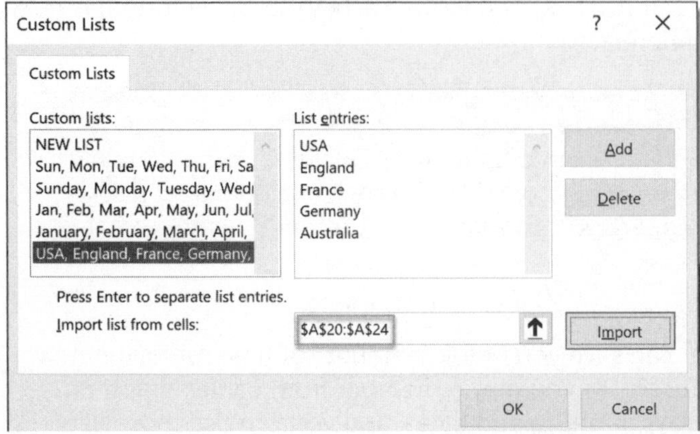

Notice that Excel has already recognized A20:A24 as the list range it's supposed to import. When you click Import, Excel adds your list added beneath any existing lists and in the List Entries box on the right side of the Options dialog, as shown above.

What good does this do you? Well, any time you need to populate that list in any workbook, all you need to do is enter a beginning value (which can be any value in the list) and then drag the AutoFill handle down, and Excel builds that list as far as you want it. This is a lot faster than copying and pasting from another workbook. Unlike dates, which increment as long as you drag, your custom lists start over when the last item is reached.

Data Validation

Data validation, which goes hand-in-hand with lists, allows you to limit cells to accept only values that fit parameters you specify. This is great for ensuring that users follow your rules regarding what they can and can't enter. For example, you might want to use data validation to limit an employee's annual wage increase to 5% or to limit the date range in a time-off request to certain periods, such as not being able to select days prior to today (because you can't take a day off if it's already passed).

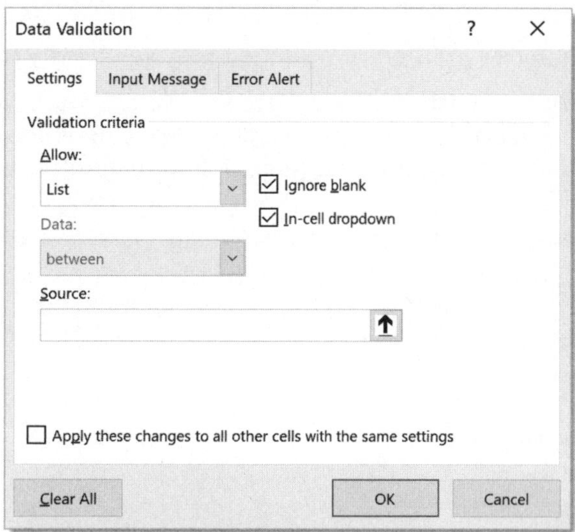

By using the Data Validation dialog, you can also use list values to give the users a drop-down list of selections, so they can't enter anything that's not in the list. For example, you could use a list of departments or part names. This is a great tool for preventing errors because when you provide users with a list they can select from, they don't have to type (and possibly misspell) the input values. This can also be great for things like order forms, where you might have detailed product names, and you don't want users to have to retype them for each order.

Note: It's a good idea to keep your data validation lists on a separate worksheet that you can hide. You don't want people changing the details!

You can find the Data Validation tool in the Data Tools group on the Data tab. A cell that has a data validation drop-down list displays a drop-down symbol on the right-hand side of the cell when you activate the cell. You can also add an input message that displays when a user selects a validated cell, as shown below.

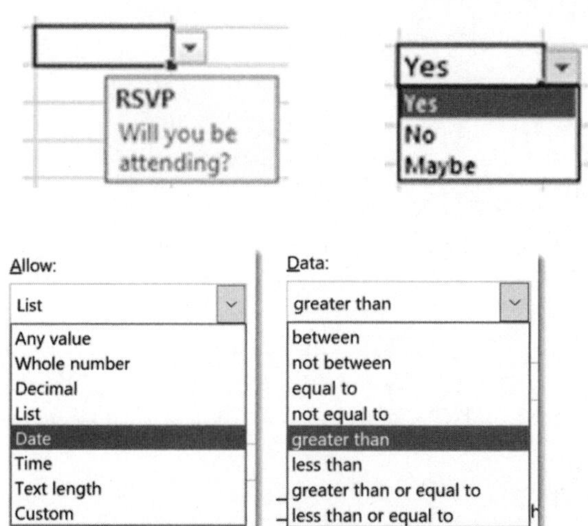

To see how to set up data validation to have a cell accept only certain values, select any cell on a blank worksheet and go to **Data > Data Validation**. For this example, to limit the value entered to only dates greater than today's date (using your system date), select Date from the list of choices in the Allow drop-down. As soon as you do, you see the Data Validation dialog change a little bit, so that date options are exposed. In the Data drop-down select Greater Than, in the Start Date field enter **=TODAY()**, and then click OK.

As you've probably guessed, the TODAY function enters today's date, and it changes each day. Now try to enter a date before today's data in that cell, and you get the not-so-subtle error message shown below.

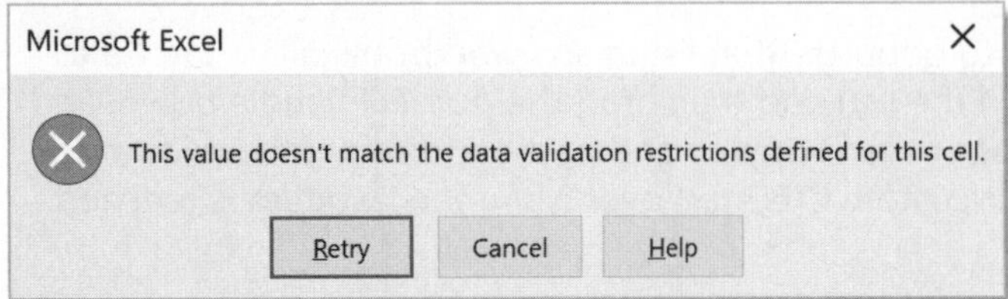

You can modify this error message to say whatever you want.

In the Data Validation dialog there are two other tabs in addition to the primary Settings tab: Input Message and Error Alert. The Input Message tab lets you define the title and input message, and Error Alert lets you pick an error style (Stop, Warning, or Information), as well as a title and an error message.

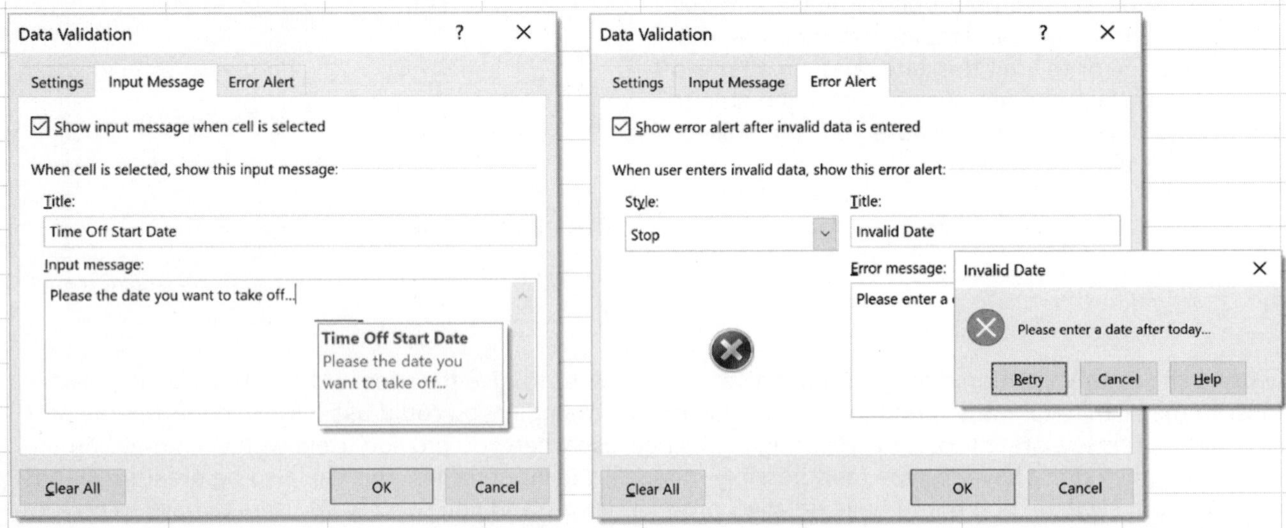

The input message appears when a user enters the data validation cell, and the error alert message appears when an invalid entry is detected. You can disable error checking and allow any entry by unchecking the Show Error Alert After Invalid Data Is Entered checkbox. However, if you're going to limit people to a list of items, you don't want to uncheck this option. After all, what is the point of giving people a list if you don't care if they stick to it?

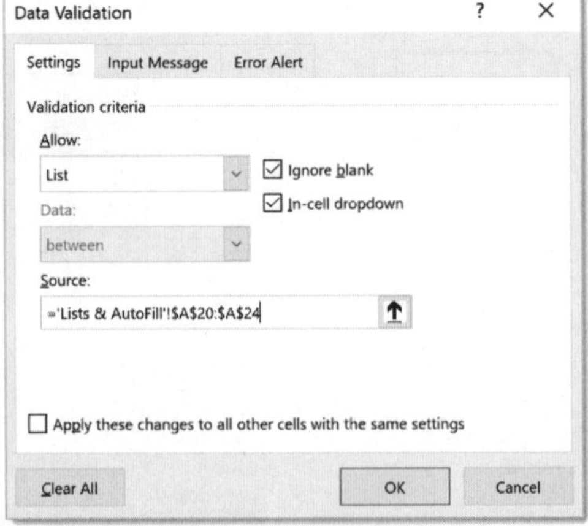

Data validation list selections don't have the same degree of flexibility as the other input options, but because you create the list, you get to determine ahead of time what can be selected. To see how it works, enter several city names in a blank area of a worksheet. While you might be tempted to put this list across columns, you learned earlier that this is not an efficient way to maintain a list; therefore, make sure that you enter your list from the top down. Now, to set up a data validation list for the information you entered, go to **Data > Data Validation**. In the Data Validation dialog, select List in the Allow box and then you can either enter the list range name or address in the Source box or you can select it with the mouse. If you want to enter the list range manually, make sure to precede it with an equals sign, or the list range will be interpreted as literal text, and that's what you'll see in your drop-down. If you have fairly static values (e.g., Yes and No, North and South), you can enter them manually, but you don't want to do this for lengthy lists, especially those with values that could change.

Dynamic Lists

If you just give the Data Validation dialog a static range address, as you just did, you need to manually adjust that list source if you ever add or remove items from the list. But there's a trick you can use to automatically update your list, no matter what you add to or remove from it. First, click anywhere in your list range and press **Ctrl+T** to convert your list to a table. Next, select the list range but don't select the table header unless you want to include it in the drop-down selection. Then go to **Formulas > Define Name**, and in the New Name dialog, enter a descriptive name in the Name box and click OK to add the name.

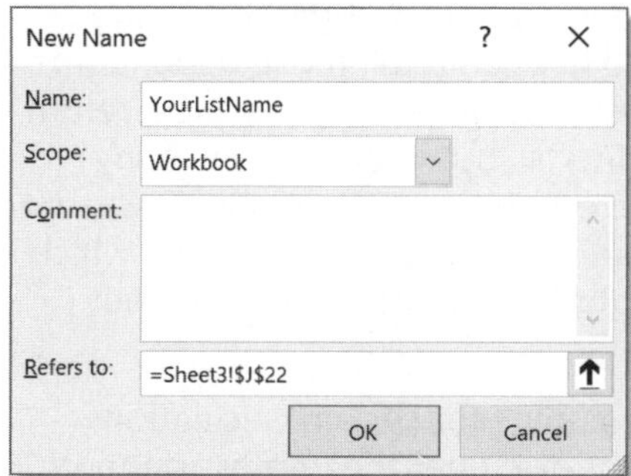

You can have multiple columns in a table, but a drop-down list can be made up of just one column, so make sure to select only a single column range for the list.

> **Hint:** When I have a workbook with a lot of lists, I always separate them into their own tables because it's easy to keep track of them that way.

Now you can go back to the worksheet where you want the data validation list to appear and go to **Data > Data Validation**. Then, in the Data Validation dialog, select List from the Allow drop-down. Next, instead of entering a range (e.g., A1:A10) in the Source box, enter ***=YourListName*** (where you replace ***YourListName*** with the actual name you want to use). When you select the drop-down, you see the same list you saw previously, but now it's dynamic.

There's obviously a lot of more to data validation that we don't discuss here, but you should already be able to see that it gives you a great many options for building end-user worksheets as well as limiting errors (including your own).

Inserting and Deleting Ranges, Rows and Columns, and Worksheets

A big part of building and working with spreadsheets is entering data and formulas. You also spend a lot of time altering data and formulas, moving things around, and even deleting things you may have already entered. But you can't just jump into a worksheet and start adding or deleting things without first understanding what implications your actions might have on the rest of the worksheet—and possibly the entire workbook. The following sections give you an idea of what you need to be aware of.

Inserting Rows and Columns

To insert rows and columns, you simply go to **Home > Insert drop-down > Insert Sheet Rows** or **Home > Insert drop-down > Insert Sheet Columns** (or press **Alt+I+R** for rows or **Alt+I+C** for columns). To see how to actually insert rows and columns, think back to the cash flow worksheet example from earlier in this chapter. What if you wanted to add some more categories to either the cash or purchases lists? It might seem logical that you would go to the first blank cell at the bottom of a list and enter a few rows there. Unfortunately, that is the long way around. If you start below the last row in each section and add your new rows and categories, you would need to update the subtotal formulas, as they wouldn't recognize the additional rows. To avoid this hassle, put your cursor anywhere inside the list range and insert the rows you need. Not only do you remain in the list, but the formulas automatically update to include the new rows. This is convenient, and, more importantly, when you let Excel do the work for you, you don't have to worry about forgetting something. You can use the same method for adding columns. If you need to move rows or columns after adding them, you can select the rows/columns and use the **Shift+click+drag** method mentioned earlier.

Deleting Rows and Columns

To delete a row or a column, select the row or column and go to **Home > Delete drop-down > Delete Sheet Rows** or **Home > Delete drop-down > Delete Sheet Columns** (or **Alt+E+D+R** for rows or **Alt+E+D+C** for columns). Doing this requires a bit of thought, though, because one seemingly innocuous deletion could cascade through an entire worksheet or workbook. Consider again the cash flow example and the date entry in cell B1, where multiple cells are dependent on that single entry. What would happen to all those dependent cells if you deleted that row? They would all lose the dates they derived from that single cell, and Excel return a **#REF!** error. In this case, you'd only be dealing with a few cells you'd need to fix, but imagine how many issues you'd have to hunt down in a big model. In addition, what you delete on one worksheet might have no effect on anything on the sheet, but there could be other worksheets that are dependent on that data, which you might not even realize. Unfortunately, by the time you do realize, it might be too late to undo it—but hopefully you can close the workbook without saving to undo the deletion.

It is very common for detailed models to rely heavily on hidden rows and columns for certain calculations that users don't need to see. Formula errors may be suppressed so that users don't get the impression that the worksheet is "broken" when they see formula errors. Then, for whatever reason, someone deletes key columns or rows; the remaining formulas may continue to recalculate, but without those missing components, they might be calculating incorrectly. This could cause an organization to make all kinds of false assumptions. Million-dollar mistakes have been made because of incorrect spreadsheets. Million-dollar mistakes don't happen all the time, but mistakes of a lesser magnitude are all too common. In fact, a Harvard study found that about 80% of spreadsheets have material errors.

Deleting Formulas

Nothing substitutes for knowing how your worksheet is designed, but sometimes you don't have a complete picture. Fortunately, Excel gives you some tools that can help you make informed decisions before you delete formulas, rows, or columns. If you ever have a question regarding whether it's safe to delete a formula, use **Formulas > Trace Precedents** and **Formulas > Trace Dependents**, which point you to all the cells that are dependent on the formula you're considering deleting, as well as all the cells that your formula depends on. If a formula reference points to another worksheet, you see just a symbol pointing off the sheet (although you aren't told what other sheet it is or where it is).

Unfortunately, there is no tool to evaluate the effects of deleting entire rows or columns beforehand, but if you see blue arrows anywhere, as shown below, it's a good idea to check out where they go before you delete anything. Generally, if you have a decent understanding of your workbook, you'll have a good idea of what's safe and what's not safe to delete. In the following example, cell A1 gets its value from another sheet, but cells A4:C4 get their value from cell A1 on the current sheet.

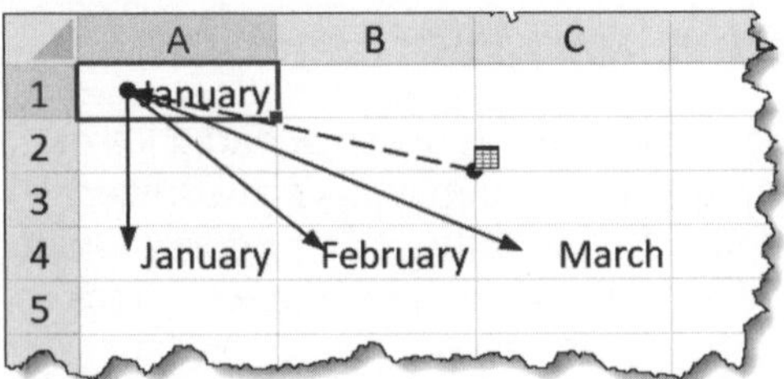

Hiding and Unhiding Rows and Columns

It is often necessary to hide rows and columns to prevent users from seeing certain internal calculations or other things you don't want them to see. To hide data on a worksheet, select somewhere in the row or column range you want to hide (you don't need to select an entire row or column) and then go to **Home > Format > Hide & Unhide > Hide Rows** or **Home > Format > Hide & Unhide > Hide Columns**.

To unhide, you need to select the range to the immediate left and right, or top and bottom of the hidden area so that the hidden area can be included. For example, to unhide column B, select columns A to C and then follow the row or column steps above. If you want to unhide a hidden row 1 or column A, you can click the **Select All** button at the intersection of the row and column headers (or press **Ctrl+A**) and then follow the row or column steps above.

The following table lists some of the keyboard shortcuts you can use for hiding and unhiding rows and columns in Excel workbooks.

Keyboard Shortcuts for Hiding Rows or Columns

Shortcut	Description
Alt+O+R+H	Hide a row
Alt+O+C+H	Hide a column
Alt+O+R+U	Unhide a row
Alt+O+C+U	Unhide a column

Deleting Worksheets

You can delete a worksheet by right-clicking on the worksheet tab and selecting **Delete**. If the worksheet contains any data, you get a warning dialog, like the one shown below. After you delete a worksheet, there is no way to undo the action except to close the workbook without saving changes. If you have AutoSave turned on, though, simply closing does not work, and you need to revert to an earlier version.

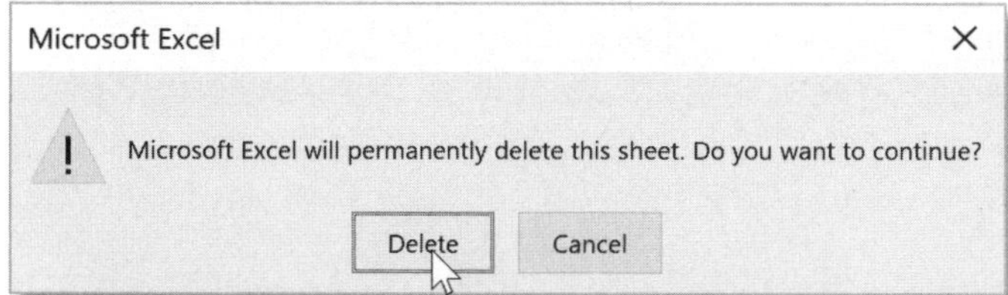

> **Note:** Excel workbooks sometimes blow up in size for no apparent reason, although the typical culprit is the used range. Whenever you enter data or apply formatting to a cell, it becomes part of what Excel sees as the used range. Let's say you import 500,000 rows of data from a database and delete all but 10,000 records. Excel still sees that 500,000 rows have been reserved. Deleting a cell's value or removing its formatting doesn't reset the used range. The only way to reset the used range is to delete all unused rows and columns and then resave the workbook.

Modifying Data on Multiple Worksheets

Earlier in this chapter, I encouraged you to make sure that a worksheet does what you want before you copy it. In the case of the cash flow report example from earlier in this chapter, you might copy that original worksheet 12 times: once for each subsequent month and again for a yearly summary. But what if you need to make one or multiple changes to one or more worksheets after you've made your copies? The good news is that you can make such changes to multiple sheets all at once by *grouping* sheets. To see how this works, start a new workbook, and once it's open, add a few more worksheets with **Alt+I+W** or by clicking the plus sign to the right of the last worksheet tab. At this point, you can choose to group all contiguous sheets or select particular sheets to group, as described in the following sections.

There are certain things you can't do to grouped sheets, including the following:

- Conditional formatting
- Table formatting
- Anything from the Insert tab other than Header & Footer and Signature lines
- Certain page setup elements, such as setting the page area (although you can apply most of the same page setup properties to all sheets at once, which can be a huge timesaver when you're getting ready to distribute a workbook)
- Object arranging
- Formula auditing
- Anything from the Data tab
- Worksheet protection

Grouping All Contiguous Sheets

To group all contiguous sheets, in the new workbook you just created, select the first sheet, hold down the **Shift** key, and click on the last sheet tab. Excel groups the first sheet, the last sheet selected, and any sheets in between. You can do the same thing by right-clicking on any sheet tab and choosing **Select All Sheets**. Note that the tabs all turn a different shade to indicate that they are now grouped; any change you make on the active sheet will also be made on the other selected sheets. Go ahead and apply some formatting, add some text, try anything you want, and then click on any of the other sheets and see what happened.

To ungroup the sheets that are grouped, all you need to do is select any sheet other than the active one.

Grouping Individual (Select) Sheets

You're not limited to grouping all the worksheets but can group individual sheets instead. One common reason to group select sheets would be in a finance model that works on a 5-4-4 monthly basis, where there are 5 weeks, 4 weeks, and 4 weeks in each month (e.g., January has 5 weeks, February has 4 weeks, March has 4 weeks, then the pattern repeats starting in April). In the 5-4-4 structure, 4 months have 5 weeks, and 8 months have 4 weeks. You could probably make changes to all the sheets at once for the 4-week months since you could naturally include the 5-week months, but what about the other way around? That is, you might want to group just the 5-week months and apply the necessary changes to those without having to interfere with the 4-week months.

To group select sheets, you hold down the **Ctrl** key (instead of the **Shift** key) and click on each sheet you want to select for grouping together. Then you can make any changes necessary. To ungroup select sheets, just activate any of the non-grouped sheets. Activating a grouped sheet does not ungroup them.

> **Caution:** Don't forget to ungroup when you're done making changes! A workbook can be ruined if someone forgets to ungroup and then goes a while without knowing it, making changes (to every worksheet) along the way.

Chapter Summary

- In this chapter, you learned about some of the concepts involved in good spreadsheet design, beginning with the initial concept and planning phase and continuing on to design.
- You saw some of the methods of quickly populating a worksheet with repeating data such as months, dates, and even sample datasets.
- You started working with some simple functions and formulas and learned how to copy them around a worksheet by using absolute and relative referencing.
- You learned how to add your own custom lists, use AutoFill, and use data validation.
- You saw how to make changes to multiple worksheets at once.

Chapter 6: Using Functions and Formulas

In Chapter 5 you learned about the general rules for good spreadsheet design and the process involved in designing a worksheet, beginning at the design phase, then building the base elements (e.g., row and column headers), and then populating the worksheet with some sample data. You also saw how to use AutoSum to add some relatively simple formulas to the worksheet. While AutoSum can do a lot for you, and you may come to rely on it in your day-to-day Excel activities, there's a whole world of functions out there that can do much more than AutoSum, and this chapter is devoted to some of Excel's most commonly used functions and formulas.

This chapter doesn't overwhelm you with obscure and industry-specific functions (e.g., the ones that might be used in statistical, scientific, or engineering applications). Rather, it talks about some of the functions that you will quickly learn to use well; in no time, you will wonder how you ever did without these functions. This chapter also discusses some of the logic that goes into functions and how you evaluate certain scenarios. Some of it might smell a bit like high school algebra—and to a certain extent it is like algebra because a lot of what you do with formulas in Excel involves evaluating conditions.

Basic Terminology

What exactly is the difference between a formula and a function? A *function* is any preprogrammed function that performs a calculation in a spreadsheet. Some functions require inputs, or arguments, that you supply, while others, like the volatile functions (e.g., TODAY, NOW) don't require any input from you. Functions are generally intrinsic to spreadsheet applications, but you can also build your own (in much the same fashion that Microsoft builds them). A formula can be either a mathematical or text equation, such as (=1+1, =A1+B1, or ="Daily Sales "&A1. Or it can be a function or a compilation of functions, such as =SUM(A1:B1) or =SUM(A1:B1)/SUM(C1:D1) or even something like =SUM(A1:B1)*.0825. Essentially, if you can think of a way to evaluate data, then you can probably combine some types of logic in Excel to do it.

If you get curious about more advanced functions and look for help in Excel message boards on the Internet, you will be truly amazed at some of the formulas that people can create. If you can think it, someone can probably come up with a formula to do it. Why emphasize this issue? Because you will (not *might* but *will*) become frustrated at some point or another when you're building formulas; that's just a reality. In fact, becoming frustrated might be a regular occurrence, but you shouldn't let that be a deterrent. Some people have a much easier time grasping formulas than others, but even the most experienced Excel users struggle with formulas from time to time, so you are certainly not alone. As soon as you let yourself know that it's okay to get frustrated, you'll generally be much better prepared to tackle advanced formulas.

The Function Library Group

Chapter 4 briefly discusses the various Formulas tab options. The following sections provide an overview of the Formulas tab functions and get into more depth with some of them.

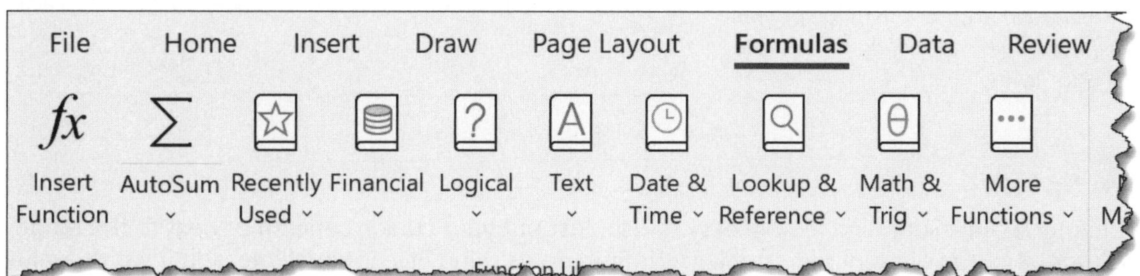

The Insert Function Option

If you don't know what function you want off the top of your head, or even what category to place it in, go to **Formulas > Insert Function**. The Insert Function dialog, shown below, appears.

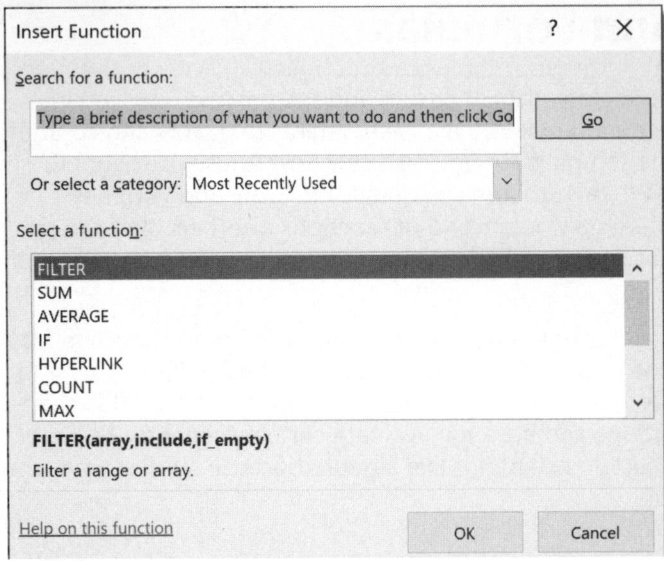

You can enter a search term, and Excel does what it can to match your request with the best result. The default category is Most Recently Used, and you typically need to change that to All before you start, or the results will be limited. However, if you know you're looking for a function in a particular category, you might want to narrow the list.

Unfortunately, the Insert Function dialog doesn't always find what you're looking for, especially if you don't know what to look for in the first place, so it is somewhat of a Catch-22 tool: You have to sort of know what you're looking for in order to find it, but if you don't know what that is, then how do you know what to ask Excel to look for? Confusing, isn't it?

> **Note:** When you're confused about what function to use, you can turn to the Internet and ask a question. The message board at www.mrexcel.com/forum is probably the best place to look if you're stumped.

If you choose a function from the Insert Function dialog, Excel brings up the Function Arguments dialog, shown at right, which can help you enter the correct values or cell references. A benefit of the Function Arguments dialog is that it evaluates each step of a function for you, so you can immediately see if you have entered an argument incorrectly. If the dialog just doesn't do enough to help you figure out how to build a function, you can always click the Help on This Function hyperlink to get more details. Excel then takes you to a Microsoft support article specific to that function, where you are likely to be able to find relevant examples.

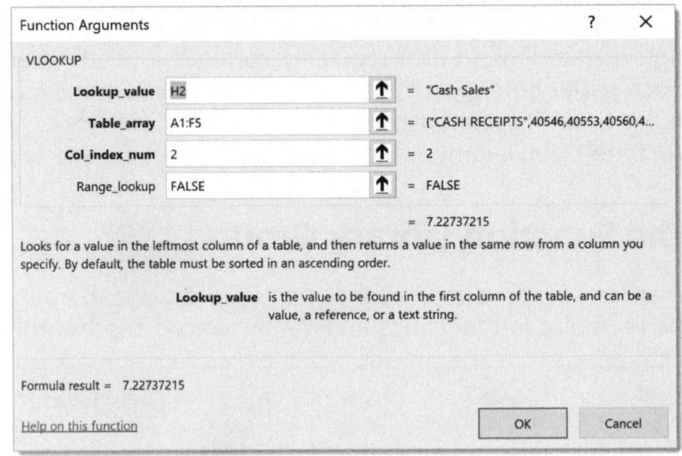

The AutoSum Option

As you saw in Chapter 5, AutoSum is incredibly easy to use. Just put your cursor beneath or next to the range you want to evaluate, choose your function, and let AutoSum do its thing. It's not infallible, and it won't evaluate datasets that have gaps, but it does a pretty good job. Although the intrinsic AutoSum functions are limited to Sum, Average, Count Number, Max, and Min, you can select **Formulas > AutoSum drop-down > More Functions** to launch the Insert Function dialog (yet another one of those things that Microsoft exposes in multiple places). You can find examples of all the AutoSum functions in the Chapter 6 companion workbook.

The Recently Used Option

Selecting **Formulas > Recently Used** is a faster way to get to your recently used functions than by launching the Insert Function dialog. As shown below, just click, and there's your list.

The Financial Option

The Financial option and the rest of the Function Library group options work the same way: Each of them displays an alphabetical list of the functions specific to that category. Financial functions can be very powerful tools for business because you can use them to perform a variety of detailed analyses, such as figuring out the depreciation of a piece of equipment you're thinking about purchasing or determining what your monthly payment might be, based on amount down, interest rate, and so on. Using these functions is generally much easier than trying to do your figuring on a calculator—and you have the bonus of being able to set up reusable models. For example, you've no doubt seen Internet-based calculators for auto or home loans; you can create the same kind of thing in Excel.

The following are a few of the functions available by selecting at **Formulas > Financial**:

- **FV**—Future value
- **IRR**—Internal rate of return
- **NPV**—Net present value
- **SLN**—Straight-line depreciation

The Logical Option

Logical functions allow you to evaluate certain criteria and return one result if the evaluation is true and another if it's false; for example, the logical function **=IF(A1="Yes",1,2)** simply says "IF A1 = Yes, then return a 1; otherwise (i.e., if A1 is anything other than Yes), return a 2." The following are some of the functions available by selecting at **Formulas > Logical**:

- **IF**—IF statements are the cornerstone of logical analysis in Excel. You'll learn a lot more about them later in this chapter.
- **AND/OR**—Both AND and OR allow you to add multiple criteria to IF statements. For example, you can create an evaluation such as "IF something is true, AND something else is false, then..." or "IF something is false, OR something else is true, then..."
- **NOT**—You can use NOT to evaluate whether something is not equal to a condition (e.g., **NOT=1**).
- **TRUE/FALSE**—Called Boolean evaluations, these functions simply test whether something is true or false.
- **IFERROR**—This can be used to remove error messages from formulas that return errors. It's generally not advisable to use IFERROR when you're first building a model because it hides all errors but doesn't resolve them, so you might not know a formula isn't working. However, it is very common to use IFERROR prior to distribution because users who see formula errors usually assume that something is broken, and when they assume that something is broken, they're less likely to trust your workbook. For example, let's say you have the formula **=A1/B1**, and it is waiting for someone to enter a value in B1. That formula will display a **#DIV/0** error until B1 is filled in. However, you don't want this error to show up because you know the formula will work correctly as soon as B1 is filled in, so you can suppress the error with **=IFERROR(A1/B1,"")**.

The Text Option

The functions available at **Formulas > Text** let you work with text in formulas. The following are some examples of text functions:

- **CLEAN**—Removes non-printable characters from a reference. This often comes in handy when you're copying data from websites or databases.
- **FIND**—Finds a text or numeric value in a text string.
- **LEFT**—Returns a specified number of characters from the left of a string. For example, **=LEFT("ABCDE",2)** returns AB.
- **RIGHT**—Returns a specified number of characters from the right of a string. For example, **=RIGHT("ABCDE",2)** returns DE.
- **MID**—Returns a specified number of characters from the middle of a string, given a starting point. For example, **=MID("ABCDE",2,2)** returns BC.
- **TEXT**—Allows you to format numeric values when they've been concatenated with text. For example, the formula **="Today's date is: "&TEXT(A1,"MM/DD/YY")**, where A1 is a valid date, returns the following: Today's date is: 01/15/18
- **TRIM**—Removes leading and trailing spaces from text strings (but does not remove spaces between words). This function can be handy when dealing with external data.
- **UPPER**—Converts all text to uppercase. There is also a LOWER function that lowercases all text, and there is a PROPER functions that capitalizes just the first letter of a word.

The Date & Time Option

The Date & Time option lets you work with dates and times, largely from a mathematical standpoint (e.g., determining the number of days between two dates). Excel stores dates and times numerically, with day 1 being January 1, 1904. So, January 1, 2018, is day number 43101, and 43101.5 would be 12:00 PM on January 1, 2018. The following are some examples of functions available by selecting **Function > Date & Time**:

- **TODAY**—Returns today's date.
- **NOW**—Returns the date and time.
- **DAY**—Returns the day number of the month, from 1 to 31.
- **NETWORKDAYS**—Returns the number of standard workdays (Monday through Friday) between two dates, including specified holidays.
- **YEAR**—Returns just the year from a date reference. For example, **=YEAR(TODAY())** returns 2018.
  Note: In the YEAR function example above, look at how it's nested with the TODAY function to use multiple functions in a single formula.

The Lookup & Reference Option

Lookup and reference formulas are perhaps the most widely used functions after the math functions (e.g., SUM, AVERAGE, COUNT). They let you look up values in a list and return relevant information from the list. For instance, you might want to look up a customer name to get his or her address or phone number. Lookup and reference functions let you do that without having to go to the source to look it up manually. For example, say that you have a large list of transactional data, such as customer orders, and you want to get the details on a specific order number. You could use VLOOKUP on the order number to return that order's relevant details, such as customer name. You could use the FILTER function to return all orders associated with that order's customer and then use the SORTBY function to sort those orders by date and product. These are some of the most commonly used functions available by selecting **Function > Lookup & Reference**:

FILTER—Filters a list based on criteria you give.

COLUMN/ROW—Returns the column/row number of a reference. For example, **=COLUMN(C1)** returns 3, and **=ROW(C1)** returns 1.

HYPERLINK—Adds a hyperlink to a location in a worksheet, workbook, other Office document, or webpage.

INDEX—Returns the value found at the intersection of a given row and column. For example, **=INDEX(A1:D5,1,1)** will return the value found in cell A1.

MATCH—Returns the relative position of an item in a range. For example, **=MATCH("ABC",A1:A10,0)** returns a value from 1 through 10, depending on where it finds the text ABC in cells A1:A10.

SORTBY—Sorts a range of values based on the values in another range. For instance, you could use the SORTBY function to return a list of all customers based in Wyoming. Office 365 only.

TRANSPOSE—Allows you to switch your data from rows to columns and vice versa.

UNIQUE—Returns only the unique values in a range. For instance, you could return a list of unique parts from a parts list. Office 365 only - this was introduced after Excel 2019 shipped.

VLOOKUP—Looks for a value in the leftmost column of a table and returns an item from the same row in the column you specify.

The Math & Trig Option

While some of the functions in the math and trig category are used mainly in businesses that deal specifically with math and trigonometry calculations, there are quite a few that you'll frequently use in the course of other types of business. These are some of the most commonly used functions available by selecting **Function > Math & Trig**:

- **ABS**—Returns the absolute value of a number, which is the number without its sign. For example, **=ABS(-10)** returns 10.
- **EVEN/ODD**—EVEN rounds positive values up to the nearest even integer and negative numbers down. ODD does the opposite.
- **CEILING/FLOOR**—CEILING rounds a number up to the nearest number you specify. For example, **=CEILING(2.6,0.25)** returns 2.75. This is good if you're pricing to the nearest *x* increment. FLOOR does the opposite.
- **INT**—Rounds a number down to the nearest integer. For example, **=INT(2.7)** returns 2.

- **RAND**—As you saw in Chapter 5, RAND generates a random number between 1 and 0. Remember that to get meaningful numbers for testing, you probably want to multiply RAND by a factor of 10 (e.g., **=RAND()*100**). If you have an Office 365 subscription, you can also use the new dynamic array function RANDARRAY, which lets you create a dynamic range instead of having to copy and paste the RAND function to whichever cells you want. For instance, =RANDARRAY(4,5) creates an array that's 4 rows tall by 5 columns wide. The benefit of this is that you enter only one formula, and Excel fills in the range for you.
- **ROUND**—Rounds a number to a specified number of digits. For example, **=ROUND(1.234,2)** returns 1.23.
- **SUM**—Returns the sum of a range. You're already familiar with this one from Chapter 5.
- **SUMIF**—Returns the sum of a range, given a single criterion. For example, **=SUMIF(A1:A10,"YES",B1:B10)** returns the sum of B1:B10, where the cells in A1:A10 = YES.
- **SUMIFS/SUMPRODUCT**—Return the sum of a range based on multiple criteria. You can find examples of both of these functions in the Chapter 6 companion workbook.

The More Functions Option

The More Functions option exposes several more categories of functions that are generally specific to a particular field, although the information functions are used quite regularly in evaluating ranges. For example, **=ISNUMBER(A1)** returns TRUE or FALSE, depending on the value in A1. This is a very useful function because sometimes what you see as numbers Excel sees as text. In cases like this, your formulas won't calculate correctly, and ISNUMBER helps you track down any improperly formatted cells. When you select **Formulas > More Functions**, you see the following categories:

- Statistical
- Engineering
- Cube
- Information
- Compatibility
- Web

Order of Operations

Before we start looking at the details of Excel's functions and formulas, you need to understand the mathematical order of operations Excel uses when it calculates functions and formulas. The primary order of operations is as follows:

1. Parentheses

2. Exponents

3. Multiplication/division

4. Addition/subtraction

By themselves, multiplication and division are equal to each other and addition and subtraction are equal to each other. However, multiplication and division are greater than addition and subtraction. That is, if both multiplication and division or both addition and subtraction appear in the same formula, they will be carried out based on whichever comes first. However, you can alter the order of any operations by adding parentheses. This is where those high school algebra concepts kick in. Consider these examples:

- The formula =2*3+4 results in 10 because 2 * 3 = 6 and 6 + 4 = 10.
- However, the formula =2*(3+4) results in 14 because 3 + 4 = 7, and 2 * 7 = 14. In this case, because the 3+4 is in parentheses, it gets calculated first.

The idea of the order of operations doesn't take long to grasp, but it is essential to understand it and then always keep it in mind because if you have an obscure calculation that doesn't generate the correct results, a lot of other dependencies that are directly or indirectly based on that calculation may also be off. Finding these types of small errors is like trying to find the proverbial needle in a haystack, so it's important to make sure you get the calculations right the first time.

Note: PEMDAS is a common mnemonic device for remembering the order of operations.

Entering Functions

Entering functions in Excel is straightforward. If you're beginning from the Insert Function dialog, you can let it do all the work for you. The following example uses the depreciation example you can find on the Financial sheet of the Chapter 6 workbook.

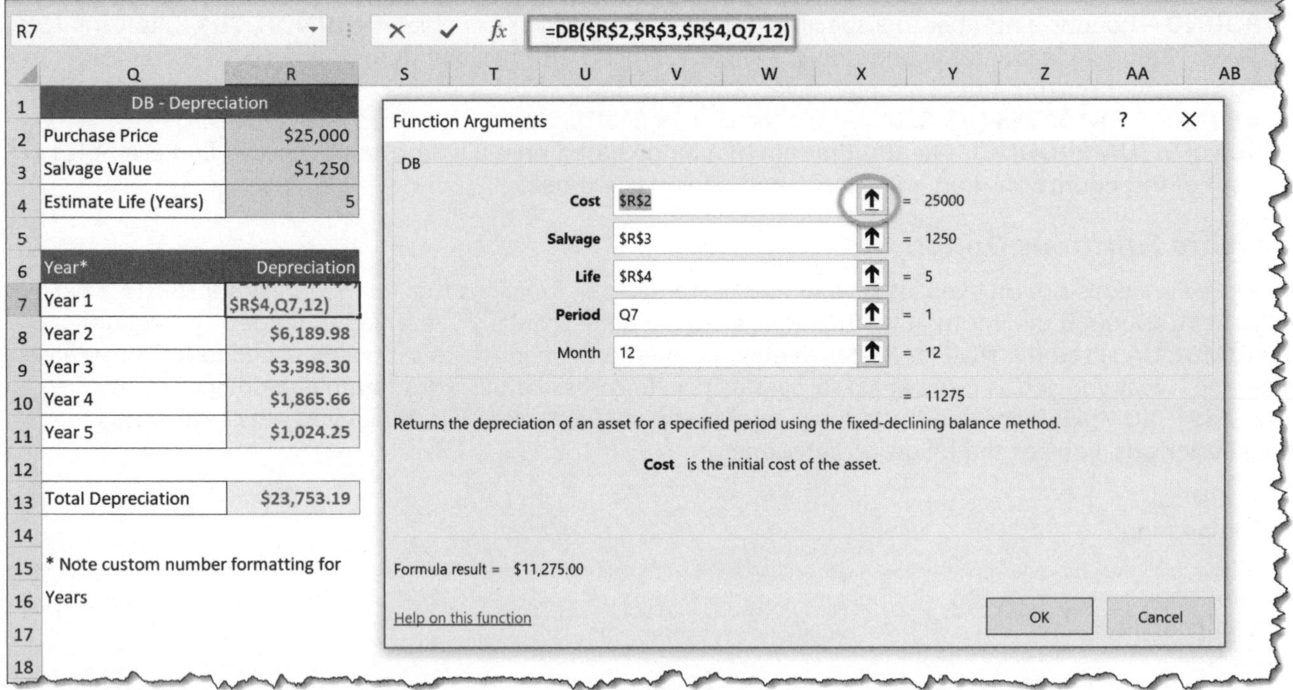

As you can see, the primary cells referenced here are R2:R4, and you want the depreciation calculations to be returned for Years 1–5, so you're going to be referencing cells Q7:Q11 for those years.

Hint: Cells Q7:Q11 have the numbers 1–5 in them, not "Year 1" and so on. This is done with the custom number format "Year "0, as shown at right.

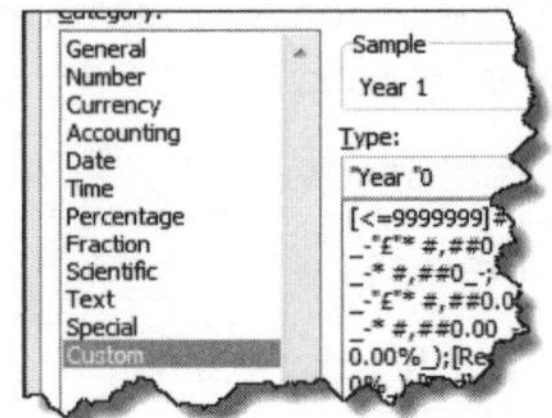

To enter this formula, go to **Formulas > Insert Function** and select the **DB** function. The Function Arguments dialog appears, and you can fill it out as follows:

- **Cost**—Click the range selection button (circled in the example above) and then click on cell R2.
- **Salvage**—Click on cell R3.
- **Life**—Click on cell R4.
- **Period**—Click on cell Q7.
- **Month**—Enter **12** or leave this blank because 12 is the default value.

Notice that the Function Arguments dialog adds absolute references for you where they are needed. As you confirm each step, you see the Function Arguments dialog evaluate it to the bottom right of the last argument. When you enter the last argument, the full function evaluates. This allows you to see if you get a valid or expected result, and if you don't, you know you have some changes to make. Next, you see the Function Arguments dialog after it's calculated a result based on all the function arguments. In this case, it's 11275. If the result is what you're expecting, you can go ahead and click OK to confirm the formula. Then you can copy or drag Year 1's result down to Year 5, and you have your extended five-year depreciation results.

As you get comfortable with using multiple argument functions, you'll probably want to build them with the Function Arguments dialog. If you're dealing with relatively simple range-limited functions, such as **=SUM(A1:A10)**, you can try to start them by hand by entering equals (=). Excel's IntelliSense functionality displays a list of functions as you start typing, and it filters your results as you enter more characters. If you see the function you want, just use your arrow keys to scroll to it and press **Tab**, and Excel enters the function for you, so you don't need to spell it out. This can save a ton of time if you remember to use it.

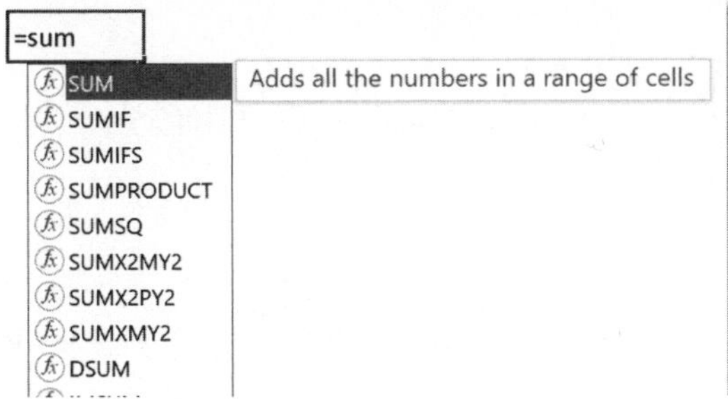

From there, you can finish your formula. Be sure to look for the function tooltip for pointers; it appears when you're writing a formula.

And don't forget that the Function Arguments dialog isn't the help you get when entering functions; if Excel recognizes the function you're entering, it gives you a tooltip once you've entered the opening parenthesis for the function. (When you press **Tab** to enter the function, Excel enters the opening parenthesis for you.) Each function argument appears in bold in the tooltip text (as shown at right) until you confirm it with a comma and move on to the next argument, at which point that argument appears in bold.

	Q	R	S	T
1	DB - Depreciation			
2	Purchase Price	$25,000		
3	Salvage Value	$1,250		
4	Estimate Life (Years)	5		
5				
6	Year*	Depreciation		
7	Year 1	=DB($R$2,$R$3,$R$4,Q7,12)		
8	Year 2	DB(**cost**, salvage, life, period, [month])		
9	Year 3	$3,398.30		
10	Year 4	$1,865.66		
11	Year 5	$1,024.25		

When you're working with formulas, you can view and edit them both in the formula bar and in the cell. In either case, you see colored references that correspond between the range references in the formula and the ranges on the worksheet, as in the example above (though if you're reading a printed version of this book, you won't be able to see the colors). This color-coding can be incredibly helpful when you're trying to build formulas, as it shows you defined reference points.

Excel Function/Formula Errors

As you've seen, when you properly enter a function/formula, Excel gives you a result. But what happens if you enter a function/formula incorrectly, or if Excel encounters a problem with a function/formula? Excel tells you about it by displaying an error message in the cell. Some error messages are straightforward and can be fixed right away, while others are a bit more obscure and can be difficult to track down (especially if a change you made on a different worksheet causes an error, and you don't see it until much later). You'll find that error management often means using logical statements to evaluate functions and/or errors to resolve them.

Errors play a big role in Excel development, as they can quickly point out problems that need to be resolved. Unfortunately, many people throw a blanket error management solution at everything, which can be misleading because it prevents Excel from telling you something's wrong. Before you start using such a shotgun approach to error management, make sure that you understand errors, what causes them, and how to sort out the root causes. The following sections discuss the most common Excel errors.

> **Note:** Prior to Excel 2007, the global error solution was **ISERROR** (e.g., **=IF(ISERROR(A1/B1),0,A1/B1))**). Unfortunately, not only does this function eliminate all errors, it also prevents Excel from telling you when you have problems. This function is also hugely inefficient as it causes Excel to calculate twice—once to evaluate the formula to see if it results in an error, and if it doesn't, then another time to return the formula's result. As you'll see shortly, when we discuss the #DIV/0! error, there's a much more selective way to address that particular error, as there is for most other errors. **IFERROR** (e.g., **=IFERROR(A1/B1,0)**) is still a shotgun approach to error management, but at least it doesn't force double calculation. It's also more efficient because it eliminates the initial **IF** statement.

#DIV/0!

You can't divide by 0—not in math and not in Excel. the #DIV/0! error is most often caused by a formula like **=A1/B1**, where B1 isn't necessarily a 0 value but just hasn't had anything entered into it yet, so it evaluates to an error. The easiest way to fix this type of error is to test for the existence of the denominator; if it exists, you can complete the formula, and if not, return a 0 or blank value (e.g., **=IF(B1,A1/B1,0)** or **=IF(B1,A1/B1,"")**).

#N/A

The #N/A error means that a referential formula can't find what you told it to find. Most people address this error with IFERROR. You can alternatively test directly for the N/A condition alone, but this still requires double calculation (e.g., **=IF(ISNA(FUNCTION),0,FUNCTION))**).

#NAME?

The #NAME? error means that Excel doesn't recognize the function name. Generally, this is the result of a typo, like **=sume(a1:a10)**, where **sume** should have been **sum**.

Note: Remember that when you're entering functions, you don't need to worry about typing them in all caps; Excel automatically converts the case for you as soon as you confirm the function.

#NULL!

The #NULL! error occurs when you tell a function to intersect two ranges that can't physically intersect. For example, **=(A1:C1 B1:B5)** returns the value in cell B2 below because that's the intersection between the two ranges. However, **=(A1:C1 B2:B5)** returns a #NULL! error because there is no intersection between the two ranges: Row 1 can't physically intersect with rows 2 through 5.

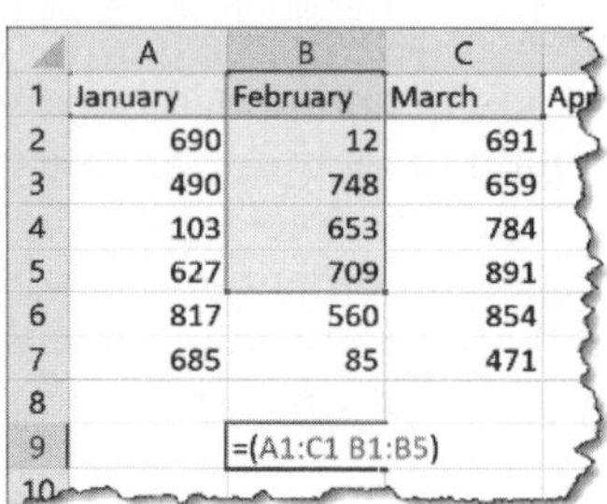

	A	B	C
1	January	February	March
2	690	12	691
3	490	748	659
4	103	653	784
5	627	709	891
6	817	560	854
7	685	85	471
8			
9		=(A1:C1 B1:B5)	

#NUM!

The #NUM! error occurs if you try to pass an invalid number to a function or if you try to get Excel to calculate a number that's too big or too small. For instance, **=1*10^308** causes an error because the largest number Excel can calculate is **=1*10^307**.

#REF!

The #REF! error generally occurs if you've deleted a range that a formula referred to and have severed the link. If you use the formula **=Sheet2!A1** and delete row 1 on Sheet2, for example, you get the error =Sheet2!#REF!. As mentioned earlier, this can get tricky in workbooks that have a lot of cross-sheet links, so you need to be very careful when you're deleting rows and columns.

#VALUE!

The #VALUE! error occurs when you try to compare two different operands, such as when you try to multiply a value by text. For instance, **=(A1*A2)** gives you an error if one cell is numeric and one is text.

Commonly Used Business Functions

The rest of this chapter explains some functions you are likely to encounter in the business world. It discusses where and when you might use these functions, shows you how to set up scenarios to use them, and shows how to put them together in more complex formulas. As you read the rest of the chapter, you should follow along with the Chapter 6 companion workbook so you can get hands-on practice using functions. The following sections present functions in the same order they appear on the Formulas tab, and I've included examples of the top four or five functions from each category, as well as some beneficial formulas.

Note: Function arguments that have brackets are optional. For instance, the [pv] and [type] arguments in the FV function are not required.

Financial Functions

There are plenty of functions in the Financial category that can help you manage your business, and there are many that you'll never even get close to using. While some of the financial functions are relatively complicated and require you to spend some time learning the ins-and-outs of the business they target (e.g., stocks, banking), a number of them are commonly used in the course of normal business operations, and these are the ones we focus on here.

FV

The FV function finds a future value. You can use it, for example, if you want to start an investment account like an IRA. Let's say you want to figure out how much your investment will be worth at the end of five years if you can get 3.2% interest over 60 months, and you put in $650 per month. (Note that this is a simple example and doesn't include compounding or variable interest rates or deposit amounts.) The following example shows how this might look in Excel.

FV - Future Value	
Description	Data
Annual Interest Rate	3.20%
Number of Payments	60
Amount of Payment	($650)
Present Value	$0
Payment Due	1
Future Value	$42,344.99

The following is the general syntax for the **FV** function:

=FV(rate, nper, pmt,[pv],[type])

where:

- **rate**—Interest rate per period
- **nper**—Number of periods in the investment
- **pmt**—Payment made each period (which is a negative amount; think of it as the amount that comes out of your checking account to go in the IRA)
- **[pv]**—Present value of the investment, which can be 0 or left out (optional)
- **[type]**—1 or 0, to indicate whether the payment is made at the beginning or end of a period (optional)

NPER

The NPER function finds the number of periods—that is, how many payments you have to make over the life of an investment if you know the interest rate and payment amount. For instance, say that you want to buy a new copier that costs $5,500. If you know the interest rate and payment periods (monthly, quarterly, etc.), you can figure out how many payments you need to make before you pay it off, as shown in the following example.

NPER - Number of Periods	
Description	Data
Annual Interest Rate	3.20%
Amount of Payment	($100)
Present Value	$5,500
Future Value	$0
Payment Due	1
Number of Periods	59.38

The following is the general syntax for the **NPER** function:

=NPER(rate, pmt, pv, [fv], [type])

where:

- **rate**—Interest rate per period
- **pmt**—Payment made each period
- **pv**—Present value
- **[fv]**—Generally 0 (optional)
- **[type]**—1 or 0, to indicate whether the payment is made at the beginning or end of a period (optional)

PMT

The PMT function tells you what your payment for something will be if you know the amount you want to finance and the interest rate. For instance, say that you need to get a new copier for the office. In this case, you've been quoted $5,500 for the copier at 3.2% interest (APR) over 60 months, but you need to figure out if you can afford the monthly payments (as shown at right). If you compare the results from this function to the results from the **NPER** function (shown above), you see that they're essentially just reverse cases of each other.

PMT - Payment	
Description	Data
Annual Interest Rate	3.20%
Number of Payments	60
Present Value	$5,500
Future Value	$0
Payment Due	1
Payment	($99.05)

The following is the general syntax for the **PMT** function:

=PMT(rate, nper, pv, [fv], [type])

where:

- **rate**—Interest rate per period

- **nper**—Number of periods in the investment
- **pv**—Present value
- **[fv]**—Future value (optional)
- **[type]**—1 or 0, to indicate whether the payment is made at the beginning or end of a period (optional)

What-If Analysis

We're going to take a slight detour here and look at one of Excel's powerful data analysis tools, Goal Seek, because it fits in with the calculations shown so far. Going back to the new copier example, let's say you have your interest rate, you know what the copier costs, you know the number of months it'll take for you to pay it off, and you know the payment amount. But what if the payment is just a bit too high? Right now, your payment is about $100 per month, but you want to know how much copier you can get for $75 per month. Instead of trying to manually adjust the scenario until you get to the price point you want, you can let Excel figure it out for you.

In the Chapter 6 companion workbook, go to the Goal Seek worksheet. You can start with the existing loan payment model and let Excel to run through scenarios until it gets to the copier you can afford. In this case, you want Excel to change the payment to $75 by adjusting the copier price until it gets there. Go to **Data > What-If Analysis > Goal Seek**. Next, select cell B6 in the Set Cell text box, enter **75** in the To Value text box, select cell B2 for the By Changing Cell text box, and click OK.

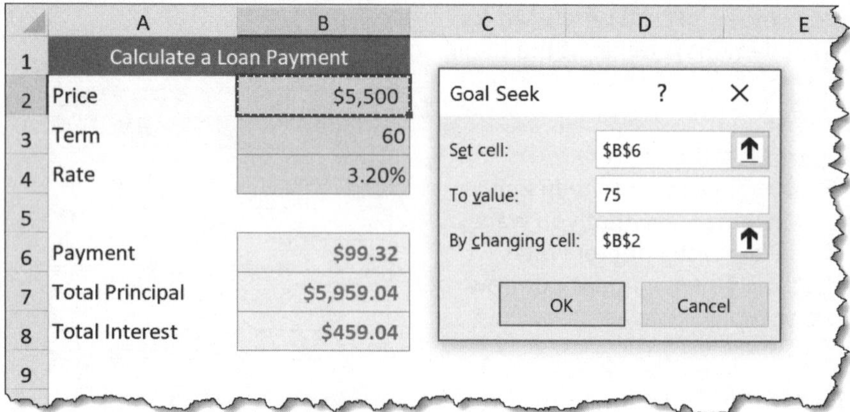

You can see here that at $75/month, with your original term and rate, you can afford a copier that costs $4,153. If you can have this information in hand before you start negotiating for that copier, then you'll be in a much stronger position. This works with buying cars, too. In fact, you can figure out any purchase that has terms involved. This is a lot easier than trying to manually adjust your values until you get to a price you can afford. Believe me, I've done more than my share of manual calculations like this and had a huge "Aha!" moment when I learned how to use Goal Seek. If you click OK in the Goal Seek Status dialog shown below, Excel confirms Goal Seek's results; if you press **Esc** or click **Cancel**, Excel leaves you where you started.

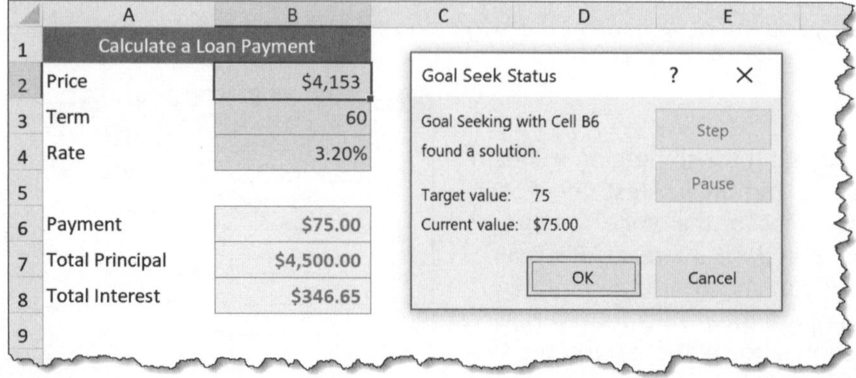

How does Excel make Goal Seek work? It's called *iterative calculation*, and Excel internally calculates multiple results to get you the result you asked for. Excel may need to perform hundreds or even thousands of internal calculations to get there, so using Goal Seek is a lot easier than your doing the calculations by hand!

RATE

The RATE function tells you what your interest rate is if you know the payments, the term of the loan, and the present value of the loan. You can use this function to find out what credit is really costing you.

The following is the general syntax for the **RATE** function:

=RATE(nper, pmt, pv, [fv], [type])

where:

RATE - Interest Rate per Period	
Description	Data
Number of Payments	60
Amount of Payment	($100)
Present Value	$5,500
Future Value	$0
Payment Due	1
Interest Rate	2.999617%

- **nper**—Number of periods in the investment
- **pmt**—Payment made each period
- **pv**—Present value
- **[fv]**—Generally 0 (optional)
- **[type]**—1 or 0, to indicate whether the payment is made at the beginning or end of a period (optional)

DB

The DB function calculates straight-line depreciation. If you buy a piece of equipment, you need to know how much you can depreciate it each year during its expected life cycle. This not only helps with taxes but also helps you figure in operating expenses for the equipment.

The following is the general syntax for the **DB** function:

=DB(cost, salvage, life, period, [month])

where:

DB - Depreciation	
Purchase Price	$25,000
Estimate Life (Years)	5
Salvage Value	$1,250
Year*	Depreciation
Year 1	$11,275.00
Year 2	$6,189.98
Year 3	$3,398.30
Year 4	$1,865.66
Year 5	$1,024.25
Total Depreciation	$23,753.19

- **cost**—Purchase price of the equipment
- **salvage**—The amount you can get for the equipment when you sell it because you need to replace it
- **life**—The number of years you can expect to use the equipment before you need to replace it
- **period**—The length of the period, generally measured in years for large equipment purchases
- **[month]**—How many months in the first year (optional); defaults to 12 months if you leave it out

Logical Functions

The functions in the Logical category help you with what-if scenarios. For instance, you could use the IF function as follows to calculate whether sales representatives sold enough to qualify for a bonus: **=IF(A1>25000,"Bonus","No Bonus")**. The following sections cover some of the most commonly used logical functions.

IF

As mentioned several times throughout this book so far, IF statements are the cornerstone to a lot of Excel logic. As you get more and more comfortable with Excel, you may find IF being one of the functions you draw on the most. But the IF statement needs to be accompanied by some significant warnings that we'll get to shortly. Just as Excel has over a million rows, but using them all probably isn't a good idea, the IF statement can do a lot of things, but trying to make it do everything isn't a good idea. Earlier versions of Excel allowed you to nest up to seven IF statements, and here's a very simple example with five nested IFs:

=IF(A1=1,1,IF(A1=2,2,IF(A1=3,3),IF(A1=4,4),IF(A1=5,5))))

The formula simply says "If A1 equals 1, then return 1. If A1 equals 2, then return 2, and so on." Imagine trying to read a formula like this if it contained some truly complex comparisons! The current version of Excel allows you to nest up to 64 levels of IF statements, so the potential for computation has increased greatly—but so has the potential for trouble.

Caution: How hard would it be to adjust the five layers of nested IF statements in the previous example, especially if they were much more complex? It would not be easy. Now imagine trying to adjust that 64 times! How many errors do you think would come out of that? You might find that 63 of 64 conditions would evaluate correctly for who knows how long, but when that 64th condition evaluated incorrectly, it might completely screw up your entire model. Then, not only would you have to find the problem itself, you would also have to fix the model for anyone else who might be using it. This is an overly dramatic assessment of nested IF statements, but if possible, you should use IF statements only for relatively simple and static text comparisons. Too often people try to get an IF statement to do something that a different function, like VLOOKUP, can do much better.

Let's look at a few examples. I don't show these examples because they're best-practice uses of IF statements but because they're incredibly common in Excel workbooks, and you need to know what you're looking at when you encounter them. If anything, these are examples of what *not* to do in Excel, and you would be much better off using lookup tables, which you'll see later in this chapter.

One of the most common uses of IF statements is to return data that matches specific criteria or that falls within a range of values. Here is a relatively common example of a nested IF statement that returns letter grades based on test scores:

	A	B	C
1	Student	Test Score	Grade
2	Bob	89.8	B
3	Tommy	52.7	F
4	Christine	99.3	A
5	Alice	63.6	D
6	Fred	73.4	C
7	Carey	98.9	A

The formula in cells C2:C7 is:

=IF(A1>=90,"A",IF(A1>=80,"B",IF(A1>=70,"C",IF(A1>=60,"D",IF(A1<60,"F")))))

The formula says "If A1 is greater than or equal to 90, then return an A. If A1 is greater than or equal to 80, then return a B, and so on, and anything less than 60 returns a F." While the formula works perfectly, there are a lot of variables that could be entered incorrectly, and they need to be ordered sequentially for the formula to calculate correctly. So, A1>=90 gets evaluated first, and if that condition is true, the formula performs the calculation associated with that condition. If that condition isn't true, the formula moves on to the next one, and so on. But if you get the conditions out of order, then one condition can invalidate the next and render the formula(s) useless. One of the inherent weaknesses with IF statements is that they need to be precise and ordered. The odds of getting them wrong increases in direct proportion to the number of conditions you're trying to evaluate.

Another common use of IF is to calculate commission statements. In this case, someone qualifies for a 2% bonus once she sells more than $25,000, 1.5% for more than $15,000, and 1% for more than $5,000. Take a look at the following example and notice what happens when the values are entered from high to low (25000 to 5000) as opposed low to high (5000 to 25000).

	A	B	C
1	Sales	Commission	Formula
2	16,000	240	=IF(A2>25000,A2*2%,IF(A2>15000,A2*1.5%,IF(A2>5000,A2*1%,0)))
3			
4	16,000	160	=IF(A2>5000,A2*1%,IF(A2>15000,A2*1.5%,IF(A2>25000,A2*2%,0)))

The first example correctly shows a $240 commission. So why does the second formula, which has exactly the same values, show only a $160 commission? It's due to the order of operations. The first formula starts at the top tier, so no matter what, the sales amount needs to start there and work its way down. So, if you sold only $2,000, you still need to pass each IF test until you get to the end, which results in $0 commission. In the second formula, by starting at the bottom, any amount sold that clears the first hurdle will be stuck there. In this case, $16,000 is greater than $5,000, and therefore the IF's test is met, the commission is calculated, and the formula exits.

Note: Bad IF statements are everywhere! You might think I'm kidding about this, but I got the commission example from training material that a major training company used. Yes, these formulas work just fine, but they're not the best way to get things done. In fact, they're just plain dangerous.

Another problem with both of these formulas is that the data in them is entered by hand, so if the conditions driving the formula ever need to be changed, the formula needs to be manually adjusted. Granted, the grades example isn't too bad, because it's not likely that those grade standards will change, but just imagine how much work you'd have to do if you had a lot of formulas as in the commission example, and you had to change the criteria.

Ideally, you'll get into the habit of using IF statements only for text comparisons like the earlier example. Yes/No/Maybe, Left/Right and other options are very common, and the nice thing about them is that they aren't likely to change very often. If you find yourself with situations like this, then by all means use IF statements; otherwise, it's time to move up to more robust alternatives, starting with LOOKUP, which we'll get to shortly. IF statements also work well for evaluating conditional formatting criteria, which we discuss in Chapter 7.

> **Note:** Instead of burying details in complex IF statements, it's much better to have them out in the open, where they can be seen and easily changed.

One of the primary reasons to move away from using IF statements for multiple criteria is so you can use table-based reference data. This gives you the ability to have your data points on a worksheet, where the values can be easily changed, as opposed to hardcoded in a formula, where finding and changing the values can be challenging. Many workbooks have been broken because numerous IF statements didn't get updated. Even worse, people make incorrect business assumptions and decisions based on them. In the commission example above, what would happen if you needed to change the 2%, and you had hundreds of formulas depending on that one? It wouldn't be fun. Keep in mind that this is a relatively small example. Imagine a formula with 64 conditions! And consider that you may not even be able to find all of the formula in the first place! Table-based dependencies are much easier to change on the fly, and this can mean a lot, especially if you're dealing with complex models and testing multiple criteria. If you're worried about people changing the data in your tables, you can always hide the worksheet. Much as I use a separate worksheet for list-based data, I use a separate worksheet for lookup tables. It's much easier to maintain a model if everything is out in the open and not buried in complex IF statements.

The Chapter 6 companion workbook provides multiple examples of logical function combinations. As with many other things in Excel, the variations you can come up with are virtually limitless. But I harp on using them sparingly because they can get so complicated that they're nearly impossible to read and maintain—even if you're able to build in the first place.

IFS

The IFS function provides an alternative to using multiple nested IF statements. You can use it, for example, to reduce the earlier IF statement for grades to the following:

=IFS(A1>89,"A",A1>79,"B",A1>69,"C",A1>59,"D",TRUE,"F")

AND

The AND function returns TRUE if all the arguments being evaluated are true. If one or more of the evaluated arguments are false, then AND returns FALSE.

OR

The OR function evaluates all the arguments and returns TRUE if any of them is true. It returns FALSE *only* if all the arguments are false.

NOT

The NOT function simply changes TRUE to FALSE or FALSE to TRUE. It is useful if you are trying to exclude something from a comparison.

IFERROR

As mentioned earlier, the IFERROR function is strictly for error management. Remember that it suppresses *all* errors, so it's generally not a good idea to use it unless you know that your model is functioning properly.

Text Functions

Text functions let you manipulate text, such as splitting apart a Full Name column into First Name and Last Name columns or vice versa. These functions are generally used in combination with one another, and some of the examples on the following pages show that.

FIND

The FIND function finds a value within a string and returns an integer corresponding to its position in the string, starting from the left. For example, with the formula **=FIND(",",A1)**, which says to find the first comma in cell A1, if the comma were in the sixth spot in the cell (e.g., "Jones, Tom"), FIND would return 6.

LEFT/RIGHT/MID

The LEFT, RIGHT, and MID functions allow you to pull text from a string—either from the left, middle, or right, respectively. They're used a lot in both parsing and concatenating names, such as converting "Smith, Bob" to "Bob Smith". For example, **=LEFT(A1,5)** would return the five characters to the left of cell A1. If you were to change the formula to **=RIGHT(A1,5)**, you would get the five rightmost characters.

&

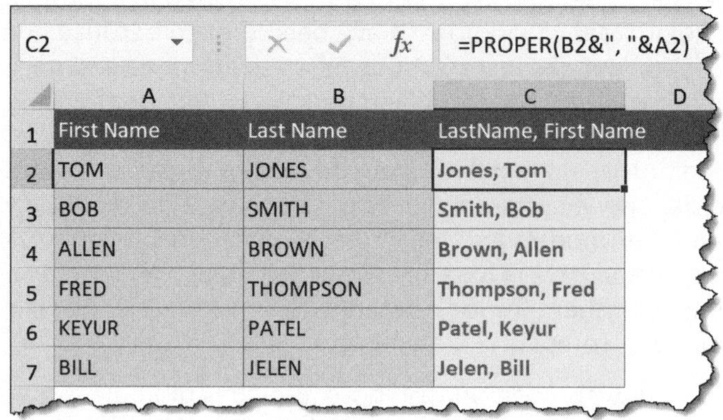

C2 | =PROPER(B2&", "&A2)

	A	B	C	D
1	First Name	Last Name	LastName, First Name	
2	TOM	JONES	Jones, Tom	
3	BOB	SMITH	Smith, Bob	
4	ALLEN	BROWN	Brown, Allen	
5	FRED	THOMPSON	Thompson, Fred	
6	KEYUR	PATEL	Patel, Keyur	
7	BILL	JELEN	Jelen, Bill	

The & function is used for concatenating, or joining, text and data. While you can also use the CONCAT and CONCATENATE functions to handle similar operations, the & function can be faster to use. You can enter it with **Shift+7**. The following example converts uppercase names to proper case and then joins last name and first name, separated by a comma and a space, which is very handy when you're dealing with customer information from a database and need to make it customer friendly:

=PROPER(B2&", "&A2)

The PROPER function converts the first letter of each word to uppercase and the rest to lowercase. It doesn't matter if the starting text string is uppercase, lowercase, or mixed case.

Parsing Functions

Parsing, which is the opposite of concatenating, means splitting text strings into different parts. In the following example, the formula splits out last and first names from full names:

=RIGHT(A10,LEN(A10)-FIND(",",A10)-1)

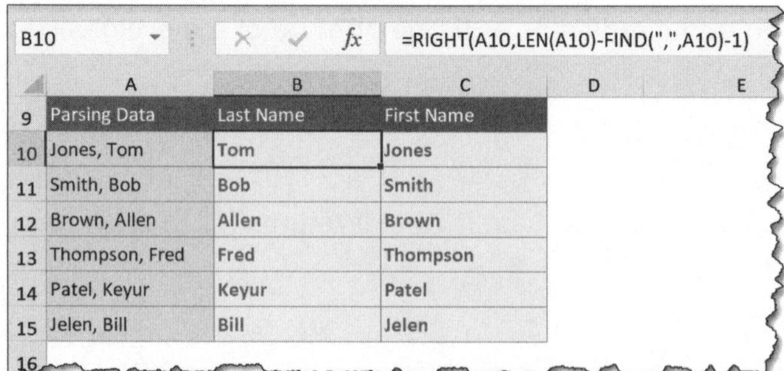

B10 | =RIGHT(A10,LEN(A10)-FIND(",",A10)-1)

	A	B	C	D	E
9	Parsing Data	Last Name	First Name		
10	Jones, Tom	Tom	Jones		
11	Smith, Bob	Bob	Smith		
12	Brown, Allen	Allen	Brown		
13	Thompson, Fred	Fred	Thompson		
14	Patel, Keyur	Keyur	Patel		
15	Jelen, Bill	Bill	Jelen		
16					

You could use the earlier **=LEFT(A1,5)** example to do the same thing, but that works only for people whose names have five characters. Instead, you use the FIND function to find a consistent character, in this case a comma, and then look for characters before and after the comma. You can also use **Data > Flash Fill**. Personally, I think it's kind of fun and challenging to come up with formulas like this. You're essentially doing math on text by finding the positions of certain characters.

You can look at this example more simply as **=RIGHT(A10,3)**. The hard part is to figure out how to get the 3. Because RIGHT goes from right to left, you need to find out where the comma is from the other direction. LEN(A10) gives you the overall length of the entire text string. FIND(",",A10) finds the comma, which you then subtract from the overall length of the text string, which returns 4. So, what's the -1 for? You need to subtract 1 to remove the space after the comma. You can select this formula in the Chapter 6 workbook and then go to **Formulas > Evaluate Formula** and then click Evaluate to watch Excel calculate the formula. It's also good practice to use the Evaluate tool to see how your formulas work from Excel's point of view.

Getting the first name, on the other hand, is much easier because you don't need to work backward:

=LEFT(A10,FIND(", ",A10)-1)

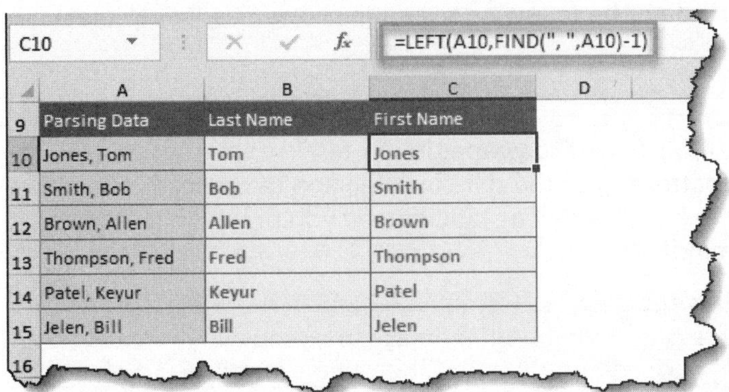

	A	B	C	D
9	Parsing Data	Last Name	First Name	
10	Jones, Tom	Tom	Jones	
11	Smith, Bob	Bob	Smith	
12	Brown, Allen	Allen	Brown	
13	Thompson, Fred	Fred	Thompson	
14	Patel, Keyur	Keyur	Patel	
15	Jelen, Bill	Bill	Jelen	
16				

TEXT

The TEXT function lets you to reapply formatting to numeric values when you've joined them in a text string (e.g., **="Report Date: "&TEXT(TODAY(),"MM/DD/YY")**). If you try to do this without the TEXT function, Excel has no idea what format you want the value to be, so it displays it in general number format. People often put a text string in one cell, and the formatted value next to it, which can look a bit awkward.

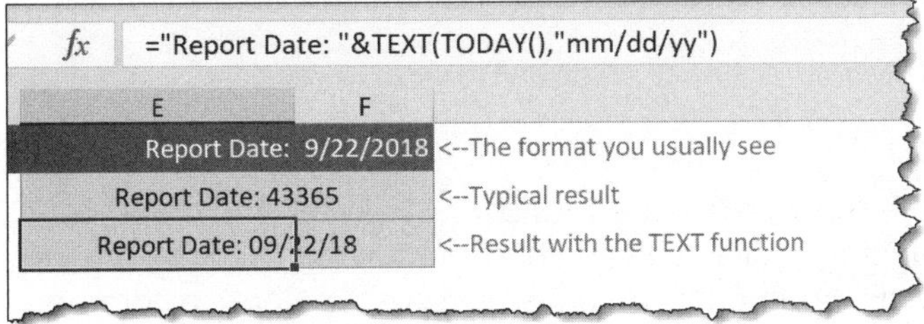

Date & Time Functions

Date & Time functions are for (wait for it...) working with dates and times. For example, you can calculate the difference between today and employee hire dates to figure out how long people have been employed. Or, for fun, you can calculate the number of days until your birthday.

TODAY

The TODAY function gives you today's date. It doesn't take any arguments, and it's volatile, meaning that it updates whenever Excel calculates. Some people try to use the TODAY and other data and time functions for static date/timestamps and then wonder what happened the next day, when the date has updated.

NOW

The NOW function gives you the date and time. It does not take any arguments and is volatile.

YEAR

The YEAR function returns the year of the date it's referencing (e.g., **=YEAR(TODAY())**).

WEEKDAY

The WEEKDAY function returns the day of the week as an integer value (1–7). For example, with the formula **=WEEKDAY(TODAY(),1)**, if it were a Wednesday, the answer would be 4. Note that WEEKDAY has a return type argument for the starting day of the week; 1 is Sunday through Saturday, 2 is Monday through Sunday, 3 is Monday through Sunday, and Monday starts as a 0 value instead of a 1.

DAYS360

The DAYS360 function lets you calculate the difference in days between two dates. It's great for kids who want to know how long it is until Christmas or their next birthday. The following example shows how to calculate the number of days until Christmas:

=DAYS360(TODAY(),DATE(YEAR(TODAY()),12,25))

Note that if you manually enter the date in the function, you need to wrap it in quotes, like this: **=DAYS("12/25/2018",TODAY())**. However, it's much better to put the date in a cell and reference it directly. This way, you don't need to hunt down and change every instance of a static date. If you're building models that rely on dates, you should especially keep this in mind!

> **Hint:** Try to limit the amount of information you manually add to formulas. It's much more efficient to be transparent and use cell references where they're out in the open and easy to change. If you have fixed values in functions, you must first find the function(s) and then find the value to replace. This is time-consuming and error prone! Missing just one vital input can lead you to make the wrong decision! This kind of error causes all kinds of problems.

EOMONTH

The EOMONTH function returns the last day of the month in reference to the date entered as an argument and how many months away you specify. For example, **=EOMONTH(TODAY(),0)** tells you the last day of the current month, and **=EOMONTH(TODAY(),6)** tells you the last day of the month six months from now. This can be handy in project planning and calculating dates because you can let Excel figure it out for you instead of having to manually enter the end date somewhere.

Lookup & Reference Functions

The functions under Lookup & Reference are some of the most widely used functions in Excel, and once you get the hang of them, you'll understand why. Lookup functions help prevent you from having to enter data repeatedly, and they help you streamline any complicated IF statements you might encounter. Here's a common scenario: A business has an invoice form for goods and services. When it comes time to enter an order for a repeat customer, someone types in the customer name and then has to go look up the customer's relevant information, such as address and phone number, and type that into the form manually. Lookup functions do all that for you, and you only need a unique identifier for the record you want to find, which in the case of customers is generally a customer ID or business name. You can also return information on sales reps, product names, part numbers, and so on. Almost any information that's table based can be set up so you can retrieve the information via formula rather than doing it manually.

LOOKUP

Remember the grades example with the long IF statement to determine the resulting grade for a student's test score? That is the perfect scenario to explain the LOOKUP function. LOOKUP functions essentially allow you to answer questions such as these: What do you want to look up? Where do you want to look for it? If Excel finds it, what do you want it to do with it?

The following example shows the grades scenario again, but this time with a table that shows the number grade scale and the corresponding letter grades. You can tell the LOOKUP formula to look up the student grades in B4:B9 and compare those values with the value in the grades table and return the result.

	A	B	C
3	Student	Test Score	Lookup
4	Bob	89.8	B
5	Tommy	52.7	F
6	Christine	99.3	A
7	Alice	63.6	D
8	Fred	73.4	C
9	Carey	98.9	A
10			
11	Number Grade Scale	Letter Grade Scale	
12	50.0	F	
13	60.0	D	
14	70.0	C	
15	80.0	B	
16	90.0	A	
17			

The LOOKUP formula in this case is **=LOOKUP(B4,$A$12:$B$16)**, and it says:

- *What do you want to look up?* The value in B4.
- *Where do you want to look for it?* The grades table, cells A12:B16. (The formula spans columns A and B because you want LOOKUP to give you the value from the second column.)
- *If Excel finds it, what do you want it to do with it?* Return the corresponding value in the second column. (Excel knows this because two columns were selected in the range, and it returns the value in the right-most column of the stated range.)

LOOKUP is the simplest of the lookup functions, and it's also the least robust, but it works perfectly in cases like this. LOOKUP tables must be sorted in ascending order to work properly. That's why you see the grades table sorted from lowest to highest. LOOKUP looks for an exact match, and if it can't find it, it returns the largest value in the table that is less than the lookup value. In this example, LOOKUP found the closest possible or approximate match to the grade that was entered.

There is also what's called an array version of the LOOKUP function, as shown in this example:

=LOOKUP(B4, {0,60,70,80,90}, {"F","D","C","B","A"})

However, you should keep in mind the same cautions with using the array method that you would consider when hardcoding any values in a function. In this case, as with the IF statement grade example, it's probably relatively benign, though, since grades and their scales aren't likely to change anytime soon. The primary advantage to the array version is that it eliminates the lookup table.

VLOOKUP

Short for *vertical lookup*, VLOOKUP looks for a value in a column and returns corresponding values to the right. VLOOKUP is the most common of all the lookup functions and probably one of the most widely used functions in Excel. VLOOKUP has a degree of flexibility that LOOKUP doesn't: First, it doesn't care which way your list is sorted, and second, you can look up a multiple-column table range and tell VLOOKUP exactly which column you want results from.

Here's the technical syntax for VLOOKUP:

VLOOKUP(lookup_value, table_array, col_index_num, [range_lookup])

where:

- **lookup_value**—Value you want to look up
- **table_array**—Range where you want to look up
- **col_index_num**—Column number in the range you want
- **[range_lookup]**—Whether you want an exact match or an approximate match (optional)

Let's look at a common example of VLOOKUP in action. Say that there is a simple table of account numbers and corresponding dollar figures for each month, as shown below. In cell A26, you can enter the value you want to find in the top table, which is 456 in this case. Then you use this formula:

=VLOOKUP($A26,$A$21:$M$23,2,FALSE)

B26 fx =VLOOKUP($A26,$A$21:$M$23,2,FALSE)

	A	B	C	E
20	Account #	January	February	April
21	123	$22	$23	$25
22	456	$32	$33	$35
23	789	$42	$43	$45
24				
25	VLOOKUP	January	February	April
26	456	$32	$33	$35

You want to search the entire table range (A21:M23), and for January, you want the second column to the right, which is the **,2,** part. With VLOOKUP, the cell you're looking at is column 1, and everything else goes to the right from there. FALSE (or 0) indicates that VLOOKUP should return only an exact match. As you might guess, when you copy the function to February, you need to change **,2,** to **,3,** and so on.

Note: Your VLOOKUP functions don't have to rely on static column offsets. Those are a pain because they have to be manually adjusted for each subsequent formula that's copied across. Instead, you can replace the column number with **COLUMN()**, as in this example:

=VLOOKUP$A8,$A$2:$M$4,COLUMN(),FALSE)

If the columns don't match, you can adjust them with **COLUMN()+1 or COLUMN()-2** and so on.

HLOOKUP

As you can probably guess, HLOOKUP is short for *horizontal lookup*. It works the same as VLOOKUP, except it looks from the top down instead of left to right. Frankly, this is an error-prone function, and it can be more of a pain than it's worth because you generally have a static row reference, and people add rows of data all the time, which can make your formula return values from the wrong row. It's just like the column reference in a VLOOKUP, but people don't usually insert columns into active datasets. (You'll rarely see someone insert a new month into a January–December model.) But I'm building on something here, which is how to use complementary functions together to overcome shortcomings.

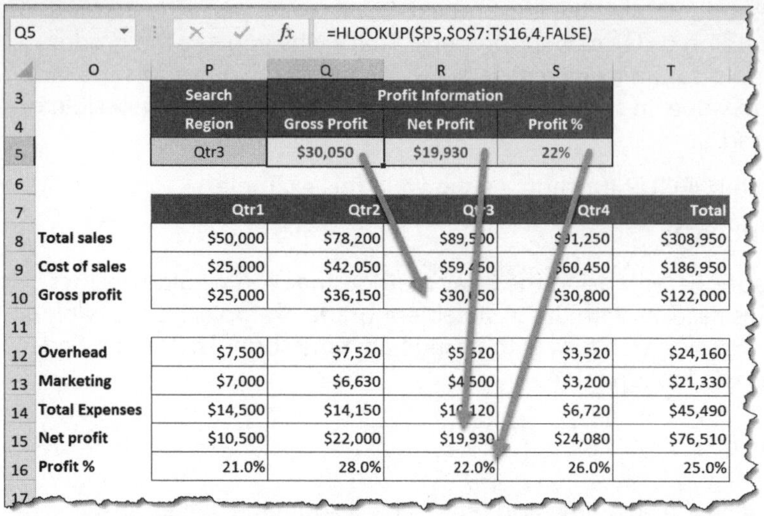

Q5 =HLOOKUP($P5,$O$7:T$16,4,FALSE)

	O	P	Q	R	S	T
3		Search	Profit Information			
4		Region	Gross Profit	Net Profit	Profit %	
5		Qtr3	$30,050	$19,930	22%	
6						
7		Qtr1	Qtr2	Q[illegible]3	Qtr4	Total
8	Total sales	$50,000	$78,200	$89,5[illegible]0	$[illegible]1,250	$308,950
9	Cost of sales	$25,000	$42,050	$59,[illegible]50	$60,450	$186,950
10	Gross profit	$25,000	$36,150	$30,[illegible]50	$30,800	$122,000
11						
12	Overhead	$7,500	$7,520	$5[illegible]520	$3,520	$24,160
13	Marketing	$7,000	$6,630	$4[illegible]500	$3,200	$21,330
14	Total Expenses	$14,500	$14,150	$1[illegible]120	$6,720	$45,490
15	Net profit	$10,500	$22,000	$19,930	$24,080	$76,510
16	Profit %	21.0%	28.0%	22.0%	26.0%	25.0%

In the example above, the formula is **=HLOOKUP($P5,$O$7:T$16,4,FALSE)**, and it's looking for the value in cell P5 (Qtr3) in the range O7:T16. When it finds it in column R, the function offsets four rows to the Gross Profit row and returns the value ($30,500). This is great if gross profit is always four rows down. But what if it moves or gets sorted? Your formula will most likely still return a valid result (no errors), but it could be wrong, and this is the kind of thing that can get you into lots of trouble. Fortunately, there's a smart addition you can make with HLOOKUP, and it works with VLOOKUP as well: You can use the MATCH function to make the HLOOKUP dynamic so it finds the "gross profit" row for you, no matter where it is (as long as it's in the same column). The MATCH function looks for a value in a row or column range, and it returns what's called an index number, which is the row or column number it finds in relation to where it started looking. You can adjust the gross profit example with MATCH like this:

=HLOOKUP($P5,$O$7:$T$16,MATCH(Q4,$O$7:$O$16,0),FALSE)

In this formula, MATCH(Q4,$O$7:$O$16,0) finds gross profit on the fourth row in the range, so it feeds a 4 to HLOOKUP. Now if someone inserts a row in the dataset, the formula won't give you the wrong results. MATCH works by looking in O7:O16 for the value that's in cell Q4. The 0 at the end means that you want MATCH to return only an exact match. If you were to put a 1 there, MATCH would find the first approximate match.

> **Caution:** You need to be very careful with the match type in your lookup functions because you can inadvertently get the wrong results if you're not careful. Unfortunately, if you do make one of these mistakes, it's technically not Excel's fault as it was doing exactly what you told it to do.

INDEX/MATCH

INDEX and MATCH is one of the most powerful function combinations you can use. Excel allows you to combine these functions into a supremely dynamic formula:

MATCH—As you saw in the dynamic HLOOKUP example, MATCH looks for a value and tries to match it in the range that you specify. What's nice about MATCH is that you can have it search both rows and columns, and it will return the row/column index number of the item it finds relative to where it's searching. When you combine it with INDEX, you can return the intersection of those two ranges—no matter where they are. This is more complicated than the lookup family of functions, but it also lets you go in all directions.

Returning to the HLOOKUP example, you could look for gross profit in column O, then look for Qtr3 in row 7, then look for the fourth row and fourth column in P7:T16. Once you have your row and column numbers, and you know the range to use to find the intersection of the fourth row and fourth column, how do you tell Excel to use them? This is where INDEX comes in.

INDEX—This function returns a value within a given range based on the intersection of the row and column that you specify. The INDEX function has the following syntax:

=INDEX(reference, row_num, [column_num])

where:

- **reference**—Range you want to look in
- **row_num**—Number of rows to reference
- **[column_num]**—Number of columns to reference (optional)

In this case, you use the following:

=INDEX(O7:T16,4,4)

- But here you are using static arguments again, and you don't want to have to manually change them. You can substitute the static values for the values that MATCH returned, and you end up with this:
- **=INDEX($O$7:$T$16,MATCH(Q20,$O$7:$O$16,0),MATCH($P21,$O$7:$T$7,0))**

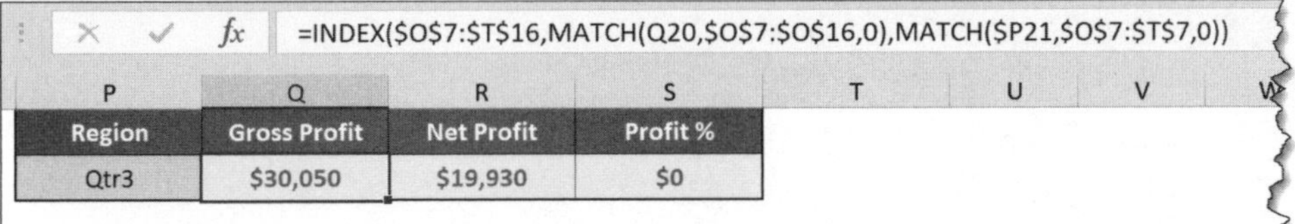

Region	Gross Profit	Net Profit	Profit %
Qtr3	$30,050	$19,930	$0

- Yes, this is a lot to absorb, but you will find these examples in the Chapter 6 companion workbook along with a breakdown of how to work them all yourself. There is also an INDEX-MATCH worksheet in the companion workbook that is dedicated solely to INDEX/MATCH and how to build the final formula in pieces. When you get comfortable with INDEX/MATCH, you might find yourself completely ignoring the lookup functions. HLOOKUP is less robust than VLOOKUP and often gets replaced with INDEX/MATCH anyway.

Note: Sometimes you need to build giant formulas that combine several other functions and formulas. The easiest thing to do is build each element/function separately. For instance, in the INDEX/MATCH/MATCH example, you might first build the first MATCH, then the second MATCH, and then the INDEX function, and then you could put in the results from the two MATCH functions. If you got the result you wanted, you could replace the row argument with the first MATCH function, followed by the second one. You'll find that it's a good idea to break down large formulas into manageable chunks!

Math & Trig Functions

From a business perspective, the ability to conditionally average, count, and sum data is fantastic for analyzing data and saving time. In the past, if you wanted to analyze your data by different criteria, you either did it by hand or used a database application. But with the amazing functionality of the functions in the Math & Trig category, you have all those tools right at your fingertips!

Note: For simplicity's sake, none of the formulas in the following examples have been cluttered with absolute references, but when you use these functions in real-life scenarios, you will want to use absolute references.

SUMIF

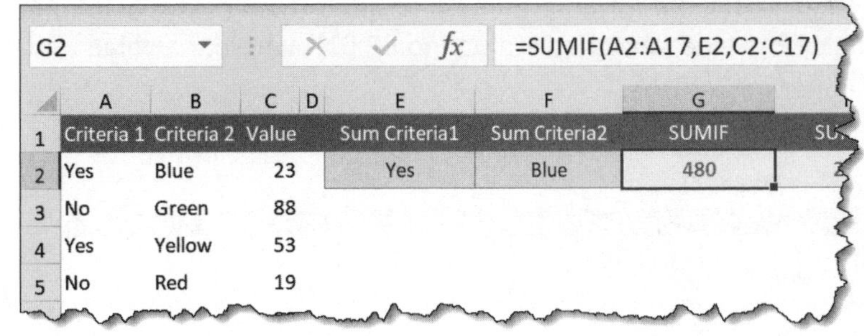

	A	B	C	D	E	F	G
1	Criteria 1	Criteria 2	Value		Sum Criteria1	Sum Criteria2	SUMIF
2	Yes	Blue	23		Yes	Blue	480
3	No	Green	88				
4	Yes	Yellow	53				
5	No	Red	19				

The SUMIF function does pretty much exactly what it sounds like: It lets you sum one range based on criteria in another. For instance, let's say you want to sum all sales for the month where the item sold was blue. In this example, you're going to sum all values in column C where the corresponding value in column A is Yes.

SUMIF has the following syntax:

SUMIF(range, criteria, [sum_range])

where:

- **range**—Range you want to evaluate
- **criteria**—Criteria you want to sum
- **[sum_range]**—Range you want to sum (optional)

Here is the formula you would use in this case:

=SUMIF(A2:A17,E2,C2:C17)

Unfortunately, this reads a little bit backward: Sum the range C2:C17, where A2:A17 equals the value in E2 (in this case, Yes).

SUMIFS

SUMIFS is like SUMIF, except it lets you sum by multiple criteria. Here is an example:

=SUMIFS(C2:C17,A2:A17,E2,B2:B17,F2)

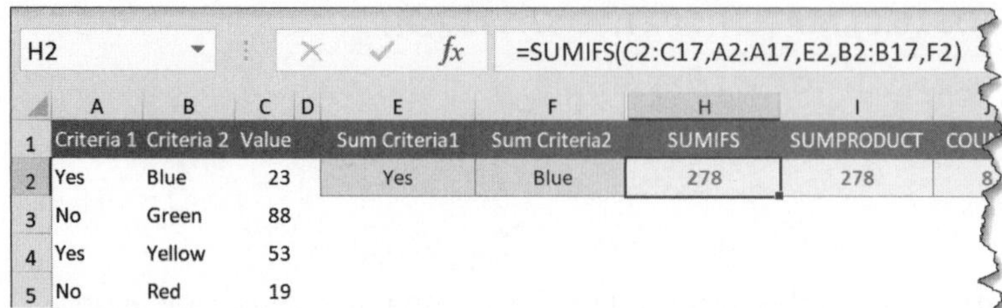

Oddly, the arguments in SUMIFS aren't in the same order as the arguments in SUMIF:

=SUMIFS(sum_range, criteria_range1, criteria1, [criteria_range2, criteria2])

where:

- **sum_range**—Range to sum
- **criteria_range1**—Range with your first set of criteria
- **criteria1**—First criterion you want to sum
- **[criteria_range2, criteria2]**—Subsequent sum ranges and criteria (optional)

In this case, you sum C2:C17 where A2:A17 equals the value in E2 (Yes) and B2:B17 equals the value in F2 (Blue). SUMIFS supports up to 127 different criteria pairs, but imagine trying to read a formula with so many criteria!

SUMPRODUCT

SUMPRODUCT can be an incredibly robust but complicated function, and it can handle up to 255 arguments. In the example in this section, SUMPRODUCT returns the same value as SUMIFS in the previous section. This chapter doesn't go into detail about how to create SUMPRODUCT formulas because it is not a one-size-fits-all function. I have included it here, however, so that you know it's available. Many times, analysis that seems impossible can be solved with SUMPRODUCT.

SUMPRODUCT breaks down the arguments that you specify, multiplies them, and generates the results as the sum of those products. It's a bit easier to see if you invoke the Function Arguments dialog and watch how Excel evaluates the formula. In the example shown below, SUMPRODUCT is evaluating A2:A17, where the value equals E2's value, and then evaluating B2:B17, where the value equals F2, and it finally comes to the sum range in C2:C17.

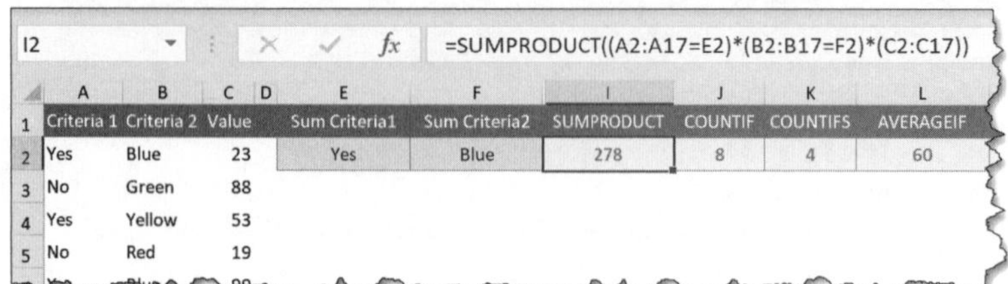

In the Function Arguments dialog, you can see that SUMPRODUCT evaluates the results of the arguments as {23;0;0;0;99;0;0;0;61;0;0;0;95;0;0;0}, which sums to 278.

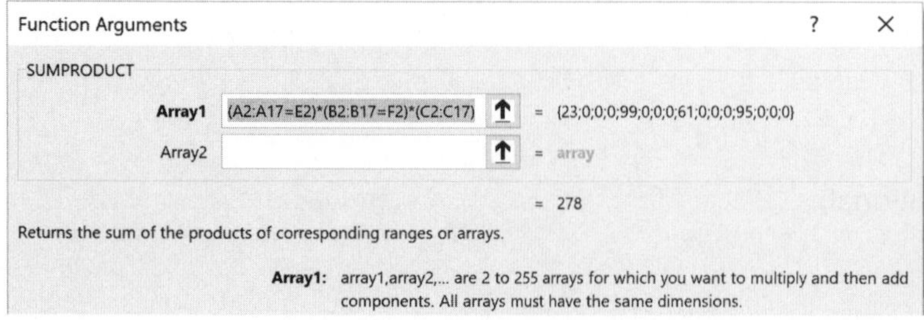

COUNTIF, COUNTIFS, AVERAGEIF, and AVERAGEIFS

COUNTIF, COUNTIFS, AVERAGEIF, and AVERAGEIFS work the same way as SUMIF but return a count or an average of the items in a range vs. their sum. The IF version of each function accepts only a single criterion, while the IFS version of each function accepts multiple criteria.

The syntax for the COUNTIF function is as follows:

COUNTIF(range, criteria)

where:

- **range**—Range you want to look in
- **criteria**—Value you want to look for

The following example counts the values in column A where the value is Yes:

=COUNTIF(A2:A17,E2)

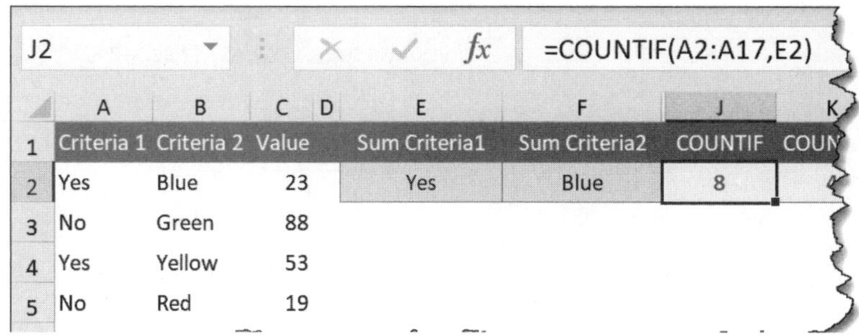

The syntax for the COUNTIFS function is as follows:

COUNTIFS(criteria_range1, criteria1, [criteria_range2, criteria2]...)

where:

- **criteria_range1**—First range to count
- **criteria1**—First value you want to look for
- **[criteria_range2, criteria2]**—Second and subsequent ranges and criteria (optional)

COUNTIFS counts only items where both ranges meet the criteria. In the following example, it counts only the values that are Yes *and* Blue:

=COUNTIFS(A2:A17,E2,B2:B17,F2)

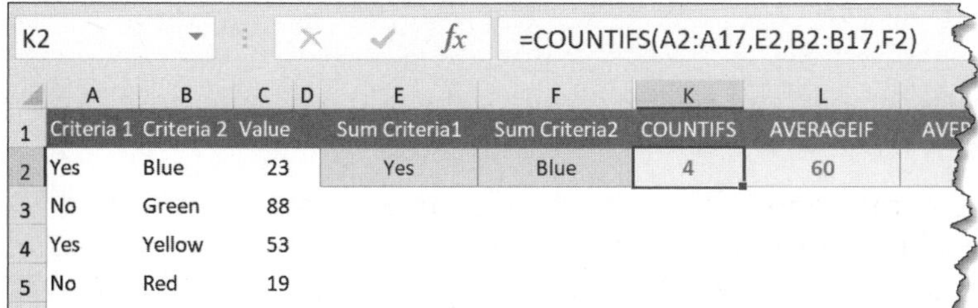

The syntax for the AVERAGEIF function is as follows:

AVERAGEIF(range, criteria, [average_range])

where:

- **range**—Range to look in
- **criteria**—Value you want to look for
- **[average_range]**—Range to average (optional)

The following example averages C2:C17, where the cells in A2:A17 equal E2 (Yes):

=AVERAGEIF(A2:A17,E2,C2:C17)

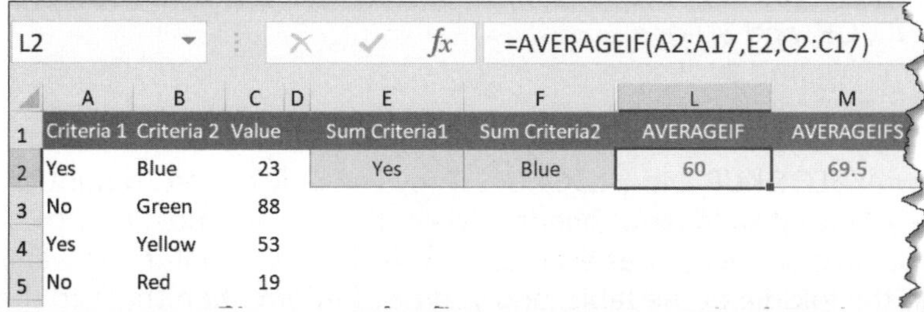

The syntax for the AVERAGEIFS function is as follows:

AVERAGEIFS(average_range, criteria_range1, criteria1, [criteria_range2, criteria2], ...)

where:

- **average_range**—Range to average
- **criteria_range1**—First criteria range to look in
- **criteria1**—First value to look for
- **[criteria_range2, criteria2]**—Second and subsequent ranges and criteria (optional)

The following example averages the values in C2:C17, where the cells in A2:A17 equal the value in E2 (Yes) *and* the cells in range B2:B17 equal the value in F2 (Blue):

=AVERAGEIFS(C2:C17,A2:A17,E2,B2:B17,F2)

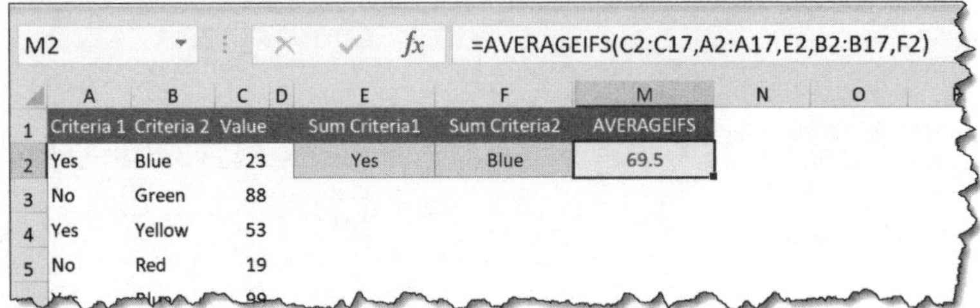

3D Formulas

Excel created 3D formulas to give you a way to perform calculations on multiple worksheets at once without cumbersome manual formulas. Remember the first-month model for the 12-month cash flow summary in Chapter 5? If you had all 12 months in place and a summary worksheet, you could summarize the total like this:

=January!A1+February!A1+March!A1+April!A1+May!A1+June!A1+July!A1+August!A1+September!A1 +October!A1+November!A1+December!A1

This would involve either typing the formula by hand (not fun) or entering = in the summary sheet, clicking on January, clicking A1, typing **+**, then clicking February and A1, and so on. This would be no fun either. 3D formulas save you from such tedium. You could use a 3D formula, for example, to replace the monstrosity above with this:

=SUM(January:December!A1)

This formula sums cell A1 in January, cell A1 in December, and cell A1 on every sheet in between those two sheets.

The following is an example from the Chapter 6 companion workbook, where there are worksheets named 3D First (the worksheet in the example), 3D Second, 3D Third, and 3D Last. So, the formula in the example is summing cell B4 on 3D Second, 3D Last, and what's in between them. You'll also see an example of a 3D AVERAGE function in the companion workbook.

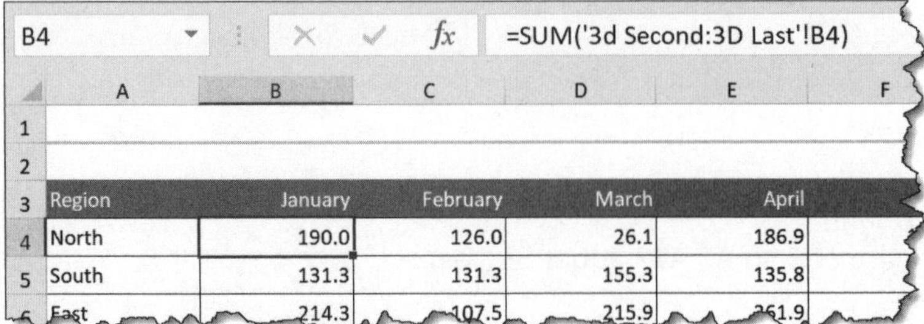

Excluding statistical functions, the following functions can support 3D formula syntax: AVERAGE, AVERAGEA, COUNT, COUNTA, MAX, MAXA, MIN, MINA, AND, OR, and SUM.

Helper Columns

Have you noticed any potential shortcomings with VLOOKUP and HLOOKUP? They can only go left to right or top to bottom. This means that whatever value you want to look for needs to be in the very leftmost or topmost portion of the range that you're going to search. In the grades example, this is fine, but what if you want to do something like search for a value that's in the middle of the table, and you need information that's to the left of it? The lookup functions can't do the job. In this case, you can use a helper column: You insert a column at the very left of your table and set a reference in that column to your unique identifier in the middle of the table. If your unique values are in column F, you add a column at the very left of your table and use **=F2** to repeat those values in the new column; then you build VLOOKUPs that reference the new column. If your data is set up in an Excel table, any new rows will automatically extend the formula, so you don't need to remember to do that.

When would you use a helper column? Let's say you have a customer table. Within the table are several companies that have multiple people with purchase authority, but they all buy under the same customer ID and name. How do you differentiate between orders placed by different people at the same company? You can use a helper column at the left of the lookup table to create a unique sub-ID:

=CompanyName&CompanyID&PurchaserLastName

You can then use this sub-ID in your lookup, where the lookup range starts with your new helper column:

=VLOOKUP(CompanyName&CompanyID&PurchaserLastName, Lookup Range, Lookup Column, 0)

Dynamic Array Functions

Released in 2019 in Office 365, dynamic array functions are a new family of functions that can dynamically resize themselves. In addition, any existing formula that has the ability to return multiple results now returns its results to the grid. This entirely new behavior for Excel gives you the ability to do things that you couldn't do previously. In fact, before these new functions, the only way to do what they can do was to write a custom routine in VBA (Visual Basic for Applications), which is the powerful programming language behind Excel. (VBA is beyond the scope of this book, but fortunately, there are many entire books devoted to VBA development.)

I've included sample workbooks for the dynamic array functions, and they cover a lot more scenarios than the following sections cover. These are the same workbooks you can get from the function references in the Excel Help files. You can find those files by selecting **Formulas > Insert Function** and then, in the Function Arguments dialog, clicking the Help on This Function link or by pressing **F1** to search the Help files.

FILTER

The FILTER function lets you filter a range by a criterion you give. In the following example, the formula filters cells C2:C11 and returns only values greater than (>) 500. The quotes at the end of the formula tell Excel to return an empty string if no values meet the criterion. If you exclude it, and no values match your criterion, Excel returns a #CALC! error. If this happens, you can adjust your criterion or display the quotes or some other value (e.g., 0) if there's no match.

=FILTER(C2:C11,C2:C11>E2,"")

C	D	E	F	G	H
Data		Criterion		FILTER	
622		500		622	
961				961	
691				691	
445				650	
378				783	
483					
650					
783					

RANDARRAY

The RANDARRAY function returns an array of random numbers between a minimum value and a maximum value you set, and you can also have Excel return integer or decimal values. The following example uses RANDARRAY to return integer values in an array that's four rows tall by five columns wide. It has a minimum value of 10 and a maximum value of 100.

=RANDARRAY(4,5,10,100,TRUE)

S	T	U	V	W
January	February	March	April	May
44	42	46	42	72
77	95	94	63	50
74	19	30	36	72
82	36	25	23	79

Remember the 10-second dataset from Chapter 5 that used **=INT(RAND()*100)**? Recall that it had to be copied to multiple rows/columns. With RANDARRAY, you define the array range in one cell, and the array range automatically spills into the destination for you. So, for example, if you wanted to create a 12-month scenario with 6 rows, you'd use **=RANDARRAY(6,12)**.

SEQUENCE

The SEQUENCE function lets you build a list of sequential values, which you might want to do when numbering rows in a table. The following example shows this formula in action:

=SEQUENCE(10)

> **Note**: SEQUENCE can do more than a sequential list of numbers. Say that you wanted 10 rows and 5 columns of numbers starting at 11 and jumping by 17. You would use =SEQUENCE(10,5,11,17).

	A
1	SEQUENCE
2	1
3	2
4	3
5	4
6	5
7	6
8	7
9	8
10	9
11	10

> **Note:** What's neat about dynamic array functions is that they exist in only one cell, but their results spill down to as far as is needed. When you select a dynamic array range, you see Excel highlight it with a shaded border. If your data is in an Excel table, the output range automatically adjusts itself as you add data to the table or remove data from the table.

SORTBY

The SORTBY function lets you sort a range of data by another range. The following example shows how to sort a list of names by age, in ascending order. Try going to the bottom of the Name/Age table in column J and adding a name. What happens? The dynamic array range automatically updates itself and puts the new name at the top of the list. If you add an age to the new name, the list automatically re-sorts itself.

=SORTBY(J2:K9,K2:K9)

J	K	L	M	N
Name	Age		SORTBY	Age
Tom	52		Fritz	19
Fred	65		Xi	19
Amy	22		Amy	22
Sal	73		Srivan	39
Fritz	19		Tom	52
Srivan	39		Fred	65
Xi	19		Hector	66
Hector	66		Sal	73

UNIQUE

The UNIQUE function returns unique values from a list.

The results here appear to be sorted, but that is because the original data was sorted. You are allowed to nest dynamic array functions just like regular array functions, so it would be valid to use =SORT(UNIQUE(Q2:Q11)) to make sure the results appear in sequence.

=UNIQUE(Q2:Q11)

Q	R	S
Item #		UNIQUE
1		1
1		2
2		3
2		4
3		5
3		
4		
4		
5		
5		

Dynamic Array Errors

As you might expect, a new class of function comes with a new class of error. The #SPILL! error occurs for several reasons, but the most common is that something is blocking the output range. Excel highlights the proposed spill area with a dotted border and displays an error flyout. If you choose the Select Obstructing Cells option (as shown below), Excel selects the cell that's preventing the formula from spilling. You can delete it or cut and paste it to a different location. As soon as the blockage is cleared, the formula automatically spills as intended.

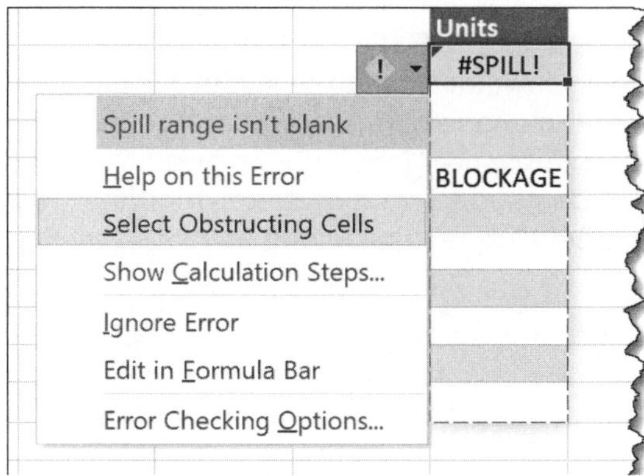

Chapter Summary

- This chapter describes the categories of business-related functions available on the Formulas tab:
    - AutoSum
    - Recently Used
    - Financial
    - Logical
    - Text
    - Date & Time
    - Lookup & Reference
    - Math & Trig
    - More Functions
- This chapter describes Excel's order of operations and how to ensure that your formulas calculate the way that you intend.
- This chapter describes the function errors that can occur in Excel and some of the ways to deal with them, as well as the potential issues involved in suppressing all errors.
- This chapter provides examples of commonly used functions and introduces Excel's exciting new dynamic array functions.

Chapter 7: Formatting, Printing, and Sharing

So far in this book, you've been primed on the creation of a workbook and how to take the necessary steps to bring it to the point where is fits your needs. You've learned how to do all the following:

- Put good spreadsheet design elements into place
- Input the primary row and column headers
- Populate a worksheet with some sample data
- Add some functions and formulas to test your sample data
- Replace sample data with live data and use referential functions such as VLOOKUP or INDEX/MATCH

If you've been following along with your own workbook, then by now you've designed the layout for the particular kind of model you're creating (e.g., finance, marketing, customer management), all your information is in your workbook, formulas have been tested, and other than some possible user input, you're good to go, right? Almost. Before you can send your workbook out in the world, you need to set it up for distribution. You need to format the workbook to make it easy for people to use, whether they're just looking at your information or are responsible for driving information back to you.

A lot of finance types might tell you that the information alone is important, and they don't worry about formatting a workbook. (If you look at a handful of corporate annual reports, you'll see what I mean.) And while the information in a workbook is important, how the information is presented determines whether it will be palatable to your recipients, so presentation is also very important. If the information is easy for people to get to and use, you'll have an easier time telling your story, but if you make it hard for people to digest your information, your story loses value. Fortunately, you often just need to make some simple adjustments to turn an otherwise boring workbook into something that looks great. This chapter talks about how you can format your workbooks for the maximum impact. It also discusses the various ways to set up a workbook for printing. This chapter also talks about the ways to share workbooks electronically and the real-time collaboration that's now possible in Excel.

This chapter shows a few different workbook scenarios and ways to improve on them. There is not one single way to properly format a workbook/worksheet. How you format a workbook largely depends on several things:

- **Your personal style**—It's your workbook. Go ahead and give it your own flair with different fonts, colors, and so on.
- **Your recipients' needs and expectations**—This is where your different fonts, colors, and so on make a difference. When you share a workbook with people, you need to be careful to make it easy for them to use. It can be tempting to splash a workbook with a ton of different colors, graphics/art, and so on, but remember to consider your audience.
- **Any technical or corporate policy limitation**—Some of the features covered in this book require an Office 365 subscription rather than the Office 2019 perpetual version, and you need to be mindful of sharing workbooks with people who might not have the same functionality you have. For instance, co-authoring—the ability to work with others in real time, is available in Office 365 but not Excel 2019.

Hint: Remember that, when in doubt, you'll never go wrong with conservative formatting, and overdoing it can be difficult on people. I always try to consider who's going to be using a workbook when I design it. For instance, I would build a finance workbook for a big company a lot differently than I'd build a fantasy football league workbook for my friends or a mortgage amortization template to figure out how much house I can afford. What a workbook should look like depends, to some extent, on your audience.

Themes

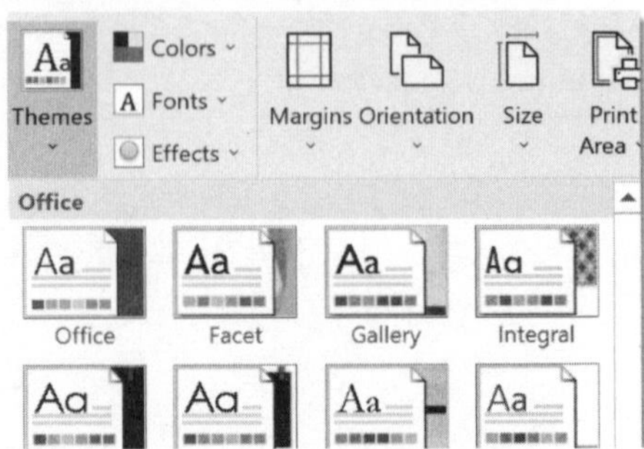

A theme provides the primary background look for a workbook, and you generally need to pick one only once—if you choose to do so at all. A theme governs some of the default formats in a workbooks, such as the color scheme that will be applied and the primary font. The default theme is the Office theme, which is relatively reserved, with a standard white background and unobtrusive colors. Go ahead and experiment with the different options, available by selecting **Page Layout > Themes** and shown below, to see what suits your needs.

Text, Cell, Row, and Column Formatting

Most workbooks have a standard font throughout, and that's how every workbook starts out. As discussed in Chapter 5, you'll save yourself a lot of time if you build a model and get the kinks worked out of it *before* you start applying a lot of formatting. Otherwise, you're likely to end up redoing it several times as you add and remove elements. I'm not saying you shouldn't add bits of formatting here and there to make it easier to navigate the model when you're designing it. However, you should try not to spend a lot of time adding finishing touches before your workbook is set up to function the way you want.

Formatting a workbook for distribution isn't necessarily very tough or time-consuming. Even if you're not especially artistic or graphically oriented, you will easily learn how to quickly draw attention to certain key points by making them a bit larger, bolded, or even a different color. You'll generally apply most of this type of differentiation on header rows and subtotal/total rows. You might also find that you want to use currency or other formatting for some of your numbers; when you do, you need to be careful to use the display formats that are best for your users. Many Excel users, for example, are tempted to use too many decimal places when two or three would probably do.

Another common problem is that users often don't clearly label what numbers have what significance. For example, if you have the number 225.99 | 45.67 | 43.98 | 1250.93 in a workbook, how does a user know which of these numbers might be dollar amounts or percentages? You don't necessarily have to add number formatting to each series of numbers, but many financial models do use a number format on at least the first row of data in each set. Again, remember your audience. Whereas that finance/accounting folks don't often use number formatting, if you try to use the same style in a sales organization, people will end up scratching their heads because they're just not used to looking at reports that way.

The following is a before example of the cash flow summary you worked with in Chapter 5.

CASH RECEIPTS	01/03/11	01/10/11	01/17/11	01/24/11	01/31/11
Cash Sales	$78.26	$41.66	$87.76	$0.16	$50.03
Collections fm CR accounts	$67.94	$63.35	$18.05	$16.65	$46.89
Loan/ other cash inj.	$21.23	$96.19	$5.38	$56.24	$61.55
TOTAL CASH RECEIPTS	$167.42	$201.20	$111.19	$73.05	$158.46
PURCHASES	01/03/11	01/10/11	01/17/11	01/24/11	01/31/11
Salaries & Wages	$55.73	$86.65	$2.02	$10.77	$69.04
Payroll expenses (taxes, etc.)	$82.33	$33.87	$59.94	$79.81	$6.49
Outside services	$29.67	$61.90	$30.91	$14.12	$33.88
Supplies (office & operating)	$18.41	$51.08	$64.02	$43.30	$90.80
Repairs & maintenance	$90.07	$3.72	$82.22	$64.60	$21.74

The following is the same sheet, formatted using fewer than 10 mouse clicks. All these changes were accomplished by selecting some ranges and then going to **Home > Cell Styles** and making selections there.

CASH RECEIPTS	01/03/11	01/10/11	01/17/11	01/24/11	01/31/11
Cash Sales	$78.26	$41.66	$87.76	$0.16	$50.03
Collections fm CR accounts	$67.94	$63.35	$18.05	$16.65	$46.89
Loan/ other cash inj.	$21.23	$96.19	$5.38	$56.24	$61.55
TOTAL CASH RECEIPTS	**$167.42**	**$201.20**	**$111.19**	**$73.05**	**$158.46**
PURCHASES	01/03/11	01/10/11	01/17/11	01/24/11	01/31/11
Salaries & Wages	$55.73	$86.65	$2.02	$10.77	$69.04
Payroll expenses (taxes, etc.)	$82.33	$33.87	$59.94	$79.81	$6.49
Outside services	$29.67	$61.90	$30.91	$14.12	$33.88
Supplies (office & operating)	$18.41	$51.08	$64.02	$43.30	$90.80
Repairs & maintenance	$90.07	$3.72	$82.22	$64.60	$21.74

This simple example should give you an idea of what you can do in a very small amount of time. You might notice in the second example that the worksheet's gridlines have been turned off (by unselecting the Gridlines checkbox on the View tab), and the applied shading and borders are clearer.

The majority of the formatting elements are on the Home tab in the Font, Alignment, Number, and Styles groups (see below).

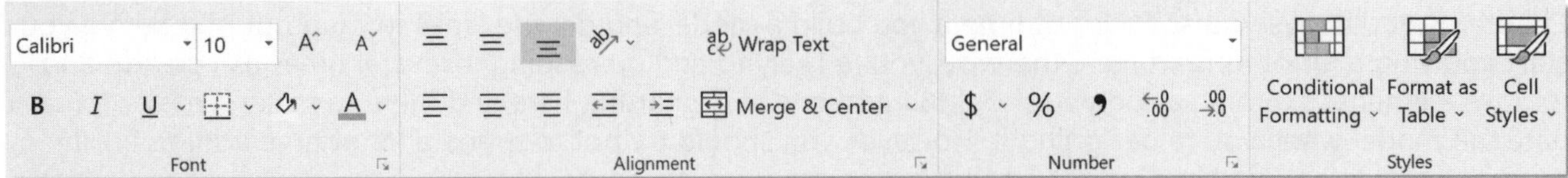

While it's important to know what your formatting options are, you should also know that it's very easy to apply so many different formats that you can't easily manage them all. You're much better off using the pre-defined options available at **Home > Cell Styles** if you want to apply different formats; if you do, when you need to change a format, you simply modify the style, and Excel automatically changes everything to which the style has been applied. Many Excel users manually apply formats throughout their workbooks and then find themselves spending hours updating those formats one by one. Efficiently using the Cell Styles options and eliminating redundant work should be something you always think about before you start applying individual formats. In fact, except when it comes to number formats and alignment, I almost always use Cell Styles.

Styles

Styles are incredibly handy to use, especially in workbooks that require input, although you are likely to need to customize them a bit to suit your tastes. The nice thing about styles is that you can quickly apply a style to either a single cell or an entire range. If you find yourself needing a lot of input from users, it might be worth the time to modify existing styles to do what you want or even create some customized styles of your own. If you want to modify a style, select **Home > Cell Styles**, right-click a style in the screen shown below and select Modify, and make any changes you like.

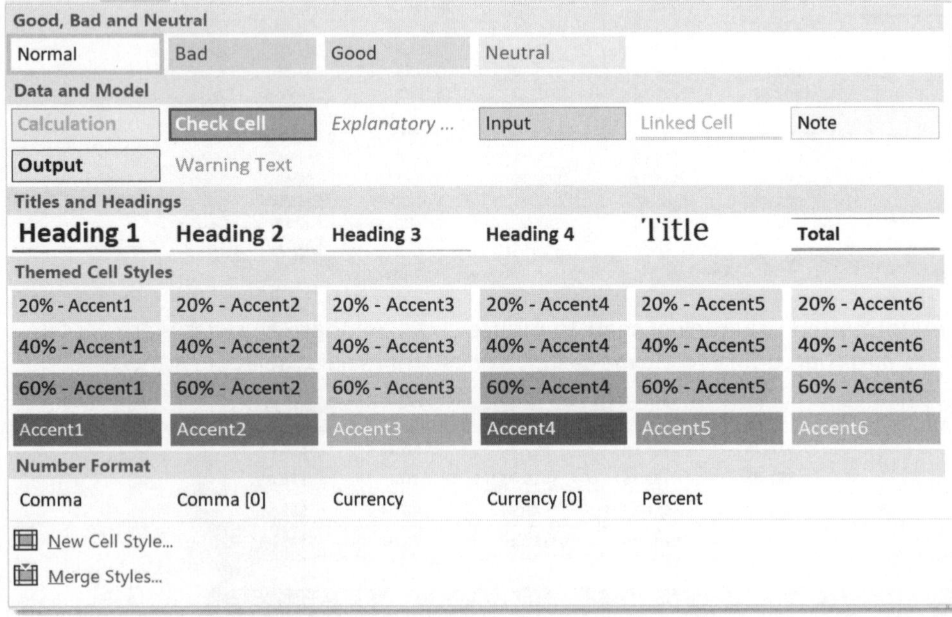

Borders

Borders can be great tools for segmenting data, but as with other elements, you need to put some thought into using them. If you just format everything with borders, you might as well just leave gridlines on. Ideally, you want to use borders to direct the flow of information and make it easy for people to quickly understand what's going on.

In the cash flow example shown below, only the total/average rows have had borders applied, but this is a very small model. In larger models, you might want to use continuous borders (i.e., with a border applied to each of the four sides) everywhere to make the information easier read. Continuous borders can also be useful on a worksheet that is going to be printed out for people who don't necessarily have the convenience of highlighting a particular row/column but need to use their fingers to follow along.

PURCHASES	January	February	March	April
Salaries & Wages	$52.59	$68.03	$25.95	$29.19
Payroll expenses (taxes, etc.)	$38.41	$40.45	$46.50	$72.33
Outside services	$74.47	$91.54	$10.28	$99.78
Supplies (office & operating)	$49.46	$19.49	$74.87	$7.68
Repairs & maintenance	$99.35	$20.97	$46.89	$25.91
Advertising	$94.89	$63.77	$90.66	$77.51
Transportation	$76.15	$98.09	$45.44	$46.96
Accounting & legal	$62.57	$54.36	$16.01	$50.24
Rent	$30.48	$44.09	$28.75	$75.54
Telephone	$16.68	$61.06	$49.45	$79.56
Utilities	$16.94	$62.28	$86.42	$69.59
Insurance	$20.28	$11.13	$16.62	$42.19

To apply borders, first select the range you want to cover and then go to **Home > Borders** and select the border style you want from the drop-down options, shown at right. It is easy to apply all of the standard borders just by clicking on them, although some borders do need to be applied in sequence. For instance, if you were to apply Thick Outside Border to a range and then apply All Borders, you would immediately wipe out the thick border. A general rule of thumb with borders is to apply inside formatting first and work outward, applying the outer border last.

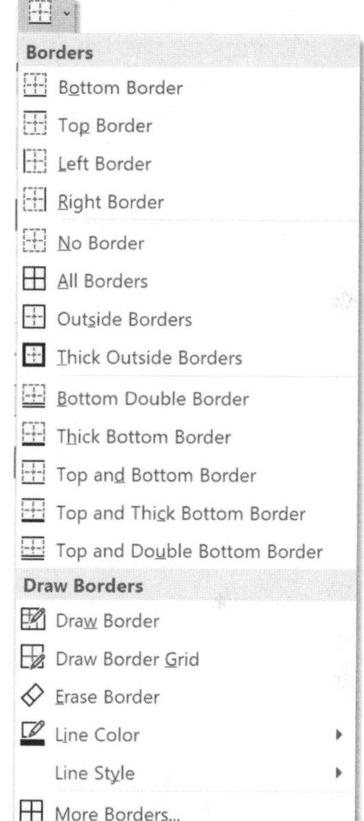

The More Borders option launches the Format Cells dialog. While the general Borders dialog also includes most of the settings you'll find here, the Format Cells dialog also makes available diagonal borders. In addition, you can modify the line styles you apply; for instance, the total rows in the cash flow example uses top and bottom double borders, which are fairly standard financial borders.

The following border tools have some advantages over other border application methods:

- **Draw Border**—This tool allows you to draw a border around the range of your choice without having to select it first. When you invoke the Draw Border tool, your worksheet suddenly looks like it has a case of the chickenpox, as it gets a bullet at each cell intersection. Next, your cursor turns into a pencil symbol. To draw a border, click where you want to start the border, drag to draw the border, and release the mouse when you're done. This is a neat trick for one-off borders where using this tool is faster than selecting a range. Note that Draw Border gives you only an outside border, not an inside border.
- **Draw Border Grid**—This tool draws all borders.
- **Erase Border**—This tool erases all borders, whether you used the Draw Border tools or placed the borders in the traditional fashion. This can be substantially faster than selecting a range and selecting No Border.

Fill Color

You should avoid using the Fill Color tool and its neighbor Font Color if you can. These tools might seem tempting since they're right there in the open on the Home tab, but they're a waste of time. As mentioned earlier, it's much better to use styles to achieve formatting because if you ever need to change a style, you only have to do it in one place at one time. If you use Fill Color and Font Color, on the other hand, you need to track down every single instance of that format and manually change it.

Fill Effects

You can apply additional formats to cell shading, and you get to them through the Fill tab of the Format Cells dialog (which you open by pressing **Ctrl+1)**, shown at right. The two options of note here are fill effects, which allow you to apply gradients to your cell shading, and patterns, which let you apply dot patterns to your cells.

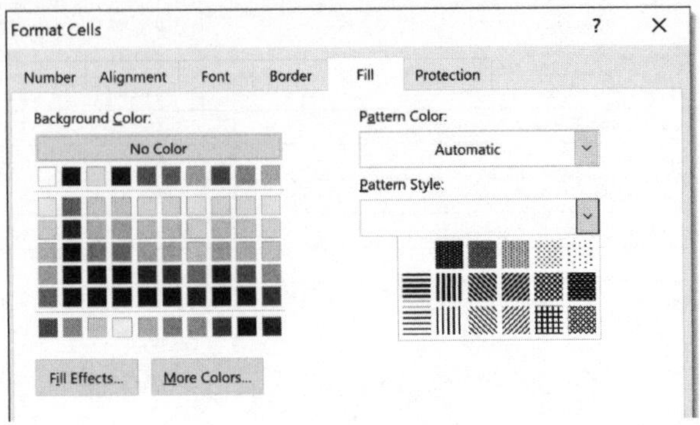

Clicking the Fill Effects button on the Fill tab of the Format Cells dialog brings up the Fill Effects dialog, shown below. Fill effects can end up being more distracting than they are helpful, as shown in the example below, and they should be reserved for non-data ranges, like dashboards, or an area where the pattern won't otherwise interfere with text. Some printers have an issue with rendering both fill effects and patterns properly, so you might not even see the output you want with certain fill effects and patterns applied. Generally, the denser the fill or pattern, the harder it is to see text that has a fill or pattern applied.

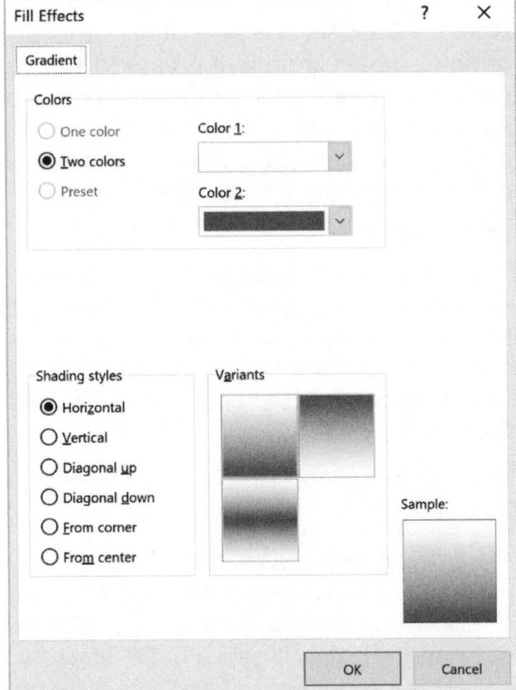

Fill Effects & Patterns can make it hard to see your data

Font Types

The Style gallery uses a mixture of font types (bold, italic, size, etc.), and it's perfectly acceptable to use a font to make something stand out. Just don't use too many different fonts on the same sheet because doing so can overwhelm your users with so much variation that the worksheet doesn't make sense.

Font Colors

Font colors come into play especially if you format rows and columns with cell shading. For darker shades, you should format with lighter colors, and for lighter shades, you should format with darker colors. Expressing too much artistic creativity can create unreadable sheets; for instance, the blue text on hot pink shading in the example below probably isn't the best combination (and will give users a headache), so check your workbook for usability before you send it out to others. (Sorry, printed book readers, that you can't see the color in the following example, but you are getting a good taste of how poorly some color combinations can print!) Another consideration is that some colors don't render too well on different monitors, so while a certain color combination might look great on your screen, it might be difficult to read on another.

CASH RECEIPTS	January	February	March
Cash Sales	$63.63	$7.81	$95.80
Collections fm CR accounts	$13.77	$35.02	$72

Alignment

Alignment can play a big role in the readability of your worksheets. One of the most common alignment mistakes is to center align everything; people tend to do this to create some visual separation between text in adjacent columns, but it can really mess up how numbers appear. Instead, try to stick with the text's default alignment, which is numbers to the right and text to the left. Here's an example where everything in the upper Cash Receipts section is centered, while the lower Purchases section has the text left-aligned and numbers right-aligned. When the numbers are centered, they don't line up properly, and the problem especially stands out in this example when some numbers display decimal points and others don't.

	A	B	C	D	E	F	G
1	CASH RECEIPTS	01/01/2019	02/01/2019	03/01/2019	04/01/2019	05/01/2019	Total
2	Cash Sales	$78	$41.66	$87.76	$0.16	$50	$257.87
3	Collections fm CR accounts	$67.94	$63	$18.05	$17	$46.89	$212.88
4	Loan/ other cash inj.	$21	$96.19	$5	$56.24	$62	$240.58
5	**TOTAL CASH RECEIPTS**	**$167.42**	**$201.20**	**$111.19**	**$73.05**	**$158.46**	**$711.33**
6							
7	PURCHASES	01/01/2019	02/01/2019	03/01/2019	04/01/2019	05/01/2019	Total
8	Salaries & Wages	$55.73	$86.65	$2.02	$10.77	$69.04	$224.21
9	Payroll expenses (taxes, etc.)	$82.33	$33.87	$59.94	$79.81	$6.49	$262.44
10	Outside services	$29.67	$61.90	$30.91	$14.12	$33.88	$170.48
11	Supplies (office & operating)	$18.41	$51.08	$64.02	$43.30	$90.80	$267.60

Hint: A caveat to centering is that if you turn on AutoFilter, either with Excel tables or standard data ranges, you might want to want to center your column headers so they're not obscured by the AutoFilter drop-downs.

Indenting/Outdenting

Indenting and outdenting are often overlooked, but they can help you handle some difficult alignment tasks. For instance, many people use leading spaces to make one row of data start a bit inside another by pressing the Spacebar a few times and then entering their text. Unfortunately, if you do this, you might make it much more difficult to use that data (text or values) down the road because you then need to get rid of the spaces. The indent/outdent tools make such situations easy to handle. Here's an example of some of the cash flow report's subcategories indented for readability.

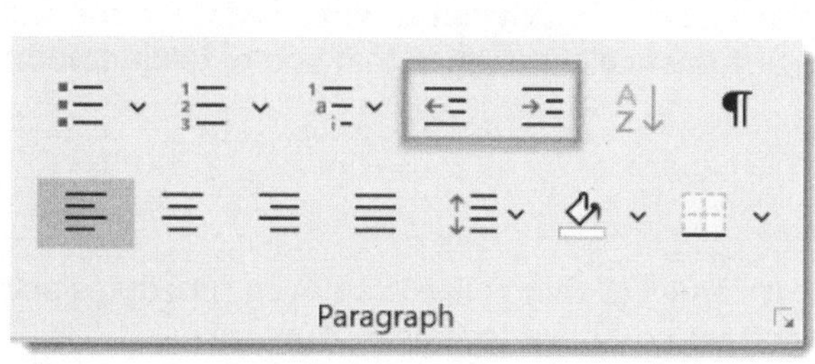

CASH RECEIPTS	January
Cash Sales	$63.63
Collections fm CR accounts	$13.77
Loan/ other cash inj.	$17.45
TOTAL CASH RECEIPTS	**$94.84**
Weekly Average	$18.97

Consider the following alignment tips:

- Try to avoid center alignment with currency figures (although some dates and percentages can be center aligned).

- Never use Merge & Center to try to align elements of your worksheets; instead, use Center Across Selection. You can do this by selecting the cell with the text you want to center, as well as the cells you want to center across. Then open the Format Cells dialog (by pressing **Ctrl+1**), go to the Alignment tab, and select Center Across Selection from the Horizontal group.
- Use the indent/outdent tools instead of spaces or extra columns for data that butts up against other data (both text and numerals).

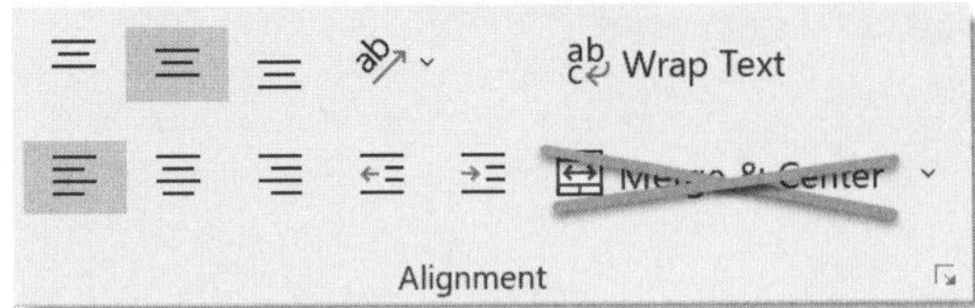

Number Formatting

We discussed the available number formats in Chapter 3. The following sections expand on the date, time, percentage, text format, special, and custom formatting options.

Dates

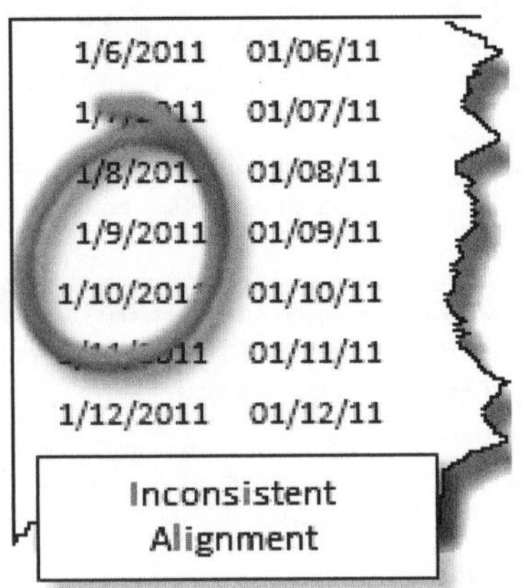

Excel's standard date format is *M/D/YYYY* (e.g., 8/1/2018), but it offers plenty of other choices—and if you don't find one that suits your needs, you can create your own custom format. Changing the Date format (or any number format, for that matter) is as simple as selecting a range, opening the Format Cells dialog (by pressing **Ctrl+1**), and selecting the format you want in the Number tab. In financial models, you'll often see *DD/MM/YY* used because it remains a consistent length, regardless of the date (e.g., 01/12/18). This can be very helpful in terms of alignment, especially if your date values are in a column.

> **Hint:** Unfortunately, one of the hardest things for new Excel users to grasp is that they don't need to enter certain symbols when entering numbers. For example, in a currency formatted cell, you would not enter $1,234.56 but simply 1234.56. You can use data validation input messages in entry cells to let people know how to enter numbers. You'd be amazed how much time this can save!

If you want to create a different date format, in the Format Cells dialog, go to the Number tab, select the Custom option, and play around until you get what you want. For instance, the long date above could be custom formatted as *dddd, mmmm dd, yyyy*. Don't worry about case in your custom settings (*M* vs. *m*, *d* vs. *D*, etc.) because Excel doesn't care.

You saw earlier that you can perform mathematical functions on dates. For example, in the cash flow example you saw the use of **=A1+1**, where A1 holds a valid date. You can also have a standard date in a cell with **=TODAY()** but format it to show the month or the day only instead of the date.

Unlike with currency and other numeric values, dates need a valid separator between day, month, and year when they're entered. You can use either the forward slash (/) or hyphen (-) as a separator. Unfortunately, periods aren't recognized, so 12.15.16 doesn't work; Excel sees this as text. If you want to enter a date in the current year, you can enter just the *day/month* (e.g., 12/31). Excel automatically assumes that you're talking about the current year and appends it for you.

Times

Times generally get less play in Excel than dates, except when it comes to things like employee schedules and timecards. Unfortunately, times can be a bit difficult to enter, and you do have to follow some rules.

Whole times, like 9:00 AM, can simply be entered as **9 a** or **9 p**, and Excel automatically converts them to valid times for you. But you have to be careful about the space between the number and a or p, as entering a time without the space ends up displaying as text. If you don't include a or p with a time, Excel converts the time to AM. You can also enter A instead of a and P instead of p, as Excel doesn't care about case here.

Fractional times must be entered with a colon between hours and minutes—for example, 10:15—and you can still enter a or p afterward to specify AM or PM.

If you're dealing with 24-hour time, you can just enter *hours:minutes* separated by a colon. Excel gets it and displays the *H:MM:SS* AM/PM equivalent in the formula bar—if your locale settings are set for the United States. (The specific format used is dependent on your locale settings.)

If you enter a time that's not possible, such as10:70 PM, Excel does not understand what you mean. Fortunately, it displays most invalid times as text, and you can reenter them at any time.

Just as with dates, you can use times in calculations—provided that the times are entered properly. For instance, you can calculate the number of hours an employee was on the job each day, including breaks, lunch, and so on. You can even use Excel to perform complex overtime calculations. (You can find plenty of Excel time resources with a quick Bing search.)

Percentages

Percentages in Excel are straightforward, and the only thing you need to do is choose how many decimal places you want to display; in most cases, two or three should suffice. Remember to apply percentage formatting *prior* to entering any data, or your number will be multiplied by 100, and you'll need to reenter it.

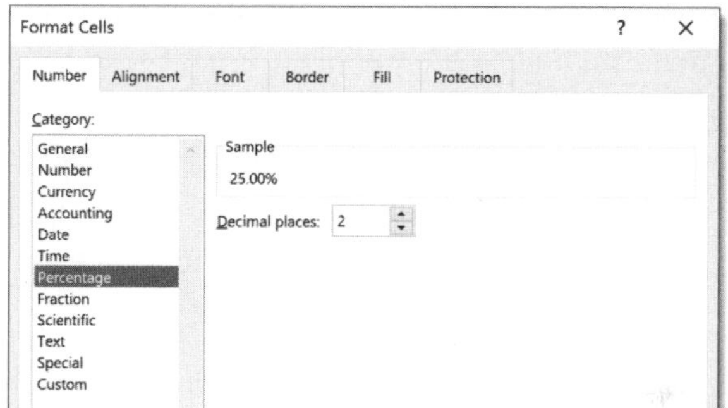

In addition, there is no negative number format for percentages, which can sometimes cause somewhat conflicting views because there are negative formats for other type of numbers. For instance, negative currency amounts might show up in parentheses and in red text—for example, ($1,234.56) (though you can't see the red if you're reading a printed version of this book)—and might look inconsistent next to percentages, which are prefixed by minus signs and appear in black text—for example, -12.5%. Fortunately, you can use conditional formatting for negative values, as discussed shortly.

Text Format

As discussed earlier in this chapter, the text format allows you to use certain value strings that you normally couldn't use if they were formatted as numbers, such as leading 0s. The TEXT function, as discussed in Chapter 6, allows you to do some text formatting, and it can be a great tool for mixing text and referential data. All you need is your text, the & to join it with your reference, and the number format of your choice (e.g., **="Today is: "&TEXT(TODAY(),"MM/DD/YY")**).

Special

Unfortunately, the predefined special formats don't get used nearly as much as they should. Invariably, if you look at a worksheet with customer information, you'll see phone numbers entered several different ways. This type of mess generally happens because the people who enter the data don't know that they can just enter plain numbers, and Excel will do the formatting for them. So, someone might enter a phone number like (760) 552-1212, and another might use the format 760.555.1212. The problem is that to do anything with data like this, you need to parse out the formatting characters to normalize the dataset. You don't want to send out a nice letter with a bunch of different number formats.

If you're going to be dealing with any degree of user input, going to the small effort of using special formats can eliminate many headaches. Fortunately, you can also use data validation to remind people how to enter their data. It's not likely that these measures will prevent data from occasionally being mis-entered, but they will catch most problems, and any time saved in not having to manipulate data that's already been entered is a win. Think about it this way: Once data has been entered in a digital environment, it should never have to be manipulated again. Sure, it can be used in calculations and references, but no one should ever need to go back and correct a manually entered format.

Note: When formatting characters (such as hyphens) are manually entered in numbers, Excel no longer sees values but sees text. It's unlikely that you would perform mathematical calculations on either phone numbers or zip codes, but this might be an issue with other data.

Custom

When nothing else fits, you can create a custom format. You can get a good idea of how to build a custom format by changing the format of a cell and then going to the Format Cells dialog, selecting the Number tab, and selecting the Custom option so you can see a sample of that format.

Format Painter

The Format Painter is one of the best tools to have in your formatting arsenal. You can use it to copy the formatting applied to a cell and then transfer that formatting to another cell. Even better, the Format Painter lets you select entire rows or columns and replicate their formatting. As a simple example, take a look at the Cash Flow - Unformatted worksheet in the Chapter 7 companion workbook. Select the first row of data (A1:G1) and apply the formatting that you want. (The formatted example uses a blue background with white text, but you can do anything you want.) When you're done, select the entire row (by clicking on the row header) and double-click the Format Painter button on the Home tab. Then click on the total rows (rows 7 and 33), and your formats are immediately applied. Press **Esc** to reset the Format Painter so it's no longer active.

When you start working with the Format Painter on some of your own worksheets, you'll quickly find out just how handy it can be. The following are some tips to keep in mind while using it:

- Single-clicking the Format Painter button on the Home tab enables the Format Painter for one click. Double-clicking, on the other hand, keeps the Format Painter enabled until you press **Esc**.
- When copying formats, it's generally easier to select an entire row or column than to select a range. Excel can remember every format in the selected row or column and apply it to your destination row(s)/column(s). If you select a range, on the other hand, you need to select a like range to apply the formatting, or you'll get some unexpected results. For example, go to the Cash Flow – Simple Format worksheet in the Chapter 7 companion workbook, select A1:A10, and then go back to the unformatted example and apply the formatting to A1. Oops! That's not quite what you wanted. Excel applied a repeating pattern, didn't it? (FYI, unless you want that formatting to stick, you should press **Ctrl+Z** now.)
- You can generally select a single cell and apply its format to multiple cells and ranges without issue.
- When you apply formatting by using the Format Painter, it wipes out any existing formatting in the destination range(s) to which you apply it.

Worksheet Tab Colors

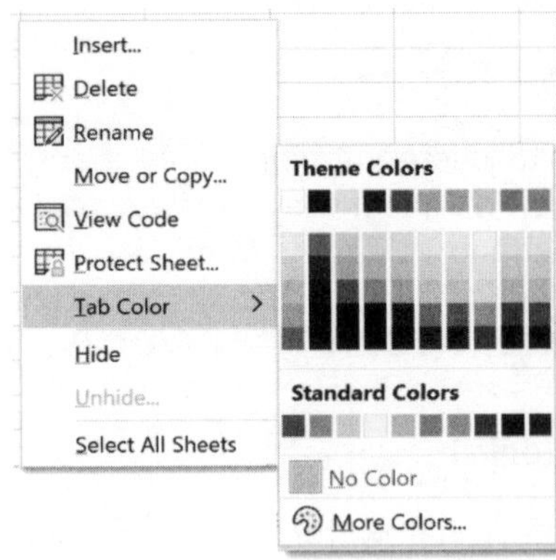

Lotus 1-2-3 allowed you to make worksheet tabs different colors, but it took Microsoft a while to finally relent and build that functionality into Excel. Why is this important? Most people generally don't see the worksheet tabs at the bottom of a workbook unless you point them out. This can be challenging if you're walking someone through a workbook on the phone and you say, "Okay, now go to the Cash Flow tab...," and they say "What?" Instead you can simply say, "Just click on the red tab at the bottom of the screen. It says Cash Flow on it." You would be amazed at how much easier it is to direct people to the worksheet tabs if you add just a little bit of color. You can also set up tab groups by color (e.g., orange could be for data input worksheets, blue for data output sheets, yellow for hidden sheets). To apply a color to a worksheet tab, just right-click on the sheet tab, click **Tab Color**, and choose a color.

Cash Flow - Unformatted | Cash Flow - Simple Format | Cash Flow - Monthly | Conditional Formatting | Custom Views & Auto-Filter | Page Break Preview | Notes

Note: While the ability to assign colors to worksheet tabs can be really helpful, if you're going to do this with any regularity, you should come up with a consistent color convention. You may end up confusing people if your sheet groupings are different each time.

Hiding Key Data

One thing you'll likely run into in your workbooks is the need to *not* display certain information. Let's say you've expanded on the weekly cash flow to have a monthly rollup, and you want to include a weekly average by month.

Many companies work on a 5-4-4 accounting schedule, which means that starting in January, each month has 5 weeks, then 4, then 4, then back to 5, until the end of the year. To get accurate weekly averages, you need to divide total monthly revenue by the number of weeks in each month. You could use =B6/5, =C6/4, =D6/4, etc., but to do that, you need to hardcode values in formulas, which you should avoid at all costs. Instead, you can put the 5-4-4 references in an unused row, usually above your data (as shown below), and reference them.

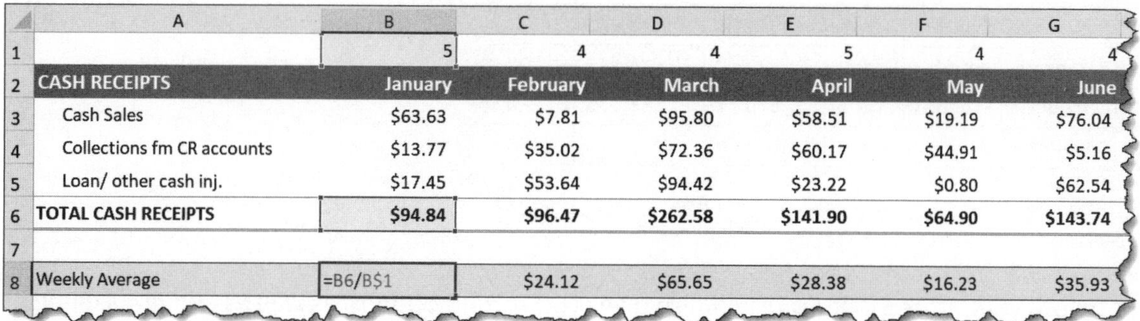

	A	B	C	D	E	F	G
1		5	4	4	5	4	4
2	CASH RECEIPTS	January	February	March	April	May	June
3	Cash Sales	$63.63	$7.81	$95.80	$58.51	$19.19	$76.04
4	Collections fm CR accounts	$13.77	$35.02	$72.36	$60.17	$44.91	$5.16
5	Loan/ other cash inj.	$17.45	$53.64	$94.42	$23.22	$0.80	$62.54
6	TOTAL CASH RECEIPTS	$94.84	$96.47	$262.58	$141.90	$64.90	$143.74
7							
8	Weekly Average	=B6/B$1	$24.12	$65.65	$28.38	$16.23	$35.93

Unfortunately, now you have some data in your worksheet that no one needs to see. You can handle this in a couple different ways:

- **Trick #1**—The most common trick is to just hide the row by selecting **Home > Format > Hide & Unhide > Hide Rows** (or pressing **ALT+O+R+H**). This doesn't work, however, if there's information on that row that does need to remain visible.
- **Trick #2—**You can format the font in these cells to look the same as their background. In the case of the cash flow example, you would just change the font to white. As you can see below, although the 5-4-4s are still there, they're no longer visible. Fortunately, what people can't see, they usually don't bother trying to find and change.

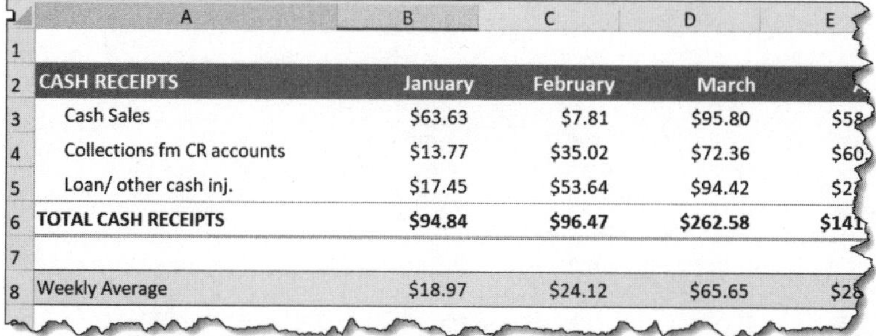

	A	B	C	D	E
1					
2	CASH RECEIPTS	January	February	March	
3	Cash Sales	$63.63	$7.81	$95.80	$58
4	Collections fm CR accounts	$13.77	$35.02	$72.36	$60
5	Loan/ other cash inj.	$17.45	$53.64	$94.42	$2
6	TOTAL CASH RECEIPTS	$94.84	$96.47	$262.58	$141
7					
8	Weekly Average	$18.97	$24.12	$65.65	$2

Caution: There are lots of ways to hide your data, but just hiding data doesn't mean it's protected from inadvertent or intentional changes. If necessary, make sure that any hidden cells are locked and always be sure to protect a worksheet before distributing it!

AutoFilter

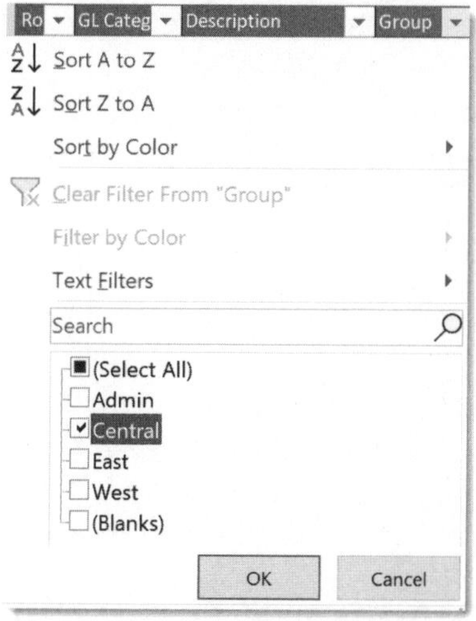

AutoFilter is one of the most powerful tools you can give users, especially in the case of a lot of data. In the previous section, you saw how to hide information from users. AutoFilter allows you to temporarily hide information that users don't want to see. In the Custom Views & Auto-Filter worksheet you just used for the custom views examples, go to **Data > Filter**. You immediately see drop-downs appear in the header row for each column. This is how Excel enables you to selectively hide or show data, based on almost any criteria you want.

In this case, say that you just want to see the information for the Central region. As shown above, select the Group drop-down, uncheck Select All, check Central, and watch what happens. This is just a simple example, but it illustrates the flexibility of AutoFilter.

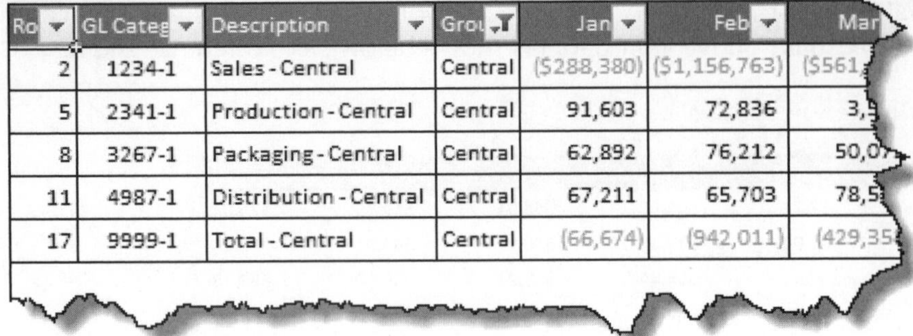

Ro	GL Categ	Description	Grou	Jan	Feb	Mar
2	1234-1	Sales - Central	Central	($288,380)	($1,156,763)	($561,
5	2341-1	Production - Central	Central	91,603	72,836	3,5
8	3267-1	Packaging - Central	Central	62,892	76,212	50,07
11	4987-1	Distribution - Central	Central	67,211	65,703	78,5
17	9999-1	Total - Central	Central	(66,674)	(942,011)	(429,35

In the examples below, you can see that AutoFilter also gives you sorting options, as well as additional filters, depending on whether your data is numeric or text. You can even sort and filter by text or cell color!

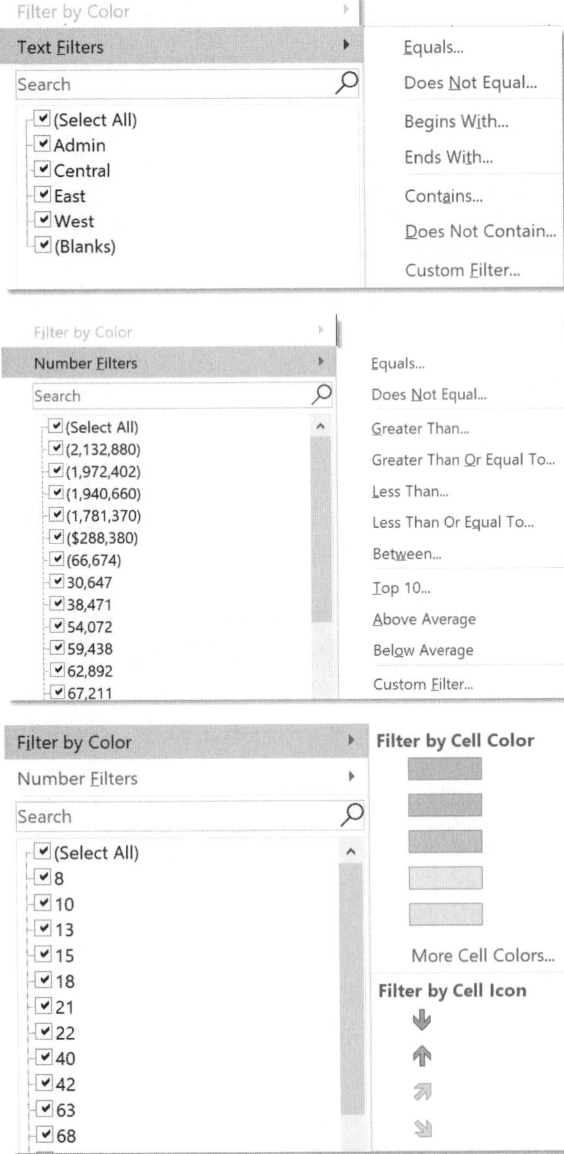

Conditional Formatting

You can add a lot of value to workbooks by identifying particular areas and pointing them out to your users. Most people highlight areas of importance in paper documents by using highlighters, and it probably wouldn't be too much of a stretch to say that almost every desk in the country has at least one highlighter in a drawer. Well, people also use highlighting in Excel: They go into a workbook and manually highlight certain cells or ranges that have particular characteristics, such as being over/under a certain value. There are a couple issues with doing this type of manual highlighting. First, finding and marking all those areas can be like finding the proverbial needle in a haystack. Also, it's easy to miss some things along the way, which means you may not accurately present your message. Finally, it's time-consuming. If one of the main points of the electronic spreadsheet is to save you time, manually highlighting cells certainly isn't a good use.

Conditional formatting allows you to define rules for cells and ranges and then apply formats to them when Excel determines that they meet the defined criteria. Let's say you have an inventory tracking sheet that helps you see when you reach certain product reordering thresholds. You could look through each line item, do a little mental count, and say, "Oh, we're down to 5 of that, so I need to reorder." Or you could set a rule in Excel to tell you when that happens by giving you a visual clue. For instance, you might tell Excel to highlight a cell green when the count of particular product is over 10, yellow when the count hits 10 pieces, and red when it gets down to 5. Setting up rules for such automatic visual clues is a lot easier than trying to manually search cells for data over and over.

Conditional formatting allows up to 64 different conditions in Excel 2019, which is a substantial increase over the 3 conditions available in earlier versions.

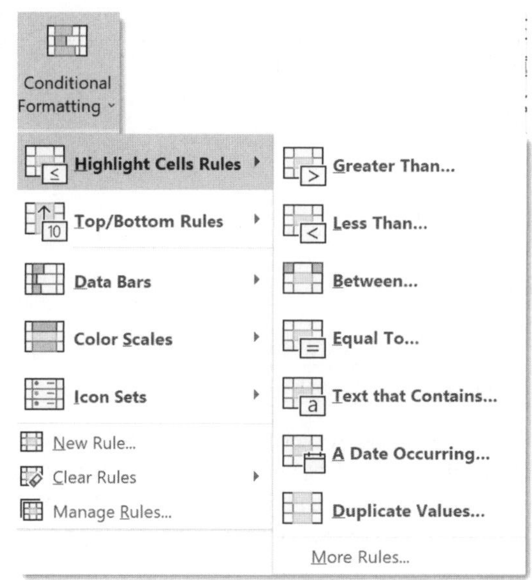

But the same rules apply to conditional formatting as to IF statements: Just because you can do something doesn't mean that you should. In this case, you'd be hard pressed to create 64 formats that are different enough from each other for your users to notice the differences between them. If the purpose of conditional formatting is to quickly showcase differences, then overwhelming the users with minute differences won't help. When you select **Home > Conditional Formatting**, you see five primary rules, as shown in the following figure and described in the following sections.

Highlight Cells Rules

In terms of trapping conditions, as in the inventory control example, you'll probably first turn to Highlight Cells Rules, as it is probably the most versatile conditional formatting option. You use this relatively straightforward option to format cells based on their values. Each option you select launches a secondary dialog, where you enter specifics. For example, the following example shows the dialog for the Less Than option and the resulting format. You can see that you can use a number of predefined formats, or you can choose Custom Format to launch the Format Cells dialog and create your own format. Each condition's dialog is slightly different. For instance, the Between option, which highlights all values between two values, has an option for the low value and another option for the high value.

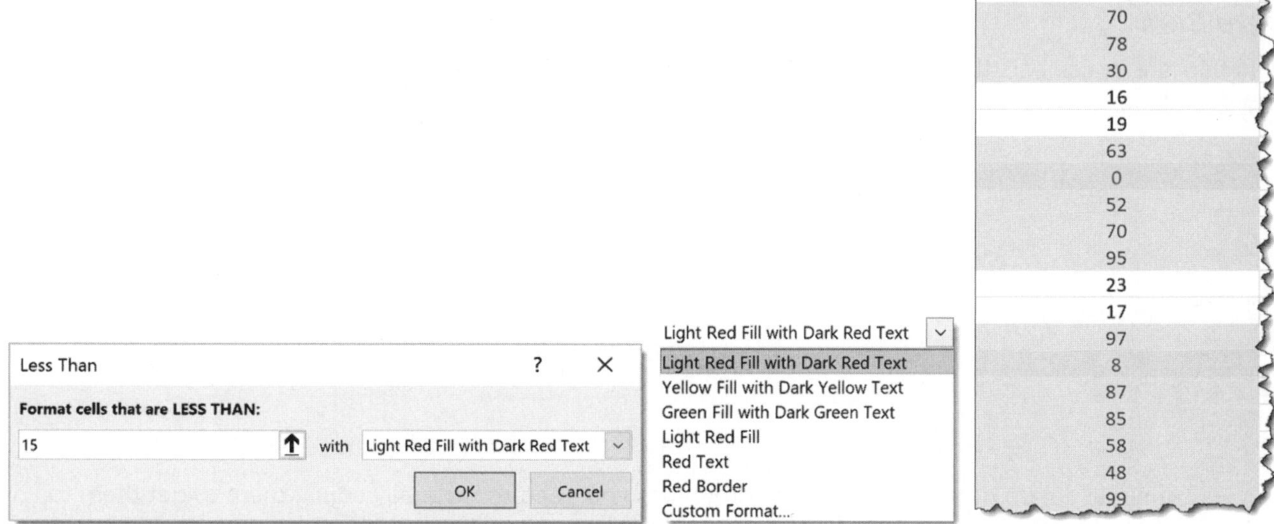

Excel now gives you two additional conditions you can add that previously had to be custom written with formulas:

- **A Date Occurring**—Allows you to format cells based on a cell's date in relationship to your system date.
- **Duplicate Values**—Allows you to identify duplicate/unique values in a range.

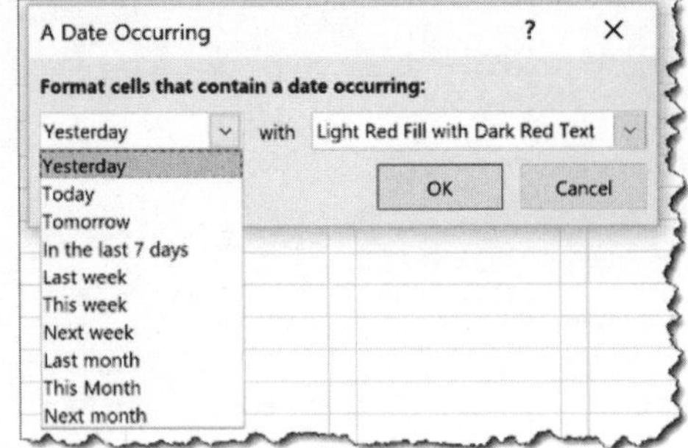

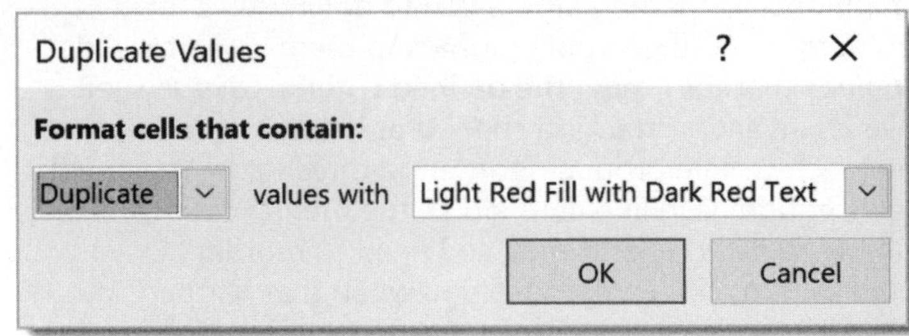

Top/Bottom Rules

Using the Top/Bottom Rules option is a very fast way to determine the ranks of certain items in a list. The Ribbon options limit you to either the top or bottom 10 or 10% and above and below the average value of the values list. With the Top/Bottom Rules option, you can easily adjust the value range in the New Formatting Rule dialog, as shown below.

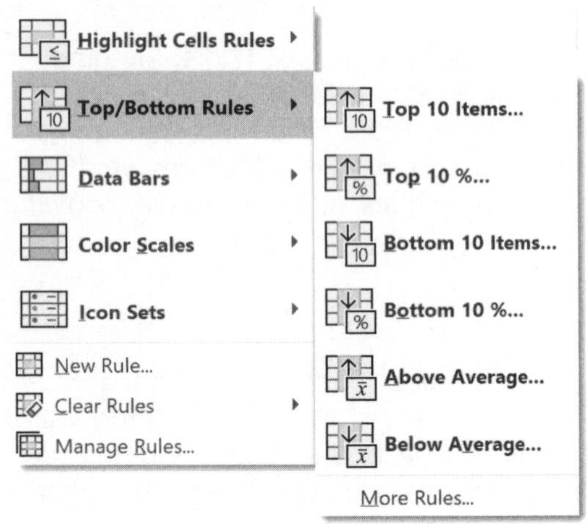

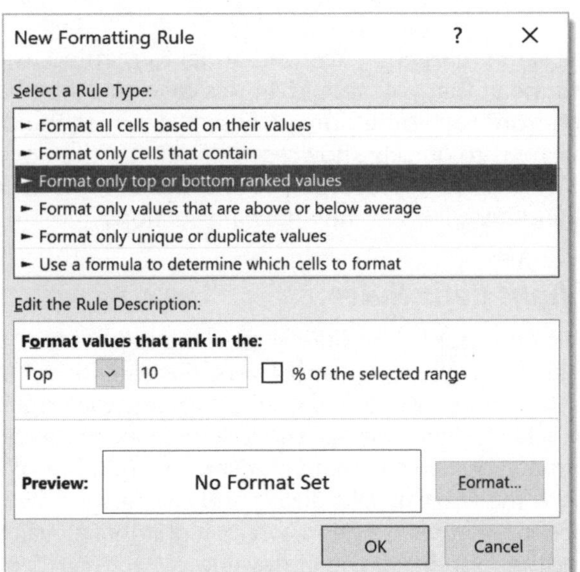

Data Bars

Data bars are in-cell bars that display horizontally and indicate, based on their length and gradient, each cell's value in relationship to the others.

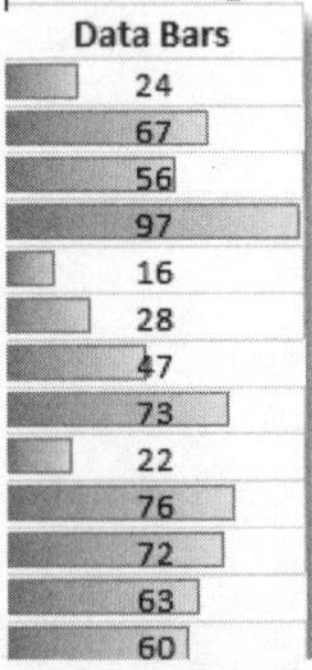

It's very simple to set up data bars. However, sometimes you need to manually adjust them to get them to scale properly and prevent certain figures from getting too much weight and others not enough. Adjusting data bars is very easy, and if the defaults aren't enough for you, you can click More Rules to find an expanded selection of options, as shown below.

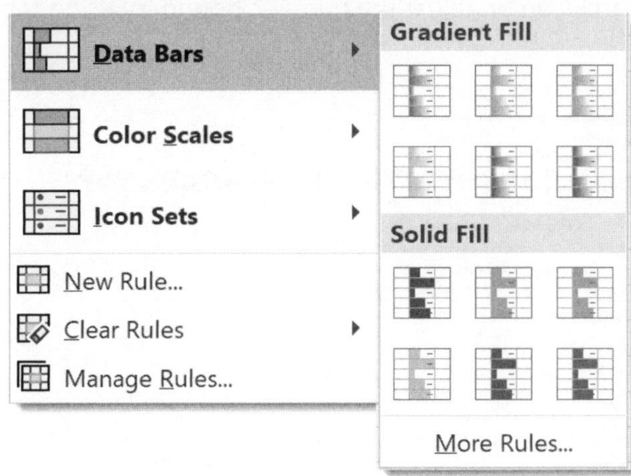

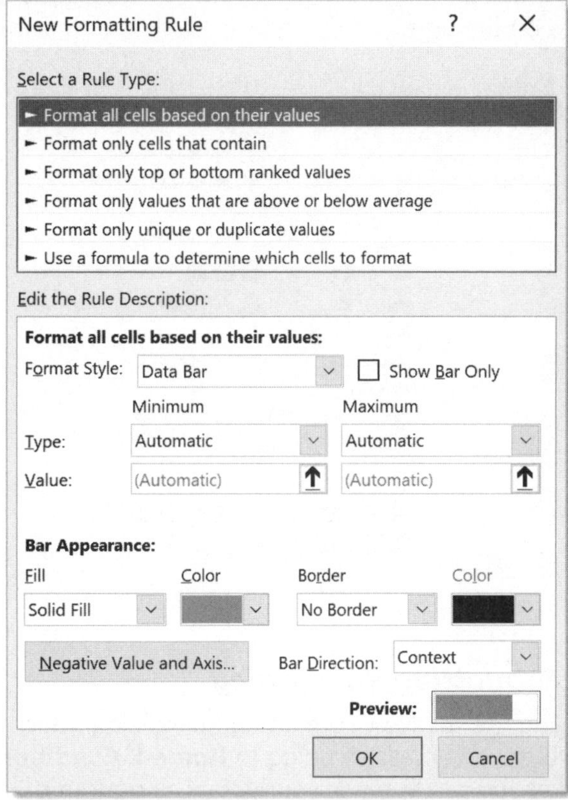

Color Scales

Color scales are like data bars except that instead of displaying an in-cell bar to represent a value, you shade the entire cell, and the intensity of the shade is determined by the cell's value in relationship to the others in the section.

If you don't like the default color selections, you can select More Rules and add your own custom colors.

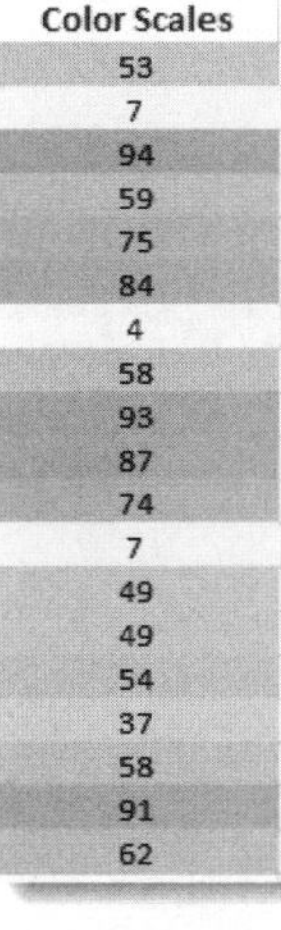

Color Scales
53
7
94
59
75
84
4
58
93
87
74
7
49
49
54
37
58
91
62

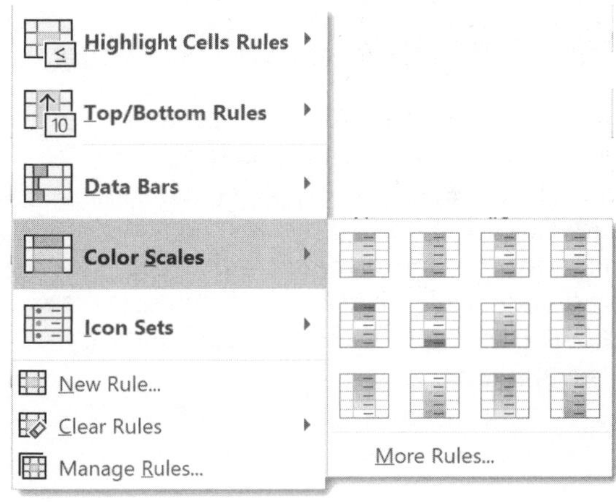

Icon Sets

You can use icon sets to add some graphics cells instead of the shading formats you've seen up to this point. When you use icon sets, it's important to keep in mind that the scale at which the various icons are applied is directly related to the number of objects in your selection. If you choose the stoplight pattern, as shown in the example below, the breaks will be at green when the value is greater than or equal to 67, yellow when the value is less than 67 but greater than or equal to 33, and red when the value is less than 33.

Basically, an icon set with three objects means splitting the values into thirds, an icon set with four objects means splitting the values into quarters, and so on.

Icon Sets
8
13
21
87
80
73
63
76
18
15
22

The built-in icon sets are shown below left. You can change the icon or adjust the numeric boundary using the settings on the right.

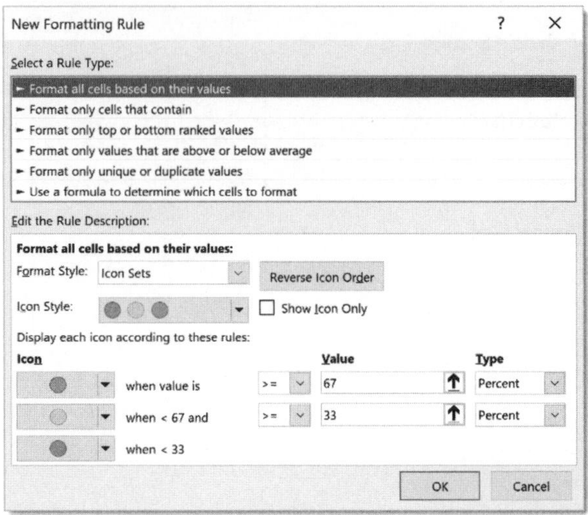

New Formatting Rule Dialog

When you use the New Formatting Rule dialog, which has already been shown several times in this chapter (and which you access by going to **Home > Conditional Formatting > New Rule**), you start with a list of six rules that you can apply to your data. The bottom of this dialog shows a preview of the formatting currently chosen. The following sections describe the six rules in the New Formatting Rule dialog.

Format All Cells Based on Their Values

The first rule, Format All Cells Based on Their Values, lets you make multiple decisions about what kind of values you want to format, what scale to use as the condition, and whether to format with a two- or three-color scale, data bars, or icon sets. The following example shows two scenarios, or rules, applied.

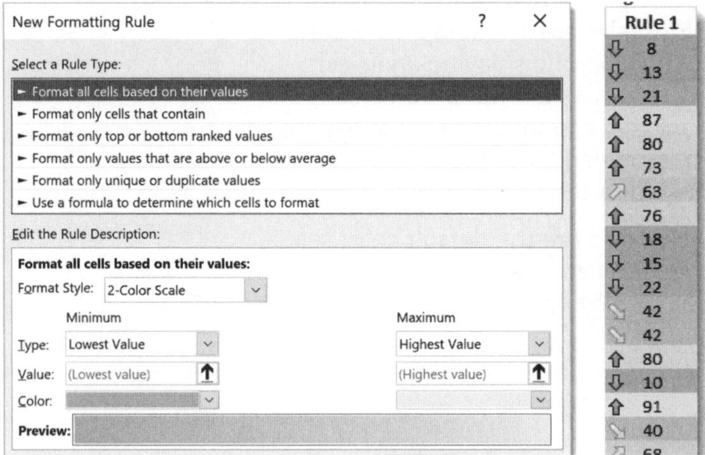

Format Only Cells That Contain

The Format Only Cells That Contain rule gives you multiple options, although, as you can see in the example below, your actual formatting options are limited.

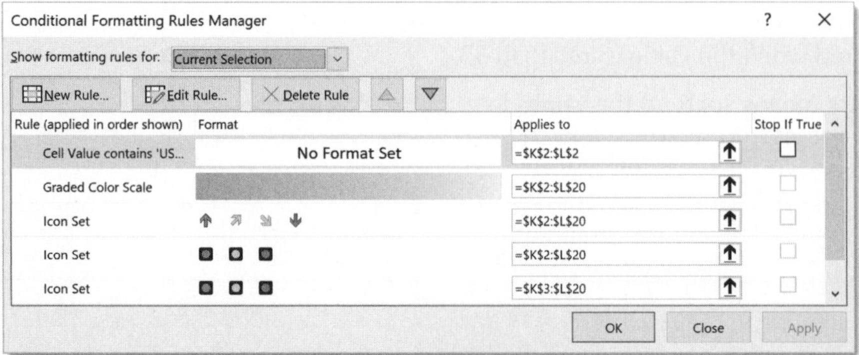

Format Only Top or Bottom Ranked Values

The rule Format Only Top or Bottom Ranked Values in the New Formatting Rule dialog is the same as the Top/ Bottom Rules option under **Home > Conditional Formatting**, but you can change the top/bottom values rather than use only the top or bottom 10, as you can do on the Home tab.

Format Only Values That Are Above or Below Average

With the rule Format Only Values That Are Above or Below Average in the New Formatting Rule dialog, you can select levels of standard deviation, as shown below.

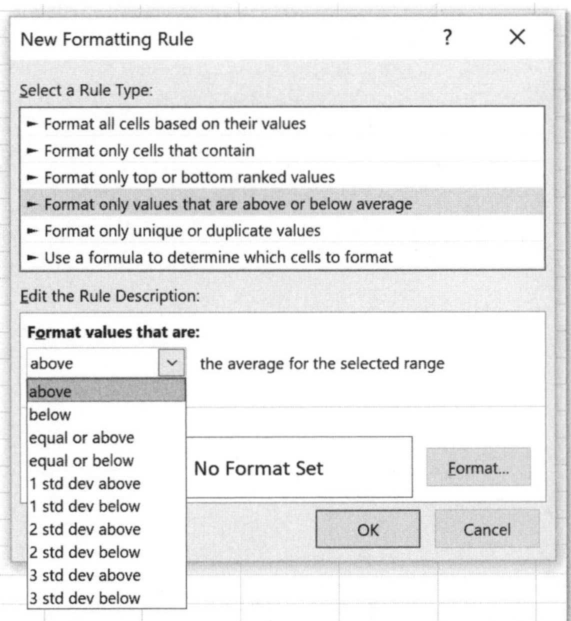

Format Only Unique or Duplicate Values

The rule Format Only Unique or Duplicate Values does the same thing as **Home > Conditional Formatting >Highlight Cells Rules > Duplicate Values**: It allows you to identify duplicate/unique values in a range

Use a Formula to Determine Which Cells to Format

The rule Use a Formula to Determine Which Cells to Format allows you to write a formula that conditional formatting needs to evaluate. In earlier versions of Excel, this was the only way to create complex evaluations, but there's little need to use this option now that there are so many more formatting options.

One handy thing you can do with this rule is shade every other row without using tables or shading manually. Select the range you want and then use the following formula:

=MOD(ROW(),2)=1

Then you can apply whatever fill you want, and every other row is shaded. Later, if you add or delete rows, the shading will be adjusted as needed.

Printing and Page Setup Options

Imagine that you're printing a worksheet, and your printer starts going wild, spitting out pages that are mostly blank. Unfortunately, this happens all the time when users forget to set up workbooks for printing. Why does this happen? Well, if you don't tell Excel what to do, it makes some assumptions on your behalf. The first is that you want to print in portrait orientation. The second is that you want to keep the document the same size it is now, or 100% scale. Finally, it assumes that you didn't want to change any of Excel's default print options. Imagine that you have a rather large worksheet that should be printed in landscape orientation (this is the orientation commonly used with financial statements and other worksheets dealing with months). When Excel sticks to its defaults, it automatically puts page breaks where it thinks they should go, so a worksheet that you want to print at 1 page wide by maybe 2 pages tall instead prints on 27 portrait orientation pages.

To see how Excel handles printing, in a blank worksheet, scroll down and across to cell AC250 or some other place that's out of the way and enter anything in a single cell; then press **Ctrl+Home** to get back to A1. In this way, you have defined Excel's print area, or the area that it will print unless you tell it otherwise. Now, go to **View > Page Break Preview**. You now see an odd grid display of your worksheet with the page number(s) overlaid above your data and a gray area to the right, which is the area outside of the print range (meaning that Excel will not print it); the figure below shows the Custom Views & Auto-Filter sheet in Page Break Preview mode. The blue dashed lines you see are the actual page breaks, and right now they're laid out based on what Excel thinks you want to do even with that single character in cell AC250. Excel doesn't know what you're printing; it only checks for a printable character and finds one in the defined print range. It doesn't care what or where it is, just that there's something there to print.

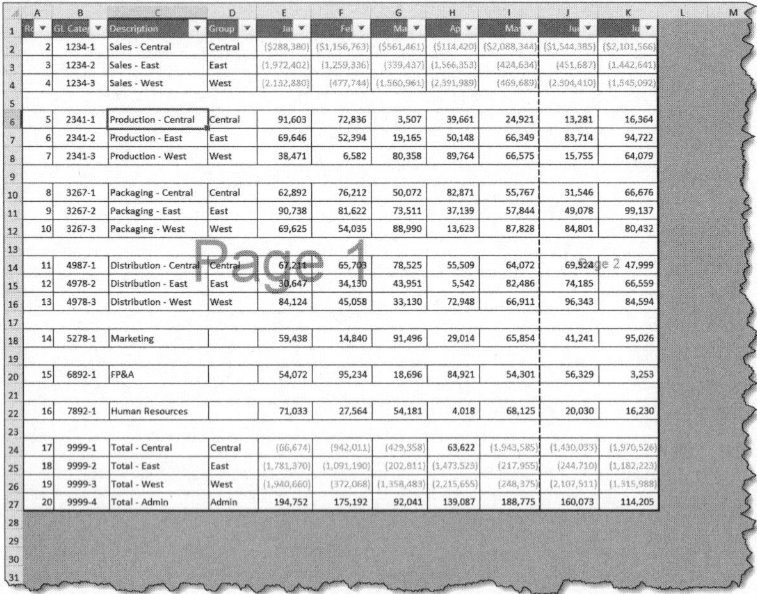

Fortunately, Excel's new automatic print preview has put a halt to a great deal of errant printing because you get a preview of what you'll print before you actually take that step. This doesn't mean you don't have to set up for printing, though, so the following sections go through the setup steps.

To follow along in the next several sections, open the companion workbook to the **Cash Flow - Simple Format** worksheet. The following sections discuss how to set printing and page setup options in Excel through the Print dialog, on the Page Layout tab, and in the Page Setup dialog.

> **Note:** It may seem silly to be talking about printing on paper when so many offices discourage it today. But even with paperless options (e.g., printing as a PDF), you need to know how to set up for printing.

Print Dialog Options

To open the Print dialog, press **Ctrl+P** or go to **File > Print**. In addition to choosing the number of copies to print and which printer to print to, you can adjust the following settings in this dialog:

- **The print area**—As shown here, you can choose to print the active worksheet, any grouped sheets, the entire workbook, or just an area that you select.
  Note: The Print Selection option comes in handy when you just need to print out a snippet of a worksheet. Print Selection does not overwrite any existing Page Setup options you might have set previously.

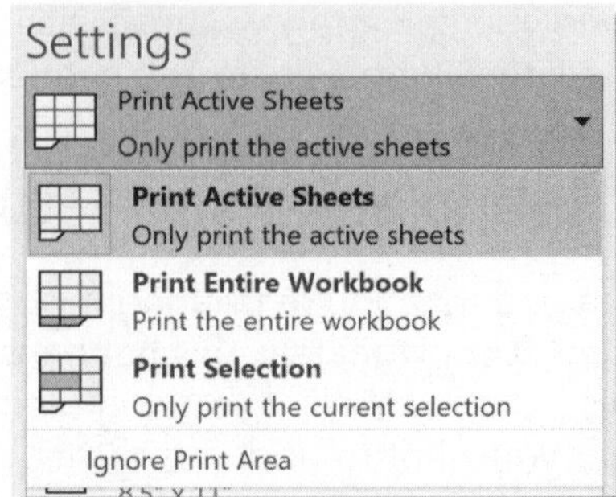

- **Pages**—If the worksheet has more than one page, you can choose which pages you want to print, so you could choose 1–3, 2–3, 4, etc.
- **Collated or Uncollated**—If you're printing multiple copies of a multi-page document, this choice can come in handy because you can choose Collated to print each complete document one at a time. If you

choose Uncollated, Excel prints each page multiple times and then proceeds to the next, and you end up with a big stack of paper that needs to be shuffled by hand. Fortunately, Collated is the default.

- **Orientation**—You can choose either Portrait or Landscape.
- **Paper size**—As shown below, you can choose one of the various standard paper sizes. The default U.S. paper size is 8.5" x 11".

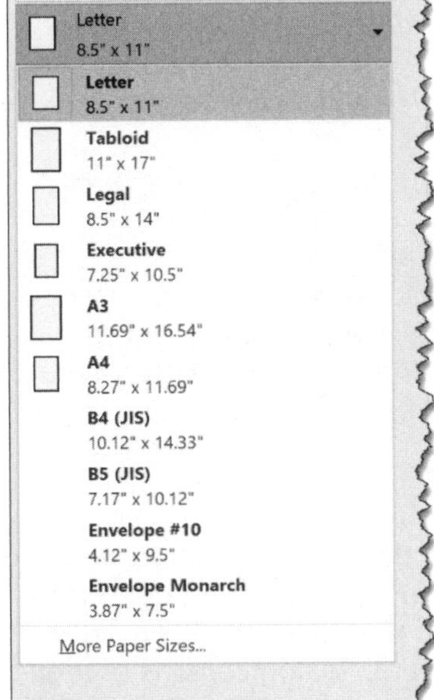

- **Scaling**—You can specify how much of the worksheet you want to fit on a page, as shown below. These are the options:
  - **Fit Sheet on One Page**—Prints one page wide by one page tall.
  - **Fit All Columns on One Page**—Prints one page wide.
  - **Fit All Rows on One Page**—Prints one page tall.

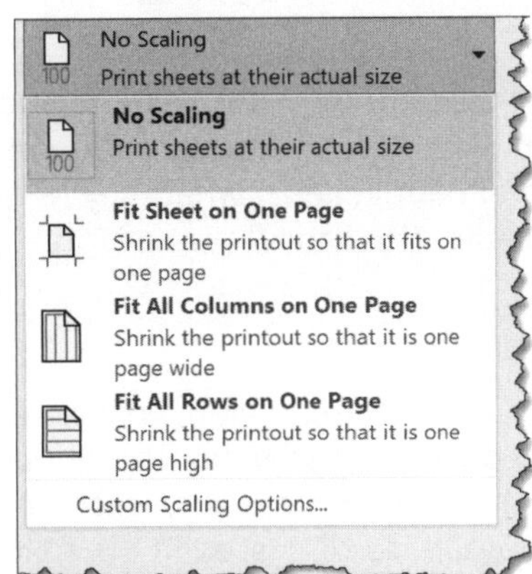

- **Margins**—You can set how close the printable area of your worksheet will be to the sides of the page. It's generally acceptable to set left and right margins at .25", but you need to be careful with top and bottom margins if you intend to use page headers and footers, which we discuss shortly.

In the case of the cash flow example, say that you want to print the worksheet one page tall by one page wide, in landscape orientation; you then need to select Landscape for the orientation and choose Fit Sheet on One Page as the scaling option. You then see the live preview automatically adjust to the new settings.

Page Layout Tab Options

The elements in the Page Setup group on the Page Layout tab are quite different from the Print dialog options because this Ribbon group doesn't deal directly with printer settings, such as collating, paper size, and what to print. It does, however, address some things that aren't exposed on the Print dialog. The following sections describe the four rightmost options in the Page Setup group (shown below).

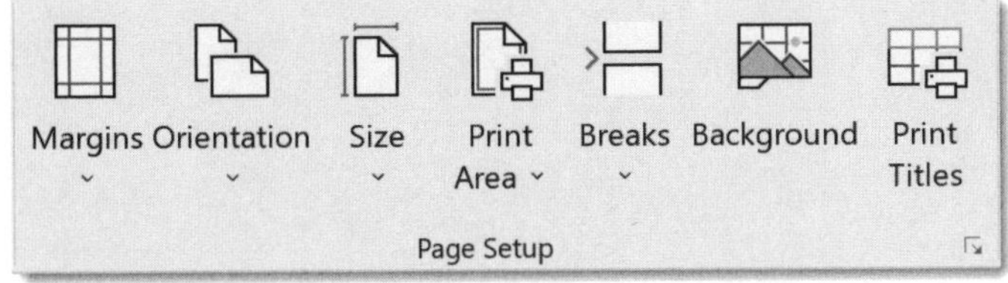

Print Area

The Print Area option lets you override Excel's default print area and set your own. By doing this, you can exclude certain areas that you don't want to print. You might, for example, have extra information on a worksheet that you don't want to print, and the Print Area option allows you to do that without having to hide those areas. You can also adjust the print area from **View > Page Break Preview** by dragging the solid blue lines up and down and left and right from their current positions.

Breaks

Where breaks occur, your pages are cut off and new pages begin. You have the choice of inserting and removing page breaks by selecting a row or column where you want a break and then selecting **Page Layout > Breaks** and then choosing the option you want. You also have the choice of resetting page breaks, but doing so does not clear any breaks that are naturally associated with the worksheet. You can also adjust page breaks by selecting **View > Page Break Preview** and dragging the breaks, but when you do this, they still fall within the confines of the current page setup; that is, you can't drag a page break past where it would normally fall (e.g., trying to force two pages into one) as Excel will just put it back, but you can drag a page break inward (e.g., creating two pages out of one). You often need to adjust page breaks so that they follow natural breaks in your data.

Background

While you can add a background behind your data, remember that people have to read past whatever you add, so make sure it doesn't obscure your data.

Print Titles

The Print Titles option allows you to choose whether you want to repeat row and column headers on each sheet. In the case of a multipage report, such as one that has dates across the top, you probably want to repeat the headers so that people know what they're looking at on later pages. When you click **Page Layout > Print Titles**, Excel launches the Page Setup dialog.

The Page Setup Dialog

In many ways, the Page Setup dialog is more complete than the Print dialog and the Page Layout tab, and you might just find yourself coming to this dialog to set up all your printing options instead of setting options in several places. To open the Page Setup dialog, click on the dialog launcher at the bottom of the Page Setup group on the Page Layout tab. As discussed in the following sections, the Page Setup dialog consists of four primary tabs, as well as some secondary options.

The Page Tab

You can use the Page tab of the Page Setup dialog to set orientation, scaling, paper size, and other options, as shown below.

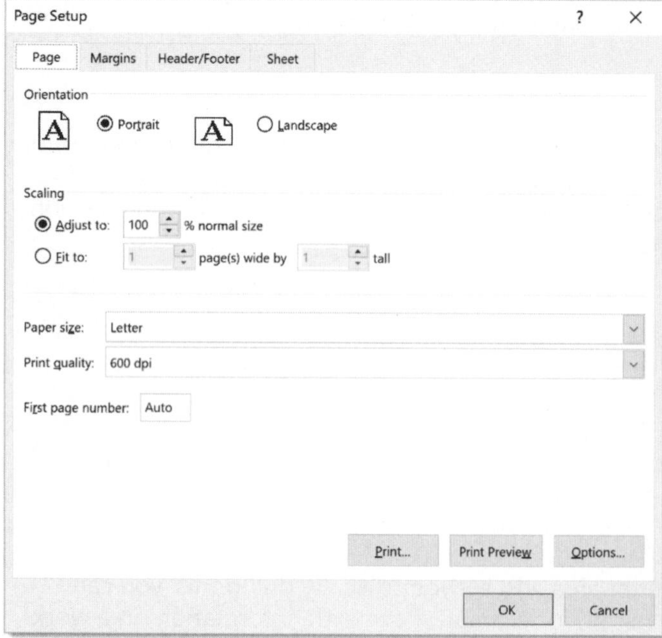

The Margins Tab

You can use the Margins tab of the Print Setup dialog to set margins, and this tab also allows you to center the worksheet on the page both horizontally and vertically. When you select either Horizontally or Vertically, you see the gridlines in the margin example move accordingly, as shown below.

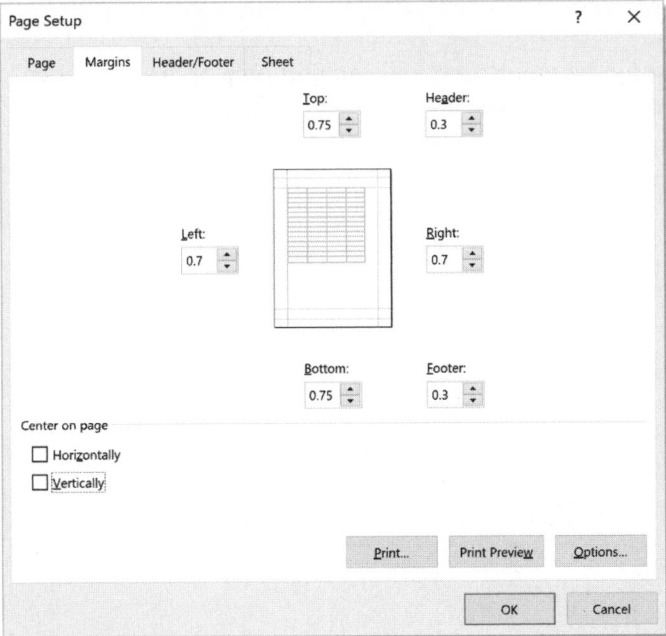

The Header/Footer Tab

The Header/Footer tab of the Print Setup dialog lets you repeat text at the top and bottom of each worksheet. Excel users often repeat the file name in the header and the date and page number in the footer. On this tab, if you click the Custom Header button, Excel opens the Header dialog (shown below), and if you click the Custom Footer button, Excel opens the Footer dialog. The buttons in both of these dialogs, from left to right, are:

- **Format Text**—It is easiest to use this option by adding any text you want, selecting that text, and clicking this button to change the format.

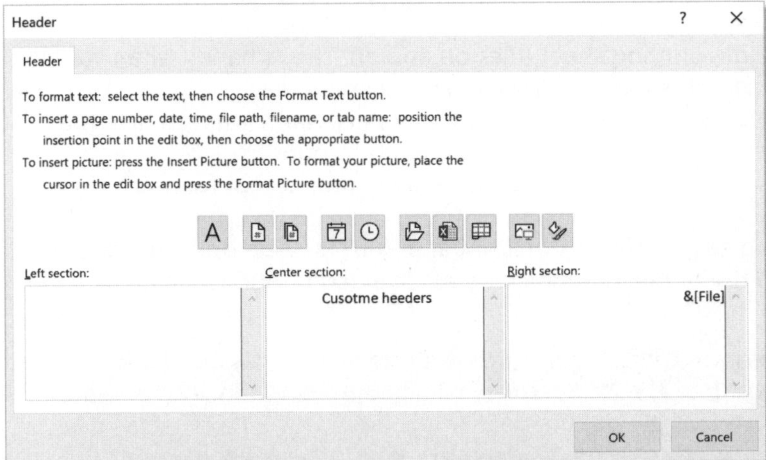

- **Insert Page Number**—Click this button to insert a page number in the header/footer.
- **Insert Number of Pages**—Click this button to insert the number of printable pages in the worksheet. You can also use combinations of AutoText entries and your own text, such as &[Page] of &[Pages].
- **Insert Date**—Click this button to insert a date in the header/footer.
- **Insert Time**—Click this button to insert a time in the header/footer.
- **Insert File Path**—Click this button to insert the file path in the header/footer.
- **Insert File Name**—Click this button to insert the file name in the header/footer.
- **Insert Sheet Name**—Click this button to insert the sheet name in the header/footer.
- **Insert Picture**—Click this button to insert a picture in the header/footer.
- **Format Picture**—Click this button to format a picture in the header/footer.

The Sheet Tab

The Sheet tab of the Print Setup dialog exposes page setup elements that you can find only on this tab, such as repeating rows and columns. You also have some other options that are worth consideration, as shown below:

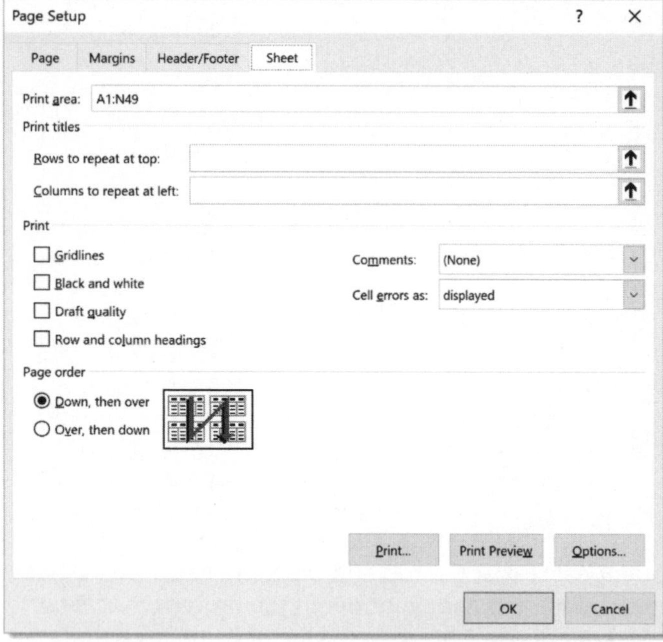

- **Print Area**—You can manually specify the print area.
- **Print Titles**—You can define how many rows or columns you might want to repeat on each page.
- **Gridlines**—You might want to select this option when you're first setting up a model because it helps you line up your elements on the printed page without using a ruler to keep track of everything.
- **Black and White**—If you have a color printer, always check this option unless you're printing a final copy. You'll save yourself a lot of ink/toner this way.
- **Row and Column Headings**—You can toggle printing sheet titles on and off. This is handy when you're testing a document and don't necessarily need the extra information but just the data.
- **Comments and Cell Errors As**—These options can be handy if you don't necessarily want to take the time to suppress anything in the worksheet itself but don't want everything to print.
- **Page Order**—You should rarely change these options unless you have a document that follows a very specific reading pattern.

The buttons at the bottom of this tab should be easy to figure out: Print and Print Preview both launch the Print dialog, and the Options button brings up the printer settings for your selected printer (which may differ from those for another printer).

> **Caution:** When you use headers and footers, be careful about including static information that will have to be changed as a document changes (e.g., Q1 2018—Financial Statement). When you print the document next quarter, your data may be up to date, but the header won't be. This type of mistake is particularly easy to overlook because you typically see the header and footer only when you print.

Sharing Your Workbook

Once your workbook is set up the way you want it, you can share it with others. What those people need to do with your workbook determines how you should distribute it. Here are several common scenarios for sharing:

- **Viewing/reference only**—Sometimes no interactions are needed or wanted. An example of this could be a price book or a product brochure, where you only need people to see the information but don't want them to manipulate it. The most secure way to share a workbook for viewing or reference only is to print and share it as a PDF, so people can't make any changes whatsoever. Email is the most common method for distributing PDFs of workbooks, but you can just as easily post them to a website or use a file sharing service, such as Microsoft's free OneDrive service.
- **Personal input only**—There are all kinds of workbooks that get distributed for personal use, such as checkbook registers, loan amortization workbooks, 401(k)/retirement calculators, and planners/schedulers.

You can find lots of examples of such workbooks if you open Excel and go to **File > New** and then search for templates. Templates may or may not be protected to keep people from deleting formulas or changing formats, but you can certainly add protection, if needed. Microsoft templates generally aren't protected, so you can make whatever changes you want, but some third-party templates may be protected. Since workbooks for personal input only are generally available to many people in an organization, the most common method for distribution is in a public file sharing service, such as a dedicated network folder, company website, or OneDrive. If you sign up for Office 365, you automatically get a OneDrive account, and that OneDrive account stays with you even if you cancel your Office 365 account. You can also sign up for a free OneDrive account.

- **Personal interaction**—For some workbooks, input is required, but there is no collaboration. Examples are employee expense or time-off reports. Basically, these workbooks collect personal information from someone. As with the personal input only workbooks, you'll most likely use a network folder, company website, or OneDrive account to make these workbooks available.
- **Collaboration**—Interaction is required on these workbooks. For example, in a project management report, multiple people might be involved, and you might need to keep progress updated in a single workbook. In most cases, you are likely to need to build a workbook that you then share, although in some cases, multiple people might build certain parts of a workbook, based on their particular skills. For instance, you might be very good at laying things out the way you want but might not be sure about how to create the formulas you need, and you can get input from someone else on that part. Or you might lay out the data input section but need some help creating summary reports. Don't be shy about asking others for their input, especially in challenging situations where you might not necessarily be an expert.

Because you're probably very familiar with how to email workbooks or post them to network or OneDrive folders, the following sections look more deeply at only the personal interaction and collaboration scenarios.

Personal Interaction: Using Microsoft Forms for Data Collection

Some of the most challenging aspects of collecting data from multiple people in Excel are figuring out how to collect the data and then aggregating it. Microsoft Forms is an online survey tool that lets you create multiple question/response surveys and direct people to them via a sharable link. The great thing about Forms is that the survey responses are automatically saved in an Excel workbook in your OneDrive account, which you can then summarize. Unlike other online survey platforms that give you canned response analysis but don't give you access to the actual responses, with Forms, your data belongs to you. Forms lets you create multiple types of questions, and each type has its own set of additional options—and you can choose whether to make answers required. Forms requires a OneDrive account.

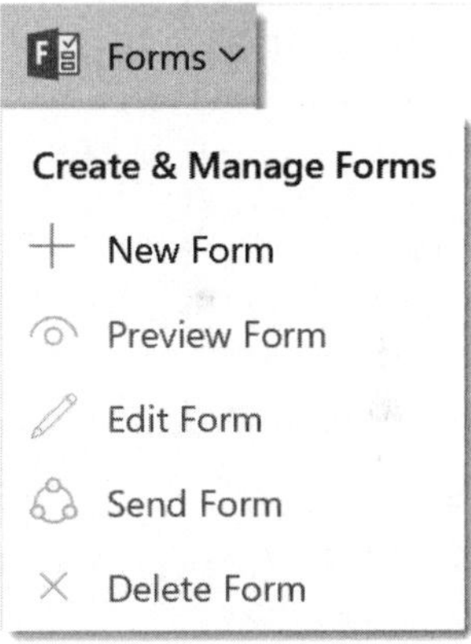

You can create a new form from Excel Online by going to **Insert > Forms > New Form**, as shown here.

Alternatively, click on the application launcher in OneDrive and select Forms, as shown below.

Forms then opens a web browser with an interactive form building tool. The default form name is your active workbook's name, and the form begins with a list of suggested questions. If you haven't named your workbook, Forms prompts you for one. When that's done, you can start adding questions, and for each one you need to select from one of seven question types, as shown below:

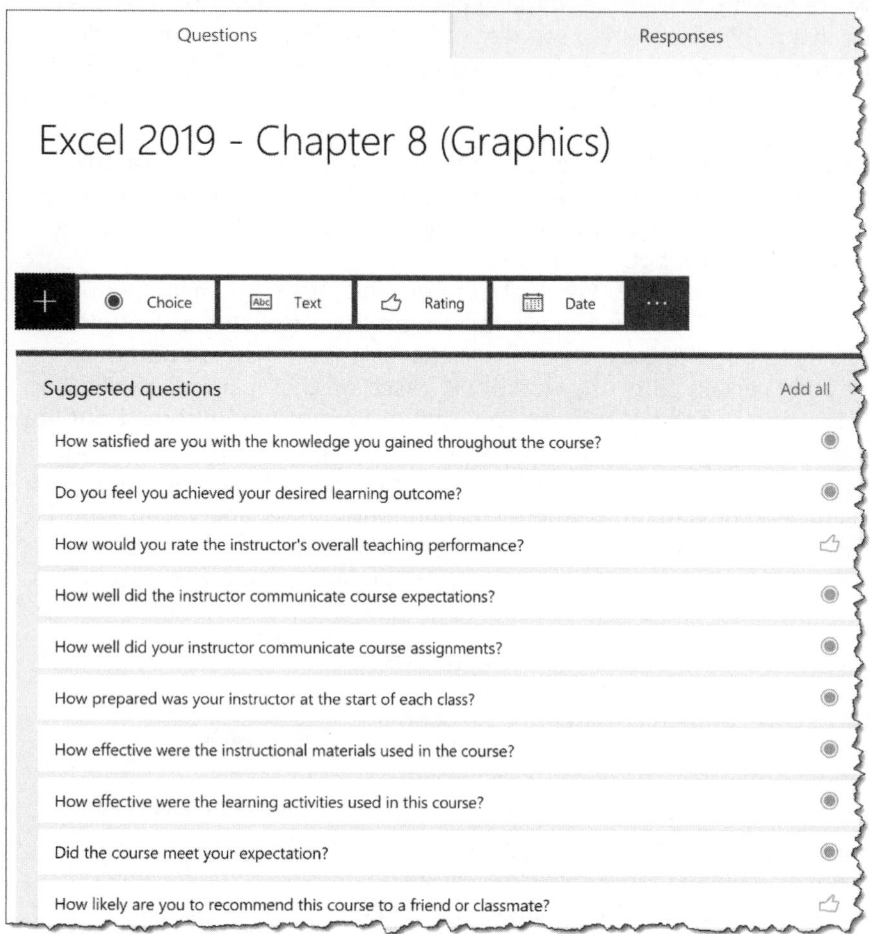

- **Multiple choice**—You can write the text for multiple answers, as shown below.

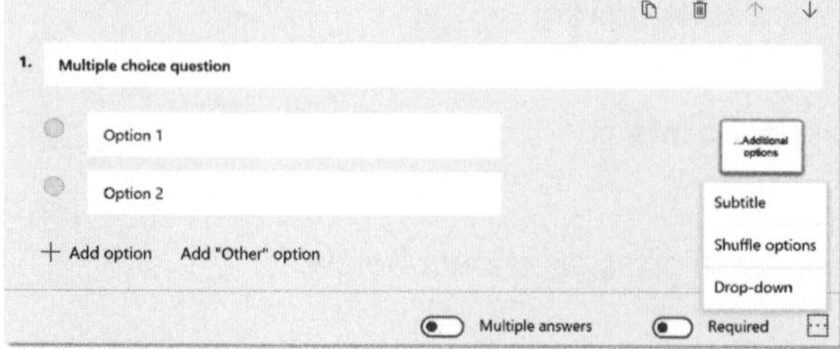

- **Text**—You can allow the user to enter long or short answers, as shown below.

- **Ratings**—You can specify 1 through 10 levels by displaying numbers or stars or other symbols, as shown below.

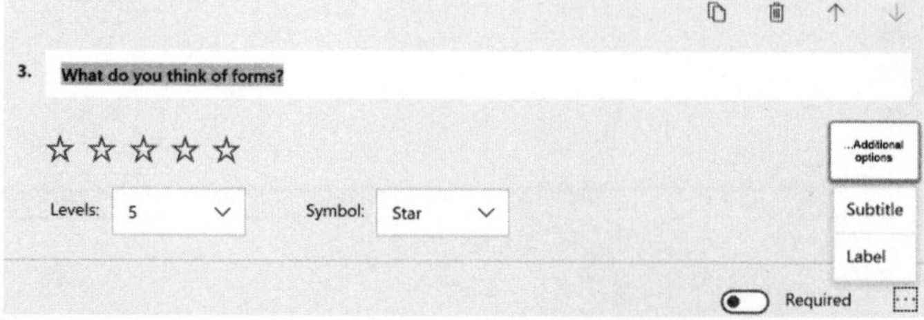

- **Date**—You can specify that a date must be entered.
- **Ranking**—You can ask users to select their top options, as shown below.

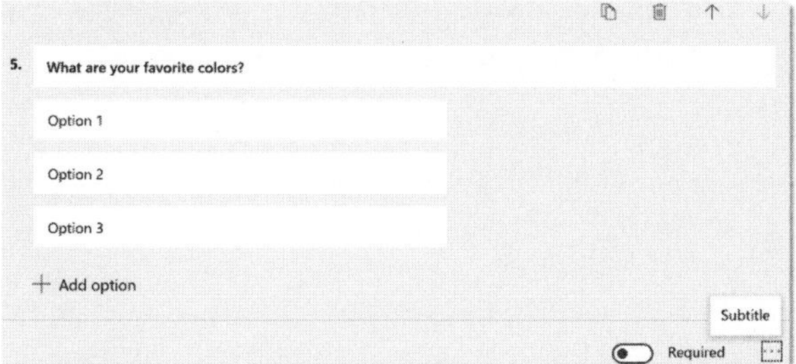

- **Likert**—You can enter the question text and the text for the five possible options, as shown below.

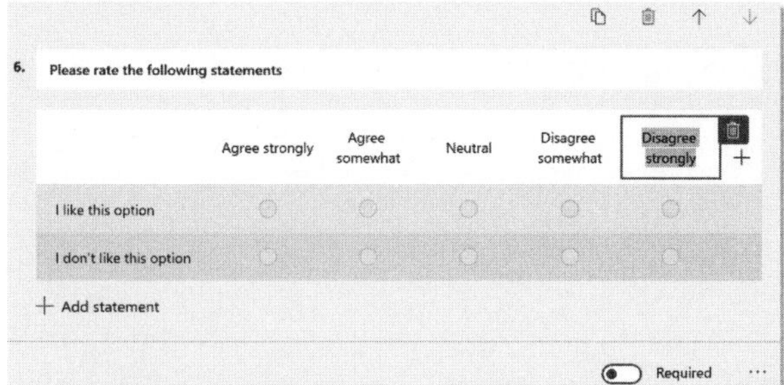

- **Net Promoter Score**—You can gauge customer response to a product or service, as shown below.

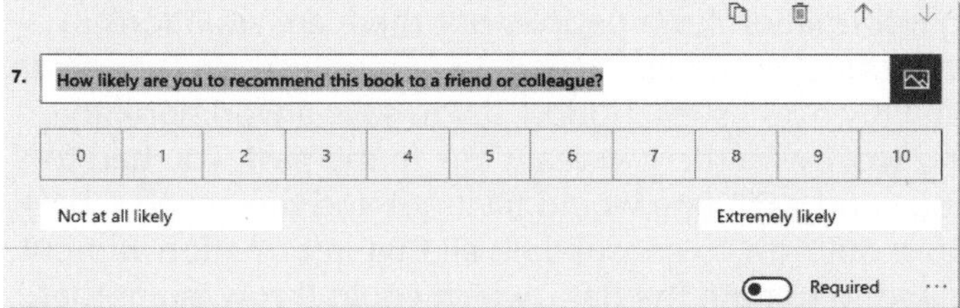

When you're done with your form, you can click the Share button (the two chain links, on the left in the figure below) in the upper-right corner of the browser pane. You can limit responses to only people in your organization or allow responses from anyone who gets a link. You can also create a scannable QR code, get HTML code tags to paste into a web page or Microsoft Sway presentation, or create an email message containing a link.

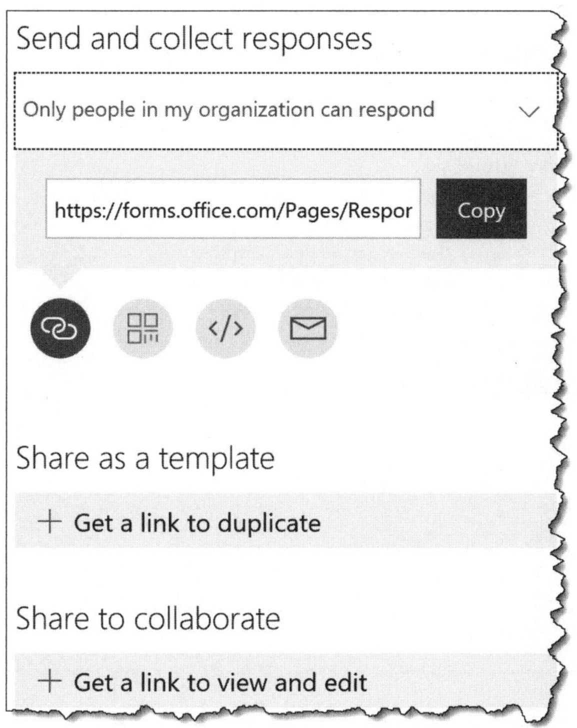

When your form is complete, Forms automatically starts collecting data as people start responding. You can click the View Results button to see the first 300 verbatim responses, click the Ideas button to have Excel create some recommended Pivot Charts for you (see Chapter 11), or click the Open in Excel button to look at the raw data.

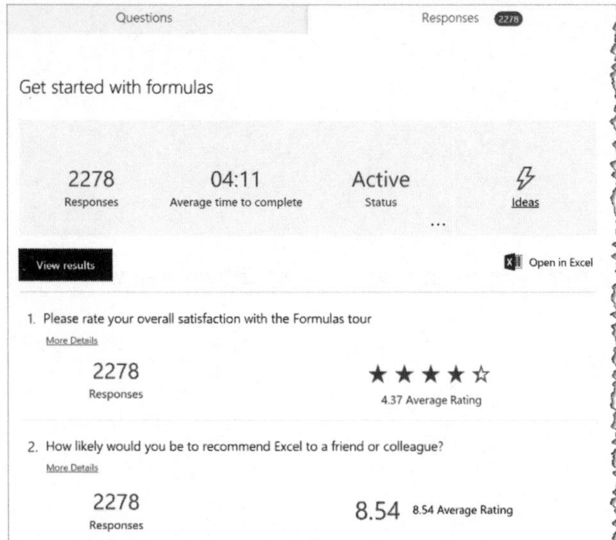

Collaboration

With Microsoft Forms, you're only interested in getting information from people, but there are situations in which you need to actively work with other people in the same workbook. This kind of multiuser collaboration is called *co-authoring*. Co-authoring in Excel requires an Office 365 subscription. If you save a workbook to your OneDrive account, you can share it with others and work with them in real time. In the past, you had to email a workbook to each person you needed input from, and each one would fill it out and then send it back. And that's where the fun began: You would have to figure out how to consolidate all that information without missing or duplicating anything. And then you might need to update the data, which could throw in another wrench or two. Fortunately, co-authoring puts all this in the past.

Just click the Share button in the upper-right corner of the Excel window, and Excel opens the Send Link dialog, shown below. You have several options of who should get the link; the example shown here includes a specific person and a personalized message. Alternatively, you can click the Copy Link button if you want to send the link to people yourself.

If you select Allow Editing, anyone who receives the link will be able to edit your workbook, although you can also limit editing rights so that the workbook is read-only by not selecting Allow Editing. When a workbook is read-only, people can make changes but can't save them without first saving as a copy of your original workbook.

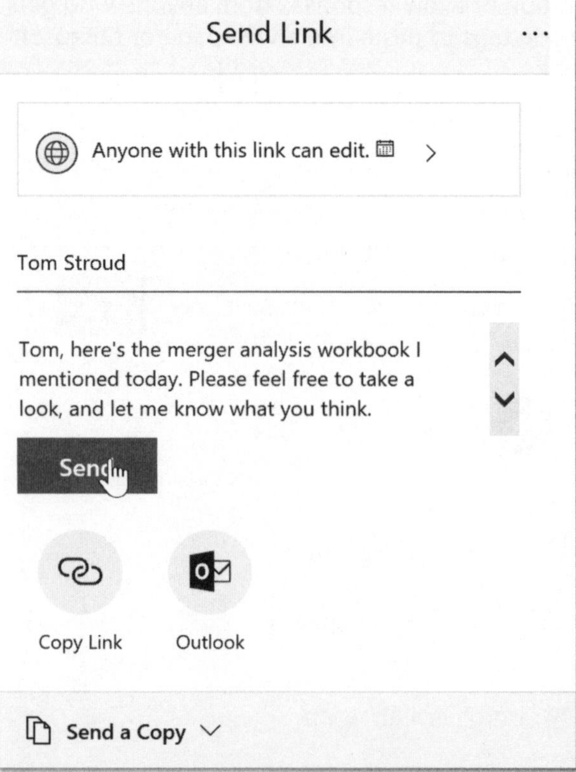

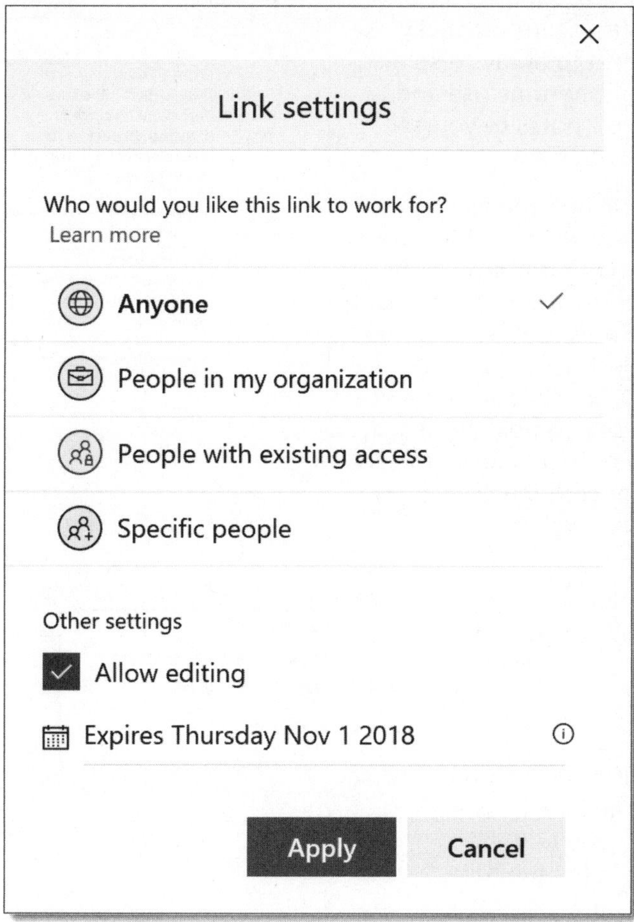

Comments and Notes

When you're working in a shared workbook, you might want to point out certain things to people or get their input on something. To do that, you can work with comments and notes.

Comments are threaded conversations attached to individual cells, and you can use @Mentions (as shown below) to call out people by name. An @Mention automatically sends an email to the person you mention by name with the comment you make and gives the person a link back to the workbook. These are referred to as *threaded comments* because you can see the entire conversation, much as in an instant message chain.

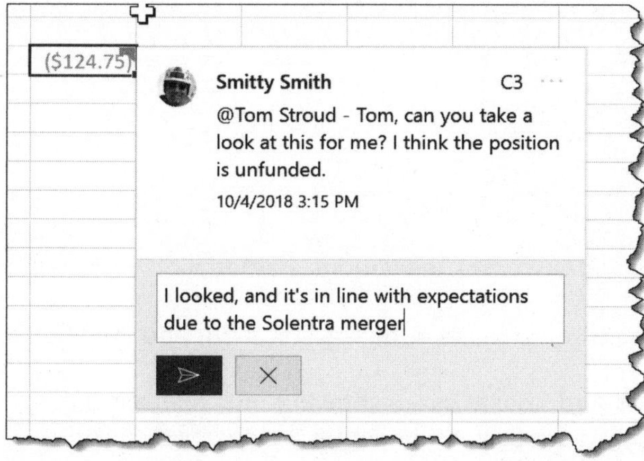

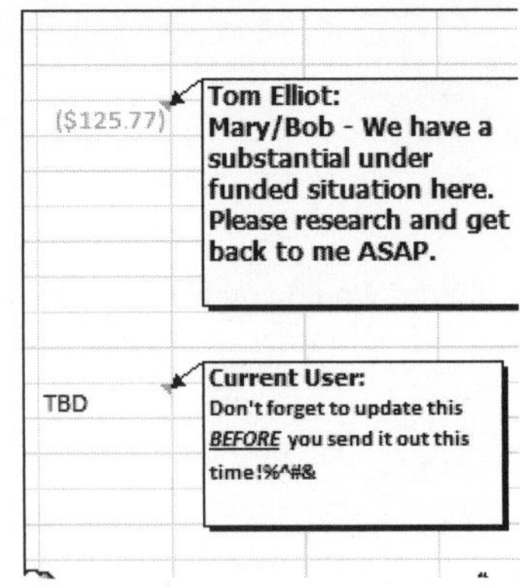

Unlike comments, notes aren't interactive. Think of notes as electronic sticky notes that you can attach to individual cells. They can be set to always display or to appear only when prompted. Notes are generally for one-time use and can be deleted after they have been resolved. You can make notes to yourself or make notes to people with whom you're sharing your workbook.

You access both comments and notes on the Review tab. When you want to add a new comment, first make sure the cell with which you want to associate a comment is the active cell and then go to **Review > New Comment**. Excel opens a text box in which you can start entering your comment text. If you want to mention someone to get his or her input, type @, and a scrollable search box with a list of people from your address book appears. Select the person's name from the list, and when you click the Send button, Excel sends that person a notification. Note that when you start typing a name in the search box, the search list automatically narrows as you type, so you don't need to type a full name. If you want to delete a comment, select **Review > Delete** or click the ellipsis (...) in the upper-right corner of the Comment pane and click Delete Thread.

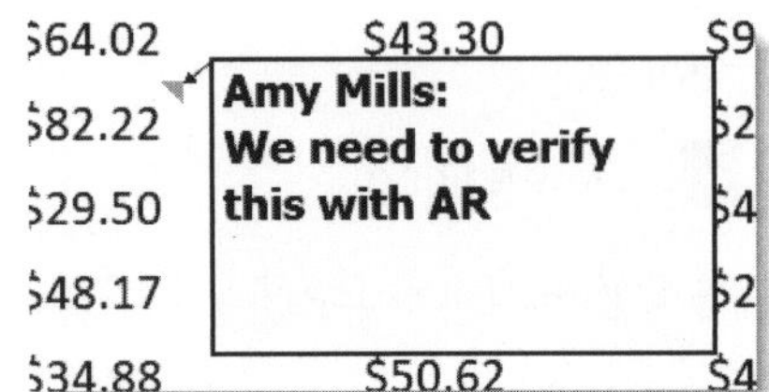

When you want to add a new note, first select the cell where you want the note and then go to **Review > Notes > New Note**. When you add a new note, you immediately see a yellow box that has an arrow leading to the active cell.

At this point, the note is the active object, so you can simply start entering text in the note. Excel automatically enters your Office user name in the note, but you can delete it if you don't need to let anyone know who wrote the note (e.g., for an instructional note). When you're done entering your note text, you can click any cell or press **Esc** until the note is deactivated (i.e., no longer has the visible object border and controls around it). Excel reactivates the grid so you can continue working in your workbook. If you want to delete a note, just select it and press Delete or go to **Review > Delete**.

Positioning Notes

When you create a note, Excel does its best to add it to the right of the active cell, but multiple notes may overlap each other, or they sometimes just don't go where you really want them. In such a case, you can just drag the note wherever you want. Notes, like many other things in Excel, should be used in moderation. You don't need them to point out the obvious, like "Enter Name Here." In fact, you probably shouldn't use notes for instructions at all but should instead use data validation input messages, which are much less obtrusive. The example below shows a validation input message on the left; this message will disappear as soon as someone starts entering information or presses **Esc**. The note on the right isn't going anywhere unless you delete or hide it, which you can do by selecting **Review > Notes > Show/Hide Note**.

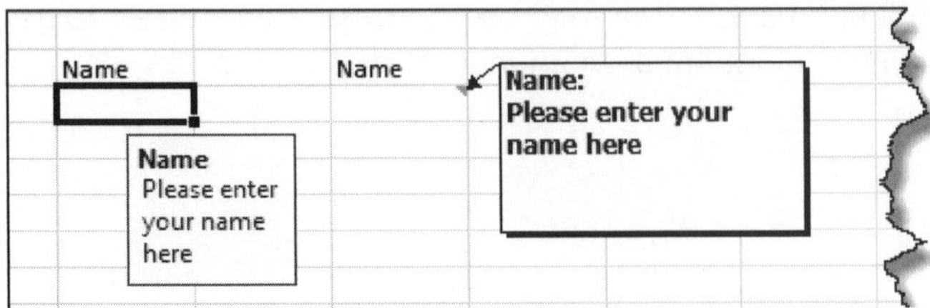

Chapter Summary

- This chapter describes how to apply and modify themes and discusses the various elements of worksheet formatting, including text, cells, rows, and columns.
- This chapter also explains how you can use number formatting to make numbers stand out and introduces conditional formatting.
- In this chapter you saw how to set up some custom views and how to make showing only relevant data easy for people with Auto Filter. You also learned about the various ways to set up a worksheet for printing and distribution.

Chapter 8: Graphics

In Chapter 7 you looked at some of the steps to take to set up a standard workbook before distributing it. This chapter takes somewhat of a step backward and goes over the many graphical elements that you can add to a workbook to help make certain key data stand out or to fulfill a specific need for graphics, such as a product brochure or a fantasy sports league brochure that includes player pictures and profiles. When developing a workbook that may be used by multiple people, you might hold back on graphics until you know that the workbook functions as the users expect it to work. It's always best to add the pretty stuff after you make sure the workbook works. This chapter discusses how to add elements such as custom logos and pictures to your documents and some of the ways you can use them. It explores the different shape objects and how to manipulate them. It also spends a good deal of time discussing Excel's SmartArt graphics, primarily because they are fantastic tools and also because there are quite a few of them, and they can be a bit overwhelming at first.

The following are some general rules of thumb for graphic use that you should keep in mind:

- Don't overdo it. Including too many graphics can dilute your message. Use what you need to tell the story—and no more.
- Images can be colorful and splashy—that's sort of the point—but don't go overboard with colors. Remember that certain color combinations can be difficult to read on different monitors, and some are just plain hard to read no matter the monitor. In addition, keep in mind that users will look at your workbook using a variety of screen sizes. What you build while looking at a 24-inch or larger monitor will look a lot different for someone who's looking at your workbook on a phone.
- Make sure an image sends the right message. You probably don't want to use the same images in a corporate report that you used in your department football pool.
- Be careful with image size. You need to watch both how much real estate an image takes up on the worksheet and the image's physical size. Almost all digital images need to be optimized before you use them. (www.tinypng.com is a great free resource for image optimization.) Images from digital cameras and even cell phones are usually well over 1 MB, but when optimized, they're usually one-tenth that size. If you don't optimize images, you might end up with a workbook that's so big it's difficult to distribute. In fact, some email systems have strict size limits on attachment size. You can also create some real issues for people (customers!) when you send out a huge workbook that by rights should have been relatively small. You will tie up the recipient's system resources in receiving your file, and you may also slow the person's PC to a crawl. This might seem like a relatively small issue, but it is one that is overlooked by most Excel users who work with a lot of graphics in their workbooks.

Pictures and Online Pictures

Pictures are some of the most common graphic tools; for example, people frequently add company logos to their Excel workbooks. To insert a picture, go to **Insert > Pictures**. Depending on how your folder view options are set, you'll see either thumbnail images of the pictures or a detailed list. With pictures, it's generally easiest to use the thumbnail preview, so you know which image you're choosing. However, the list and detail views allow you to see how big images really are. Either way, browse to your picture's location, select the picture, and click Insert.

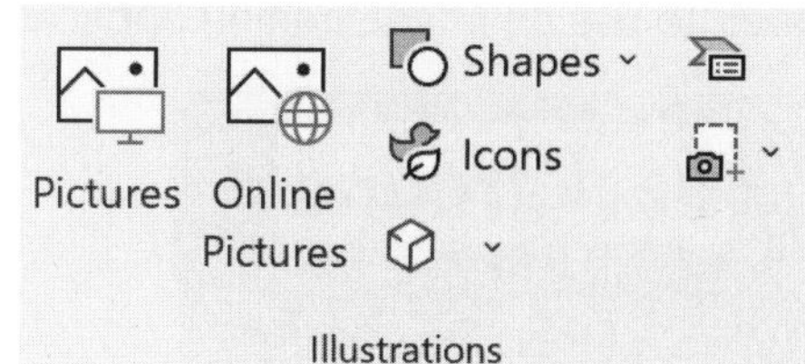

If you don't have a picture but want to browse a collection of royalty-free images, go to **Insert > Online Pictures**, and you see the options shown below. From this page, you can select an image to see a variety of related pictures. When you find one you like, click it and then click Insert.

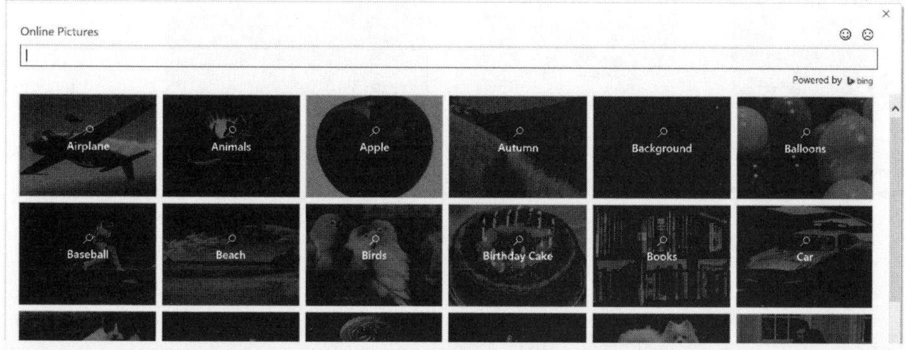

Note: If you have a picture image that's anything over 250 KB, I recommend compressing it before moving forward. Let's say you have a 250 KB corporate logo, and you put it on 10 sheets. You don't have 1 original image and 9 small copies; rather, you have 10 250 KB images, and you can end up with serious file size implications in no time at all. If you don't have a photo editing application, you can get the outstanding *www.paint.net* for free. You can also use *www.tinypng.com*, a free image compression site.

When you initially bring an image into Excel, it is the active object, so you see it selected on your worksheet. From there you can move and size it as needed. As shown below, Excel has a lot of tools on the Picture Format tab that you can use to manipulate how the image interacts with your sheet. The following sections describe the groups available on the Picture Format tab.

Note: The Picture Format tab, which appears only when you have a picture selected on a worksheet, is the same in other Office applications as in Excel, so if you get the hang of it here, you'll know how to use it in other Office applications as well.

The Adjust Group

You use the Adjust group on the Picture Format tab, shown below, to alter the physical attributes of images. You can, for example, adjust the color or contrast or add artistic effects. The following sections describe the options available in the Adjust group.

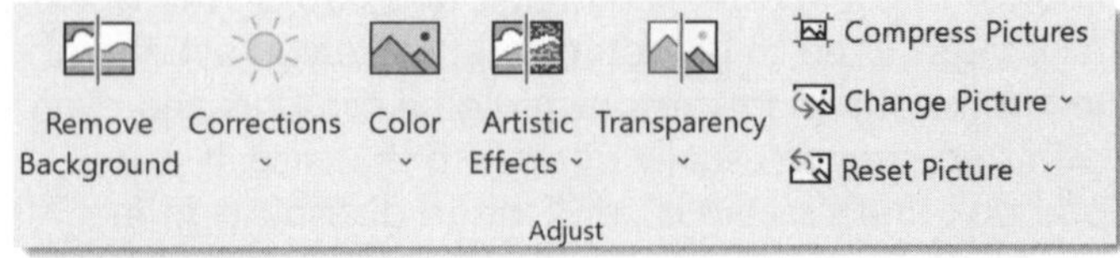

Remove Background

The **Picture Format > Remove Background** option can be useful if you have a background that's not compatible with your image, and you want to make some minor adjustments. For instance, say that you have a logo with a white background, but your worksheet or dashboard area is dark. In this case, the logo will stick out like a sore thumb unless you remove the logo's background (as shown in the following example). Excel does what it can to help you, but if you need better background removal than you can achieve with Excel, you need to use an image editing application.

The following image shows several of the different effects that you can apply.

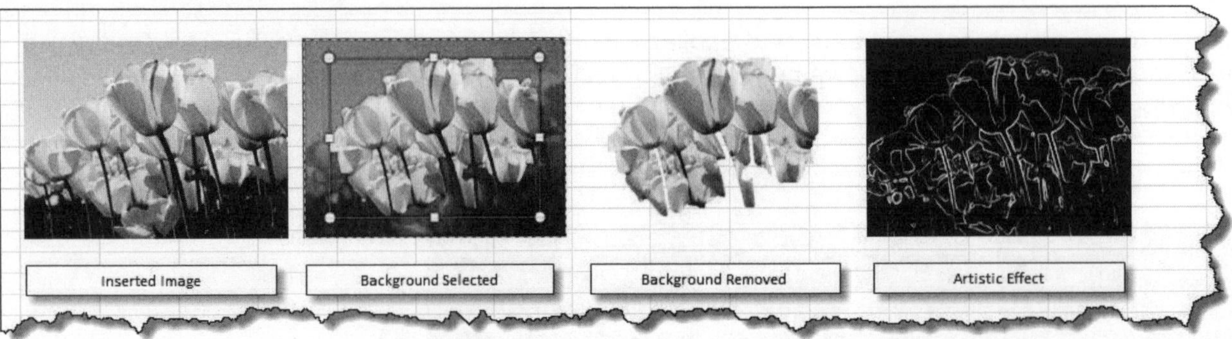

Corrections, Color, Artistic Effects, and Transparency

As soon as you insert an image, Excel analyzes it to determine what kind of standard corrections it can make for you. As you can see from the artistic effect sample above, some of the corrections are pretty interesting. This is one of those areas where everyone's taste will be a bit different, so when you have some time, insert a few images (either your own or some of the Office samples) and make some of the adjustments Excel suggests. In practice, you might never alter an image beyond sizing it, but it's good to know that there are a lot of things you can do with it. The images at right provide examples of corrections, color, artistic effects, and transparency. With an image selected, you can hover over each of the effects to see it instantly previewed. If you like the preview, you can click on it to apply it.

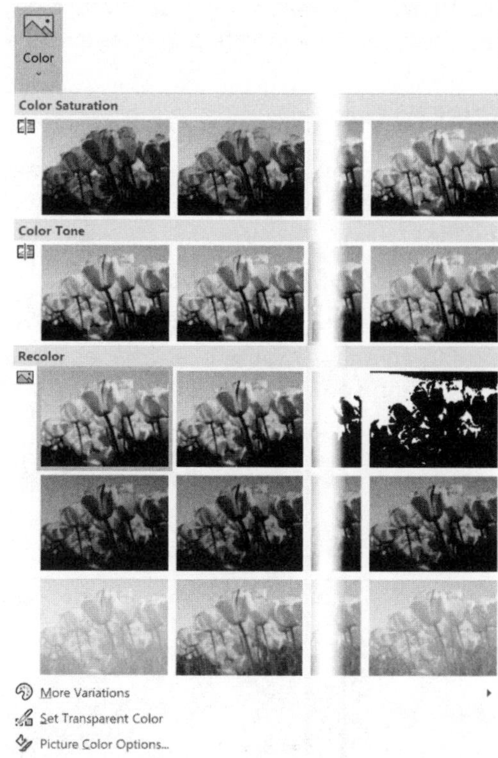

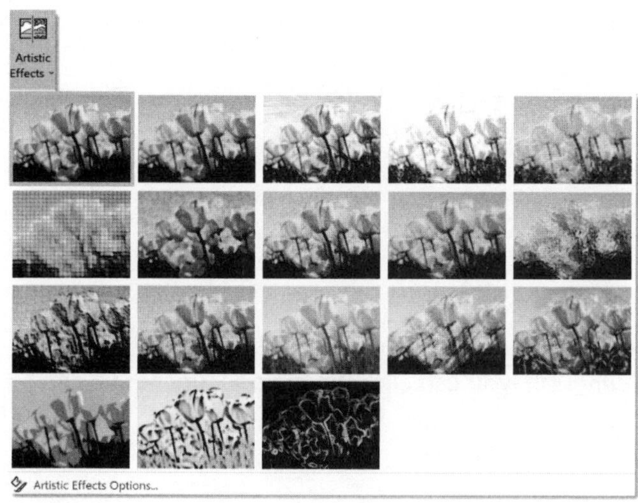

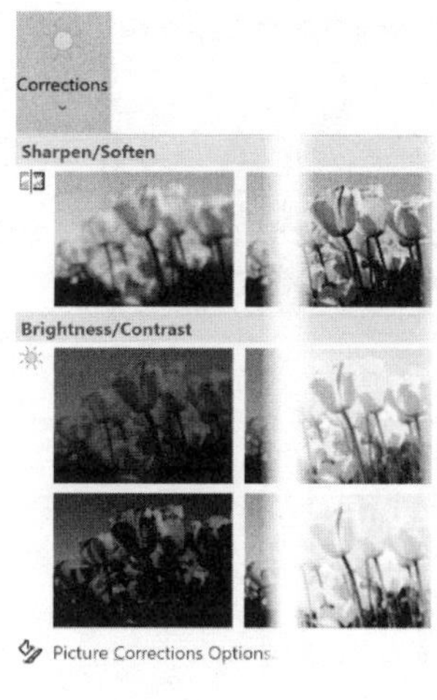

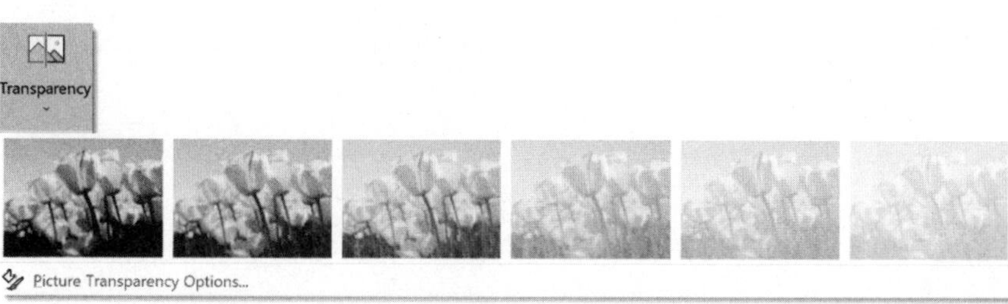

Compress Picture

If you have a large image, you can certainly try the **Picture Format > Compress Pictures** option, but you end up having no idea what size the resulting image is because you don't have access to those attributes within Excel. If you use this option, just stick with the defaults and see how it works

Hint: Consider Compress Pictures an emergency tool, not something you use routinely. In general, you should compress images before you bring them into Excel (or any other application, for that matter).

Change Picture

The **Picture Format > Change Picture** option brings up the Insert Picture dialog in the same location where you most recently inserted an image; this dialog lets you swap one image for another.

Reset Picture

If you made any artistic changes to an image, you can use the **Picture Format > Reset Picture** option to reset it to the state it was in when you first inserted it.

The Picture Styles Group

The Picture Styles group on the Picture Format tab, shown below, offers a variety of picture frames you can put around an image. Sometimes images placed directly on Excel's stark white background just look a bit pitiful, and adding some depth can help them stand out, as shown in the following examples.

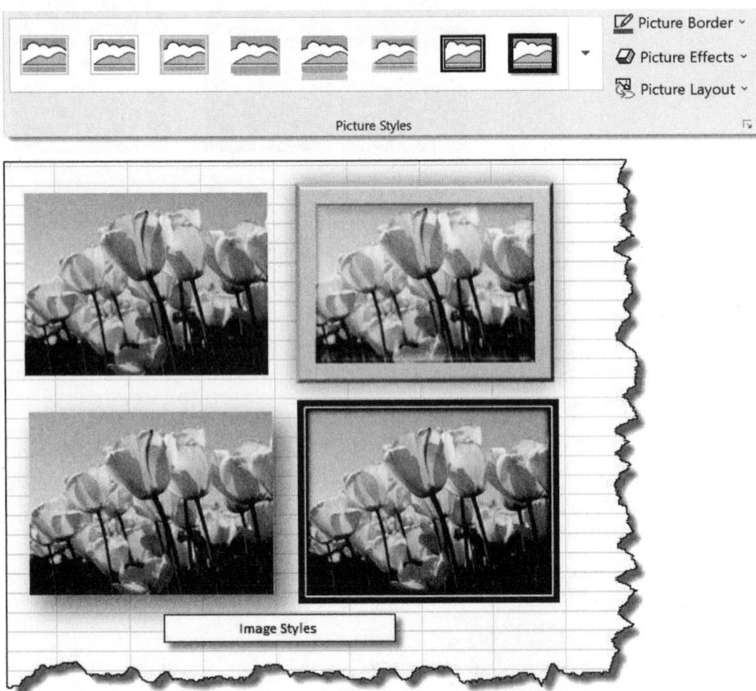

You can also create your own effects by using the Picture Border, Picture Effects, and Picture Layout tools on the right side of the Picture Styles group. And if that's not enough, you can click the dialog launcher to get more options, shown below.

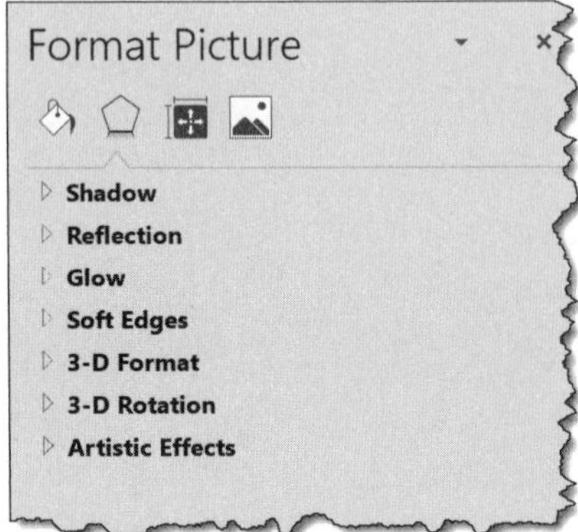

The Accessibility Group

More and more organizations are requiring accessibility features in their documents. For example, screen readers can read special text, called *alt text*, for visually impaired users. The Accessibility group on the Picture Format tab allows you to add alt text to your images so that visually impaired users can get an idea of what pictures are shown on a worksheet. Alt text is completely invisible in Excel, and it doesn't cause any visual complications with your images.

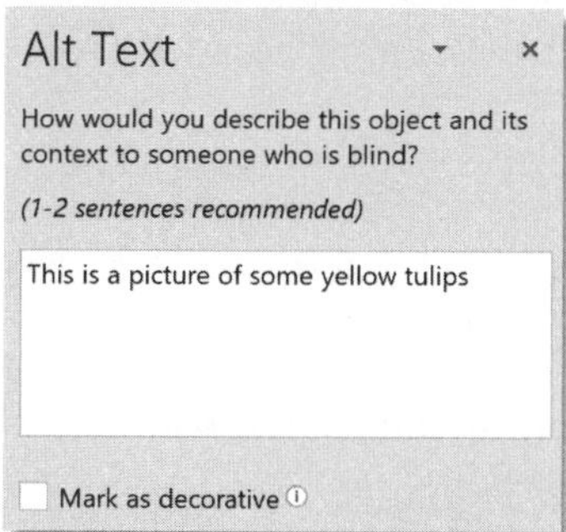

Accessibility is so important to Microsoft that it includes an accessibility recommendation in the status bar, as shown below. You can also go to **File > Info > Check for Issues > Check Accessibility** to get help from Excel on making your workbooks accessible.

The Arrange Group

The tools in the Arrange Group on the Picture Format tab, shown at right and described in the following sections, are primarily for dealing with multiple images that you want to organize in relation to each other.

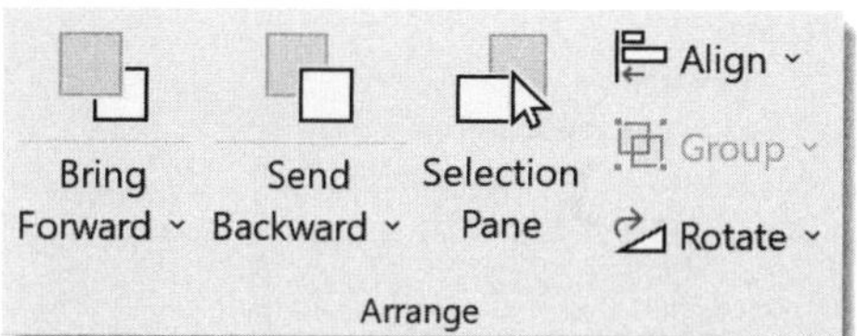

Bring Forward and Send Backward

If you want to overlay certain images, you can use the Bring Forward and Send Backward options to move images in front of or behind one another.

Align

Earlier in this chapter you saw four images of flowers grouped in a square configuration. If you wanted to make sure that those images were precisely placed in line with each other, you could use the Align tools. The Align options are enabled only when you have two or more objects selected; if you have three or more objects selected, the Align options also include tools for distributing the objects, as shown below.

Align
Align Left
Align Center
Align Right
Align Top
Align Middle
Align Bottom
Distribute Horizontally
Distribute Vertically
Snap to Grid
Snap to Shape
View Gridlines

Snap to Grid

The Snap to Grid option aligns an image with the worksheet's gridlines. If you move an object around when this option is on, you see that the image automatically jumps to the nearest gridline intersection, so you don't have to try to place it right on the lines with just the mouse.

Note: Alt+click temporarily disables the Snap to Grid option.

Snap to Shape

The Snap to Shape option allows you to quickly line up objects with other objects.

Group

After you've aligned all your objects, you can group them so that you can move the entire group at once instead of moving one item at a time.

Rotate

The Rotate option lets you rotate or flip objects in standard directions, as shown below.

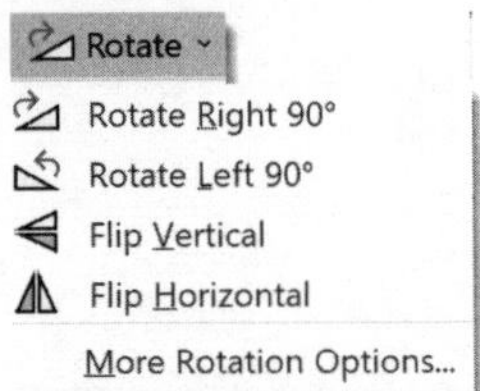

If the standard directions aren't enough for you, you can click More Rotation Options to launch the Format Picture pane, shown below, which provides many more options.

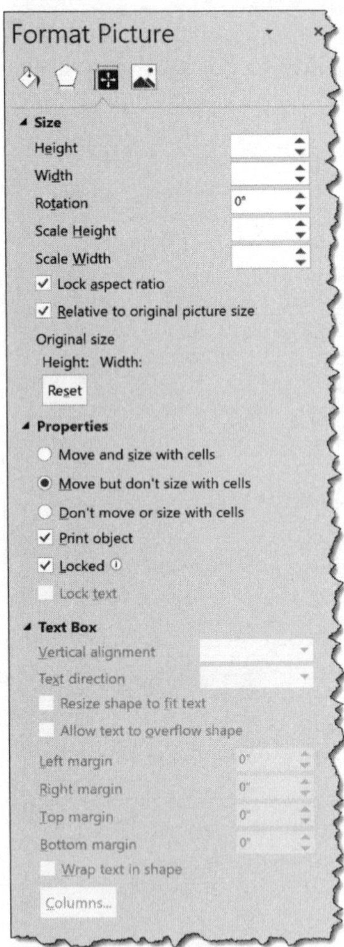

The Size Group

You are most likely to manipulate images, including adjusting the size, by using the mouse. However, there are a few tools that you might want to use from time to time, and they are in the Size group on the Picture Format tab, shown below.

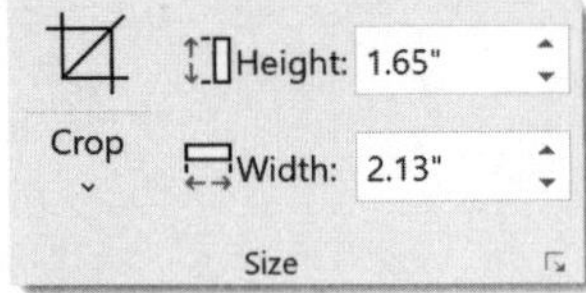

Crop

You are very likely to use the Crop tools if you take a lot of screenshots, paste images from the Internet, or have any images that need to be trimmed in some way. You can simply use the cropping tools to get rid of what you don't want. The following options are available under **Picture Format > Crop drop-down**:

- **Crop**—Wherever you see cropping handles, which are the dark handle lines on the borders of an image, you can drag them to crop the image from that direction. You can crop from top, bottom, left, and right. When you're ready, press **Esc** to accept the crop. If you're not happy with the results, you can press **Ctrl+Z** and start over.
- **Crop to Shape**—This cool tool lets you crop an image into the exact shape of any of Excel's shape objects. Here's an example of the artistic flowers from earlier in the chapter, cropped into an arrow.

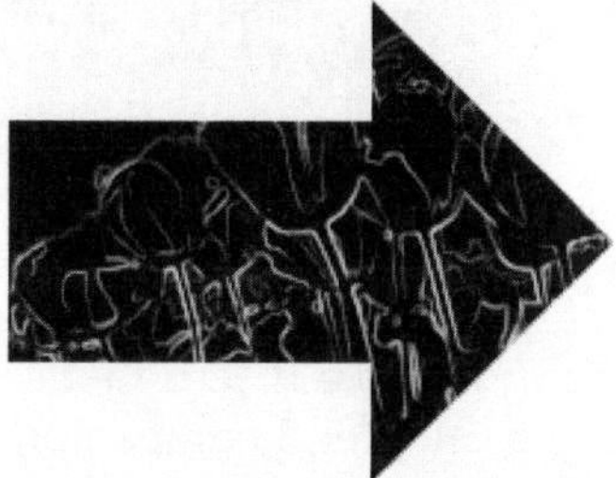

- You can be very creative with this tool, but on the other hand, you might be tempted to spend a lot of time designing creative images for a spreadsheet that might not warrant it. Or, worse, you might come up with some artistic rendering that only you can appreciate. As always, keep your users and usability in mind.
- **Aspect Ratio**—This tool allows you to crop an image by a predefined ratio, which can be helpful if you don't want to manually crop an image and mess with getting the size just right.

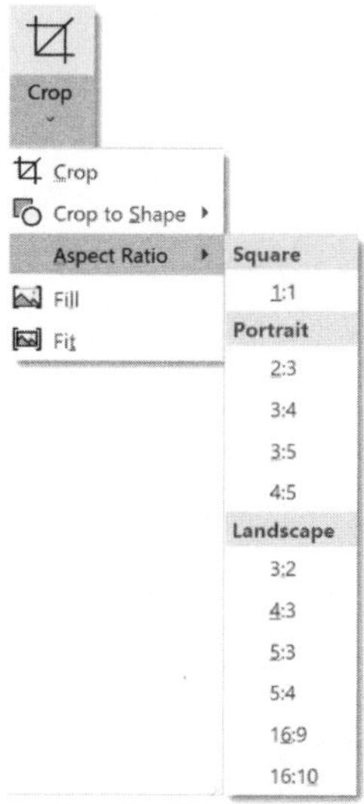

- **Fill and Fit**—Fill lets you reduce or enlarge an image and automatically adjust it to fit precisely within the new dimensions. On the other hand, Fit makes the image fit into the new dimensions but maintains its original aspect ratio, which means it doesn't get stretched out of proportion. To use either of these tools, first click on the fill type you want to use and then select the image and resize it the way that you want. Finally, go back to the Crop menu and select either Fill or Fit, and the correct effect is applied.

Height and Width

You can use the Height and Width spin buttons to increase or decrease an image's size instead of dragging its handles into a new position or to a new size. When you resize an image by using the sizing handles, the picture increases/decreases proportionately, meaning that if you adjust the height, the width automatically adjusts appropriately. When you size pictures by using the spin buttons, you can adjust height and width independently of each other.

Note: Consider the following tips related to sizing images using the sizing handles:

- If you drag any of an image's center handles, you size the image in only that direction, and the image will end up being out of proportion.
- If you drag an image by any of its diagonal handles, you size the image proportionately.
- You can use **Ctrl+drag** to proportionately increase an image at all four corners. (This is a neat trick!)
- If you use **Ctrl+drag** on the center handles, you end up resizing the image disproportionately in both directions.

Shapes

Shapes, also called *drawing objects*, have two specific functions. The first function is primarily aesthetic: A shape can serve as nothing more than an object on a worksheet. You very often use shapes in this capacity to draw attention to something, like circling information instead of telling someone to look at cell AB23, drawing an arrow to point to something, or using a teaching callout to point out a new feature the first few times you use it.

This is a callout shape. You can use it to give people instructions.

The second function of shapes is automation: You can assign macros to shapes in workbooks to implement various types of automation. For instance, you can have a shape of an arrow assigned to a macro that can take the user to the next worksheet. To give you some ideas of how to use shapes, the Chapter 8 companion workbook includes the dashboard shown below; a dashboard can function as a starting point for a workbook, and you can use it to lay out all the elements for your users. A dashboard can be as simple as a list of instructions for filling out a form or a group of navigation buttons, or it can be more complicated and include buttons that can open other applications, get data from them, and return the data to Excel. The opportunities are limitless.

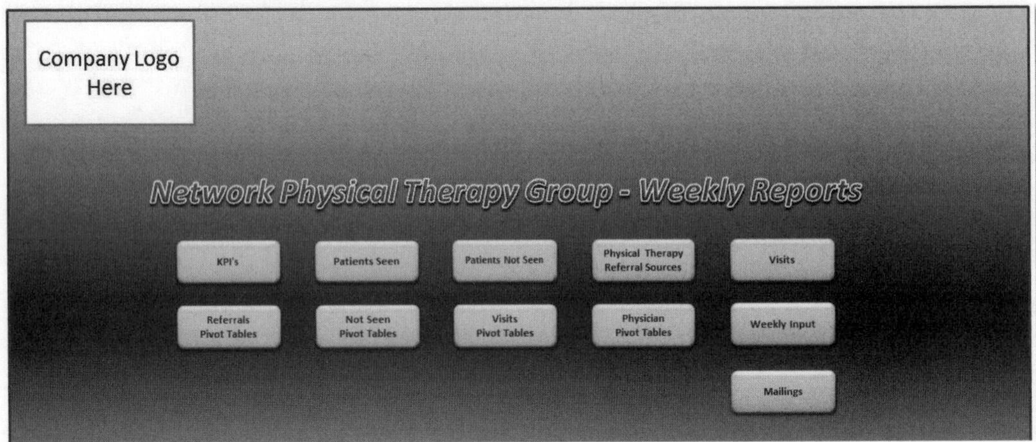

Shape Types

There are shapes for every occasion under **Insert > Shapes**, and they all have the capacity to be formatted with any of the styles available on the Shape Format tab. Most of them can be used as text boxes as well, so don't think that text boxes need to be boring. For example, you could use a star shape as a text box. There are eight shape categories, as shown in the figure below.

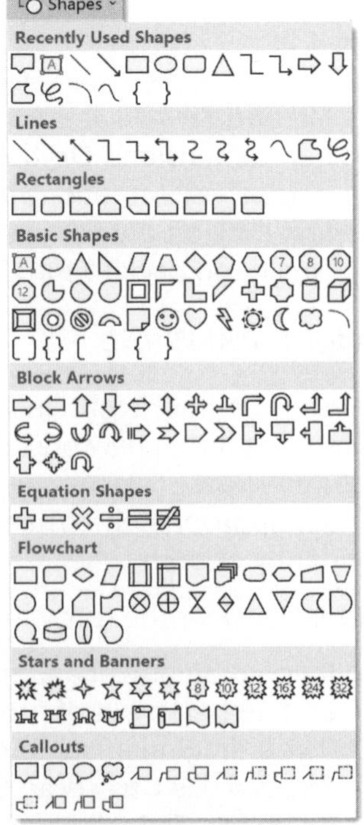

Considering that Excel is a far cry from a professional graphics editing application, Microsoft has done a fantastic job of bringing you some remarkable graphics tools. You can create very nice additions to your worksheets in ways that only high-end graphic designers could have done just a few versions ago.

The buttons you see in the dashboard example in the Chapter 8 companion workbook are nothing more than rounded rectangles from the Shapes drop-down, with an intense effect added. After I formatted them, I assigned to them macros that do different things. You can assign macros to almost any object—anything from the Shapes gallery and pictures and images as well. You can even make your company logo do something if it's clicked. If you have macros to assign, you can right-click on an object and select the Assign Macro option. Excel opens the Assign Macro dialog, and you can select the macro you want to assign from the Macro Name list.

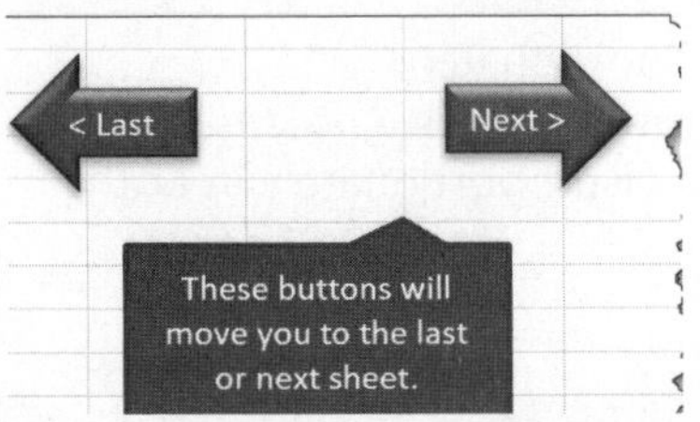

If you want to use buttons for navigation to other sheets, you can insert hyperlinks. To do this, right-click a shape and choose **Link > Insert Link**. Once the Edit Hyperlink dialog loads, select the Place in This Document button on the left, and then select the worksheet you want to activate when the button is clicked. Finally, you can change the cell address if it's something other than A1, which is the default selection.

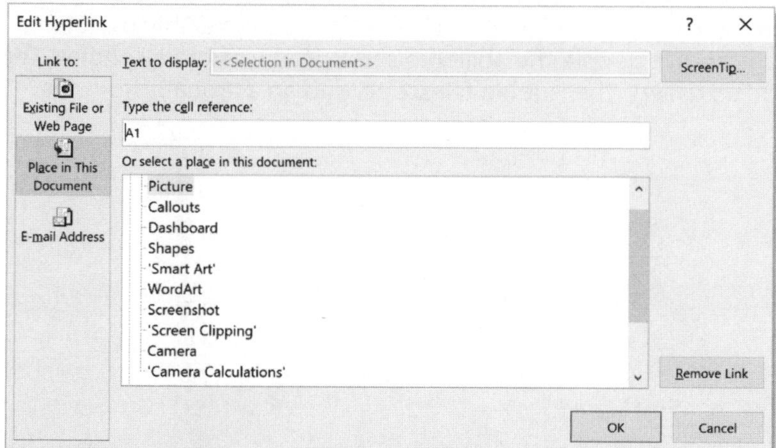

Recall from Chapter 4 that shapes generally start out being very plain and boring, but in this chapter you've seen that Excel gives you some fantastic tools to help you build appealing shapes. If you can increase a workbook's visual appeal and functionality/ease of use, then you'll increase people's willingness to use it. Sometimes little things, like the buttons people click, can do a lot for a workbook's appeal. There are so many shapes that you just need to take some time on your own to play with one or two of them from each category. You'll soon get ideas about where certain objects might work in your workbooks.

Icons

Icons, introduced in Excel 2016, are a set of premade images. A bonus is that they are scalable-vector graphics, which means you can adjust their size, color, and effects, and they will not become distorted if you resize them. Following is an example of the Icons gallery. Notice that there's a categories list on the left.

The following is an example of using several icons combined with a text box.

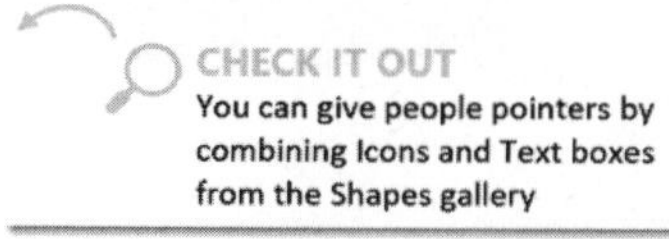

3D Models

Did you know you can insert a 3D image into Excel and then move it around to see all its facets? It's pretty cool: Go to **Insert > Illustrations > 3D Models > From Online Sources** and then select an image from the gallery. After you insert a 3D model, you can click on it and rotate it in any direction by just clicking the gyroscope button in the middle of a 3D model and moving your cursor. 3D models might be incredibly useful in a parts catalog or sales brochure, where you want to give people the ability to see a product from all angles. The images below show the online sources 3D Models gallery, the Hubble telescope, and an astronaut from the Space collection.

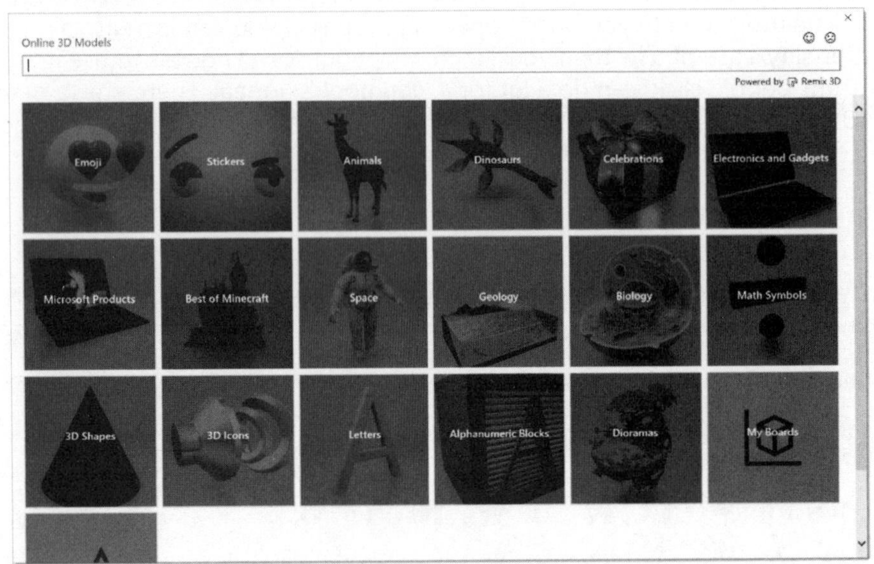

3D models even have their own contextual menu, as shown below.

SmartArt

In the past, when someone needed an organizational diagram, a bunch of people would sit around a conference table brainstorming, and when they reached a consensus, the designated note-taker would take the scribbled ideas to marketing or the art department, explain everything to someone there, and that person would then create the art, generally not knowing or caring about the contents but just knowing that it needed to look good. These days, if you're sitting in an office trying to build some organizational diagram and don't have or want to use a marketing department, you can use SmartArt to do the job yourself. Microsoft has done a great job of identifying some very common organizational diagrams and charting models and bringing them to you in an easy-to-use format.

SmartArt isn't quite as intuitive to use as shapes, so it's worth discussing some scenarios and when you would use certain diagrams. In the following sections, we go through one representative diagram in each category, detailing the steps to create, format, and edit it until it's everything you could ever want in a diagram. As we review each diagram, we discuss different parts of the creation process, so that by the time we get to the last section, you'll know how to change every element of SmartArt diagrams.

Each SmartArt graphic consists of individual elements, and they can accept text entered directly through a text dialog editor associated with the entire image. Generally, the amount of text you enter determines the number of objects your graphic displays. For example, if you start with a five-circle process chart but enter only four items, Excel will delete the unused fifth item. Some of the objects lend themselves to a good deal of descriptive text, while others can accommodate just key points, and details should follow in related documents.

One thing to keep in mind when you're building SmartArt diagrams is accurately depicting your process, structure, timeline, and so on so that it will make sense to others. When you're doing this kind of storytelling, you want to get your point across as effectively as possible. A diagram that holds meaning only for you is great posted on your wall, but what about when you're trying to communicate thoughts or concepts to others? When you're working with SmartArt, you want to let the graphic do a lot of the work for you, and that generally means being as concise as possible with the graphic text. You have plenty of room to expand on the ideas later. When you're trying to convey a great visual impression, don't clutter it up!

After you choose a SmartArt design, you simply click OK, and Excel creates an empty object on the sheet for you, right in the center of your screen. This object has the focus, and you can start working with it right away. If you click off it, the SmartArt stays in place, but the text dialog disappears until you once again select the object. You can enter text in the text dialog, or you can enter it directly in the text boxes on the diagram itself.

Hint: When you first set up a SmartArt diagram, it's probably better to use the text dialog, and save editing individual elements until you're done. By then you should only need to make minor changes to one or two parts.

You can move and size both the text dialog and the SmartArt diagram by using their borders and drag handles. The text dialog defaults to a position on the left, but if you move a diagram to the far left of the worksheet, Excel does its best to keep the text dialog close to the diagram.

Note: The following examples are included in the Chapter 8 companion workbook. For each of the following categories of SmartArt, you'll find the initial empty diagram, a diagram with just text entered, and the final diagram with formatting applied.

SmartArt Categories

To insert SmartArt on a worksheet, go to **Insert > SmartArt**. Excel opens the Choose a SmartArt Graphic dialog (shown below), which includes a number of categories, each with quite a few unique options. Each category shows a list of the options available, and when you choose any of them, Excel automatically displays a color preview on the right.

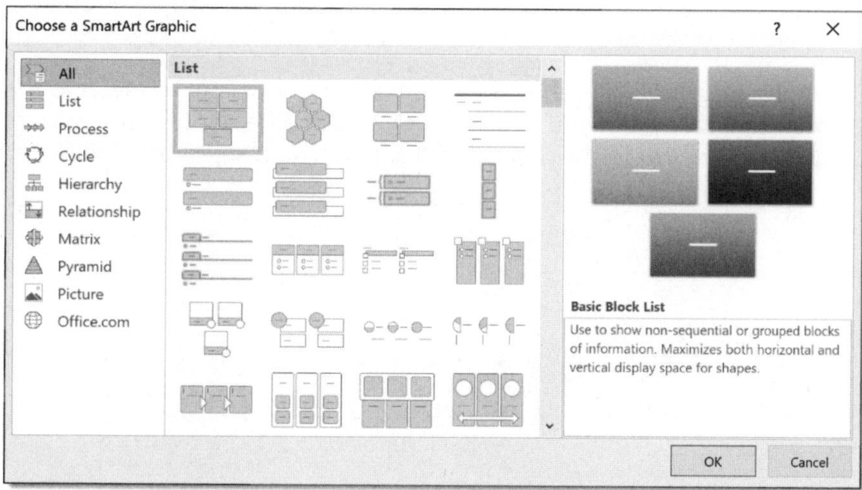

The List Category

You can use lists to show blocks of information that are usually segmented into related groups. You can use lists of anything you want: ideas, tasks, people, departments, processes and subprocesses, and so on. Using

SmartArt lists is a great way to add flair to a document that might otherwise have just a boring numbered or bulleted list. The following example shows a basic SmartArt list, followed by the same list with three text items entered, and then a final formatted rendering just a few mouse clicks later.

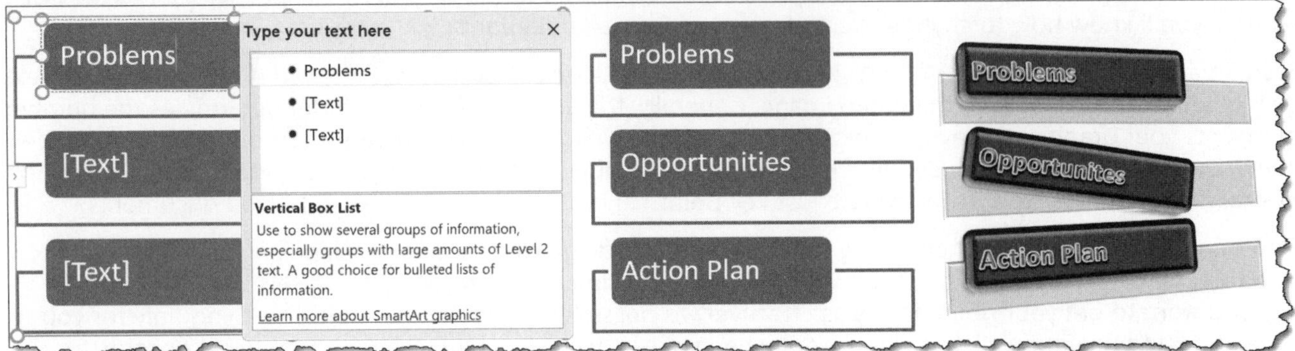

Notice the text dialog floating over the first list in the example above. This is where you enter the list details. As soon as you click off that list, the text dialog disappears. It reappears when you click the list again. Keep in mind that you can format, resize, and even rotate many diagram elements if you want. For example, the third diagram in this example shows the center text box rotated to a diagonal position; you probably wouldn't want to do this in most instances, but it's an example of what you can accomplish with SmartArt lists. What features you use depends on how you want to present your information.

The Process Category

The SmartArt Process options are generally designed to document some sort of flow. Process diagrams can detail anything that has several steps to be completed in order, such as how to get from Point A to Point B, the order in which an order goes from marketing to sales to production to fulfillment, or the steps to take to create a cup of coffee or to refill the toner in the copier.

To use process SmartArt, select the diagram you want from the Choose a SmartArt Graphic dialog and let Excel place it on the sheet for you. Next, you can start entering text for bullet points; as shown in the example below, and you can also add some alternating headers.

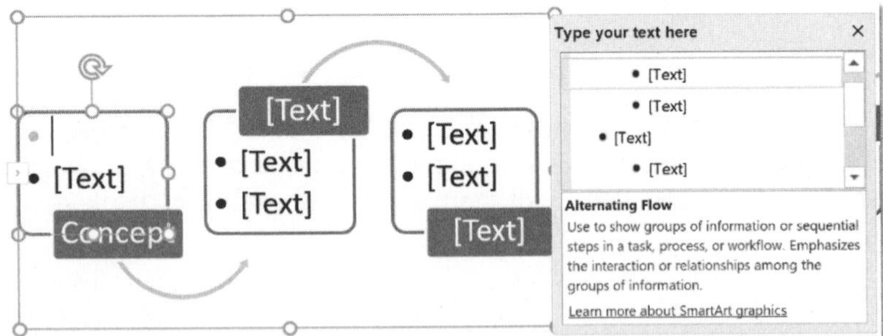

If you click on the very first [Text] option in the diagram, you can enter your text just by typing. To move to the next item in the list, you can press the **down arrow** key, but you need to click on the different groups/headers to get to them. You can also select a SmartArt shape, go to the SmartArt Design tab, and select the Text Pane option, shown below.

Then, as you type, you can see what you are entering previewed in the corresponding text box on the diagram. When you're done entering text, you can leave it as is, or you can adjust the individual elements however you want. As you can see in the example below, there are many formatting options available. The best way to get familiar with them is to play with them on your own.

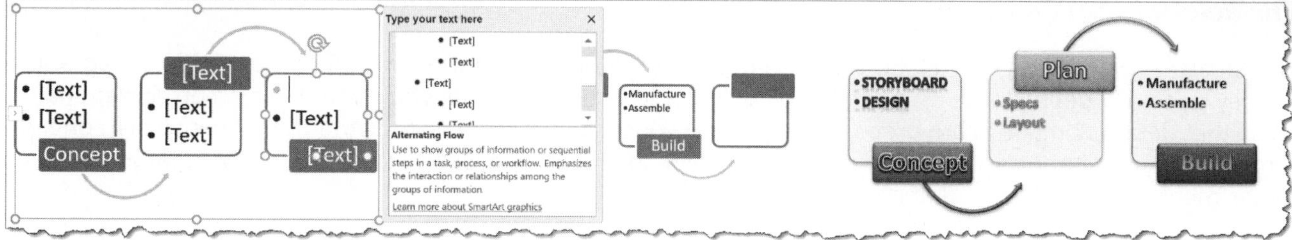

The Cycle Category

The diagrams in the Cycle category are used to represent continuing flows of actions, such as a manufacturing process in which a piece of raw material gets run through a series of procedures and is finished, and then another piece of material goes through the same process right away. Another example would be farming: The farmer prepares the fields and plants seeds, the seeds grow into plants, and the plants are harvested and sent to market. Whereas a process flow has a start and an end, a cycle is continuous until someone shuts off the power or in some other way puts an end to the process.

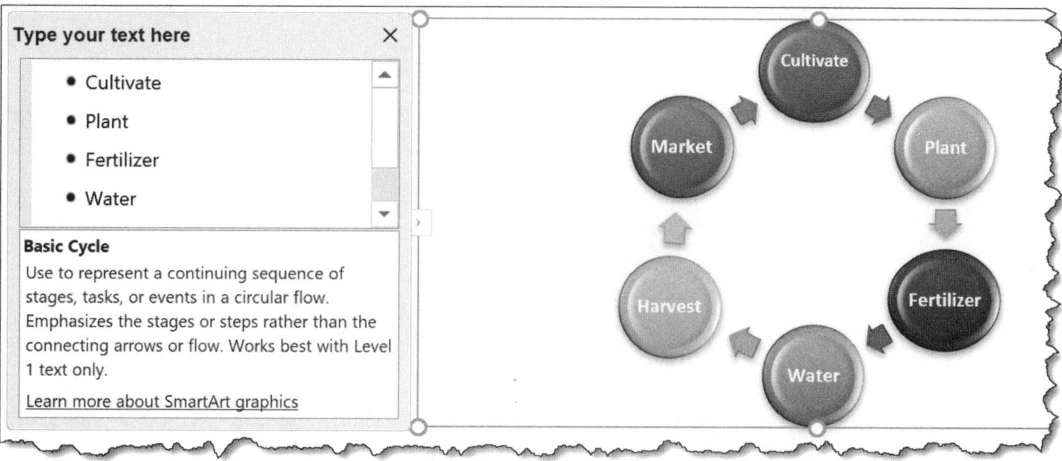

The Hierarchy Category

The Hierarchy SmartArt category can be used to create what are commonly called org (or organizational) charts. Such a chart essentially defines parent/child relationships, and there is always something or someone at the top. For instance, a corporation might be the parent object, and multiple departments within that organization might be listed underneath. Within those departments are managers, supervisors, and staff, all with different levels of responsibility and job functions. Within those areas of responsibility may be certain processes and procedures that need to be followed, and so on. Hierarchical diagrams often represent the top levels of an entity and progress into deeper detail with every level. There might be 20 or more org charts that define the structure of a single organization.

A traditional org chart goes from the top down, but another common theme is from side to side. You've probably seen something like this if you've ever looked at a sports bracket, where a group starts with 16 teams, then whittles down to 8 and then to 4 and then to 2, and finally down to a single champion.

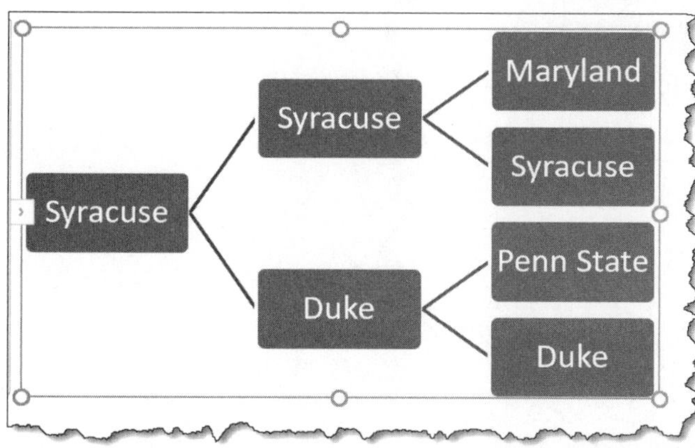

The Relationship Category

The SmartArt graphics in the Relationship category are a bit less structured than the other types of diagrams as they generally define loose associations between objects. For instance, you might have an organizational chart that details company core processes (e.g., marketing, sales, production, distribution, finance). No one department is more important than the others, and each one plays a vital role in the organization (although each department will likely beg to differ).

An example of a relationship diagram is a Venn diagram, which uses two or more circles overlapping to various degrees, depending on the depth of the relationship between the objects. (The symbol for the Olympics is technically a Venn diagram.)

The Matrix Category

The options in the Matrix SmartArt category generally show individual parts in relationship to each other or in relationship to a greater whole or concept. This SmartArt category is often used in brainstorming, where you have disparate functions that are all related to a central theme. Matrix diagrams are generally limited to four or fewer elements.

The Pyramid Category

Everyone's seen the old USDA Food Pyramid, which detailed the healthy amounts of food types we should eat each day. Depending on their direction, pyramids roll up or down from greatest importance to least.

The Picture Category

The SmartArt Picture category of options includes some very creative diagrams in which you can customize each object with an image, as opposed to just a colored shape. For instance, you could have pictures of individual departments, with the employee of the month in the middle. Or, as shown below, you could showcase your products with their respective prices.

Formatting SmartArt

The following sections briefly look at some of the formatting options you have available when working with SmartArt.

Adding Another Shape

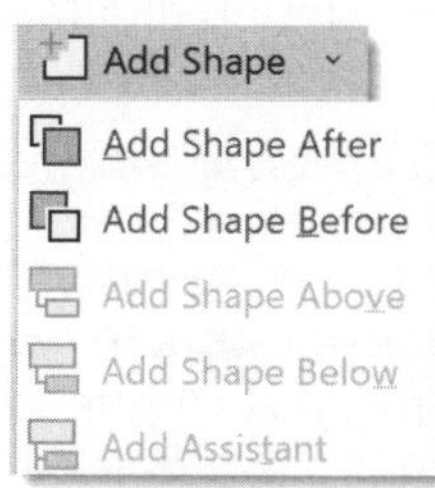

What do you if you have created a cycle SmartArt diagram and want to add another shape to your process? You need to go to **SmartArt Design > Add Shape**. Then, depending on the type of diagram you have and which object you have selected, you also have to make some choices about where the new shape will go, as shown at right.

Adding a Bullet

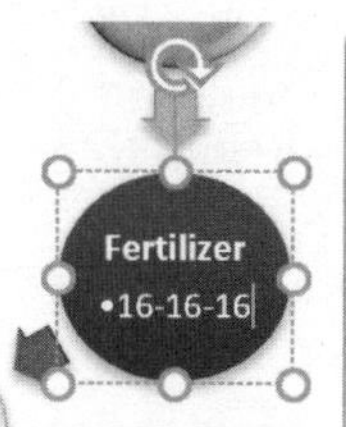

In a cycle SmartArt diagram, a shape's subheader, shown at right, is called a *bullet*.

Changing Colors

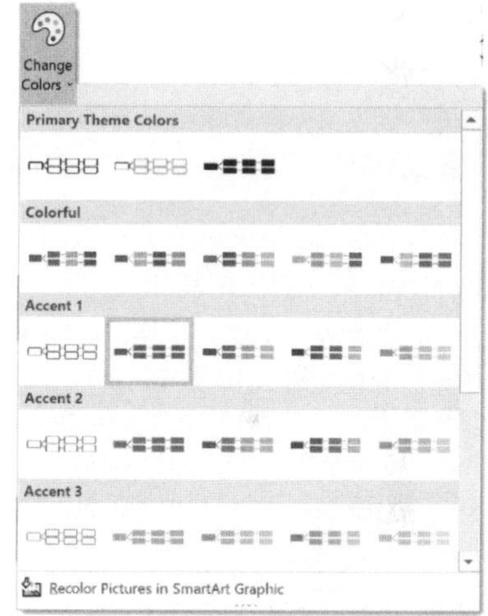

When you have the correct number of shapes, and all your text is entered, it's time to add a color scheme. To do this, go to **SmartArt Design > Change Colors** and select the color scheme that's best for you from the options shown below. The Change Colors command has live preview, so you can hover over the combinations one at a time to see your image change.

Changing Styles

You can adjust the default style from the SmartArt Styles group on the SmartArt Design tab, where each SmartArt type has its own style selections. The following example shows the selections for the Horizontal Hierarchy style.

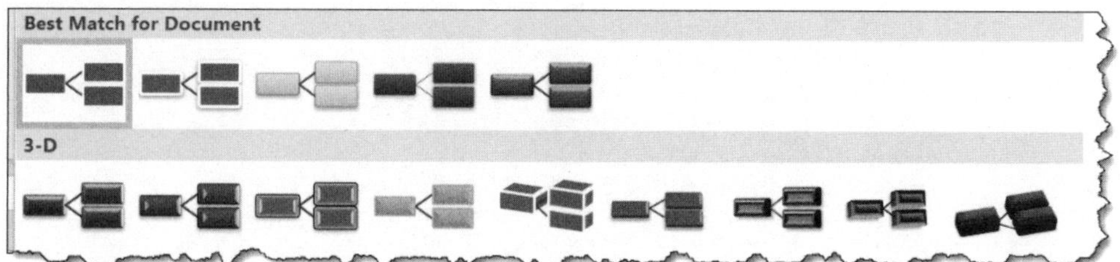

Making Additional Changes

If you want to change fonts and other attributes, you can make changes to individual objects or to all the objects in a piece of SmartArt. To change an individual shape, click just that shape and go to the Font group on the Home tab. To change all the text in the entire graphic, select the group pane and go to the Font group on the Home tab. This is one of the rare times when you need to manually apply changes from the Font group because SmartArt doesn't support styles the way that cells do.

Note that with some SmartArt shapes, you can customize fonts and other attributes, but they might lose those changes if you switch to a SmartArt style that doesn't support the configurations you've applied. If you click through the SmartArt gallery for each shape, for example, you can see which ones support multiple colors. As mentioned earlier, it's a good idea to hold off on making formatting changes until you've finalized your general design and text.

Changing Shapes

It's possible that when you create SmartArt, you might get a shape close to where you want it, but it just doesn't work for you, and you want to change it. In this case, go to the Layouts or Styles group on the SmartArt Design tab and scroll through the selections. These feature have live preview, so you can see what your changes look like on the fly. For example, the following image shows two different themes, which you preview just by hovering over them in the gallery.

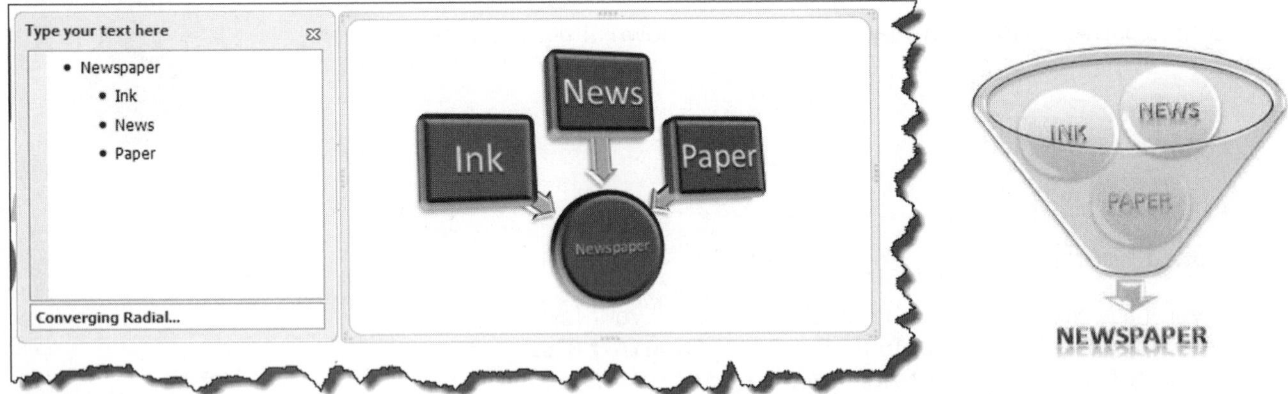

Format Object Menu

What if after you've made many changes, you still don't think your masterpiece is complete? You can dive into the Format Shape pane and adjust individual elements. To get there, right-click on the object in question and select Format Shape from the bottom of the context menu. As you can see below, there are quite a few options available. The best way to get to know all these options and the possible combinations is to experiment and see what you can create.

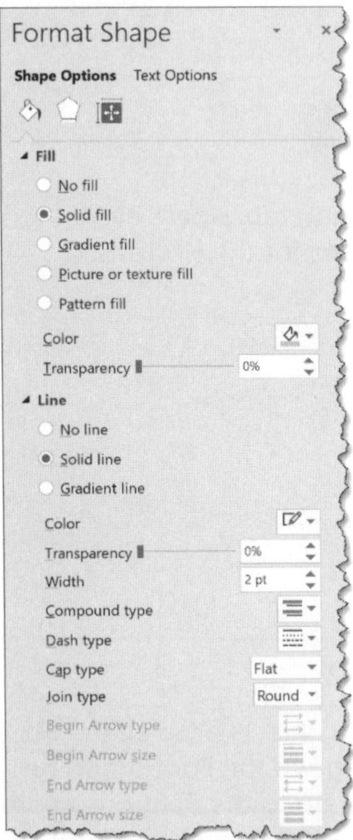

Converting to a Shape

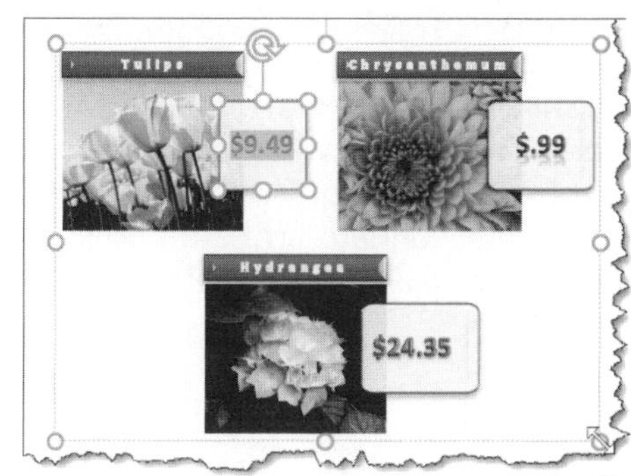

When you're ready to share your workbook that includes SmartArt graphics, you probably want to prevent people from changing those graphics. There are two ways to accomplish this. First, if you want to be able to make changes later, you can protect the worksheet. When you do this, your SmartArt stays SmartArt, and you can still interact with it all. The other option is to go to **SmartArt Design > Convert to Shapes** to convert the diagram into a series of grouped shapes. The following example shows SmartArt converted to shapes; you can still change the pricing and the text, but you can't add or remove shapes or bullets unless you copy one of the existing shapes and add it manually.

WordArt

Perhaps you've noticed that the text in SmartArt is plain old worksheet text. Sure, you can change the font type, color, or size, but those options still aren't as creative as the SmartArt graphics themselves. Fortunately, WordArt complements SmartArt very well. Select the SmartArt shape you want to change, select the SmartArt Format tab, and from the WordArt Styles group, select the format you want from the gallery shown below. You can make further adjustments to the shape's text fill, outline, and effects.

The following image shows a simple WordArt example.

Your text here

Following is an example of a basic matrix shape that has a WordArt style applied.

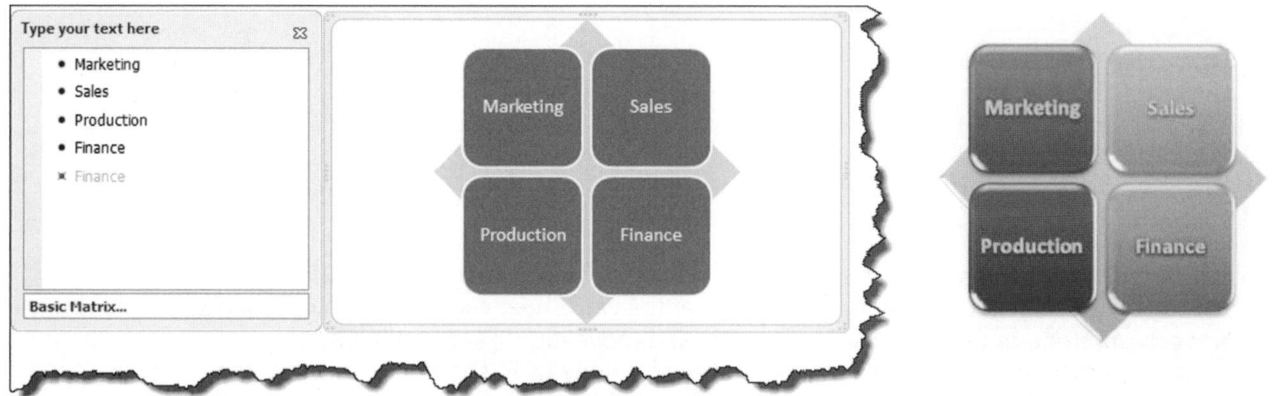

WordArt lets you give your text some flair beyond what's available in the standard Format Cells dialog. However, WordArt is applicable only to updating font attributes in pictures, shapes (including charts), and SmartArt. WordArt styles don't apply to text in the Excel grid, which is probably a very good thing from a usability standpoint.

I've talked several times in this book about being conservative with how you dress up and present your work in Excel. You should be as careful with WordArt as you are with other features in Excel, but if you've built a nice custom graphic, you can use WordArt to tastefully give its text a bit of flair. If you have an existing object with text you want to adjust, you can click to select it and go to the WordArt Styles group on the Shape Format tab and experiment with the options. You generally select an option from the WordArt Styles gallery on the left before you use the Text Fill, Text Outline, or Text Effects options. If you don't have an existing object, you can go to **Insert > Shapes** to add a text box and then enter your text; then you can select the shape and apply WordArt settings. As with SmartArt objects, you should finalize your WordArt text before you start formatting it. Text boxes with WordArt behave just like any other text boxes: You can resize, rotate, change font size, and even change standard font attributes, like bold, italic, underline, and so on. Live preview helpfully lets you see what changes will look like before you commit to them.

Take some time to play with WordArt to get a feel for the many possibilities. Making final touches by adding WordArt to your graphics can make a world of difference in a workbook.

Screenshot

You can use the **Insert > Screenshot** option if you need to create a users' manual or some type of training material that walks someone through a process with screenshots. The Screenshot tool can be really helpful, and I captured many of the images in this book with it.

When you go to **Insert > Screenshot**, you see a small menu that displays images of your open Office windows, as shown below.

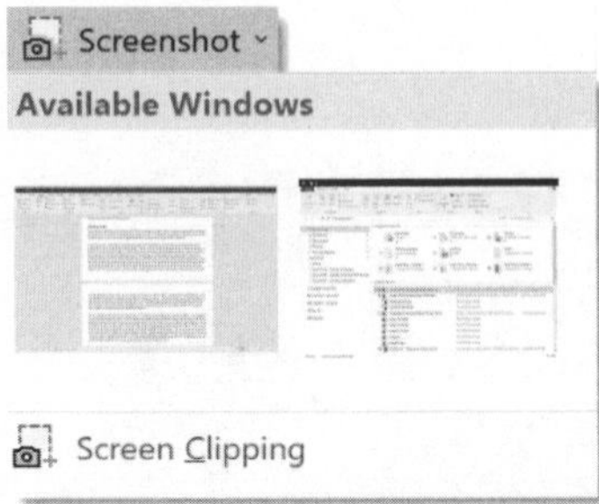

You can select any of the images in this menu to place a full-screen image of that Office window in Excel. Unfortunately, the image might initially take up the entire worksheet window, so you probably want to resize it a bit. You can grab one of the corner sizing handles and move it until you get it where you want it. If you grab the middle handles, you resize the shape—but not proportionally. To show only a part of the image, with the image selected, go to **Picture Format > Crop**. You immediately see the image's sizing handles turn into cropping handles. Start from any side and crop the image down to just the area that you want to keep. As you crop in each direction, the Crop tool shades the area that it's going to remove. When the image area is the size you want, all you need to do is press **Esc** to finish the cropping. When the image is the final size that you want, you can add some shapes like arrows or callouts to help describe certain processes, add labels, or point out other specifics. The image below shows a screenshot of this chapter, which could be cut down to one page by using the Crop tool.

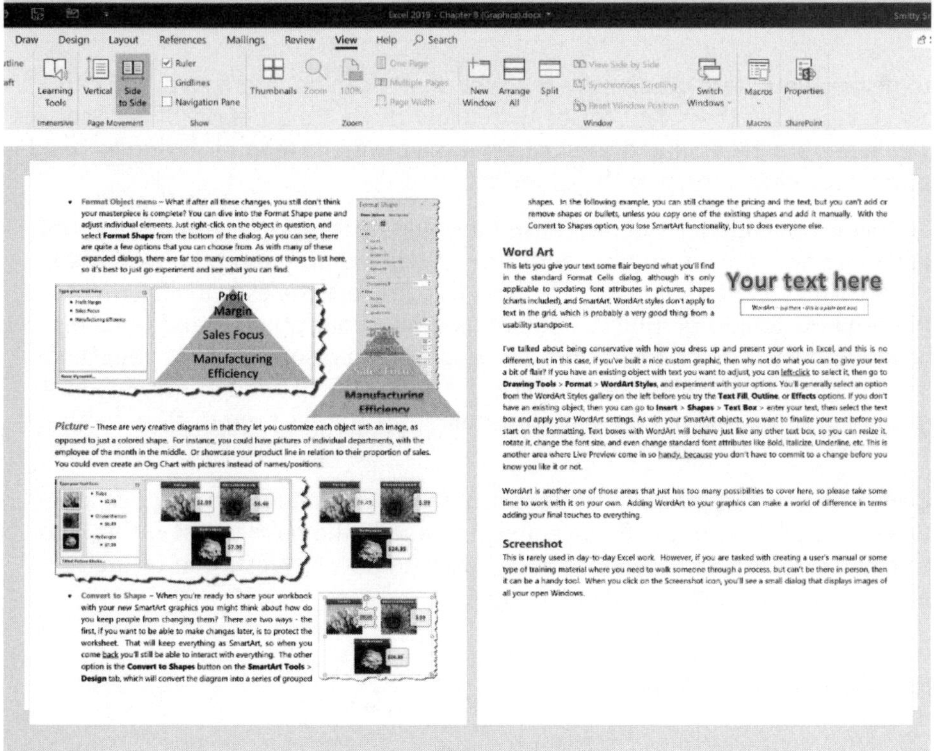

Screen Clipping

When you select the Screenshot tool, you get a Screen Clipping option at the bottom of the drop-down menu. The Screen Clipping option circumvents the screenshot/cropping process just described and allows you to grab just the area that you want from the start. When you select the Screen Clipping option, your cursor turns into a cross, which you can drag around the specific area you want to capture. Here is an example of a screen clipping of this section (with a border added for effect).

Screen Clipping

When you select the Screenshot

Clipping option circumvents the

want from the start. When you se

around the specific area you wan

to pick which one to take a scree

Hint: If you're using OneNote, an even better way to crop is to use the **Shift+Windows+S** shortcut to use the OneNote screen clipping tool because you can switch to the application you want to capture and then use the shortcut to grab it. When you're done, just switch back to Excel and use **Ctrl+V** to paste it in.

Chapter Summary

- In this chapter you learned about the different ways you can bring more meaning to your workbooks than just through figures and text. Excel lets you use comments, custom pictures and logos, shapes, SmartArt, and even live action images of other worksheets.
- This chapter describes the many different SmartArt types and provides examples of where to use them. It also discusses using WordArt.
- This chapter shows how to create screenshots and crop certain areas from them.

Chapter 9: Charts

Using charts is an amazing way to display your data graphically. In Excel, charts can be interactive: You can add filters and slicers to let people change what they want to see with a few clicks. It's the basis of "self-service business intelligence," where you give people the ability to see just what they want instead of having to build multiple reports for others to see the information the way they want to see it.

Throughout this book, we've been following a relatively common workbook progression: determining your needs and developing an initial layout; adding data, formulas, and formatting; and preparing the workbook for sharing with other people. At this point, you have already seen how to complete the essential elements of a workbook, and you have also seen how to add graphical elements to make your points stand out. This chapter continues that theme, showing how to add charts, which are graphical representations of your data, and can make it easier for you to tell your story quickly. Like graphics, charts are best added at the very end of your workbook's development. Once you have all the data and formulas in place, it's time to start creating snapshots of it.

The following image shows company revenue plotted against gross profit in what's called a *magnitude*, or *combo*, chart. This kind of chart was made popular in the finance industry, and in the past, building this kind of chart was a complicated affair. Fortunately, the Excel team actively listens to user requests and created a combo chart type so you can build this kind of chart in just a few clicks.

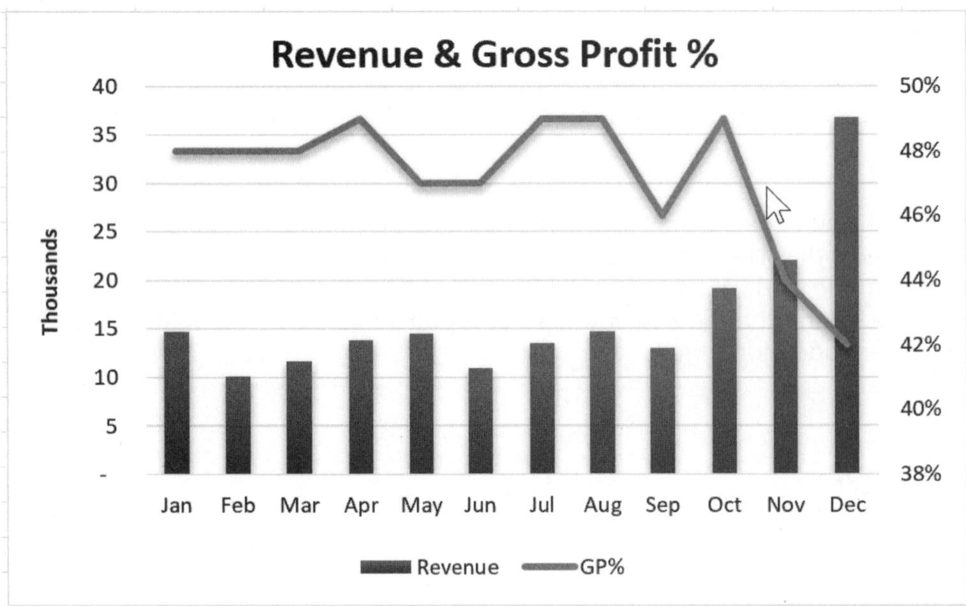

Not everyone can look at a series of numbers and immediately identify a trend or pattern. Most people could probably see some of the same trends given some time, but using charts can help people come to such conclusions more quickly. You have a story to tell with your numbers, and charts are a fantastic way to help you tell it better. Unfortunately, charts are also some of the most inefficiently used tools in Excel. It's not because charts are inherently difficult to build; in fact, they're remarkably easy to make. The issue is largely that people don't know how to properly build them. Building a chart is one of the most time-consuming tasks in Excel, and there are admittedly quite a few elements in a chart to change. The mistake people make is that they build the same chart over and over and make the same changes to each individual copy of the chart, not realizing that it only needs to be built once and can then be reused.

This chapter discusses the broad theory of charts, including the types of charts available and when you might use them. It also show how to build charts from all nine of Excel's standard chart categories and how to save each one of those chart types as a favorite template that you can use again and again. Along the way, this chapter also covers some of the key tools that you can use to turn plain old boring Excel charts into something that people will think came from the marketing department. Who says data has to be boring?

Planning to Use Charts

You can use a chart any time you think a graphical representation of data would tell a better story than the data itself. However, as with a lot of other elements we've discussed throughout this book, charts should be used judiciously. While charts can tell a great story, they are meant to augment the underlying data, and using too many of them—particularly if they have only minute differences or have little relevance to the subject—can quickly overwhelm a workbook. By the same token, if you don't include enough charts, you might not get your point across. You need to strike a balance and present what's most appropriate for your audience.

Just as important as the content of a chart is how you place charts in relationship to the worksheet, your data, and other charts. Some people prefer to intersperse charts with data, others keep data hidden and show only charts, others prefer chart sheets (i.e., Excel worksheets that are each dedicated to a single chart), and some prefer dashboard-type views in which charts are clustered together with or without supporting data. Regardless of the format you choose, you need to hold yourself accountable to providing a layout that's as user friendly as possible. If you overwhelm your audience with charts thrown all over the place, the valuable information they can impart is lost. It's important to consider the message you trying to send.

Before you create charts, you need to make sure your data structure can support them; otherwise, you'll end up with a confusing mess. In general, your data needs to be in a row/column format and consistently formatted and labeled. This means that data types can't be mixed within the same column or row (e.g., currency and dates mixed in the same column or in merged cells). Here's an example of properly formatted data and a new column chart based on this data.

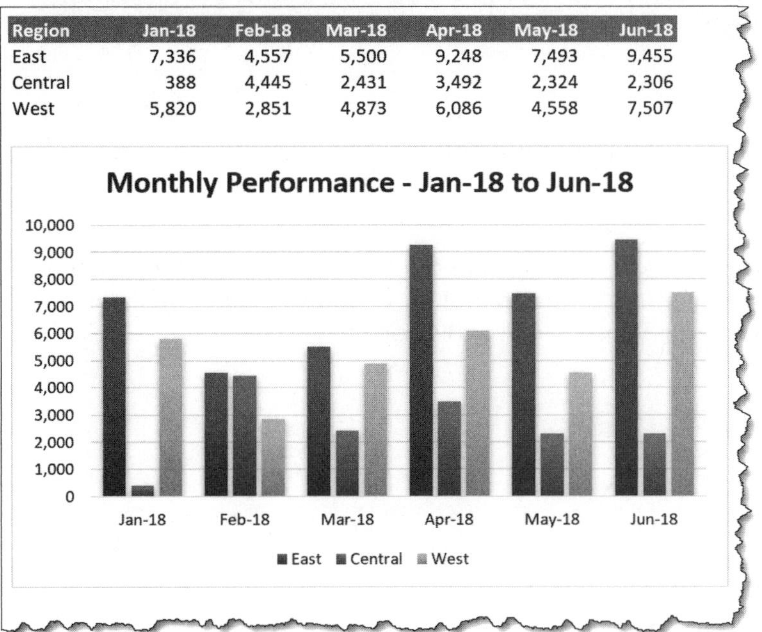

Region	Jan-18	Feb-18	Mar-18	Apr-18	May-18	Jun-18
East	7,336	4,557	5,500	9,248	7,493	9,455
Central	388	4,445	2,431	3,492	2,324	2,306
West	5,820	2,851	4,873	6,086	4,558	7,507

When your data is in the correct format, you can determine which chart type would best show what you want to show with the chart.

Chart Terminology and Components

The following sections provide a general overview of the elements that make up a standard chart. This is by no means a comprehensive look at chart components, but it's enough to get started before we look at each of the major chart types.

Plot Area

The only absolutely necessary component of any chart is the data. Charts don't need to have any secondary descriptive elements, like chart title, legends, or axis labels, although these certainly help in many cases—especially when you have several charts, and you want users to be able to quickly note differences between them.

Horizontal and Vertical Axes, Labels, and Titles

Excel automatically adds horizontal and vertical axes, labels, and titles based on the information you have in your column headers and data range. For the vertical axis, Excel analyzes your data and determines the appropriate data range to display, based on the high and low data values. Excel does everything it can to display horizontal labels as true to form as possible, but many times it's forced to cram everything together, and you need to choose a different scale to display (as discussed later in this chapter). In addition to the data labels, you can also add data titles. In the following example, I used Months for the horizontal (x) axis title and Revenue (000's) for the vertical (y) axis title.

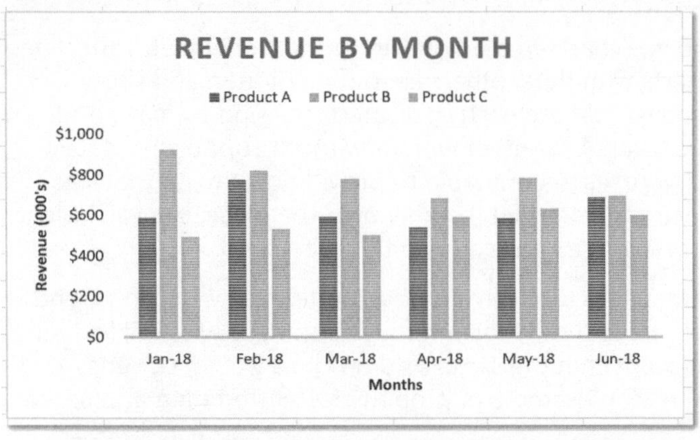

Hint: If you're not sure what kind of chart you need, you can go to **Insert > Recommended Charts**, and Excel will give you some suggestions, based on the data you currently have selected.

x Axis/y Axis

Remember that the horizontal axis is called the *x axis*, and the vertical axis is called the *y axis*.

Legend

The legend provides a summary of your row headers. Legend entries are color-coded to their chart equivalents. In the following example, the legend is at the bottom of the chart. In it, quantity is blue, and it corresponds to the first column of data, which is also blue, revenue is red, and so on.

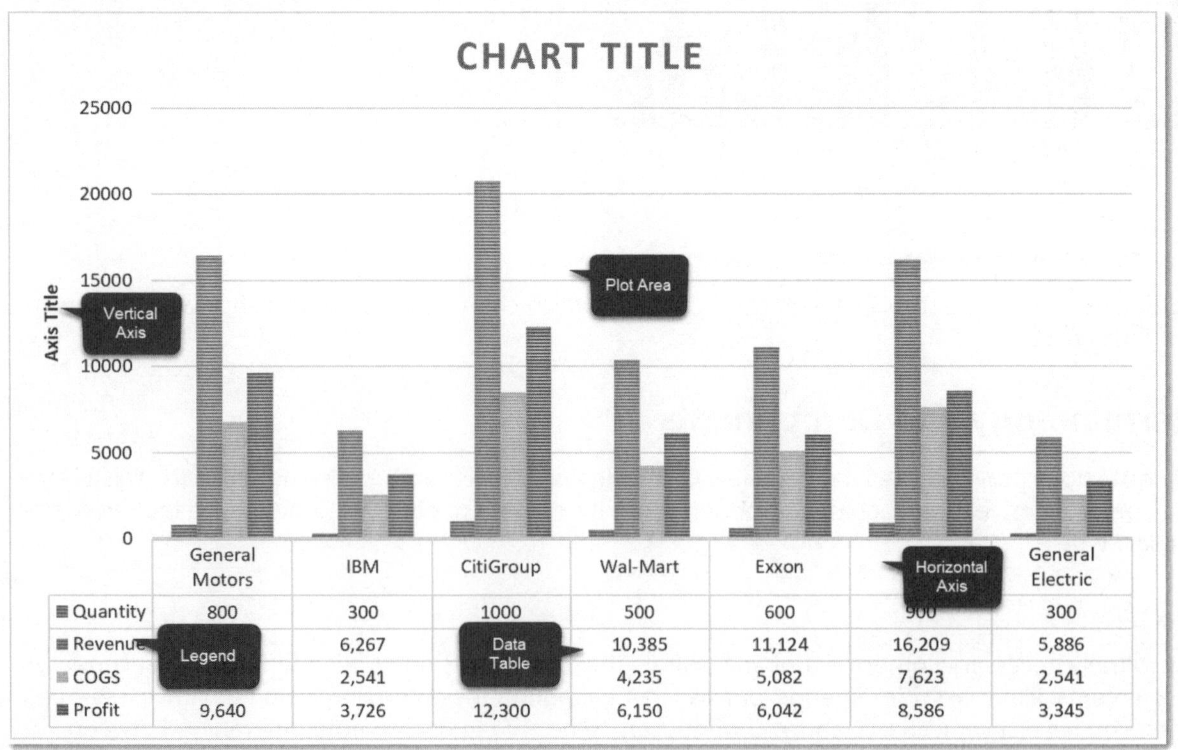

	General Motors	IBM	CitiGroup	Wal-Mart	Exxon		General Electric
Quantity	800	300	1000	500	600	900	300
Revenu		6,267		10,385	11,124	16,209	5,886
COGS		2,541		4,235	5,082	7,623	2,541
Profit	9,640	3,726	12,300	6,150	6,042	8,586	3,345

Chart Title

Excel automatically adds a blank text box labeled Chart Title when you create a chart. You can manually input your own text to replace it, or if you have a title row for your data, you can link that to the chart title by using a formula so it doesn't have to be entered by hand. For instance, you could use the formula **="Quarterly Report - "&TEXT(TODAY(),"MM/DD/YY")** in a cell and link to it. To do this, click the Chart Title text box, go to the formula bar, enter =, click the cell that contains the value you want to use for the chart title, and click the checkmark box to the left of the formula bar.

Data Tables

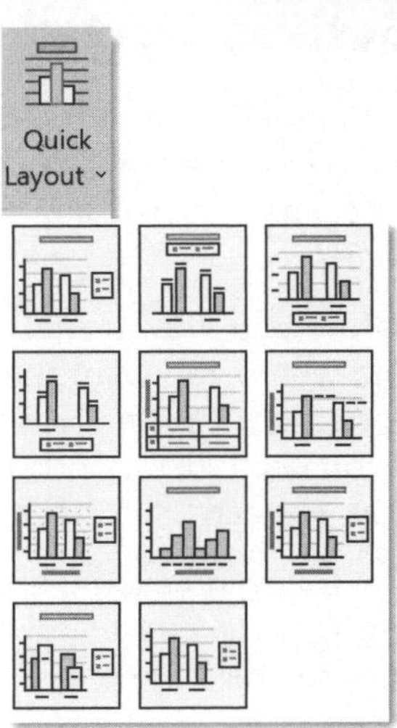

A data table allows you to include the chart data with a chart. The chart example above, for instance, shows a data table at the bottom of the chart. It's not necessary to include a data table with every chart, but it's just one of the many layout options Excel makes available to you. After you have created a chart, you can change the display options by selecting **Chart Design > Quick Layout**, as shown at right. Play with the various options to see what they do. Don't worry about getting a chart perfect for now; you can always adjust individual parts later.

How Data Maps to a Chart

The example below helps you see how various chart elements relate to the data that's being charted.

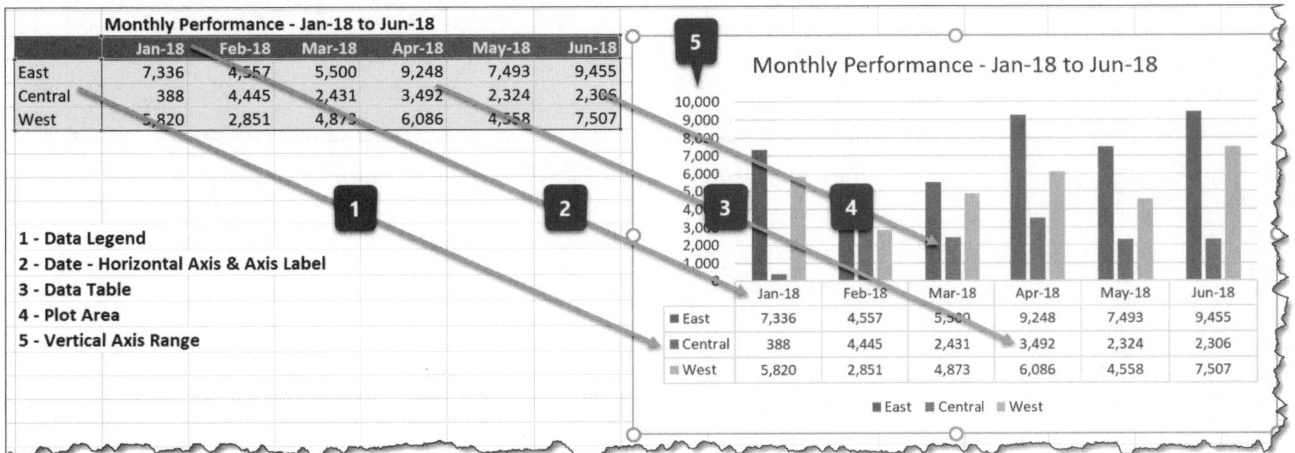

As you can see in this example, the first row of data (East) is represented in the first column in each period (Jan–Jun), followed by the second, and so on. A bar chart would be similar, as it's basically a column chart laid on its side.

Chart Area Visualizations

Remember from Chapter 6 that editing a formula causes Excel to highlight all the formula elements in both the formula and the ranges it references. A chart acts in a similar fashion when you select the chart's plot area. If your data is within view of the chart, you see the chart data area highlighted in different colors and sections that correspond to your data. In addition, when the chart data is highlighted, you can use the drag handles to decrease or expand the current chart area.

> **Note:** Excel only lets you resize chart elements in ways that it can actually chart, so don't be surprised if you can't drag in every direction.

Formatting

Excel carries over cell formatting to your chart, so if you were to change the date or number format in the data, Excel would automatically reflect that change in the chart output. For example, if you were to format the data range as currency with two decimal points, the chart data and legend would display in the same format. In general, you want to keep chart number formats as small as possible and use extraneous data such as decimals only when really necessary. Little things as small as decimal points can add up, eventually cluttering up a chart.

Getting Started with Charts

In Chapter 4 you got a quick look at chart types and some of the basics of charts, but this chapter goes over them in more detail. In this chapter you will learn about more specifics, starting with the dataset, the chart type, chart formatting, and the final placement of a chart in relationship to the worksheet and any other charts.

Before you draw a chart, you should have a general idea of what you want the data to say, where the data is, and where you want the chart to be (e.g., the current worksheet, a different sheet, a chart sheet). After you've done that, it's time to pick your data. If you want to chart an entire range, you can select any cell in that range; if you want just a portion of the range, you need to select only the range(s) you want to chart. (Don't forget that you can use **Ctrl+click** to select multiple, non-contiguous ranges.)

The following example shows a contiguous data range. However, only a portion of this data is going to be used for the chart, and it is selected manually. If you don't manually select the data you want to chart, Excel tries to chart the entire range, which may not be what you want.

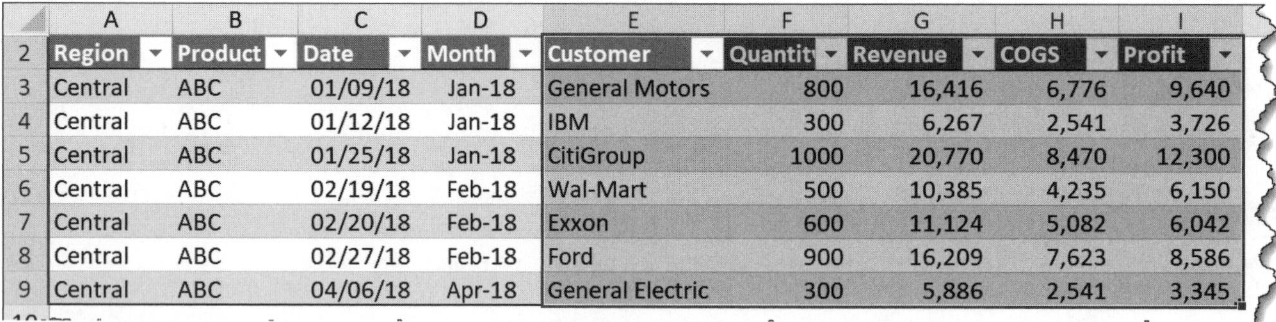

	A	B	C	D	E	F	G	H	I
2	Region	Product	Date	Month	Customer	Quantit	Revenue	COGS	Profit
3	Central	ABC	01/09/18	Jan-18	General Motors	800	16,416	6,776	9,640
4	Central	ABC	01/12/18	Jan-18	IBM	300	6,267	2,541	3,726
5	Central	ABC	01/25/18	Jan-18	CitiGroup	1000	20,770	8,470	12,300
6	Central	ABC	02/19/18	Feb-18	Wal-Mart	500	10,385	4,235	6,150
7	Central	ABC	02/20/18	Feb-18	Exxon	600	11,124	5,082	6,042
8	Central	ABC	02/27/18	Feb-18	Ford	900	16,209	7,623	8,586
9	Central	ABC	04/06/18	Apr-18	General Electric	300	5,886	2,541	3,345

Next, you need to decide on a preliminary chart type. Excel has nine primary categories of charts:

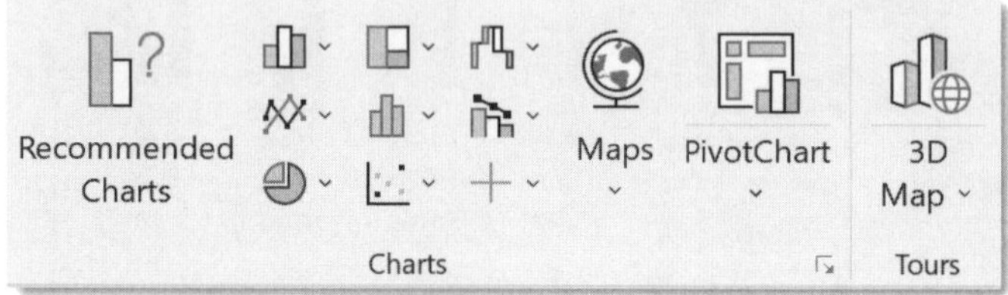

- Column and bar charts
- Line and area charts
- Pie and doughnut charts
- Hierarchy charts, such as treemaps and sunbursts
- Statistic charts, such as (histograms and box and whisker plots
- Scatter (x/y) and bubble charts
- Waterfall, stock, funnel, stock, surface, and radar charts
- Combo charts
- Map charts

Excel also offers some more obscure chart types that have very specific uses. The following sections cover the most common chart types.

> **Note:** All of the examples in this chapter are included in the Chapter 9 companion workbook. In the companion workbook, you'll find data for each example, an initial unformatted chart, a formatted chart, and several other examples to give you some ideas.

Column and Bar Charts

Column charts display data in vertical columns, and bar charts display data in horizontal columns. Both of these chart types are especially good at displaying multiple data points for several groups, such as revenue, expense, and profit by company. Because column and bar charts are almost identical (just oriented differently), this section goes into detail about only column charts, but there is a bar chart example in the Chapter 9 companion workbook.

The most common column charts are the 2-D and 3-D styles; the only difference between the two styles is that an additional illustration gives a 3-D column chart a three-dimensional feel. 3-D charts can be difficult to use with a lot of data, though, because the additional illustration area takes up needed space.

Note: In any chart style—not just column and bar charts—unless you really need 3-D for some reason, stick to 2-D chart types. Excel gives you enough formatting options that 2-D chart styles should work in most cases.

The following sections walk through how to set up a column chart and deal with a data range that is too big to plot accurately. If you allow Excel to choose the data range, it might not choose the same thing you would choose. The following example shows Excel trying to bite off more than it can chew. Here you would really want to plot the customer name and the financials associated with customer, but Excel gives you a lot more than that. At this point, you could go back and re-select just the data you want, or you could just hide the rows and columns you don't need to see.

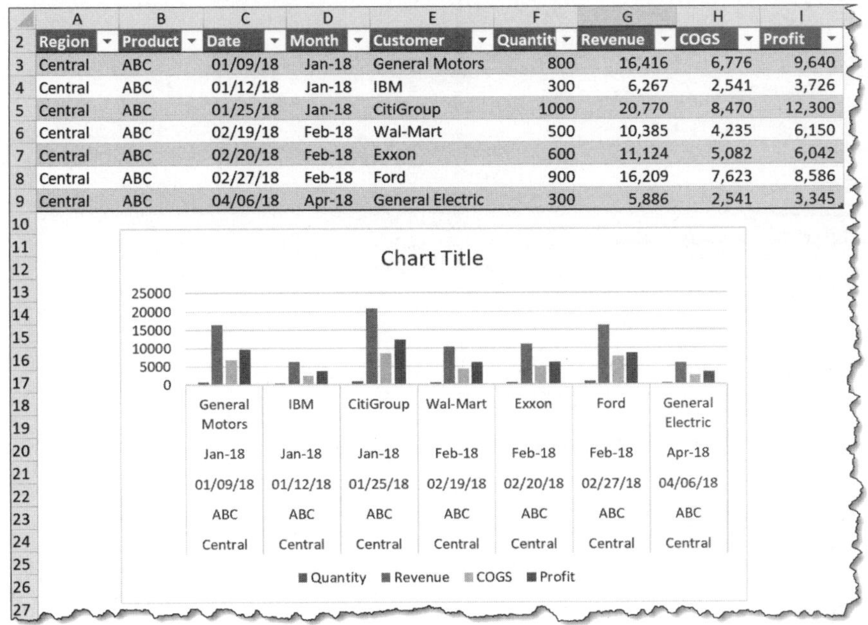

Region	Product	Date	Month	Customer	Quantity	Revenue	COGS	Profit
Central	ABC	01/09/18	Jan-18	General Motors	800	16,416	6,776	9,640
Central	ABC	01/12/18	Jan-18	IBM	300	6,267	2,541	3,726
Central	ABC	01/25/18	Jan-18	CitiGroup	1000	20,770	8,470	12,300
Central	ABC	02/19/18	Feb-18	Wal-Mart	500	10,385	4,235	6,150
Central	ABC	02/20/18	Feb-18	Exxon	600	11,124	5,082	6,042
Central	ABC	02/27/18	Feb-18	Ford	900	16,209	7,623	8,586
Central	ABC	04/06/18	Apr-18	General Electric	300	5,886	2,541	3,345

Excel's default behavior is to plot only visible ranges. This means you can hide rows and columns, and as you do, the corresponding data in the chart is hidden as well. For instance, in the data range in the example above, you could hide the first four columns (A–D), and the chart would show the information you want to show. This hidden range method works great if you don't need to see what's hidden, if you are only going to be basing one chart on a particular data range, or if multiple charts will be sharing the same visible range. If you have multiple charts that need to access both hidden and displayed data, you probably need to instead select the specific range for each chart. Here's the same chart as above but with columns A:D hidden. It's much more concise now.

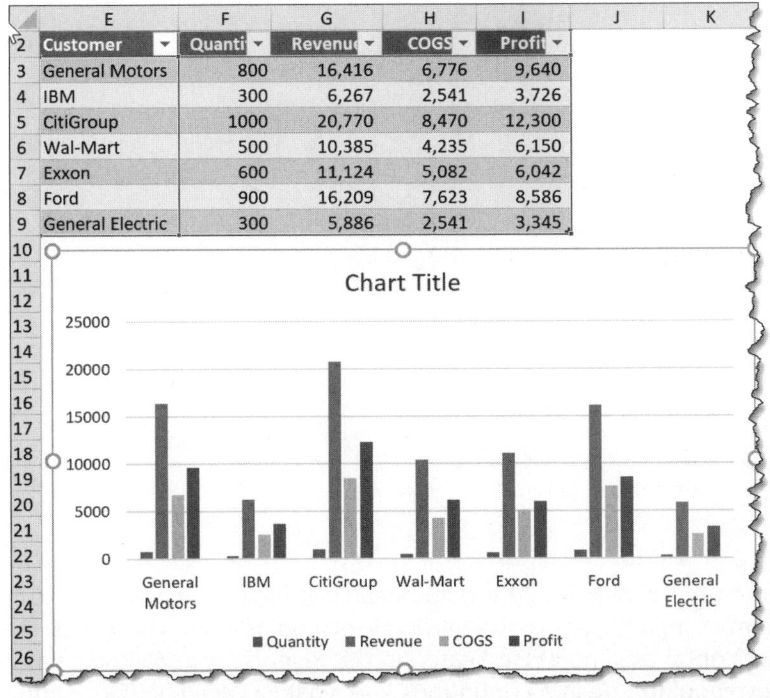

Customer	Quanti	Revenu	COGS	Profit
General Motors	800	16,416	6,776	9,640
IBM	300	6,267	2,541	3,726
CitiGroup	1000	20,770	8,470	12,300
Wal-Mart	500	10,385	4,235	6,150
Exxon	600	11,124	5,082	6,042
Ford	900	16,209	7,623	8,586
General Electric	300	5,886	2,541	3,345

Creating a Column or Bar Chart

Now that you know a bit more about charts and their data, you're ready to try building a column chart. You'll use the same dataset as in the last example, but this time you'll select only the data you want plotted—company and financial data. Go to the Charts group of the Insert tab and select the column chart type you want. If you hover over the various charts in each chart group, Excel gives you a live preview of each one. If you're not sure what chart would be best, go to **Insert > Recommended Charts**, and Excel analyzes your data and recommends several options, as shown below. Select the one you like best, click OK, and Excel adds it for you.

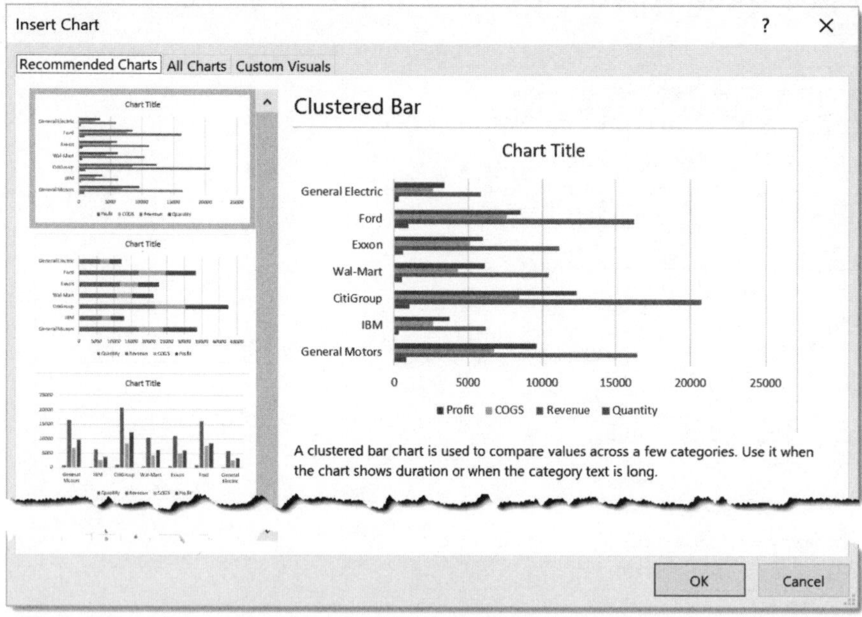

Changing the Chart Type and Style

If you don't like a chart that you or Excel have inserted, you can select the chart, go to **Chart Design > Change Chart Type**, and browse through your options. As you select each option, you get a live preview in the Charge Chart Type dialog, shown below, but your actual chart isn't change until you click OK.

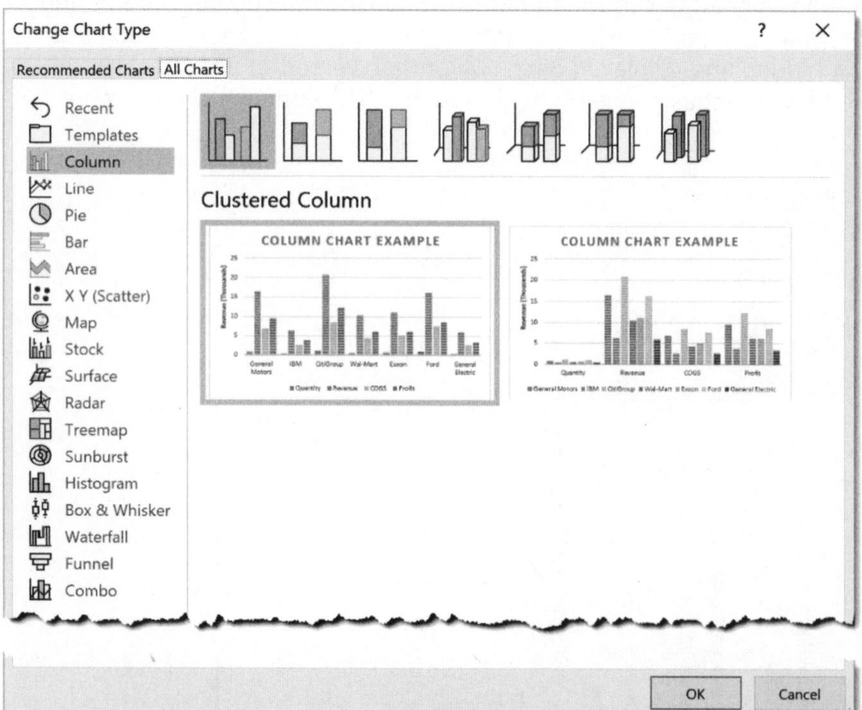

It's pretty easy to see when a chart type is not the right choice for your data because it looks visibly awkward. For example, the following example of the current company data is awkwardly displayed as a line chart that doesn't actually tell the viewer anything. The horizontal data points indicated in the legend aren't following a timeline and aren't related to each other, so they shouldn't be in a continuous line. That is, each line (Quantity,

Revenue, etc.) shows a relationship between corporations even though there isn't one. IBM's revenue and CitiGroup's revenue share no common link, so a chart shouldn't make it seem like they do. In this case, a column chart is a much better choice.

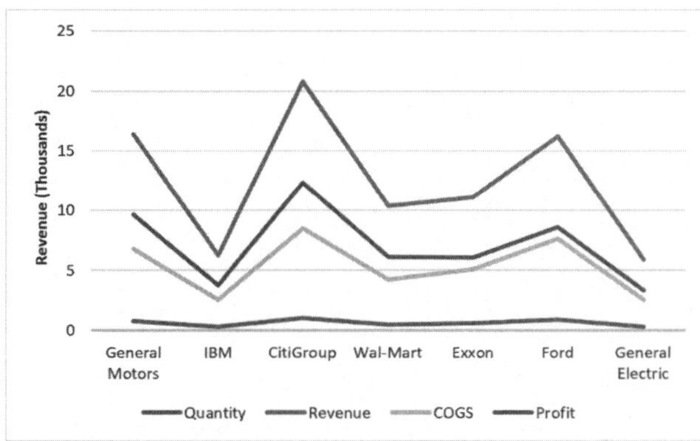

Inspecting a Chart

After you create a chart or Excel creates one for you, you need to ensure that it's correct. Much as you need to validate a workbook for accuracy, you need to ensure that a chart is sending the right message.

While it's generally pretty easy to spot errors in charts because of their visual nature, you shouldn't just assume that a chart is correct without really examining it. Is your data properly plotted? Are your data points properly represented on each axis (horizontal and vertical)? Is your legend correct? Does your chart accurately represent your data? Are you happy with the chart type, or would a different chart type better tell a story? Now is the time to address changes—before you invest too much time in the chart. If the underlying data is in good shape, then your chart is likely to come out very close to what you need.

Using the Chart Design Tab

If you don't like some or any of your major chart elements, you can change them. While you're getting a chart set up, it can be a good idea to see what the chart looks like with another design, such as in 3-D mode instead of 2-D or as a bar chart rather than a column chart. Now is when your major formatting should take place, and the following sections review all the formatting options Excel makes available on the Chart Design tab.

The Add Chart Element Tool

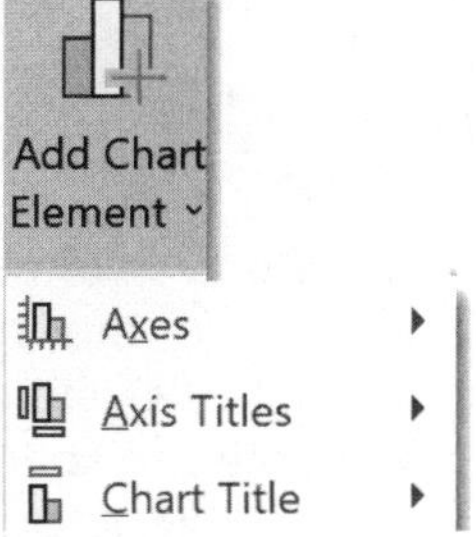

The Add Chart Element tool gives you options for adding individual elements to your charts. For each option you can even find a More Options option, which launches a formatting task pane on the right side of the Excel pane.

The Add Chart Element tool includes the following options

- **Axes**—Choose how to format the x (horizontal) and y (vertical) axes (if you are displaying the axes).
- **Axis Titles**—Choose to display primary horizontal axis titles, primary vertical axis titles, or both. If your axis information is detailed enough, you probably don't need these.
- **Chart Title**—Choose whether and where to include a chart title. Nothing says your chart has to have a title, but it's a good idea to include one if it's not immediately apparent what your chart is trying to say.
- **Data Labels**—Indicate whether and where to label each bar or column. Data labels can be helpful if you don't have a lot of data, but they can quickly clutter up a chart and be obscured by the chart lines themselves, as shown below.

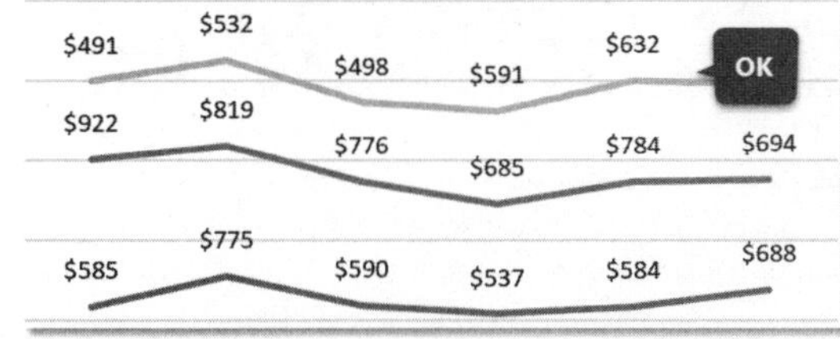

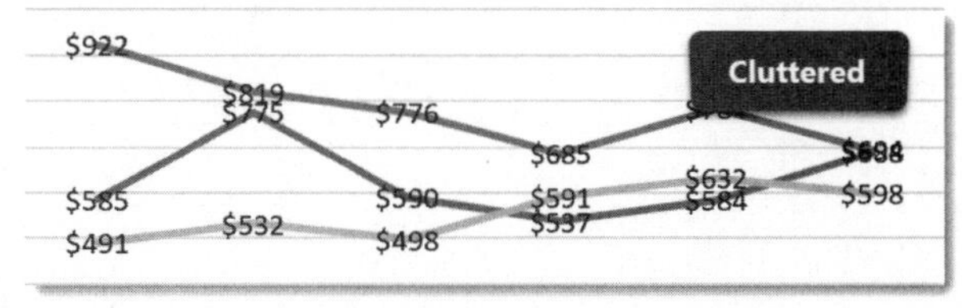

- **Data Table**—Choose whether to include a data table with the chart and whether to include legend keys. Including a data table can be a good way to cross-reference your data and the chart, but it often adds more clutter than is helpful, as in the example below.

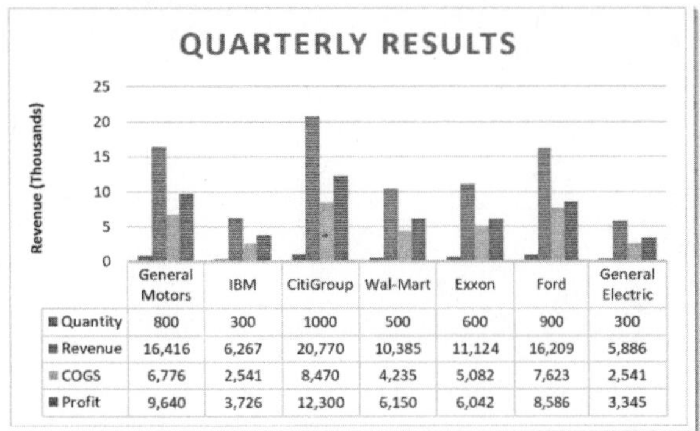

- **Error Bars**—Choose whether to include error bars, which are primarily used in statistical charts to show standard error, percentage error (as shown below), or standard deviation. Choose More Error Bars Options to apply error bars to individual chart items.

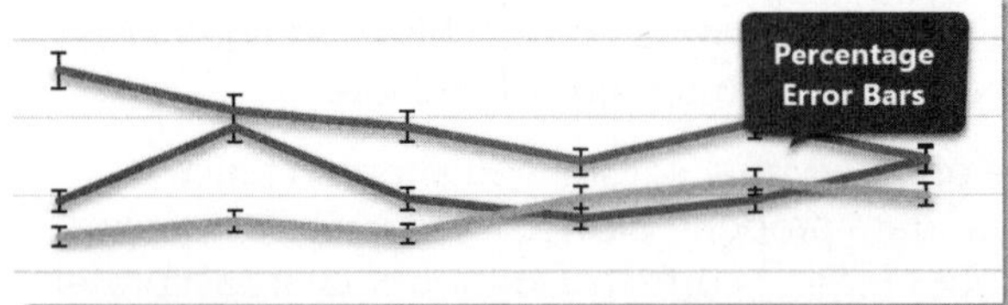

- **Gridlines**—Choose whether to display gridlines, and if you do, choose whether to display minor gridlines, major gridlines, or both. By default, charts have horizontal gridlines at the major data points, but you can also display them on minor points and display vertical gridlines.
- **Legend**—Choose whether to display a legend at the top, bottom, left, or right side of your chart. As with chart titles, you might not need a legend if your data is descriptive enough.
- **Lines**—Choose whether to add vertical lines to your data points where they change, as shown below. Choose Drop Lines to extend to the bottom of the plot area or High-Low Lines to draw lines between the data points.

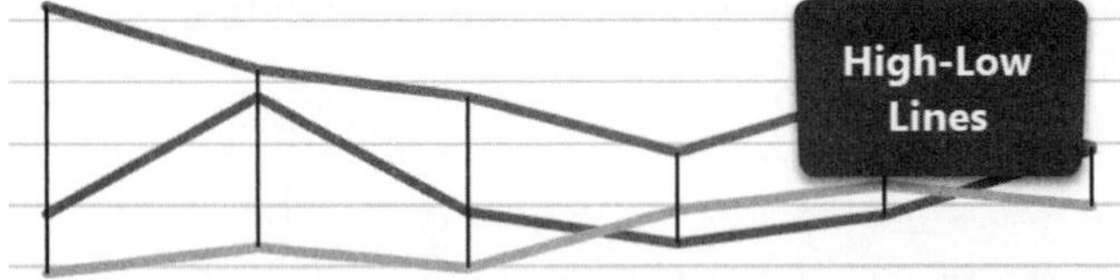

- **Trendline**—For any chart group you select, choose whether Excel should calculate linear, exponential, forecast, or moving average trendlines. The linear trend is the most common, but you might find circumstances where the others prove useful as well. When you select any of the trendline options, you are prompted to specify the dataset to which the trend should apply. While a trendline doesn't show any level of scientific accuracy (although the calculations behind it do), it is a good indicator of performance and can help you make informed decisions. Here's an example with a trendline added for each of three regions. The trendlines clearly show that the East region is performing better than its counterparts.

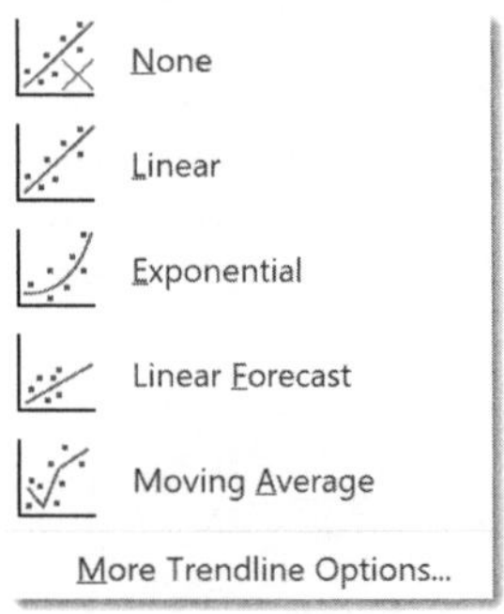

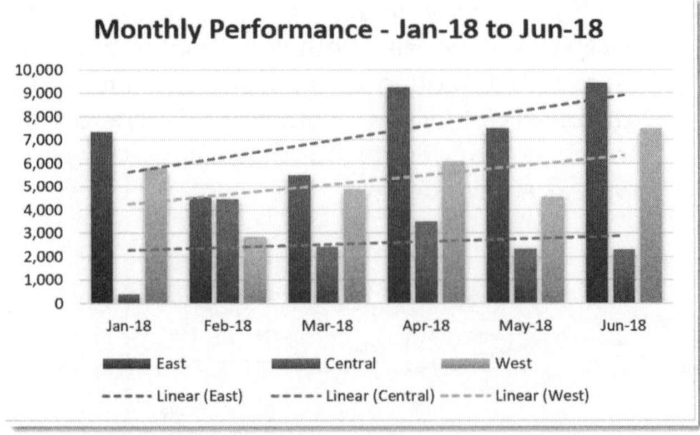

- **Up/Down Bars**—Choose whether to display vertical bars between different data points. Up and down bars work only on 2D line charts. I'm not a big fan, as I think they just clutter things up, as shown below.

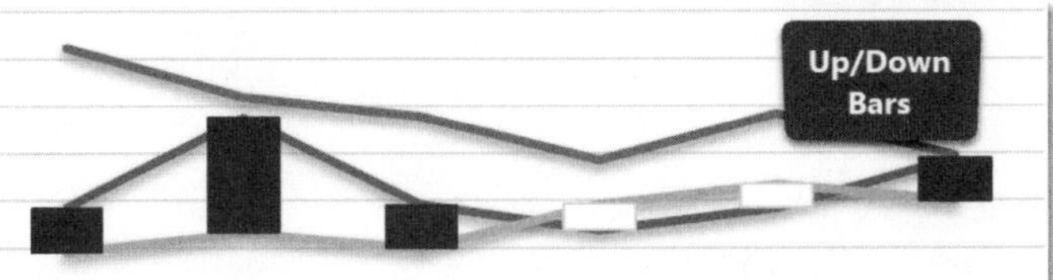

The Quick Layout Tool

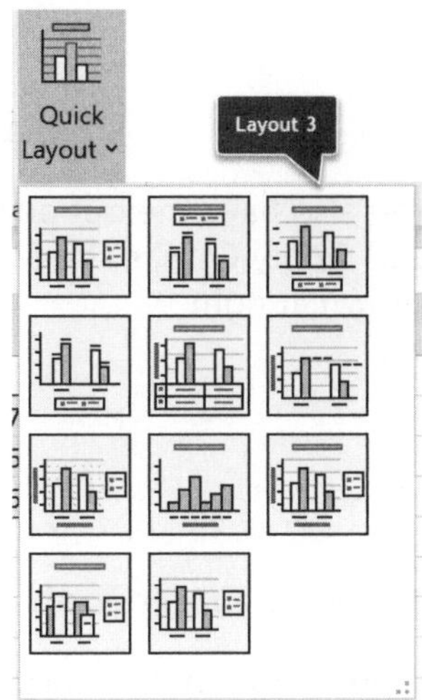

Quick Layout lets you choose from several predefined layouts. For instance, Layout 3, shown at right in the Quick Layout gallery, displays the chart title at the top and a legend at the bottom.

The Change Colors Tool

Much as you can change Excel's color scheme by selecting **Page Layout > Colors**, you can change the chart's general color scheme by selecting **Chart Design > Change Colors**.

The Chart Styles Gallery

If you don't like the chart style that Microsoft picks or want to change a style you applied, you can choose a different one. Applying a style can be a lot easier than trying to format a chart by hand. Just pick one that's close to what you want and then customize it to get exactly what you want.

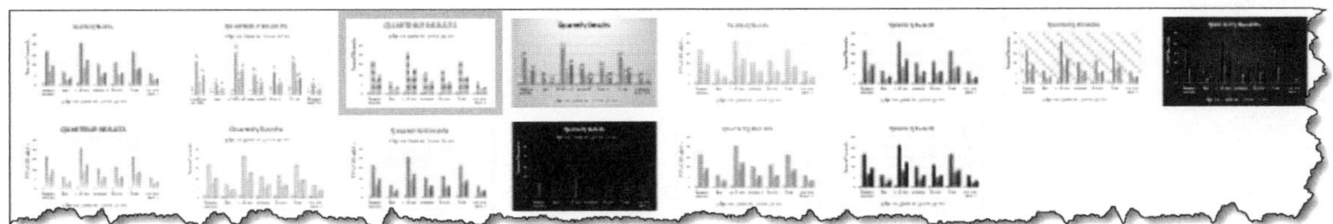

The Switch Row/Column Tool

Sometimes your data might look better with rows as columns and vice versa. The Switch Row/Column tool can help you see which presentation is most helpful. In the following case, the example on the left makes more sense.

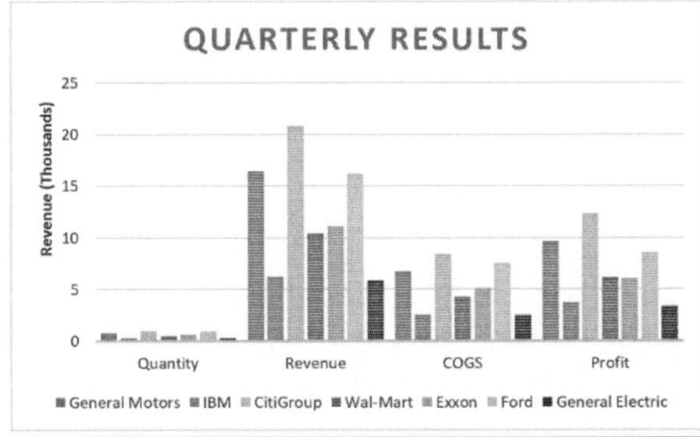

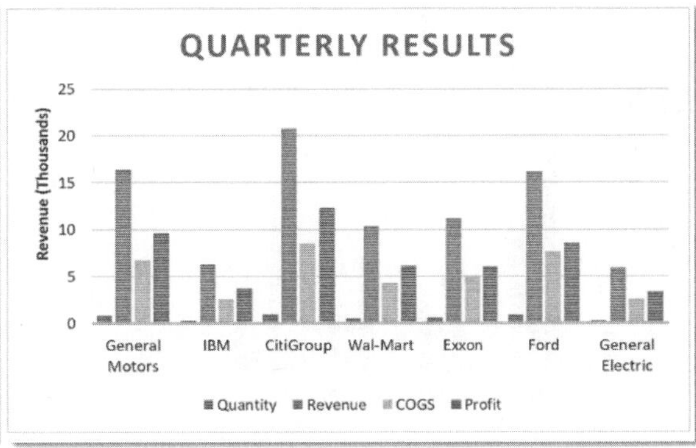

The Select Data Tool

When you click the Select Data tool, Excel opens a new dialog, shown here, that lets you individually deselect items on your chart.

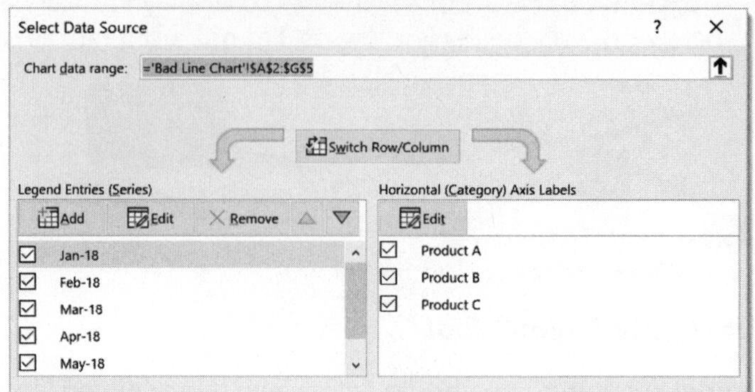

You also have the option to chart hidden or empty cells. If you click Hidden and Empty Cells in the Select Data Source dialog, Excel gives you the dialog shown at right.

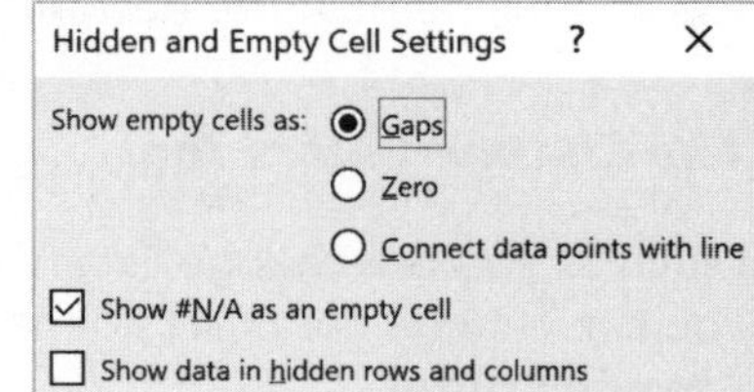

The Move Chart Tool

If you decide that a chart would look better on its own sheet, you can move it to another sheet. For instance, you might have your data on one sheet, create a chart, and then move the chart to a dashboard or summary sheet away from the data. To do this, you click the Move Chart tool, and Excel opens the dialog shown below.

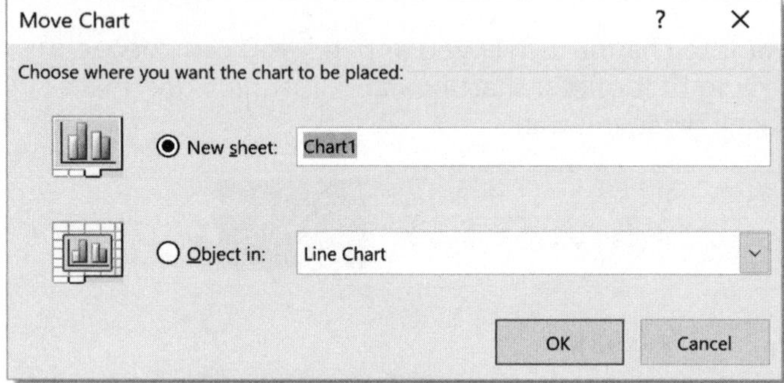

Putting Together the Tools on the Chart Design Tab

The following examples show before and after shots of a default column chart that Excel creates and the same chart a few mouse clicks later, with some formatting adjustments made using the tools just described. If you experiment with the Chart Design tab tools a bit, you'll quickly see how easy it is to change the default chart formats.

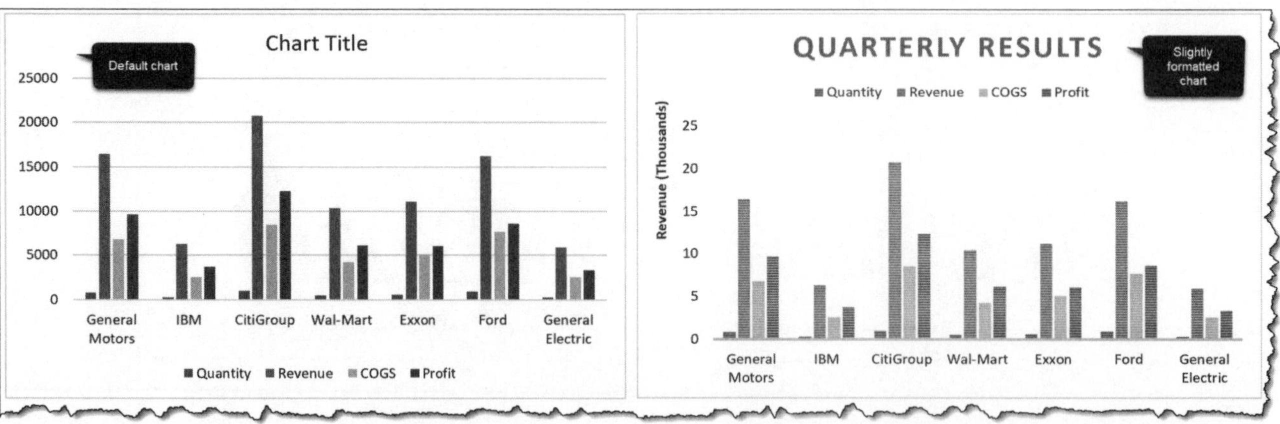

Throughout this book I've several times mentioned the great work Microsoft does in adding graphical options to almost everything you can do in Excel (and all of Office, for that matter). Because it's impossible to please everyone, in many places Microsoft defaults to the basics and allows you to create your own options if you want. This is certainly true with charts, so one thing this chapter focuses on is not only how to create a general chart theme(s) that you like but also how to get Excel to use your favorite chart themes instead of its defaults. And nothing says you have to limit yourself to one theme; in fact, you can have several. You might want to use a very professional style for your company financials but a more relaxed style for displaying sales performance to your team.

Changing a Chart's Display Units

Often when you create a chart, you're dealing with large numbers that take up too much space on the chart's axes. In the past, the only way to change this was to create a false dataset that reduced these values, usually by dividing them by a factor of 10. Fortunately, enough people requested a change that Microsoft added the ability to automatically reduce those values by the scale you determine. The following example shows the same column chart example from before but with a realistic dataset involving revenues and costs in the millions of dollars. You can see that updating the y axis labels increases the overall size of the chart data.

To make this change, right-click anywhere on the y axis label area, select Format Axis, and then select the scale that's appropriate for your values from the Format Axis pane (shown at right), which opens on the right. The change is dramatic, and it's significantly easier than having to alter your data to accommodate the scale change.

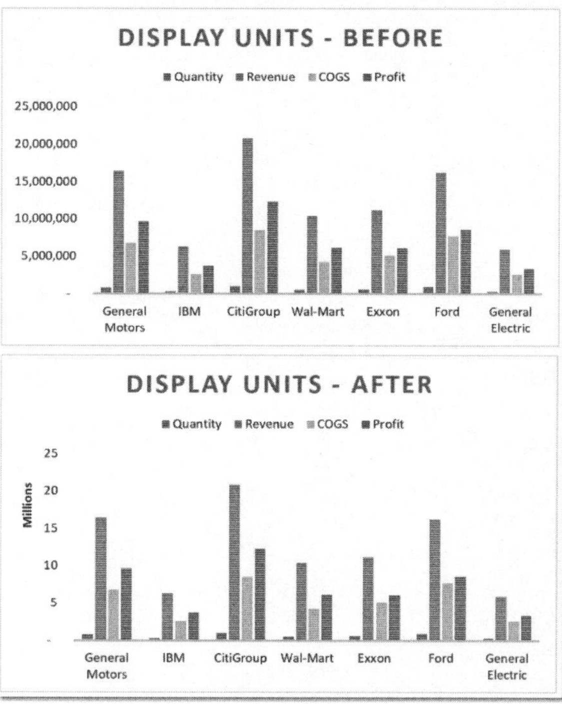

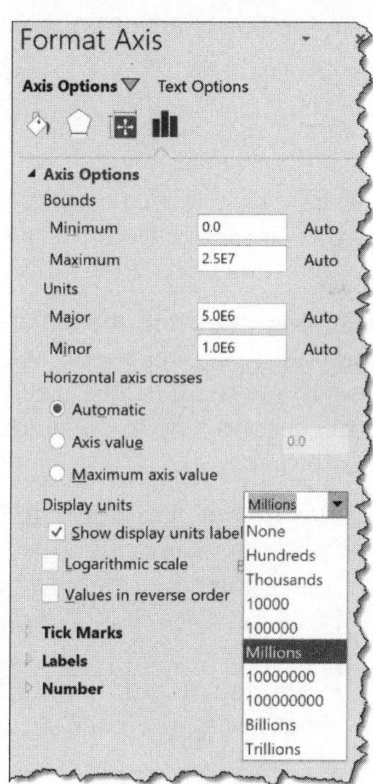

Using Chart Chicklets

If you click on a chart, you see the three small buttons shown here appear on the right of the chart. You can use these buttons to make adjustments more quickly than you can make the same adjustments from the Ribbon. The top button displays a Chart Elements flyout, which lets you add or remove chart elements such as a chart title or legend. The second button launches a chart styles and color picker, and the third displays the filter options. The most exciting of these buttons is the filter button because it allows you to quickly add or remove items from your chart by using a very intuitive interface; you can see its flyout below.

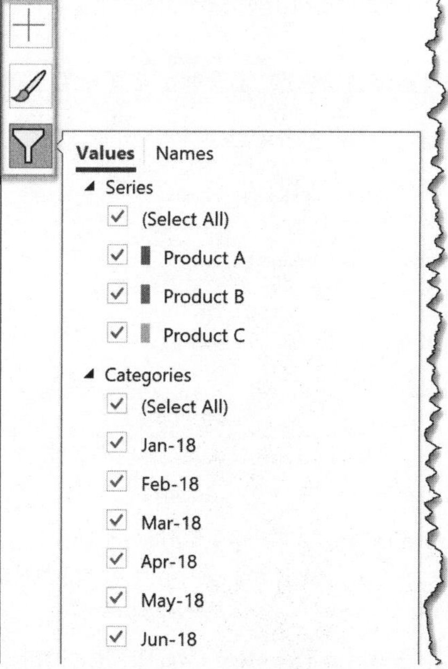

Line Charts

Line charts, which are probably as common as column charts, display data in a series of horizontal lines. Line charts are generally used to show data over a given period, such as weeks or months. With a line chart, the horizontal (x) axis can only be a category (text), such as the corporations in the column chart examples shown earlier in this chapter, or dates that are all evenly spaced across the axis. Excel automatically spaces dates equally, regardless of their interval, so January, February, and March will have the same distance between points as 1/7, 1/14, 1/21, and so on.

Creating a Line Chart

In Excel, you create a line chart the same way you create any other chart. If you want to plot an entire dataset, you just put the cursor anywhere in the data range, and Excel automatically selects the entire range. If you want to plot something less than the entire dataset, select just the range you want plotted, go to the Charts group on the Insert tab, and pick the chart you want from the line chart options shown here.

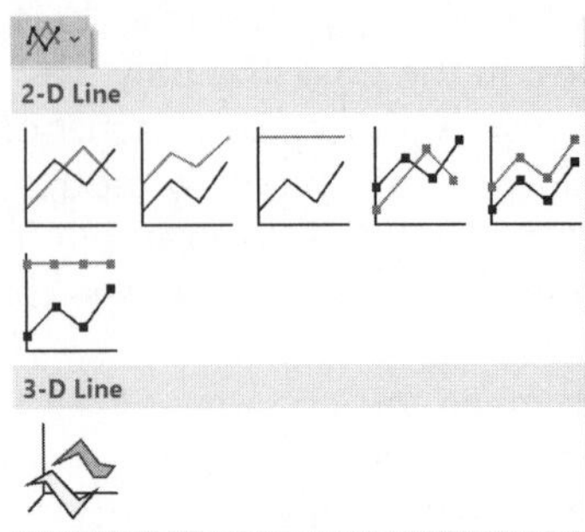

The following is an example of a line chart. As you can see, line charts are easy to understand if they don't try to show too much.

After you've gotten the initial chart drawn and your design elements selected, it's time to move on to the layout phase, which is the second step in creating a charting masterpiece.

> **Hint:** I encourage you to work with the examples in the Chapter 9 companion workbook as you read through this chapter and change them as you see fit so you can begin to understand the options available and refine your charting style.

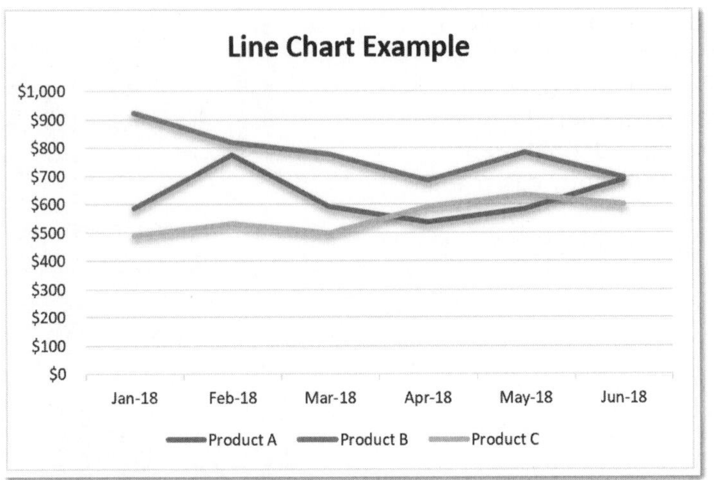

Creating a Default Line Chart

In the following example, on the left you see a dataset and the default line chart Excel creates for you.

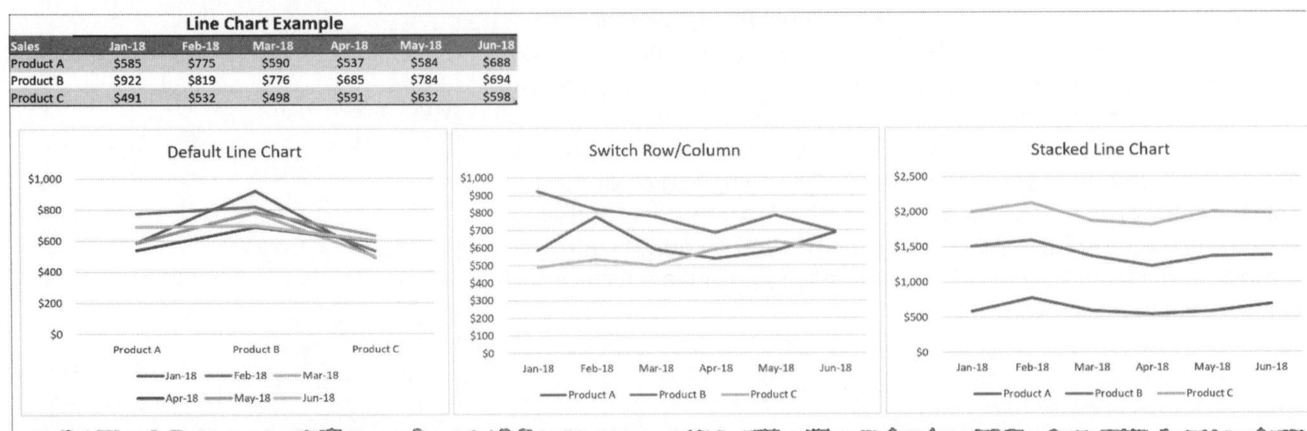

Line Chart Example

Sales	Jan-18	Feb-18	Mar-18	Apr-18	May-18	Jun-18
Product A	$585	$775	$590	$537	$584	$688
Product B	$922	$819	$776	$685	$784	$694
Product C	$491	$532	$498	$591	$632	$598

Unfortunately, Excel hasn't gotten the chart quite get. Excel can only make its best guess as to what you want (and sometimes it's completely clueless), so you need to be prepared to make some corrections from time to time.

Fortunately, it is very easy to turn this line chart into something you can actually work with. Go to **Chart Design > Switch Row/Column**, and you instantly get the layout you want, as shown in the middle of the example above. In addition, Excel lets you create line charts with lines that overlap, as shown in the examples so far, or line charts with stacked lines, as shown on the right side of the example above. You can pick between these options and more by selecting **Chart Design > Change Chart Type**.

Formatting a Line Chart: The Chart Format Tab

Assuming that your chart is everything you want it to be from data and type standpoints, you can drag it to where you want it, keeping an eye out for how large or small it will have to be when you place it. It's generally a good idea to get a chart in place and think about how big it needs to be before you start formatting it because the chart's overall size can impact some features, especially font size. For example, if you format a chart and then shrink it, you might end up having to reformat it. However, you generally won't have a problem if you start small and then increase the chart's size. The following sections discuss the primary formatting tools and options available in the Chart Format tab.

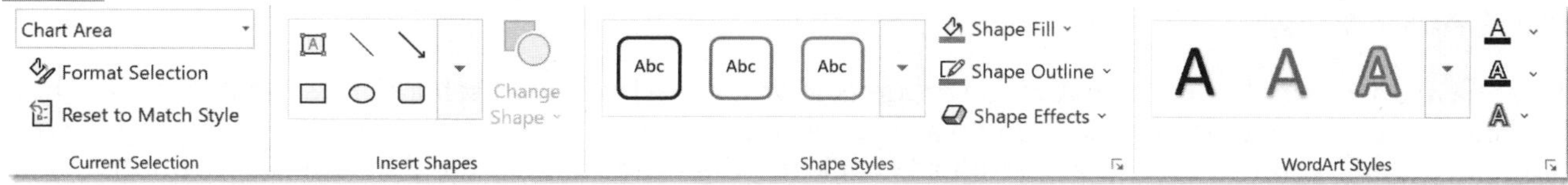

The Current Selection Group

You can use the drop-down at the top of the Current Selection group (shown below) to scroll through individual chart elements in a list as opposed to clicking on them in the chart. If you select one of the elements, it becomes active in the chart, and you can make changes to it. Whether you use this drop-down is a matter of preference and efficiency; for example, you might choose to use it if you happen to be closer to the Ribbon than to the chart. It can also be useful if you have a lot of data points plotted and are having a hard time selecting them on the chart.

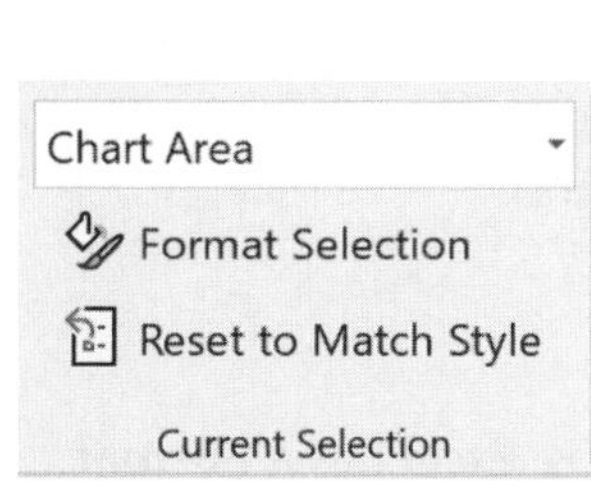

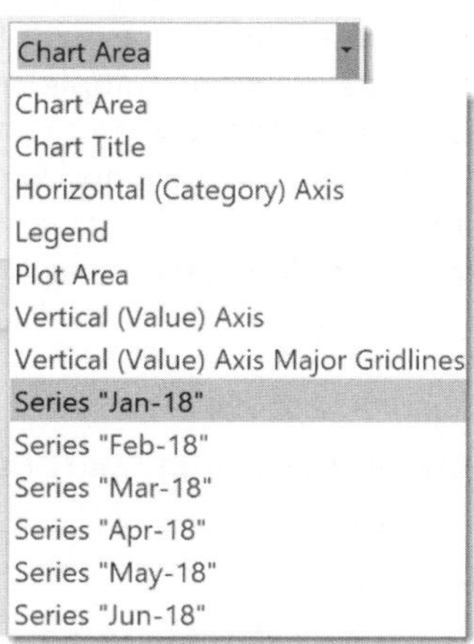

The Insert Shapes and Shape Styles Groups

Excel doesn't limit you to textured fills and backgrounds. You can actually insert your own pictures, shapes, or text boxes in charts. For instance, you might want to draw an arrow with a label to point out a particular item of interest on a chart. The commentary text boxes in some of the chart examples in the companion workbook might give you an idea of what you can do with these options. After you draw a shape, you can adjust it in the Shape Styles group, which gives you options similar to those on the Shape Format tab when you insert a shape from the Insert tab.

The WordArt Styles Group

You can apply WordArt styles to text on your charts but try not to get too carried away, as you don't want to detract from the chart's overall message. In this group you have the same as options you have after you add a shape to a worksheet (described in Chapter 8).

The Accessibility Group

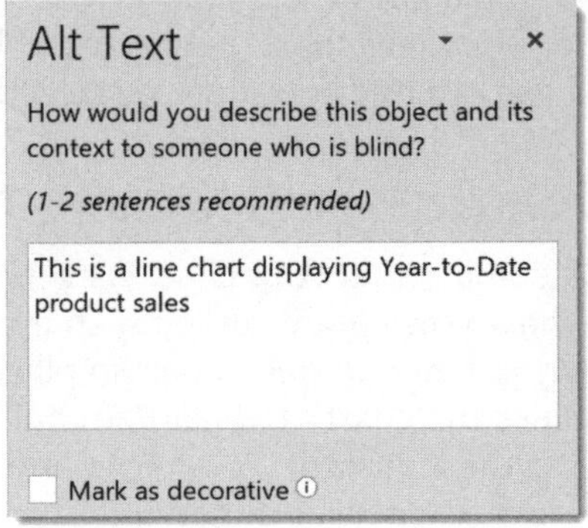

As described in Chapter 8, the Alt Text tool is an accessibility feature that allows you to add to a chart descriptive text that a screen reader can narrate for those with vision limitations.

The Arrange Group

If you have only a single chart, the Arrange group (shown below) isn't very useful, but it's great when you have multiple charts that you need to arrange on a sheet. Instead of trying to manually align the charts so they're neat and orderly, you can select them with **Ctrl+click** and then choose from the different Align options. For instance, say that you have nine charts lined up in a 3 x 3 pattern. You can select the top three charts and select **Chart Format > Align > Align Top**. Then you repeat this process for the next two rows of charts. Then you can select the three charts on the left and select **Chart Format > Align > Align Left**. You can make similar alignment choices for the next two columns. When you're done with this, you can select all the charts and use **Chart Format > Group** to keep the charts from moving around on you (and to keep others from moving the charts around).

The Size Group

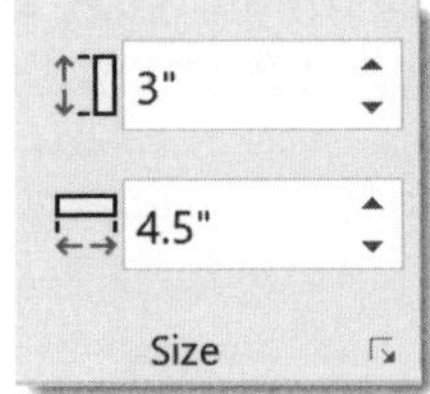

The Size group is another option that you probably won't use on a single chart; with just one chart, you are more likely to use the chart's sizing handles. But as with the Arrange options, the Size group options are really handy for dealing with multiple charts. You can pick a single chart, take note of its height and width in the Size group, and then select the rest of your charts. Next, you can plug in the same height and width settings you just noted, and all your charts end up the same size. You probably want to take this step before you arrange everything because resizing can definitely move things around.

The Format Chart Area Pane

In addition to giving you a variety of tools in the **Chart Design** and **Chart Format** tabs, Excel has a **Format Chart Area** pane that gives you even more formatting options.

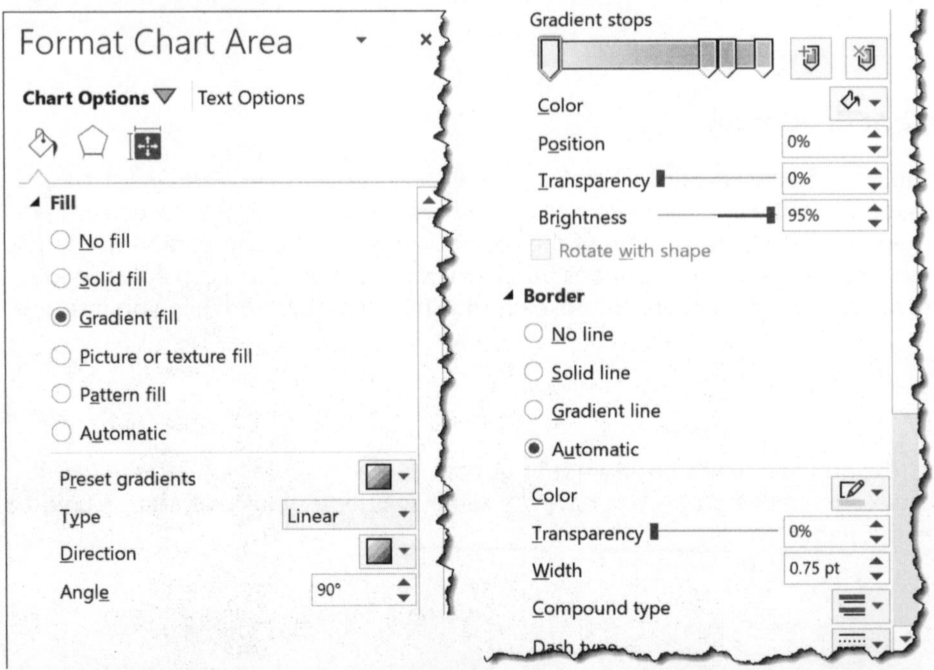

You can get to these options by right-clicking on the body of a chart (not its axis legends or plot area) and selecting Format Chart Area. As shown above, at the top of the pane are a Chart Options group and a Text Options group. In this example, in the Chart Options group, the paint bucket icon allows you to set fill and border options, and the hexagon icon lets you set effects, such as shadow, glow, soft edges, and 3-D format. The square icon lets you set chart size and properties options. Then, if you switch to the Text Options group, you see options for text fill and outline, text effects, and text boxes.

Fill Options

The Fill group offers a number of options, but it can get overwhelming very quickly. It's important to make sure the elements you add to a chart don't actually end up detracting from the chart's overall message by distracting the audience. Again, it's important to take a conservative approach with your designs. While we all want charts to look great, there's a difference between making a purely artistic statement and actually letting your figures speak to the issue(s) that you're trying to communicate.

Following are some examples of the fill options you can apply. The first is a gradient fill, and the second fill is a picture selected from Microsoft's free online photo gallery. You can also choose a file you have on your computer, such as a company logo. Play around with it, and you'll see that there are a lot of settings for you to explore as you define your charts.

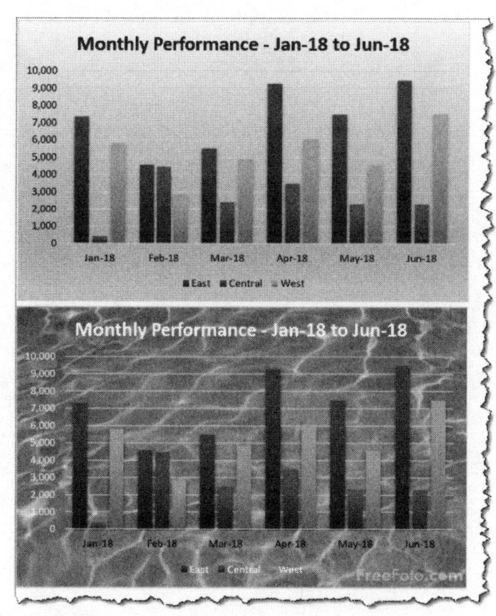

Border Options

The Format Chart Area pane gives you different border options both for the chart's external border and for the chart's plot area.

> **Note:** As you can probably tell by now, you have virtually limitless choices when you put together charts. Despite the fact that there are so many options, many corporate charts look surprisingly similar. Most people don't realize how easy it is to customize charts and make them look unique. Fortunately, you're learning not to be bound by those misconceptions.

Area Charts

An area chart allows you to compare like data over a given timeline. This type of chart generally obscures more information than it shows, and you should use this type only if there are enough differences between the datasets to differentiate them well. You might need to select a few different styles in order to get all your data points to display.

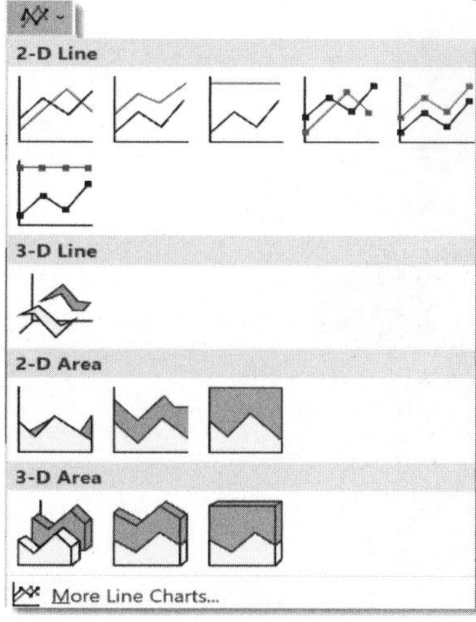

The example below shows the corporate dataset used in the column chart example earlier in this chapter. As you can see, it's not the kind of data that's a good fit for an area chart because unrelated data is plotted all on one line.

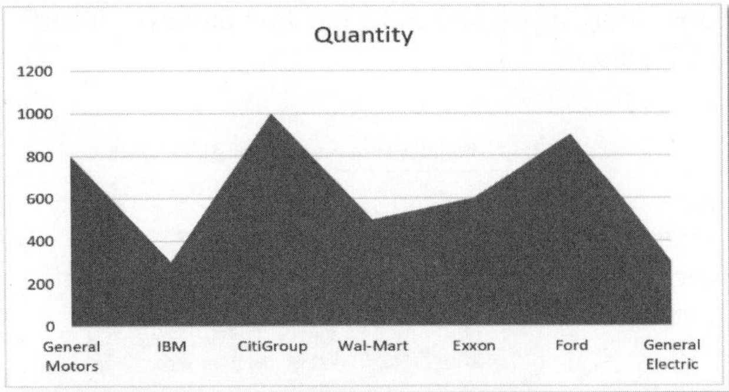

A better dataset for this chart type would be the Product A, B, and C data shown in the next example.

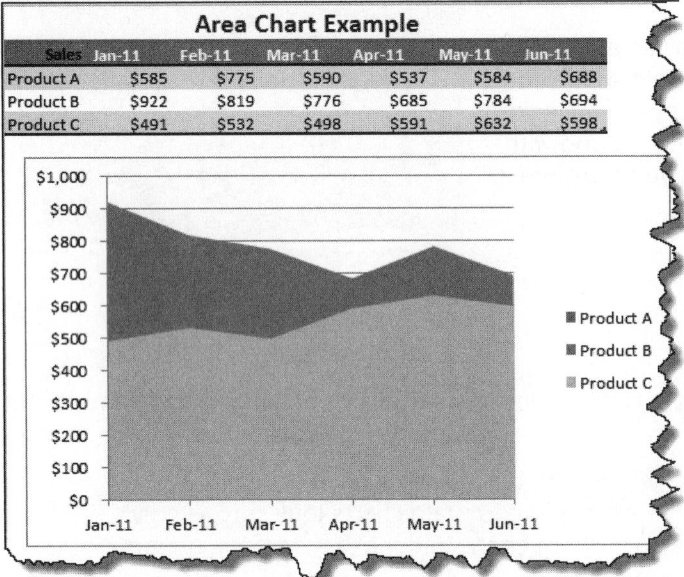

Area Chart Example

Sales	Jan-11	Feb-11	Mar-11	Apr-11	May-11	Jun-11
Product A	$585	$775	$590	$537	$584	$688
Product B	$922	$819	$776	$685	$784	$694
Product C	$491	$532	$498	$591	$632	$598

But what's wrong with this example? Right, there should be three products represented, but you see only two. Unfortunately, Product A's data is hidden behind the data for Products B and C. The best way to solve this is to convert the chart to either a stacked area or 3D area chart, as shown in the next example.

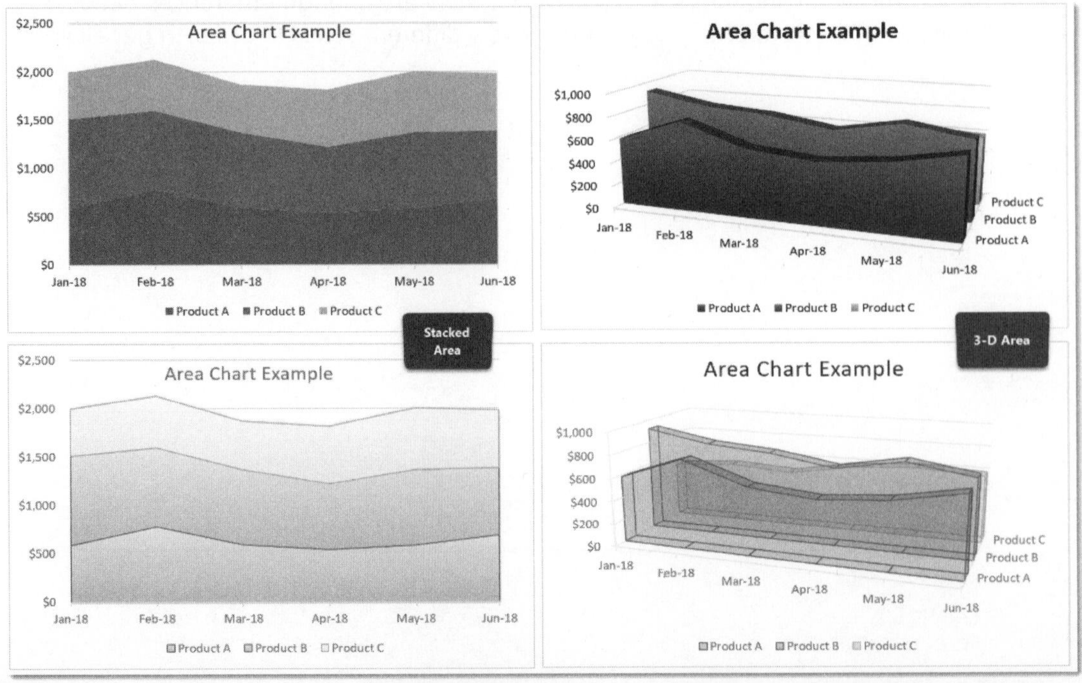

Here you can see that the stacked area chart shows each dataset in relationship to the total of the three, while the 3-D chart shows each dataset as its own independent measure. You can change the chart style by going to the Chart Styles group on the Chart Design tab and selecting one of the styles. You can also select a transparent theme (as shown in the bottom right of the example above), which lets you see all the data points.

After you've adjusted a chart's primary elements, you can continue with some additional formatting steps, such as applying shape and WordArt styles. That's where you see these examples go from a white background and default font to "finished" examples. You certainly don't need to take the additional step of modifying those elements; in fact, you will probably leave a chart rather nondescript as often as you will take the additional steps to fully format one. Consider, for example, a chart that's bound for both the company stock prospectus and your company's annual report. These might be exactly the same charts, but a prospectus dictates a very spartan approach, while the annual report may need some marketing department flair. There are so many possible chart formatting options available that you just need to experiment on your own.

As you can see in the following examples, 3-D area charts can be a bit challenging to format, and it is difficult to make the smaller values in the back stand out clearly, even with transparency. It can be easy to spend more time trying to get an area chart to look right than it's worth. In addition, these charts can be difficult for users to fully comprehend unless the dataset is completely straightforward. If you find yourself with data that is even the least bit ambiguous, an area chart probably isn't the right chart choice; a line chart is usually a much better option.

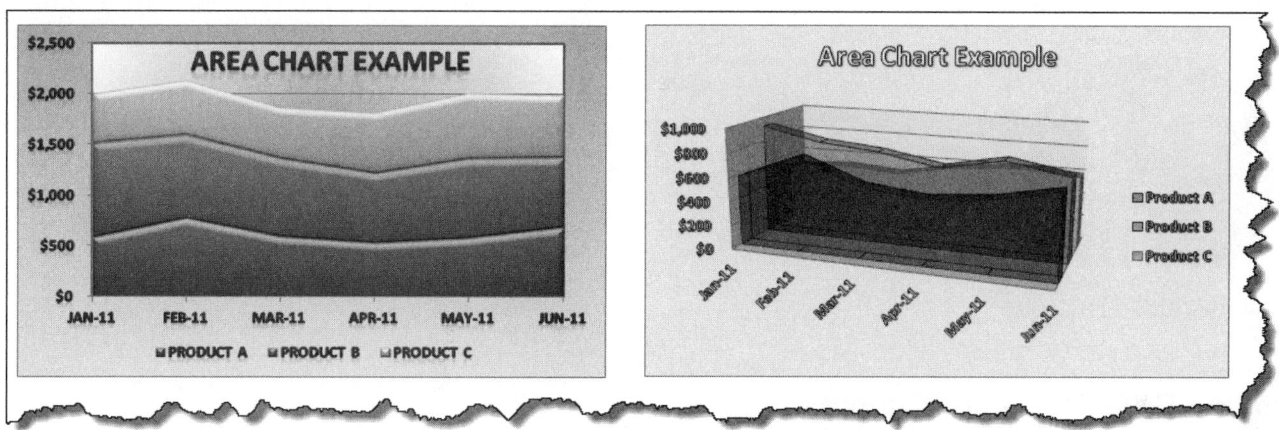

Pie Charts

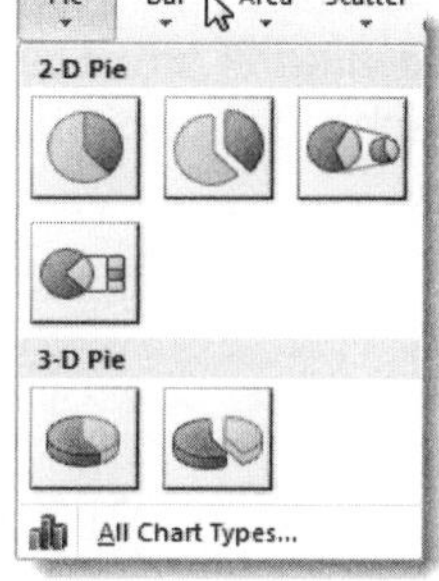

A pie chart can show only one data point per item, so the sole purpose of this chart type is to represent the overall share that each element has of the total pie.

The example at right shows revenue by company, which means revenue is the single data point for each company. This is a very basic example of a pie chart—and it is a good example of a situation in which a pie chart actually works. Pie charts can get out of hand if you try to add too many data points.

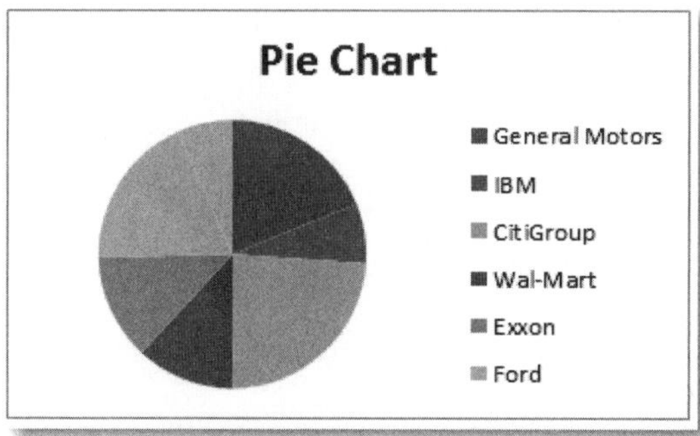

Adding Detail

The first thing you can do with a pie chart to give it more detail is expand the slices; you can expand the slices as a group or individually. To expand all the slices as a group, simply select the plot area (anywhere in the pie) and drag outward in one motion. If you want to move individual slices, when you first select the pie chart's plot area, you see every intersecting point highlighted. Select each one and drag it out individually to where you want it.

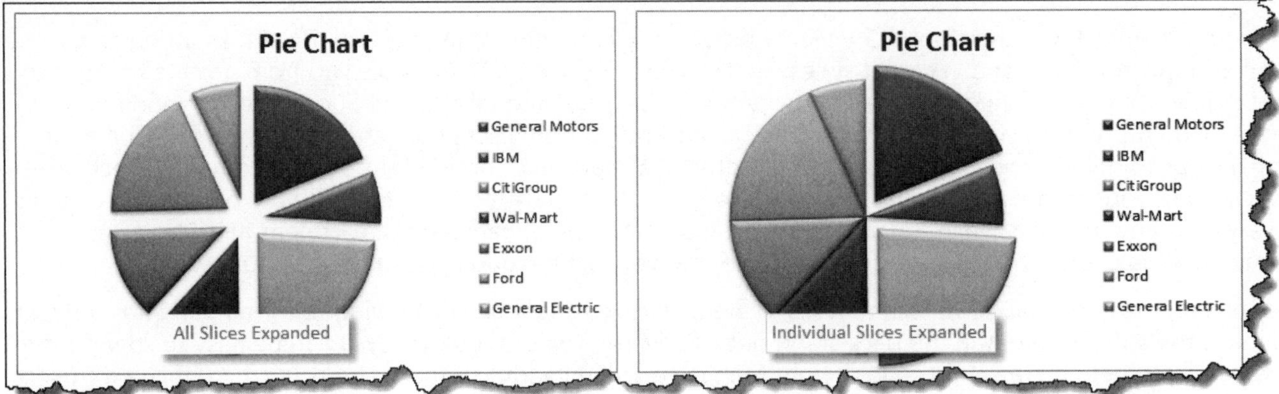

This is what a pie chart looks like when all points are selected:

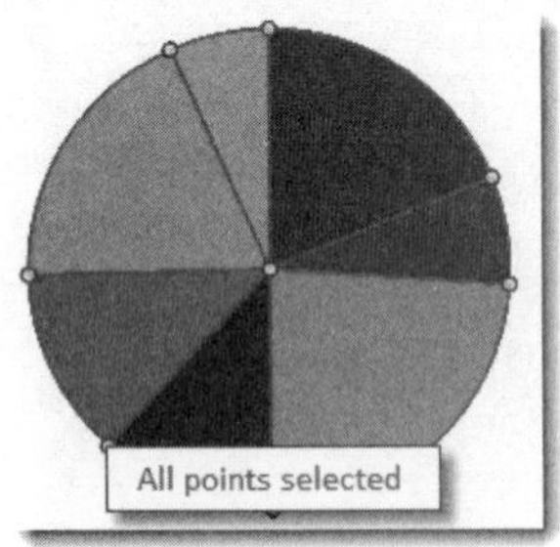

And here's what it looks like when a single slice is selected:

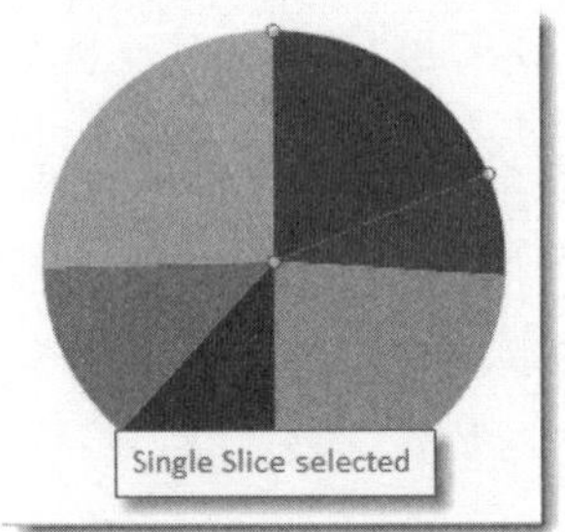

Adding Data Labels and Callouts

You can add detail to a pie chart's plot area, which generally means adding labels of some sort. The earlier pie chart examples include no indication of the value of each section of the pie. If you add data labels or callouts, Excel adds a text box showing each slice's value. The following example includes data callouts that display each slice's individual percentage as compared to the whole.

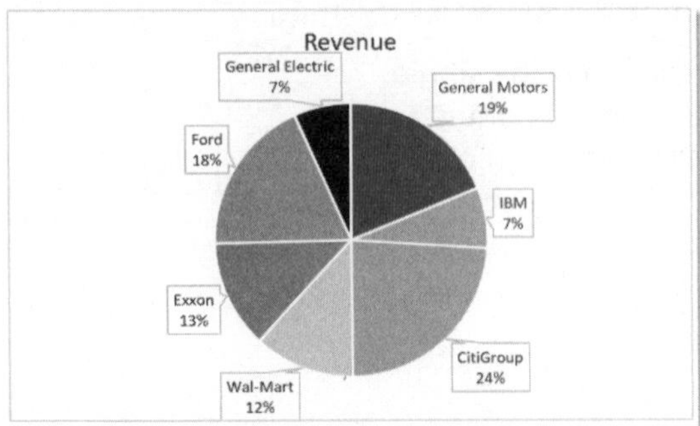

The following example shows the flyout you use to add data labels or callouts.

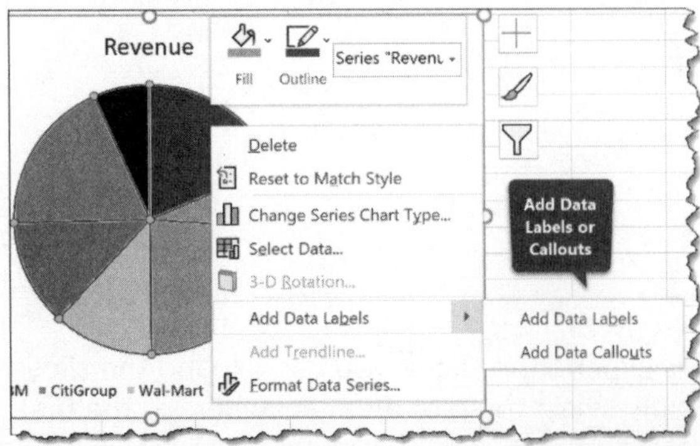

After you've added either data labels or callouts, if you right-click the plot area again, you see that the menu now includes the option Format Data Labels, and if you select it, a new Format Data Labels pane (shown below) flies out on the right. You can use this pane to adjust what the labels display and where. You can also adjust the number format—to Percentage (%), Currency ($), etc.—in the Number section of the pane.

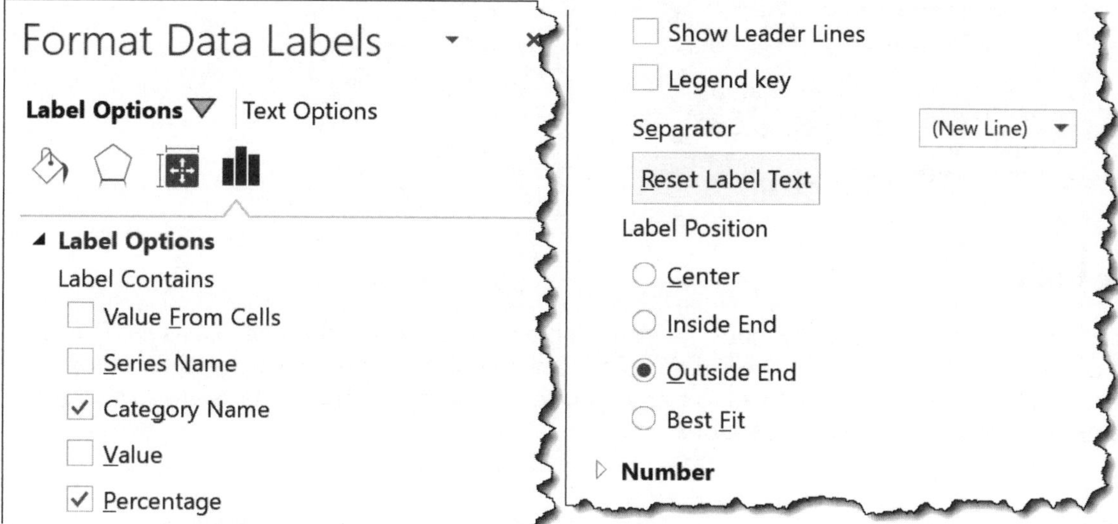

Formatting the Chart Area

With pie charts, the main problem has long been aligning the data labels so that they're not crowded into each other, as shown on the left in the example below.

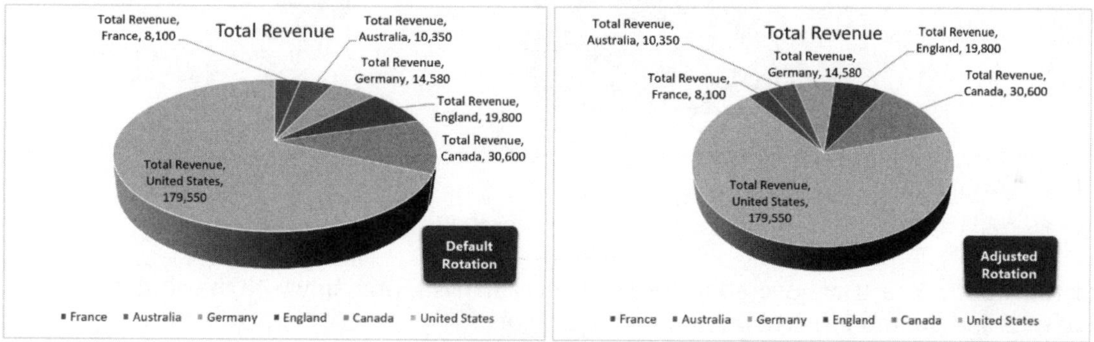

In the past, you were generally required to move and place most of the label elements by hand in order to space them properly. But now you can right-click the chart, select the 3-D Rotation option, and adjust the Rotation and Perspective settings in the Format Chart Area pane until they look good. You'll still probably need to make some manual adjustments, but this beats having to do it all yourself, and that's one of the points of this chapter: Given how time-consuming creating charts can be, any amount of time you can save helps you become more efficient.

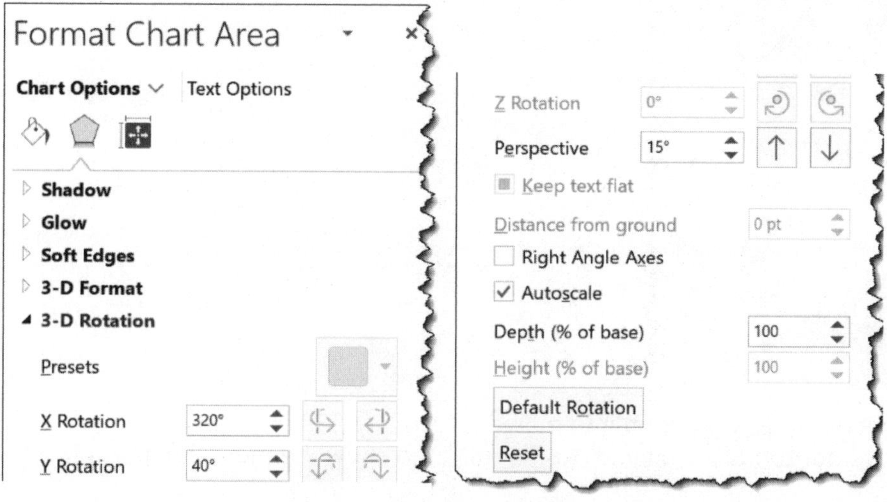

Note: Charts generally have titles that you have to change manually, but you can link a chart title to a cell so that it automatically updates. Pick the cell where you want the title (in the example below, it's cell A1). Then click on the chart title, enter = in the formula bar, and click on the cell where you want the title (in this case A1). Excel then builds the cell reference for you: **='Column & Bar Chart'!$A$1**

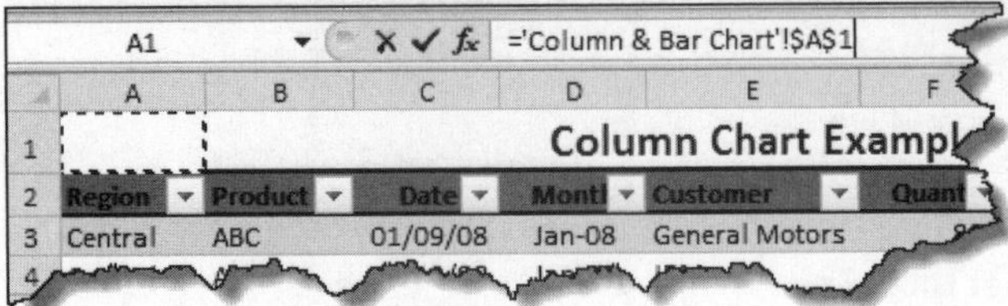

Hierarchy Charts

Treemap and sunburst charts are essentially modern twists on pie charts, and they can be just as easily misused. Hierarchy charts should be limited to fewer than 10 or 15 data points, or your message can get lost. You don't have a whole lot of options when it comes to formatting these charts, but these charts are so straightforward that you really don't need too many options.

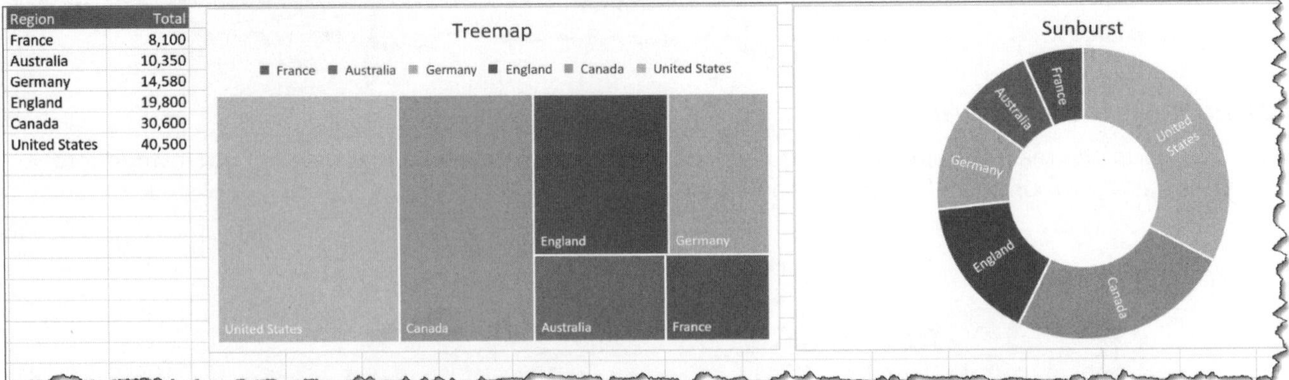

Statistic Charts

As the name indicates, statistic charts are geared toward statistical analysis, primarily with the classic histograms and Pareto charts and the more recent box-and-whisker plots:

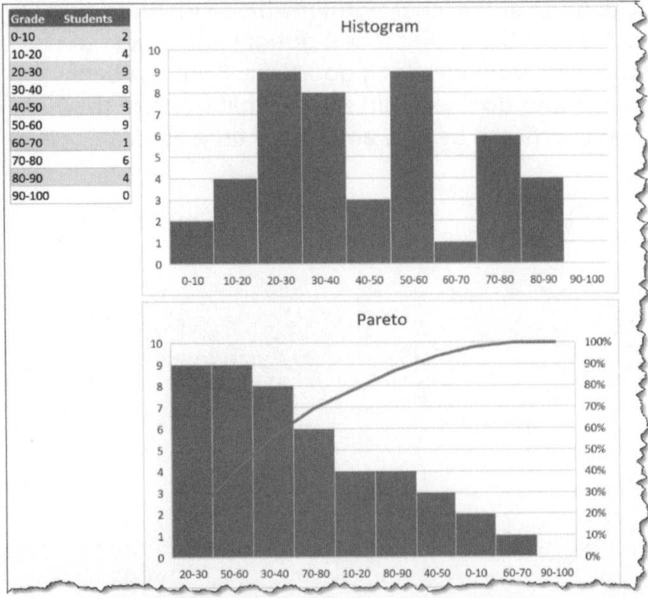

- **Histograms**—Show the distribution of data grouped into bins.
- **Pareto charts**—Show the relative portion of each factor to the total and show the most significant factors in the data.

- **Box-and-whisker plots**—Display the variation within a set of data, where the data points relate to each other in a similar way. The data is displayed in quartiles, which highlight the mean values and any outliers. The outliers are the whiskers (i.e., the lines that extend past the mean). This example shows the average grades between several classes.

Course	Class1	Class2	Class3
English	30	36	32
Math	46	98	49
Physics	89	61	64
French	33	93	94
Geometry	58	65	26
English	78	28	69
Math	35	25	57
Physics	81	44	31
French	46	81	31
Geometry	29	89	40
English	60	50	68
Math	55	73	32
Physics	38	70	37
French	33	60	60
Geometry	51	96	37

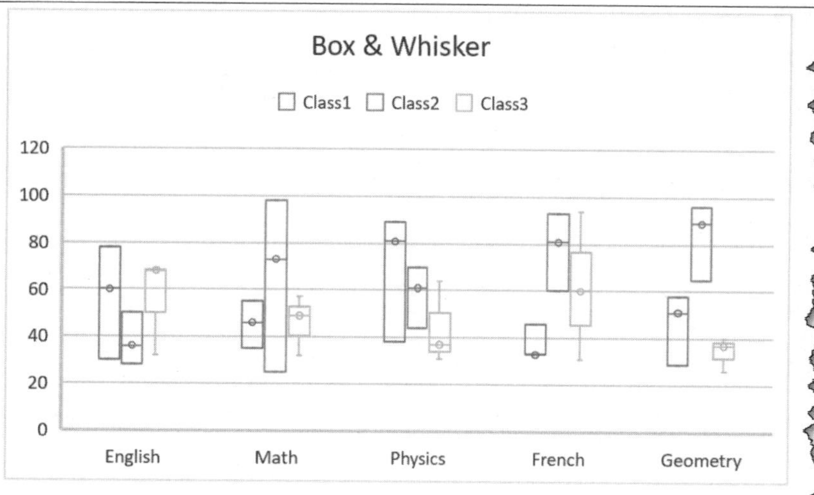

Scatter and Bubble Charts

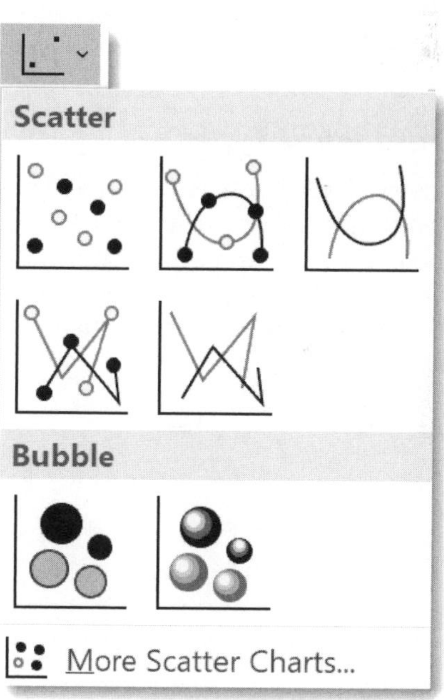

Scatter charts are a lot like line charts, except that whereas line charts are good for comparing datasets over a given time period, scatter charts are good for comparing pairs of data against each other. Scatter charts can also plot two series of data as one.

Whereas a line chart's horizontal (x) axis must either be text or a date, a scatter chart can plot a numeric value on the horizontal axis. This means you can plot two numeric values against each other.

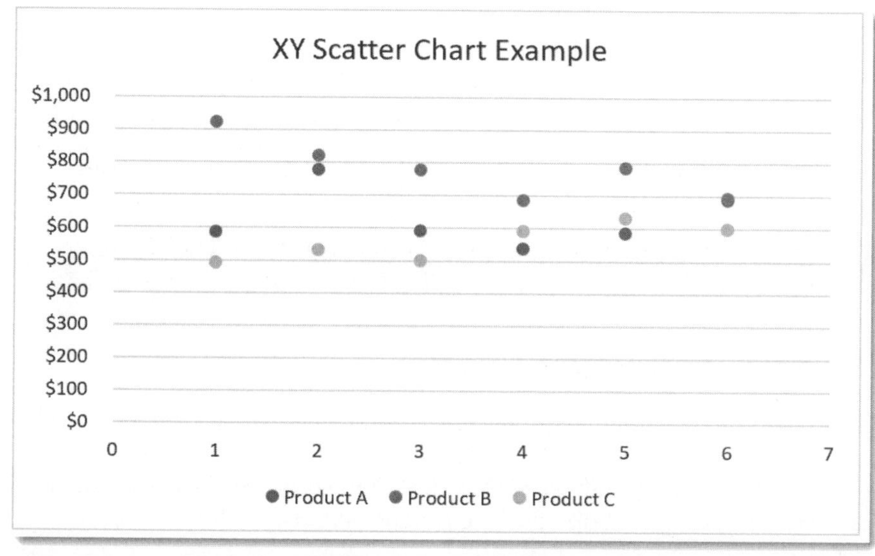

The following example plots average temperature and precipitation over a given period. Unfortunately, in practice, this is not a great use for a scatter chart because the rainfall amounts hover below 1 and are much lower than the temperature ranges, so the chart doesn't tell a very good story. It would be much better to display this information with a combination chart (which we'll get to shortly), where you could plot temperature and rainfall amounts separately to better show the relationship between temperature and rainfall.

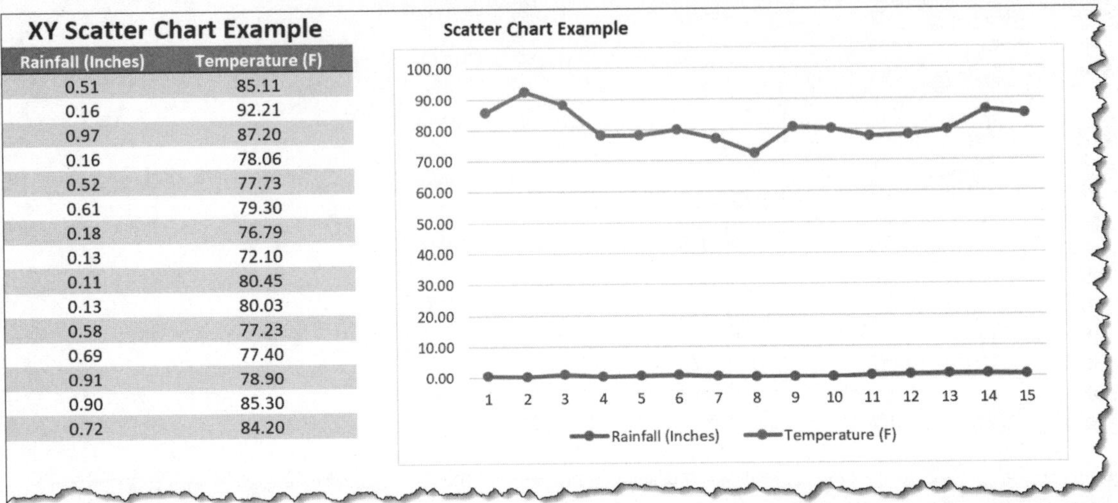

XY Scatter Chart Example

Rainfall (Inches)	Temperature (F)
0.51	85.11
0.16	92.21
0.97	87.20
0.16	78.06
0.52	77.73
0.61	79.30
0.18	76.79
0.13	72.10
0.11	80.45
0.13	80.03
0.58	77.23
0.69	77.40
0.91	78.90
0.90	85.30
0.72	84.20

> **Note:** Why did I point out this less-than-optimal use for a chart? I see things like this all the time, and I want you to know you have options and aren't stuck with only a not-so-great choice.

Data Point Types

As with line charts, with scatter and bubble charts, you can use a line, markers, or both to plot your data. You might choose to show markers if you have quite a few data points and the addition of lines might make the chart hard to read (as shown on the left in the example below). This is especially true with scatter charts because lines might wrap all over the place when following the data points (as shown on the right in the example below); this isn't much of a problem with line charts because their data is plotted along consistent intervals.

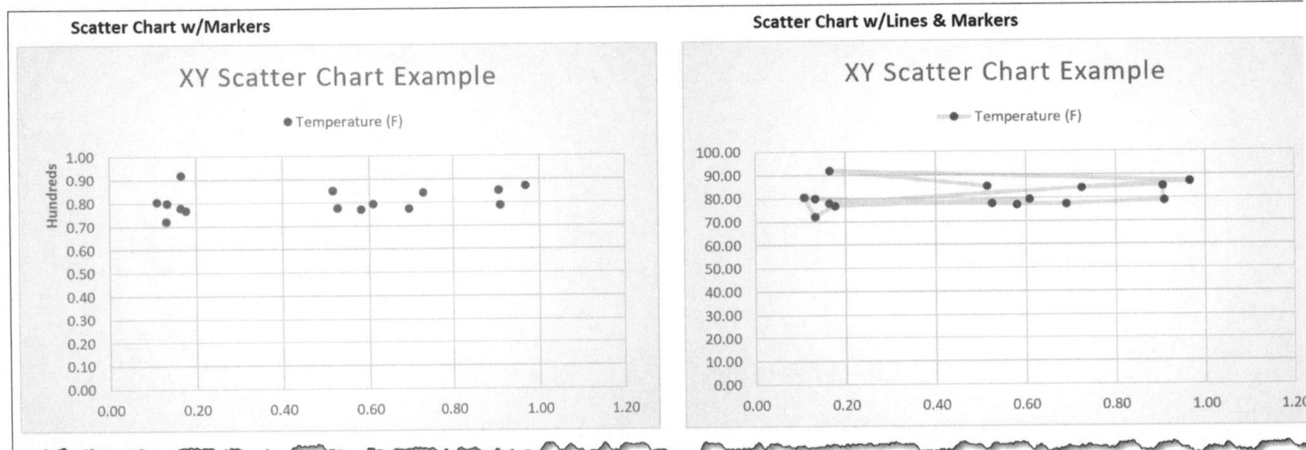

To select the line or marker options you want, with the chart selected, go to the **Chart Design > Change Chart Type** and select a new chart type.

> **Hint:** To quickly create a standard column chart, place the cursor in any cell in the chart data range and press **Alt+F1**. Then right-click the chart and choose the **Change Chart Type** option to change it.

Waterfall, Funnel, Stock, Surface, and Radar Charts

Waterfall and stock charts are largely used with financial data. Funnel charts generally display data in a largest-to-smallest order to show the stages in a process. For instance, you might show how many sales leads you have by status, such as prospect, initial conversation, negotiation, closed deal, and so on. Surface and radar charts show data in multiple dimensions. The following sections provide details on each of these types.

Waterfall

Here's an example of a waterfall chart with some top-line revenue and expense categories. For the Gross Margin and Net Income, right-click the column and choose Set As Total.

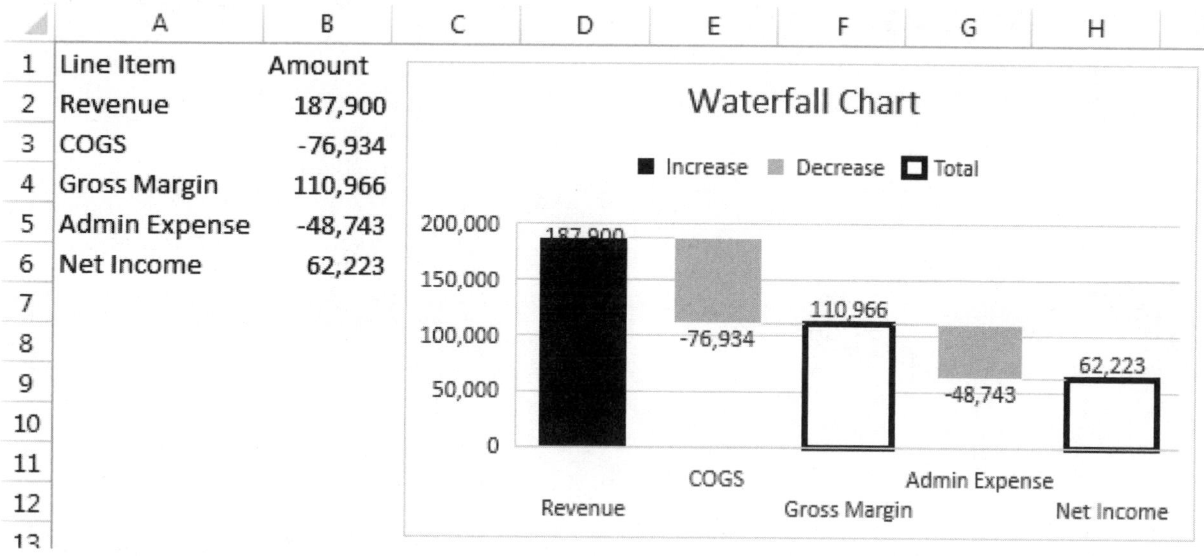

Funnel Charts

Here's an example of a funnel chart that shows customer lead status.

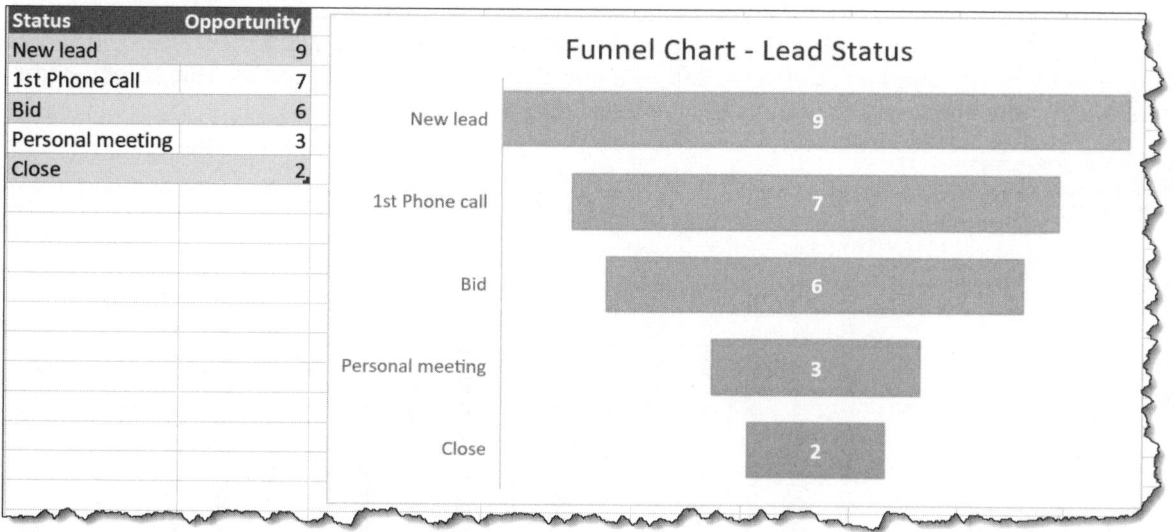

Stock Charts

Here's an example of a stock chart showing Q4 2018 volume, open, high, low, and close values for Microsoft.

Date	Volume	High	Low	Close
12/21/18	110,945,000	$103.00	$97.46	$98.23
12/20/18	70,221,500	$104.31	$98.78	$101.51
12/19/18	68,110,780	$106.88	$101.35	$103.69
12/18/18	48,033,550	$104.51	$102.52	$103.97
12/17/18	56,837,160	$105.80	$101.71	$102.89
12/14/18	46,961,130	$109.26	$105.50	$106.03
12/13/18	30,600,890	$110.87	$108.63	$109.45
12/12/18	36,169,700	$111.27	$109.04	$109.08
12/11/18	42,342,240	$110.95	$107.44	$108.59
12/10/18	40,463,870	$107.98	$103.89	$107.59
12/07/18	44,391,210	$109.45	$104.30	$104.82
12/06/18	47,866,160	$109.24	$105.00	$109.19
12/04/18	44,572,140	$112.64	$108.21	$108.52
12/03/18	34,293,960	$113.42	$110.73	$112.09
11/30/18	33,652,230	$110.97	$109.36	$110.89
11/29/18	27,792,540	$111.12	$109.03	$110.19

Surface and Radar Charts

The following charts are examples of a surface chart and a radar chart, both based on some random values for asset allocation by department.

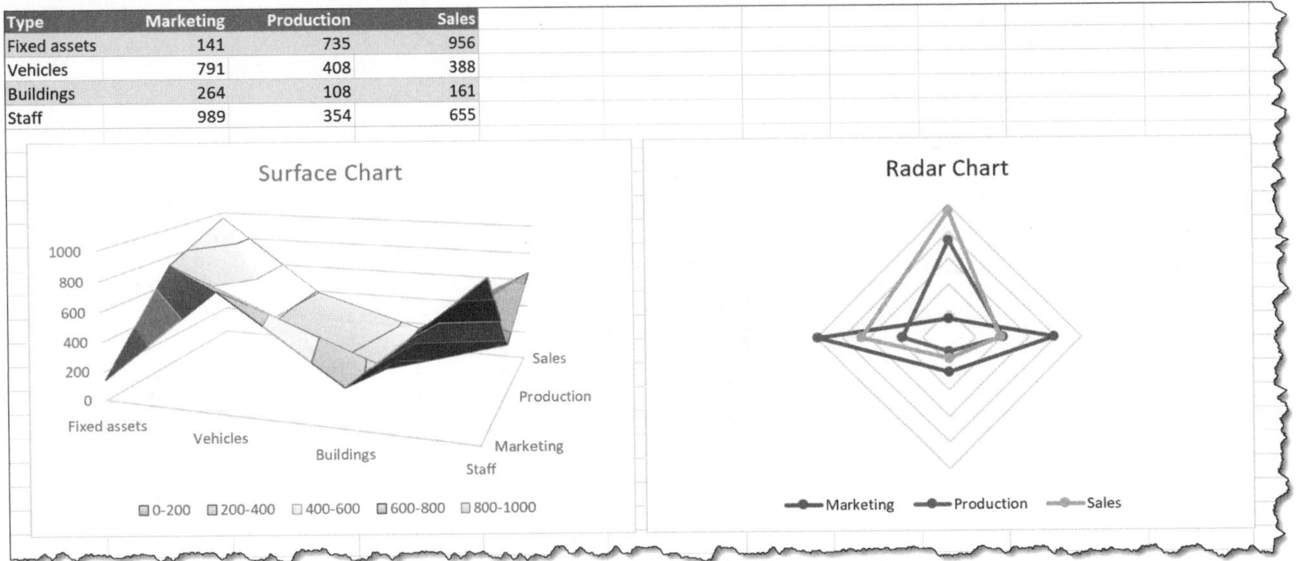

Type	Marketing	Production	Sales
Fixed assets	141	735	956
Vehicles	791	408	388
Buildings	264	108	161
Staff	989	354	655

Combo Charts

Also called *magnitude charts*, combo charts let you plot disparate values—such as rainfall and temperature data, as mentioned earlier—in relationship to each other. The following example shows temperature plotted as a column chart on the primary axis and rainfall plotted as a line chart on the secondary axis. This combo chart shows the data much more effectively than does the earlier scatter chart example.

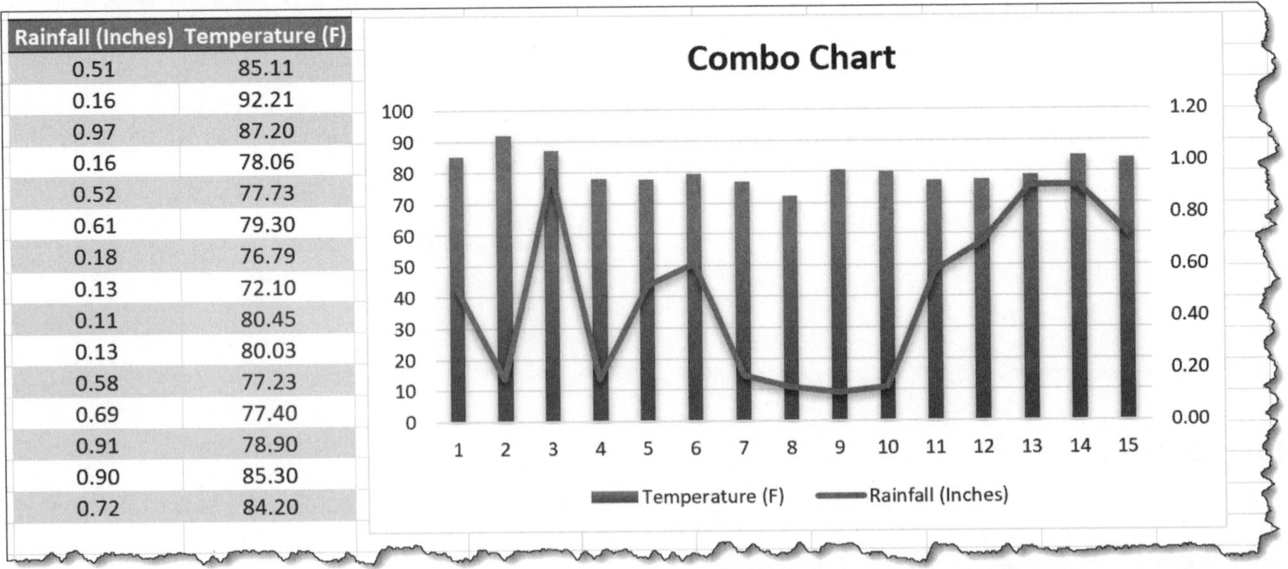

Rainfall (Inches)	Temperature (F)
0.51	85.11
0.16	92.21
0.97	87.20
0.16	78.06
0.52	77.73
0.61	79.30
0.18	76.79
0.13	72.10
0.11	80.45
0.13	80.03
0.58	77.23
0.69	77.40
0.91	78.90
0.90	85.30
0.72	84.20

In the past, setting up such a combo chart was difficult and time-consuming. Fortunately, the Microsoft charting team took on this long-standing request and created the combo chart type for it.

The easiest way to create a combo chart is to press **Alt+F1** to have Excel create a default chart for you. As shown below, in this chart you can just barely see how rainfall is plotted; it's such a small number in relationship to temperature that it's barely visible. So to change it to a combo chart, go to **Chart Design > Change Chart Type**. Then, in the Change Chart Type dialog, as shown below, select Combo and then change the chart type to Line and check the Secondary Axis option. These few clicks give you the great chart shown above.

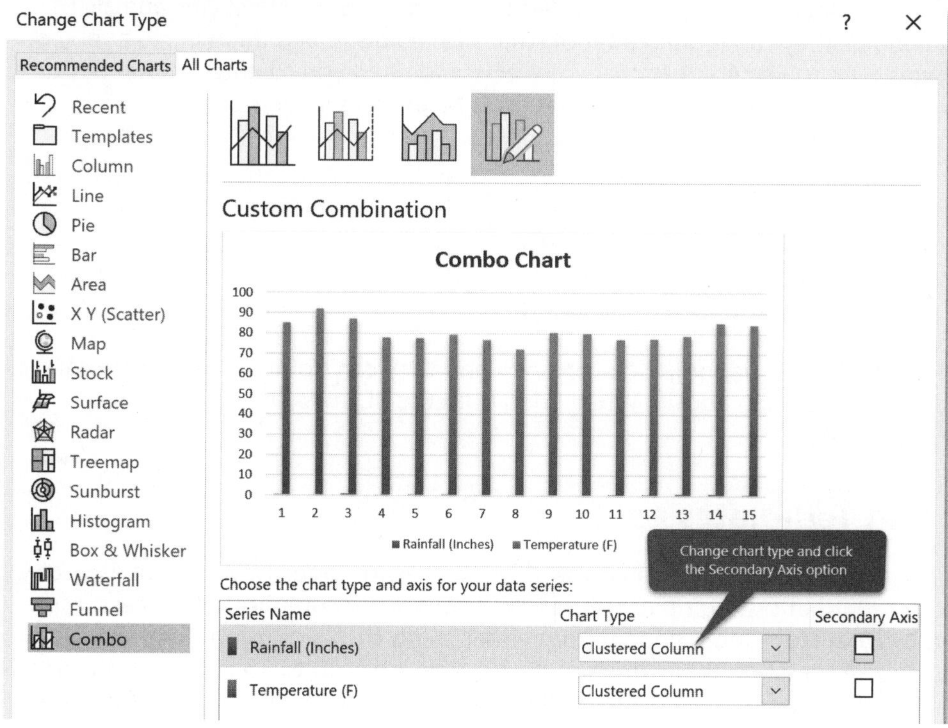

Map Charts

Map charts are my favorite new charts, and they fit very nicely with Excel's new Geography data types. The following example shows a map chart of U.S. states and populations. The tri-fold map icon to the left of each state name indicates linked data types. In this example, you can see that I used **=[@State].Population** for the Population column, which pulls linked data from the State column. If you refresh the linked data, the chart automatically updates.

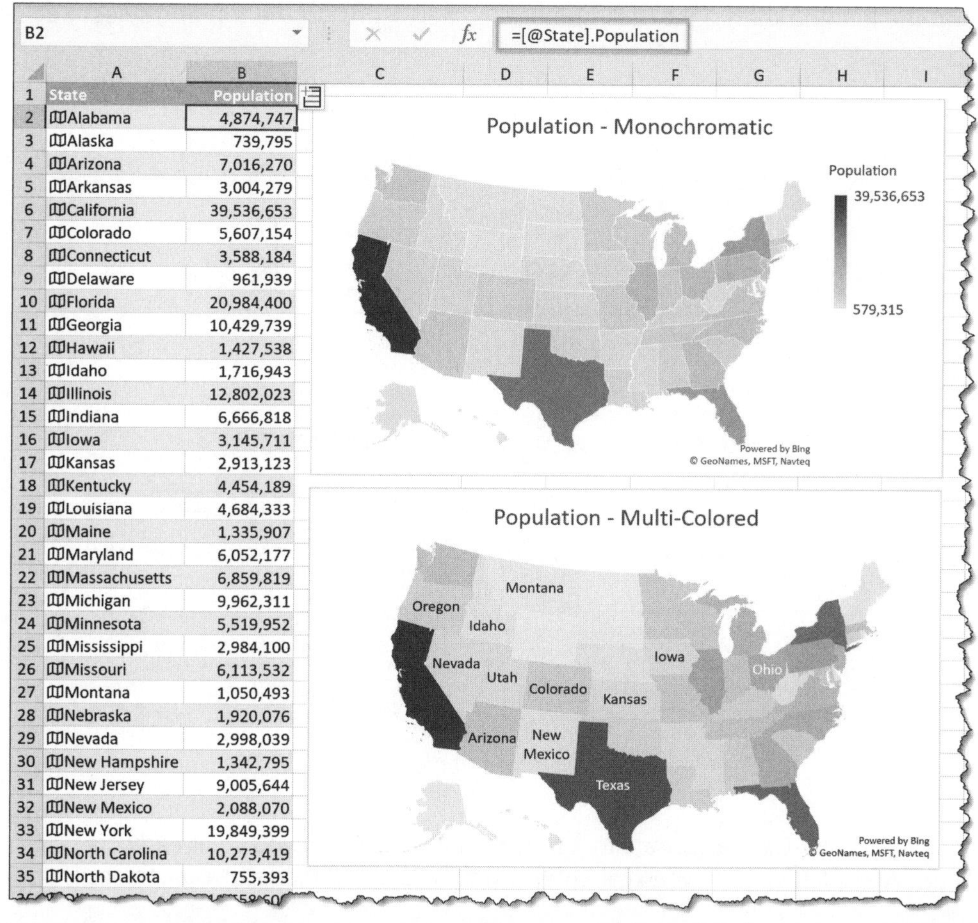

	State	Population
2	Alabama	4,874,747
3	Alaska	739,795
4	Arizona	7,016,270
5	Arkansas	3,004,279
6	California	39,536,653
7	Colorado	5,607,154
8	Connecticut	3,588,184
9	Delaware	961,939
10	Florida	20,984,400
11	Georgia	10,429,739
12	Hawaii	1,427,538
13	Idaho	1,716,943
14	Illinois	12,802,023
15	Indiana	6,666,818
16	Iowa	3,145,711
17	Kansas	2,913,123
18	Kentucky	4,454,189
19	Louisiana	4,684,333
20	Maine	1,335,907
21	Maryland	6,052,177
22	Massachusetts	6,859,819
23	Michigan	9,962,311
24	Minnesota	5,519,952
25	Mississippi	2,984,100
26	Missouri	6,113,532
27	Montana	1,050,493
28	Nebraska	1,920,076
29	Nevada	2,998,039
30	New Hampshire	1,342,795
31	New Jersey	9,005,644
32	New Mexico	2,088,070
33	New York	19,849,399
34	North Carolina	10,273,419
35	North Dakota	755,393

Map charts, which are driven by Bing's mapping engine, are limited to country, region, state, city, and zip/postal code maps. Note that sometimes they can require a bit of what's called *disambiguation* in case you confuse the engine. For example, if you were to just enter Portland, Excel would need you to enter a state because there are two well-known cities named Portland in the United States (in Maine and in Oregon).

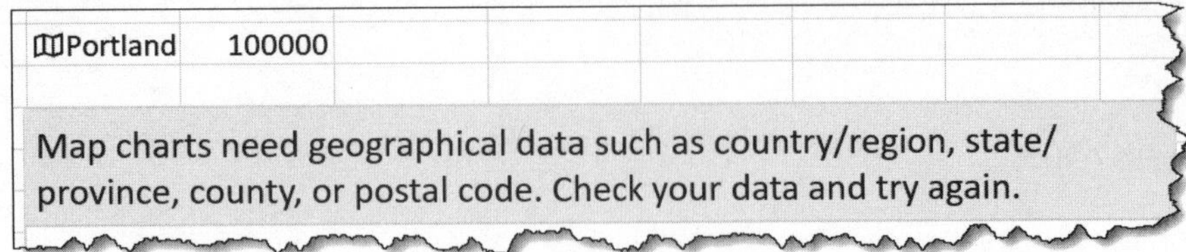

Map charts are intended to provide high-level geographic overviews, and they can't plot at the street address level. However, you can do that with the 3D Map add-in. While I don't discuss 3D maps here, you can see www.support.office.com/Excel for details.

Using Default Charts and Templates

If you've followed along with either the Chapter 9 companion workbook or a workbook of your own as you've read this chapter, you've no doubt seen that setting up charts can be a somewhat complicated process, especially if you're not used to doing it. What stops most people from either using charts or using them efficiently is getting bogged down in constantly re-creating them. Imagine that a report has 10 to 15 charts, and you have to create each one by hand. Even if it takes you only 5 to 10 minutes per chart (which is a perfectly reasonable time frame), that's a good chunk of your morning gone. Of course, Excel gives you a better way: You can use default charts and templates, which you can use over and over again.

Default Charts

When you use the **Alt+F1** trick to create a chart, Excel gives you a clustered column chart. If you primarily use a different type of chart, such as a line chart or pie chart, you can change the default chart to that type so that every new chart you create defaults to that one. To do this, click any chart and then go to **Chart Design > Change Chart Type**. In the Change Chart Type dialog, as shown below, select the chart type you want to be the default from the chart list on the left and then right-click one of the chart icons on the top and select **Set as Default Chart**.

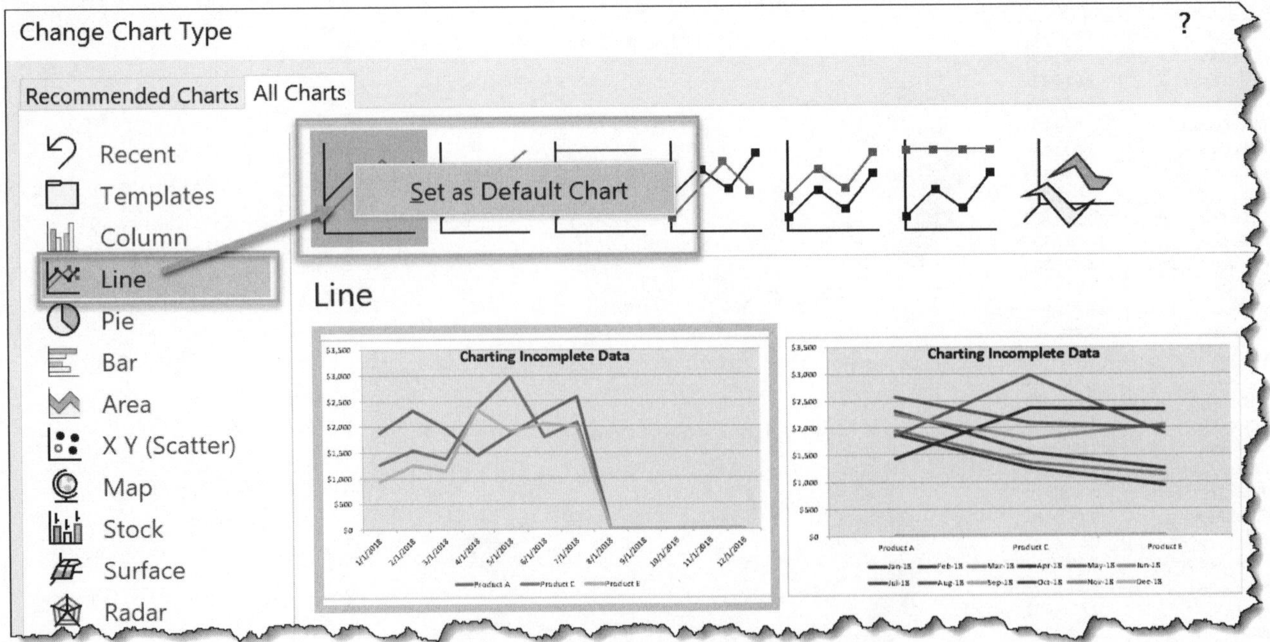

Chart Templates

Chart templates let you quickly change any standard chart to a fully formatted design you've already created. For example, if you used the **Alt+F1** trick to have Excel enter a standard column chart, you can apply a column chart template that has all the formatting pre-applied. To start, when you have a chart that's formatted the way you want (this is where all the up-front work comes in), right-click the chart and select the Save As Template option. When the Save Chart Template dialog then prompts you for a file name, enter a descriptive name, as shown below, and click Save.

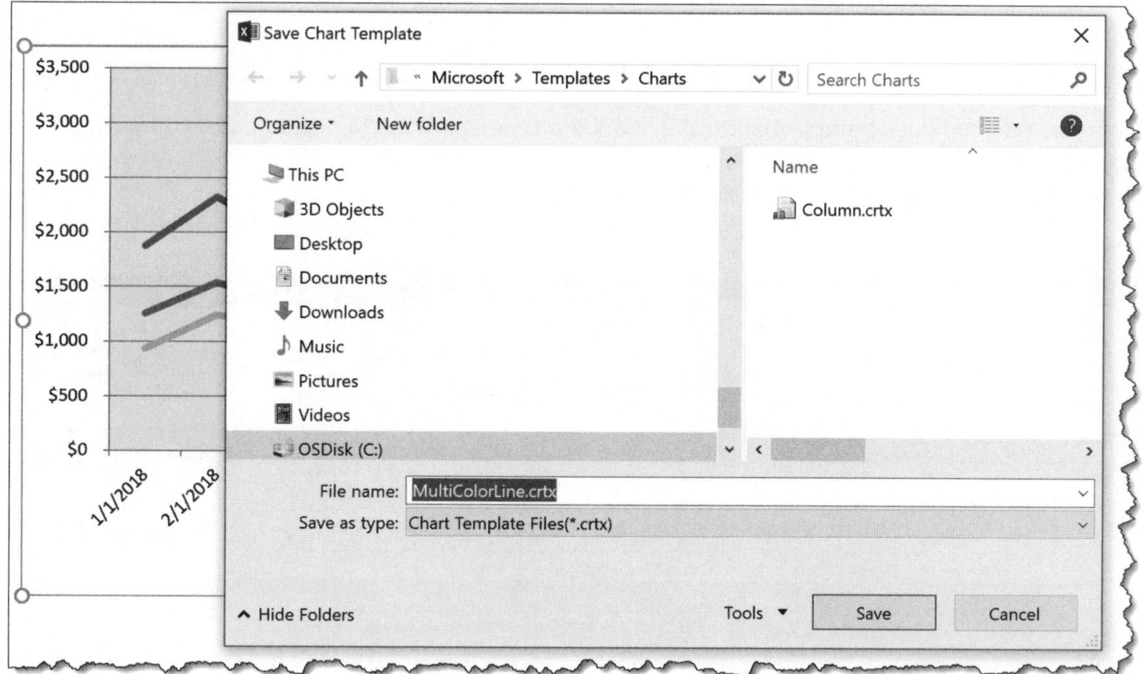

If you ever want to apply that chart style to a chart in the future, simply select the chart you want to change, go to **Chart Design > Change Chart Type**, and in the Change Chart Type dialog select Templates and then select the template you want to apply. I generally have at least one chart type template saved for each of the nine primary chart types, and using them saves an incredible amount of time compared to having to re-create charts all the time.

Hint: Be sure to give your templates descriptive names, or you'll end up wasting time trying to figure out which is which.

Sparklines

While sparklines aren't technically a part of charts, they fill a remarkably similar need, so this is a good place to discuss them. Sparklines are mini-charts in cells that represent the data selected. Whereas a chart is great on its own, sparklines make the most sense when they're displayed right next to their data. The amazing thing about sparklines is that they are truly easy to set up and use. Don't be surprised if you find yourself using them quite a bit. They are also a great substitute for a chart in situations where a chart might not be appropriate due to size limitations. As with charts, when the data behind a sparkline changes, the sparkline immediately updates itself because it's linked to your data.

To get to the dialog shown below, select cells O20:O22, go to **Insert > Line**, and select cells C20:N22 as the data range.

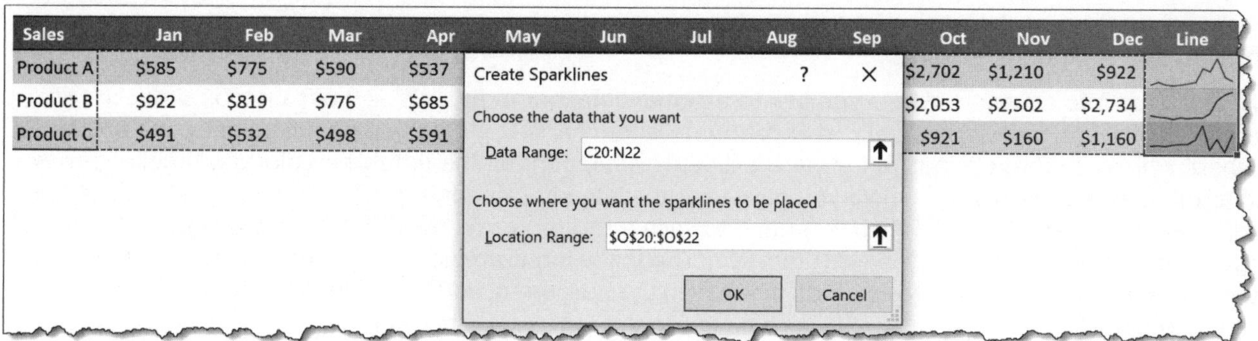

After you click OK, Excel places the sparkline(s) on your sheet, and the Sparkline tab is activated (as shown below).

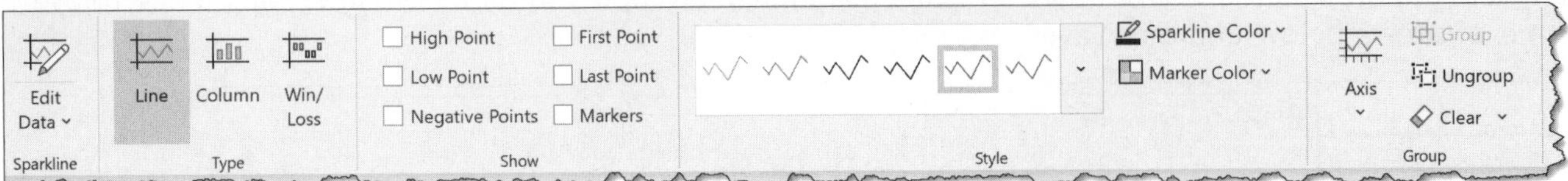

You can use this tab to edit the data points, change the sparkline type, show certain data points, and select a style for the sparkline. Once again, Excel gives too many options to detail here, but feel free to experiment with the examples in the Chapter 9 workbook or create your own.

The following example shows some of the variations you can create by using sparklines.

Sales	Jan	Feb	Mar	Apr	May	Jun	Jul	Aug	Sep	Oct	Nov	Dec	Line	Columnn	Win/Loss
Product A	$585	$775	$590	$537	$584	$688	$793	$1,888	$1,650	$2,702	$1,210	$922			
Product B	$922	$819	$776	$685	$784	$694	$776	$758	$1,104	$2,053	$2,502	$2,734			
Product C	$491	$532	$498	$591	$632	$598	$868	$1,765	$269	$921	$160	$1,160			

Sales	Jan	Feb	Mar	Apr	May	Jun	Jul	Aug	Sep	Oct	Nov	Dec	Line	Columnn	Win/Loss
Product A	$585	$775	$590	$537	$584	$688	$97	$2,428	$250	$2,392	$1,727	$278			
Product B	$922	$819	$776	$685	$784	$694	$175	$1,955	$1,837	$1,101	$1,574	$2,388			
Product C	$491	$532	$498	$591	$632	$598	$2,009	$1,061	$387	$1,866	$123	$1,676			

Sales	Jan	Feb	Mar	Apr	May	Jun	Jul	Aug	Sep	Oct	Nov	Dec	Line	Columnn	Win/Loss
Product A	$585	$775	$590	$537	$584	$688	$104	$1,406	$1,919	$2,654	$959	$643			
Product B	$922	$819	$776	$685	$784	$694	$1,584	$222	$684	$271	$283	$2,176			
Product C	$491	$532	$498	$591	$632	$598	$2,256	$2,529	$683	$77	$2,643	$2,447			

Dealing with Charting Problems

This section discusses a few chart tips and tricks that don't necessarily fall into the realm of your everyday charting activities but that might come in handy.

Dealing with Hidden and Empty Cells

You can use the Hidden and Empty Cells tool to tell Excel how to deal with empty cells or #N/A errors in your data. You can also choose to show data in hidden rows in columns if you want. To use this tool, right-click on a chart's plot area and choose the Select Data option. In the Select Data Source dialog that appears (see below), click the Hidden and Empty Cells button, and select your options.

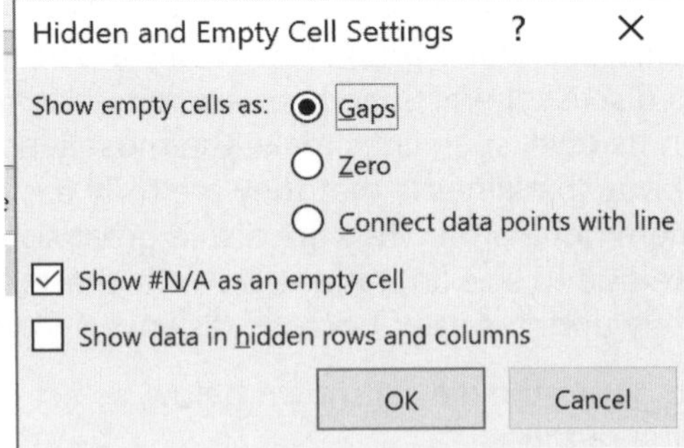

What to Do About 0 Values

You'll often run into situations where you link to external data, but it displays as 0 because Excel doesn't see any data for it. Unfortunately, when Excel encounters 0s for charts, it plots the data a flat line at the bottom of the chart, which can throw things out of perspective. This happens all the time when plotting timeline series, such as days, weeks, or months, where you have year-to-date information but no data for the portion of the period that hasn't yet occurred. When you run into such a situation, you need to tell Excel to ignore the missing data, which you can do with the **NA()** function. The following example shows some linked data that goes to zero because there's no data for periods that haven't yet occurred. You therefore need to tell Excel to ignore the missing data.

In this case, start by selecting cell C9 and then drag across the entire linked range. Then enter **=IF(C3=0,NA(),C3)** and press **Ctrl+Enter** to paste the formula into the selected cells. The formula tells Excel that if the linked cell's value is empty or 0, it should convert the result to **#N/A**, which charts will ignore. Otherwise, Excel should return the cell's value and plot it.

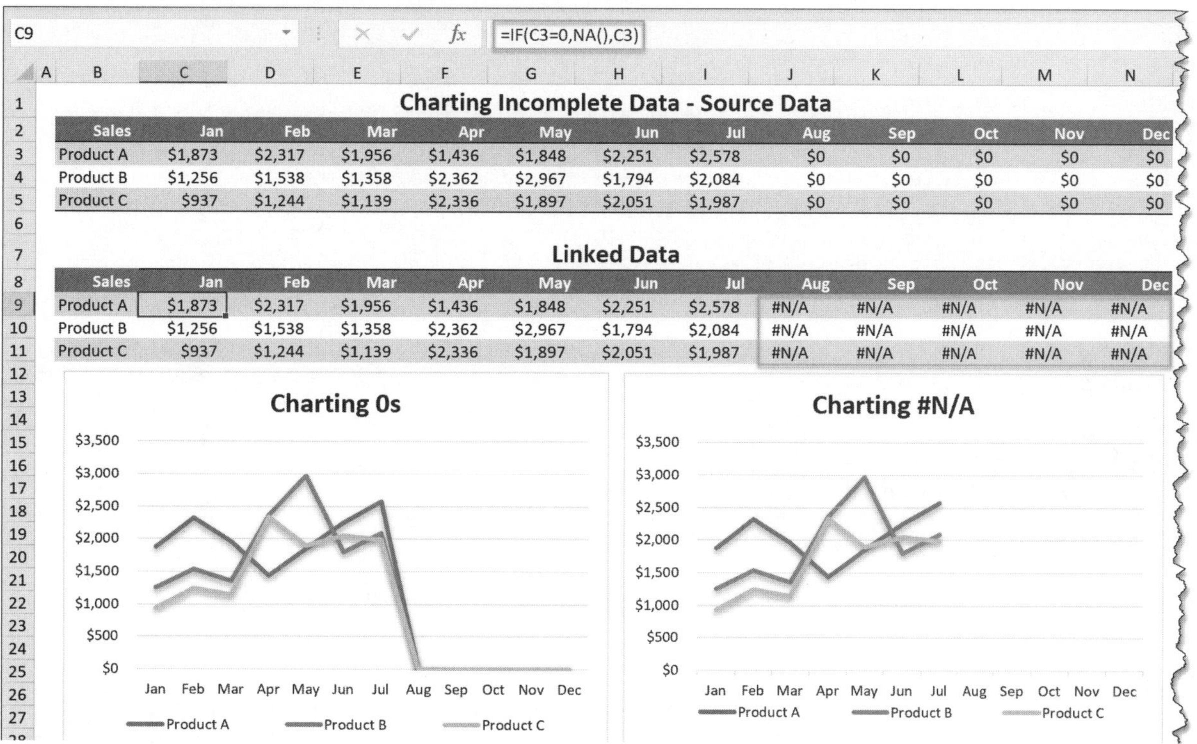

Sales	Jan	Feb	Mar	Apr	May	Jun	Jul	Aug	Sep	Oct	Nov	Dec
Product A	$1,873	$2,317	$1,956	$1,436	$1,848	$2,251	$2,578	$0	$0	$0	$0	$0
Product B	$1,256	$1,538	$1,358	$2,362	$2,967	$1,794	$2,084	$0	$0	$0	$0	$0
Product C	$937	$1,244	$1,139	$2,336	$1,897	$2,051	$1,987	$0	$0	$0	$0	$0

Sales	Jan	Feb	Mar	Apr	May	Jun	Jul	Aug	Sep	Oct	Nov	Dec
Product A	$1,873	$2,317	$1,956	$1,436	$1,848	$2,251	$2,578	#N/A	#N/A	#N/A	#N/A	#N/A
Product B	$1,256	$1,538	$1,358	$2,362	$2,967	$1,794	$2,084	#N/A	#N/A	#N/A	#N/A	#N/A
Product C	$937	$1,244	$1,139	$2,336	$1,897	$2,051	$1,987	#N/A	#N/A	#N/A	#N/A	#N/A

Interactive Charts

A chart's default nature is to ignore hidden rows and columns, although as you just saw, you can force charts to display hidden data. By default, Excel does not plot hidden data. You can use slicers and/or AutoFilter to create interactivity with charts by selectively choosing which data to display. This is great in interactive reporting tools, such as dashboards, where you might want to give users flexibility but don't want to prepare 27 different scenarios. Interactivity would be great in the following example, which includes too much data for the chart to be meaningful.

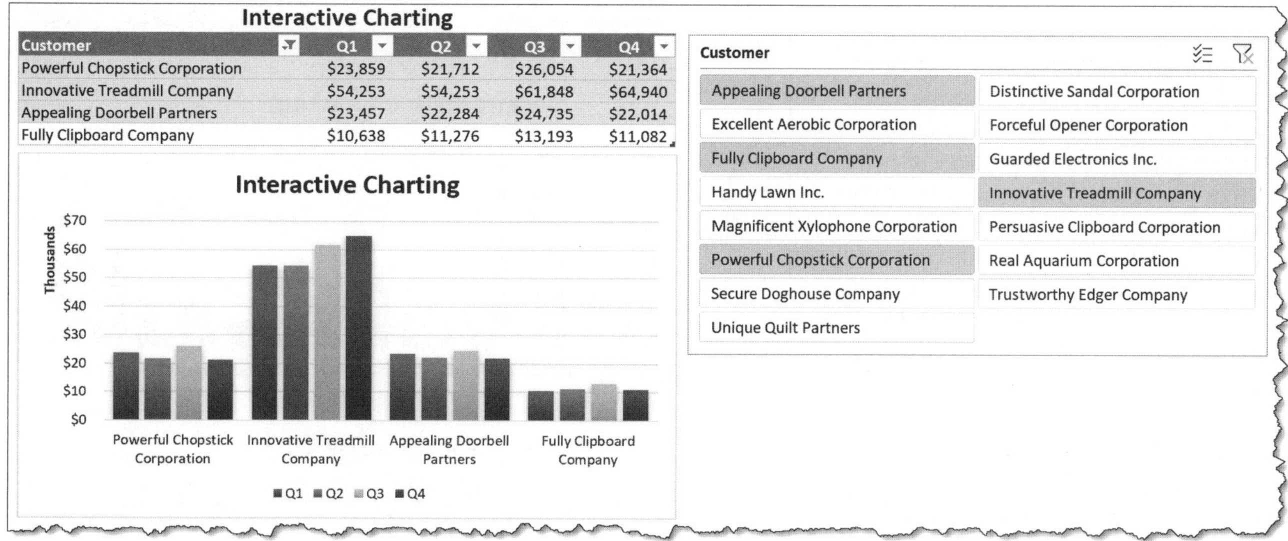

Customer	Q1	Q2	Q3	Q4
Powerful Chopstick Corporation	$23,859	$21,712	$26,054	$21,364
Innovative Treadmill Company	$54,253	$54,253	$61,848	$64,940
Appealing Doorbell Partners	$23,457	$22,284	$24,735	$22,014
Fully Clipboard Company	$10,638	$11,276	$13,193	$11,082

Slicers

Slicers let you filter data with buttons that display your options. To create the slicer shown in the following example, select any cell within the customer table, go to **Table Design > Insert Slicer**, and select the Customer field from the Insert Slicers dialog. Now, when you click the buttons in the Customer slicer, only the filtered data is plotted on the chart. Slicers are an extension of Excel's filter functionality, which you can also use to find this type of information, but clicking the buttons in a slicer is generally more intuitive.

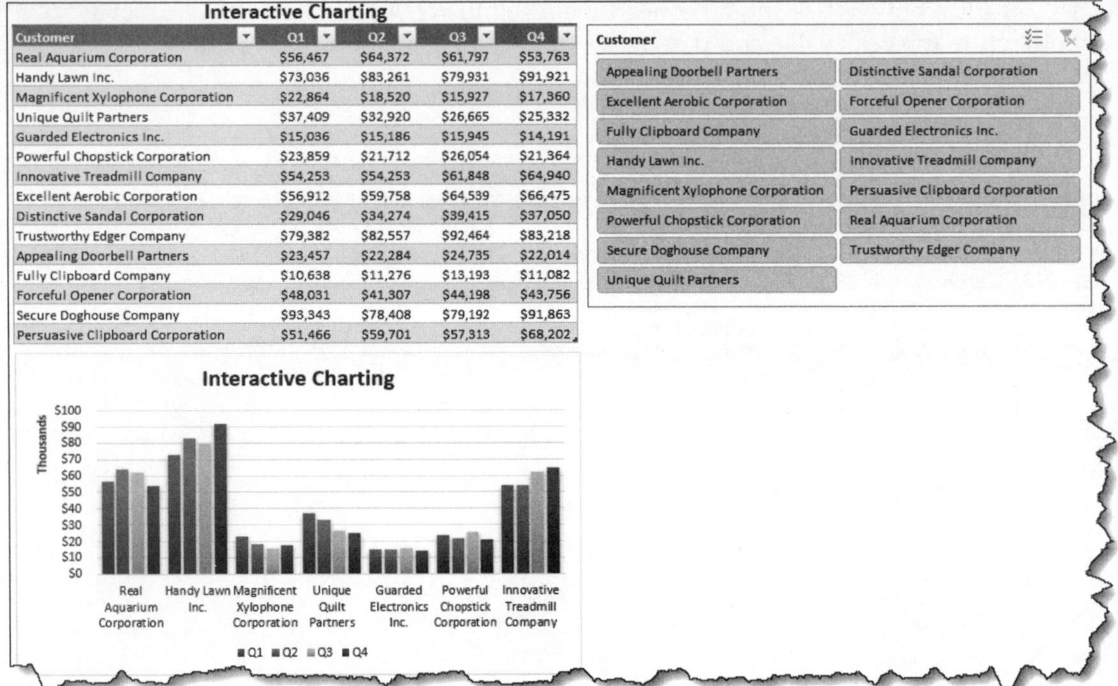

Quickly Adjusting Chart Data Ranges

So far, you've seen that you don't necessarily need to select an entire data range in order to have Excel chart it. If you want to chart an entire data range, all you need to do is have the active cell somewhere within the data range, and Excel automatically includes the entire range. You've also seen that if a data range has areas that you don't want to chart, you need to select the chart range for Excel. But what if you want to adjust the plot range after a chart has been created? It's a lot easier than you might think. Just as Excel highlights data ranges that contain formulas, it highlights a chart's data ranges for you when you select the chart plot area, so you need look no further than the range highlights in the data itself. Going back to the interactive charting example, you can just drag the area selections to the range that you want, either expanding or decreasing the plot data range. In the example here, I dragged the fill handle from the bottom of the chart data range up a few rows to adjust the plotted range.

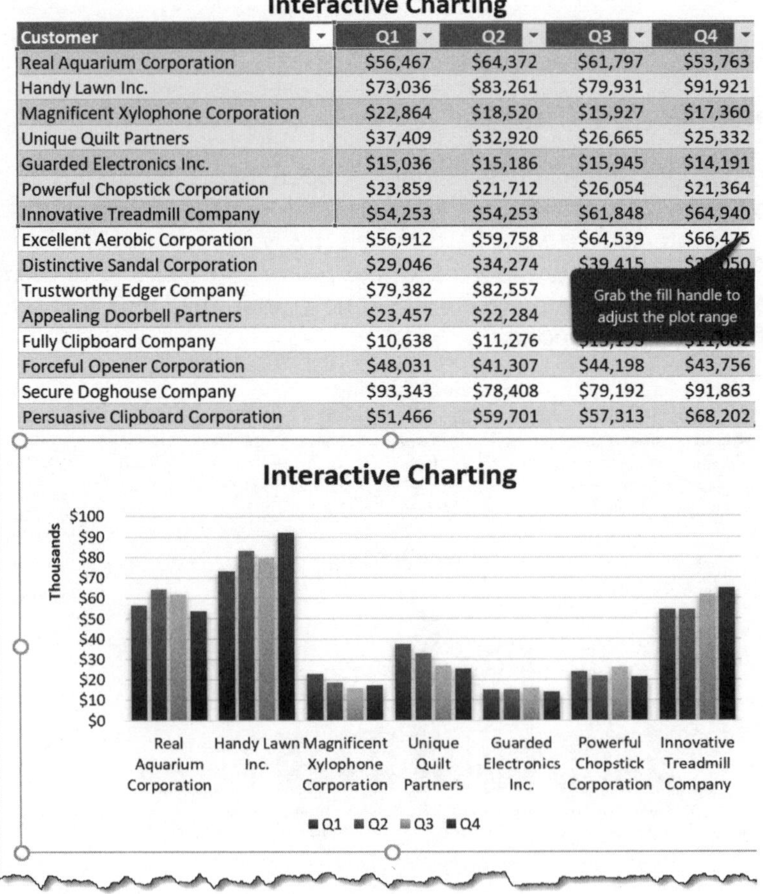

Charting Non-Contiguous Ranges

Chart elements don't need to be contiguous in order to work. For instance, in the following example, I used **Ctrl+click** to select just the header row and data specific to the Central region. Be aware that if you decide to use complex ranges like this, Excel does not readily expose your data range by highlighting it, as it would with a standard data range. To view a complex data range, you need to select the chart and then select **Chart**

Design > Select Data. Excel then shows your data range bordered by dancing ants and opens the Select Data Source dialog, where the data range is highlighted in the Chart Data Range box, as shown below.

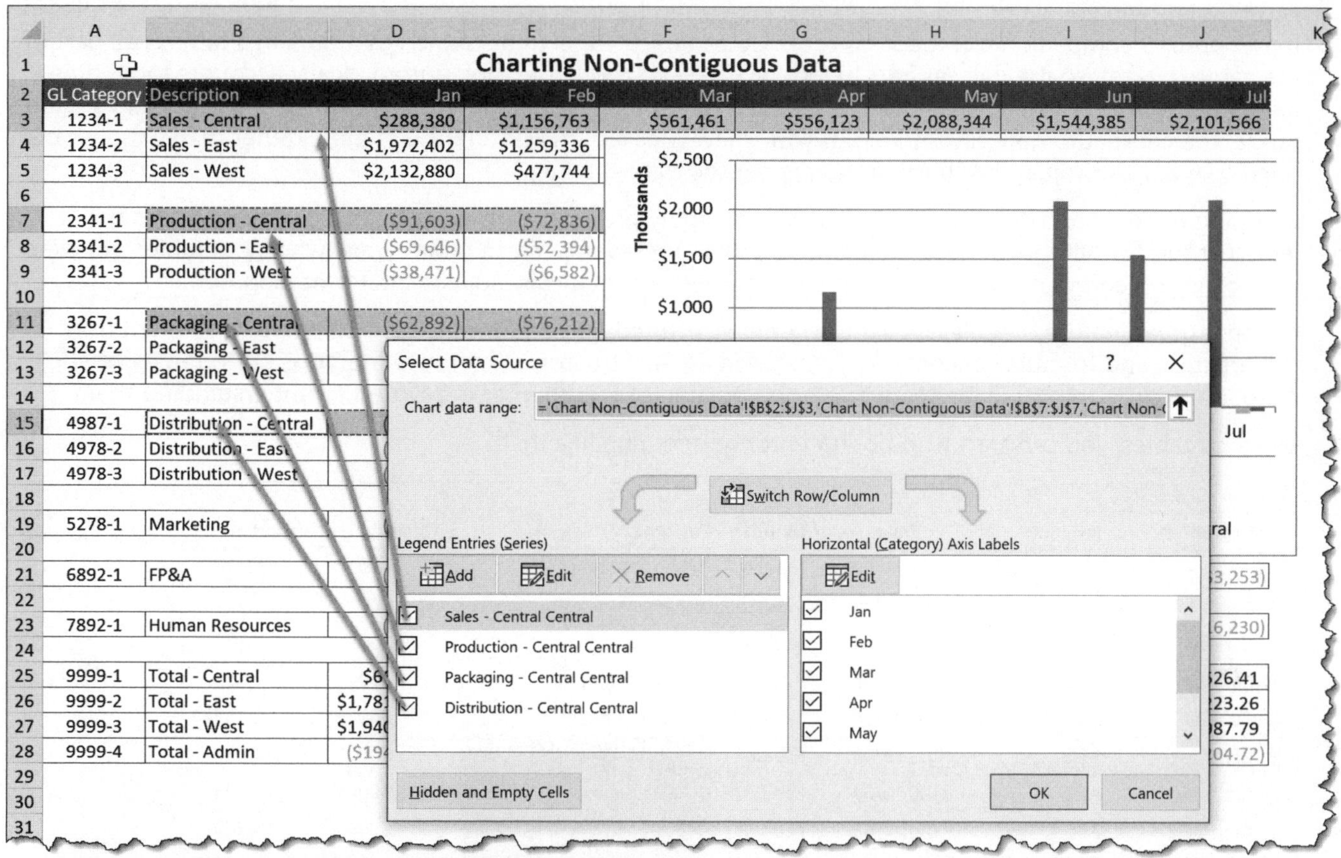

Note: Jon Peltier is a Microsoft Excel MVP and is widely recognized as the best charting guru on the planet. His website, www.peltiertech.com, is full of advanced charting techniques and tutorials that you should definitely check out.

Chapter Summary

- This chapter shows that you do not have to settle for the plain old boring charts that so many people feel compelled to create and share. In this chapter you learned about the various types of charts you can use in Excel. You saw how to create each type and what types of data are best in different scenarios.
- This chapter shows that charts work best when the data is laid out in a cohesive row/column format; this idea is directly tied to good spreadsheet design, so the concepts reinforce each other.
- This chapter shows ways to quickly draw charts either embedded in a worksheet or as independent chart sheets.
- This chapter discusses some of the multitude of ways you can format charts, including by changing styles and adding customized backgrounds and WordArt elements.
- This chapter shows to create templates that allow you to reuse your favorite chart designs over and over again instead of creating charts from scratch each time.

Chapter 10: Excel Tables and Subtotals

Excel tables help you work with datasets in a structured fashion; you may have noticed that all the samples in the Chapter 9 companion workbook were set up as tables. Excel understands that data in a table is all part of the same dataset, so if a dataset gets bigger or smaller, Excel knows and automatically accounts for it internally. For instance, if you have a chart based on a table, when you add or remove data from that chart's data range, the chart automatically updates. If your chart is based on just a range of data, rather than a table, you need to manually adjust the chart's data range if the data changes.

In addition, like charts, tables allow you to quickly apply predefined formats from a dedicated styles gallery. Just this formatting alone is often enough of a timesaver to make tables worthwhile, but tables get even better: As you add or remove data from a table, Excel automatically adjusts the formatting, too.

Another great feature of tables is that they offer *structured references*, which are completely different from the function and formula concepts you've learned so far. Structured reference methods do to tables what AutoSum can do to simple ranges, and a good portion of this chapter is devoted to understanding them.

By using tables, you can start with boring unformatted data like this:

	A	B	C	D	E	F	G
1	**Region**	**Product**	**Date**	**Month**	**Customer**	**Quantity**	**Revenue**
2	Central	ABC	01/09/08	Jan-08	General Motors	800	16,416
3	Central	ABC	01/12/08	Jan-08	IBM	300	6,267
4	Central	ABC	01/25/08	Jan-08	CitiGroup	1000	20,770
5	Central	ABC	02/08/08	Feb-08	CitiGroup	100	1,817
6	Central	ABC	02/09/08	Feb-08	General Motors	300	5,157
7	Central	ABC	02/19/08	Feb-08		500	10,385
8	Central	ABC	02/20/08	Feb-08		600	11,124
9	Central	ABC	02/27/08	Feb-08		900	16,209
10	Central	ABC	03/18/08	Mar-08	Wal-Mart	800	16,696

Unformatted table data

And turn it into the following in just a few mouse clicks:

	A	B	C	D	E	F	G
1	Region	Product	Date	Month	Customer	Quantity	Revenue
2	Central	ABC	01/09/08	Jan-08	General Motors	800	$16,416
3	Central	ABC	01/12/08	Jan-08	IBM	300	$6,267
4	Central	ABC	01/25/08	Jan-08	CitiGroup	1,000	$20,770
5	Central	ABC	02/08/08	Feb-08	CitiGroup	100	$1,817
6	Central	ABC	02/09/08	Feb-08	General Motors	300	$5,157
7	Central	ABC	02/19/08	Feb-08	Wal-Mart	500	$10,385
8	Central	ABC	02/20/08	Feb-08		600	$11,124
9	Central	ABC	02/27/08	Feb-08		900	$16,209
10	Central	ABC	03/18/08	Mar-08		800	$16,696
11	Central	ABC	03/22/08	Mar-08	Wal-Mart	300	$5,355

Data formatted as a table

Table-Related Shortcuts

Shortcut	Description
Ctrl+L	Create a table
Ctrl+T	Create a table
Ctrl+Shift+T	Add a total row

The ideal data candidate for an Excel table is any data that is cohesive and formatted using rows and columns. Essentially, each row should be a unique item, such as a sales order or product information, and each individual column should contain data all of the same data type. For instance, you don't want to mix product price and sale date in the same column. Unlike charts, tables may contain numeric data, but they don't have to. Data that has poor or no structure won't do you any good as a table—but then it probably won't be much use to you in Excel at all.

Excel Table Basics

The following sections go over some of the basics of working with tables.

Converting Data to a Table

Converting data to a table is remarkably easy. With the active cell somewhere in the data range you want to turn into a table, simply go to **Home > Format as Table**, select the table style that you want, and you have a fully formatted table in a few mouse clicks. You can also use **Ctrl+T** to create a table with the default formatting. If all you want to do is quickly apply formatting to a dataset, then there's no reason to go any further than this.

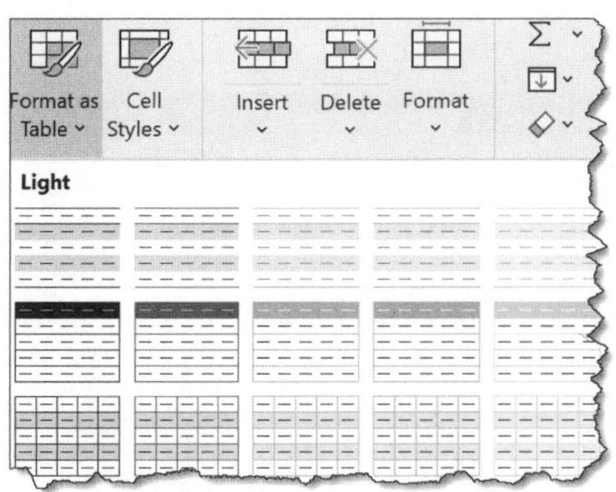

You can change a table's format from the Table Styles gallery any time: Just select the table, go to the Table Design tab on the Ribbon, and choose a new style from the Table Styles gallery.

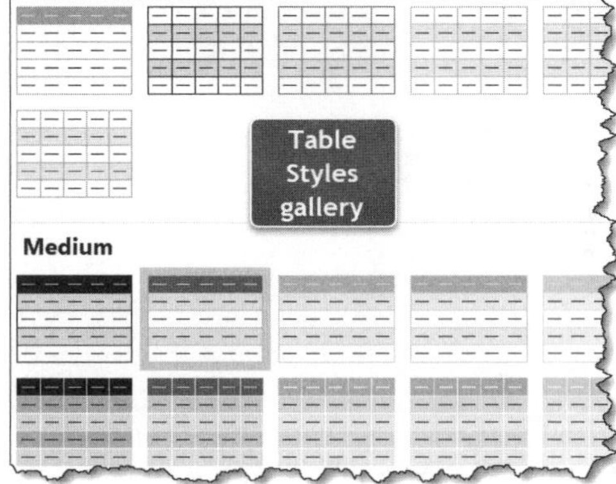

If the available formats don't suit your needs, you can right-click on one that's close and select Duplicate to set it up the way you want. In the Modify Table Style dialog that appears next, select each table element you want to change, click Format, and apply the format you want. When you're done formatting everything, just click OK. As with customizing anything else in Excel, it can take some time to set up a new table format the first time, but you only need to do it once because you can reuse your new format as often as you like.

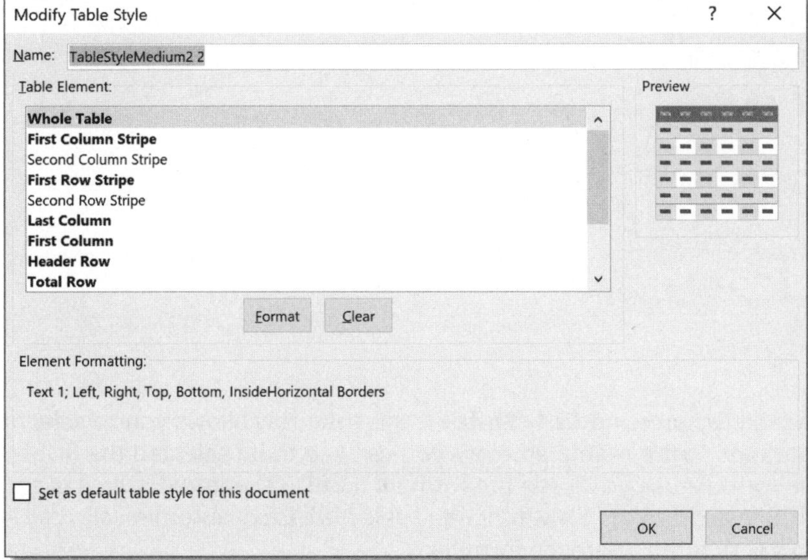

AutoFilter

The most recognizable element of Excel tables (aside from the obvious formatting) is that AutoFilter is applied automatically. You've already seen the power that AutoFilter gives you, but we'll review it briefly here, in the context of Excel tables. In the following example, table data has been filtered based on the Central region, product ABC, and 2018. Remember that you can quickly tell which columns in a table are filtered if you see an Active Filter symbol (which looks like a funnel) in the Filter drop-downs; if a column has a down arrow, AutoFilter has not been applied to that column. AutoFilter plays a big role when it comes to narrowing data to what you want to see, and it's very flexible.

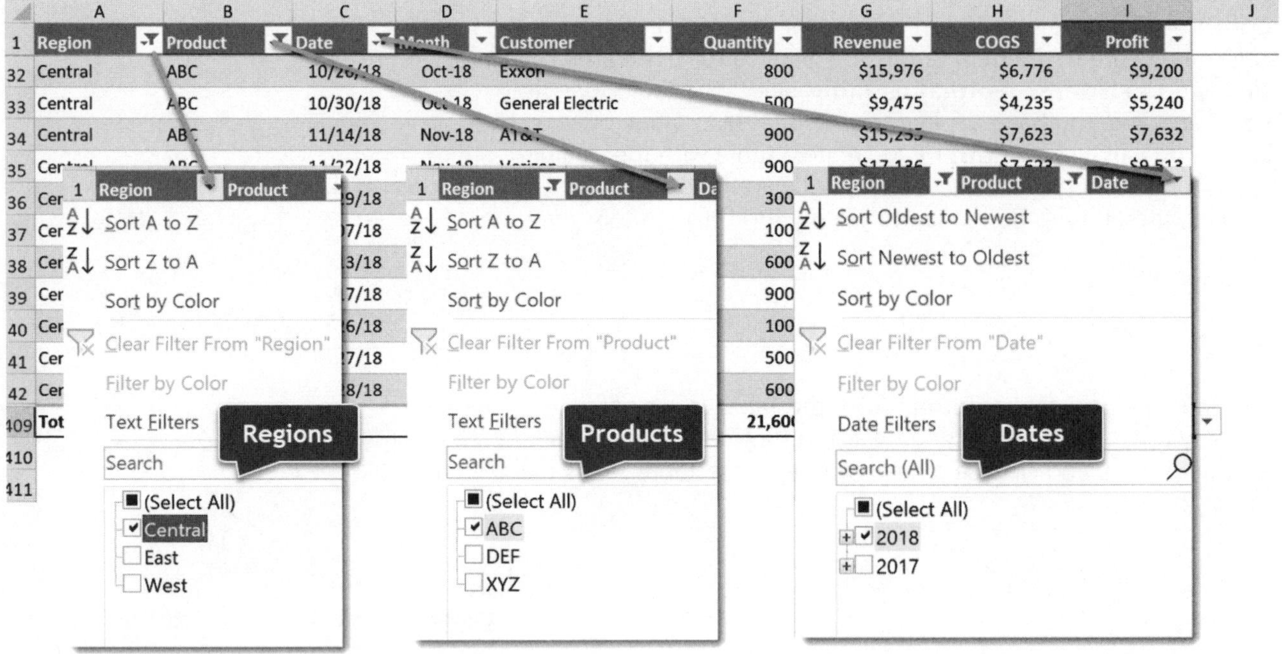

Slicers

Unfortunately, AutoFilter can be a bit challenging in some situations, but Excel also allows you to use slicers, which are a bit easier to use than AutoFilter. To create a slicer, select any cell in a table, go to **Table Design > Insert Slicer** and select the table column(s) you want to include. You can then move and size the slicers wherever you want. The following example shows three slicers that have been resized and arranged to fit together well.

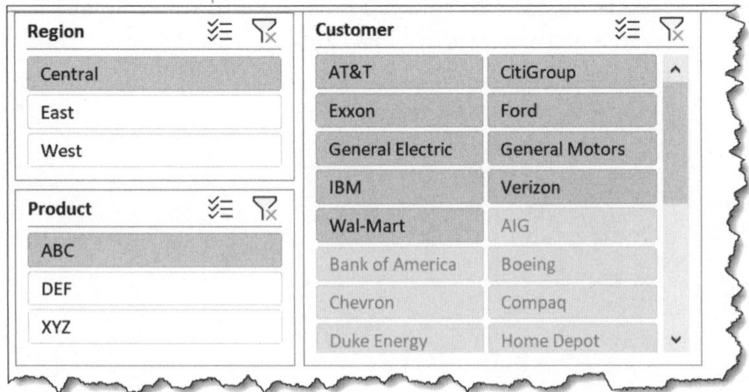

Total Rows

You can add a total row at the bottom of a table by pressing **Ctrl+Shift+T**; this total row allows you to select functions from the same drop-down as AutoSum. In the example below, you can see that I selected the SUM function. However, if you look closely at the formula bar, you'll see the formula that Excel entered, which is a SUBTOTAL function (=SUBTOTAL(109,[Profit])) instead of the SUM function I selected. Excel automatically converts the SUM function for you to create this structured reference formula.

The 10 portion of the formula above tells Excel to ignore hidden rows, and the 9 tells Excel that you want a sum formula. You could change the 9 to a 1 to tell Excel that you want to use the AVERAGE function. You could delete the 10 to tell Excel to include hidden rows in any calculations. Following is a list of SUBTOTAL numbers and their associated Excel functions.

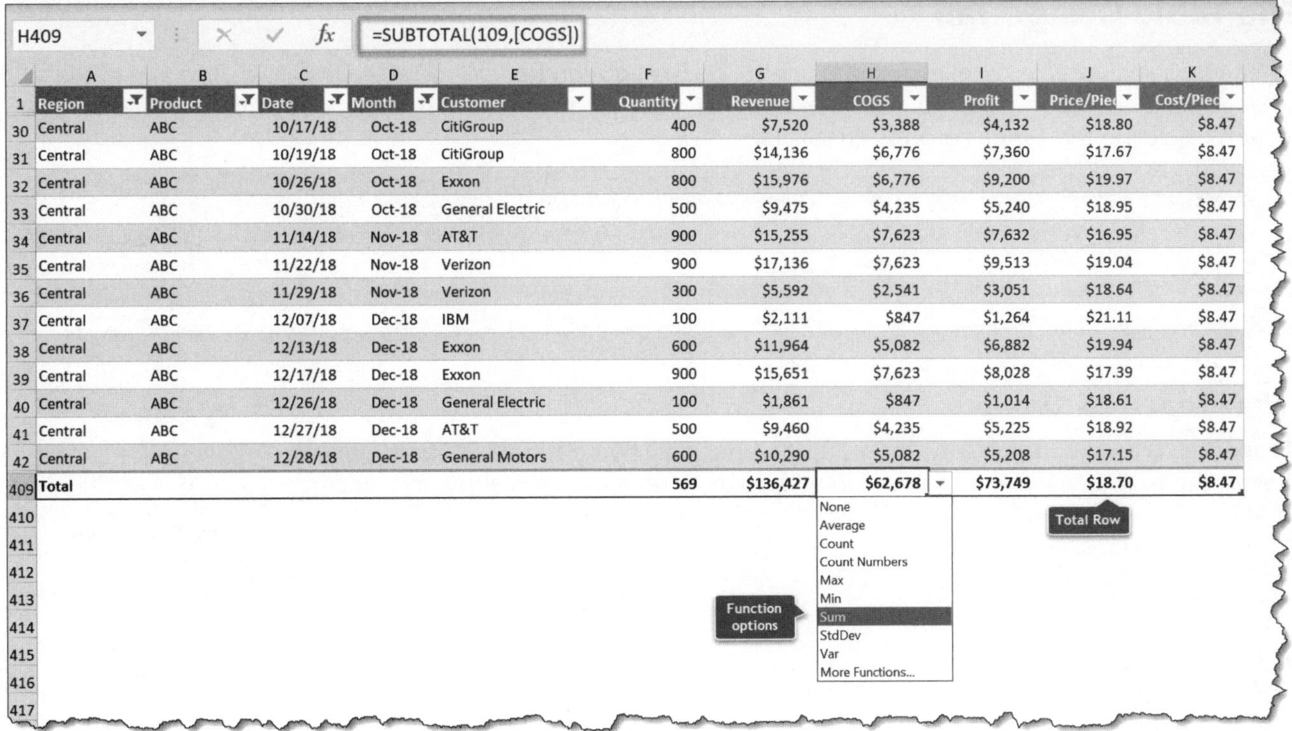

Subtotal Functions

Function Number	Excel Function
1	AVERAGE
2	COUNT
3	COUNTA
4	MAX
5	MIN
6	PRODUCT
7	STDEV
8	STDEVP
9	SUM
10	VAR
11	VARP

When you're done adding your first formula, you can use the fill handle to drag the formula to the left or right and extend it to the other total row cells. Note that when you're using structured reference formulas, you can't just copy/paste from column to column because the column reference (in this case [Profit]) won't update as it would if you were dealing with a normal Excel function, like =SUBTOTAL(109,I2:I408). We'll talk more about structured references later in this chapter, but the most important thing to know for now is that Excel replaces standard cell references with the column header. Excel automatically knows that [Profit] represents the data in I2:I408. As you add or remove data from the table, Excel automatically updates the [Profit] range—and any other formulas you've applied—for you. This is great because you don't need to worry about hunting down formulas that might have cell references (e.g., I2:I408) and update them manually.

The SUBTOTAL Function

SUBTOTAL is a special function that wraps other functions, such as SUM, AVERAGE, and COUNT, and can be set to include only visible rows. This works especially well with tables and their integrated AutoFilter because as you filter data, only the visible rows are included in the totals. This is very similar to interactive charting, where you can use a filter to adjust what charts display. SUBTOTAL also works with slicers.

The Table Design Tab

When you select a table, Excel exposes a new contextual Ribbon tab called Table Design. It's like any of the other contextual ribbon elements you've seen so far, but it deals strictly with table elements. The following sections describe the various groups on this tab.

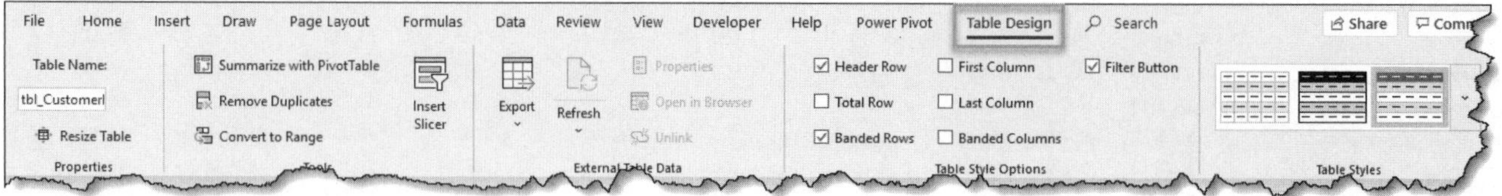

The Properties Group

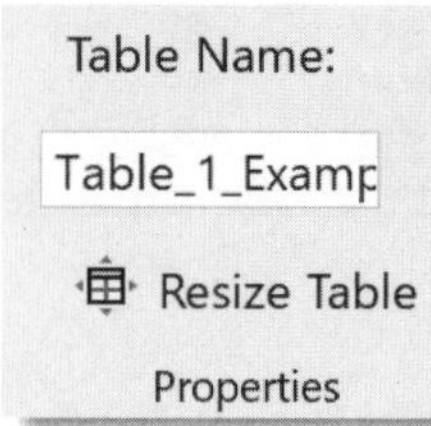

Properties is a very straightforward group that has only two options: Table Name and Resize Table. You can use the Table Name text box to rename your tables, as explained next.

Table Name

By default, Excel names each new table you create sequentially with a nondescript Table*xx* name. Ideally, you should give your tables descriptive names so you can keep track of them. Table names need to start with a letter or an underscore, and they can't include spaces or the characters /, \, *, [,], :, and ?. So, for example, Expense Tracking wouldn't work, but Expense_Tracking (note the underscore) would. If you enter an invalid name, Excel tells you about it.

Table names are stored in the Name Manager dialog, which you can get to by selecting **Formulas > Name Manager**. Here is an example of the Name Manager dialog, where you can see a list of all the tables in the Chapter 10 companion workbook. Notice that they're ordered alphabetically, and you can also see the named slicers in the list.

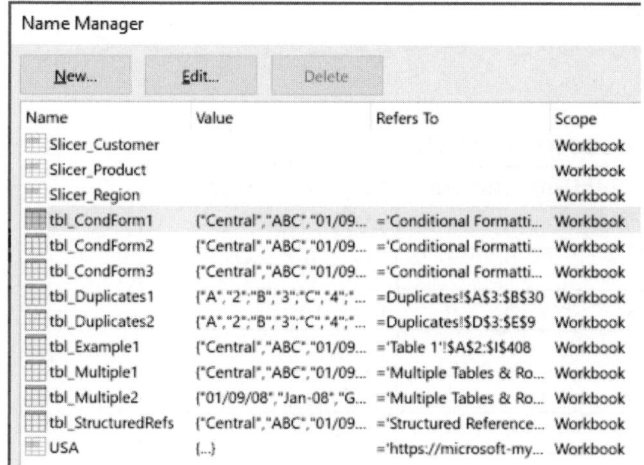
Name Manager

New... Edit... Delete

Name	Value	Refers To	Scope
Slicer_Customer			Workbook
Slicer_Product			Workbook
Slicer_Region			Workbook
tbl_CondForm1	{"Central","ABC","01/09...	='Conditional Formatti...	Workbook
tbl_CondForm2	{"Central","ABC","01/09...	='Conditional Formatti...	Workbook
tbl_CondForm3	{"Central","ABC","01/09...	='Conditional Formatti...	Workbook
tbl_Duplicates1	{"A","2";"B","3";"C","4";"...	=Duplicates!$A$3:$B$30	Workbook
tbl_Duplicates2	{"A","2";"B","3";"C","4";"...	=Duplicates!$D$3:$E$9	Workbook
tbl_Example1	{"Central","ABC","01/09...	='Table 1'!$A$2:$I$408	Workbook
tbl_Multiple1	{"Central","ABC","01/09...	='Multiple Tables & Ro...	Workbook
tbl_Multiple2	{"01/09/08","Jan-08","G...	='Multiple Tables & Ro...	Workbook
tbl_StructuredRefs	{"Central","ABC","01/09...	='Structured Reference...	Workbook
USA	{...}	='https://microsoft-my...	Workbook

Hint: I tend to prefix my table names with ***tbl_***, use ***pt_*** for PivotTables, and use ***pc_*** for Pivot Charts. You don't have to use the same prefixes, but using such a convention makes it much easier to keep track of things.

Resize Table

You aren't very likely to use the Resize Table option because Excel automatically expands the table range if you add data to any contiguous row or column (to the right of the table only). You would use this option, however, to add data that isn't contiguous. For example, if you have a table whose range is D1:H100, and you want to include column I, just start typing a new column header in I1, and the table automatically expands. But if you want to add column C or column J, you need to select **Table Design > Resize Table** and then select your new table range. You can type the new range or enter it by selecting it with your mouse.

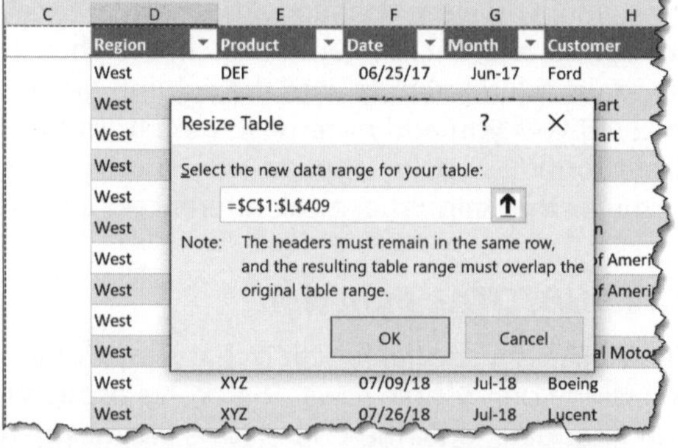

Note: If you have a total row and want to add a new row to your table between the last row and the total row, then you can go to the last cell in the last column above the total row and press **Tab**. Excel adds a row and puts the cursor in the first column of that row. You can add or delete rows anywhere in the rest of the table by right-clicking any table cell and choosing from either the Insert or Delete options.

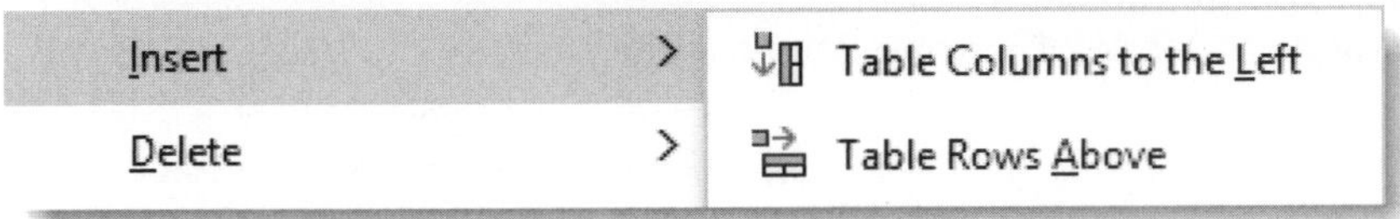

The Tools Group

There are four options in the Tools group on the Table Design tab: Summarize with PivotTable, Remove Duplicates, Convert to Range, and Insert Slicer.

Summarize with PivotTable

Tables give you access to a very powerful tool in Excel: PivotTables. In fact, Chapter 11 is devoted to PivotTables, so we're not going to spend much time on them here. Basically, when Excel creates a table, it also takes internal stock of your data and its structure, and it sets it up for seamless transition to a PivotTable.

Remove Duplicates

Remove Duplicates is another fantastic tool. In the past, if you wanted to identify duplicate data, you had to go through some fairly laborious steps, many of which involved VBA; use conditional formatting to identify the duplicates; or use fairly complex formulas—and then if you wanted to remove the duplicates, you had to find a mechanism to delete the ones you had identified. More often than not, it was faster to put that data into a database to remove the duplicates and then pull the remediated data back into Excel. You can imagine how long that took, but the alternative in many cases was to manually identify duplicates and remove them by hand. The Remove Duplicates tool make it simple to remove duplicates right in Excel—with no formulas or other gymnastics required.

The Remove Duplicates tool on the Table Design tab is the same as the Remove Duplicates tool on the Data tab, but it's included as a native table option to save you the time of switching to another Ribbon group while you're working in a table. When you click it, the dialog shown here appears.

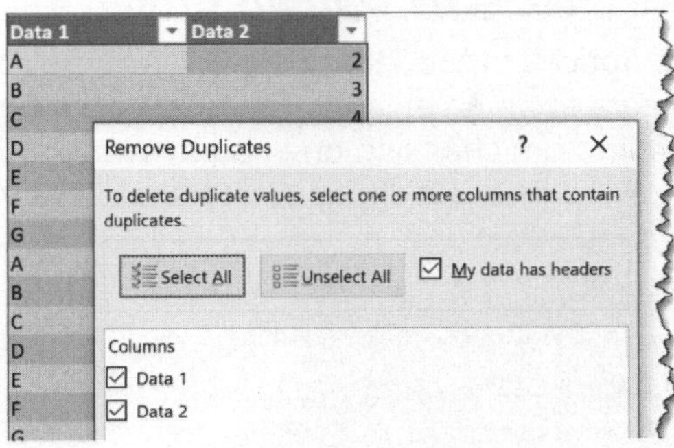

By default, Excel selects all the columns in your data range or table. Unfortunately, that's typically not what you want, though. In this example, if you leave both columns checked, you'll get a message that Excel can't find any duplicates even though it's easy enough to see that there are some. Why? Even though there are duplicates in column A, when Excel looks at both columns A and B together, it doesn't see any duplicates. If you uncheck the Data 2 checkbox in the Remove Duplicates dialog box, Excel gets rid of the column A duplicates. As an added bonus, the list it returns to you is sorted!

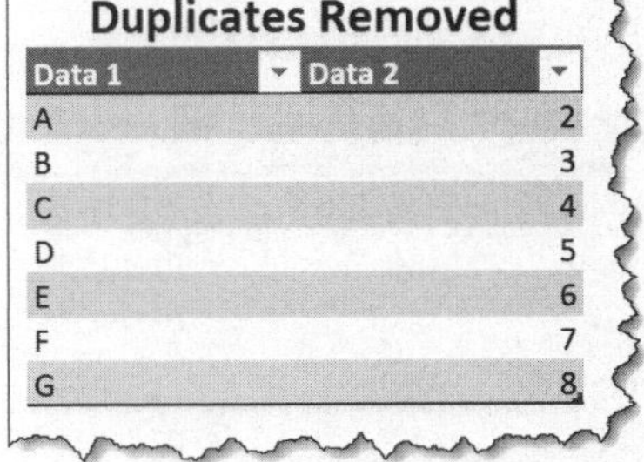

Duplicates Removed

Data 1	Data 2
A	2
B	3
C	4
D	5
E	6
F	7
G	8

Convert to Range

If you love table formatting but don't really need the added functionality that tables offer, the Convert to Range option is for you. It simply lets you remove the table elements from your data but retain the table formatting. Just be aware that if you add new rows or columns after using this tool, the table formatting won't apply. To format the new data the same as the original data, you need to convert the data to a formatted table again and then convert it back to a range.

The External Table Data Group

The External Table Data group on the Table Design tab allows you to export your table data to outside applications, most notably SharePoint and Visio, as shown here.

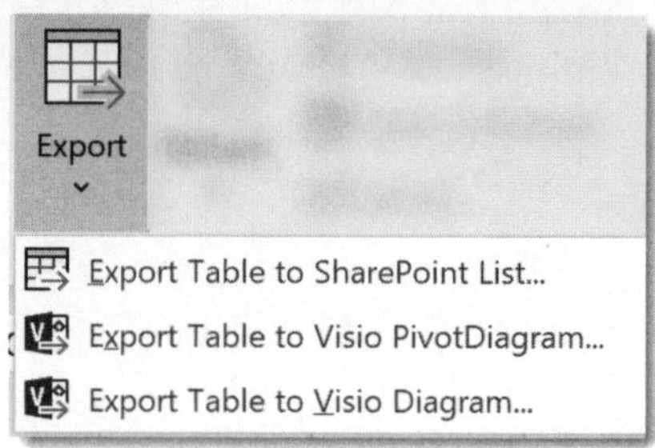

SharePoint

If you're not in a corporate setting, then it's unlikely that you'll deal with SharePoint. If you do need to export a table to SharePoint, however, you need to know the server URL for publishing the table, and you also need to have the proper network access to be able to do so. If you have that information and select **Table Design > Export > Export Table to SharePoint List**, Excel walks you through the export process with relative ease. If you don't have the necessary information, you probably need to have someone from your SharePoint services/IT department handle the export for you.

Visio

Visio is another application that very few users outside a corporate setting are likely to have installed. If you do have Visio, though, you know that it's an excellent application. Although Visio is a very complex application, it is remarkably easy to use it without having to delve into the complexities. Visio gives you the ability to draw all kinds of diagrams, such as flowcharts and process charts, organizational charts, floor plans, network maps, and database designs. If you have any data that could benefit from the addition of a diagram, you should explore Visio.

The Table Style Options Group

The options in the Table Style Options group let you refine the table style you selected when you first converted data to an Excel table. The following example shows the choices in this group. There is no performance loss or gain from choosing one option over another. In most cases, you'll want to select at least Header Row. The following example shows what it looks like if you have rows unbanded and all the column options selected.

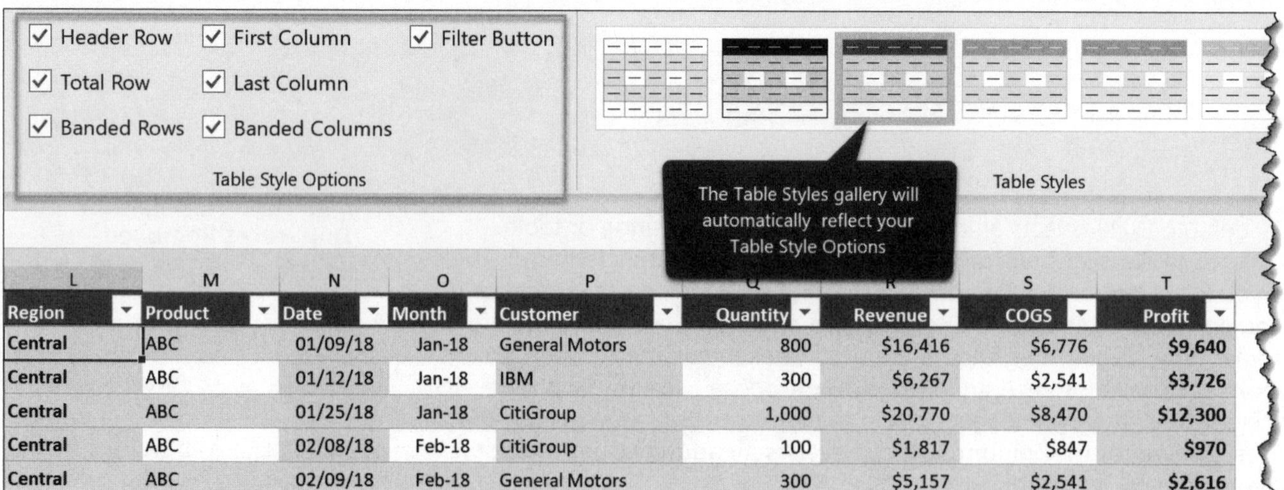

To avoid making your table look too busy, you should generally choose only Banded Rows or Banded Columns but not both.

The Table Styles Group

The options in the Table Styles group allow you to apply the color theme of your choice. You can choose these table formatting options when you convert data to a table, or you can insert a default table and format it later. You can choose from Light, Medium, or Dark, and the style colors you see are dependent on your default theme. The default is the Office theme, but you can select **Page Layout > Themes** to choose any theme you like or create your own.

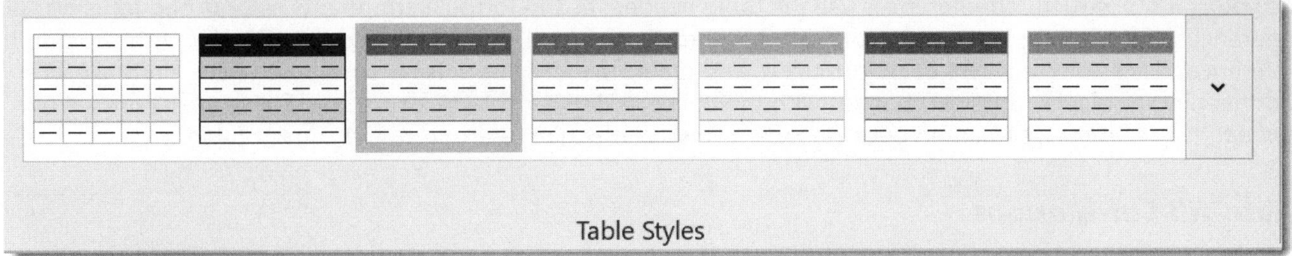

Conditional Formatting with Tables

Tables work very nicely with conditional formatting, including data bars, color scales, and icon sets. The example below shows conditional formatting data bars applied.

Conditional Formatting - Data Bars

Region	Product	Date	Month	Customer	Quantity	Revenue	COGS	Profit
Central	ABC	01/09/18	Jan-18	General Motors	800	$16,416	$6,776	$9,640
Central	ABC	01/12/18	Jan-18	IBM	300	$6,267	$2,541	$3,726
Central	ABC	01/25/18	Jan-18	CitiGroup	1,000	$20,770	$8,470	$12,300
Central	ABC	02/08/18	Feb-18	CitiGroup	100	$1,817	$847	$970
Central	ABC	02/09/18	Feb-18	General Motors	300	$5,157	$2,541	$2,616

The Excel team added something called *persistent formatting* to tables, and it's incredibly useful. Thanks to persistent formatting, if you apply formatting to an Excel table and then add another row, Excel automatically extends the formatting to the new row. If you're working with non-table data and try formatting a new row of data manually, you'll quickly get an idea of how much persistent formatting can simplify your Excel life. Seemingly trivial performance enhancements like this might not seem like much, but when you spend a lot of time in Excel, they really start to add up.

Microsoft has done an amazing job of continuously updating Excel, and many things that could be done only with VBA in the past are now easy to do with tools included with Excel. In fact, you can make suggestions for what you'd like to see changed or updated in Excel by going to https://excel.uservoice.com. The Excel team actively reads all suggestions and acts on the ones that get the most votes.

Structured References

Tables work with structured references, which are similar to the formula/function syntax you've seen so far. Whereas native Excel functions use range references, structured references use a table's column headers, as you saw with the =SUBTOTAL(109,[Profit]) formula earlier. A normal formula would have an explicit range address like I2:I408, but Excel automatically knows that's the Profit column. If you add or remove rows, Excel automatically reflects that internally, and you don't need to adjust anything. The following example uses calculated columns for profit, price per piece, and cost per piece formulas. It also includes the =SUBTOTAL(109,[Column Name]) functions at the bottom.

I409 | =SUBTOTAL(109,[Profit])

	Region	Product	Date	Month	Customer	Quantity	Revenue	COGS	Profit	Price/Piece	Cost/Piece
34	Central	ABC	11/14/18	Nov-18	AT&T	900	$15,255	$7,623	$7,632	$16.95	$8.47
35	Central	ABC	11/22/18	Nov-18	Verizon	900	$17,136	$7,623	$9,513	$19.04	$8.47
36	Central	ABC	11/29/18	Nov-18	Verizon	300	$5,592	$2,541	$3,051	$18.64	$8.47
37	Central	ABC	12/07/18	Dec-18	IBM	100	$2,111	$847	$1,264	$21.11	$8.47
38	Central	ABC	12/13/18	Dec-18	Exxon	600	$11,964	$5,082	$6,882	$19.94	$8.47
39	Central	ABC	12/17/18	Dec-18	Exxon	900	$15,651	$7,623	$8,028	$17.39	$8.47
40	Central	ABC	12/26/18	Dec-18	General Electric	100	$1,861	$847	$1,014	$18.61	$8.47
41	Central	ABC	12/27/18	Dec-18	AT&T	500	$9,460	$4,235	$5,225	$18.92	$8.47
42	Central	ABC	12/28/18	Dec-18	General Motors	600	$10,290	$5,082	$5,208	$17.15	$8.47
409	**Total**					**527**	**$414,348**	**$182,952**	**$231,396**	**$19.17**	**$8.47**

Note: You don't need to use Freeze Panes with tables to lock the header row in place. Tables automatically convert the ABC header row and display the table headers when you scroll down.

The example above uses the following formulas:

- *Profit column:* =[@Revenue]-[@COGS]
- *Price/Piece column:* =[@Revenue]/[@Quantity]
- *Cost/Piece column:* =[@COGS]/[@Quantity]

As you can see, structured references use the table headers as the formula arguments as opposed to using cell references. If this example were not formatted as a table, the Profit formula would be =G2-H2. With structured references, Excel knows where each formula is, and it automatically updates the cell references internally without needing to display physical changes with them, like =G3-H3, =G4-H4, and so on. These are examples of *unqualified references*, so named because Excel knows that you're referring to the current table.

Auto-fill Calculations

When you enter a formula in a table, Excel automatically fills it down through the entire column, so you don't need to copy/paste as you would need to with a standard formula. If you change a formula in a column, Excel also updates the rest of the formulas for you. However, if you enter a formula that's inconsistent with what you already have in the column, Excel stops auto-filling formulas for you because it no longer knows which one you want to use. This also happens if you enter a value in a column that contains formulas. If you select **File > Options** to open the Excel Options dialog, select the Formulas tab, and select the Enable Background Error Checking checkbox, Excel lets you know where these inconsistencies happen, as shown in the example here.

Total Rows

As discussed briefly earlier in this chapter, tables give you the ability to add a total row that contains multiple functions. The following example has a total row that uses AVERAGE for the Quantity, Price/Piece, and Cost/Piece columns and SUM for Revenue, COGS, and Profit.

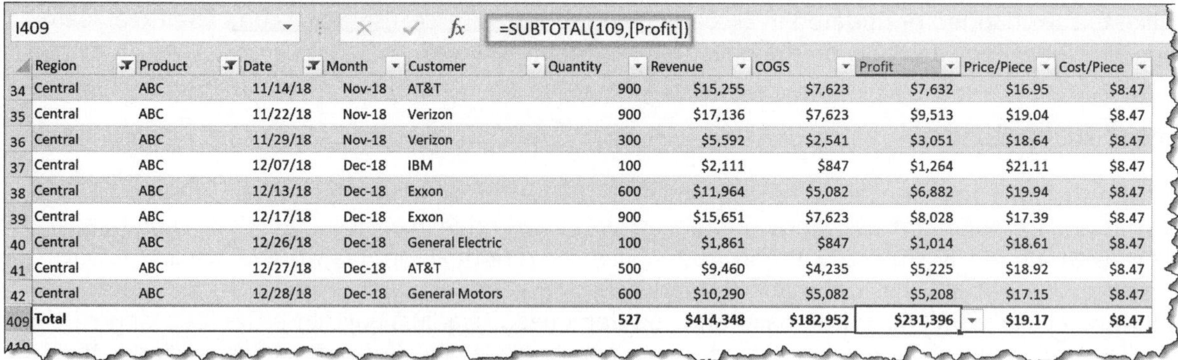

I409 =SUBTOTAL(109,[Profit])

	Region	Product	Date	Month	Customer	Quantity	Revenue	COGS	Profit	Price/Piece	Cost/Piece
34	Central	ABC	11/14/18	Nov-18	AT&T	900	$15,255	$7,623	$7,632	$16.95	$8.47
35	Central	ABC	11/22/18	Nov-18	Verizon	900	$17,136	$7,623	$9,513	$19.04	$8.47
36	Central	ABC	11/29/18	Nov-18	Verizon	300	$5,592	$2,541	$3,051	$18.64	$8.47
37	Central	ABC	12/07/18	Dec-18	IBM	100	$2,111	$847	$1,264	$21.11	$8.47
38	Central	ABC	12/13/18	Dec-18	Exxon	600	$11,964	$5,082	$6,882	$19.94	$8.47
39	Central	ABC	12/17/18	Dec-18	Exxon	900	$15,651	$7,623	$8,028	$17.39	$8.47
40	Central	ABC	12/26/18	Dec-18	General Electric	100	$1,861	$847	$1,014	$18.61	$8.47
41	Central	ABC	12/27/18	Dec-18	AT&T	500	$9,460	$4,235	$5,225	$18.92	$8.47
42	Central	ABC	12/28/18	Dec-18	General Motors	600	$10,290	$5,082	$5,208	$17.15	$8.47
409	**Total**					**527**	**$414,348**	**$182,952**	**$231,396**	**$19.17**	**$8.47**

Here are the formulas for each column in this example:

- *Quantity column:* =SUBTOTAL(101,[Quantity])
- *Revenue column:* =SUBTOTAL(109,[Revenue])
- *COGS column:* =SUBTOTAL(109,[COGS])
- *Profit column:* =SUBTOTAL(109,[Profit])
- *Price/Piece column:* =SUBTOTAL(101,[Price/Piece])
- *Cost/Piece column:* =SUBTOTAL(101,[Cost/Piece])

External References to Table Ranges

If you're outside a table and try to reference the table in a formula, Excel automatically appends the table name to your formula. This is similar to how Excel adds a sheet name when you try to reference a sheet other than the active sheet in a formula. Say that you need to create a formula for profit by subtracting COGS from revenue. The result is the same as the $57,904 profit figure that was calculated in the totals row in the preceding example, but the syntax has been expanded to include the table name (tbl_StructuredRefs in this case):

Profit=tbl_StructuredRefs[[#Totals],[Revenue]]-tbl_StructuredRefs[[#Totals],[COGS]]

In this syntax, tbl_StructuredRefs is the table name. [#Totals] is called a *special item specifier*, and it refers specifically to the total row. The [Revenue] and [COGS] references are called *column specifiers*, and they refer to the specific table columns, as identified by the column headers. This is an example of a fully qualified reference, which is necessary to let Excel know explicitly which table you're referring to.

Deleting Table Rows and Columns

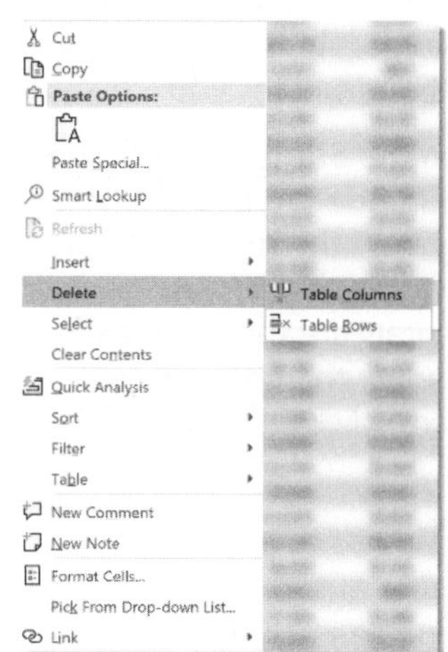

To delete table rows or columns, you can right-click anywhere in a table and select **Delete > Table Rows** or **Delete > Table Columns**, as shown below. You can also use **Home > Insert** and **Home > Delete** .

Rows and columns in tables behave differently than rows and columns in the Excel grid. If you delete a row or column from a table, the surrounding rows or columns aren't affected. But if you delete a row or column from outside a table, and they intersect with the table, that row or column is deleted from the table as well. This is good because tables behave independently of the grid, so you can delete rows or columns without affecting any data outside the table.

Subtotals

Subtotals are a fantastic tool for summarizing data without having to resort to lengthy formulas. Microsoft has built in a very robust series of subtotal functionality to do the work for you. In addition, you can use *nested subtotals*, in which you can subtotal one series of data and then add additional layers. To follow along with this section, open the worksheet called Subtotals in the Chapter 10 companion workbook.

Note: Unfortunately, subtotals aren't supported in tables. However, you can use PivotTables to get subtotal functionality. PivotTables are discussed in Chapter 11.

When you apply subtotals, Excel adds some new numbered buttons to the left of the row headers, as shown in the following example. In this example, you can click 1 to display only the grand total row, 2 to display the group you selected to subtotal (in this case, Region), and 3 to display all your data. If you add additional levels of subtotals, you see additional numbered buttons. The + and - buttons beneath the numbered buttons allow you to expand or collapse the details for each individual group. Clicking on the middle button, for example, would display all the data for the East region but leave the other regions collapsed.

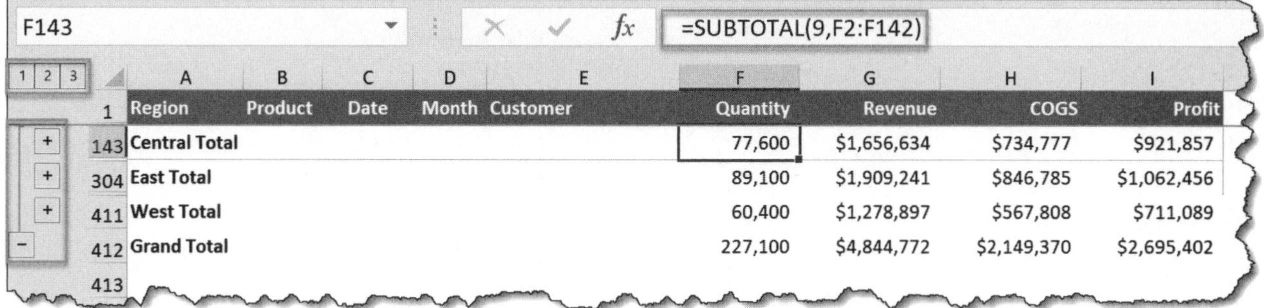

	A	B	C	D	E	F	G	H	I
1	Region	Product	Date	Month	Customer	Quantity	Revenue	COGS	Profit
143	Central Total					77,600	$1,656,634	$734,777	$921,857
304	East Total					89,100	$1,909,241	$846,785	$1,062,456
411	West Total					60,400	$1,278,897	$567,808	$711,089
412	Grand Total					227,100	$4,844,772	$2,149,370	$2,695,402
413									

The first rule of thumb with subtotals is that your data needs to be sorted in the order that you want to subtotal. If your data isn't ordered correctly, you are likely to experience some unexpected results. The order is generally easy to fix with smaller datasets, but if you have a large dataset, you might not realize that the subtotals are incorrect, or at the very least you'll have a hard time spotting any anomalies that are created.

Hint: Because subtotals don't physically alter your data, you can remove them at any time, sort your data as needed, and reapply the subtotals.

Adding a Subtotal

After you've sorted your data and are ready to apply a subtotal, go to **Data > Subtotal**, and you see this dialog. Note that you don't need to select the data range; as long as your data is in contiguous rows and columns, Excel selects the range for you.

In the Subtotal dialog box, select an option for the At Each Change In option; in this case, select Region to have Excel group the regions. Next, specify the function to use, which in this case should be SUM. (Your function options for subtotals are the same as for total rows in Excel tables.) Then select the columns you want to include in your subtotal and click OK. Excel adds a subtotal as shown here.

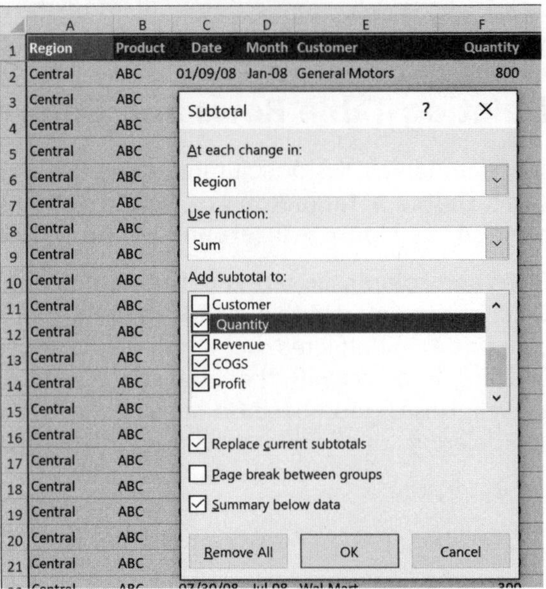

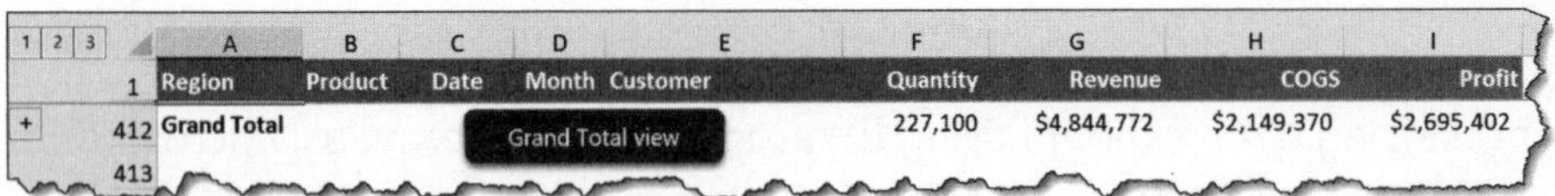

Adding Layers of Subtotals

Very few people know it, but you can have more than one level of subtotals. First, you need to apply the primary subtotal, and then you can apply subgroups, in descending order of importance. So, if you want to subtotal by region and then product, you need to apply the subtotals in that order. The key to applying secondary subtotals is the Replace Current Subtotals checkbox in the Subtotal dialog (shown here). To see how you use it, let's look at an example of applying another layer of subtotals.

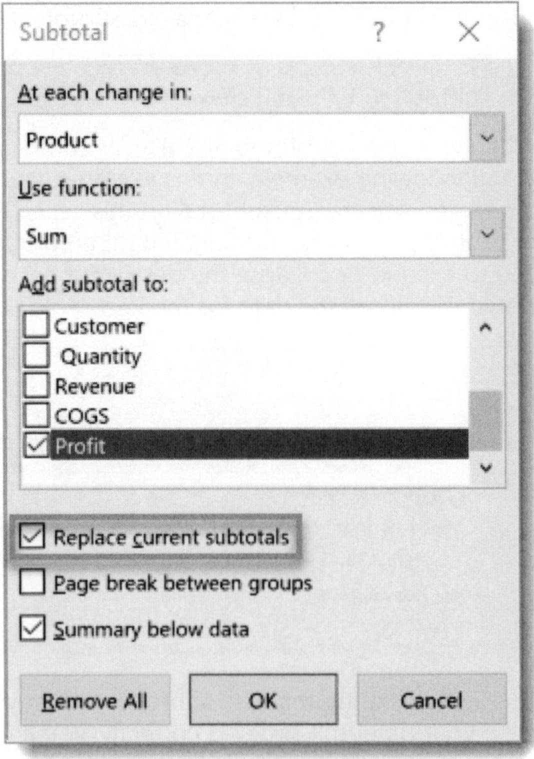

In the following example, you already have a subtotal on region, and you want to add one for the product category. As soon as your secondary subtotals have been applied, you see another numbered button (in this case, 4) added to the subtotals grouping in the upper-left corner, as shown below.

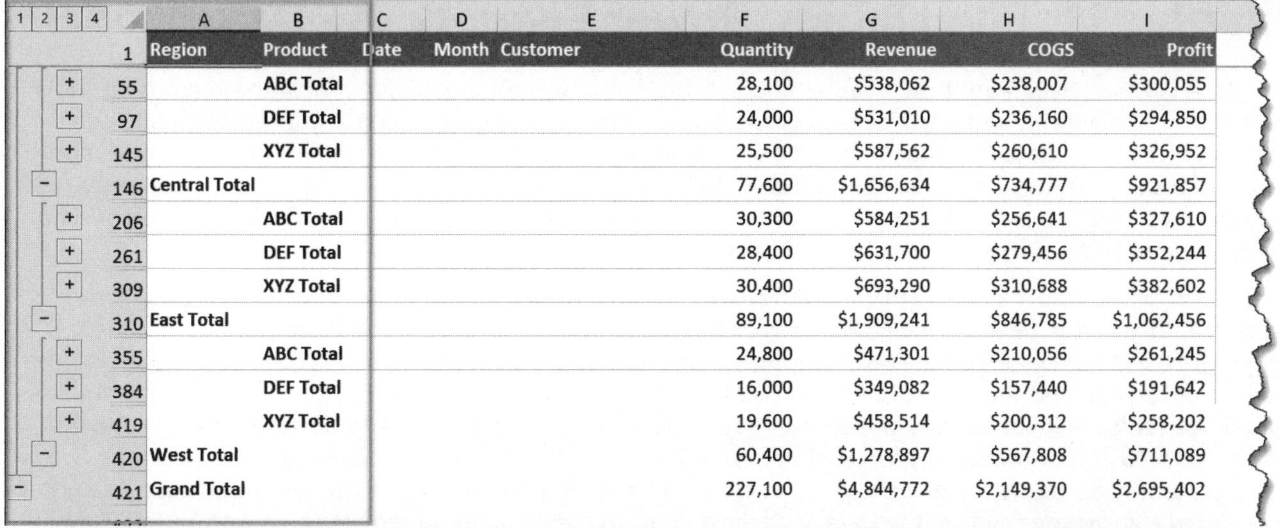

	Region	Product	Date	Month	Customer	Quantity	Revenue	COGS	Profit
55		ABC Total				28,100	$538,062	$238,007	$300,055
97		DEF Total				24,000	$531,010	$236,160	$294,850
145		XYZ Total				25,500	$587,562	$260,610	$326,952
146	Central Total					77,600	$1,656,634	$734,777	$921,857
206		ABC Total				30,300	$584,251	$256,641	$327,610
261		DEF Total				28,400	$631,700	$279,456	$352,244
309		XYZ Total				30,400	$693,290	$310,688	$382,602
310	East Total					89,100	$1,909,241	$846,785	$1,062,456
355		ABC Total				24,800	$471,301	$210,056	$261,245
384		DEF Total				16,000	$349,082	$157,440	$191,642
419		XYZ Total				19,600	$458,514	$200,312	$258,202
420	West Total					60,400	$1,278,897	$567,808	$711,089
421	Grand Total					227,100	$4,844,772	$2,149,370	$2,695,402

Note: You might notice that the Date, Month, and Customer columns are blank at this point. That's because only the subtotaled columns can be displayed. If you were to add another subtotal group for customer, the Customer column would display as well.

Mixing Functions in Subtotals

Unfortunately, when you apply subtotals, you can select only one function at a time, so you can't, for example, ask Excel to apply an average and a sum at the same time. But after a subtotal has been applied, you can manually adjust the formulas to apply another function. Let's say you don't want to use Sum of Quantity but want to use Average instead. You can use **Home > Find & Select > Replace** (or press **Ctrl+H**) to change the function. In this case, you could select column F and press **Ctrl+H**, and then in the Find and Replace dialog, you would insert **(9** in the Find What textbox, **(1** in the Replace With textbox, and click Find All (because 9 represents Sum, and 1 represents Average). The example below shows what this looks like.

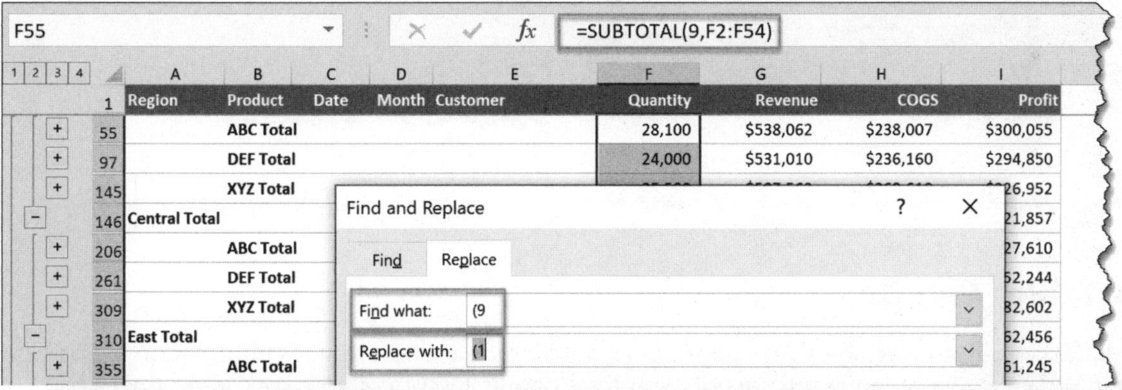

Note: Why do you enter **(9** instead of just **9**? Many times, when you use Find and Replace, you need to create a unique string so that you don't unintentionally replace something else. For example, if there were a 9 in the formula ranges, and you entered just **9** and **1** in the Find and Replace dialog, you would alter the ranges as well. Such little changes are often hard to spot until it's too late!

Chapter Summary

- In this chapter, you learned about Excel tables and saw that you can use them to quickly format your data, or you can go further and take advantage of the additional tools that they offer, including the following:
  - Integrated filtering and sorting
  - Structured references
  - Total rows
  - Styles, including banded rows and columns
  - The ability to automatically add rows and columns to a dataset
- This chapter discusses how you can quickly remove duplicates from your data, and it also reviews Excel's Subtotal feature, which gives you the ability to quickly summarize multiple data points with different functions (SUM, AVERAGE, COUNT, etc.).

Chapter 11: PivotTables, Power Pivot, & the Data Model

In Chapter 10, we talked about Excel tables and subtotals, and we got a glimpse of how these amazing tools don't want to play nicely with each other. Fortunately, Excel's PivotTables overcome that problem and can make you look like a data rock star with just a few clicks. PivotTables are the foundation of self-service reporting solutions in that they let you slice and dice data in ways that would otherwise require a database programmer. You can also create Pivot Charts, which are fantastic because you can use slicers to filter your data, and any charts that you have associated with your PivotTables update dynamically.

PivotTables also support a new kind of slicer called a *timeline*, which lets you filter your PivotTables by day, week, month, quarter, or year. Finally, PivotTables take advantage of two powerful integrated tools called Power Pivot and the Data Model. Power Pivot gives you the ability to import millions of rows of data, and the Data Model sits behind the scenes, allowing you to create relationships between tables and then use any field from those tables in PivotTables. For example, you could have a customer list with customer details and an orders list of customer transactions in customer number order. If you create a relationship between the two tables on the Customer Number field, you can create a PivotTable that shows customer details such as address and related transactions. Before the Data Model, you had to create an intermediate table with formulas to join the relevant data and then create a PivotTable from that. The Data Model makes things much more efficient.

The following PivotTable example took a few minutes to create. It would take a whole lot longer to get similar information with formulas, and the solution wouldn't be nearly as flexible.

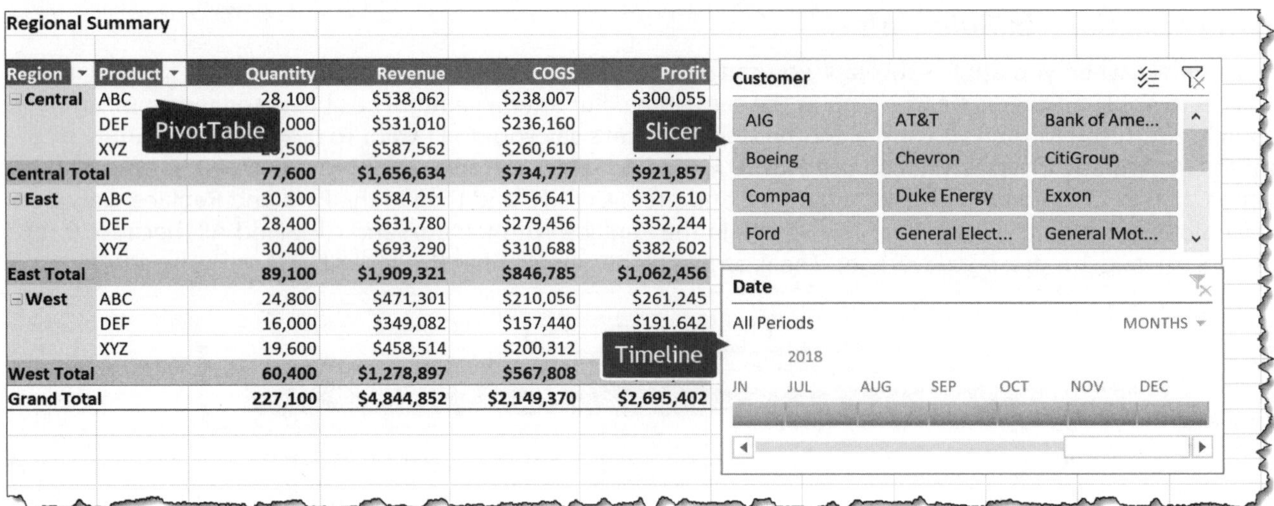

Regional Summary

Region	Product	Quantity	Revenue	COGS	Profit
Central	ABC	28,100	$538,062	$238,007	$300,055
	DEF	,000	$531,010	$236,160	
	XYZ	,500	$587,562	$260,610	
Central Total		77,600	$1,656,634	$734,777	$921,857
East	ABC	30,300	$584,251	$256,641	$327,610
	DEF	28,400	$631,780	$279,456	$352,244
	XYZ	30,400	$693,290	$310,688	$382,602
East Total		89,100	$1,909,321	$846,785	$1,062,456
West	ABC	24,800	$471,301	$210,056	$261,245
	DEF	16,000	$349,082	$157,440	$191.642
	XYZ	19,600	$458,514	$200,312	
West Total		60,400	$1,278,897	$567,808	
Grand Total		227,100	$4,844,852	$2,149,370	$2,695,402

What PivotTables Can Do

To get an idea of the power of PivotTables, let's take a quick look at the corporate sales information example we've used so far. You can work along in this section with the Chapter 11 companion workbook, where you'll find data as well as PivotTable and Pivot Chart examples. Note that the data in the workbook is in a flat-file format, which is absolutely necessary for PivotTables. To refresh your memory, flat-file data is simply data that's arranged in a row/column format, with each row representing an individual record. While flat-file data should generally have some type of unique identifier, such as a part or order number, as the next example shows, it's not necessary, as each row represents a unique transaction.

	A	B	C	D	E	F	G	H
1	Region	Product	Date	Customer	Quantity	Revenue	COGS	Profit
2	Central	ABC	01/09/18	General Motors	800	$16,416	$6,776	$9,640
3	Central	ABC	01/12/18	IBM	300	$6,267	$2,541	$3,726
4	Central	ABC	01/25/18	CitiGroup	1000	$20,770	$8,470	$12,300
5	Central	ABC	02/08/18	CitiGroup	100	$1,817	$847	$970
6	Central	ABC	02/09/18	General Motors	300	$5,157	$2,541	$2,616
7	Central	ABC	02/19/18	Wal-Mart	500	$10,385	$4,235	$6,150

PivotTables are so powerful that when you get used to using them, you'll wonder how you ever did without them. One of the reasons that people may be afraid of PivotTables is the misperception that if something goes wrong, you've just screwed up your data. Fortunately, nothing could be further from the truth: When you create a PivotTable, Excel takes a snapshot of your data and re-creates it (in a *PivotTable cache*), so your original data doesn't get altered in any way whatsoever.

There are a few ground rules for PivotTables, but they're pretty much the same as the spreadsheet design rules you've already learned:

- Your data should have unique column headers. (If you're using an Excel table, Excel won't let you have duplicate column headers.)
- There should be no gaps in your data—that is, no missing rows or columns.
- Data types cannot be mixed. For example, you can't mix currency values in the same column with dates.

To see how easy it is to create a PivotTable, in the Chapter 11 companion workbook, select any cell in the Excel Table worksheet data range and then go to **Insert > PivotTable**. (Excel automatically recognizes the data range for you, so you don't need to select the entire table range.) The Create PivotTable dialog, shown here, appears.

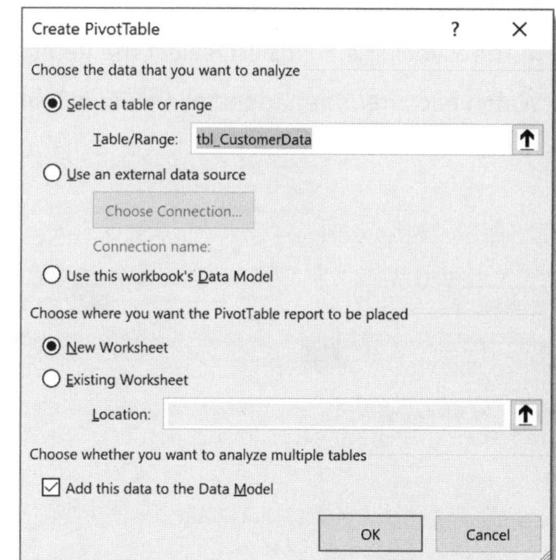

Note: You don't need to use an Excel table for PivotTable data, as any Excel data range works, as long as it meets the PivotTable report ground rules just mentioned.

In the Create PivotTable dialog, you have a choice of using external data, which comes in handy if you're creating an interactive workbook for users but don't necessarily want to include all your data. Next, you can choose to place the PivotTable in the same worksheet as your data or in a new worksheet, which is the default. It's generally easiest to keep your PivotTables separate from your data, and the benefit of doing so is that you also keep your data and users separated. When you start combining PivotTables and charts into dashboards, you'll see that you can have PivotTables created from multiple worksheets or data sources. Finally, you have the option of including your data in the Data Model. It doesn't hurt anything to add it, but if you don't, you can always add it later from the PowerPivot tab, as we'll discuss later in this chapter.

As soon as you click OK in the Create PivotTable dialog, Excel creates a new worksheet and activates the PivotTable Analyze and Design contextual tabs. On the left-hand side of the worksheet you see a PivotTable window, and on the right side you see the PivotTable Fields list, which is where all your data fields will be listed and where you set up your PivotTable. At this point, Excel hasn't created a PivotTable for you. It has merely analyzed your data and loaded it and your headers into a PivotTable cache, waiting for you to pull everything together.

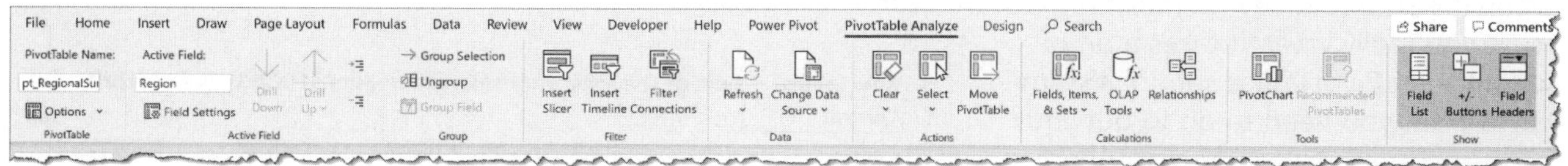

You need to determine which fields you want in your PivotTable and simply select each one of them, as illustrated in the figure below, where the numerals correspond to the following steps:

1. Start with a new PivotTable.

1. In the PivotTable Fields list, select the items you want by clicking the check box next to each one.

1. Watch each item get added to the PivotTable as you click it.

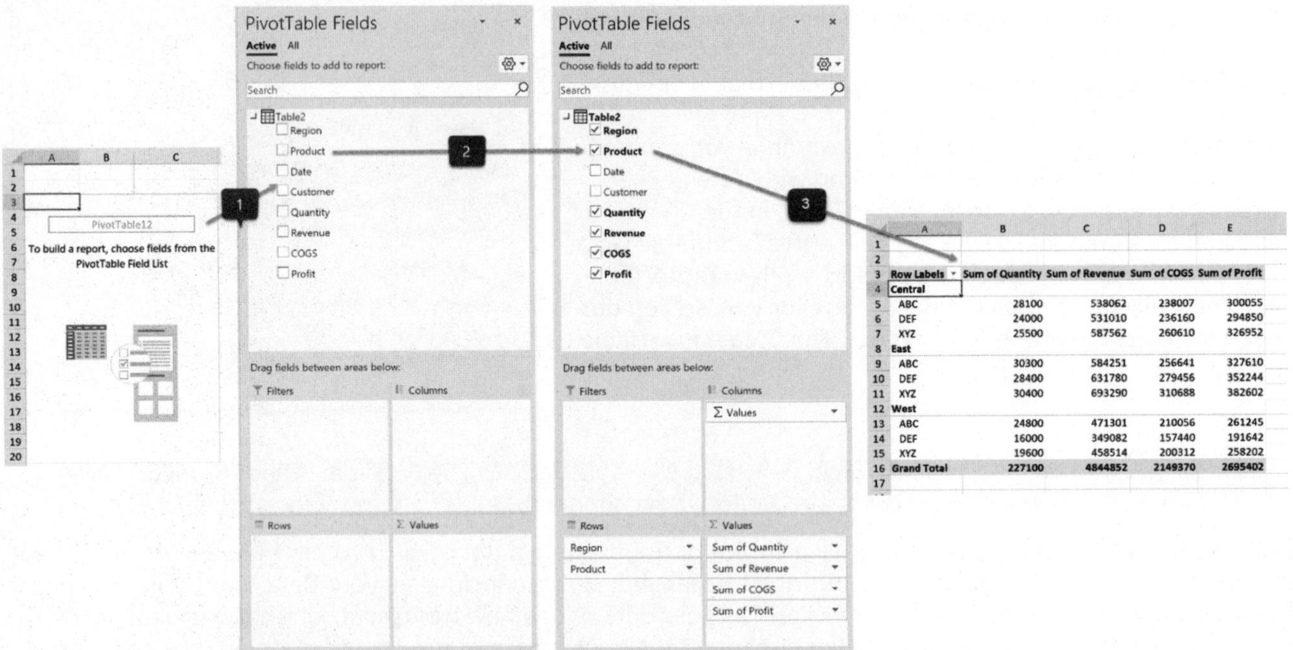

If you decide you don't want a field included in your PivotTable, you can either uncheck it or drag it out of the PivotTable Fields list.

Excel automatically detects your numeric data and places it in the Values section at the bottom of the PivotTable Fields list. Similarly, it detects your text-based data and put that in the Rows section for you. Now you can see why it's so important to make sure your data types are consistent: If they're not, Excel won't necessarily put the right fields in the right sections for you. If Excel does put a numeric field in the Rows section, you can drag it out and put it in the Values section. You can also reorder items by dragging them above or below each other.

Now is the point in building a PivotTable when it's time to dive into making it do what you really want. It takes a bit of work to get PivotTables set up; it's similar to what you need to do to get your charts set up the way you want them. You often need to do some experimentation, and even the most seasoned Excel users need to make some adjustments to get a PivotTable to do what they want.

The following example shows the PivotTable Excel gives you after you've made the selections shown above. Excel's default PivotTable view appears in compact form, which means it keeps your Rows fields grouped in the same column.

	A	B	C	D	E
1					
2					
3	Row Labels	Sum of Quantity	Sum of Revenue	Sum of COGS	Sum of Profit
4	Central				
5	ABC	28100	538062	238007	300055
6	DEF	24000	531010	236160	294850
7	XYZ	25500	587562	260610	326952
8	East				
9	ABC	30300	584251	256641	327610
10	DEF	28400	631780	279456	352244
11	XYZ	30400	693290	310688	382602
12	West				
13	ABC	24800	471301	210056	261245
14	DEF	16000	349082	157440	191642
15	XYZ	19600	458514	200312	258202
16	Grand Total	227100	4844852	2149370	2695402

This PivotTable is about as plain and boring as it gets, but if you look closely, you'll see that Excel has manipulated the data in a way that would be very difficult for you to try to re-create manually. Take a look at how region, product, date, and customer have been stacked here compared to how they appear in the source Excel data.

You might also notice that Excel has added an AutoFilter button to the Row Labels header cell, which you can use to narrow the list of fields or choose from various sorting options. For instance, you can uncheck a region, as shown at right, if you don't want it displayed.

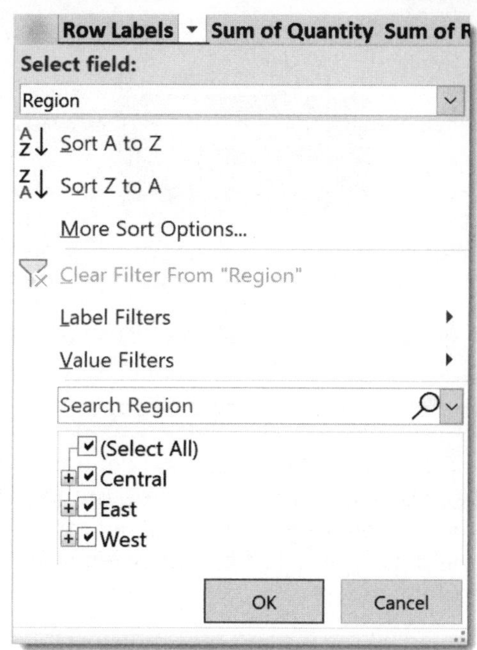

> **Note:** You might have noticed the Defer Layout Update check box at the bottom of the PivotTable Fields pane. It's useful when you're designing a PivotTable that has a large data source, and every change takes a while to recalculate. Just deselect this check box until you're ready to refresh, and then click the Update button.

Getting Started with PivotTables

In this section, you'll give the PivotTable Fields pane a workout and see how easy it is to add or remove things in a PivotTable. If you want to remove fields, you can just uncheck them from the list, or you can drag them from pane to pane.

Next, we'll examine each section of the PivotTable Fields pane so you can see what you can expect from it. The first thing you'll notice is that the pane is broken down into an upper group and a lower group. The upper group, the Fields section, represents the data fields that you can add to a PivotTable. The lower group, the Report section, represents the different PivotTable locations where you can place that data.

The Fields Section

As you saw in the earlier examples, the Fields section of the PivotTable Fields list is where you add or remove items from your PivotTables. When you're dealing with the Data Model, you can also see fields from other tables listed here.

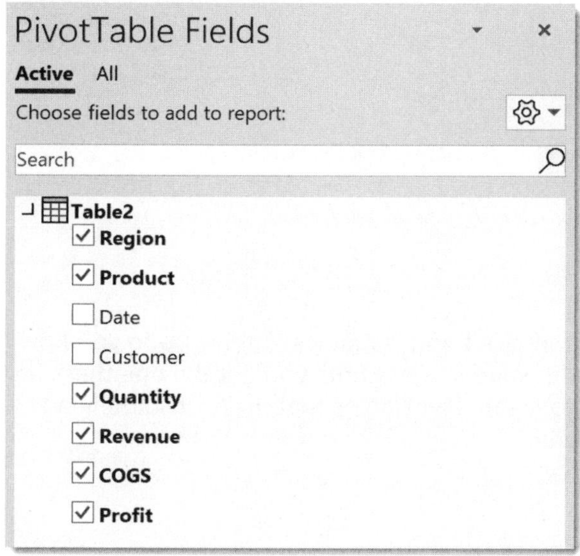

The Report Section

The Report section is where you do the vast majority of your PivotTable work. After you add an item from the Fields section, you need to make sure the PivotTable displays the right values and that it's formatted the way you want.

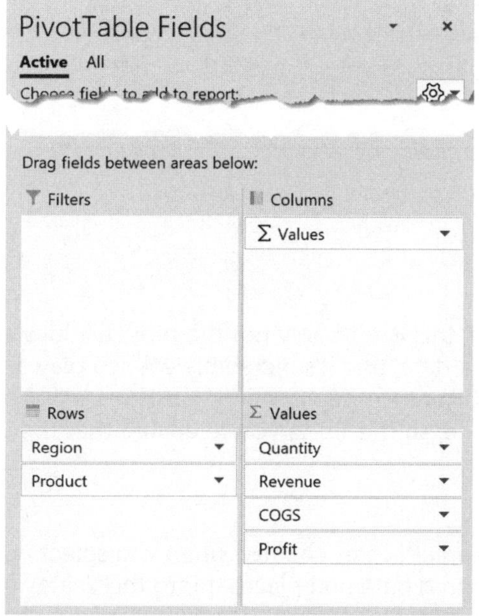

The Filters Group

Filters is the first group in the Report section. It lets you narrow down your view by removing certain elements from the PivotTable and placing them above it. The following example shows Region moved out of the Rows section and used as a report filter. All you need to do is drag it from the Rows section up into the Report Filter group.

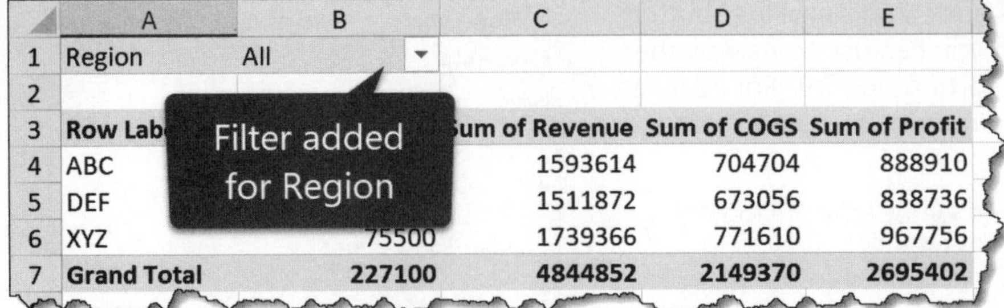

	A	B	C	D	E
1	Region	All			
2					
3	Row Lab		um of Revenue	Sum of COGS	Sum of Profit
4	ABC		1593614	704704	888910
5	DEF		1511872	673056	838736
6	XYZ	75500	1739366	771610	967756
7	Grand Total	227100	4844852	2149370	2695402

Note: You can use slicers instead of filters; quite often slicers are easier to use than filters.

The Columns and Rows Groups

The Columns and Rows groups determine how your data will be presented—either horizontally or vertically. When you experiment with these groups a bit, you'll find that you can create some very interesting scenarios. Some of them might be useful, but others won't be, and you'll probably reverse them almost immediately. Some data should just be presented in certain ways, and figuring out how is one of the learning curves with PivotTables.

Learning all the ins and outs of PivotTables and spending a bit of time adjusting each individual PivotTable is well worth it: Whereas you would spend untold hours working on a formula-based report, you can change a PivotTable view almost effortlessly to get different views of the data. And once you get used to building PivotTables, you'll just get faster and faster with them.

You can move any item in the Report section of the PivotTable Fields list by dragging it from one group to another, such as from Rows to Columns or vice versa. The following example shows a PivotTable containing the same information as above but now with the Columns and Rows sections swapped.

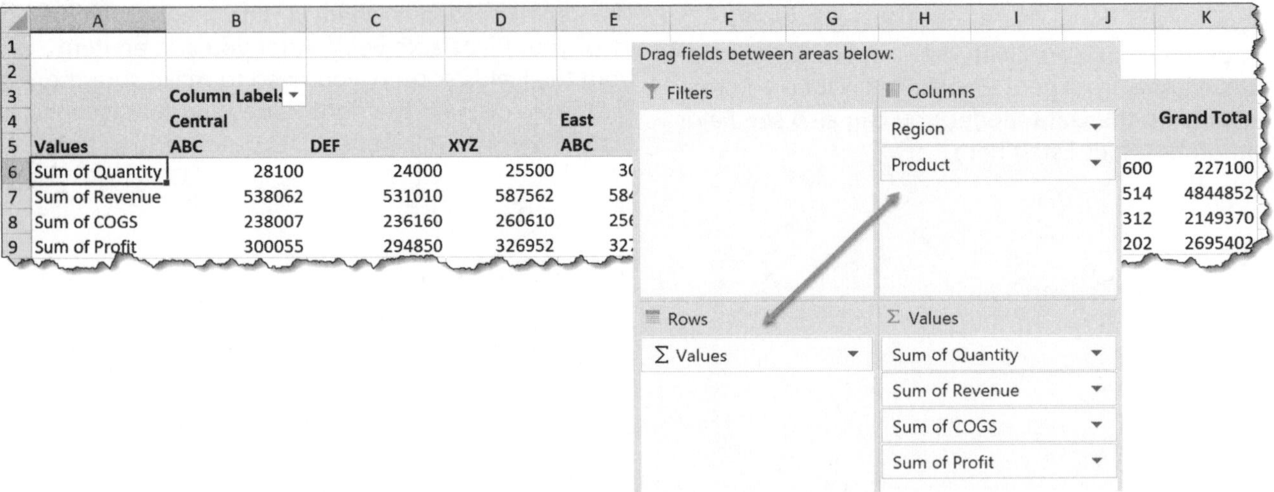

	A	B	C	D	E	K
3		Column Labels				
4		Central			East	Grand Total
5	Values	ABC	DEF	XYZ	ABC	
6	Sum of Quantity	28100	24000	25500	3(	600 227100
7	Sum of Revenue	538062	531010	587562	58·	514 4844852
8	Sum of COGS	238007	236160	260610	25(	312 2149370
9	Sum of Profit	300055	294850	326952	32	202 2695402

As you can see, this is probably not the most useful view, but the nice thing is that it's entirely up to you how you present the data, and it's incredibly easy to play around with various views until you get the one that's just right. It is important to keep in mind that Excel will allow you to create PivotTables that make absolutely no sense to any one, so it is up to you to ensure that they are useful.

Values

As discussed earlier in this chapter, when you select numeric data in the PivotTable Fields list, Excel automatically evaluates that data and places it into the Values pane. By default, Excel applies a sum to the Value field, although it will give you a count if you have mixed data types in a column. To change the calculation, click the drop-down arrow to the right of a category and choose the Value Field Settings option and then, in the dialog that appears, change the current calculation in the Summarize Values By tab.

Note: When you click the drop-down arrow to the right of a category, you also see some Move options, which just give you further ways to move elements. However, it's faster to just drag and drop items instead of going through this menu.

In this case, if you change the Quantity field from Sum to Average, you immediately see the results reflected in your data, as shown below.

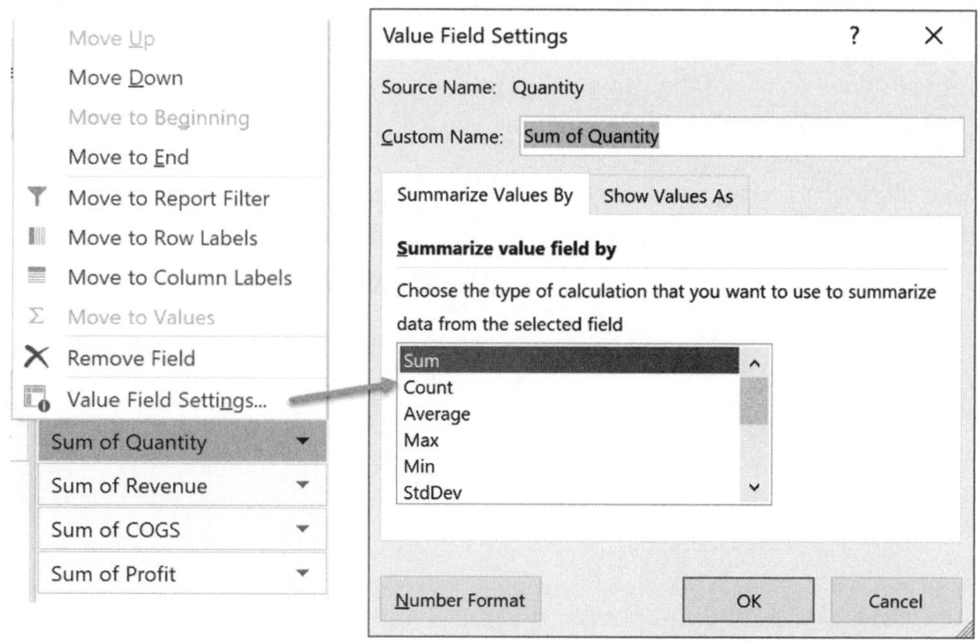

Row Labels	Average Quantity	Sum of Revenue	Sum of COGS	Sum of Profit
Central				
ABC	530	538062	238007	300055
DEF	585	531010	236160	294850
XYZ	543	587562	260610	326952
East				
ABC	514	584251	256641	327610
DEF	526	631780	279456	352244
XYZ	647	693290	310688	382602
West				
ABC	564	471301	210056	261245
DEF	571	349082	157440	191642
XYZ	576	458514	200312	258202
Grand Total	**558**	**4844852**	**2149370**	**2695402**

If you click a number field and Excel adds it to the Rows section instead of the Values section, you should check your underlying numbers. It's quite possible that they're formatted as text, and you'll need to convert them to numbers. This happens all the time, and "Convert numbers stored as text to numbers" is a very popular topic on https://support.office.com.

Field Names

Excel automatically names your fields, starting with the function name and followed by the field name, such as Sum of *X* or Average of *Y*. You shouldn't bother changing the field names until you've gotten your PivotTable set up the way you want it, though. It can be frustrating to rename a field, decide you want to use a different calculation, and then have Excel automatically rename it on you. I usually wait until the end and press **Ctrl+H** to find and replace the function name (e.g., Sum of) with nothing (just leave it blank).

Show Values As

Normally when you place a value field in a PivotTable, Excel displays only its value. But what if you want to see how that value ranks with the rest? Instead of the default Summarize Values By options, you can use the Show Values As tab of the Value Field Settings dialog to create different data views, such as % of Grand Total, % of Column/Row Total, or even Running Total. You can choose from the following options:

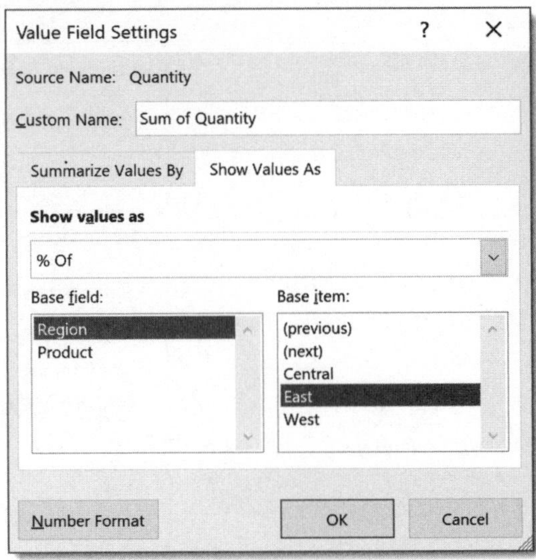

- % of Grand Total
- % of Column Total
- % of Row Total
- % of
- % of Parent Row Total
- % of Parent Column Total
- % of Parent Total
- Difference From
- % Difference From
- Running Total In
- % Running Total In
- Rank Smallest to Largest
- Rank Largest to Smallest
- Index

When you're done adding fields and have them set up the way you want, you can click the Number Format button (or press **Ctrl+1**) to launch the Format Cells dialog, which allows you to format your PivotTable data. It's generally advisable to format your data and the rest of the report after you have the PivotTable arranged the way that you want it; otherwise, you might find yourself making multiple unnecessary changes as you adjust the PivotTable to display the data you want.

The PivotTable Analyze Tab

The following sections discuss the various groups and options on the PivotTable Analyze tab, which you activate by selecting any cell in a PivotTable.

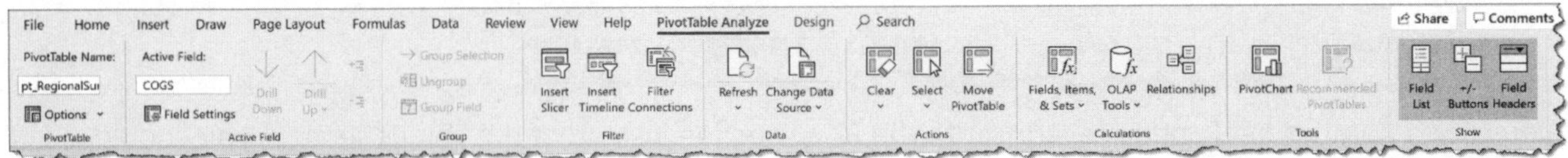

The PivotTable Group

You use the PivotTable group on the PivotTable Analyze tab to name your PivotTable and set some more detailed options. Naming PivotTables is just as important as naming tables because you need to be able to tell them apart. Under Options in the PivotTable group, you have three distinct choices, as shown here and discussed in the following sections.

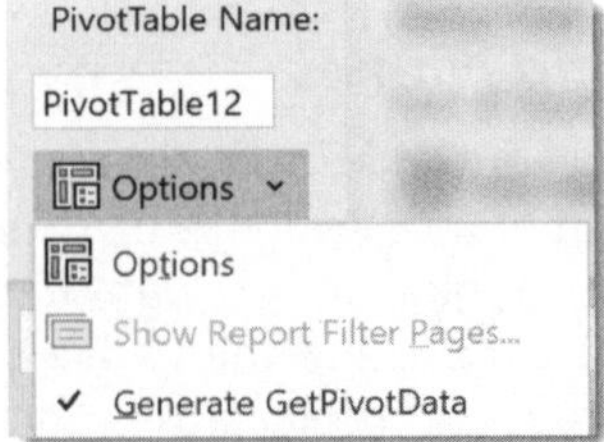

Options

When you select **PivotTable Analyze > Options**, the PivotTable Options dialog appears. As shown below, this dialog has six individual tabs. Most of them are relatively straightforward, and there are just too many options to go into individually, so you should experiment with them yourself. The following are some of the noteworthy settings:

- **Layout & Format tab**—The most important thing in the Layout & Format tab is the Autofit Column Widths on Update option, which you should uncheck. If it is checked, Excel resizes your columns whenever you refresh your data. This can be incredibly inconvenient if you've manually resized a lot of columns already.

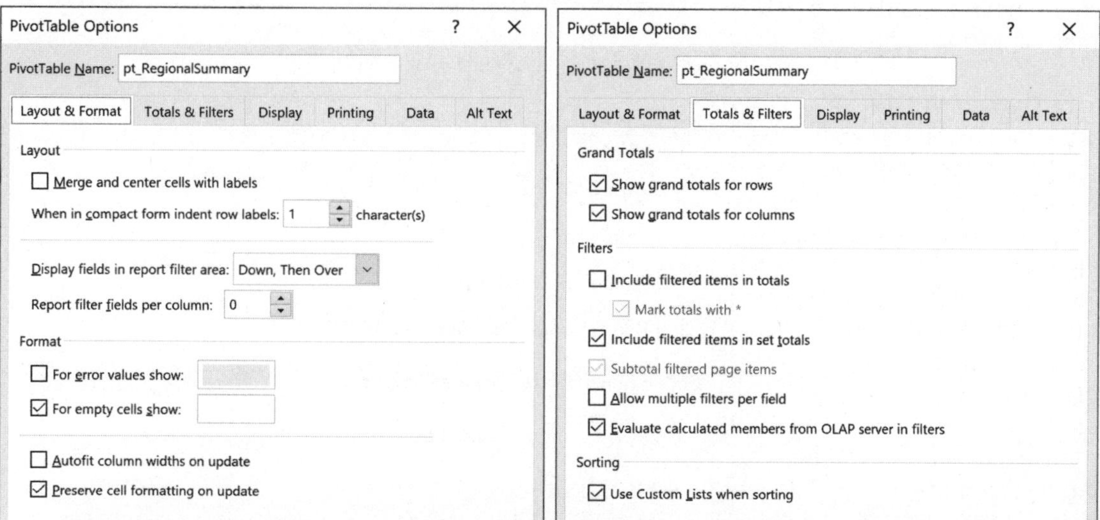

Note: What does *refresh* mean? A PivotTable is just a snapshot of your data, so if you change something in your raw data, you need to go back to your PivotTable and tell it to display the new information. Fortunately, this is really easy: Just select the PivotTable and go to ***PivotTable Analyze > Refresh***. (or **Refresh All** if you have multiple PivotTables.

- **Totals & Filters tab**—The Totals & Filters tab lets you specify how you want to display or edit totals and/or any filters that you might have applied. If you've taken advantage of custom lists, described earlier, keep the option Use Custom Lists When Sorting selected.
- **Display tab**—On the Display tab, I generally uncheck the Show Expand/Collapse Buttons option, as I find these buttons to be distracting; these buttons do the same thing as the expand/collapse buttons with subtotals in that they show or hide the detail rows for each group. You can select the Classic PivotTable Layout option to revert to the way PivotTables worked in earlier Excel versions so that you can drag data points onto the physical PivotTable instead of using the PivotTable Fields list. On this tab, you can also choose to sort the PivotTable Fields list in alphabetical order (A to Z) or stick with the order in which your source data is sorted.
- **Printing tab**—The Printing tab is straightforward and simply gives you options for displaying the grouping buttons and labels when you print a PivotTable.

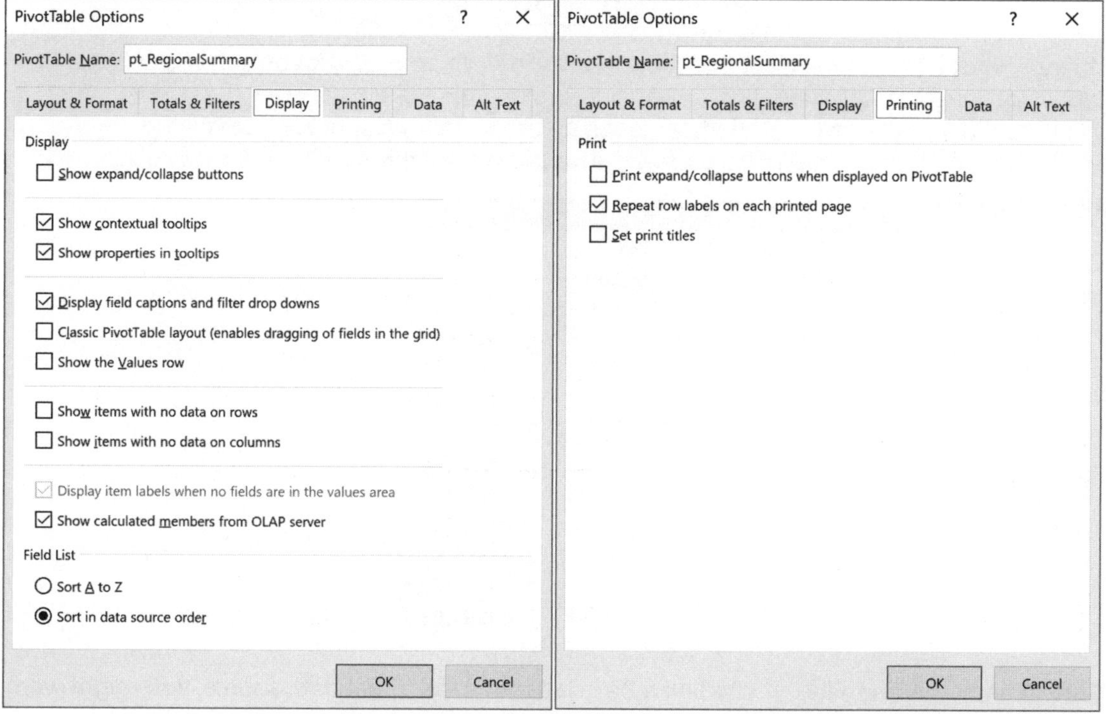

- **Data tab**—The Data tab offers several options that are important, especially if you plan on distributing your PivotTables:
  - **Save Source Data with File**—If you've used external data as your data source, and if you want your users to be able to manipulate your PivotTable(s), you should leave this option checked. Otherwise, your PivotTable(s) may not have a data connection, which might cause a PivotTable to fail under certain circumstances. If you only want users to have a snapshot, or if you have an unusually large dataset that can be challenging to distribute, uncheck this option.

  - **Enable Show Details**—This option allows you to drill down into the data that supports the PivotTable. If you double-click on a PivotTable data item, Excel creates a new automatically filtered worksheet with just that item's underlying details. Drill-down functionality is a fantastic tool, but there may be times when you don't want to share the underlying PivotTable data with end users. Unchecking the Enable Show Details option prevents users from drilling down, and Excel gives a confusing message to a user who tries to drill down.

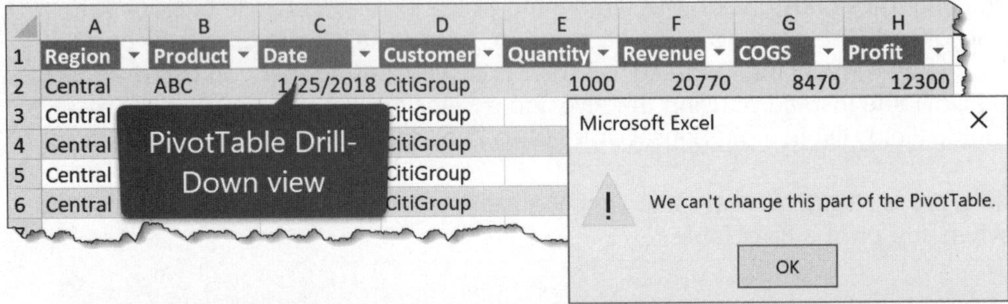

Note: While there's no option on the PivotTable Ribbon tabs for drilling down, if you select a cell in a PivotTable that has data in the Data Model or is connected to an OLAP cube, you can click the magnifying glass icon to drill deeper into your underlying data, as shown below in the Explore dialog. Note that this restructures your existing PivotTable, so make sure to save your workbook before you start.

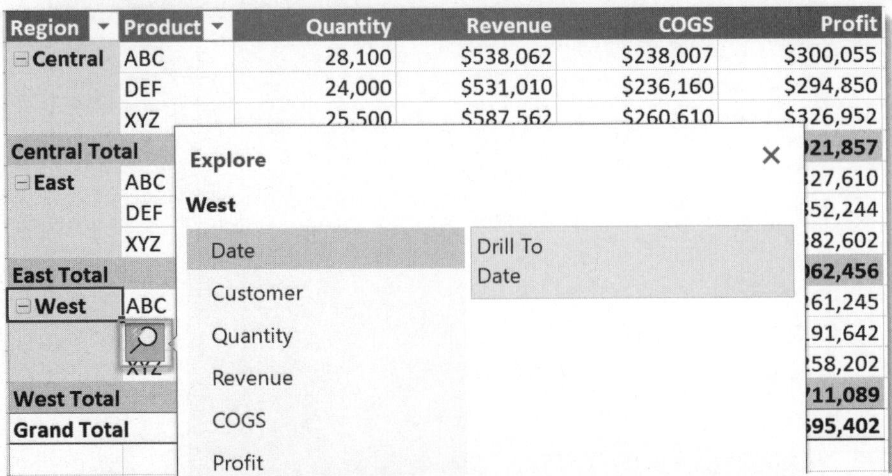

  - **Refresh Data When Opening File**—If you link a PivotTable to an external data source, you might want to enable this option. However, if your data rarely needs to be refreshed or it takes a long time to refresh, you'll probably want to opt for manually refreshing your dataset. Keep in mind that if you enable this option and share your workbook with users who don't have access to your data source, they'll receive error messages when trying to open the workbook.

- **Alt Text tab**—The Alt Text tab is where you enter text that a screen reader can read for people with visual impairments so they can understand the worksheet's contents.

Show Report Filter Pages

You can select **PivotTable Analyze > PivotTable > Options > Show Report Filter Pages** to create individual worksheets for any filters that you have in place. In the Chapter 11 companion workbook you can see that three sheet views were created for the individual report regions. The Show Report Filter Pages tool is amazing when you have a lot of detail that you want to show in individual PivotTables. For instance, you might want to have an individual report for each of your sales managers.

Generate GetPivotData

You can select **PivotTable Analyze > PivotTable > Options > Generate GetPivotData** to interact with PivotTable data via the GetPivotData function. If you exit the PivotTable by clicking on any cell outside the PivotTable range and then use = and link back to any cell in the PivotTable, you see a GetPivotData function created for you. This function isn't very friendly, so unless you're interested in experimenting, I recommend avoiding it.

The Active Field Group

The Active Field group shows you which field item is active at any given time.

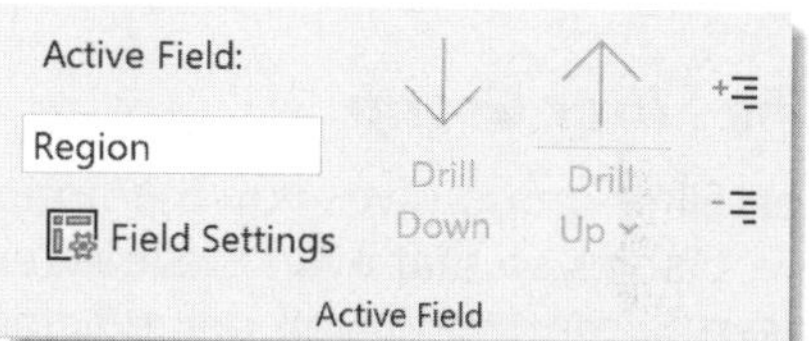

Field Settings

If you select **PivotTable Analyze > Field Settings**, Excel opens a dialog. If you're in a text field, it opens the Field Settings dialog, and if you're in a value field, it opens the Value Field Settings dialog.

The Field Settings dialog contains two tabs for the selected field item, as shown here:

- **Subtotals & Filters**—On this tab you can set automatic subtotals, no subtotals, or custom subtotals. You can also choose to add a new manual AutoFilter, but this works only if you don't have any slicers connected to the PivotTable. (Frankly, the benefits of slicers outweigh the manual filtering option.)
- **Layout & Print**—On this tab you can set your PivotTable print options.

The Value Field Settings dialog lets you change how your numeric items are displayed. These are the same options you get if you click on any of the Value items in the PivotTable Fields list and select Value Field Settings.

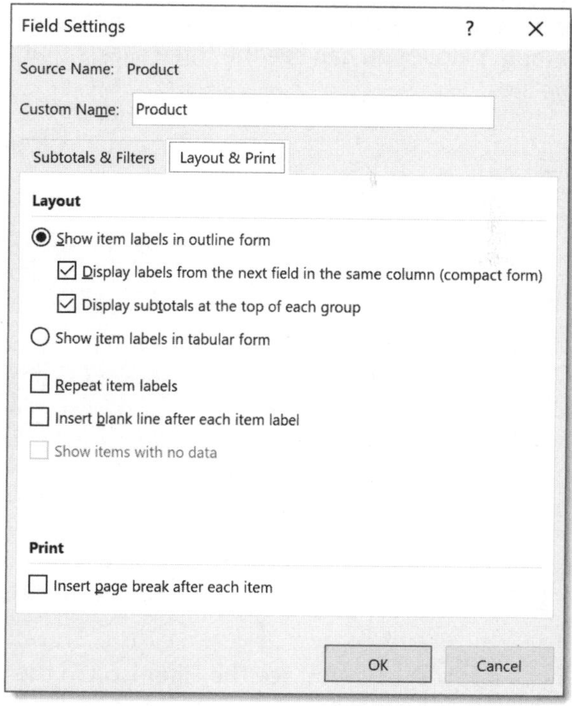

Drill Down/Drill Up

If you're in a cell that can be drilled into, you can select **PivotTable Analyze > Drill Down** or **PivotTable Analyze > Drill Up** to drill down or drill up.

Expand Field/Collapse Field

The Expand Field and Collapse Field options are enabled only if you're in a Rows item area. These options allow you to expand or collapse an entire Rows group as opposed to clicking the individual Expand/Collapse buttons in the PivotTable itself.

The Group Group

The Group group on the PivotTable Analyze tab allows you to add groups within groups. For instance, you can group individual dates into months, years, or quarters. As you experiment with defining deeper levels of details in PivotTables, you might find this ability to group handy for isolating certain data. You see different options depending on the PivotTable Fields list item you select. The example at right shows dates grouped by month.

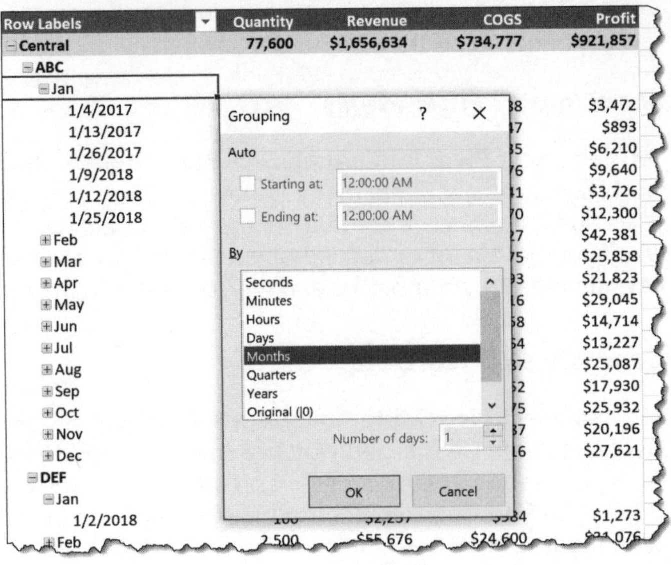

The Group options can be frustrating because not everything can be grouped, and Excel throws an irritating error message at you if it can't group something. The most common reason for this error is having mixed data types in a column you try to group. If Excel won't group your dates, look for a cell with an invalid date such as April 31 .

The Filter Group

The Filter group gives you the option to insert slicers and timelines, which are great tools that let you set up PivotTables so that even the least experienced user can manipulate them with ease. When you first select the Insert Slicer option, you get a dialog that lists your PivotTable Fields list items. You can add a slicer for each item that you select in the PivotTable Fields list. Based on the selections in the following example, Excel create slicers for customer, product, and region. After Excel creates the slicers, it lumps them on top of each other in the middle of the worksheet. It's up to you to move them around and resize them as you want them. In the example below, you can see the three slicers that have been formatted, sized, and arranged on top of a single timeline.

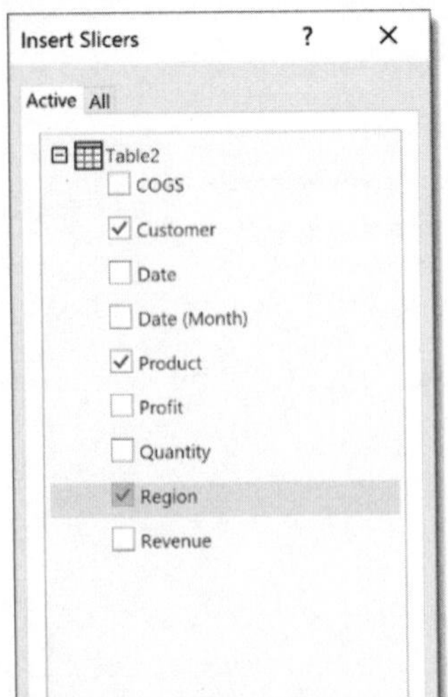

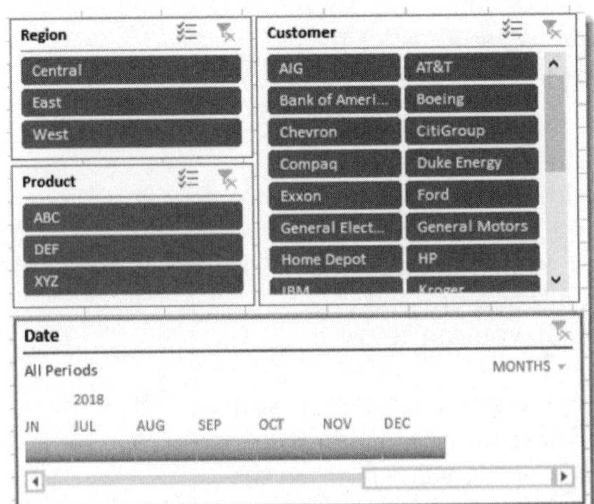

As you apply slicers, you see the Filter icon in the upper-right corner of each slicer change, and you see each slicer selection highlighted. Slicers are dependent on each other, so as you select an item from one, the others reset to display only what's available in that group. You'll get a better sense of how slicers work by experimenting with them in the Chapter 11 companion workbook on the PivotTable 1 and Slicers & Timeline worksheets.

The Slicer Tab

As soon as you create a slicer or timeline, you see a contextual Ribbon tab called Slicer.

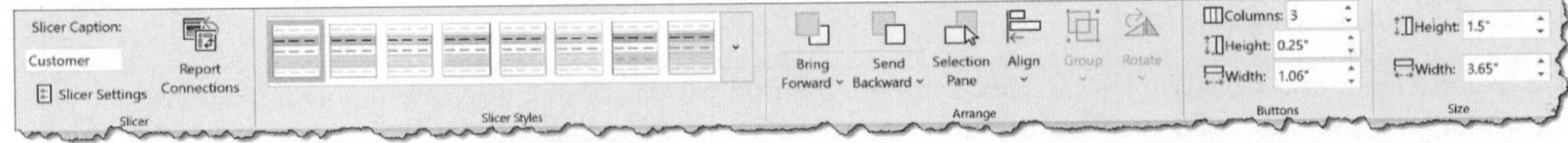

The tools on this tab allow you to format, name, move, and size your slicers in relation to the grid and any other worksheet objects, such as charts or timelines. You can use **Ctrl+click** to select multiple slicers, which can be helpful because you can format, align, and resize them at the same time with the tools in the Arrange group on the ribbon. This way, you don't have to spend a lot of time trying to get them aligned perfectly with the mouse. The image below shows the default placement for multiple slicers. Unfortunately, Excel doesn't know where you want to place your slicers, so it just drops them in one spot for you.

The Slicer tab includes the following options:

- **Slicer Settings**—When you activate the Slicers toolbar, you see the Slicer group on the left. The Slicer Settings option lets you control how data is displayed in each slicer. For instance, you can change the slicer's display header or change the default sort order. The most important option here is the Hide Items with No Data group of checkboxes. If you remove data from your PivotTable, your slicers will keep displaying them by default, which can be confusing to people, so you might want to turn off the Hide Items with No Data option.

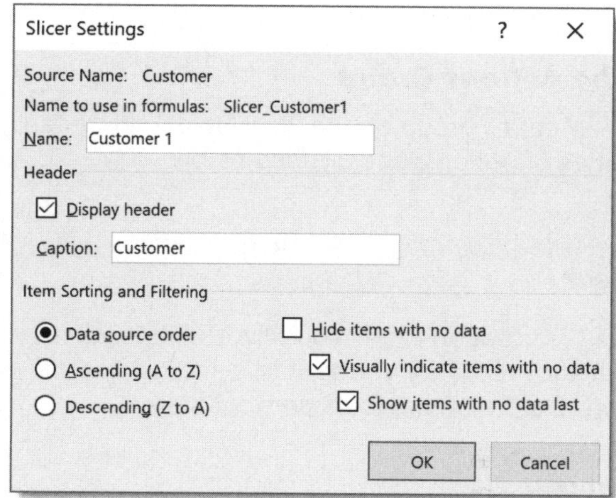

- **Report Connections**—You can use a single slicer to link to multiple PivotTables, provided that they're all connected to the same data source. This can be very handy when you build dashboards that have PivotTables that support Pivot Charts but you want to keep the PivotTables on a separate sheet. When you connect slicers to your PivotTables, they update behind the scenes, and your charts update as a result. You can see an example of this in the Create a Dashboard in Excel workbook included with the Chapter 5 companion workbook.
- **Slicer Styles, Arrange, Buttons, and Size**—The rest of the options on the Slicer tab deal with styles, arrangement, and size. You should definitely experiment with the Columns option, as slicers default to only one column, and they don't resize when you widen them.

The Timeline Tab

Timelines are like slicers, but they allow you to dynamically filter PivotTables by date. Next to slicers, they're probably my favorite PivotTable feature, primarily because they're really user-friendly. After you add a timeline, you can select it to activate the Timeline tab, which provides options similar to those available for slicers. You can also connect multiple PivotTables to a single slicer, provided that the data source is the same.

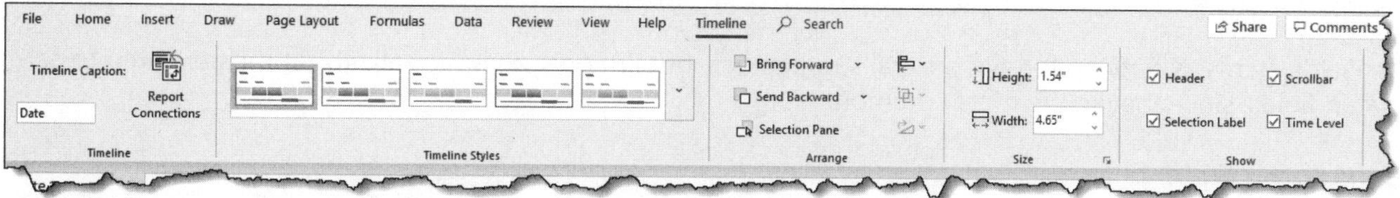

Timelines also give you the ability to display years, quarters, months, or days, as shown below. As you select each option, the timeline automatically adjusts to reflect your selection.

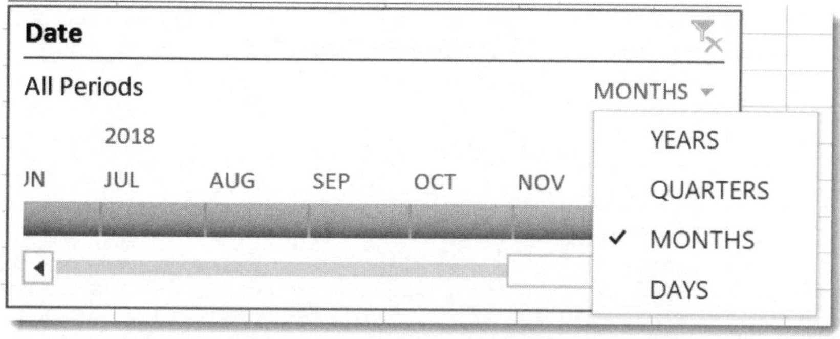

The Data Group

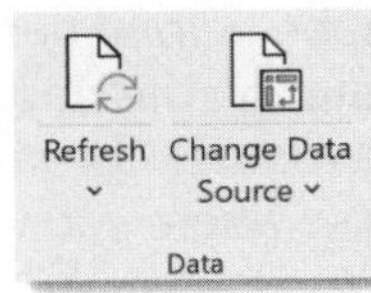

The options in the Data group of the PivotTable Analyze tab, shown below, allow you to refresh or change your PivotTable's data source. You probably won't change data sources too often, but you will likely find yourself refreshing as you add or remove data from your dataset. Refreshing is very common if you're connecting to data from the Web or a company database. If you have a large dataset, you should be prepared to wait, as Excel will be tied up until the data has refreshed.

The Actions Group

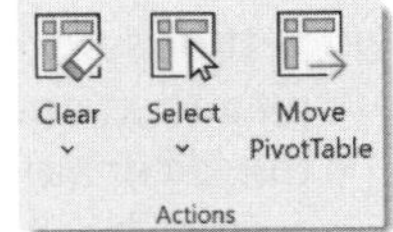

The Actions group on the PivotTable Analyze tab, shown here, is another straightforward series of options, as described below.

Clear

The Clear option resets your PivotTable to where you started, leaving you with a clean slate and a PivotTable Fields list ready for you to start selecting items. If you activate Clear by accident, you can press **Ctrl+Z** to restore the PivotTable to its previous state.

Select

The Select option allows you to select various items on a PivotTable, including labels, values, and even the entire PivotTable. The **PivotTable Analyze > Select > Enable Selection** option allows you to manually select PivotTable groups by clicking on them. This comes in handy if you want to apply groupings from the Group options, described earlier in this chapter.

Move PivotTable

The Move PivotTable option lets you move a PivotTable to another worksheet. You can also just select a PivotTable and then use **Ctrl+X** to cut it, select the destination worksheet, and use **Ctrl+V** to paste it. If you don't select the entire PivotTable, you'll end up pasting as values only, which will disconnect the PivotTable from its source.

The Calculations Group

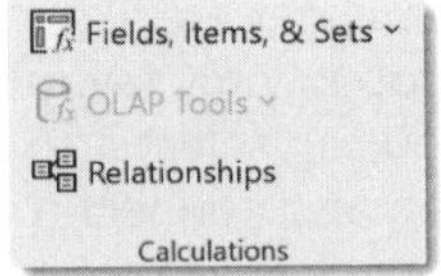

The Calculations group, shown here, lets you add calculations to a PivotTables if you can't add them to your source data, which is common when you're downloading data from the Web or from an internal database.

The Fields, Items, & Sets option has several sub-options, but I'm only going to talk about those related to calculated fields, since they're the most common.

Calculated Field

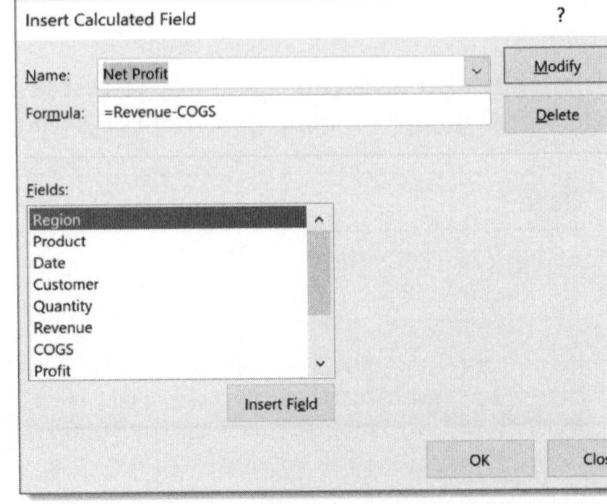

A calculated field lets you create calculations that might not be available in your source data. For example, you can calculate profit by subtracting cost of goods sold from revenue. To insert a calculated field, select **PivotTable Analyze > Fields, Items, & Sets > Calculated Field**, and the Insert Calculated Field dialog, shown here, appears.

The following example uses the existing customer data and re-creates the existing Profit column with a calculated column called Net Profit. A calculated column is a lot like a structured reference formula in an Excel table, and you just need to click each field you want to add from the PivotTable Fields list and then enter an operator, such as +, -, *, or /. You can also add Excel functions, but doing so takes some practice.

When you look at the Calculated Field worksheet in the Chapter 11 companion workbook, you can see that Excel doesn't actually create a formula within the PivotTable for you; it just creates the calculation as a new field that you need to select. Once you select it, the calculated field automatically updates, and when you refresh the PivotTable, the calculated field updates as well.

Calculated Item

By selecting **PivotTable Analyze > Fields, Items, & Sets > Calculated Item**, you can combine two or more fields and create a new one, such as a total for the Central and West regions.

Solve Order

If you have created calculated items, you can select **PivotTable Analyze > Fields, Items, & Sets > Solve Order** to see the order in which those items are being calculated.

List Formulas

You can select **PivotTable Analyze > Fields, Items, & Sets > List Formulas** to create a summary report displaying all the calculated fields that you have in a PivotTable. The following example shows the net profit calculation created earlier.

	A	B	C	D
1	*Calculated Field*			
2	Solve Order	Field	Formula	
3	1	Net Profit	=Revenue-COGS	
4	2	Field1	=Quantity*Revenue	
5				
6	*Calculated Item*			
7	Solve Order	Item	Formula	
8				

The Tools Group

You can use the Tools group on the PivotTable Analyze tab to create Pivot Charts. This group also includes the Recommended PivotTables option, although this is a strange place for that option as you need to have already created a PivotTable in order to see this option in the first place.

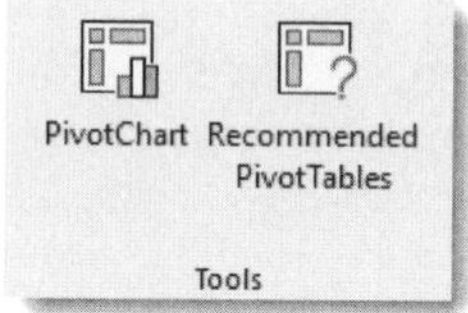

Pivot Charts

Excel allows you to create Pivot Charts, which are charts based on your PivotTable data. As you can see in the following example, Pivot Charts look similar to regular Excel charts.

> **Note:** As with any other charts, when you create Pivot Charts, you'll generally want to collapse your data down to the smallest group possible because having too much visible data can make a chart difficult to read. For instance, you wouldn't want to try to plot thousands of rows in a chart. Instead, you can use a PivotTable to reduce the visible data so that it make sense in your chart.

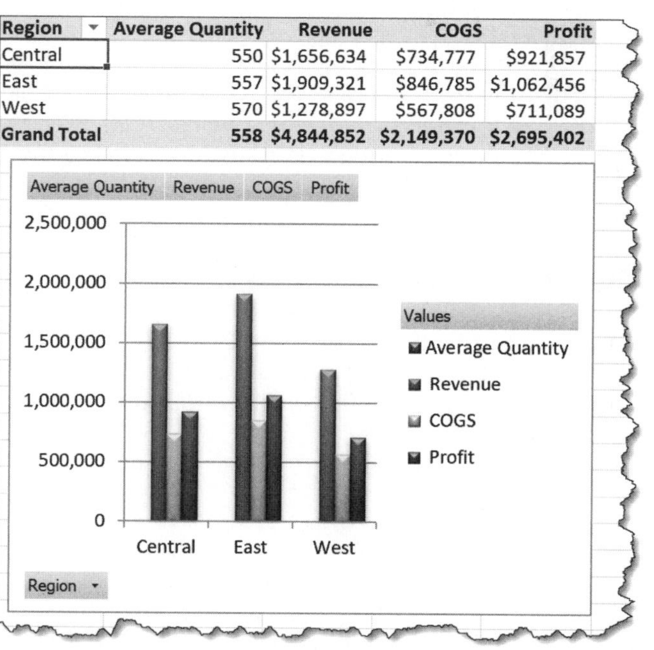

Region	Average Quantity	Revenue	COGS	Profit
Central	550	$1,656,634	$734,777	$921,857
East	557	$1,909,321	$846,785	$1,062,456
West	570	$1,278,897	$567,808	$711,089
Grand Total	**558**	**$4,844,852**	**$2,149,370**	**$2,695,402**

Unlike a regular Excel chart, a Pivot Chart displays the PivotTable's underlying Field list and Values list items as buttons. The Values field items are displayed at the top of the chart; they simply indicate which Values fields are included in your chart. The Field list items are at the bottom left, and you can interactively filter each of them. You can manipulate both series of items by right-clicking them—but be careful because doing this will also adjust your PivotTable. If you have any expanded fields, you can toggle between expanded/collapsed states with the +/- buttons in the lower-right corner.

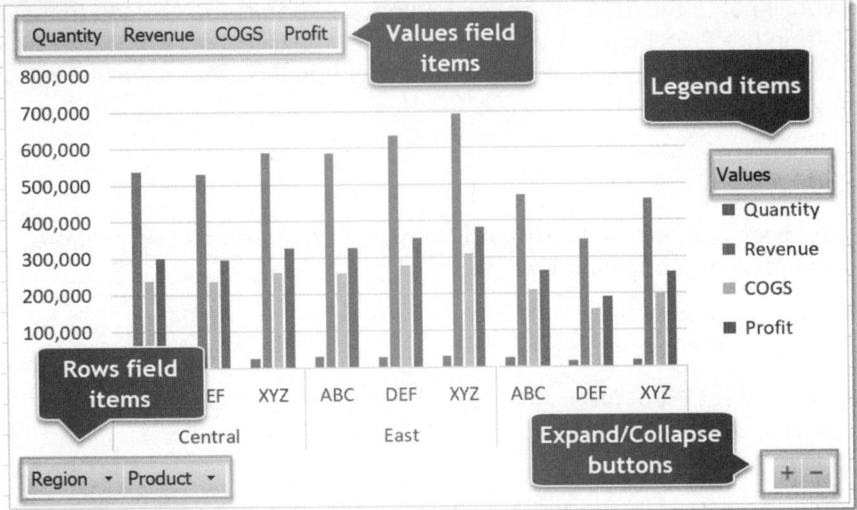

This is another one of those areas that just has too many potential variables to discuss here, but you should certainly experiment with the Pivot Chart sheet in the Chapter 11 companion workbook. If you have a Pivot Chart selected, you can go to PivotChart Analyze and click on the Field Buttons arrow to see your display options. I generally remove the field buttons with the Hide All option and use slicers instead.

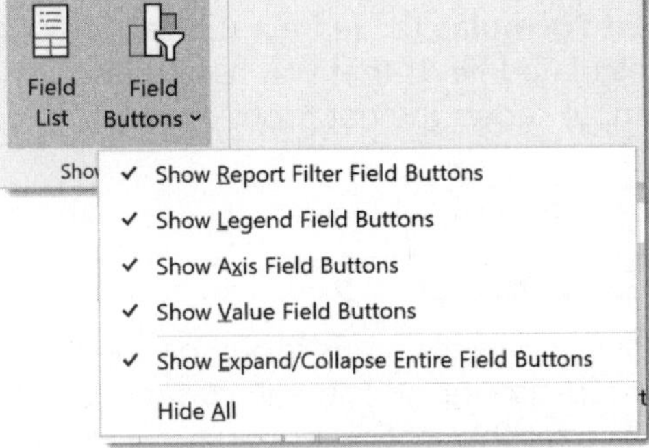

The Show Group

The Show group on the PivotTable Analyze tab merely exposes the PivotTable features that you can view. To start, you'll probably want to leave them all visible. When you distribute your PivotTable, you might want to hide the PivotTable Fields list, though, just to avoid giving your users such an easy way to change your PivotTable. This group of options is almost identical to the Show/Hide options for Pivot Charts.

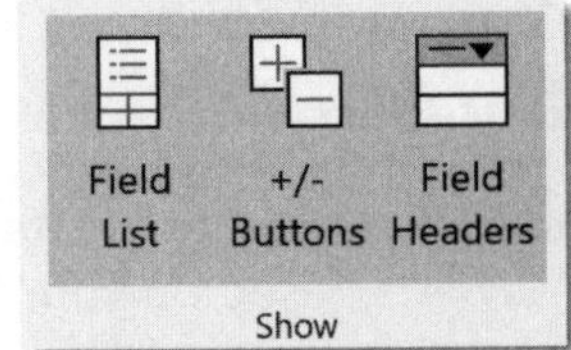

The PivotTable Design Tab

As mentioned earlier, you are likely to make many adjustments to a PivotTable when you're initially constructing it, and you probably shouldn't apply design elements until you're done. But when you're ready to apply those elements, you use the Design tab, whose groups are described in the following sections.

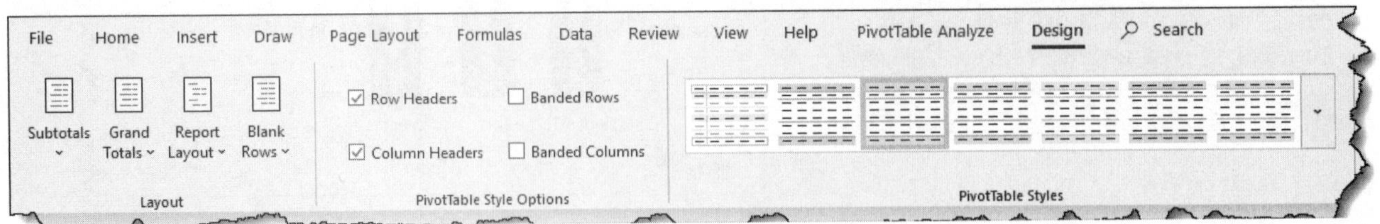

The Layout Group

The options in the Layout group on the PivotTable Design tab allow you to define how you want your PivotTable data to be displayed. These options, shown here and described in the following sections, are more personal than they are functional, and they don't alter a PivotTable's data in any way.

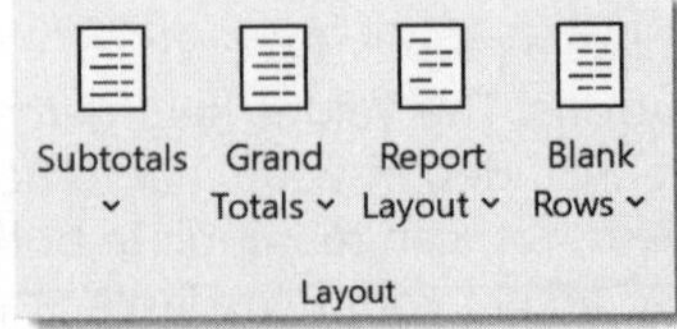

Subtotals

You can use the Subtotals option to turn off subtotals or show them at the top or bottom of each data series.

Grand Totals

You can opt to use grand totals for rows and/or columns.

Report Layout

You can define the display structure you want for your PivotTable. In the Chapter 11 companion workbook you can see examples of all the Report Layout options, shown below. Compact form is good for data with a lot of field items. Outline form and tabular form can both be a bit unwieldy if you have a lot of field items.

By default, PivotTables don't repeat data, but you can toggle Repeat All Item Labels under the Report Layout option to turn them on or off. This option isn't used very often because it makes PivotTables look like flat-file source data.

Show in Compact Form
Show in Outline Form
Show in Tabular Form
Repeat All Item Labels
Do Not Repeat Item Labels

Blank Rows

The Blank Rows option just lets you insert a blank row after each line item. If you have a lot of data, this might make it easier to read, but you need to be careful when you print because the Blank Rows option can create extra pages.

The PivotTable Style Options Group

The PivotTable Style Options group on the PivotTable Design tab gives you the option to toggle headers and banding. While you can change these without applying a PivotTable style, they generally work best in conjunction with styles.

☑ Row Headers ☐ Banded Rows
☑ Column Headers ☐ Banded Columns
PivotTable Style Options

The PivotTable Styles Group

The PivotTable Styles group on the PivotTable Design tab is nearly identical to the Excel table styles in that it's a predefined gallery of style options you can select for your PivotTable. The nice thing is that if you add or remove items from a PivotTable, the applied style automatically adjusts with the changes. This holds true when you apply filters or add calculated fields. If you find that the PivotTable Styles group doesn't have an option that suits your needs, you can create your own by clicking the down arrow on the right and then selecting New PivotTable Style.

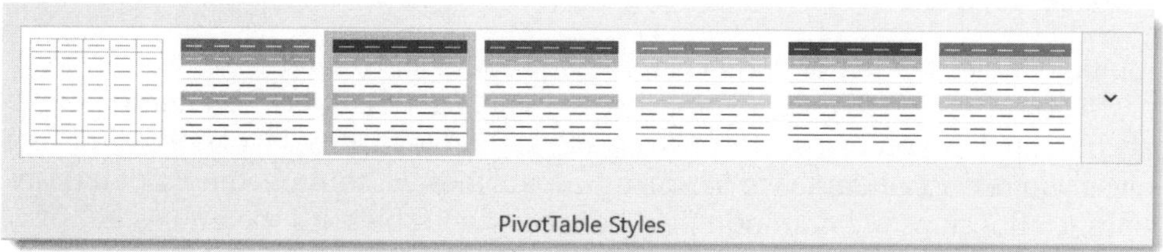

Setting PivotTable Default Options

My preferred PivotTable style is the tabular form, and I always turn off the Autofit Column Widths on Update option. As you work with PivotTables, you'll find that you tend to have preferences like these, and you can set them as your defaults. You used to have to apply such formatting changes to every PivotTable you built, which was a huge pain. Fortunately, enough people complained about it that the PivotTable team at Microsoft developed a way to keep your preferred PivotTable settings. You can now set your default options by hand, or even better, you can set up a PivotTable the way you want it and have Excel import your settings. After you do that, those settings are automatically applied to any new PivotTable you create.

To set default options, select any cell in a PivotTable and go to **File > Options** and in the Excel Options dialog that appears (shown below), select the Data tab and go to the Data Options section. Then click the Edit Default Layout button, shown below to open the Edit Default Layout dialog.

Excel Options

General
Formulas
Data
Proofing
Save
Language
Ease of Access
Advanced
Customize Ribbon
Quick Access Toolbar

Change options related to data import and data analysis.

Data options

Make changes to the default layout of PivotTables: Edit Default Layout...

☑ Disable undo for large PivotTable refresh operations to reduce refresh time

Disable undo for PivotTables with at least this number of data source rows (in thousands): 300

☑ Prefer the Excel Data Model when creating PivotTables, QueryTables and Data Connections

☑ Disable undo for large Data Model operations

Disable undo for Data Model operations when the model is at least this large (in MB): 8

☐ Enable Data Analysis add-ins: Power Pivot, Power View and 3D Maps

☐ Disable automatic grouping of Date/Time columns in PivotTables

If you click the Import button in the Edit Default Layout dialog, Excel imports your current PivotTable's settings and uses them for all PivotTables you create in the future. Or you can manually adjust your settings by changing the options in the Edit Default Layout dialog. You can restore Excel's original settings any time by clicking the Reset to Excel Default button, shown here.

As simple as this capability to change default options may seem, it took an amazing amount of engineering effort to accomplish. But it was well worth it, as this one update alone will save you hours when you start working with a lot of PivotTables.

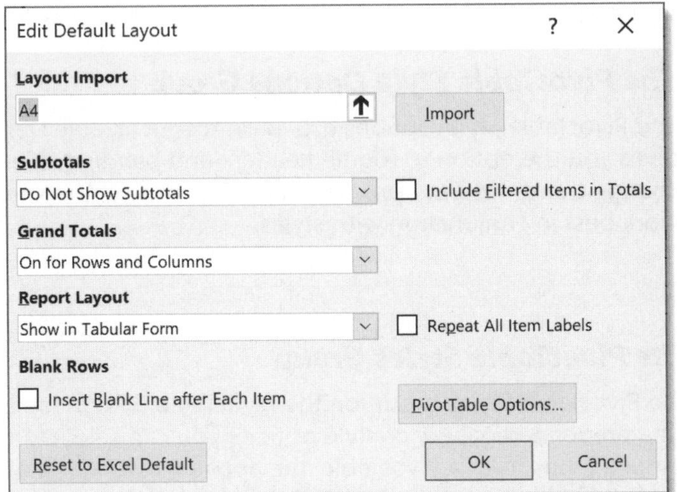

Power Pivot and the Data Model

The Data Model lets you add multiple tables in memory and create relationships between them. You can work with it alone or in conjunction with Power Pivot, which is an amazing big data tool that's now built into Excel. The Data Model, which is largely unseen, lets you use any field from a linked table in your PivotTables. This is a game-changer for Excel, as it gives you relational database modeling capabilities without needing a database application. All you need to create relationships is a common field between two tables. It's the equivalent of how you use the VLOOKUP function to look up a unique value in one table and return data from another table that shares that unique value. The example at the top of the next page shows the PivotTable Fields pane with several different tables displayed. These tables have been connected, which means you can select any field from any one of them to use in your PivotTables.

You can follow along in this section with the Student Data Model workbooks and the Chapter 11 companion workbook. There's a data-only workbook (Student Data Model - Data Only) that you can use to create a Data Model yourself, and there's a workbook with completed Data Model relationships (Student Data Model - Complete). There are four separate sheets in each workbook:

- Student Details (Student ID)
- Classes (Class Number)
- Grades (Student ID)
- Semesters (Semester ID)

Each of these sheets contains one table, and each table has a unique ID (shown in parentheses above) you can use to tie together the four tables.

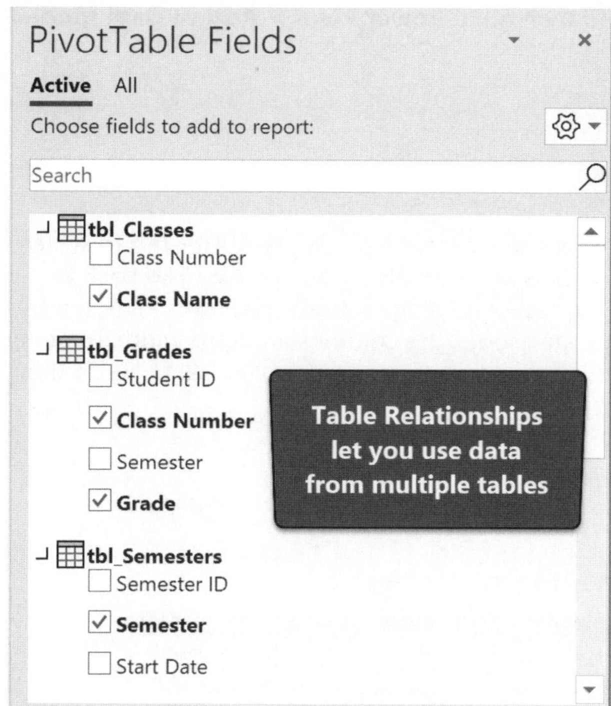

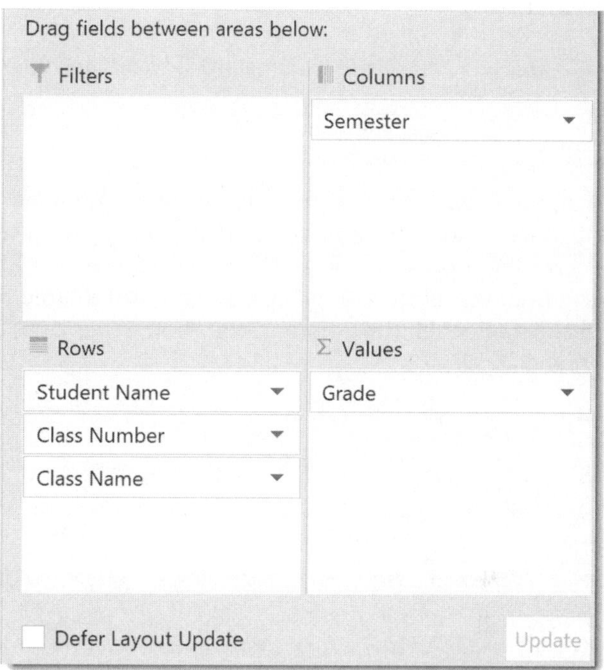

Say that you want Excel to create relationships between these tables based on Student ID, Class Number, and Semester ID. Because there are multiple tables to add in this case, the quickest way is through Power Pivot, but you need to enable it before you can use it. Go to **File > Options** and in the Excel Options dialog that appears, select the Add-Ins tab. Then, next to Manage, select COM Add-ins and click Go. In the Add-ins dialog that appears, check Microsoft Power Pivot for Excel and click OK. Power Pivot is now enabled and ready to be used.

All the data in the Student Data Model sample workbooks is self-contained for simplicity, but you can link to multiple data sources by using Power Pivot. For instance, you could connect to a customer database for customer details and orders, to an HR database for sales rep details, and to an internal list for all your products. When you tie the tables together, you can create some outstanding reports that you otherwise wouldn't be able to create without a database.

The following example shows a PivotTable that takes fields from each of those four tables. You can see that it incorporates Student Name from the Students table, Class Number from the Grades table, Class Name from the Classes table, Grade from the Grades table, and Semester from the Semesters table. Without the Data Model relationships, you wouldn't be able to use any of these fields together in a PivotTable.

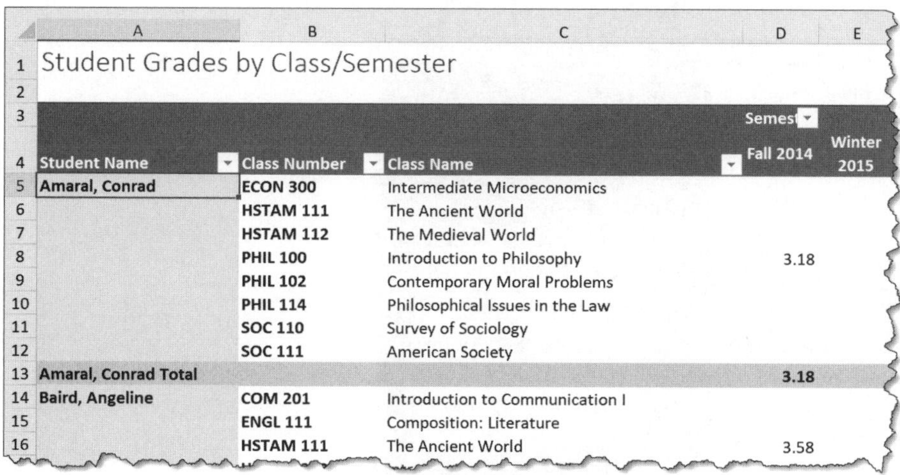

Student Grades by Class/Semester

Student Name	Class Number	Class Name	Fall 2014	Winter 2015
Amaral, Conrad	ECON 300	Intermediate Microeconomics		
	HSTAM 111	The Ancient World		
	HSTAM 112	The Medieval World		
	PHIL 100	Introduction to Philosophy	3.18	
	PHIL 102	Contemporary Moral Problems		
	PHIL 114	Philosophical Issues in the Law		
	SOC 110	Survey of Sociology		
	SOC 111	American Society		
Amaral, Conrad Total			3.18	
Baird, Angeline	COM 201	Introduction to Communication I		
	ENGL 111	Composition: Literature		
	HSTAM 111	The Ancient World	3.58	

I'm not going to go in depth about Power Pivot, as there are entire books devoted to it, such as *Power Pivot and Power BI* by Rob Collie (see https://www.mrexcel.com/store/), but I'll walk through setting up table relationships from within Power Pivot, which has an intuitive drag-and-drop relationship interface, and then creating a PivotTable with fields from multiple linked tables.

Select the first table in the Student Data Model workbook and then go to **Power Pivot > Add to Data Model**, as shown below.

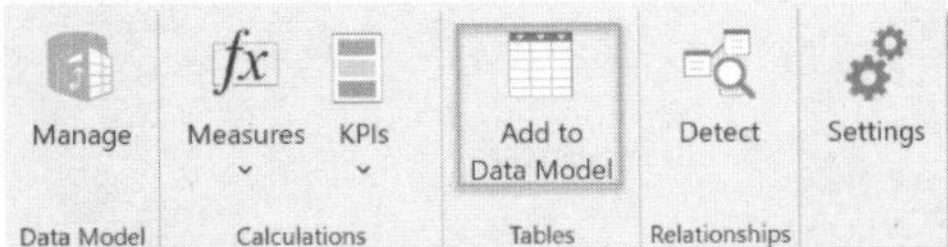

Excel opens Power Pivot in a new pane, which you can ignore for the moment (so just press **Alt+Tab** to switch back to Excel). Add the remaining tables to the Data Model in the same way. Now you can **Alt+Tab** back to the Power Pivot pane. If you accidentally close Power Pivot, you can open it again from the Power Pivot tab by clicking Manage. Note that when you first add a table to the Data Model, the columns are fixed width, but you can click to select all the columns and then hover over any column intersection and double-click to resize the columns.

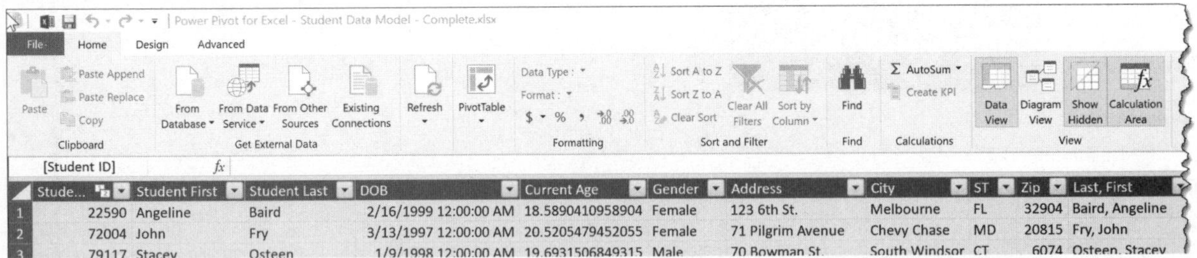

Next, in Power Pivot, go to **Home > View > Diagram View**. As shown below, Power Pivot opens a new pane that shows your tables.

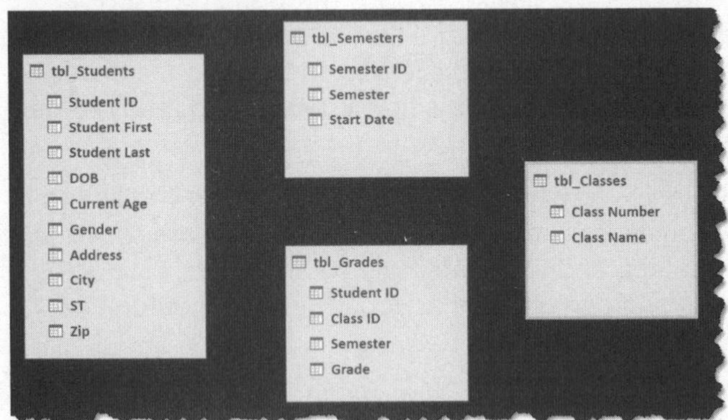

Now it's time to determine which fields should be linked between your tables. From tbl_Students, drag Student ID on top of Student ID in tbl_Grades, and Power Pivot creates a line between the two tables. If you hover over that line, Power Pivot highlights the linked fields for you, as shown below.

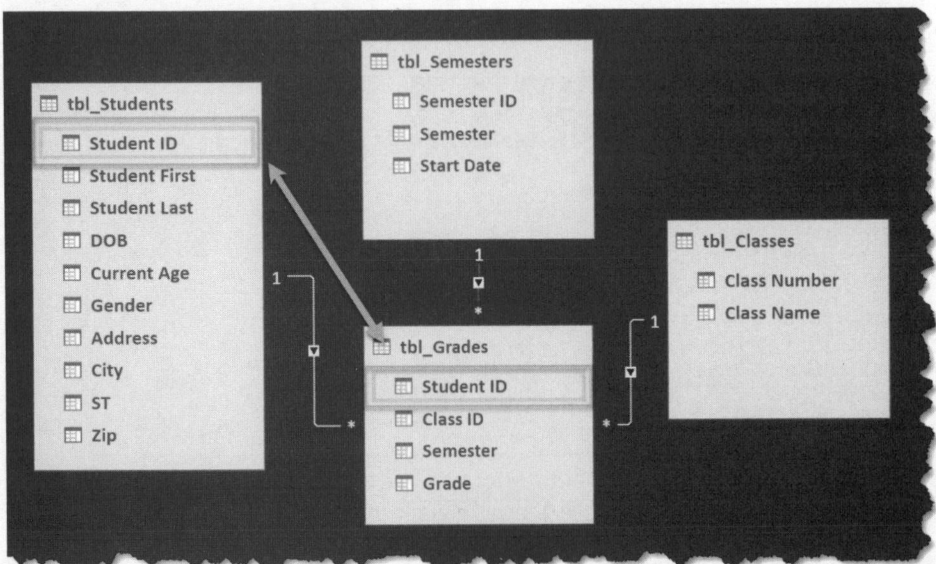

Similarly, drag Class ID from tbl_Grades to Class Number in tbl_Classes and then drag Semester from tbl_Grades to Semester ID in tbl_Semesters. The 1 in the relationship line indicates the relationship type, or cardinality, between the tables. There are multiple records for each student in the Grades table, while each record in the Students table represents a single student. In database terminology, this is called a *many-to-one relationship* because many records in one table match up with a single record in another.

Note: Notice that the field names aren't the same between tables. I set them up this way to show that Power Pivot only cares about the underlying table data, not the field name. In practice, it's a good idea to make sure your field names are consistent between tables to make it easier to know what should link to what, but that's not always practical.

You can move or resize any of the tables within the pane if you don't like the layout that Power Pivot created. When you're done, you can click the Data View button next to Diagram View to display your tables.

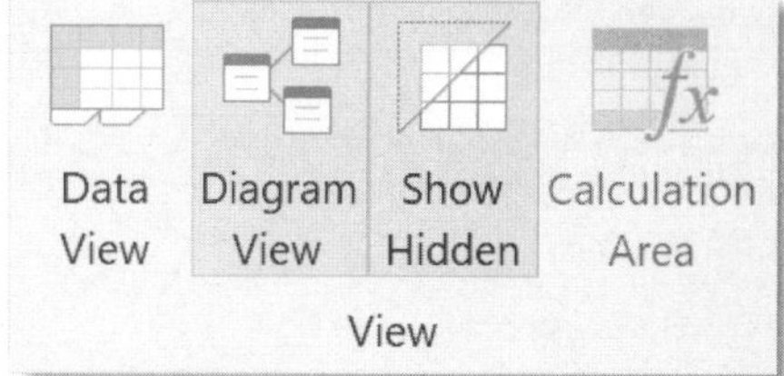

Here's an example with the tables rearranged so the *many* table (tbl_Grades) is on the left, and the *one* tables are on the right. How you set it up is personal preference, but when you create data models with a lot of tables, this kind of arrangement makes it easier to see how your relationships flow.

If you accidentally create a relationship that you don't want, you can click on the relationship line in the Diagram view and then press Delete. If you're in Excel, you can go to **PivotTable Analyze > Relationships**. Then, in the Manage Relationships dialog that appears (and is shown below), select the one you no longer want and click Delete. You can also edit existing relationships in this dialog.

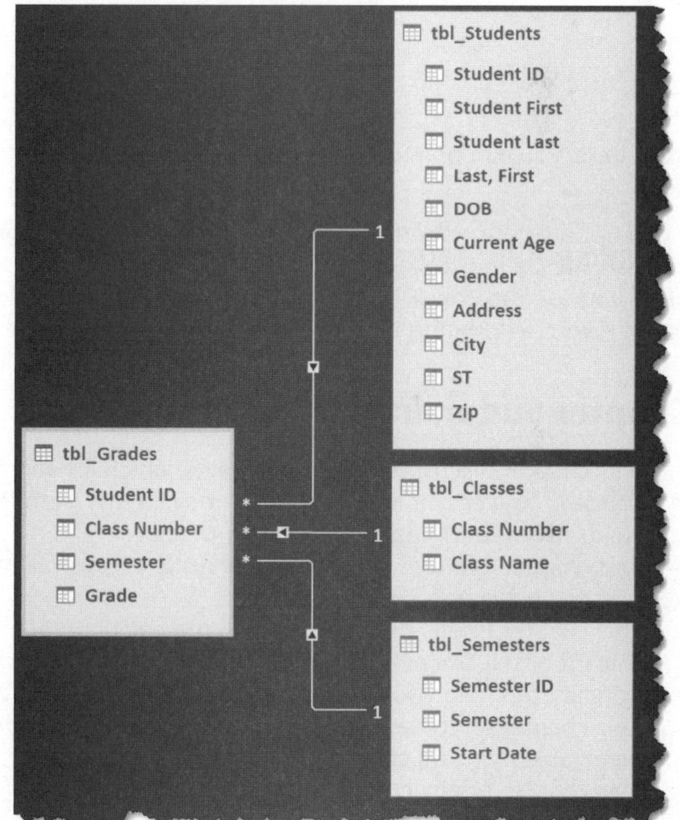

Manage Relationships

Create | Edit | Delete

Active	Table 1	Cardinality	Filter Direction	Table 2
Yes	tbl_Grades [Class ID]	Many to One (*:1)	<< To tbl_Grades	tbl_Classes [Class Number]
Yes	tbl_Grades [Semester]	Many to One (*:1)	<< To tbl_Grades	tbl_Semesters [Semester ID]
Yes	tbl_Grades [Student ID]	Many to One (*:1)	<< To tbl_Grades	tbl_Students [Student ID]

Now you can exit Power Pivot (by clicking the X in the upper-right corner) and start taking advantage of your new relationships.

Back in Excel, select any of the linked tables and go to **Insert > Pivot Table**. Next, in the Pivot Table Fields list, click the All option, and you see all your linked tables, as shown below. If you expand them, you see their respective table fields, and you can use any of them in your PivotTable.

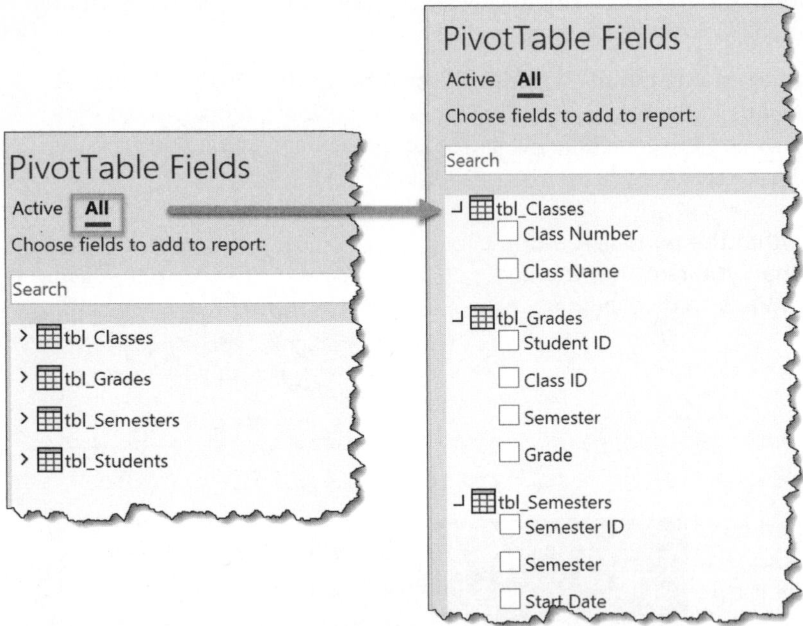

From here, you can practice on your own and review the Student Data Model - Complete workbook version as well.

If you update your underlying data and have Power Pivot open, you can go to **Power Pivot > Home > Refresh All**. Or, in Excel, you can select your PivotTable and go to **PivotTable Analyze > Refresh > Refresh All**. If you use the Power Pivot option, you see a status dialog that shows your progress. This can be very useful if you're updating a lot of records and multiple tables.

Chapter Summary

- This chapter discusses Excel PivotTables, which let you quickly manipulate flat-file data in amazing ways.
- You saw how easy it is to add and remove items from PivotTables by either clicking items in the PivotTable Fields list or dragging and dropping them.
- This chapter explores the different ways to create valuations with a click of a button, such as changing a sum to an average.
- This chapter briefly discusses how to use calculated fields, slicers, and timelines to make data analysis a snap. It also looks at adding Pivot Charts to your data and how a PivotTable's filtering and grouping functionality can help you expand and contract your chart data.
- This chapter discusses the PivotTable options for subtotals and grand totals, as well as how to format a PivotTable by using styles.
- This chapter briefly covers Power Pivot and the Data Model, which allow you to create database-type table relationships to use data from multiple tables in a single PivotTable.

Chapter 12: External Data and Mail Merge

In Chapters 10 and 11 you learned about using Excel tables, PivotTables, Power Pivot, and the Data Model. All these tools give you excellent ways to organize and analyze data without having to create a lot of formulas or complicated scenarios. When you use them, you can let Excel do the heavy lifting for you. What we haven't talked about yet is how to get your data into Excel and get it ready to do what you want. That's the topic of this chapter.

It has always been possible to import data into Excel from different sources, and the Excel team continues to add new data connectors. For instance, you can pull data from web pages or databases (like Microsoft Access, SAP, or Oracle), and you can connect to online sources such as Salesforce or Facebook. The challenging part is the transformation step—that is, cleaning up the data so it does what you want. Seemingly simple things like removing unnecessary rows or columns from data when you update it used to require a lot of manual manipulation, or if you knew what you were doing, you could automate the process with VBA code. Fortunately, this has gotten a whole lot easier with the evolution of Power Query, which you access through the Get & Transform Data group on the Data tab. Power Query has taken Excel's data import and modeling capabilities to the next level, and in this chapter we discuss a few ways to get data from external sources, create some rules for it, and use the data and the rules to create dynamic reports with some of the tools you've seen so far, such as Excel's new data types, map charts, and PivotTables. This chapter also shows you how to connect to an external data source and then use Microsoft Word's Mail Merge feature to create a custom mailing.

> **Note:** Power Query was originally introduced in Excel 2010 as an add-in that you needed to download and activate. It was so popular that it was added to Excel 2013 as a native add-in (which still needed to be activated). Since Excel 2016, Power Query has been integrated with Excel and the Data tab. When you import data using Get & Transform options, the Power Query engine is what makes it all possible.

The Get & Transform Group

Regardless of the data source you plan to use, you start on the Data tab, in the Get & Transform Data group, shown below. This is the beginning of what database people call ETL—which stands for *exchange, transform, load*—in which you first exchange the data between sources, then transform it to suit your needs, and finally load it into Excel. The following sections discuss some of the important options in the Get & Transform Data group on the Data tab.

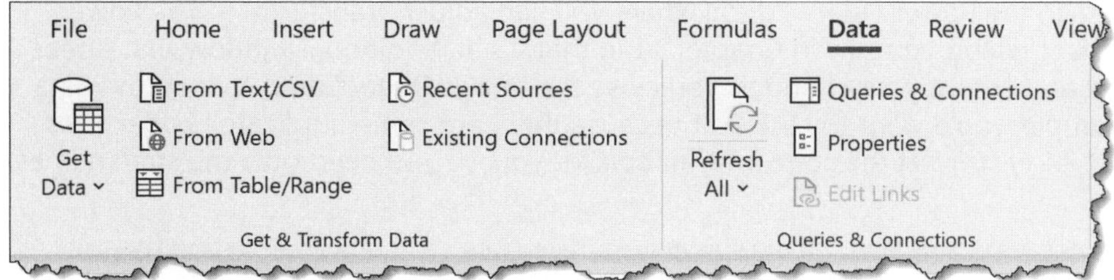

From Web

To see how to get data from the Internet, let's look at getting a list of U.S. states from Wikipedia. Go to **Data > From Web**, and in the From Web dialog that appears, enter the URL of the site you want to pull data from. This example, as shown below, uses the URL https://en.wikipedia.org/wiki/List_of_states_and_territories_of_the_United_States, and you can follow along in the States worksheet of the Chapter 12 companion workbook.

After you click OK, the Power Query engine analyzes the website and breaks up what it can into tables/sections that can be individually downloaded. That's right: Power Query can differentiate different parts of websites, so you get only what you need. U.S. states aren't going to change anytime soon, so this particular example won't need to have data refreshed, but you could refresh it if you wanted to, and Power Query would remember your initial selection. This is particularly helpful for datasets that vary in size because Power Query gets the entire range (usually, but it's not infallible).

In the example below, I've selected what Power Query has identified as the fourth table, and it shows a preview on the right-hand side. The default display is Table view, which is what you see when the data is imported to Excel; Web view displays the web page and allows you to select a range. You can choose the view that works best for you, but in general, you're likely to stick with Table view.

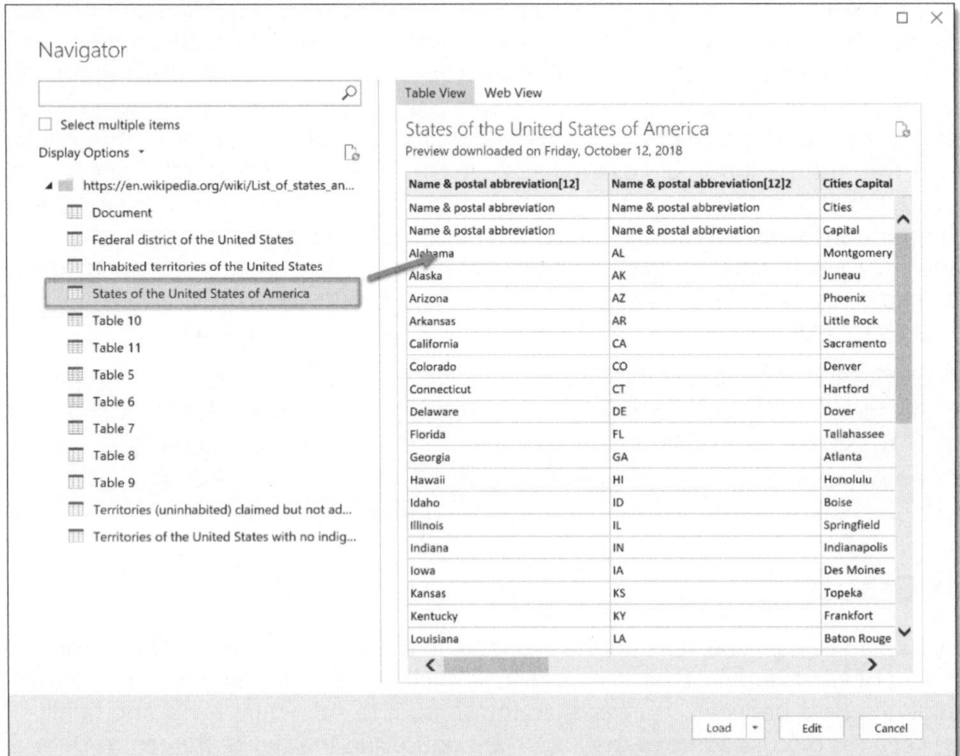

Next, you should either click Load to load the data directly to Excel (which you can do if it doesn't need any changes) or Edit to load the data in the Power Query Editor, where you can adjust (transform) it. The Power Query Editor is like the Power Pivot dialog you saw in Chapter 11 in that it's an additional window that opens alongside Excel. After you make and accept your changes, you close the Power Query Editor to load the data and return to Excel. For this example, you'd want to click Edit because there are some duplicate header rows you don't need, and you can let Excel convert the state information for you, so you need only the state names and not the extra columns.

> **Note:** As with Power Pivot, there are books dedicated to Power Query, so I don't go into detail here but just give you enough to know what it does so you can explore on your own.

At the top of the Power Query pane, you see the Power Query Ribbon. Under that is the Power Query formula bar, which is very much like the formula bar in Excel, but this one uses a different formula language, called M. Fortunately, you don't need to know how it works unless you want to because the Power Query Editor has a powerful recorder that does most of the groundwork for you. You use the options on the Ribbon to transform your data, and your steps are automatically recorded in the Applied Steps section on the right. If you don't like how a step turns out, you can click the X next to it to delete it. If you want to, you can view and edit the M code on your own by clicking the Advanced Editor option on the Power Query ribbon. The data preview pane, the largest part of the window at the bottom left, shows the data that Power Query has identified to import. As you make changes to the data, you see the preview pane update.

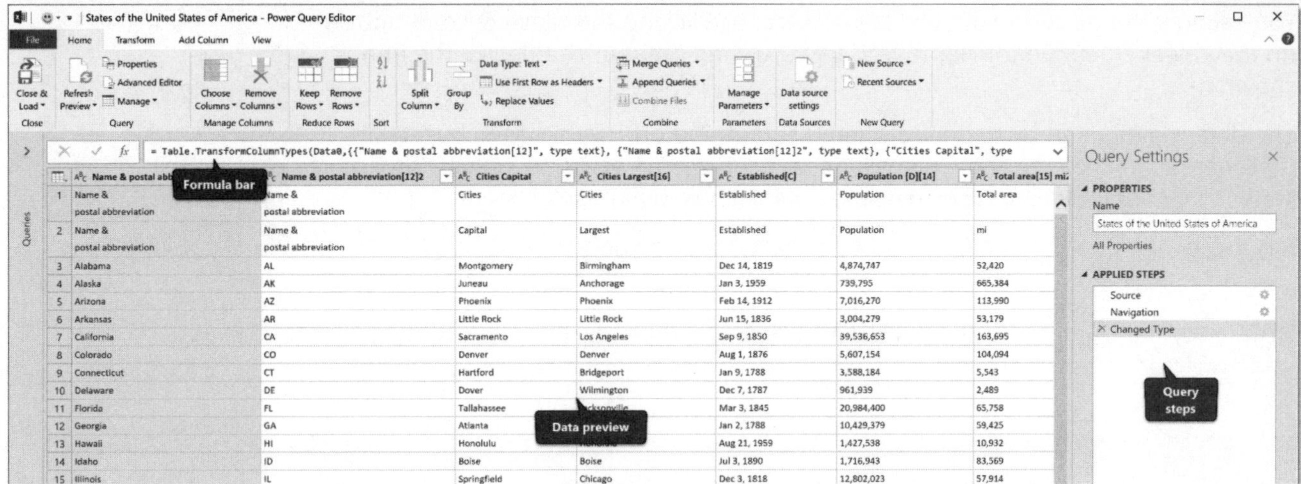

To remove the duplicate header rows, go to **Home > Remove Rows > Remove Top Rows**, as shown below, and then select the number of rows to remove. In this case, you want the header row but not the next two rows, so you fill out the Remove Top Rows dialog as shown below.

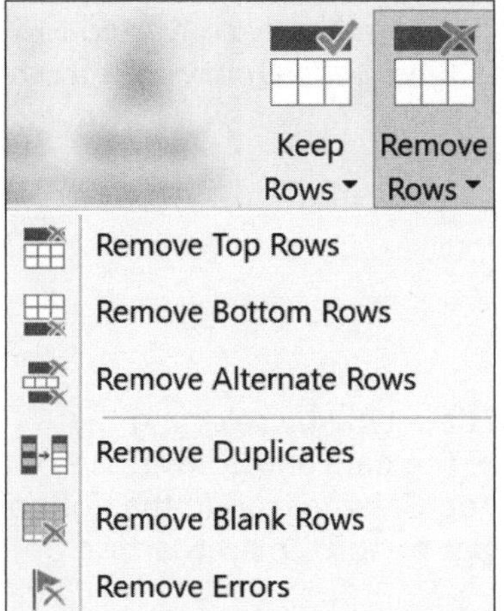

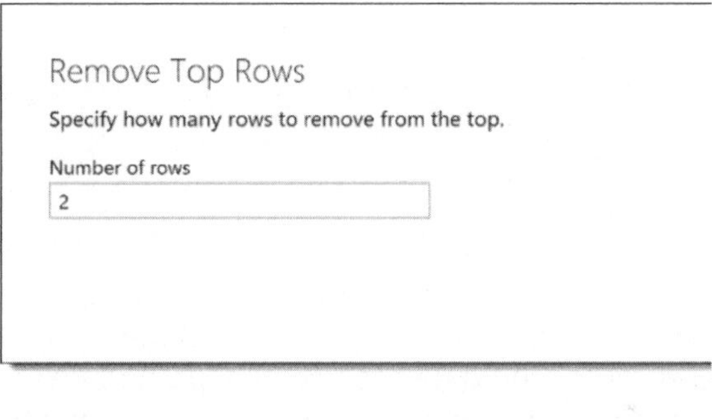

You immediately see Power Query update your data with the top rows removed, and the step is recorded in the Applied Steps section.

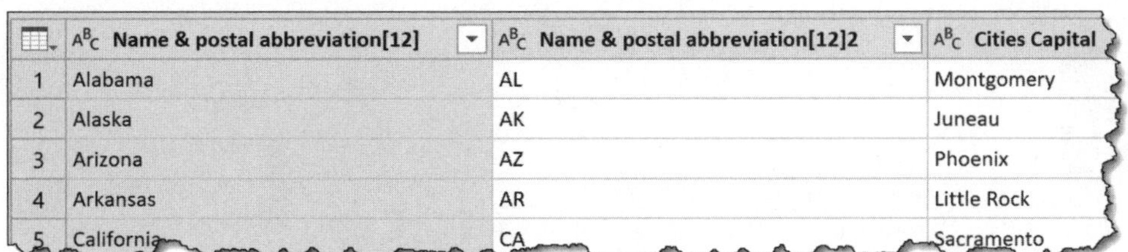

	Name & postal abbreviation[12]	Name & postal abbreviation[12]2	Cities Capital
1	Alabama	AL	Montgomery
2	Alaska	AK	Juneau
3	Arizona	AZ	Phoenix
4	Arkansas	AR	Little Rock
5	California	CA	Sacramento

Next, to remove the additional columns, select the first column and go to **Home > Remove Columns > Remove Other Columns**, and Excel removes all columns except the one selected. You can also remove individual columns by right-clicking on any column header and choosing the Remove Columns option, or you can **Ctrl+click** to select multiple columns to delete.

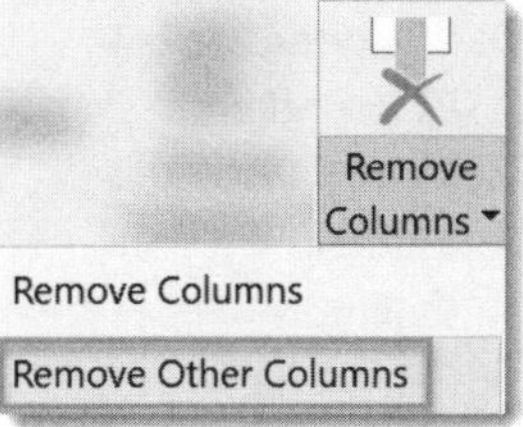

Next, double-click the remaining header row and rename it **States**.

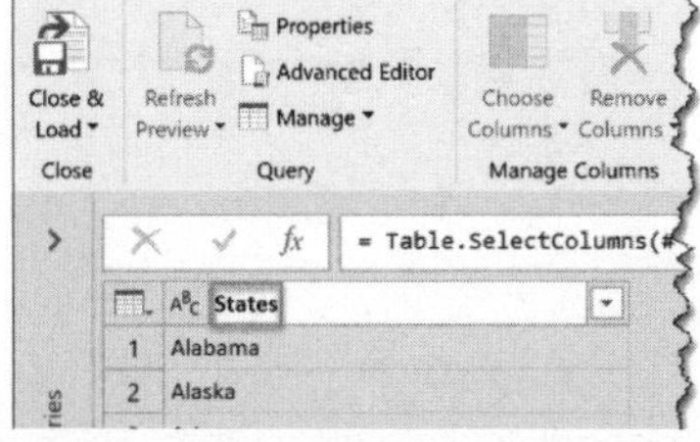

You can load the resulting data back into Excel by clicking the Close & Load button on the Power Query Editor Home tab, and you then see it in a table like the one shown here.

The data is almost ready to go, but there's something odd with Massachusetts in that there's an [E] at the end. That will be an issue when you try to convert the list of states to Geography data types because "Massachusetts[E]" isn't a state.

Right-click the query in the Queries & Connections page and choose Edit.

Fortunately, you can go to **Home > Replace Values** and replace [E] with nothing, as shown below.

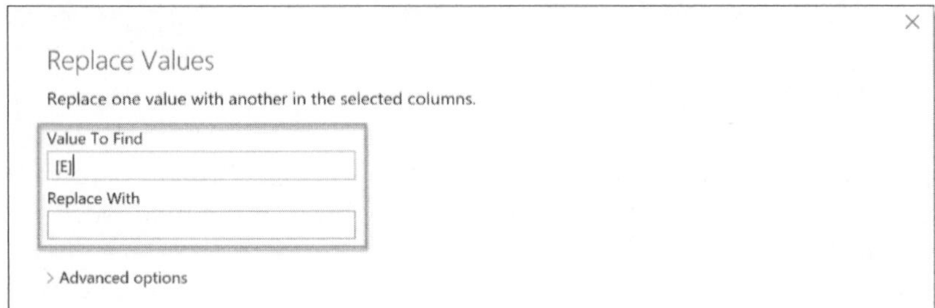

Finally, click Close & Load to get the updated list of states back to Excel, and it is automatically converted to an Excel table. When your underlying data changes, you can select the table and then go to **Query > Refresh**, as shown below.

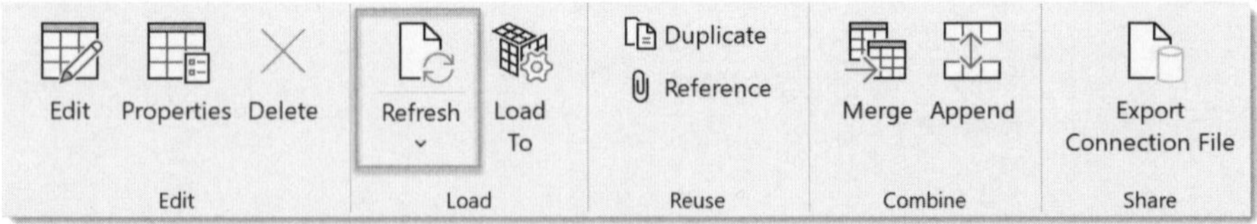

Once the list of states has been loaded into Excel, you can convert it to a linked data type by selecting the list of states and going to **Data > Geography**. Excel's intelligent services analyze the data and convert it to Geography data types. When the data has been converted, you can select the Add Column icon to the right of the table and choose the Population option to add a new column. The next step is to add a map chart, so go to **Insert > Maps > Filled Map**. You now see a map like the one shown below.

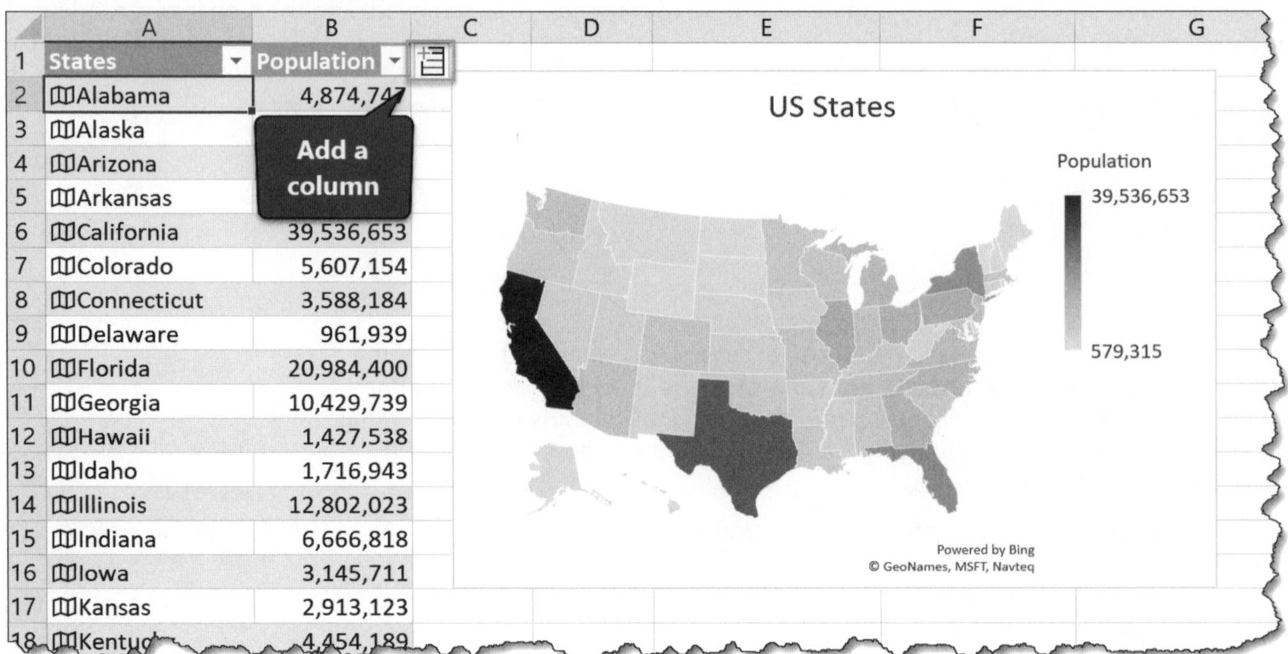

Getting Data from a Database

You can import data into Excel from an Access database. This example uses the Northwind Traders sample database. It's included with this chapter's sample files, and you can also get to it from Access by searching for it in **File > New**. To get started, go to **Data > Get Data > From Database > From Microsoft Access Database**.

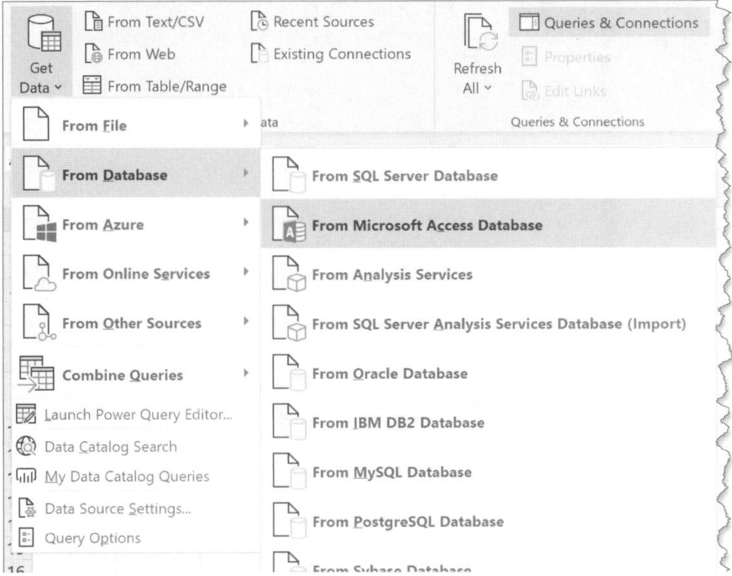

Power Query launches the Navigator pane, and you can then select the table you want to import (in this case Sales Analysis) and click Transform Data to load the data into the Power Query Editor.

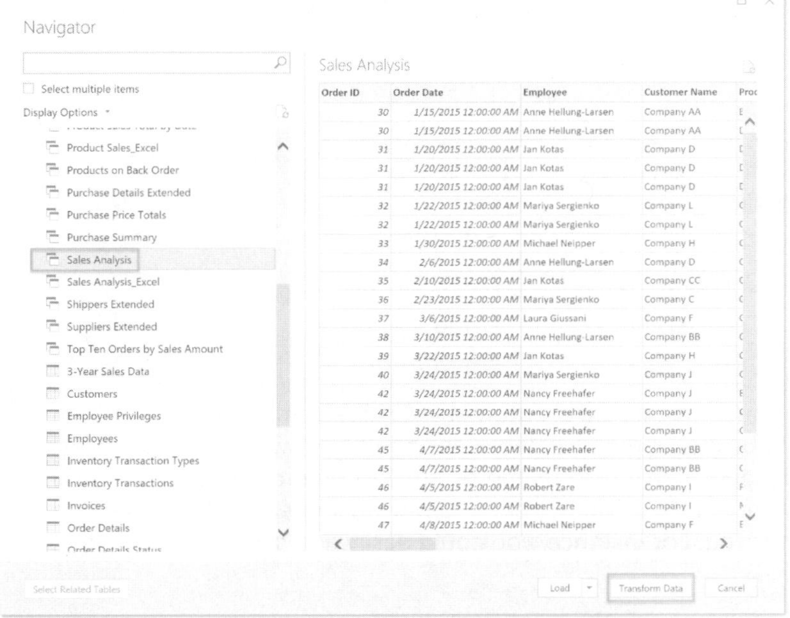

For this example, you only want to focus on the sales reps, what they sold, when, and their respective sales amounts, so go ahead and select all the columns to the right of State/Province and then go to **Home > Manage Columns > Remove Columns**.

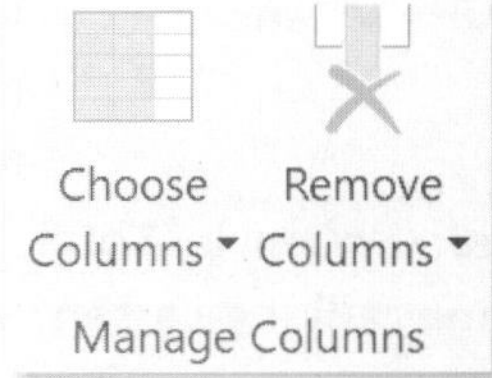

Next, remove the Order ID column.

If you look at the formula bar, you see the Remove Columns steps that Power Query has recorded for you, as shown below.

```
= Table.RemoveColumns(#"_Sales Analysis",{"Country/Region", "Employee ID", "Product ID", "Customer ID", "Year", "Month", "Quarter", "Month Name", "Category", "Product", "Customer", "MonthOfQuarter", "Order ID"})
```

If you need to adjust which columns are removed, you can manually edit them here, or you can delete the Removed Columns step from the Applied Steps section of the Query Settings pane and redo it.

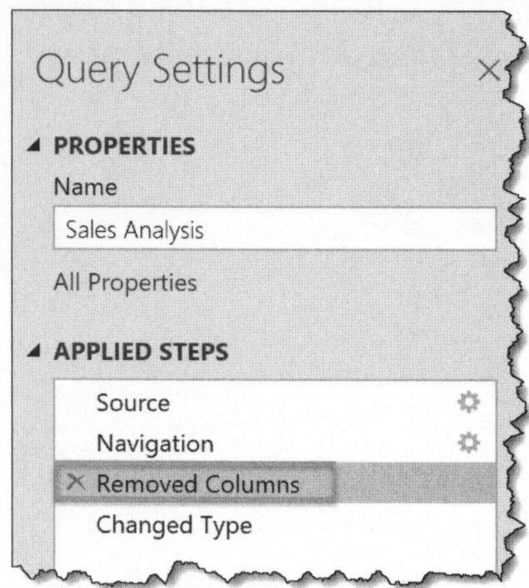

Next, select the Order Date column and go to **Home > Transform > Data Type > Date**.

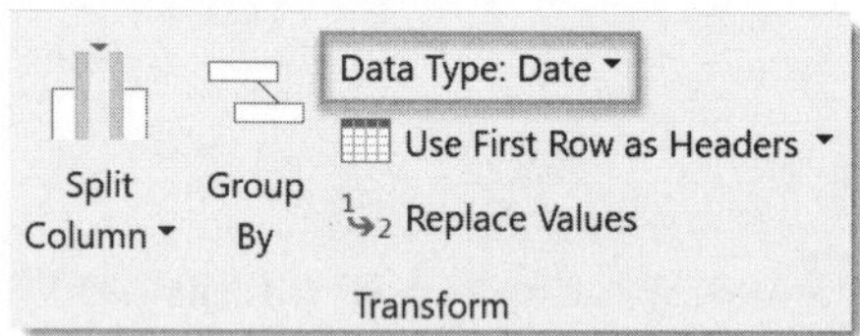

Finally, click **Close & Load** to bring the data back to Excel. In the following figure, you can see the imported sales data with only the columns you wanted. If you refresh the data, Power Query will remember your column selection.

	A	B	C	D	E
1	Order Date	Employee	Customer Name	Product Name	Sales
2	1/15/2015	Anne Hellung-Larsen	Company AA	Beer	1400
3	1/15/2015	Anne Hellung-Larsen	Company AA	Dried Plums	105
4	1/20/2015	Jan Kotas	Company D	Dried Pears	300
5	1/20/2015	Jan Kotas	Company D	Dried Apples	530
6	1/20/2015	Jan Kotas	Company D	Dried Plums	35

The first thing you'll notice about the Access query is that Excel automatically creates the data as an Excel table. From here you can summarize the data by creating a PivotTable, as shown below. This entire process has substantial benefits over having to pull static reports that are created by an IT or finance department because you can manipulate the data however you want it, and you don't need to rely on someone else making changes to existing reports or creating new ones for you. For instance, you could easily add slicers to the PivotTable to filter by employee or product name.

Employee	Product Name	Total Sales
Andrew Cencini	Northwind Traders Chocolate	$127.50
	Northwind Traders Dried Apples	$1,590.00
	Northwind Traders Dried Pears	$900.00
Andrew Cencini Total		**$2,617.50**
Anne Hellung-Larsen	Northwind Traders Beer	$1,400.00
	Northwind Traders Boysenberry Spread	$2,250.00

Getting Data from Facebook

You can use Excel to import Facebook data, such as your post activity. If you go to **Data > Get Data > From Online Services > From Facebook**, Excel takes you through a series of prompts, and you need to log in to your Facebook account. One of the prompts, as shown below, is a security prompt that says Excel will be using a third-party service for the connection. You can check the Don't Warn Me Again for This Connector option if you don't want to be prompted again. Then click Continue.

Next, choose which data you want to download from Facebook. You can leave me in the first textbox, as shown below, because Power Query will give you a chance to log in to Facebook in the next step. Click OK.

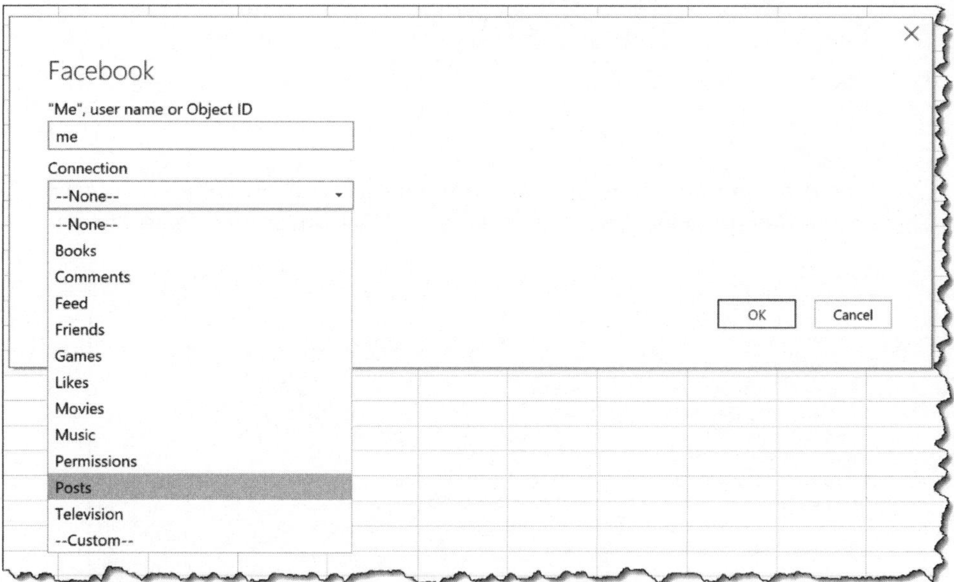

In the next screen, shown below, click the Sign In button.

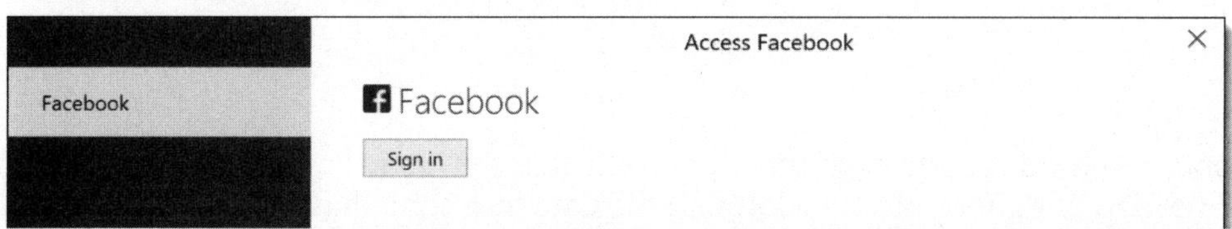

Next, you are asked to provide your username and password, as shown in the following example.

When you click Log In, Power Query retrieves your information and returns a preview, as shown below. From here you can go through the steps you've already seen to load the data into Excel or edit it.

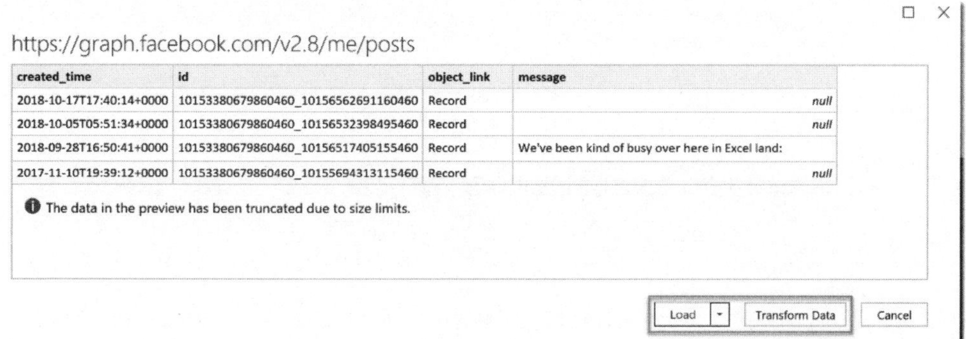

created_time	id	object_link	message
2018-10-17T17:40:14+0000	10153380679860460_10156562691160460	Record	null
2018-10-05T05:51:34+0000	10153380679860460_10156532398495460	Record	null
2018-09-28T16:50:41+0000	10153380679860460_10156517405155460	Record	We've been kind of busy over here in Excel land:
2017-11-10T19:39:12+0000	10153380679860460_10155694313115460	Record	null

The Queries & Connections Group

All your queries and connections are listed in the Queries & Connections pane, which you can activate by selecting **Data > Queries & Connections**.

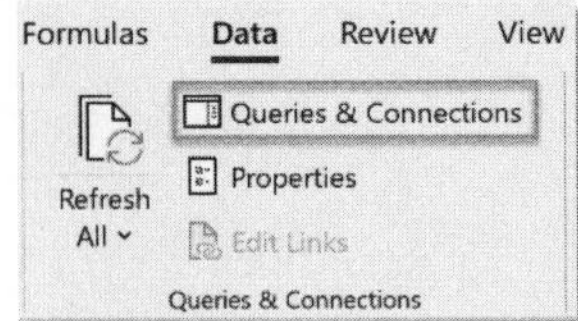

If you hover over a query, as shown below, a summary pane appears to the left that gives you an overview of the data and query properties. This can be helpful when you receive a workbook from someone and want to see how it's put together.

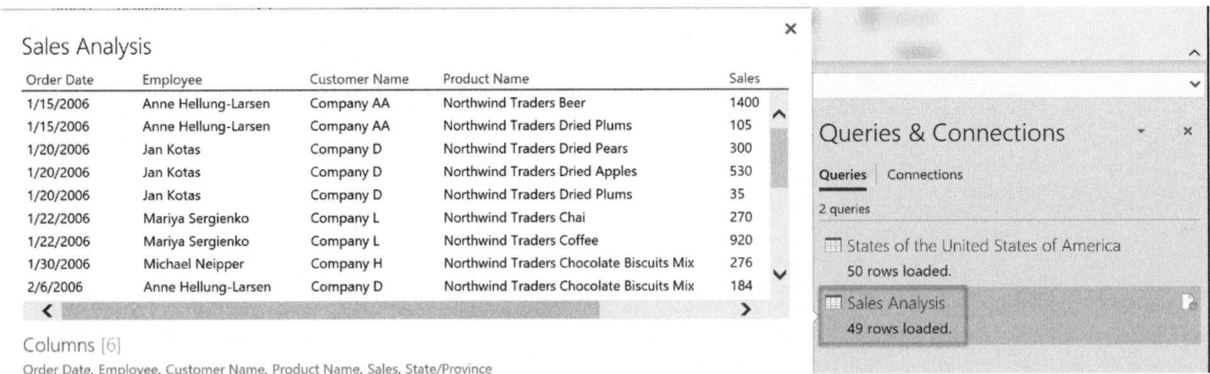
Sales Analysis

Order Date	Employee	Customer Name	Product Name	Sales
1/15/2006	Anne Hellung-Larsen	Company AA	Northwind Traders Beer	1400
1/15/2006	Anne Hellung-Larsen	Company AA	Northwind Traders Dried Plums	105
1/20/2006	Jan Kotas	Company D	Northwind Traders Dried Pears	300
1/20/2006	Jan Kotas	Company D	Northwind Traders Dried Apples	530
1/20/2006	Jan Kotas	Company D	Northwind Traders Dried Plums	35
1/22/2006	Mariya Sergienko	Company L	Northwind Traders Chai	270
1/22/2006	Mariya Sergienko	Company L	Northwind Traders Coffee	920
1/30/2006	Michael Neipper	Company H	Northwind Traders Chocolate Biscuits Mix	276
2/6/2006	Anne Hellung-Larsen	Company D	Northwind Traders Chocolate Biscuits Mix	184

Columns [6]
Order Date, Employee, Customer Name, Product Name, Sales, State/Province

Unpivoting Data

One of the toughest things about receiving reports from other people is that they may or may not be what you need, and you sometimes have to put effort into transforming the data into something you want. In the past, you needed to write VBA code to do this, but Power Query has an Unpivot feature that can make this a snap. This section walks through the process with a 12-month cash flow statement for a fictitious company, which is included in the Chapter 12 companion workbook. As you look at the example, you'll see that the data you really need starts on row 19 (the first GL Code/Revenue line). The dataset also has unnecessary summary rows, as well as blank rows between sections (e.g., rows 26 and 27). Most importantly, the data is presented in a pivoted state, so you can see the detail, but you can't manipulate it with additional PivotTables. What you need to do is get the data back into a transactional state, with one row for each GL code and month. So, for example, in the Total Revenue section, you will turn the 6 summary rows into 72, creating a new row for each transaction (6 rows × 12 months = 72).

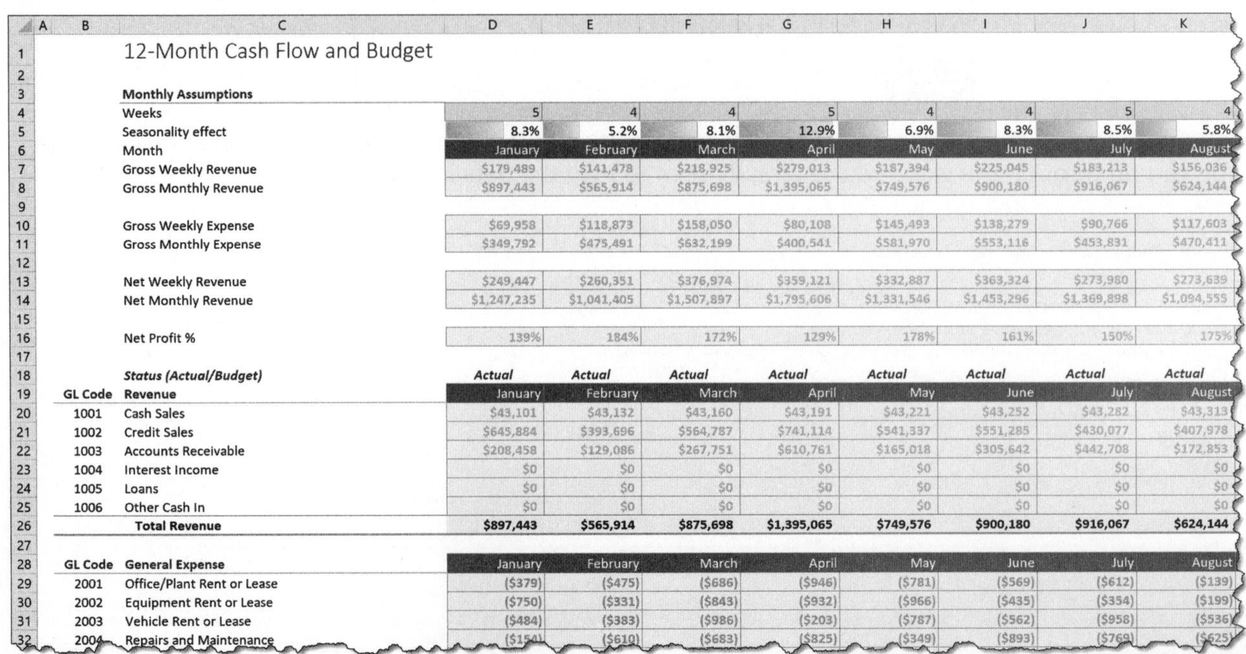

	B	C	D	E	F	G	H	I	J	K
1		12-Month Cash Flow and Budget								
2										
3		**Monthly Assumptions**								
4		Weeks	5	4	4	5	4	4	5	4
5		Seasonality effect	8.3%	5.2%	8.1%	12.9%	6.9%	8.3%	8.5%	5.8%
6		Month	January	February	March	April	May	June	July	August
7		Gross Weekly Revenue	$179,489	$141,478	$218,925	$279,013	$187,394	$225,045	$183,213	$156,036
8		Gross Monthly Revenue	$897,443	$565,914	$875,698	$1,395,065	$749,576	$900,180	$916,067	$624,144
9										
10		Gross Weekly Expense	$69,958	$118,873	$158,050	$80,108	$145,493	$138,279	$90,766	$117,603
11		Gross Monthly Expense	$349,792	$475,491	$632,199	$400,541	$581,970	$553,116	$453,831	$470,411
12										
13		Net Weekly Revenue	$249,447	$260,351	$376,974	$359,121	$332,887	$363,324	$273,980	$273,639
14		Net Monthly Revenue	$1,247,235	$1,041,405	$1,507,897	$1,795,606	$1,331,546	$1,453,296	$1,369,898	$1,094,555
15										
16		Net Profit %	139%	184%	172%	129%	178%	161%	150%	175%
17										
18		***Status (Actual/Budget)***	*Actual*	*Actual*	*Actual*	*Actual*	*Actual*	*Actual*	*Actual*	*Actual*
19	GL Code	Revenue	January	February	March	April	May	June	July	August
20	1001	Cash Sales	$43,101	$43,132	$43,160	$43,191	$43,221	$43,252	$43,282	$43,313
21	1002	Credit Sales	$645,884	$393,696	$564,787	$741,114	$541,337	$551,285	$430,077	$407,978
22	1003	Accounts Receivable	$208,458	$129,086	$267,751	$610,761	$165,018	$305,642	$442,708	$172,853
23	1004	Interest Income	$0	$0	$0	$0	$0	$0	$0	$0
24	1005	Loans	$0	$0	$0	$0	$0	$0	$0	$0
25	1006	Other Cash In	$0	$0	$0	$0	$0	$0	$0	$0
26		**Total Revenue**	**$897,443**	**$565,914**	**$875,698**	**$1,395,065**	**$749,576**	**$900,180**	**$916,067**	**$624,144**
27										
28	GL Code	General Expense	January	February	March	April	May	June	July	August
29	2001	Office/Plant Rent or Lease	($379)	($475)	($686)	($946)	($781)	($569)	($612)	($139)
30	2002	Equipment Rent or Lease	($750)	($331)	($843)	($932)	($966)	($435)	($354)	($199)
31	2003	Vehicle Rent or Lease	($484)	($383)	($986)	($203)	($787)	($562)	($958)	($536)
32	2004	Repairs and Maintenance	($154)	($610)	($683)	($825)	($349)	($893)	($769)	($625)

The following steps show what you need to do in the Power Query Editor:

1. Go to **Data > From Table/Range**.

2. Select the range B1:O84. (There's no reason to import the last total row or the YTD summary column since you'll be re-creating those when you're done.)

3. In the Power Query Editor, select the filter for column 1 and un-check null to remove the null rows.

4. Go to Home > Transform > Use First Row as Headers.

5. Select the GL Code column filter, scroll to the bottom of the filter list, and uncheck GL Code. (The order in which you apply these steps is important; if you had deleted GL Code first, you wouldn't be able to have the current row headers.) At this point, the data looks as shown below, with 14 columns and 49 rows.

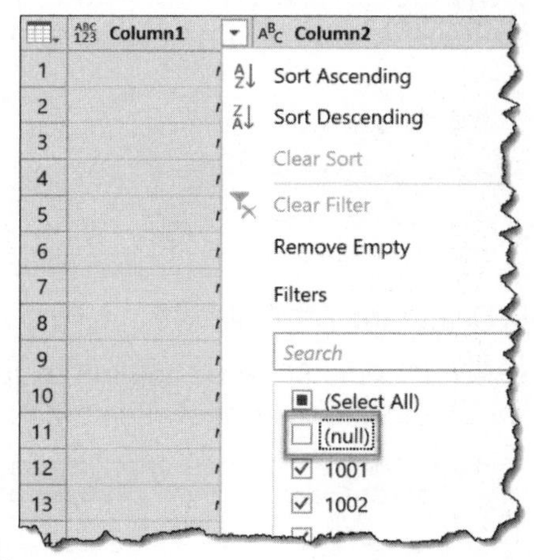

1.

	GL Code	Revenue	1/1/2018 12:00:00 AM	2/1/2018 12:00:00 AM
1	1001	Cash Sales	43101	43132
2	1002	Credit Sales	645883.975	393695.775
3	1003	Accounts Receivable	208458.25	129086.1
4	1004	Interest Income	0	0
5	1005	Loans	0	0
6	1006	Other Cash In	0	0
7	2001	Office/Plant Rent or Lease	-379	-475
8	2002	Equipment Rent or Lease	-750	-331
9	2003	Vehicle Rent or Lease	-484	-383
10	2004	Repairs and Maintenance	-154	-610

6. Next, select the 12 date columns (which you can do by selecting the first one and then pressing **Shift+right arrow** until you've selected them all). Next, go to **Transform > Unpivot Columns**.

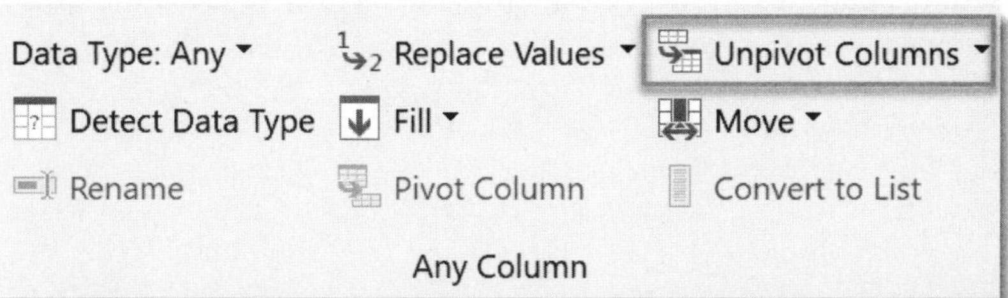

- The data should now look as shown below, with 4 columns and 588 rows. The Unpivot transformation creates a new row for each transaction, essentially taking you back to the state the data was in before it was pivoted.

	GL Code	Revenue	Attribute	Value
1	1001	Cash Sales	1/1/2018 12:00:00 AM	43101
2	1001	Cash Sales	2/1/2018 12:00:00 AM	43132
3	1001	Cash Sales	3/1/2018 12:00:00 AM	43160
4	1001	Cash Sales	4/1/2018 12:00:00 AM	43191
5	1001	Cash Sales	5/1/2018 12:00:00 AM	43221
6	1001	Cash Sales	6/1/2018 12:00:00 AM	43252
7	1001	Cash Sales	7/1/2018 12:00:00 AM	43282
8	1001	Cash Sales	8/1/2018 12:00:00 AM	43313
9	1001	Cash Sales	9/1/2018 12:00:00 AM	43344
10	1001	Cash Sales	10/1/2018 12:00:00 AM	43374
11	1001	Cash Sales	11/1/2018 12:00:00 AM	43405
12	1001	Cash Sales	12/1/2018 12:00:00 AM	43435
13	1002	Credit Sales	1/1/2018 12:00:00 AM	645883.975
14	1002	Credit Sales	2/1/2018 12:00:00 AM	393695.775

7. To format the date, select the Attribute column (which is what Power Query named the column it added when you unpivoted) and go to **Home > Transform > Data Type > Date**. Oops, Power Query shows an error. What happened? When you promoted the first row as headers, Power Query converted those values to text, so you can't format them as dates. But you can add a new column and get the date from the Attribute column. So, go to the Applied Steps pane, delete the last step (Changed Type2) and then go to **Add Column > Column from Examples**. Power Query adds a new column to the right. Enter **1/1/2018** in the first cell and

choose the Attribute option, as shown below. This tells Power Query that you want to get the date part of the Attribute field, and it will auto-fill the rest of the column for you. Click OK to accept the changes and then double-click the column header and rename it **Date**.

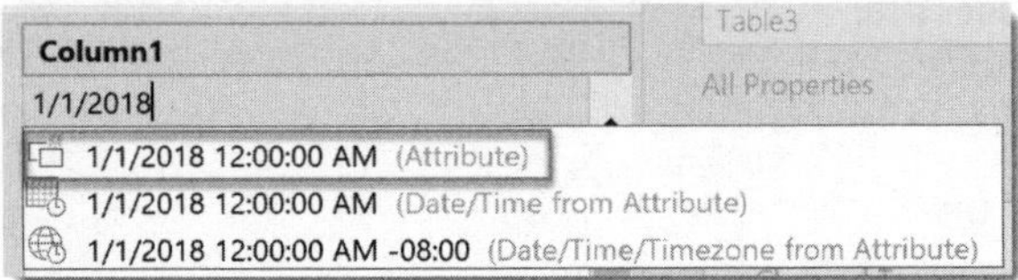

8. Delete the Attribute column by clicking on it and going to **Home > Manage Columns > Remove Columns**.

9. Rename the Revenue column to something that better describes it, such as **GL Description**, and your data should now look as shown below.

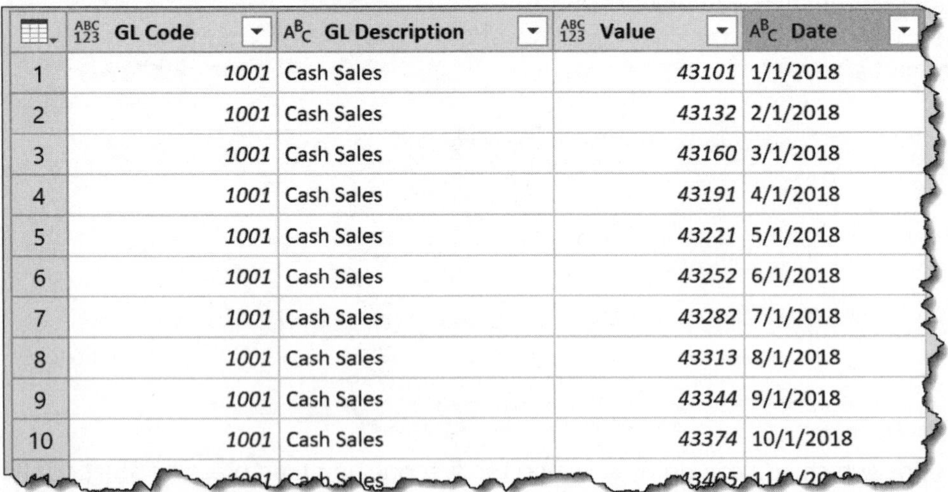

	GL Code	GL Description	Value	Date
1	1001	Cash Sales	43101	1/1/2018
2	1001	Cash Sales	43132	2/1/2018
3	1001	Cash Sales	43160	3/1/2018
4	1001	Cash Sales	43191	4/1/2018
5	1001	Cash Sales	43221	5/1/2018
6	1001	Cash Sales	43252	6/1/2018
7	1001	Cash Sales	43282	7/1/2018
8	1001	Cash Sales	43313	8/1/2018
9	1001	Cash Sales	43344	9/1/2018
10	1001	Cash Sales	43374	10/1/2018

10. Finally, rename your table in the Query Settings pane, as shown below, and you're ready to close the query and load it to Excel.

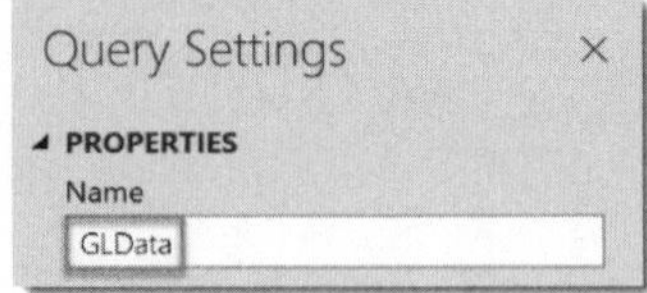

Putting Data to Work

Next you would need to go to Power Pivot to add the data to the Data Model, which I've already done in the Chapter 12 companion workbook. Adding the data to the Data Model is important for the next step, where you'll tie the new data to a chart of accounts to be able to use parent categories in a summary PivotTable.

The focus of this chapter is not on creating table relationships (which we discussed in Chapter 11) but on making adjustments to your PivotTable(s), so I've created a few PivotTable worksheets for you (Cash Flow Pivot Summary1 and Cash Flow Pivot Summary2). Here's the current PivotTable.

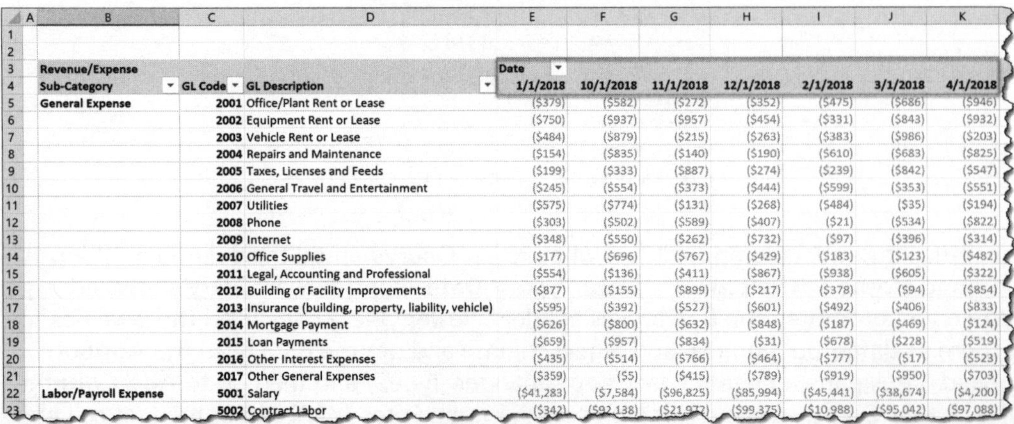

Revenue/Expense Sub-Category	GL Code	GL Description	1/1/2018	10/1/2018	11/1/2018	12/1/2018	2/1/2018	3/1/2018	4/1/2018
General Expense	2001	Office/Plant Rent or Lease	($379)	($582)	($272)	($352)	($475)	($686)	($946)
	2002	Equipment Rent or Lease	($750)	($937)	($957)	($454)	($331)	($843)	($932)
	2003	Vehicle Rent or Lease	($484)	($879)	($215)	($263)	($383)	($986)	($203)
	2004	Repairs and Maintenance	($154)	($835)	($140)	($190)	($610)	($683)	($825)
	2005	Taxes, Licenses and Feeds	($199)	($333)	($887)	($274)	($239)	($842)	($547)
	2006	General Travel and Entertainment	($245)	($554)	($373)	($444)	($599)	($353)	($551)
	2007	Utilities	($575)	($774)	($131)	($268)	($484)	($35)	($194)
	2008	Phone	($303)	($502)	($589)	($407)	($21)	($534)	($822)
	2009	Internet	($348)	($550)	($262)	($732)	($97)	($396)	($314)
	2010	Office Supplies	($177)	($696)	($767)	($429)	($183)	($123)	($482)
	2011	Legal, Accounting and Professional	($554)	($136)	($411)	($867)	($938)	($605)	($322)
	2012	Building or Facility Improvements	($877)	($155)	($899)	($217)	($378)	($94)	($854)
	2013	Insurance (building, property, liability, vehicle)	($595)	($392)	($527)	($601)	($492)	($406)	($833)
	2014	Mortgage Payment	($626)	($800)	($632)	($848)	($187)	($469)	($124)
	2015	Loan Payments	($659)	($957)	($834)	($31)	($678)	($228)	($519)
	2016	Other Interest Expenses	($435)	($514)	($766)	($464)	($777)	($17)	($523)
	2017	Other General Expenses	($359)	($5)	($415)	($789)	($919)	($950)	($703)
Labor/Payroll Expense	5001	Salary	($41,283)	($7,584)	($96,825)	($85,994)	($45,441)	($38,674)	($4,200)
	5002	Contract Labor	($342)	($92,138)	($21,972)	($99,375)	($10,988)	($95,042)	($97,088)

Do you notice anything strange about this PivotTable and how the data is laid out? First, the dates are out of order (January, October, November, December, February, etc.). This is because the Power Query step you took to get the date from the Attribute field did add the date, but it formatted it as text, which is why the dates are sorted in that order. Fortunately, you can manually move PivotTable fields, and they'll stay put when you refresh the data. In the Cash Flow Pivot Summary1 worksheet, select the October, November, and December columns by hovering your mouse over the 10/1/2018 column, and when the cursor turns into a down arrow, drag across to select the next two columns. Then click any edge of the selection border and drag the columns to the right, just before the Grand Total column.

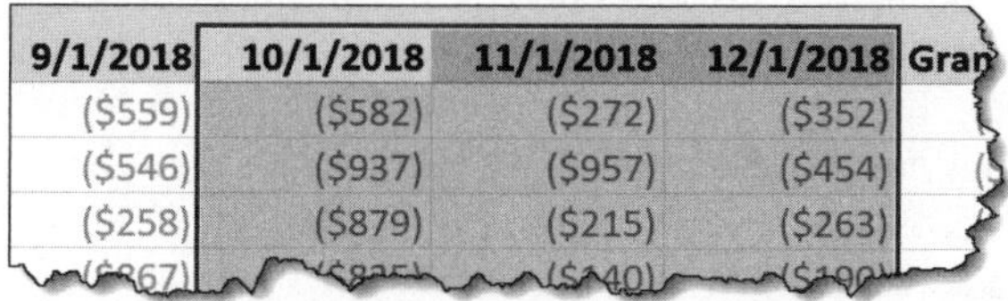

9/1/2018	10/1/2018	11/1/2018	12/1/2018	Gran
($559)	($582)	($272)	($352)	
($546)	($937)	($957)	($454)	
($258)	($879)	($215)	($263)	

The next challenge is that the PivotTable fields are listed alphabetically, so Revenue is in the middle of the Expense fields. Select the Revenue section and drag it up to the top, so it's just beneath the Sub-Category row. You'll notice that a bold line appears every once in a while as you're dragging; it indicates the destination when you release the mouse. You'll also find that Excel doesn't let you drop the selection within another group; it only lets you drop it outside the other groups. The PivotTable should now look as shown below.

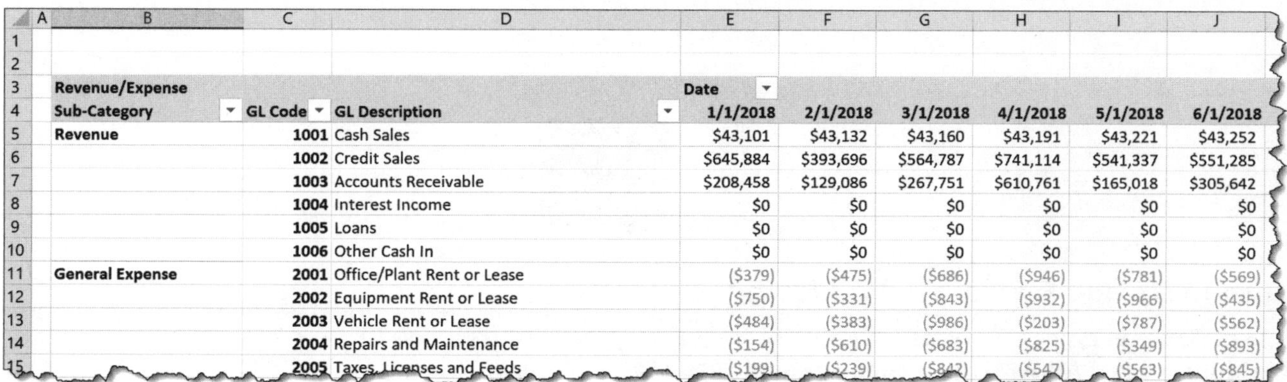

	B	C	D	E	F	G	H	I	J
1									
2									
3	Revenue/Expense			Date					
4	Sub-Category	GL Code	GL Description	1/1/2018	2/1/2018	3/1/2018	4/1/2018	5/1/2018	6/1/2018
5	Revenue	1001	Cash Sales	$43,101	$43,132	$43,160	$43,191	$43,221	$43,252
6		1002	Credit Sales	$645,884	$393,696	$564,787	$741,114	$541,337	$551,285
7		1003	Accounts Receivable	$208,458	$129,086	$267,751	$610,761	$165,018	$305,642
8		1004	Interest Income	$0	$0	$0	$0	$0	$0
9		1005	Loans	$0	$0	$0	$0	$0	$0
10		1006	Other Cash In	$0	$0	$0	$0	$0	$0
11	General Expense	2001	Office/Plant Rent or Lease	($379)	($475)	($686)	($946)	($781)	($569)
12		2002	Equipment Rent or Lease	($750)	($331)	($843)	($932)	($966)	($435)
13		2003	Vehicle Rent or Lease	($484)	($383)	($986)	($203)	($787)	($562)
14		2004	Repairs and Maintenance	($154)	($610)	($683)	($825)	($349)	($893)
15		2005	Taxes, Licenses and Feeds	($199)	($239)	($842)	($547)	($563)	($845)

Mail Merges

A big challenge for many businesses is figuring out how to communicate with customers. Say that you have a customer list, and you've written a letter that you want to send to your customers. How do you merge the two? This chapter's sample workbook is connected to the Northwind Traders database, with a customer list imported, as shown below, and you can use this as the data source for a customer letter. It is also possible to connect directly to a database from Word if the data is set up the way you want it.

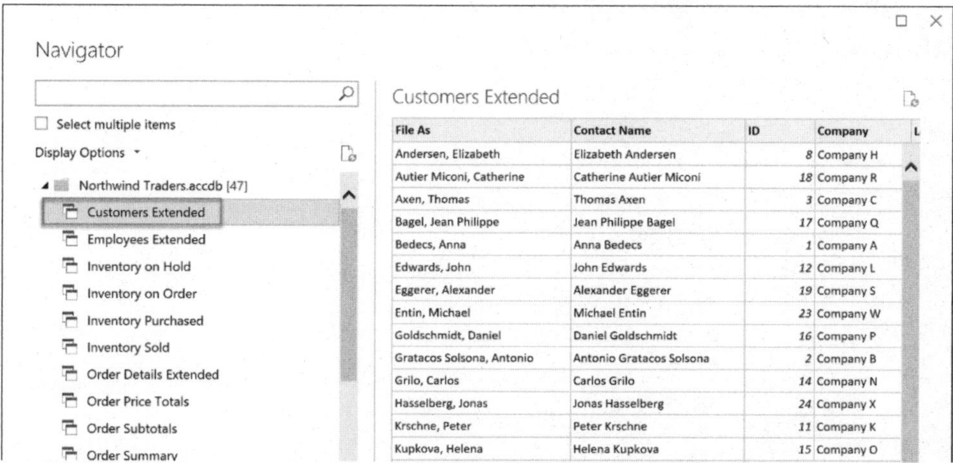

File As	Contact Name	ID	Company
Andersen, Elizabeth	Elizabeth Andersen	8	Company H
Autier Miconi, Catherine	Catherine Autier Miconi	18	Company R
Axen, Thomas	Thomas Axen	3	Company C
Bagel, Jean Philippe	Jean Philippe Bagel	17	Company Q
Bedecs, Anna	Anna Bedecs	1	Company A
Edwards, John	John Edwards	12	Company L
Eggerer, Alexander	Alexander Eggerer	19	Company S
Entin, Michael	Michael Entin	23	Company W
Goldschmidt, Daniel	Daniel Goldschmidt	16	Company P
Gratacos Solsona, Antonio	Antonio Gratacos Solsona	2	Company B
Grilo, Carlos	Carlos Grilo	14	Company N
Hasselberg, Jonas	Jonas Hasselberg	24	Company X
Krschne, Peter	Peter Krschne	11	Company K
Kupkova, Helena	Helena Kupkova	15	Company O

You very often need to clean up data when it comes from external sources, as discussed later in this chapter. Fortunately, the Northwind Traders customer information is in pretty good shape, so you don't need to clean it up before you use it. Using this data, you are ready to open Word to create the mail merge document and get it ready to receive your Excel data.

Creating a Word Document to Use for a Mail Merge

Before you can run a mail merge, you need a Word document to populate with your customer information. In this case, you can use the Blue Curve Letterhead template letter (shown below) from the Word template gallery. I've included the template in the companion files, so you can follow along from there. You can also find it and other business templates in Word if you go to **File > New** and search for "letters," or you can use a pre-existing letter of your own. If you want to browse templates for all Office applications, go to https://templates.office.com.

To start, I deleted the template form fields, since you'll be replacing them with mail merge fields. I also updated the letter to suit the needs of this example. In this case, it's a notification that a customer's annual spending level has entitled that customer to a personal shopping concierge. (If you open the template from **File > New**, rather than using the file provided with the companion files, you'll need to do that as well.)

Setting Up and Running a Mail Merge

The mail merge process involves a number of steps. First, open Word and go to **Mailings > Start Mail Merge > Step-by-Step Mail Merge Wizard**.

Word opens a new pane on the right. Select Letters and click Next: Starting Document at the bottom of the pane. The figures below show the steps in the wizard and how you need to fill them out.

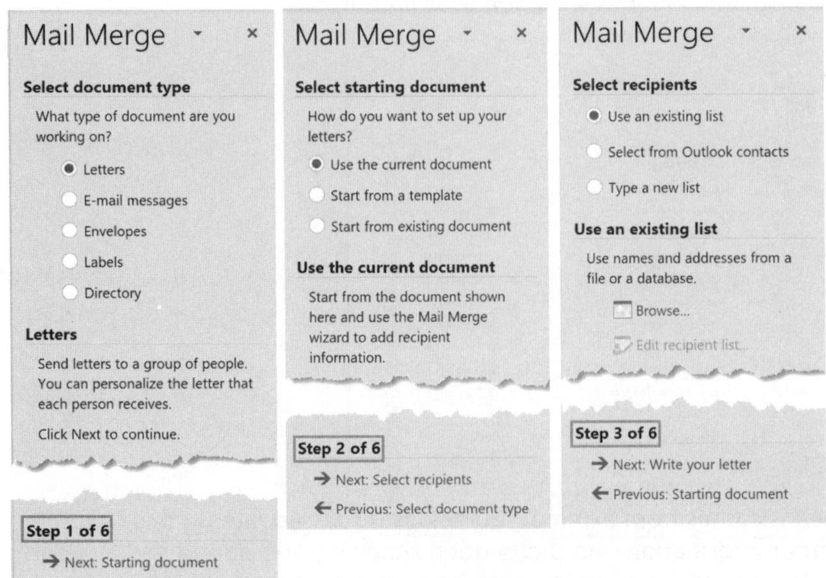

Since you've already opened the Word template, there's no need to do anything other than allow Word to proceed with the Use the Current Document option, so choose the Next: Select Recipients option at the bottom of the Mail Merge dialog.

The next step is to select your data source, which is where you get Excel involved. I've set up a Customers worksheet in the Chapter 12 companion workbook, so choose Use an Existing List, and then click Browse. Excel loads the Select Data Source dialog, where you can browse to wherever you've saved the sample files and select the companion workbook.

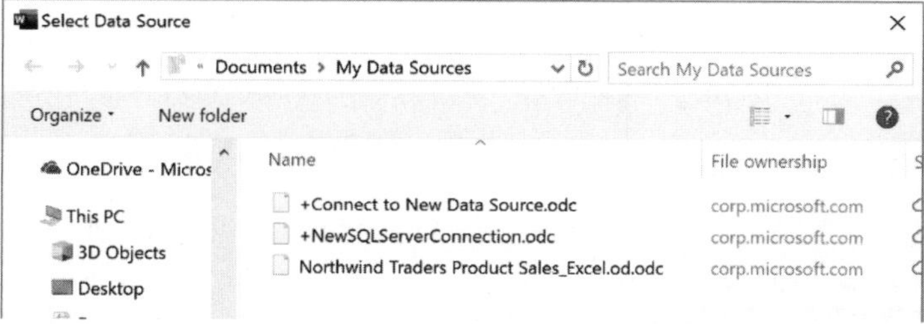

After you click OK, you see a Select Table dialog where you can select the Customers worksheet and click OK.

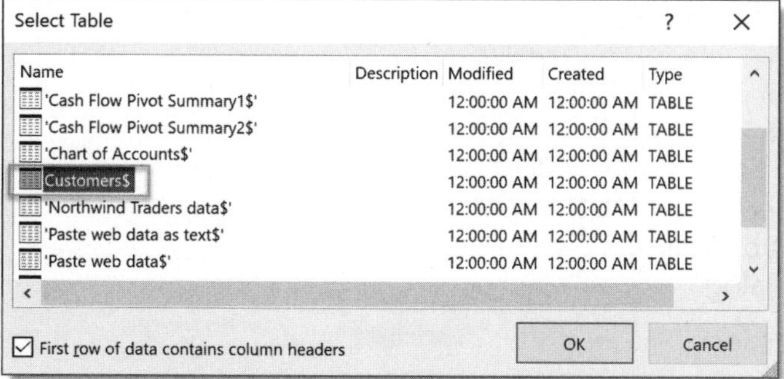

Word gives you a preview of the data. If there are any specific records you don't want to include in the mail merge, you can uncheck them here. If everything looks good, click OK to keep going.

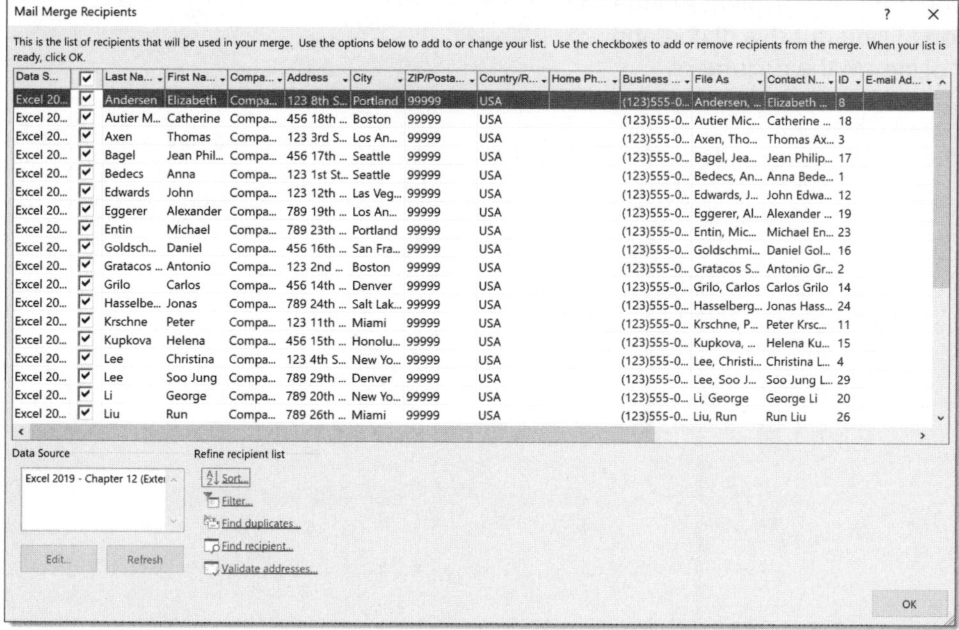

Field Mapping

It is crucial to ensure that you correctly map your data source fields to the Word document. This process, called *field mapping*, is integral to being able to successfully perform mail merges. Put your cursor above the "Dear ," line in your letter and choose the Address Block option either from the Mail Merge pane or the ribbon. Word opens the Insert Address Block dialog, shown below, analyzes your source data, and attempts to pre-populate the fields for you. This is where it's important to have good column names in Excel, like Address, City, State, Zip Code, and so on. If you don't, Word will have a hard time mapping your data fields, and you'll have to do it by hand. In the following example, you can see that Word did a pretty good job matching fields, but it missed State, so click the Match Fields button and choose the correct column for that field. In this case, it's State/Province.

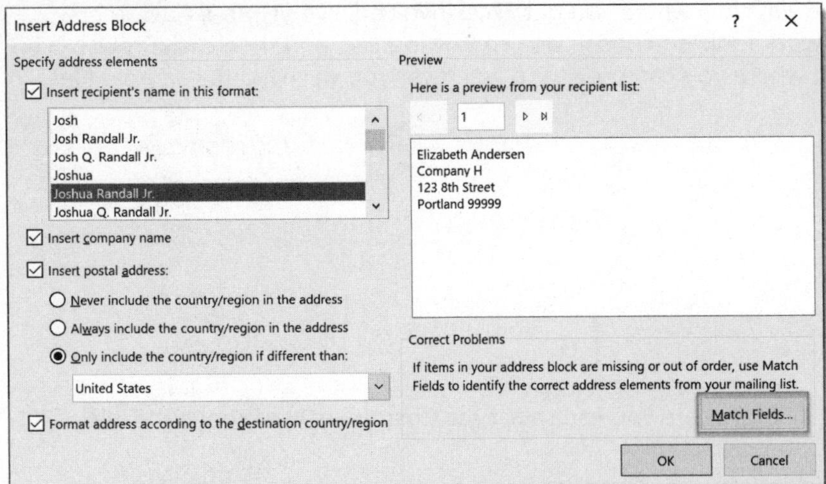

When you're done, Word places «AddressBlock» in the document. That may not look like much, but behind the scenes, Word knows that's a Mail Merge field. If you'll be using the same mail merge data again, you should check the Remember This Matching for This Set of Data Sources on This Computer option at the bottom of the Match Fields dialog.

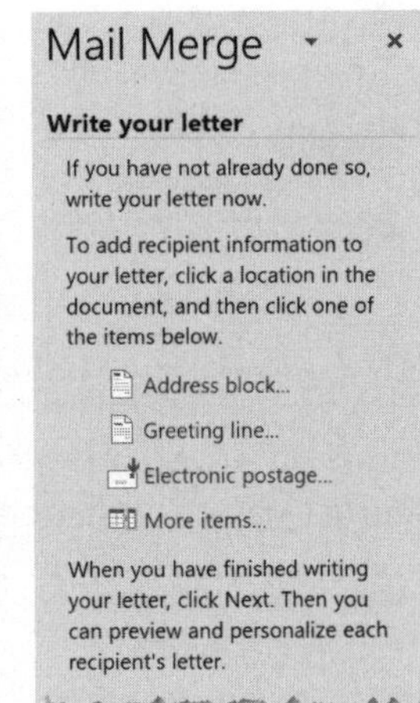

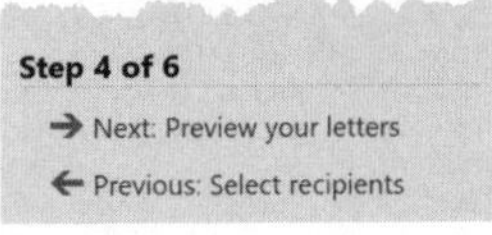

Next, you add a greeting line, so select the "Dear ," section and choose the Greeting Line option from the Mail Merge pane.

You see the Insert Greeting Line dialog, as shown below, where you can choose how you want the recipient's name to be displayed. When you're done filling out this dialog and click OK, Word adds «GreetingLine» in the document.

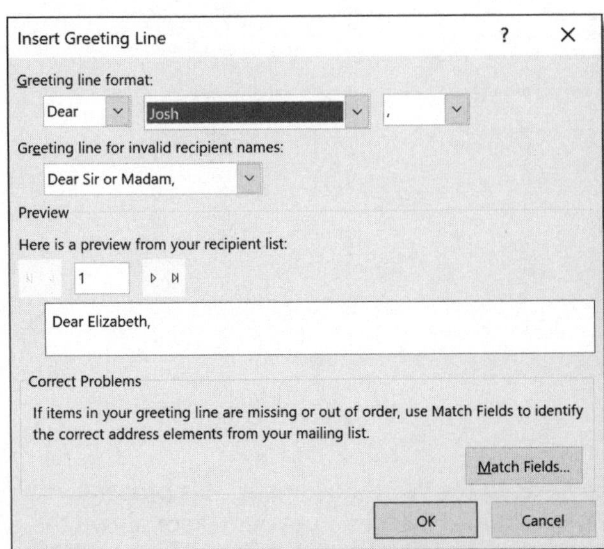

At this point, you may have additional fields to add. For instance, you might want to show someone his or her current account balance or the last item he or she purchased. What merge fields you add depends on the purpose of your letter and your data. In the following example, I've added a few more fields—for the customer's annual purchase amount and the personal concierge's contact information.

«AddressBlock»

Adding multiple merge fields

«GreetingLine»

Your annual purchases of «Annual_Purchases» have raised you to our Valued Customer status, which is an honor accorded to only a select few. This gives you access to your own personal concierge, «Concierge», who you can reach directly at «Concierge_Email», or (800) 555-1212 ext. «Concierge_Extenstion».

If you have any questions at all, please don't hesitate to reach out to me directly.

Previewing the Letter

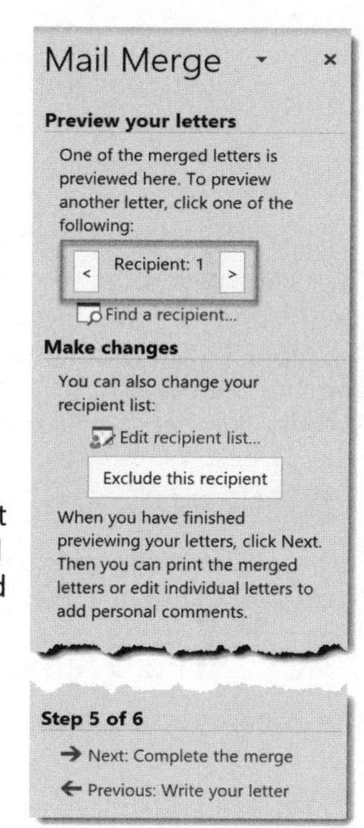

The next step is to cycle through your letter to make sure it looks okay. You can use the arrows in the Mail Merge pane to go through them, or you can use the record selectors on Word's Mailings tab. If you find any issues with the data, you can select the Edit Recipient List option to change the data in Excel. You can also choose to exclude certain recipients. If your source data is consistent, you'll probably only need to look through a few records to make sure they're displaying the way you want. While you're doing this, you can also change the design, layout, or wording of your letter, and you can add new fields, if needed.

While you're previewing this letter, you should immediately notice that, as shown below, the Annual Purchases field is not formatted. But if you look back at the customer list in Excel, you see that it is formatted there. To fix this, you need to use *field switches*, which allow you to apply formatting directly in Word. You might think that you could just add a $ before the merge field and be done with it—and you could, but what about the comma to separate hundreds and thousands? Field switches take all this into account.

Your annual purchases of 9615.6727 have raised you to our Valued Customer status, w is an honor accorded to only a select few. This gives you access to your own personal concierge, Debbie Tibbets, who you can reach directly at d.tibbets@northwindtraders.cc (800) 555-1212 ext. 1234.

Press **Alt+F9** to toggle the MergeField view. As shown below, it looks like a lot of gibberish, but when you take a closer look at it, you see a definite logic.

```
{ DATE \@ "M/d/yyyy" }

{ ADDRESSBLOCK \f "<<_FIRSTO_>><< _LASTO_>><< _SUFFIXO_>>
<<_COMPANY_
>><<_STREET1_
>><<_STREET2_
>><<_CITY_>><<, _STATE_>><< _POSTAL_>><<
_COUNTRY_>>" \l 1033 \c 2 \e "United States" \d }

{ GREETINGLINE \f "<<_BEFORE_ Dear >><<_NICKO_>> <<_AFTER_ ,>>" \l 1033 \e "Dear
Sir or Madam," }

Your annual purchases of { MERGEFIELD Annual_Purchases } have raised you to our Valued
Customer status, which is an honor accorded to only a select few. This gives you access to
your own personal concierge, { MERGEFIELD Concierge }, who you can reach directly at {
MERGEFIELD Concierge_Email }, or (800) 555-1212 ext. { MERGEFIELD
Concierge_Extenstion }.
```

MergeField view

For example, you can see where Word created a mergefield for the date at the top of the letter. If you change the "M/d/yyyy" format, you'll see the change as soon as you toggle the MERGEFIELD view back off by pressing **Alt+F9** again. In Chapter 6, we discussed using the TEXT function in Excel to convert numeric entries; field switches are very similar to that, and you can use them to format dates, phone numbers, zip codes, Social Security numbers, and so on. The following example shows how to change the date format.

{ DATE \@ "MMMM d, yyyy" } → January 4, 2019

Just as you can apply formatting to a date field, you can apply formatting to a currency field, which you need to do with the Annual Purchases field, like this:

{ MERGEFIELD Annual_Purchases \# "$###,0.00"}

The example below shows the result.

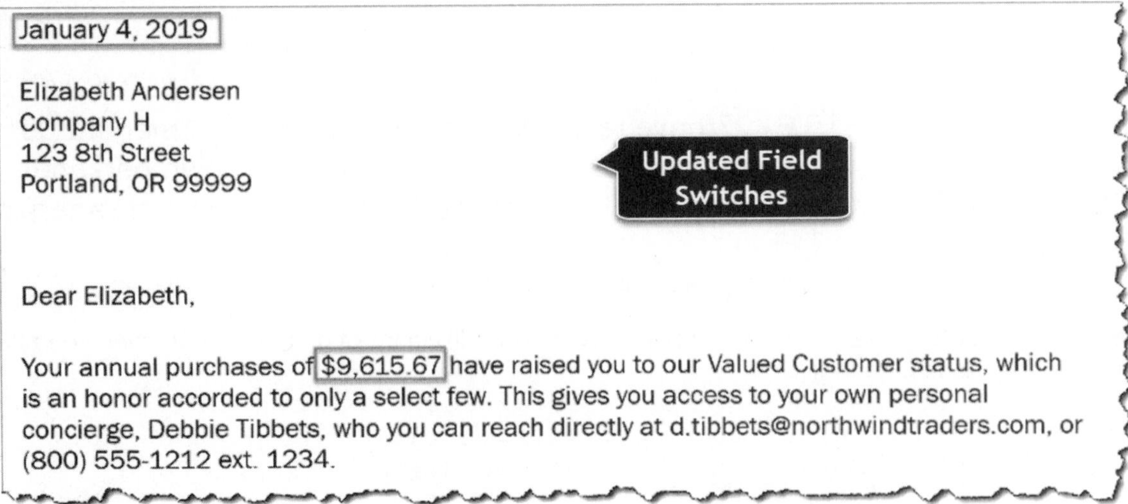

January 4, 2019

Elizabeth Andersen
Company H
123 8th Street
Portland, OR 99999

Dear Elizabeth,

Your annual purchases of $9,615.67 have raised you to our Valued Customer status, which is an honor accorded to only a select few. This gives you access to your own personal concierge, Debbie Tibbets, who you can reach directly at d.tibbets@northwindtraders.com, or (800) 555-1212 ext. 1234.

Completing the Merge

To complete the mail merge you've been working with throughout the past several sections, select the Print option and follow the dialogs to select which records you want to print.

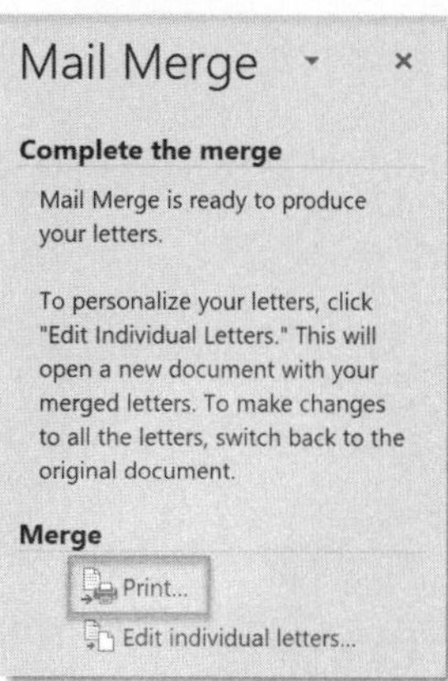

You can choose to print all, print the current record, or print a range, where you input the starting and ending record numbers. Next, select your printer or PDF, followed by where you want to save the merged document. When the merge is complete, all the records are displayed in Word.

Additional Mail Merge Steps

When your mail merge is complete, you can come back to it any time and rerun it. If you're physically mailing your letter as opposed to emailing it, you also have the option of creating envelopes or mailing labels. I should also point out that you're not limited to creating customer correspondence with a mail merge. You can use any list-based data to create things like nametags for an event, recipes, or asset tags for corporate equipment.

When you reopen a Word document that has been set up for a mail merge, you get a prompt about updating the data source, as shown below.

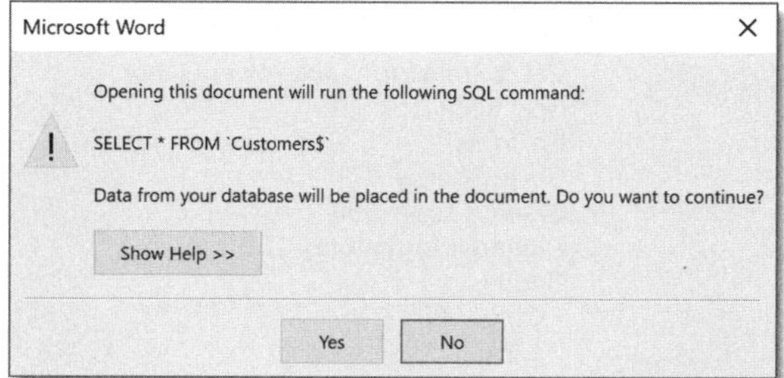

If your data source gets disconnected because it's been moved, you get an error message, but Word gives you a chance to reconnect, as shown below. You will run into this issue when you try to use the mail merge companion file for this chapter, so you'll need to browse to wherever you saved the companion files to reconnect.

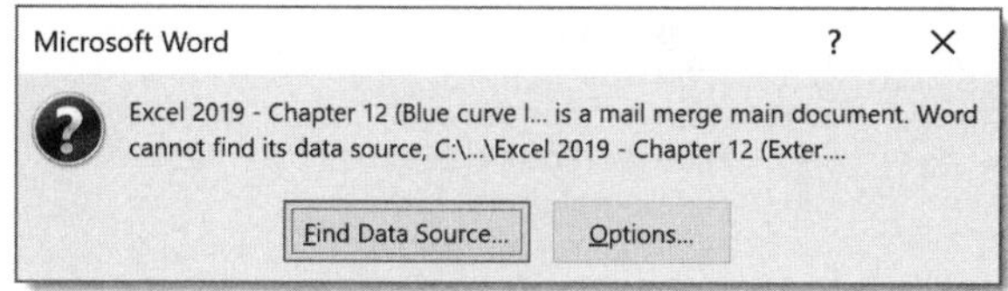

Chapter Summary

- In this chapter you learned how to use Excel to retrieve data from other data sources with Power Query. While this chapter doesn't cover every external data source, it gives you a good idea of where you can look and how to do it. When you get the hang of retrieving data, it's remarkably uncomplicated, provided that the data source is readily accessible. (However, not all Internet data is formatted to be readily retrieved.)
- This chapter shows the steps involved in creating a mail merge document in Microsoft Word, beginning with choosing a template from the Word Template Gallery, linking the document to some Excel data, and adjusting the template based on how Word formats the data from Excel.
- Finally, this chapter looks at how to use field switches and the MergeField view to format Excel data that loses its original formatting when Word merges it into a document.

Index

Power Pivot AND Power BI
The Excel User's Guide to the Data Revolution
2nd Edition
Summary Facts
Rob Collie & Avichal Singh

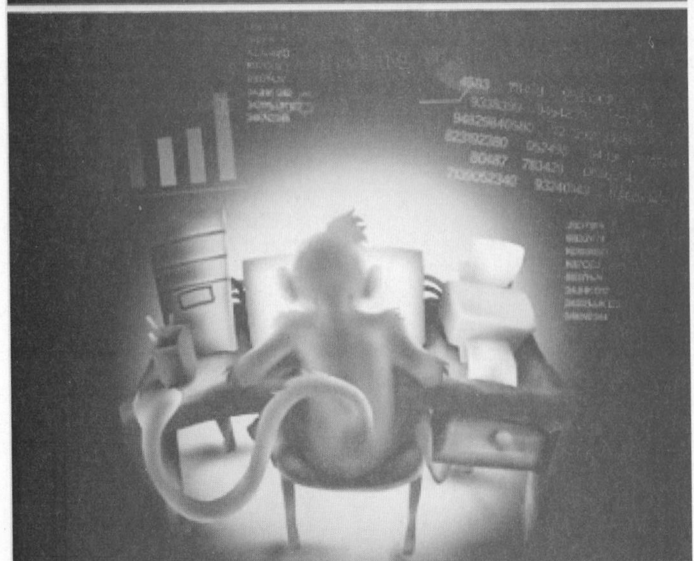

NATIONAL GEOGRAPHIC LEARNING | CENGAGE Learning

FOUNDATIONS

READING EXPLORER

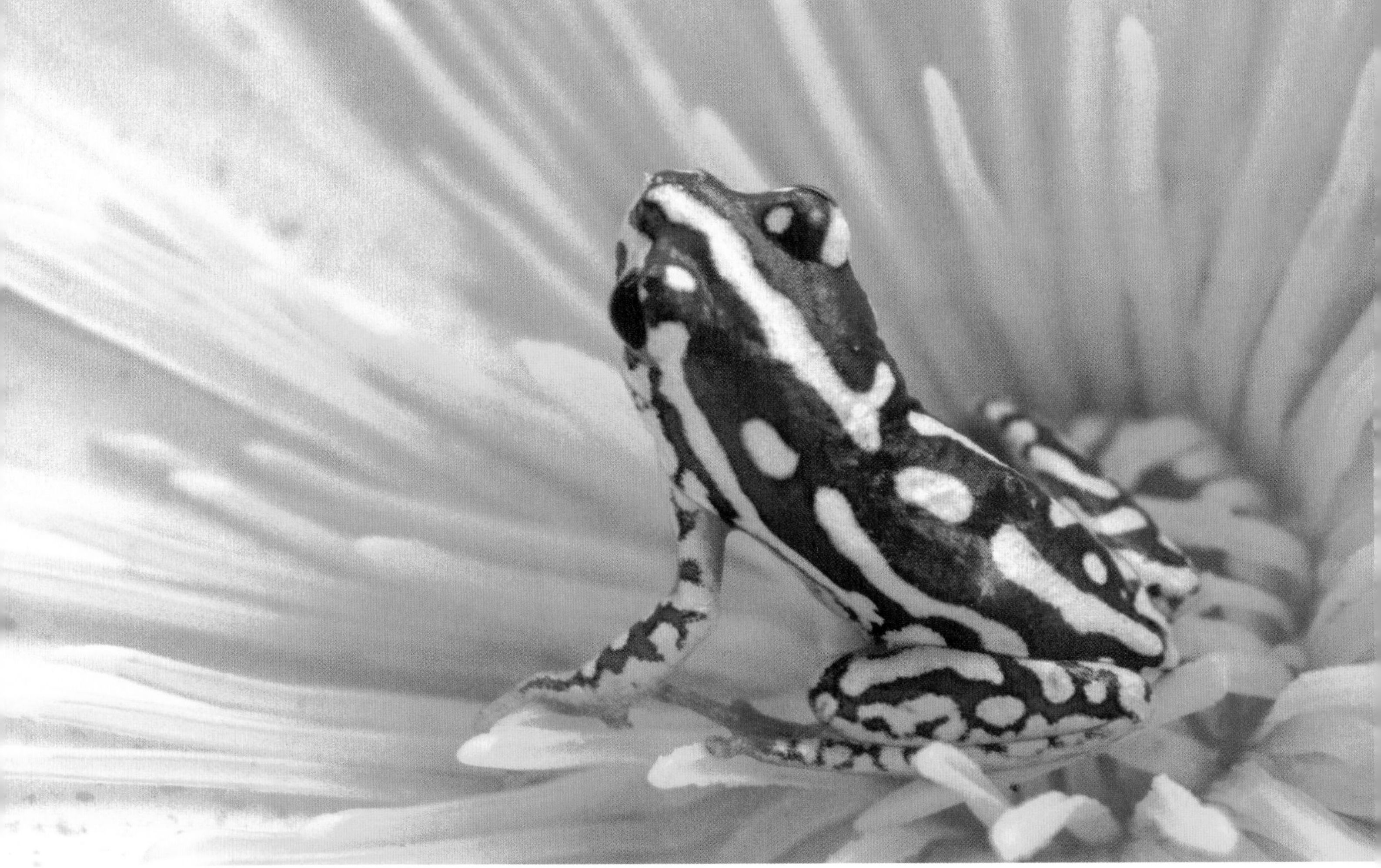

BECKY TARVER-CHASE • DAVID BOHLKE

Second Edition

Australia • Brazil • Japan • Korea • Mexico • Singapore • Spain • United Kingdom • United States

Reading Explorer Foundations
Second Edition

Becky Tarver-Chase and David Bohlke

Publisher: Andrew Robinson

Executive Editor: Sean Bermingham

Senior Development Editor: Derek Mackrell

Development Editor: Claire Tan

Assistant Editor: Melissa Pang

Director of Global Marketing: Ian Martin

Product Marketing Manager: Lindsey Miller

Senior Director of Production: Michael Burggren

Senior Content Project Manager: Tan Jin Hock

Manufacturing Planner: Mary Beth Hennebury

Compositor: SPi Global

Cover/Text Design: Creative Director: Christopher Roy, Art Director: Scott Baker, Designer: Alex Dull

Cover Photo: Frans Lanting/ National Geographic Creative

Student Book with Online Workbook:
ISBN-13: 978-1-305-25450-3

Student Book:
ISBN-13: 978-1-285-84700-9

National Geographic Learning
20 Channel Center Street
Boston, MA 02210
USA

Cengage Learning is a leading provider of customized learning solutions with office locations around the globe, including Singapore, the United Kingdom, Australia, Mexico, Brazil, and Japan.

Cengage Learning products are represented in Canada by Nelson Education, Ltd.

Visit National Geographic Learning online at **ngl.cengage.com**

Visit our corporate website at **www.cengage.com**

Printed in the United States of America
8 9 10 11 12   23 22 21 20 19

Contents

Scope and Sequence

Unit	Theme	Reading
1	**Mysteries**	**A:** Have Aliens Visited Us? **B:** The Lost City of Atlantis
2	**Favorite Foods**	**A:** The History of Pizza **B:** The Hottest Chilies
3	**Cool Jobs**	**A:** Training Grizzlies! **B:** Getting the Shot
4	**Shipwrecks**	**A:** I've Found the *Titanic*! **B:** Treasure Ship
5	**Science Investigators**	**A:** At the Scene of a Crime **B:** The Disease Detective
6	**Explorers and Pioneers**	**A:** Who Was Sacagawea? **B:** Polar Pioneer
7	**Mind's Eye**	**A:** The Meaning of Dreams **B:** Seeing the Impossible
8	**Animal Wonders**	**A:** A Penguin Family **B:** Do Animals Laugh?
9	**Incredible Domes**	**A:** A Love Poem in Stone **B:** The Great Dome of Florence
10	**Wild Weather**	**A:** A Warming World **B:** Freaky Forces of Nature
11	**Giants of the Past**	**A:** The Mammoth's Tale **B:** Sea Monsters
12	**Technology**	**A:** The Robots Are Coming! **B:** How Will We Live in 2035?

Reading Skill	Vocabulary Building	Video
A: Scanning **B:** Skimming	**A:** Usage: *research* **B:** Usage: *solid*	Loch Ness Mystery
A: Identifying the Parts of a Passage **B:** Pronoun Reference	**A:** Word Partnership: *basic* **B:** Word Partnership: *painful*	A Taste of Mexico
A: Finding the Correct Definition of a Word in a Dictionary **B:** Understanding the Use of Commas	**A:** Thesaurus: *difficult* **B:** Word Partnership: *spend*	Right Dog for the Job
A: Identifying a Paragraph's Main Idea **B:** Recognizing Compound Subjects and Objects	**A:** Usage: *agree* **B:** Usage: *coast/beach*	Saving Ocean Life
A: Inferring Meaning **B:** Identifying the Purpose of a Paragraph	**A:** Word Partnership: *space* **B:** Word Link: *-ous*	Virus Detectives
A: Creating a Timeline of Events **B:** Understanding Compound Nouns	**A:** Usage: *village/town/city* **B:** Usage: *drive/ride*	Native Americans
A: Creating a Concept Map **B:** Understanding Compound Sentences	**A:** Word Partnership: *problem* **B:** Word Partnership: *mistake*	Parasomnia
A: Paraphrasing **B:** Identifying Supporting Details	**A:** Word Partnership: *enter* **B:** Word Partnership: *similar*	Penguins in Trouble
A: Understanding Complex Sentences **B:** Recognizing Prepositions	**A:** Word Partnership: *promise* **B:** Thesaurus: *material*	Brunelleschi's Dome
A: Identifying Text Types **B:** Identifying Cause and Effect	**A:** Word Partnership: *temperature* **B:** Usage: *drop vs. fall*	Storm of the Century
A: Recognizing Active and Passive Sentences **B:** Organizing Information in a Chart	**A:** Usage: *further/farther* **B:** Usage: *probably/definitely/possibly*	Days of the Dinosaurs
A: Supporting Ideas with Examples **B:** Understanding Prefixes and Suffixes	**A:** Word Partnership: *operate* **B:** Word Partnership: *future*	Deep-sea Robot

Welcome to Reading Explorer!

In this book, you'll travel the globe, explore different cultures, and discover new ways of looking at the world. You'll also become a better reader!

What's new in the Second Edition?

New and updated topics

Explore the animal world, the lives of explorers and pioneers, and amazing feats of architecture.

3B

Getting the Shot

Before You Read

National Geographic photographer Joel Sartore photographs an Adélie penguin chick in Antarctica.

A. Discussion. Look at the photo above and read the caption. Then discuss these questions with a partner.

1. What kinds of things do you usually take photos of?
2. Do you think a photographer's job is easy?

B. Skim. Skim the interview on pages 42–43. Then write each interview question above its answer in the passage.

a. I want to be a photographer. Do you have any advice for me?
b. What kind of photographers is the *National Geographic Magazine* looking for?
c. Is it difficult to get a job as a photographer today?
d. How did you become a *National Geographic* photographer?

Unit 3B 41

New Reading Skills section

Learn how to read strategically—and think critically as you read.

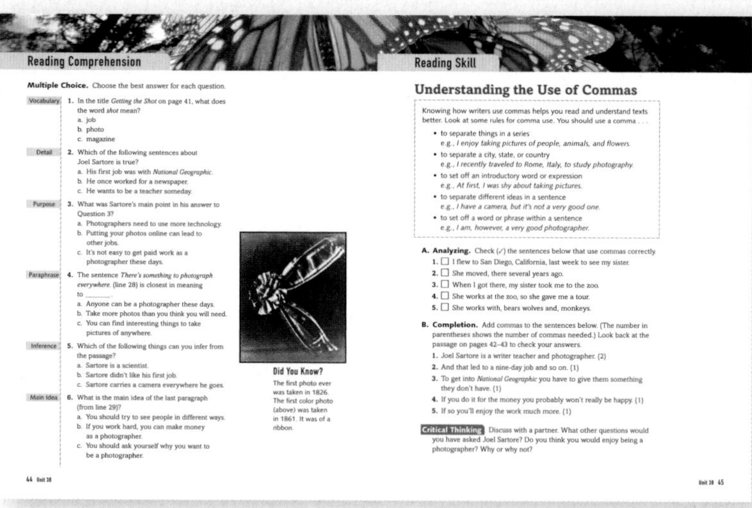

Reading Comprehension

Multiple Choice. Choose the best answer for each question.

Vocabulary 1. In the title *Getting the Shot* on page 41, what does the word *shot* mean?
a. job
b. photo
c. magazine

Detail 2. Which of the following sentences about Joel Sartore is true?
a. His first job was with *National Geographic*.
b. He once worked for a newspaper.
c. He wants to be a teacher someday.

Purpose 3. What was Sartore's main point in his answer to Question 3?
a. Photographers need to use more technology.
b. Putting your photos online can lead to other jobs.
c. It's not easy to get paid work as a photographer these days.

Paraphrase 4. The sentence *There's something to photograph everywhere.* (line 28) is closest in meaning to ______.
a. Anyone can be a photographer these days.
b. Take more photos than you think you will need.
c. You can find interesting things to take pictures of anywhere.

Inference 5. Which of the following things can you infer from the passage?
a. Sartore is a scientist.
b. Sartore didn't like his first job.
c. Sartore carries a camera everywhere he goes.

Main Idea 6. What is the main idea of the last paragraph (from line 29)?
a. You should try to see people in different ways.
b. If you work hard, you can make money as a photographer.
c. You should ask yourself why you want to be a photographer.

Did You Know?
The first photo ever was taken in 1826. The first color photo (above) was taken in 1861. It was of a ribbon.

Reading Skill

Understanding the Use of Commas

Knowing how writers use commas helps you read and understand texts better. Look at some rules for comma use. You should use a comma . . .

- to separate things in a series
  e.g., *I enjoy taking pictures of people, animals, and flowers.*
- to separate a city, state, or country
  e.g., *I recently traveled to Rome, Italy, to study photography.*
- to set off an introductory word or expression
  e.g., *At first, I was shy about taking pictures.*
- to separate different ideas in a sentence
  e.g., *I have a camera, but it's not a very good one.*
- to set off a word or phrase within a sentence
  e.g., *I am, however, a very good photographer.*

A. Analyzing. Check (✓) the sentences below that use commas correctly.

1. ☐ I flew to San Diego, California, last week to see my sister.
2. ☐ She moved, there several years ago.
3. ☐ When I got there, my sister took me to the zoo.
4. ☐ She works at the zoo, so she gave me a tour.
5. ☐ She works with, bears wolves and, monkeys.

B. Completion. Add commas to the sentences below. (The number in parentheses shows the number of commas needed.) Look back at the passage on pages 42–43 to check your answers.

1. Joel Sartore is a writer teacher and photographer. (2)
2. And that led to a nine-day job and so on. (1)
3. To get into *National Geographic* you have to give them something they don't have. (1)
4. If you do it for the money you probably won't really be happy. (1)
5. If so you'll enjoy the work much more. (1)

Critical Thinking Discuss with a partner. What other questions would you have asked Joel Sartore? Do you think you would enjoy being a photographer? Why or why not?

44 Unit 3B — Unit 3B 45

Expanded Viewing section

Apply your language skills when you watch a specially adapted National Geographic video.

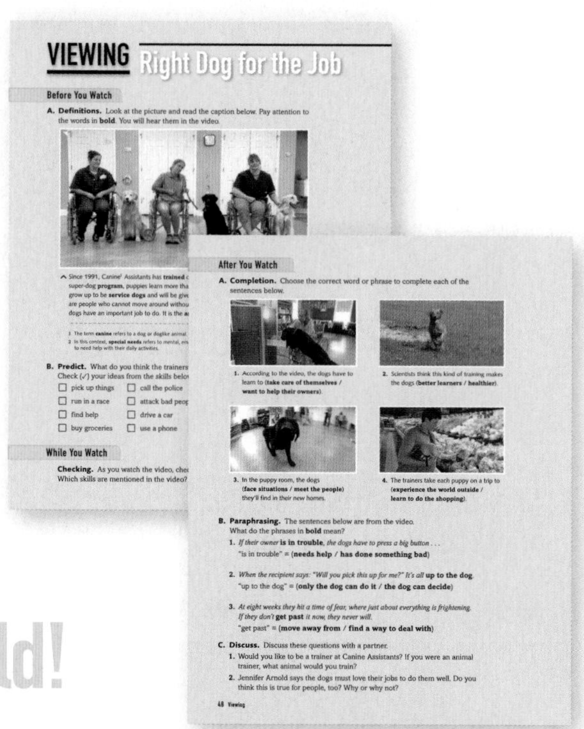

VIEWING Right Dog for the Job

Before You Watch

A. Definitions. Look at the picture and read the caption below. Pay attention to the words in **bold**. You will hear them in the video.

After You Watch

A. Completion. Choose the correct word or phrase to complete each of the sentences below.

1. According to the video, the dogs have to learn to (**take care of themselves / want to help their owners**).
2. Scientists think this kind of training makes the dogs (**better learners / healthier**).
3. In the puppy room, the dogs (**face situations / meet the people**) they'll find in their new homes.
4. The trainers take each puppy on a trip to (**experience the world outside / learn to do the shopping**).

B. Predict. What do you think the trainers ... Check (✓) your ideas from the skills below ...

☐ pick up things ☐ call the police
☐ run in a race ☐ attack bad people
☐ find help ☐ drive a car
☐ buy groceries ☐ use a phone

While You Watch

Checking. As you watch the video, check ... Which skills are mentioned in the video?

B. Paraphrasing. The sentences below are from the video. What do the phrases in **bold** mean?

1. *If their owner* **is in trouble**, *the dogs have to press a big button . . .*
   "is in trouble" = (**needs help / has done something bad**)
2. *When the recipient says: "Will you pick this up for me?" It's all* **up to the dog**.
   "up to the dog" = (**only the dog can do it / the dog can decide**)
3. *At eight weeks they hit a time of fear, where just about everything is frightening. If they don't* **get past** *it now, they never will.*
   "get past" = (**move away from / find a way to deal with**)

C. Discuss. Discuss these questions with a partner.

1. Would you like to be a trainer at Canine Assistants? If you were an animal trainer, what animal would you train?
2. Jennifer Arnold says the dogs must love their jobs to do them well. Do you think this is true for people, too? Why or why not?

48 Viewing

Now you're ready to explore your world!

1

Mysteries

At the top of Mauna Kea, in Hawaii, a mysterious red cloud hangs above a snowy mountaintop.

Warm Up

Discuss these questions with a partner.

1. Do you think there are things that science cannot explain? If yes, give an example.
2. What do you think about when you read or hear the word *mystery*?

Sometimes **pilots** see mysterious lights in the sky. Others have seen **aircraft** that look like **disks** or "flying saucers." We call these "UFOs" (unidentified flying objects). Some people think UFOs are **alien** spaceships visiting Earth.

Before You Read

A. Definitions. Look at the photo and read the caption. Then match each word in **bold** with its definition.

1. pilots	•	•	a. machines that fly
2. aircraft	•	•	b. people who fly airplanes
3. disks	•	•	c. from other places or planets
4. alien	•	•	d. objects with a round shape

B. Skim. Quickly skim pages 9–10. What is the passage mainly about? Circle **a**, **b**, or **c**. Then read the passage to check your answer.

a. UFO sightings around the world

b. a famous place to see UFOs

c. famous movies about UFOs

Have Aliens Visited Us?

Many people have stories about seeing aliens. Here are two.

Judy Varns works for a group called the Mutual UFO Network. The **purpose** of this group is to **research** UFO sightings.[1] Varns thinks a place called Area 51, in Nevada in the U.S., may be the best place on Earth to see UFOs. One day, she took some photos in the **area** and saw something she thinks is a UFO. "We saw this little disk-shaped thing in our photos. It's kind of exciting," she says.

Pat Travis lives near Area 51. One night, she saw a **strange** light in the sky. The light's **movements** were very unusual. Travis saw the lights move sideways[2] and up and down. She saw them make many strange moves. Travis thinks it was a UFO.

1 When someone has a **sighting** of something unusual, they see it.

2 Moving **sideways** is moving from left to right or right to left.

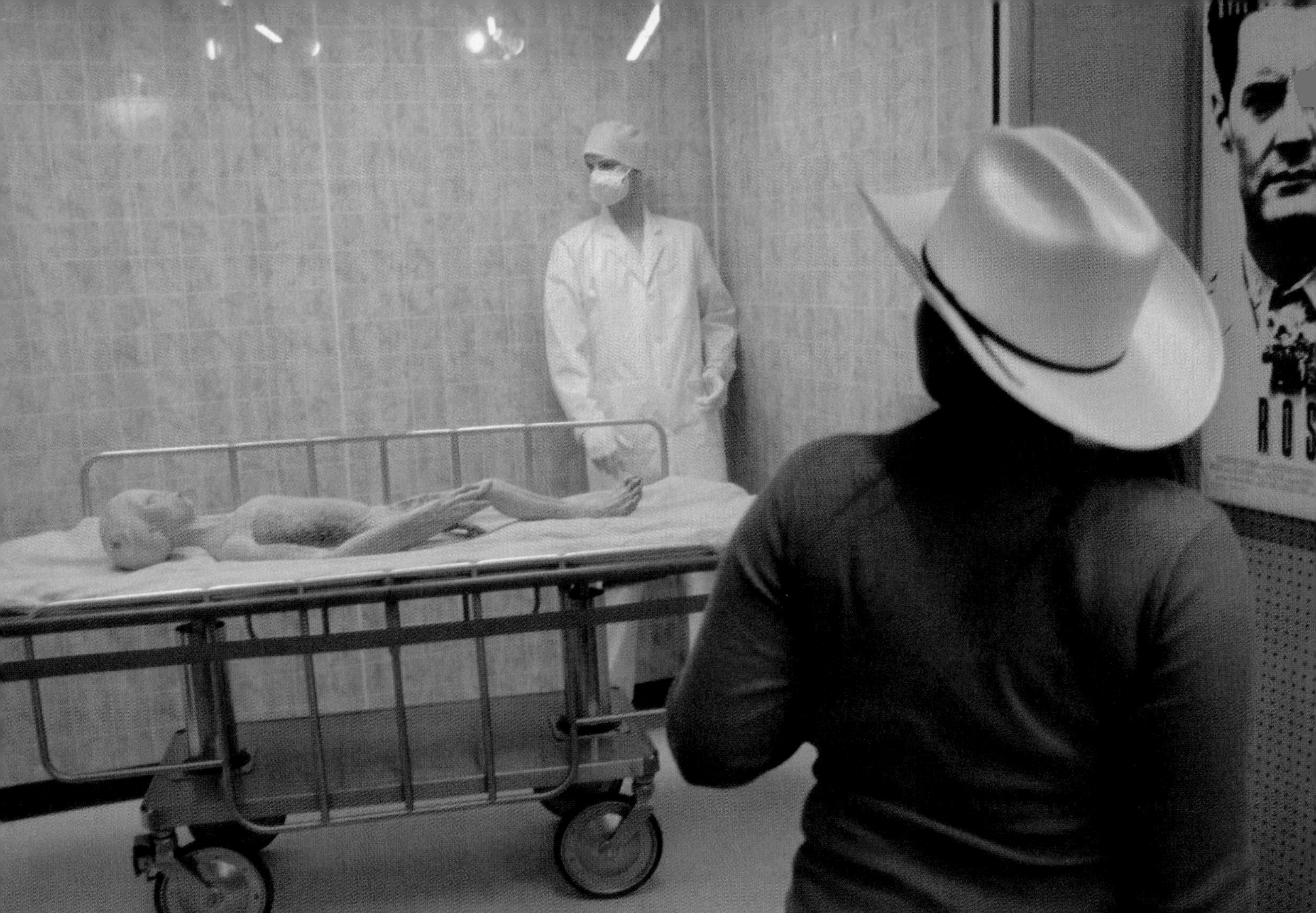

A fake alien body lies in a display in Roswell, New Mexico, where people think an alien ship landed on Earth. Some believe the ship and aliens were taken to Area 51.

Secrets of Area 51

Some people think Area 51 is where the U.S. Air Force[3] keeps **secrets**, like UFOs that came to Earth and the aliens inside them. But really, Area 51 is a place the U.S. Air Force uses to test new **technology**, such as new kinds of aircraft.

James McGaha is a pilot who flew airplanes at Area 51. "There is absolutely[4] no UFO activity at Area 51," he says. "No flying saucers, no live aliens, no dead aliens."

So what did Varns and Travis see? Bill Fox worked at Area 51, too. He thinks he knows the answer. "We did build some strange-looking airplanes," he says. "I could see why some people would think they were UFOs."

So are UFOs real? You'll have to **decide** for yourself. But if you do visit Nevada, keep your eyes on the skies!

3 An **air force** is the part of an army that fights in the air.

4 **Absolutely** means "totally."

Reading Comprehension

Multiple Choice. Choose the best answer for each question.

Detail

1. Which of these sentences about Judy Varns is true?
   a. She works at an airport in Area 51.
   b. She helped Bill Fox build new airplanes.
   c. She works for a group that studies UFO sightings.

Main Idea

2. What is the main idea of the second paragraph (from line 9)?
   a. Pat Travis lives near Area 51.
   b. Pat Travis thinks she saw a UFO.
   c. Pat Travis has seen many unusual things.

Vocabulary

3. In line 18, the word *kinds* means __________.
   a. a lot
   b. types
   c. people

Detail

4. What was James McGaha's job at Area 51?
   a. He flew airplanes.
   b. He made airplanes.
   c. He took secret photos.

Paraphrase

5. What does *"I could see why some people would think they were UFOs."* (lines 24–25) mean?
   a. I agree with people who believe in UFOs.
   b. I saw UFOs near Area 51 with my own eyes.
   c. I understand why some people think they saw UFOs.

Inference

6. Which person is likely to say "*I believe UFOs are real, and could be alien spaceships.*"?
   a. Bill Fox
   b. Judy Varns
   c. James McGaha

Did You Know?

There is a UFO sighting somewhere on Earth every three minutes.

Scanning

You scan a text when you want to find specific information. When you scan, you only look for the information you want. You don't read the rest of the text. For example, for the question *Where is Area 51?*, look through the text for a place name, possibly a word beginning with a capital letter (*Nevada* or *U.S.*).

A. Scan. Look back at the passage on pages 9–10. Find and underline these words in the passage as quickly as you can.

1. Earth
2. sideways
3. flew
4. saucers
5. dead
6. skies

B. Scan. Read the questions below. Think about what answers you need to look for. Then scan the passage on pages 9–10, and write the answers. Try to find the answers as quickly as you can.

1. Who works for the Mutual UFO Network? __________
2. Who lives near Area 51? __________
3. What does the U.S. Air Force test at Area 51? __________
4. What is James McGaha's job? __________
5. What did Bill Fox build? __________

Critical Thinking Discuss with a partner. Do you think UFOs are real? Why or why not? What other things do you think could explain what Judy Varns and Pat Travis saw?

A model of a saucer-shaped aircraft, the Couzinet Aerodyne RC-360, built in France, in 1952.

Vocabulary Practice

A. Matching. Read the information. Then match each word in **red** with its definition below.

Crop Circles

A farmer wakes up to find something very **strange** in his field. Someone or something has made strange shapes in the field by pushing down his crops.[1] The shapes can only be seen from the sky! These are called crop circles.

Where do these crop circles come from? Some people think that UFOs make the crop circles when they land. But **research** shows most crop circles are made by people. The **technology** to make them is very simple—just a rope and some wood.

What is the purpose of making crop circles? Some people make them so others will believe in aliens. Some people make crop circles just for fun. Today, some farmers even make them to mark out each different **area** of their farms.

1 **Crops** are plants grown in large amounts.

A crop circle is made when something pushes the crops down, leaving empty spaces in the field.

1. ______________: hard to understand or explain
2. ______________: the reason you do something
3. ______________: a part of a place, or of some land
4. ______________: the use of science and machines to do things
5. ______________: the work of trying to find facts about something

B. Words in Context. Complete each sentence with the correct answer.

1. When you **decide** what to have for lunch, you ________ what you want.
   a. don't know b. know
2. A **secret** is something you want __________ to know about.
   a. very few people b. a lot of people
3. An example of **technology** is __________.
   a. a computer b. a song
4. The **purpose** of your English textbook is to __________.
   a. have 160 pages b. help you read better
5. An example of **movement** is __________.
   a. something you hear b. something you do

Usage

Research can be used as a verb or a noun. *Professor Baker **researches** UFOs. His **research** will take five years.*

Before You Read

^ Many believe that Atlantis had rings of land with water between them. A temple stood right in the center of the island.

A. Matching. Look at the picture and read the information below. Then match each word in **bold** with its definition.

Long ago, the Greek writer Plato wrote about Atlantis—an **island** that **sank** into the sea. In his story, the people of Atlantis were very **rich**. But they were also very **greedy**. They wanted too much, so they lost everything.

1. ____________: went underwater
2. ____________: having a lot of money
3. ____________: land with water around it
4. ____________: wanting a lot of money, things, or food

B. Scan. Quickly scan the passage on the next page. Remember that names of people and places usually start with capital letters.

1. What names of people can you find? Underline them.
2. What names of places are mentioned? Circle them.

The Lost City of ATLANTIS

Most people have heard the story of the **lost** island of Atlantis. But is any part of the story true?

Over two thousand years ago, the Greek writer Plato wrote about Atlantis, an island in the Atlantic Ocean. The island's people were very rich. They built a big city with many great buildings. At the center of the island, they built a beautiful golden temple.[1] But the people became greedy—they had many things, but they still wanted more. So the gods became angry, and the island was **struck** by earthquakes[2] and very large waves. **Finally**, the whole island sank into the sea.

Many explorers have looked for Atlantis. In 2004, explorer Robert Sarmast **reported** finding the remains[3] of a city under the sea near Cyprus. However, Sarmast and other scientists later found out the **structures** he found under the sea were **natural**, not man-made.

Many people think Atlantis is simply a story. The purpose of the story is to teach people not to be greedy. Richard Ellis wrote a book about Atlantis in 1999. He says "there is not a **piece** of **solid** evidence"[4] for a real Atlantis.

So was the island real or not? We only know one thing: The mystery of Atlantis will be with us for a long time.

1 A **temple** is a building where people practice a religion.
2 An **earthquake** is the shaking of the ground caused by movement of the Earth.
3 The **remains** of something are the parts that are left after most of it is gone.
4 **Evidence** is anything that makes you believe that something is true.

Many people believe very tall waves struck the city before it sank.

Reading Comprehension

Multiple Choice. Choose the best answer for each question.

Gist

1. Another title for this passage could be __________.
   a. Atlantis Sinks
   b. Is Atlantis Real?
   c. I Found Atlantis!

Detail

2. In Plato's story about Atlantis, the people were ________.
   a. angry at the gods
   b. wealthy but greedy
   c. greedy but beautiful

Sequence

3. What happened after Robert Sarmast said he found Atlantis?
   a. He wrote a book about his findings.
   b. Richard Ellis said that Atlantis was not real.
   c. He found out the structures were not man-made.

Main Idea

4. What is the main idea of the third paragraph (from line 12)?
   a. Scientists found out the structures were natural.
   b. Explorers found a city under the sea near Cyprus.
   c. People are looking for Atlantis, but no one has found it.

Vocabulary

5. We can replace the word *simply* (line 17) with ________.
   a. just
   b. easy
   c. sometimes

Paraphrase

6. Which sentence is closest in meaning to *"there is not a piece of solid evidence" for a real Atlantis.* (lines 20–21)?
   a. There is only one reason to believe the Atlantis story is true.
   b. The story of Atlantis is made up of many small pieces.
   c. There is nothing to make us believe the Atlantis story is true.

Did You Know?

The story of Atlantis was first written down in Plato's *Dialogues* in 360 B.C. Even today, Plato is known as one of the great thinkers of all time.

Reading Skill

Skimming

You skim a passage when you look at the whole passage quickly to see what it is about. You do not read every word. Instead, look at the title, headings, photos, and captions. Read the first line of each paragraph, and quickly read the conclusion.

A. Skim or Scan. Look at these reasons for reading. For each reason, should you skim or scan? Check (✓) the correct boxes.

	Skim	Scan
1. to see if a story is funny or serious	☐	☐
2. to find the names of countries mentioned	☐	☐
3. to find a quote (" ") by a scientist	☐	☐
4. to see if the author feels positive about the topic	☐	☐

B. Skim. Quickly skim the passage below. What is it mainly about? Circle **a**, **b**, or **c**.

a. Kimura has found Atlantis in the Pacific Ocean.
b. Kimura believes he has found a lost land near Japan.
c. Kimura has shown that the strange structures he found were made by humans.

The Lost Continent in the Pacific Ocean

People believe that thousands of years ago, like Atlantis, the lost continent of Mu sank because of an earthquake. Today, no one knows if there really was a place called Mu, or where it was.

However, Professor Masaaki Kimura thinks he knows where the remains of Mu are. He believes they are near the Yonaguni Islands of Japan. Kimura thinks the strange structures he has found were made by people. Some other researchers don't think so. No one is sure, but the research continues.

A diver explores the strange steplike structures in the waters near the Yonaguni Islands.

Critical Thinking Discuss with a partner. Can you think of times you scan or skim things outside of class? What kinds of texts do you usually scan or skim?

Vocabulary Practice

A. Completion. Choose the correct words to complete the information below.

Leeds Castle, in England, has a long history. The **1.** (**structure** / **piece**) of the castle is very old, and today, it is empty—except, some say, for the ghost[1] of a big black dog. Some believe that people who see the dog are **2.** (**struck** / **lost**) with bad luck.

But one woman **3.** (**struck** / **reported**) that the dog brought her very good luck. She was sitting by a window in the castle one day. She looked up and saw a big black dog walk through a **4.** (**solid** / **natural**) wall. She got up to look for it—and then a **5.** (**piece** / **natural**) of the window where she was sitting fell into the water below. Thanks to the ghost dog, the lucky woman got out of the castle safely!

1 A **ghost** is the spirit of a dead person or animal.

Is there really the ghost of a dog in Leeds Castle?

B. Words in Context. Read the sentences and circle true (**T**) or false (**F**).

1. When an area is **struck** by a storm, it is suddenly hit by the storm. **T F**
2. Something that is **natural** is made by humans. **T F**
3. If something is **lost**, you know where it is. **T F**
4. When you **report** something has happened, you say it never happened. **T F**
5. You use the word ***finally*** to say something happened after a long time. **T F**

Usage
The word **solid** is used to describe objects that are fixed in shape and volume. **Solid** can also describe information that can be trusted.

VIEWING Loch Ness Mystery

Before You Watch

A. Definitions. Look at the picture and read the caption. Then match the words in **bold** with their definitions below.

This photograph was **published** in London's *Daily Mail* newspaper on April 21, 1934. According to the report, the photograph was taken in Loch Ness, a famous **lake** in Scotland, where a strange **creature** is said to live. Some people are **certain** that the **monster** is real. Others are not so sure.

1. published •	• a. an animal of any type
2. lake •	• b. sure, believing completely in something
3. creature •	• c. an animal of strange or frightening shape or size
4. certain •	• d. put in a book, newspaper, magazine, or online for all to see
5. monster •	• e. a large body of water that is on land and not part of the sea

B. Discuss. Look at the picture again. Then discuss the questions below with a partner.

1. What do you think the picture shows?
2. Do you think it's real?

While You Watch

Checking. As you watch the video, check your answers in **Before You Watch B**. Were your ideas correct?

After You Watch

A. Sequencing. Number these events in the order they really occurred.

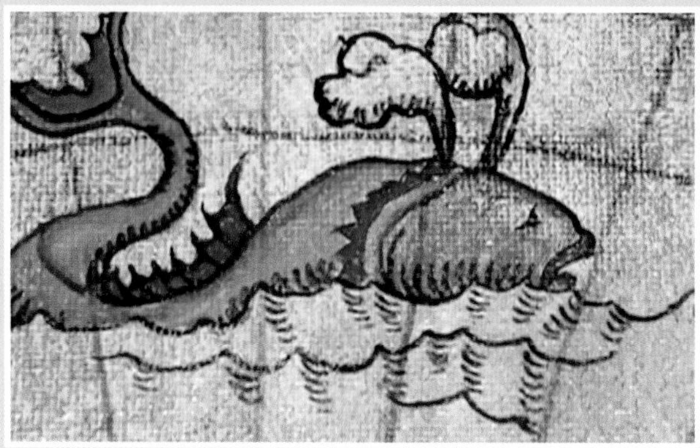

☐ People first reported strange movements in the lake.

☐ This photograph was published in newspapers.

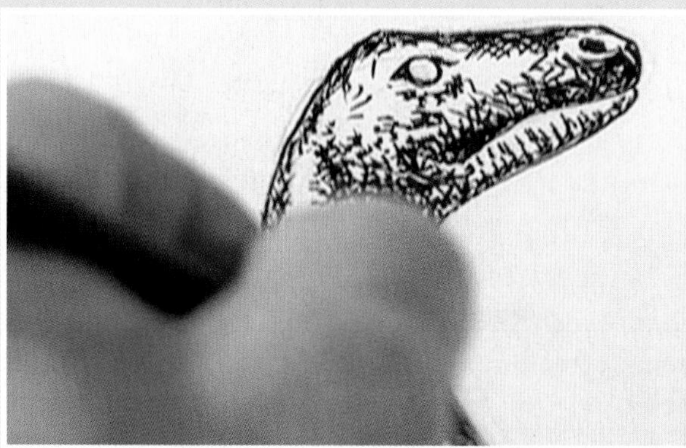

☐ The Loch Ness story continued to grow.

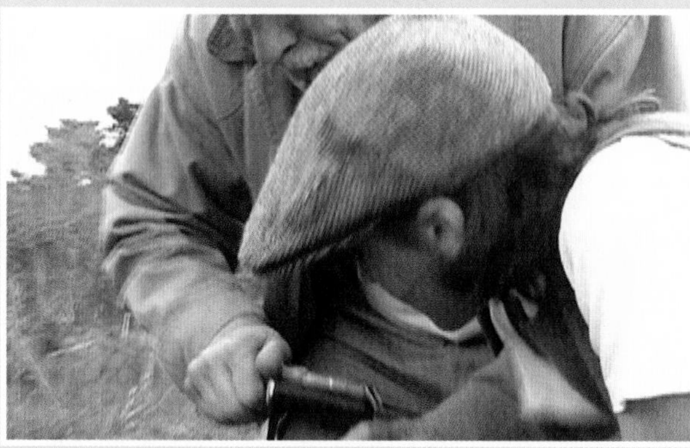

☐ Christian Spurling told people the true story.

☐ "Duke" Wetherall took a photo of "Nessie."

COURIER, TUESDAY, MAY 2, 1933.

ORPHANAGE

il's Confidence Trustees

S TO SCHEME

monthly meeting of the ncil, it was unanimously e draft scheme of the ents (Scotland) Com- the government of the

STRANGE SPECTACLE ON LOCH NESS

What was it?

(FROM A CORRESPONDENT).

Loch Ness has for generations been credited with being the home of a fearsome-looking monster, but, somehow or other, the "water-kelpie," as this legendary creature is called, has always been regarded as a myth, if not a joke. Now, however, comes the news that the beast has been seen once more, for, on Friday of last week, a well-known business man, who lives

CORRESI

INVERNESS TOW

TO THE EDITOR OF TI

Sir,—May I crave columns to express m or harangue, which C has made in your la justified protest aga meeting of the H stead of replying to parently gone out of I think, a most unjus

☐ Newspapers in the 1930s published stories about the monster, but they had no pictures.

B. Discuss. Discuss these questions with a partner.

1. Do you believe there is a creature in Loch Ness? Why do you think so many people have reported seeing Nessie?
2. Look back at the mysteries mentioned in this unit. Which things can scientists explain? Which things can't they explain?

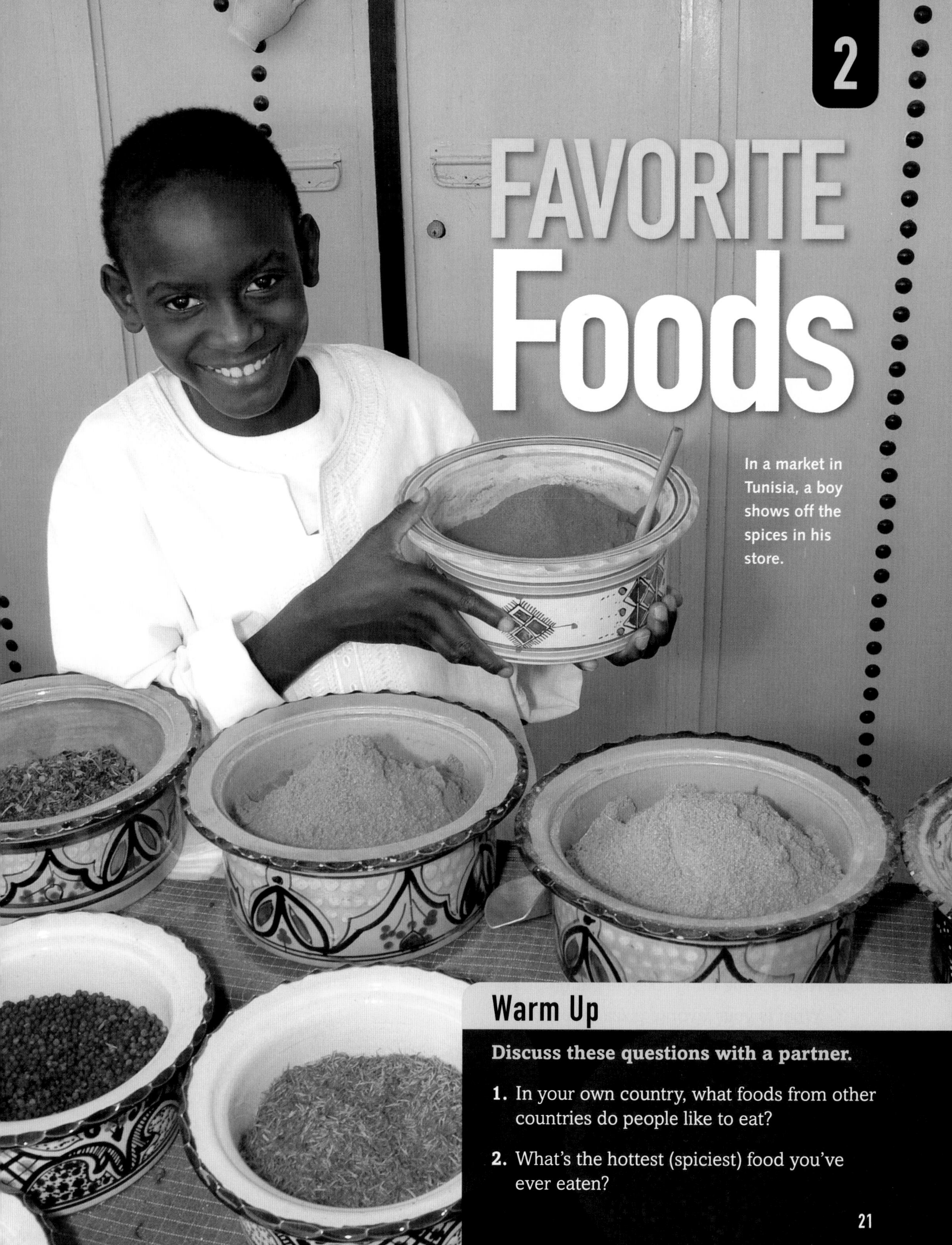

2

FAVORITE Foods

In a market in Tunisia, a boy shows off the spices in his store.

Warm Up

Discuss these questions with a partner.

1. In your own country, what foods from other countries do people like to eat?
2. What's the hottest (spiciest) food you've ever eaten?

Many people believe pizzas were first made by the Greeks. Pictures like this one show the Romans made them, too. They made large, round pieces of bread and put food, olive oil, and spices on them.

Before You Read

A. Quiz. What do you know about pizza? Look at the pictures and captions on pages 22–24. Then answer the questions below.

1. Who made the first pizza?

2. Name some things people put on pizza.

3. What is your favorite pizza topping?

B. Predict. Read the title and subheadings on pages 23–24. Check (✓) the questions you think the passage answers.

☐ Where is pizza from?

☐ What kind of pizza do most people like?

☐ When did people first put tomatoes on pizza?

2A

The History of PIZZA

^ The foods that people put on top of their pizzas are called "toppings." Lombardi's, in New York City, is said to be the first pizza restaurant in the U.S.

Today, pizza is one of the world's favorite foods. All over the world, people make different pizzas, with different **ingredients**. But where does pizza come from? And who made the first one?

The First Pizza

People have been making pizza for a very long time. In the Stone Age,[1] some people mixed flour[2] with water to make dough. Then they **cooked** it on hot rocks. Over time, people started using the cooked dough as a plate, covering it with **various** other foods, herbs, and spices.[3] They had made the world's first pizza.

1 The **Stone Age** is a very early time in human history when people used things made of stone.

2 **Flour** is powder made from the seeds of wheat or corn.

3 **Herbs** and **spices** are used to add taste to food.

A New Ingredient

Then—in the early 1500s—European explorers brought the first tomatoes back from the Americas. Tomatoes are a **basic** ingredient in many pizzas today. At first, however, most Europeans thought eating tomatoes would make them sick. So, for about 200 years, few people ate them.

Slowly, people learned that tomatoes were safe to eat, as well as **tasty**. In the early 19th century, cooks in Naples, Italy, started the **tradition** of putting tomatoes on baking dough. The **flat** bread soon became a favorite food for **poor** people all over Naples. In 1830, a cook in Naples took another big step in the history of pizza—he opened the world's first pizza restaurant.

A World Food

Today, about five billion pizzas are made every year around the world. In the U.S. alone, people eat about 350 slices every second! People may not know it, but every piece is a slice of history.

Today, people across the globe can eat pizza cooked in the same way it has been for centuries.

Reading Comprehension

Multiple Choice. Choose the best answer for each question.

Main Idea

1. What is the main idea of the passage?
   a. Stone Age people made the first pizza.
   b. Pizza was an important food in Naples, in Italy.
   c. Pizza has a long history and has changed over time.

Detail

2. What does *people started using the cooked dough as a plate* (lines 7–8) mean?
   a. People put other foods on top of the dough.
   b. People cooked the pizza dough on hot rocks.
   c. People used the same pizza dough again and again.

Paraphrase

3. In lines 16–17, the phrase *safe to eat, as well as tasty* could be replaced with ______.
   a. only safe when they tasted good
   b. safe to eat, and they tasted good
   c. good to eat if they were cooked well

Vocabulary

4. In line 17, the word *century* refers to ______.
   a. 50 years
   b. 100 years
   c. 200 years

Detail

5. Who were the first people to put tomatoes on pizza?
   a. people in the U.S.
   b. people in Naples, Italy
   c. people in the Stone Age

Inference

6. Which of the following sentences is likely to be true?
   a. Tomatoes were a basic ingredient in pizzas in the 1700s.
   b. The first pizzas in Naples didn't cost much money.
   c. Europeans in the 1500s didn't like the taste of tomatoes.

Did You Know?

The world's largest pizza was made in Italy. It was about 40 meters (131 feet) across.

Reading Skill

Identifying the Parts of a Passage

A reading passage can have several parts. Look at every part to get a complete understanding of the passage. This is very useful when previewing a passage or predicting what it contains. These parts include:

7A

THE FLOWER TRADE

Aalsmeer, Netherlands

When you purchase fresh-cut flowers, do you think about where they came from? It might **make sense** to think they were grown somewhere nearby. The reality, though, is that the cut flower trade is increasingly international. Today, thanks to airplanes and high-tech cooling systems, even the most delicate[1] flower can be **exported**, and sold in a florist thousands of kilometers away from where it was grown.

The heart of the global flower trade, Aalsmeer processes 19 million flowers every day.

The Cut Flower Leader

The country that **dominates** the world cut flower trade is the Netherlands. It **handles** about 60 percent of the world's cut flowers. And its auction houses[2] are very large indeed—Aalsmeer, near Amsterdam, is an auction house in the sense that Tokyo is a city, or Everest a mountain. About 120 soccer fields would fill its main building. Nineteen million flowers are sold here on an average day, including roses, lilies, and of course, tulips.

1 Something **delicate** is easy to damage and needs to be treated carefully.

2 **Auction houses** are companies that hold public sales where the price of an item is not yet decided and customers compete to buy it.

Unit 7A 101

The **title** is a kind of **heading**. It tells you what the whole text is about.

Subheadings above **paragraphs** tell you what they are about.

The **main text** contains the most important information.

Photos and **illustrations** show information visually.

Globes and **maps** show you where in the world a place is. They also give you more visual information about a place.

Captions explain the pictures.

Footnotes give meanings for harder vocabulary words or more information.

A. Identifying. Look back at the passage on pages 23–24. Which parts of a passage are used there? Check (✓) the parts you can find.

- ☐ a title ☐ photos ☐ a globe
- ☐ subheadings ☐ illustrations ☐ a map
- ☐ a main text ☐ captions ☐ footnotes

B. Scan. Look back at the passage again, and answer the questions below.

1. How many paragraphs are there? (**3** / **5**)
2. How many headings are there? (**4** / **6**)
3. Does every picture have a caption? (**Yes** / **No**)
4. How many footnotes are there? (**3** / **5**)
5. Is there a globe or map? (**Yes** / **No**)

Critical Thinking Discuss with a partner. Why do you think pizza is so popular? Do you think pizza is good for you? Why or why not?

Vocabulary Practice

A. Words in Context. Complete each sentence with the correct answer.

1. If you are **poor**, you have _______________ money.
   a. a lot of   b. only a little
2. An example of something **flat** is _______________.
   a. a piece of paper   b. a ball
3. To **cook** food, you usually make it __________.
   a. cold   b. hot
4. A **tradition** is _______________ way to do something.
   a. a new   b. an old
5. An example of a **basic** food is _______________.
   a. bread or rice   b. chocolate cake

A hamburger

B. Completion. Complete the information below with words from the box. One word is extra.

cook	flat	ingredient	tasty	traditional	various

Who Made the First Hamburger?

Around the world, there are **1.** __________ people who say the first hamburger was made in their country. For example:

Some say that in the 1200s, Mongolian soldiers had no time to **2.** __________ their food. So they put meat under their saddles[1] to make it soft and flat, like the patties in hamburgers today.

Others in Hamburg, Germany, say hamburgers came from "Hamburg steak"—a(n) **3.** __________ German dish. The main **4.** ____________ in this dish is salty meat, which is put on bread.

One story says, in 1885, a man named Charles Nagreen was selling meatballs at a U.S. fair. The meatballs were very **5.** _____________, but were hard to eat while walking. So Nagreen put them between pieces of bread. Without knowing it, he had made a new type of food.

Which story is true? No one knows for sure.

1 A **saddle** is a seat for a rider that is placed on a horse's back.

Word Partnership
Use ***basic*** with:
(*n.*) basic **skills**, basic **needs**, basic **training**, basic **questions**.

Scientists use Scoville heat units (SHU) to rate a chili pepper's "heat" level.

Before You Read

A. True or False. Look at the information above. Then mark each sentence below as true (**T**) or false (**F**).

1. The Trinidad Moruga Scorpion is hotter than the Dorset Naga. **T F**
2. The Scoville is a type of chili pepper. **T F**
3. Tabasco peppers are hotter than jalapeños. **T F**
4. Sweet bell peppers have a very high SHU level. **T F**

B. Scan. In Assam, India, a woman named Anandita Dutta Tamuly likes to eat very hot chilies. Quickly scan the passage on the next page. Which of the chilies above is she famous for eating?

The Hottest Chilies

You may have **experienced** the feeling—your mouth feels like it's on fire, and the heat causes your eyes to water. You've just eaten one of nature's hottest foods—the chili pepper!

Chili peppers, also called chilies, are found in **dishes** around the world. They are in dishes like Indian curries, Thai tom yum soup, and Mexican enchiladas. Chilies come from the capsicum **plant**. They are "hot" because they **contain** something called *capsaicin*.

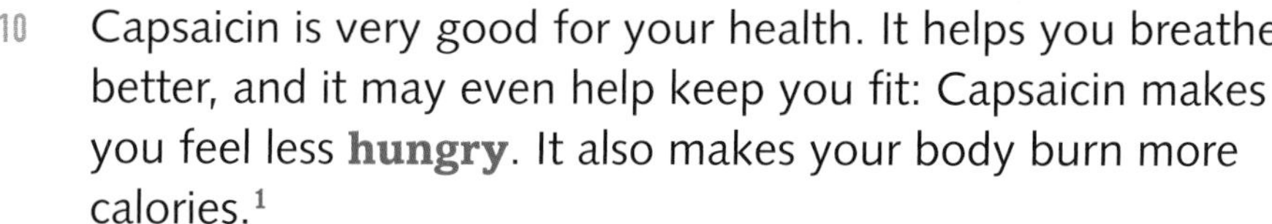

Capsaicin is very good for your health. It helps you breathe better, and it may even help keep you fit: Capsaicin makes you feel less **hungry**. It also makes your body burn more calories.[1]

We can **measure** the heat of chilies in units called Scoville heat units (SHU). The world's hottest chili is the Carolina Reaper. It sometimes measures up to 2 million SHU!

Anandita Dutta Tamuly eats a tray full of Naga Jolokia, "Ghost Peppers."

Eating a hot chili can be **painful**, but some people really like to eat them. **Recently**, Anandita Dutta Tamuly, a woman from Assam, India, became famous for eating chilies. She ate 51 hot peppers in just two minutes! The peppers she ate were Naga Jolokia ("Ghost Peppers"). They grow in Assam and are the third hottest chilies in the world.

"I found eating chilies was a great way to stay healthy," says Tamuly. She began eating chilies when she was a child. She eats chilies when she is sick, too. "Every time I have a cold or flu, I just munch on[2] some chilies and I feel better. To be honest,[3] I barely notice them now."

1 **Calories** are units used to measure the energy value of food.
2 If you **munch on** food, you eat it, often noisily.
3 If someone is **honest**, they tell the truth.

Reading Comprehension

Multiple Choice. Choose the best answer for each question.

Gist

1. What is the reading mainly about?
   a. how to eat very hot chili peppers
   b. interesting facts about hot chili peppers
   c. ideas for cooking using chili peppers

Purpose

2. What is the purpose of the third paragraph (from line 10)?
   a. to explain why eating chilies is painful
   b. to show the effect of chilies on the mind
   c. to inform you about how chilies are good for you

Detail

3. How is capsaicin good for your health?
   a. It helps you breathe better.
   b. It makes you feel happier.
   c. It makes you feel hungrier.

Detail

4. How many SHUs are in the world's hottest chili pepper?
   a. up to 1,000,000
   b. up to 2,000,000
   c. up to 3,000,000

Detail

5. Which of the following sentences about Anandita Dutta Tamuly is true?
   a. She is making a movie about chilies.
   b. She uses chilies to help sick people.
   c. She started eating chilies as a child.

Paraphrase

6. In line 27, the phrase *I barely notice them now* can be replaced with ______.
   a. I usually don't eat hot chilies anymore
   b. I feel the heat of the chilies even more now
   c. I almost don't feel the heat of the chilies now

Did You Know?

It's a tradition in Mexico to put chilies on Christmas trees.

Pronoun Reference

Pronouns are words such as *he, she, it, they,* and *them,* and usually refer to a noun earlier in a passage. To understand a passage, it is important to know what each pronoun refers to.

Sara bought chilies. **She** *put* **them** *in my favorite curry.* **It** *was too hot to eat!*

A. Reference. In each sentence, draw an arrow between the pronoun in **bold** and the word it refers to, as in the example above.

1. The jalapeño is a popular chili from Mexico. **It** takes its name from Jalapa, in Veracruz.
2. My brother and sister asked my mother not to put chilies in the food **she** made.
3. After Europeans brought chilies from the Americas, **they** spread very quickly around the world.
4. The cayenne pepper is hotter than the sweet bell pepper, but **it** isn't as hot as the Carolina Reaper.
5. Indians put chili peppers in many of their dishes. They often add **them** to curries.

People in the Americas were eating chilies as early as 7,500 B.C.

B. Reference. Look back at the passage on page 29. Find the following sentences in the passage, and write the word each pronoun in **bold** refers to.

1. **It** helps you breathe better. (lines 10–11) it = ________
2. She began eating chilies when **she** was a child. (line 24) she = ________
3. To be honest, I barely notice **them** now. (line 27) them = ________

Critical Thinking Discuss with a partner. What do you like or dislike about chili peppers? Why do you think Anandita Dutta Tamuly ate so many Naga Jolokia peppers?

Vocabulary Practice

A. Completion. Complete the information below with words from the box.

contains	dishes	measure	painful	recently

They may not look very tasty, but some types of cactus plants can be eaten and are very healthy. In Mexico, *nopalitos*—young stems of the cactus—have been eaten for hundreds of years.

Eating cactus has **1.** ____________ become more and more popular outside of Mexico. There are many tasty and healthy **2.** ____________ that use cactus stems. One easy way to cook them is in a pan, in some oil. This is how to do it.

- Clean and cut up the cactus stems. Watch out for the sharp parts of the plant! You don't want to cut yourself. That could be quite **3.** ____________.
- Next, **4.** ____________ how much oil you need. Heat the oil in a pan. Add the pieces of cactus. Add some salt and cover the pan to let the cactus cook.
- The cactus **5.** ____________ a strange liquid. Cook the cactus until all the liquid comes out and dries up. After that, the rest of the cactus stem can be eaten.

In a Mexican market, a man cuts and cleans cactus stems.

B. Definitions. Match the words in **red** with their definitions.

1. **plant** •
2. **hungry** •
3. **measure** •
4. **recently** •
5. **experience** •

- • a. a short time ago
- • b. having a need for food
- • c. a living thing that grows in the ground
- • d. to find out something's length, height, etc.
- • e. to do or see something, or have it happen to you

Word Partnership

Use ***painful*** with: (*n.*) painful **cut**, painful **experience**, painful **reminder**, painful **memory**.

VIEWING A Taste of Mexico

Before You Watch

A. Definitions. Look at the picture and read the caption. Pay attention to the words in **bold**. Then match them with their definitions below.

The land around the **historic** city of Oaxaca (/wəˈhɑːkə/) in Mexico is very hard for people to move across. So, many of the native[1] **cultures** in this region—some that have **developed** for over 13,000 years—have been kept safe. This means their traditions, as well as their unique foods, are still around today. In fact, it is this **complex** mix of native traditions and cultures that makes Oaxacan food—for example, the seven types of *mole*[2] it is famous for—one of a kind.

1 If something is **native** to a place, it originally comes from there.

2 **Mole** is a kind of sauce that has chilies and often chocolate in it.

1. ________________: famous or important in history
2. ________________: grew; slowly started to exist
3. ________________: having many parts, often different from each other
4. ________________: the ideas and traditions of different groups of people

B. Predict. You will hear the following words in the video.

traditions dishes ingredients chocolate dances national treasures

What do you think the video will be about? Discuss your ideas with a partner.

While You Watch

Checking. As you watch the video, check your answers in **Before You Watch B.** Were your ideas correct?

After You Watch

A. Completion. Complete the word web with words and phrases from the box.

chilies	cooking school	Europe	history	hotel	ingredients	mole	national

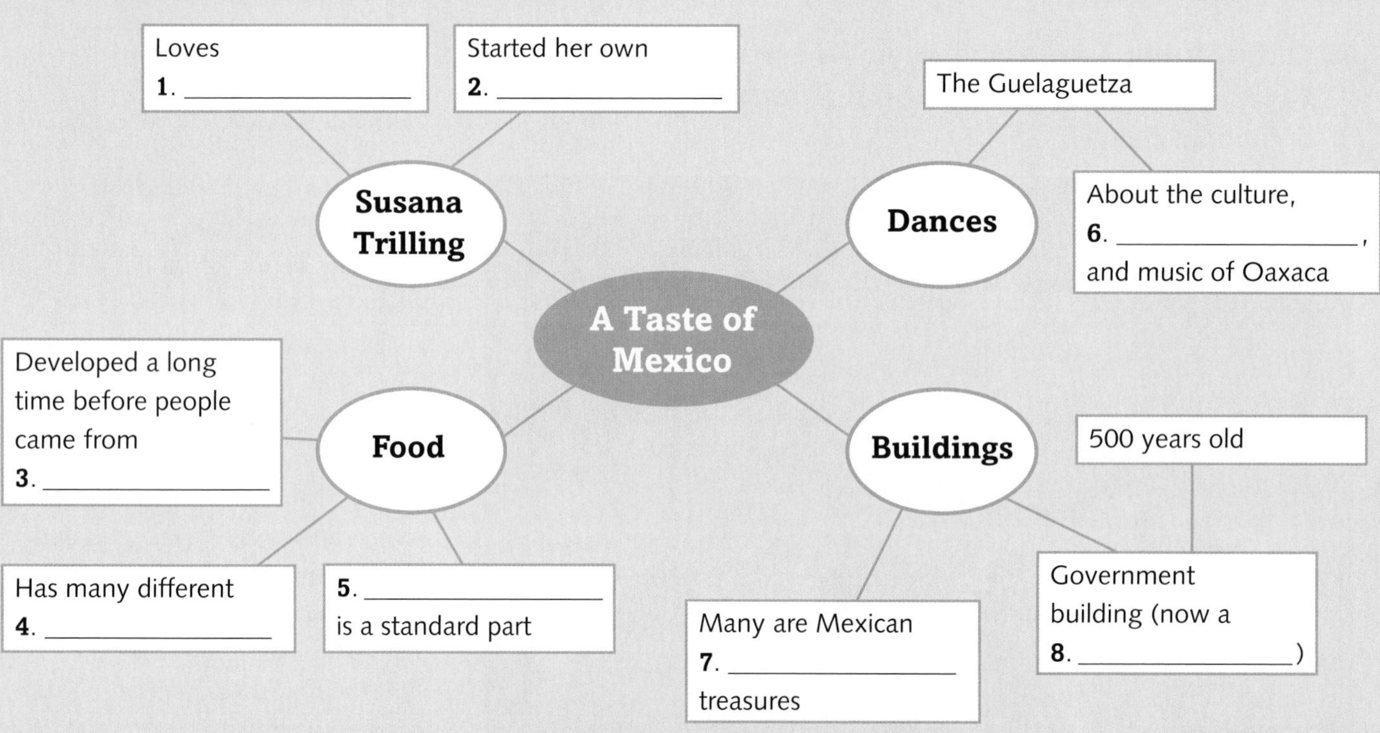

B. Discuss. Discuss these questions with a partner.

1. What traditions about food do you have in your country?
2. If you could go to a cooking school, what kind of cooking would you want to learn?

A Zapotec woman makes traditional tamales. The Zapotec people are one of Oaxaca's native cultures.

3

Cool JOBS

Hi-tech suits keep climate scientists safe from the extreme cold as they are lowered onto the Arctic ice.

Warm Up

Discuss these questions with a partner.

1. What are the people in the photo doing? Would you like this job?
2. What interesting—or "cool"—jobs can you name? What makes them "cool"?

Training GRIZZLIES!

Before You Read

A. Definitions. Look at the photos and read the captions on pages 36–37. Then match each word below with its definition.

1. wrestle •	• a. a baby lion, wolf, or bear
2. paw •	• b. a person in a TV show, movie, or play
3. actor •	• c. the foot of an animal, like a dog or bear
4. cub •	• d. to teach a person or an animal
5. train •	• e. to use your body to fight someone or push them down

B. Scan. When he was 16, Russell Chadwick had an unusual summer job. Scan the first two paragraphs on page 37. Answer the questions below. Read the passage to check your answers.

1. What did Russell Chadwick do that summer?

____

2. Where did Russell Chadwick work?

____

Author Doug Chadwick roars next to Tank, a bear from the Wasatch Wildlife Training Center. At the center, Lynne and Doug Seus train animals to be actors in TV shows and movies.

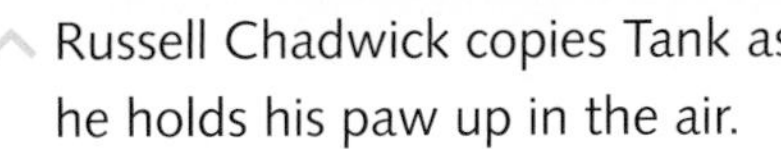

Russell Chadwick copies Tank as he holds his paw up in the air.

Russell Chadwick wrestles with a little bear cub.

Russell Chadwick **remembers** the summer he turned 16. It was the summer he wrestled with grizzly bears!

It all started when Russell worked as an animal trainer at Wasatch Rocky Mountain Wildlife. Wasatch Wildlife is an animal-training center in Utah, in the U.S. At the center, Doug and Lynne Seus train animals to be actors.

Doug and Lynne asked Russell to help **take care of** two four-month-old grizzly bear cubs named Little Bart and Honey Bump. That's more **difficult** than it sounds. Baby bears are big!

Russell's job was to play with the bears. This teaches them to be **comfortable** with humans. Playing with the bears was fun, but Russell had to remember that bears are **wild** animals.

"One time, Honey Bump took a bite[1] out of my back, and I had to wrestle her to the ground. But it also showed me how smart[2] she is. She knew she had done something wrong and '**apologized**' by putting her head in my lap."[3]

Russell found that bears can understand more than just "sit" and "stay." For example, when Russell said "Peekaboo!" to one baby bear, he **covered** his eyes with his paws, just like a human child.

Russell didn't get much money for doing this job. But he **enjoyed** the experience. He also learned a lot from it. When you've wrestled with a grizzly bear, things like work and exams don't seem so difficult anymore!

1 A **bite** refers to a small piece of food, or something you grab with your teeth.
2 If someone is **smart**, they are good at learning things.
3 Your **lap** is the front area formed by your thighs when you are sitting down.

Reading Comprehension

Multiple Choice. Choose the best answer for each question.

Gist

1. What is the reading passage mainly about?
   a. how to get a summer job in Utah
   b. why wild animals make good actors
   c. what Russell Chadwick did for his summer job

Vocabulary

2. In line 1, we could change the word *turned* to ______.
   a. became
   b. grew up
   c. went around

Detail

3. Which of these sentences about Doug and Lynne Seus is NOT true?
   a. They are movie actors.
   b. They are animal trainers.
   c. They work at Wasatch Rocky Mountain Wildlife.

Detail

4. What was the main thing that Doug and Lynne Seus wanted Russell Chadwick to do?
   a. play with the bears
   b. teach the bears to sit and stay
   c. teach the bears to live in the wild

Reference

5. In line 20, *he* refers to ______.
   a. Doug Seus
   b. a baby bear
   c. Russell Chadwick

Main Idea

6. What is the main idea of the last paragraph (from line 22)?
   a. Tests and homework are good ways to get ready for a summer job.
   b. Russell Chadwick's experience helped him get ready for other things in his life.
   c. Russell Chadwick didn't get enough money for his summer job.

Did You Know?

When they stand on their back legs, grizzly bears can be over 2.4 meters (8 feet) tall.

Reading Skill

Finding the Correct Definition of a Word in a Dictionary

When you look up a word in a dictionary, there is often more than one definition. To find the correct definition, first identify what part of speech the word is (e.g., noun, verb, adjective, adverb). Then look at the other words in the sentence to help you find the correct definition.

A. Matching. Identify the part of speech of the word ***smart*** in each sentence below. Then match each sentence to the correct definition.

1. The actor's clothes are very **smart**. ______
2. I bought a **smart**phone. ______
3. Smoke makes my eyes **smart**. ______
4. The bear is very **smart**. ______

smart \ˈsmaːrt\
adjective
a. good at learning
b. fashionable
c. controlled by computers
verb
d. to hurt

B. Completion. Circle the part of speech for each underlined word. Then look up the word in a dictionary, and write down its definition.

1. At the <u>center</u>, Doug and Lynne Seus train animals. (lines 5–6)
   part of speech: **noun / verb**
   definition: ______________________________
2. That's more difficult than it <u>sounds</u>. (line 9)
   part of speech: **noun / verb**
   definition: ______________________________
3. Honey Bump took a bite out of my <u>back</u>. (line 14)
   part of speech: **noun / adverb**
   definition: ______________________________
4. I had to wrestle her to the <u>ground</u>. (lines 14–15)
   part of speech: **noun / adjective**
   definition: ______________________________

Animal trainer Doug Seus works with Tank, a grizzly bear actor.

Critical Thinking Discuss with a partner. What animals do you think are easy to train? Would you like a summer job like Russell Chadwick's? Why or why not?

Vocabulary Practice

A. Matching. Read the information below. Then match each word in **red** with its definition.

There are many jobs that animal-lovers would be good at. For example, some people work as caregivers. Their job is to **take care of** animals. Caregivers need to feed, wash, and play with the animals they work with.

People who **enjoy** teaching animals to do tricks could become trainers. Trainers can work in a pet store, an animal park, or a zoo, but if they want to train people's pets, they have to be **comfortable** teaching the owners, too.

Some animal-lovers become veterinarians. Being an "animal doctor" can be fun sometimes. However, a vet's work is often quite **difficult**.

A zoo vet holds a baby orangutan.

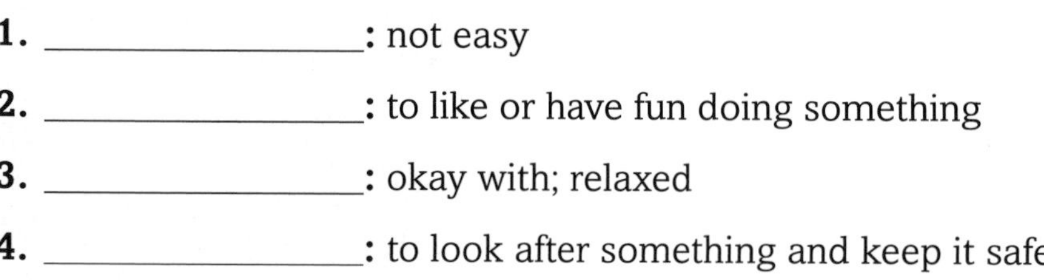

1. ________________: not easy
2. ________________: to like or have fun doing something
3. ________________: okay with; relaxed
4. ________________: to look after something and keep it safe

B. Words in Context. Choose the correct word or phrase to complete each sentence below.

1. If you **remember** something, you __________.
   a. think of it again   b. forget all about it
2. Examples of **wild** animals are __________.
   a. dogs and cats   b. lions and bears
3. If you **cover** something with your hands, you put your hands ________ it.
   a. under   b. over
4. Something that is **difficult** is ________ to do.
   a. hard   b. easy
5. If you **apologize**, you say that you are ________.
   a. happy   b. sorry

Thesaurus
difficult Also look up:
(*adj.*) *hard, tough, challenging*

3B

Getting the Shot

Before You Read

National Geographic photographer Joel Sartore photographs an Adélie penguin chick in Antarctica.

A. Discussion. Look at the photo above and read the caption. Then discuss these questions with a partner.

1. What kinds of things do you usually take photos of?

2. Do you think a photographer's job is easy?

B. Skim. Skim the interview on pages 42–43. Then write each interview question above its answer in the passage.

a. I want to be a photographer. Do you have any advice for me?

b. What kind of photographers is the *National Geographic* magazine looking for?

c. Is it difficult to get a job as a photographer today?

d. How did you become a *National Geographic* photographer?

Monarch butterflies at rest completely cover a tree.

An interview with Joel Sartore

Joel Sartore is a writer, teacher, and photographer. His words—and ***images****—show his* ***passion*** *for photography and for the world around us.*

Question 1: ________________________________

My first job was for a newspaper. After a few years there, I met a *National Geographic* photographer. He liked my photos and said I should send some to the magazine. So I did. That led to a one-day job. And that led to a nine-day job, and so on.

Question 2: ________________________________

To get into *National Geographic*, you have to give them something they don't have. It's not **enough** just to be a great photographer. You also have to, for example, be a scientist, or be able to dive under sea ice, or **spend** several days in a tree.

Joel Sartore

At the cutest-baby contest in Barrow, Alaska, the babies wear coats made of seal and wolf fur.

Question 3: ______________________________

It's now more difficult to work for magazines. Technology now makes it easy to take good pictures, which means there are more photos and photographers. Also, the web is full of photos from all around the world that are free, or **cost** very little. These photos are often good enough to be put in books and magazines that once **paid** for photographers and their photos.

Question 4: ______________________________

Advice?[1] Well, work hard. Be passionate about every project you work on. Take lots of pictures in different **situations**. Look at others' photos thoughtfully and learn from them. And be curious[2] about life. There's something to photograph everywhere.

But be a photographer for the right reasons. If you do it for the money, you **probably** won't really be happy. Do you want to make the world a better place, or make people see things in a different way? If so, you'll enjoy the work much more.

---

1 If you ask someone for **advice**, you ask them what you should do.

2 If you are **curious** about something, you want to know more about it.

Reading Comprehension

Multiple Choice. Choose the best answer for each question.

Vocabulary

1. In the title *Getting the Shot* on page 41, what does the word *shot* mean?
   a. job
   b. photo
   c. magazine

Detail

2. Which of the following sentences about Joel Sartore is true?
   a. His first job was with *National Geographic*.
   b. He once worked for a newspaper.
   c. He wants to be a teacher someday.

Purpose

3. What was Sartore's main point in his answer to Question 3?
   a. Photographers need to use more technology.
   b. Putting your photos online can lead to other jobs.
   c. It's not easy to get paid work as a photographer these days.

Paraphrase

4. The sentence *There's something to photograph everywhere.* (line 28) is closest in meaning to ________.
   a. Anyone can be a photographer these days.
   b. Take more photos than you think you will need.
   c. You can find interesting things to take pictures of anywhere.

Inference

5. Which of the following things can you infer from the passage?
   a. Sartore is a scientist.
   b. Sartore didn't like his first job.
   c. Sartore carries a camera everywhere he goes.

Main Idea

6. What is the main idea of the last paragraph (from line 29)?
   a. You should try to see people in different ways.
   b. If you work hard, you can make money as a photographer.
   c. You should ask yourself why you want to be a photographer.

Did You Know?

The first photo ever was taken in 1826. The first color photo (above) was taken in 1861. It was of a ribbon.

Reading Skill

Understanding the Use of Commas

Knowing how writers use commas helps you read and understand texts better. Look at some rules for comma use. You should use a comma . . .

- to separate things in a series
  e.g., *I enjoy taking pictures of people, animals, and flowers.*
- to separate a city, state, or country
  e.g., *I recently traveled to Rome, Italy, to study photography.*
- to set off an introductory word or expression
  e.g., *At first, I was shy about taking pictures.*
- to separate different ideas in a sentence
  e.g., *I have a camera, but it's not a very good one.*
- to set off a word or phrase within a sentence
  e.g., *I am, however, a very good photographer.*

A. Analyzing. Check (✓) the sentences below that use commas correctly.

1. ☐ I flew to San Diego, California, last week to see my sister.
2. ☐ She moved, there several years ago.
3. ☐ When I got there, my sister took me to the zoo.
4. ☐ She works at the zoo, so she gave me a tour.
5. ☐ She works with, bears wolves and, monkeys.

B. Completion. Add commas to the sentences below. (The number in parentheses shows the number of commas needed.) Look back at the passage on pages 42–43 to check your answers.

1. Joel Sartore is a writer teacher and photographer. (2)
2. And that led to a nine-day job and so on. (1)
3. To get into *National Geographic* you have to give them something they don't have. (1)
4. If you do it for the money you probably won't really be happy. (1)
5. If so you'll enjoy the work much more. (1)

Critical Thinking Discuss with a partner. What other questions would you have asked Joel Sartore? Do you think you would enjoy being a photographer? Why or why not?

Vocabulary Practice

A. Completion. Choose the correct words in **red** to complete the information below.

Stories Behind the Shots

Joel Sartore took this photo of an ocelot at the Omaha Zoo in Nebraska, U.S.A. Sartore **1.** (**spent** / **paid**) a lot of time with the animal, but getting the shot was not easy. "They hardly ever hold still," says Sartore. "So I really had to act quickly when he looked into my camera's lens." Many animals will stand still only long **2.** (**probably** / **enough**) to get food. After they eat enough and are not hungry anymore, the photo shoot is over.

Behind this **3.** (**passion** / **image**) is another great story. At an aquarium in Baltimore, Maryland, U.S.A., Sartore came across a very angry frog. While he tried to take a photo of it, it tried to bite him. He never thought he would be in a **4.** (**situation** / **cost**) where he was afraid of a frog! "First time for everything," says Sartore.

B. Words in Context. Read the sentences below. Then mark each sentence as true (**T**) or false (**F**).

1. Something that's **probably** true is likely to be true. **T F**
2. When you're **paid** for a photo, you get money for it. **T F**
3. If something is free, it **costs** a lot. **T F**
4. If you have **passion** for something, you like doing it very much. **T F**
5. If you have **enough** money, you don't need any more. **T F**

Word Partnership

We use **spend + time** to mean we allow time to pass when doing something (e.g., *I **spent** an hour at the mall.*). We use **spend + money** to mean we use money to pay for something (e.g., *I **spent** $100 on a new camera.*).

VIEWING Right Dog for the Job

Before You Watch

A. Definitions. Look at the picture and read the caption below. Pay attention to the words in **bold**. You will hear them in the video.

^ Since 1991, Canine[1] Assistants has **trained** over 1,500 dogs. In Canine Assistants' super-dog **program**, puppies learn more than just tricks. These very **smart** dogs will grow up to be **service dogs** and will be given to people who need them. The **recipients** are people who cannot move around without help or have other special needs.[2] These dogs have an important job to do. It is the **animal trainers**' job to teach them to do it.

1 The term **canine** refers to a dog or doglike animal. For example, wolves and foxes are also canines.

2 In this context, **special needs** refers to mental, emotional, or physical problems that cause some people to need help with their daily activities.

B. Predict. What do you think the trainers in the video teach the dogs to do? Check (✓) your ideas from the skills below.

- ☐ pick up things
- ☐ run in a race
- ☐ find help
- ☐ buy groceries
- ☐ call the police
- ☐ attack bad people
- ☐ drive a car
- ☐ use a phone
- ☐ turn lights on
- ☐ be comfortable with people
- ☐ perform in contests
- ☐ get along with other animals

While You Watch

Checking. As you watch the video, check your answers in **Before You Watch B**. Which skills are mentioned in the video? Are your answers correct?

After You Watch

A. Completion. Choose the correct word or phrase to complete each of the sentences below.

1. According to the video, the dogs have to learn to (**take care of themselves / want to help their owners**).

2. Scientists think this kind of training makes the dogs (**better learners / healthier**).

3. In the puppy room, the dogs (**face situations / meet the people**) they'll find in their new homes.

4. The trainers take each puppy on a trip to (**experience the world outside / learn to do the shopping**).

B. Paraphrasing. The sentences below are from the video. What do the phrases in **bold** mean?

1. *If their owner* **is in trouble**, *the dogs have to press a big button . . .*
   "is in trouble" = (**needs help / has done something bad**)

2. *When the recipient says: "Will you pick this up for me?" It's all* **up to the dog**.
   "up to the dog" = (**only the dog can do it / the dog can decide**)

3. *At eight weeks they hit a time of fear, where just about everything is frightening. If they don't* **get past** *it now, they never will.*
   "get past" = (**move away from / find a way to deal with**)

C. Discuss. Discuss these questions with a partner.

1. Would you like to be a trainer at Canine Assistants? If you were an animal trainer, what animal would you train?
2. Jennifer Arnold says the dogs must love their jobs to do them well. Do you think this is true for people, too? Why or why not?

4

Shipwrecks

A shipwreck lies half-covered by the sands of the Namib Desert in Namibia.

Warm Up

Discuss these questions with a partner.

1. Do you know about any famous shipwrecks?
2. What do you think happened to the ship in the photo?

Called the "Ship of Dreams," the *Titanic* was the biggest passenger ship of its time. Its makers said it was "unsinkable," but the great ship sank on its very first trip.

April 10, 1912
The *Titanic* leaves England, traveling toward New York.

April 14, 11:40 p.m.
The *Titanic* smashes into an **iceberg**.

April 15, 12:00–2:20 a.m.
Water begins to fill the ship's lower levels. **Passengers**, mostly women and children, get into small lifeboats. But there aren't enough lifeboats.

Before You Read

A. True or False. Look at the picture and read the information above. Pay attention to the words in yellow. Then mark each sentence below as true (**T**) or false (**F**).

1. An iceberg caused the *Titanic* to sink.	**T**	**F**
2. Most of the male passengers got into lifeboats.	**T**	**F**
3. Over 1,500 passengers died.	**T**	**F**
4. Nobody knew where the ship was for 100 years.	**T**	**F**

B. Scan. Read the title and the first sentence of each paragraph on pages 51–52. How many times did Robert Ballard explore the *Titanic*? Then read the whole passage to check your answer.

I've Found the TITANIC!

April 15, 2:20 a.m.
The ship breaks into two and sinks. 1,514 people die that night.

August 31, 1985 The *Titanic*'s resting place is found after 73 years. Explorers use deep-sea **submarines** to study the **shipwreck** lying on the ocean floor.

As a boy, Robert Ballard liked to read about shipwrecks. He read a lot about the *Titanic*. "My lifelong **dream** was to find this great ship," he says.

On August 31, 1985, Ballard's dream came true. He found the wreck of the *Titanic*. The ship was in two main parts lying four kilometers (2.4 miles) under the sea. Using video cameras and an undersea robot,[1] Ballard looked around the ship. He found many **items** that told the sad story of the *Titanic*'s end. For example, he found a child's shoes, a reminder[2] of the many **deaths** that happened that night in 1912.

1 A **robot** is a machine controlled by a computer.

2 A **reminder** of something makes you remember it.

In 1986, Ballard visited the *Titanic* again. This time, he **reached** the ship in a small submarine. A deep-sea robot—a "swimming eyeball"—took photos inside the ship. When other people saw the photos, they wanted to visit the ship, too.

Deep-sea explorer Robert Ballard with one of the submarines he used to explore the *Titanic*

When Ballard **returned** in 2004, he found the *Titanic* in very bad **condition**. Other explorers had taken away about 6,000 items, like clothes, dishes, and shoes. Some even took pieces of the ship. They think these things should be moved to a safer place, but Ballard doesn't **agree**.

Ballard believes that taking things from the *Titanic* is like robbing a grave.[3] **Instead**, he wants to put lights and cameras on and around the shipwreck. This way, people can see the great shipwreck and remember what happened to it. "As long as she needs protection,"[4] says Ballard, "the *Titanic* will always be part of my life."

---

3 **Robbing a grave** is taking things from where a dead body is kept.

4 If someone gives you **protection**, they keep you safe from danger.

"As long as she needs protection, the *Titanic* will always be part of my life."

— Robert Ballard

Lights from a submarine break the darkness of the deep sea to show the bow (the front) of the *Titanic*.

Reading Comprehension

Multiple Choice. Choose the best answer for each question.

Gist

1. What is the reading mainly about?
a. how visitors to the *Titanic* leave it in bad condition
b. Robert Ballard's hopes that more people will visit the *Titanic*
c. how Robert Ballard found the *Titanic* and wants to keep it safe

Detail

2. The first time he explored the *Titanic*, Ballard did NOT ______.
a. take photos inside the shipwreck
b. find a child's shoes in the shipwreck
c. use a robot to look around the shipwreck

Detail

3. Which of the following sentences about Ballard is true?
a. He read about the *Titanic* when he was a child.
b. He swam into the *Titanic* wreck to take photos.
c. On his second trip to the *Titanic*, he found the ship in bad condition.

Detail

4. According to the passage, what did people see that made them want to visit the *Titanic*?
a. the submarine Ballard used
b. photos from inside the ship
c. items that were taken from the ship

Reference

5. Who does *they* refer to in line 20?
a. Robert Ballard and his team
b. other visitors to the *Titanic* shipwreck
c. people from the *Titanic* who are still alive

Inference

6. Which statement would Ballard probably agree with?
a. People should not remove anything from the *Titanic*.
b. Lights and cameras will hurt the remains of the *Titanic*.
c. The *Titanic* wreck should be moved out of the water completely.

Did You Know?

Each lifeboat on the *Titanic* could hold 65 people. Sadly, when the ship sank, many lifeboats were not full. One boat, for example, only had 35 people in it.

Identifying a Paragraph's Main Idea

The main idea of a paragraph is its central idea. To determine the main idea, skim the paragraph and ask yourself, "What point is the author trying to make?" The first and last sentences of a paragraph, as well as its heading (if it has one), can also give you clues about the main idea.

A. Multiple Choice. What is the main idea of the text below? Circle **a**, **b**, or **c**.

a. The *Carpathia* took over three hours to get to the *Titanic*.
b. The *Carpathia* answered the *Titanic*'s call and helped save lives.
c. The *Carpathia* was too far away to help stop the *Titanic* from sinking.

On April 15, 1912, at 12:20 a.m., the British ship *Carpathia* got a message from the *Titanic*. The "Ship of Dreams" was sinking. The *Carpathia* was 93 kilometers (58 miles) away. It traveled at top speed to where the *Titanic* was, even though there were dangerous icebergs in the ocean. It arrived at 3:30 a.m., over an hour after the *Titanic* sank. Still, the *Carpathia* was able to pick up 711 people. The ship then went to New York, arriving there on April 18.

B. Matching. Look back at the passage on pages 51–52. What is the main idea of each paragraph?

Paragraph 1: a. Ballard read a lot about the *Titanic*.
b. Ballard's dream was to find the *Titanic*.

Paragraph 2: a. Ballard found items like a child's shoe.
b. Ballard finally found the shipwreck he was looking for.

Paragraph 3: a. Ballard reached the ship in a small submarine.
b. Ballard returned and took photos of the ship.

Paragraph 4: a. Other explorers had taken things from the *Titanic* wreck.
b. Ballard thinks taking items from the ship hurts the wreck.

Paragraph 5: a. Ballard wants to protect the *Titanic*.
b. Ballard wants to put lights and cameras around the ship.

Critical Thinking Discuss with a partner. Robert Ballard thinks no one should take things from the *Titanic*. Do you agree with him?

Vocabulary Practice

A. Completion. Complete the information using words from the box. One word is extra.

conditions	deaths	items	reach	returned

Why were there so many **1.** ____________ on the night the *Titanic* sank? One reason is that the **2.** ____________ in which people waited to be saved were very bad. The air and water were very cold. Scientists believe most of the people who fell into the water died from the cold in less than 15 minutes. However, the main reason is that there were not enough lifeboats. There were 2,223 people on the ship, but lifeboats for only 1,186 people. Also, many people could not **3.** ____________ the boats before the ship sank. In the end, only 705 people **4.** ____________ safely to land.

At first, most people could not believe the news of the *Titanic*'s sinking.

B. Words in Context. Complete each sentence with the correct answer.

1. If people **agree**, they have __________ about a subject.
   a. the same idea b. different ideas
2. If you drink tea **instead of** coffee, you drink __________.
   a. tea b. both tea and coffee
3. An example of an **item** of clothing is __________.
   a. warmth b. a jacket
4. A lifelong **dream** is something you have ________ all your life.
   a. wanted to do b. tried to stop doing
5. If you **reach** a place, you are __________ get there.
   a. able to b. not able to
6. If you **return** to somewhere, you go there __________.
   a. for the first time b. again

Usage

If you **agree with** someone, you have the same idea or opinion as that person.
If you **agree to** do something, you say that you will do it.

In the 1500s, the fastest way to travel from Europe to India was to pass the **coast** of southern Africa. But **sailors** feared this area, named **Skeleton** Coast for the many animal **bones** found there. It is now famous for its large number of shipwrecks.

Before You Read

A. Matching. Look at the picture and read the caption. Match each word in **bold** with its definition.

1. ____________: land next to the sea
2. ____________: people who work on a ship
3. ____________: hard pieces inside a body that give it shape
4. ____________: the shape that all the bones in your body make

B. Predict. Read the first sentence of each paragraph on the next page. Check (✓) the information you think you'll read about. Then read the passage to check your answers.

- ☐ how a ship became wrecked
- ☐ what was found on the shipwreck
- ☐ maps that show where the ship is
- ☐ a fight over gold coins

Part of the treasure of the *Bom Jesus*. Almost 23 kilograms (50 pounds) of gold coins were found in the sand.

*On a **beach** along the Skeleton Coast, the sand is filled with diamonds. But in April 2008, workers found something very different: a piece of lost history—a shipwreck and its treasure.*[1]

The story began when a worker from the nearby diamond mines found a piece of **metal** on the beach. It was a piece of copper. Soon, they found more copper and many gold coins.[2] The workers then found that these came from the remains of a large ship. The shipwreck was the real treasure.

Archeologists[3] studied the shipwreck. They thought the ship probably came from Portugal about 500 years before. However, it was difficult to find information about it. In 1775, many maps and books about the ships of the time were lost in a fire in Lisbon. "That left a big **hole** in our history," says Portuguese archeologist Alexandre Monteiro.

Finally, Monteiro found out that a group of ships left Lisbon for India in 1533. One of them, the *Bom Jesus*, **carried** 300 people and a large **amount** of treasure. The Portuguese sailors planned to use the treasure to buy **expensive** Indian spices. Archeologists now believe the wreck might be the *Bom Jesus.* This is because many of the gold coins found were Spanish. Monteiro found an old **letter** in the Spanish royal archives.[4] The letter said that Spain gave Portugal money for the trip. Two thousand Spanish coins were put on the *Bom Jesus*. This could explain why so many Spanish coins were found in a Portuguese shipwreck.

So what happened to the ship? The *Bom Jesus* probably got lost in a storm. Then it smashed into rocks near the coast and sank. There were few human bones found, so the sailors were probably able to get off the ship. But even if they swam onto the beach, they would have found themselves in a strange, **distant** land. They had no way to get home. They might as well have been on Mars. To this day, no one knows what happened to them.

1 **Treasure** is something expensive and hard to find.

2 A **coin** is a small piece of metal used as money.

3 An **archeologist** studies old things, to find out about the past.

4 The term **royal archives** refers to a place where old papers, etc., owned by the king are kept.

Reading Comprehension

Multiple Choice. Choose the best answer for each question.

Detail

1. What did the worker first find on the beach?
   a. a diamond
   b. a piece of gold
   c. a piece of copper

Paraphrase

2. Which sentence is closest in meaning to *The shipwreck was the real treasure.* (line 8)?
   a. There were a lot of expensive items on the ship.
   b. The shipwreck was a very important discovery.
   c. The coins on the ship weren't real, but it was an important ship.

Purpose

3. What is the purpose of the third paragraph (from line 9)?
   a. to describe how a fire destroyed a part of the ship
   b. to describe what books and maps were like in the 1500s
   c. to explain why it's difficult to know much about the ship

Detail

4. What is NOT true about the *Bom Jesus*?
   a. It was a Portuguese ship.
   b. It was returning from India.
   c. It was carrying Spanish money.

Fact or Theory

5. Which statement is a fact?
   a. All the sailors were able to swim to land.
   b. There were 2,000 Spanish coins on the *Bom Jesus*.
   c. The ship got lost in a storm and smashed into rocks.

Inference

6. Why does the author say the sailors *might as well have been on Mars.* (lines 30–31)?
   a. to show how bad the sailors' situation was
   b. to compare the Skeleton Coast to what Mars looks like
   c. to say that the sailors had found a beautiful but strange place

Did You Know?

There are over a thousand shipwrecks on the Skeleton Coast.

Reading Skill

Recognizing Compound Subjects and Objects

A sentence can have a single subject or a compound subject. A compound subject is a subject that contains two or more nouns. Sentences can also contain compound objects. Look at the examples below.

Compound subject: (*Ballard and his team*) *found the* Titanic *in 1985.*

Compound object: *Ballard used (cameras and a robot) to look at the ship.*

A. Analyzing. Find and circle examples of compound subjects and objects in the passage below. In each example, underline the different subjects or objects.

On July 17, 1956, the *Andrea Doria* left Italy for New York. The ship was carrying over 1,700 passengers and crew members. A week later, the *Stockholm* left New York for Sweden. That night, the *Andrea Doria* and *Stockholm* crossed paths with tragic results. Just after 11:00 p.m., the *Stockholm* smashed into the side of the *Andrea Doria*. The *Andrea Doria* began to slowly sink. The *Stockholm* helped with the rescue of the passengers, but there would be 52 deaths that night. Were darkness and bad weather the cause of the accident? It remains a mystery to this day.

The *Andrea Doria* and the *Stockholm* crash into each other in the North Atlantic Ocean.

B. Scan. Find examples of compound subjects and objects in the passage on page 57. Fill in the blanks.

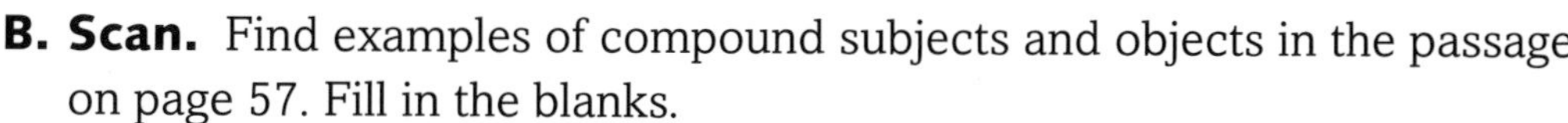

1. Compound object: ____________ and ____________ (paragraph 2)
2. Compound subject: ____________ and ____________ (paragraph 3)
3. Compound object: ____________ and ____________ (paragraph 4)

Critical Thinking Discuss with a partner. What do you think should happen to the treasure from ships like the *Bom Jesus*? Should the people who find it get to keep it? Why or why not?

Vocabulary Practice

A. Definitions. Read the information. Then complete the sentences below with the correct form of the words in **red**.

Silver Shipwreck

On August 2, 2013, a company called Odyssey Marine Exploration removed over 50,000 kilograms (120,000 pounds) of silver from a shipwreck off the coast of Ireland—the heaviest **amount** of the **metal** ever taken from a shipwreck. The ship, the *S.S. Gairsoppa,* was **carrying** tea, iron, and silver from the **distant** lands of India, when it sank in 1941. Today, that much silver is worth almost $75 million. In addition to the silver, the company also found some newspapers and **letters** written by the sailors.

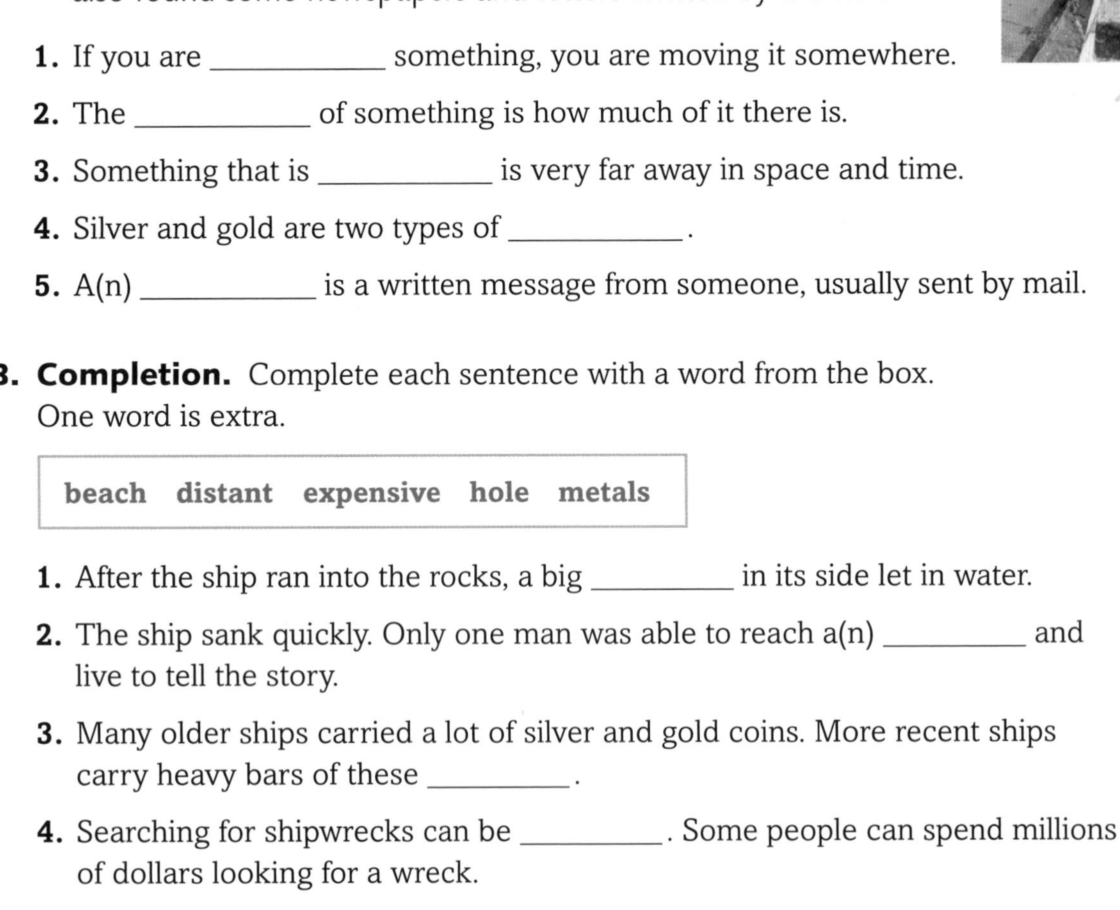

Silver from the *S.S. Gairsoppa*

1. If you are ___________ something, you are moving it somewhere.
2. The ___________ of something is how much of it there is.
3. Something that is ___________ is very far away in space and time.
4. Silver and gold are two types of ___________.
5. A(n) ___________ is a written message from someone, usually sent by mail.

B. Completion. Complete each sentence with a word from the box. One word is extra.

beach	**distant**	**expensive**	**hole**	**metals**

1. After the ship ran into the rocks, a big _________ in its side let in water.
2. The ship sank quickly. Only one man was able to reach a(n) _________ and live to tell the story.
3. Many older ships carried a lot of silver and gold coins. More recent ships carry heavy bars of these _________.
4. Searching for shipwrecks can be _________. Some people can spend millions of dollars looking for a wreck.

Usage
Coast refers to a piece of land along or near the ocean, while **beach** refers to a piece of land near a large body of water that is filled with sand or small stones.

VIEWING Saving Ocean Life

Before You Watch

A. Definitions. Look at the picture and read the caption. Pay attention to the words in **bold**. You will hear them in the video. Match the words with their definitions below.

^ Trawling is a way of fishing in which giant **nets** with heavy **weights** are put into the ocean. These nets are pulled along the **bottom** of the ocean, so the fish can't get away. Many fishermen[1] like trawling because they can bring in a lot of fish at a time. However, the nets and the weights **scrape** up everything on the ocean floor, and a lot of plants and animals that the fishermen don't need are hurt, too. Today, experts are trying to find ways to **protect** ocean life from trawling ships. One of these ways is to sink an old ship, and leave the shipwreck on the ocean floor.

1 **Fishermen** are people who make money by fishing.

1. nets •
2. weights •
3. bottom •
4. scrape •
5. protect •

• a. to keep safe
• b. the lowest part
• c. heavy things used to hold something down
• d. pieces of cloth, string, etc., tied together to hold things
• e. to remove a layer off something by moving something rough or sharp across it

B. Predict. How do you think a shipwreck can help save ocean life? Discuss your ideas with a partner.

While You Watch

Checking. As you watch the video, check your answers in **Before You Watch B**. Were your ideas correct?

After You Watch

A. Completion. Choose the correct word or phrase to complete each sentence below.

1. This shipwreck was once a (**war** / **passenger**) ship.

2. The shipwreck protects ocean life by (**tearing up trawl nets** / **damaging the trawler ships**).

3. Before they sink an old ship, workers take off all the (**metal** / **wood**).

4. After a few years, the shipwreck (**moves to a new place** / **falls apart**).

5. According to the video, another way to protect the ocean floor may be to (**build concrete walls** / **grow more sea plants**).

6. Sobel believes people are (**smart** / **scared**), so they'll do the right thing to protect the ocean.

B. Discuss. Discuss these questions with a partner.

1. Jack Sobel says, "I'm an optimist. I think we'll be successful." What do you think he means?
2. What other ways can we protect ocean life? Are there things you can do to help?

5

Science INVESTIGATORS

An investigator looks at a piece of broken glass. Crime scene investigators are scientists who work with the police.

Warm Up

Discuss these questions with a partner.

1. What do you think the investigator in the photo is looking for?
2. What kinds of people, besides crime scene investigators, use science in their jobs?

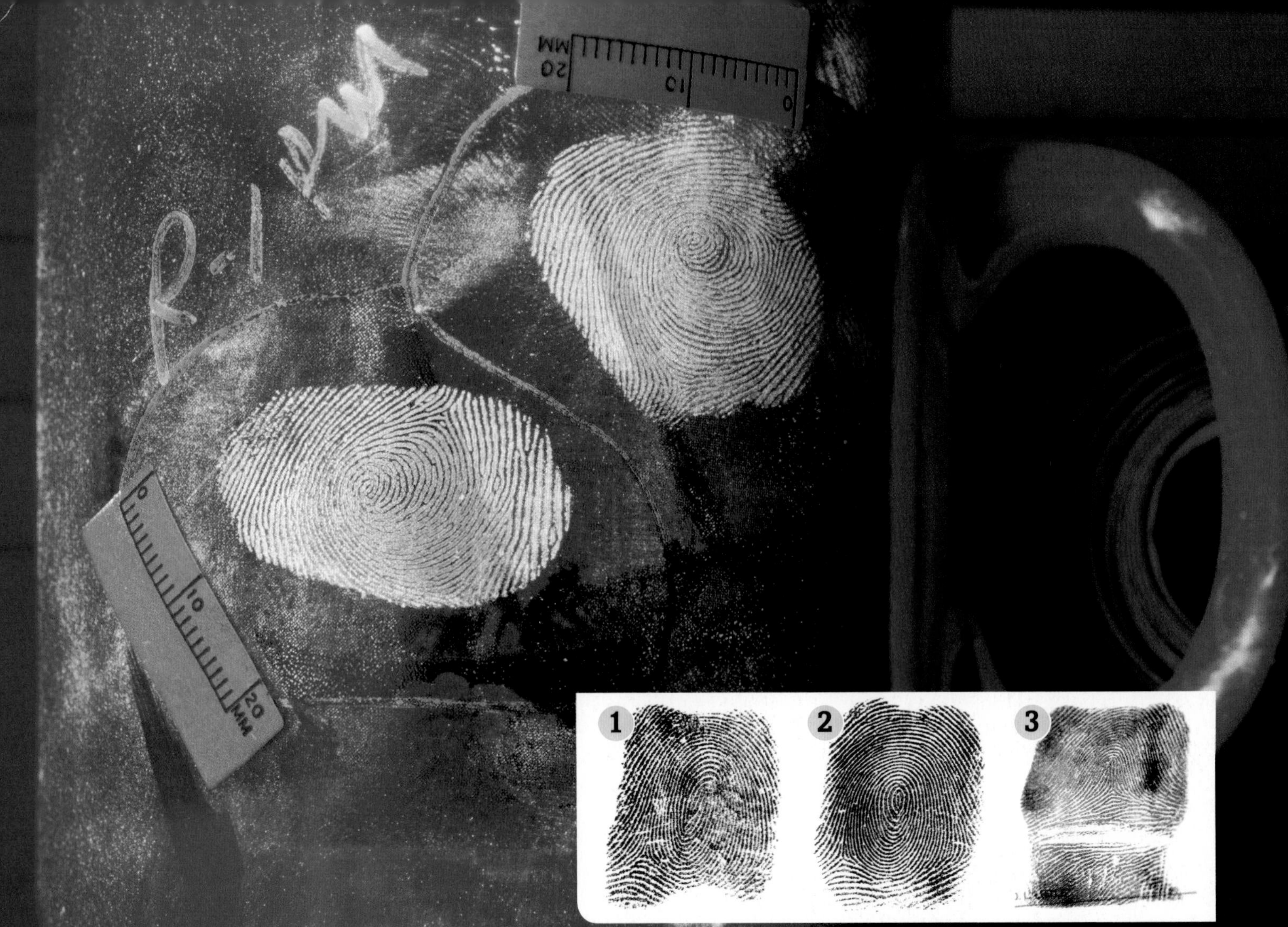

1 The lines on this fingerprint form patterns that are called **loops**.

2 These lines form around a single point. These are called **whorls**.

3 The lines here form **arches**. Many people have this pattern.

Before You Read

When there's a crime,[1] the police often call a **crime scene investigator**. This person helps the police study the **scene**, looking for evidence.[2] One thing they look for is **fingerprints**. Everyone has a different **pattern** of fingerprints.

A. Discussion. Look at the pictures and information above. Pay attention to the words in **bold**. Then answer the questions.

1. Who do crime scene investigators help?
2. Besides fingerprints, what else do you think a crime scene investigator could look for?
3. Look at your own fingers. What patterns can you find?

B. Scan. Quickly scan the passage on pages 65–66. Underline all the clues the crime scene investigator finds.

1 A **crime** happens when someone does something bad, or breaks the law.

2 **Evidence** refers to things that can help the police find out who did the crime.

At the Scene of a Crime

Your phone rings. The police officer says someone broke into[1] a store and took some expensive items. They need you right away. It is your job to study the whole scene for **clues** that will help **catch** the thief.[2] You are a crime scene investigator, and the game is on.

Outside the store, you see a broken window, some glass on the street, shoeprints, and marks made by a **vehicle's** tires.[3] You look at the shoeprints. They're large, so you're likely looking for a man. You photograph the shoe's pattern. This can tell you the type of shoe. You then measure the **space** between the shoeprints. You now know how long the man's **steps** were. This gives you an idea of how tall he was.

As you follow the shoeprints over to the tire marks, they get farther away from each other. They lead to the passenger's side of the vehicle. Now you know the man probably didn't work alone. You photograph the tire marks. They can help you find out what type of vehicle it was, and the **direction** it went in.

^ A crime scene investigator begins looking for fingerprints in places the thief is likely to have touched, like the front door.

1 If someone **breaks into** a place, they go inside though they are not allowed to be there.

2 A **thief** is someone who takes something that they do not own.

3 A **tire** is the outside of a car wheel. It is usually black and made of rubber.

The print left by a shoe can say a lot about the person wearing it. So at a crime scene, the print is measured. Then it is studied under colored light that makes the pattern clearer.

On the Case

The most important clues will come from a person's body. The person who broke in left a little of himself behind. In the store, you find some fingerprints. Using a computer, you can **compare** these prints against millions of others.

In the store, there is a lot more glass. Then you find something else—a hair. You keep this because you know hair contains a person's DNA.[4] You can compare this with other people's DNA, too. If you find a match for the fingerprint or the DNA, you will know who was in the store.

Will you find the thief? You now have a lot of information, so it's **possible**. For a crime scene investigator, it's all in a day's work.

4 A person's **DNA** contains information about that person. It tells a person's body things like what color its eyes or hair should be.

Reading Comprehension

Multiple Choice. Choose the best answer for each question.

Gist

1. What is this reading mainly about?
a. how an investigator used clues to find a famous thief
b. what a crime scene investigator finds at a crime scene
c. how thieves are using new technology to break into places

Vocabulary

2. What can the word *likely* in line 8 be replaced with?
a. carefully
b. probably
c. comfortably

Detail

3. In the passage, why was the investigator interested in a shoeprint?
a. because it had a very strange pattern
b. because it showed how tall the thief was
c. because it showed the direction the thief went

Detail

4. Which of the following do the tire marks NOT show?
a. the direction the thief went
b. how heavy the thief's car was
c. the type of car the thief used

Detail

5. What are the most important clues that the investigator finds?
a. fingerprints and a hair
b. shoeprints and tire marks
c. video from the store's camera

Inference

6. How would the author probably answer the question, "Will the thief be caught?"
a. Yes, he will.
b. Maybe.
c. I don't think so.

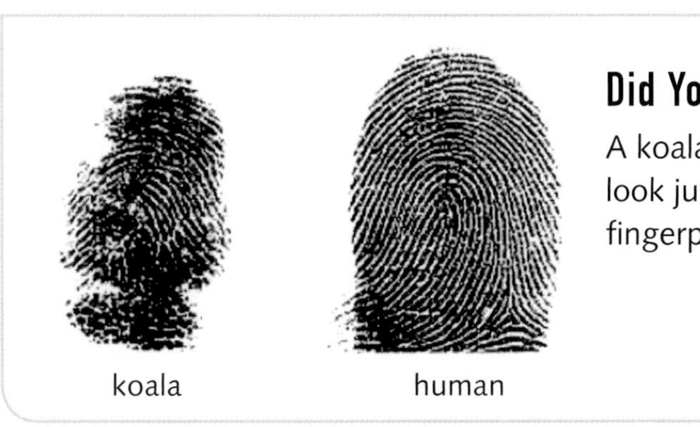
koala human

Did You Know?

A koala's fingerprints look just like a person's fingerprints.

Inferring Meaning

A text does not always state everything directly. Sometimes you need to infer meaning by "reading between the lines." You can infer meaning by using what you already know about the topic, clues in the text, and common sense. For example, in the passage on pages 65–66, we know the shoeprints were large, so it is likely that they were a man's.

A. Inference. Look at some facts from the passage on pages 65–66. What can you infer?

1. There was more broken glass inside the store than outside.
   a. The thief broke the window from the inside.
   b. The thief broke the window from the outside.

2. The space between shoeprints near the tire marks got farther apart.
   a. The thief was walking slower, and then stopping.
   b. The thief was walking faster, maybe running.

3. The shoeprints led to the passenger's side of the car.
   a. The thief drove the car.
   b. Someone else drove the car.

A burglar breaks a window while breaking into someone's house.

B. Inference. How sure are you of these things? Check (✓) the things you can infer from the passage.

1. ☐ The crime happened at night.
2. ☐ Some things were missing from the store.
3. ☐ The fingerprints belong to the thief.
4. ☐ The hair belongs to the thief.
5. ☐ The investigator will look for a match for the fingerprints.
6. ☐ The investigator will find a match for the fingerprints.

Critical Thinking Discuss with a partner. Can the information from fingerprints and DNA ever be wrong?

Vocabulary Practice

A. Completion. Choose the correct words to complete the information below.

We know that one of the best ways to **1.** (**catch** / **step**) a thief is by collecting fingerprints from a crime scene and then **2.** (**comparing** / **stepping**) them to others with a computer. But how difficult is it to get the prints?

Try this: Press a finger onto a drinking glass. If your fingers are oily or wet, the print will be better. Then cover the print with a small amount of powder. You can use things you have in your kitchen, such as flour or cocoa powder.

Now remove some of the powder with a small, dry paintbrush. Go in a circular **3.** (**direction** / **space**) until you see the print. Then place some tape over the print. Take the tape off and put it on a piece of paper. If **4.** (**catching** / **possible**), use colored paper. You should now see the fingerprint clearly.

Powder covers the pattern of the fingerprint, so it can be seen clearly.

B. Words in Context. Choose the best answer for each question below.

1. In which of these situations would a **clue** be helpful?
   a. when doing a puzzle   b. when building a house
2. Which of these do you use to take a **step**?
   a. your hands   b. your feet
3. Which of these things is an example of a **vehicle**?
   a. a house   b. a bus
4. Which of these things has more **space**?
   a. a large room   b. a box filled with books

Word Partnership
Use ***space*** with: (*adj.*) **open** space, **empty** space, **office** space, **living** space, **public** space.

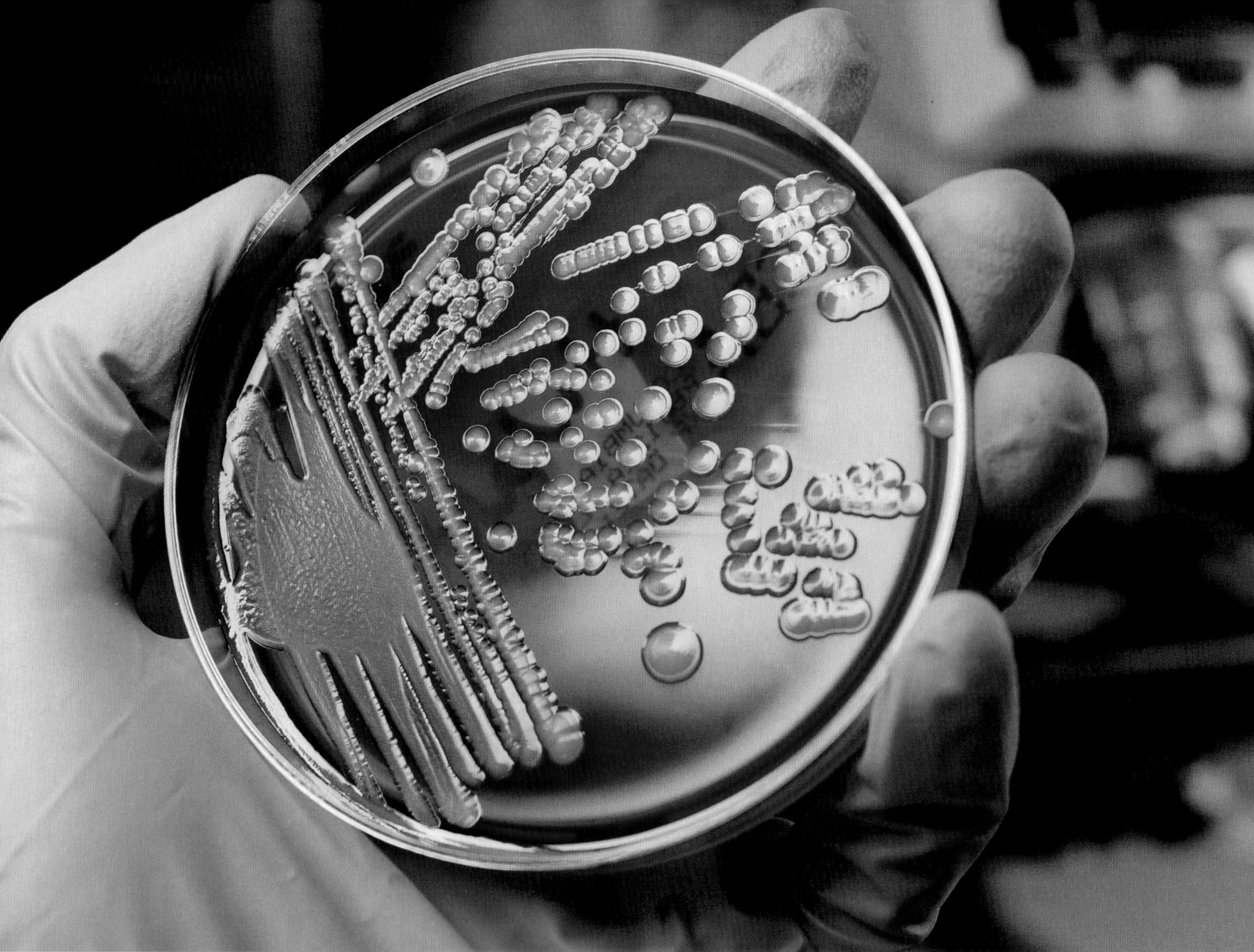

Before You Read

^ **Bacteria** are so small, you need a **microscope** to see them. *E. coli* is a type of bacteria that can be found in both animals and humans. Many **strains** of *E. coli* won't hurt you, but some can make you very **ill** or cause death.

A. Matching. Look at the photo and read the caption. Then match each word in **bold** with its definition.

1. ____________: kinds or groups of bacteria
2. ____________: sick
3. ____________: a kind of very small living thing
4. ____________: a machine that shows a larger view of something very small

B. Predict. Look quickly at the photos and headings on page 71. Check (✓) the information you think you'll read about. Then read the passage to check your answers.

☐ how a doctor found the cause of an illness

☐ how *E. coli* has caused many deaths around the world

☐ how more people want to become doctors

The Disease Detective

5B

Six children were in the hospital. They were very sick, but the doctors didn't know what to do. They called Dr. Richard Besser, an **expert** on strange illnesses.[1] Dr. Besser knew just what to do.

Dr. Richard Besser is an expert on illnesses that move and kill quickly.

Finding a Cause

First, Dr. Besser needed to find the cause of the illness. He used a microscope to look for **germs** like bacteria in the children's bodies. Dr. Besser found that all the children had a strain of the bacteria *E. coli*. Then he looked at the bacteria's DNA. The DNA showed him that this strain of *E. coli* was **dangerous** to humans.

Where Did It Come From?

Dr. Besser knew *E. coli* could move from animals to humans. **Perhaps** the children had **touched** animals that carried the bacteria? Besser found other *E. coli* cases in the area where the children lived. But it wasn't enough.

Besser then made a **list** of what the sick children had eaten. They had all eaten cheese, apple juice, and fish. He then made a list of what healthy children in the area had eaten, and compared his lists. They had eaten the cheese and fish, but not the apple juice.

Case Closed

Besser went to where the apple juice was made. He saw that there were animals around the apple trees, and he saw the workers using **dirty** apples that had fallen on the ground. More importantly, he saw that the apples were not washed before the juice was made, and that the juice was not heated. Doing these things would **kill** the bacteria. Besser then knew it was the apple juice that made the children sick.

Besser's *E. coli* case has a happy ending. The children got better. And what Besser learned that day now helps keep others safe.

1 A **disease** or an **illness** is something that makes you sick.

Reading Comprehension

Multiple Choice. Choose the best answer for each question.

Gist

1. Another title for this passage could be ________.
   a. Good vs. Bad Bacteria
   b. Looking for Answers
   c. A Death at the Hospital

Sequence

2. Which of the following things happened first?
   a. Dr. Besser found out what made the children sick.
   b. Dr. Besser made a list of what the sick children ate.
   c. Dr. Besser went to where the apple juice was made.

Detail

3. Which of the following is NOT true about *E. coli*?
   a. It's a kind of plant.
   b. It can make people sick.
   c. It moves from animals to people.

Reference

4. Who does *they* refer to in line 18?
   a. the sick children
   b. the healthy children
   c. both the sick and the healthy children

Cause and Effect

5. What made the children sick?
   a. old fish
   b. dirty apples
   c. smelly cheese

Inference

6. What advice would Dr. Besser probably agree with?
   a. Never drink apple juice from a supermarket. You should make it yourself.
   b. Stay away from animals that live near trees. They will make you sick.
   c. Don't eat fruit from the ground. Wash the fruit before you eat it.

Did You Know?

There are about two kilograms (four pounds) of bacteria in a human body.

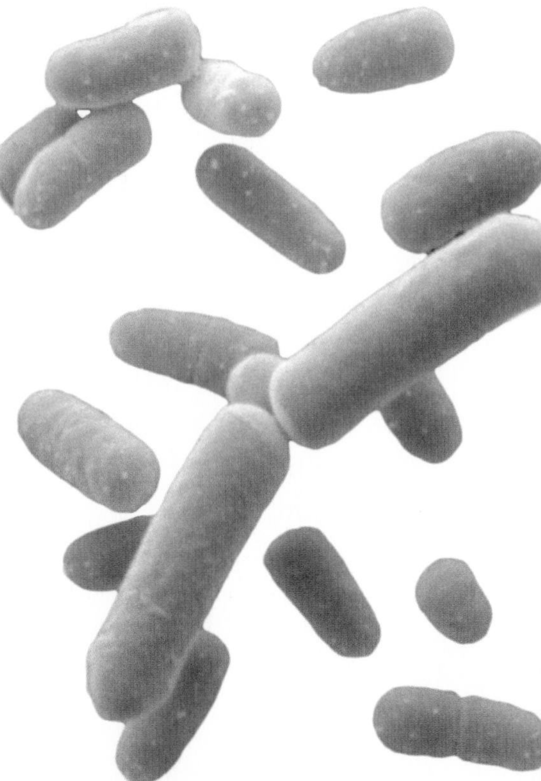

Identifying the Purpose of a Paragraph

Identifying a paragraph's purpose (or purposes) helps you understand the organization of a passage. The first line of a paragraph and its heading (if it has one) can give you clues about its purpose. These purposes can include:

- to introduce a topic
- to answer a question
- to give an example
- to describe a solution
- to continue a point
- to give data and statistics
- to make an argument
- to summarize ideas

A. Identifying Purpose. Look back at the photo and caption on page 70. Check (✓) the purpose(s) of the information in the caption.

- ☐ to introduce a topic
- ☐ to give statistics
- ☐ to help explain a photo
- ☐ to ask a question
- ☐ to give a definition
- ☐ to provide facts

B. Identifying Purpose. Look back at the passage on page 71. What is the main purpose of each paragraph?

1. Paragraph 1
a. to give background information
b. to summarize what will come later

2. Paragraph 4
a. to list a sequence of actions
b. to answer a question

3. Paragraph 5
a. to introduce a new topic
b. to answer a question

4. Paragraph 6
a. to describe the end of an event
b. to predict what will happen

Critical Thinking Discuss with a partner. How do you think we can keep safe from germs?

A good way to keep safe from germs is to wash your hands often.

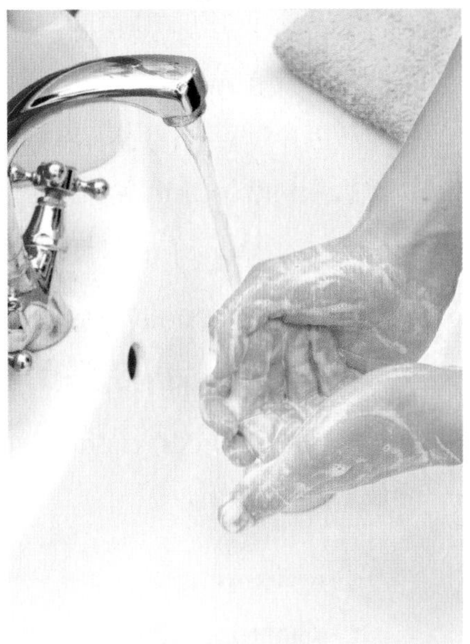

Vocabulary Practice

A. Completion. Complete the information below with the correct form of words in the box. One word is extra.

dangerous	dirty	expert	kill	touch

When a bee stings a person, the bee's "poison"[1] goes into their body. To most people, a bee sting is painful, but it's not really **1.** ____________. However, for some, a little bee sting can **2.** ____________. In fact, every year, there are many people who die from bee stings.

But scientists are learning that bee stings can also be used to help people. Dr. Chris Kleronomos is a(n) **3.** __________ on natural medicines. He is trying to help a young man named Erick. Erick has a disease that causes his muscles to hurt. He experiences a lot of pain when people **4.** __________ him. Dr. Kleronomos uses the bee's poison to take away Erick's pain. It may sound strange, but for people like Erick, it seems to be working.

1 A **poison** is something that causes illness or death if you eat or drink it.

B. Words in Context. Read the sentences below. Mark each sentence as true (**T**) or false (**F**).

1. In a restaurant, most people are happy to eat off a **dirty** plate. **T F**
2. **Perhaps** is another way to say *maybe* or *possibly*. **T F**
3. A **list** usually has just one thing on it. **T F**
4. An **expert** on a subject knows a lot about it. **T F**
5. **Germs** can make people sick. **T F**

Word Link

The suffix **-ous** (meaning "full of") can be added to some nouns to make adjectives. For example: *danger → dangerous, mystery → mysterious, adventure → adventurous.*

VIEWING Virus Detectives

Before You Watch

A. Definitions. Look at the picture and read the caption. Pay attention to the words in **bold**. You will hear them in the video. Match the words with their definitions below.

Nathan Wolfe is a scientist who studies viruses. A virus is very small. It lives inside other creatures—like bacteria, plants, animals, and people. Some viruses are **deadly**, and can **kill**. Many diseases caused by viruses are difficult to **cure**, but we can **prevent** them from getting into our bodies. In today's globalized[1] world, scientists in different countries can work together more easily to help sick people, but viruses can also **spread** more quickly than ever.

1 When we say the world is **globalized**, we mean technology has made it easy for people to move around and talk to people from other parts of the world.

1. ______________: to stop something from happening before it happens
2. ______________: very dangerous, able to cause death
3. ______________: to increase and happen over a greater area
4. ______________: to make a sick person completely well again
5. ______________: to cause death

B. Discuss. Nathan Wolfe is the leader of a group of scientists that study viruses. Where do you think these scientists go to study viruses? Discuss your ideas with a partner.

While You Watch

Checking. As you watch the video, check your answers in **Before You Watch B**. Were your ideas correct?

After You Watch

A. Completion. Choose the correct word or phrase to complete each sentence below.

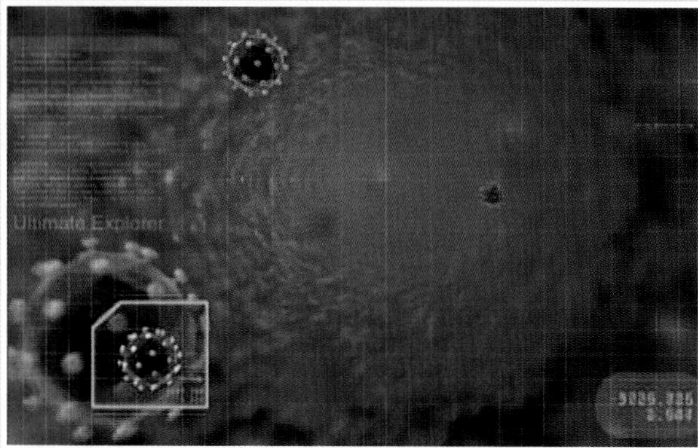

1. Nathan Wolfe and his team study how viruses move from (**animals** / **plants**) into people.

2. According to the video, people who eat (**uncooked food** / **wild animals**) are more likely to get sick from viruses.

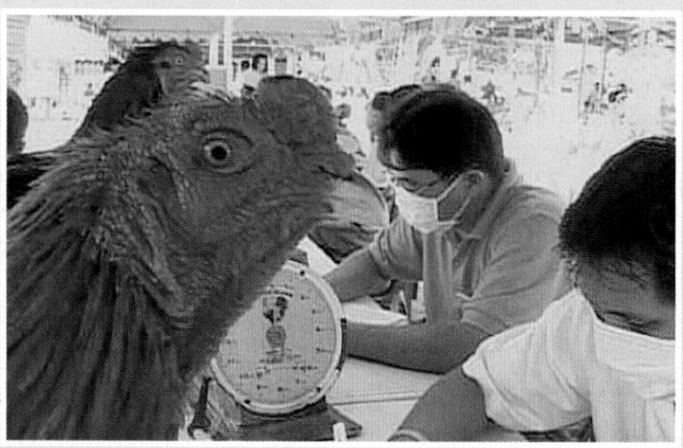

3. Wolfe's team believes that many diseases started in a (**warm** / **cold**) place.

4. According to the video, if a deadly virus begins to spread, (**the whole world** / **people living close to animals**) will be in danger.

B. Inferring Meaning. Answer the questions below. Then discuss your answers with a partner.

1. Can viruses be found in chickens?
2. What is one way viruses get from animals into humans?
3. How does a virus spread from country to country?

C. Discuss. Discuss these questions with a partner.

1. What do you think a day in the life of a scientist like Nathan Wolfe is like? Would you like to work with his team?
2. How do you think people can help prevent viruses from spreading?

A virus can go into a person's blood and make copies of itself.

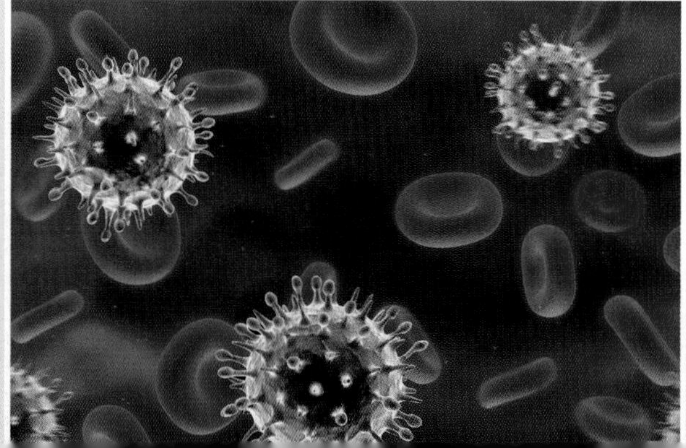

6

EXPLORERS AND PIONEERS

Early European settlers moving across the land in wagons, spread out across North America.

Warm Up

Discuss these questions with a partner.

1. Pioneers are people who explore new places or do things that have never been done before. Do you know about any famous pioneers?
2. Who were the first people to explore, or live in, your country? What stories do you know about them?

Before You Read

In 1804, mapmakers Lewis and Clark began to explore the western part of North America. Sacagawea, a Native American woman from the Shoshone **tribe**, went with them. Today, there are many **statues** of her in the U.S. Her face is also on an American **coin**.

A. Matching. Look at the picture and read the caption. Then match the correct form of each word in **bold** with its definition.

1. ____________: a piece of metal, usually round, used as money
2. ____________: a group of many families with the same language, traditions, and beliefs
3. ____________: a piece of art made of stone, metal, or wood, usually showing a person or an animal

B. Skim. Skim the passage on the next page. Check (✓) the information given in the passage. Then read the passage to check your answers.

- ☐ how Sacagawea helped the explorers
- ☐ how Sacagawea lived after the trip
- ☐ how people remember Sacagawea today

Who was Sacagawea?

The Sacagawea dollar coin was first made in 2000.

There are more statues of her than of any other American woman. Her face is on a U.S. coin. **Clearly**, she was an important person. But what do we know about the real Sacagawea?

Sacagawea was part of a Native American tribe called the Shoshone. At the age of 13, she was taken away by people from the Hidatsa tribe. She was living **among** the Hidatsa when Meriwether Lewis and William Clark met her in 1804.

Meriwether Lewis and William Clark were mapmakers. These pioneers were exploring the western part of the U.S. Because Sacagawea spoke two different Native American languages, they asked her to **travel** with them, along with her husband and baby son.

Sacagawea became an important part of the group and helped the explorers in many ways. For example, on May 14, 1805, a strong storm tipped over[1] one of their boats. Sacagawea stayed **calm**. She acted quickly and was able to **save** many of the maps and other things from the water. Her **actions** saved important **knowledge** from being lost.

As they traveled, Sacagawea helped Lewis and Clark talk to the Native American people in each **village** they visited. She helped the explorers make friends among the Native Americans, so they could trade with them. She also helped Lewis and Clark find a way across the mountains to the Pacific Ocean, and helped them find food on the way.

Sacagawea died when she was about 25. Sadly, we don't know much more about this amazing woman. But two hundred years later, she is remembered as an important woman in U.S. history.

Lewis and Clark traveled from St. Louis to the Pacific Ocean and back again.

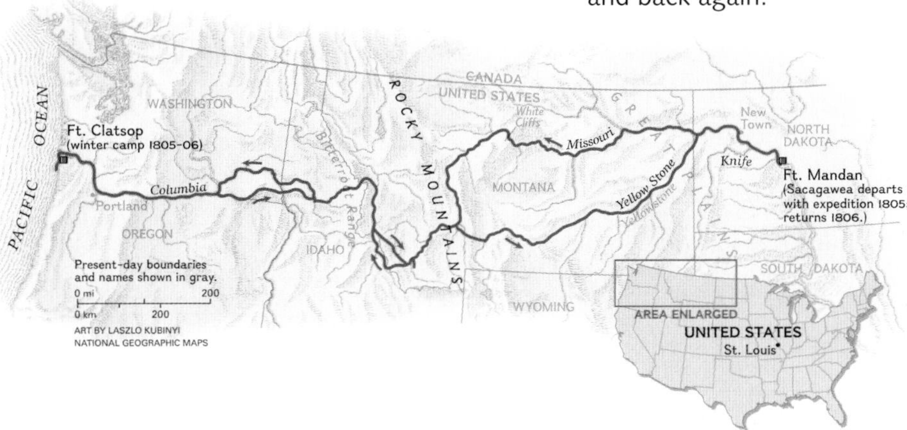

1 When something **tips over**, it turns and falls on its side.

Reading Comprehension

Multiple Choice. Choose the best answer for each question.

Gist

1. The reading is mainly about why ______.
   a. not much is known about Sacagawea
   b. Sacagawea left Lewis and Clark's group
   c. Sacagawea was an important woman in U.S. history

Detail

2. Which of these sentences about Sacagawea is NOT true?
   a. She took her child with her on the trip.
   b. She asked Lewis and Clark if she could come on the trip.
   c. She started living with the Hidatsa tribe when she was 13 years old.

Detail

3. When the explorers' boat tipped over, Sacagawea ______.
   a. lost all the food they were carrying
   b. was able to save Meriwether Lewis
   c. was able to save maps from the water

Detail

4. Which of the following did Sacagawea do to help Lewis and Clark?
   a. She helped them draw maps of the places they saw.
   b. She helped them make friends with the native people.
   c. She saved their lives when wild animals attacked them.

Vocabulary

5. The word *trade* (line 19) means ______.
   a. fight
   b. tell stories
   c. buy and sell things

Inference

6. Which of the following sentences is likely to be true?
   a. The author thinks Sacagawea was too young to travel.
   b. The author would like to know more about Sacagawea.
   c. The author believes the story of Sacagawea is not true.

Did You Know?

Lewis kept a journal of the trip. He wrote nearly 5,000 pages.

Creating a Timeline of Events

When you read a passage that has a series of events, it can be useful to place them on a timeline. This gives you a clear picture of what things happened in the order that they happened. Look carefully at ages, dates, and years. But be careful—events may not always appear in the passage in the order that they happened.

A. Scan. Find and underline these events in the reading passage on page 79.

a. The Hidatsa take Sacagawea from her people at age 13.

b. About 200 years ago, Sacagawea dies at about age 25.

c. In 1805, Sacagawea saves maps and other items during a storm.

d. Sacagawea lives among the Shoshone people during her childhood.

e. In 1804, Sacagawea meets Lewis and Clark.

f. With Sacagawea's help, Lewis and Clark reach the Pacific Ocean.

g. Sacagawea joins Lewis and Clark on their trip.

B. Sequencing. Label the timeline with the events in **A**.

	a					

1804

Critical Thinking Discuss with a partner. What do you think Sacagawea's life was like after the expedition? Why do you think we don't know much about Sacagawea's life?

During the trip, Sacagawea visited her own tribe. Her brother, who was now the chief, was very happy to see her.

Vocabulary Practice

A. Completion. Complete the timeline below with words from the box. Two words are extra.

actions	among	calm	clearly	save	travel	village

Amy Johnson sits aboard her plane.

Amy Johnson—A Pioneer of Flight

1903 Amy Johnson is born in Hull, England.

1928 She takes flying lessons. She is **1.** ________ not a natural—at first, she is quite bad at it. But she doesn't give up and after a lot of hard work, finally learns to fly.

1930 Johnson becomes the first woman to fly solo[1] from England to Australia. The world starts to take notice of her, and her **2.** ________ inspire many other pilots. When she returns to England, the king and queen are **3.** ________ the many people who send their congratulations.[2]

1931 Johnson is the first person to **4.** ________ from London to Moscow in one day. She then flies across Siberia to Tokyo.

1936 Johnson becomes the first person to fly solo from England to South Africa.

1941 Johnson's plane crashes in the River Thames in London. People from a nearby ship try to **5.** ________ her, but they are too late.

1 If someone flies **solo**, they fly alone.

2 **Congratulations** are nice messages sent, or things people say, to someone who has done something well.

B. Words in Context. Complete each sentence with the correct word or phrase.

1. Many people think life in a **village** is too ______.
   a. quiet b. noisy
2. If you are **among** friends, you are ______ the group.
   a. inside b. outside
3. If you have great **knowledge** of a subject, you ______.
   a. know it well b. know nothing about it
4. A person ______ is an example of someone who is **calm**.
   a. in the middle of a fight b. who is resting

Usage
A **town** is usually bigger than a **village**. A **city** is usually bigger than a **town**. *About 90 people live in that **village**. Seven thousand people live in my **town**. Tokyo is the world's biggest **city**.*

Polar PIONEER

In 1937, Matthew Henson was invited to be a member of the Explorers Club. He was the first African American to be invited.

Before You Read

A. Completion. Read the definitions. Then complete the information below with the correct form of the words in **bold**.

on foot: by walking

sleds: objects used for traveling over snow

team: a group of people working together

member: one of the people that makes up a group

In 1909, Matthew Henson became the first man to reach the North Pole. He did this as a **1.** __________ of a **2.** __________, led by explorer Robert Peary. To get to the North Pole, the explorers traveled by ship, in **3.** __________ pulled by dogs, and **4.** __________.

B. Scan. Quickly scan the passage on pages 84–85. In total, how many times did Peary and Henson try to reach the North Pole? Read the passage to check your answer.

Matthew Henson: Arctic Explorer

Robert Peary and Matthew Henson both wanted to be great explorers. When Peary needed someone to **join** him on his trip to the North Pole, he thought of Henson. They had once worked together in Central America. At the time, it was unusual for an African American to be a **well-known** explorer. Henson wanted to change that. So, though he knew the trip would be hard, he agreed to go.

First, they traveled by ship to Greenland. The members of Peary's team lived among the Inuit people there. The Inuit called Henson "Maripaluk—Matthew, the Kind One." Henson learned their language. The Inuit taught him how to live outdoors on the ice, find food, build igloos,[1] make snowshoes, and **drive** dogsleds through the snow and ice.

1 An **igloo** is a round house made of ice.

Robert Peary, the explorer, stands in Greenland with his sled dogs.

Among other things, the explorers' ship, the *Roosevelt*, carried over 200 sled dogs.

To the Top of the World

Between 1891 and 1906, the Peary-Henson team made seven **attempts** to get to the North Pole. Each time, they learned hard lessons about the dangers there. Sleds broke. Dogs died. Men got hurt. They got close to the North Pole, but they always had to go back.

In 1909, they decided to make one more attempt. Peary and Henson found themselves within 56 kilometers (35 miles) of the North Pole. Peary sent Henson **ahead**. Henson made a **trail** through the snow for Peary to **follow**. Peary followed 45 minutes later. "I think I am the first man to sit on top of the world," Henson told Peary.

The team returned home as **heroes**. Both men's dreams had come true: They were the first explorers to reach the North Pole.

"I think I am the first man to sit on top of the world."

—Matthew Henson, April 6, 1909

Reading Comprehension

Multiple Choice. Choose the best answer for each question.

Main Idea

1. What is the main idea of the second paragraph (from line 8)?
   a. The Inuit have a difficult life in Greenland.
   b. Henson learned how to speak the Inuit language.
   c. Henson learned many things from the Inuit.

Detail

2. Which of the following sentences about Matthew Henson is true?
   a. He was from Central America.
   b. The Inuit called him "the Kind One."
   c. He was the leader of the team on this trip to the North Pole.

Reference

3. The word *their* in line 10 can be replaced by _____.
   a. the Inuit's
   b. the team's
   c. Peary and Henson's

Vocabulary

4. The phrase *hard lessons* (line 16) refers to ______.
   a. things that are hard to understand
   b. ways they learned to break up hard ice
   c. things they learned because bad things happened

Paraphrase

5. The sentence *Peary sent Henson ahead.* (line 21) is closest in meaning to ______.
   a. Peary sent Henson a message
   b. Peary asked Henson to go first
   c. Peary and Henson traveled together

Inference

6. Which of these statements would Henson likely agree with?
   a. He and Peary were a good team.
   b. Bringing dogs to the North Pole was a bad idea.
   c. The explorers could have reached the North Pole without the help of the Inuit.

Did You Know?

Peary and Henson's 1909 expedition to the North Pole included 19 dogsleds, 133 dogs, and 24 men, including 17 Inuit. Only Peary, Henson, and four Inuit men got to the North Pole.

Reading Skill

Understanding Compound Nouns

A compound noun is a word created by putting two words together. It can be formed from different parts of speech, such as a noun + a noun (e.g., *homework*), an adjective + a noun (e.g., *whiteboard*), or a preposition + a noun (e.g., *afternoon*).

A. Noticing. Look back at the second paragraph of the passage on pages 84–85. Find and write the four compound words in the paragraph. Take notice of what smaller words are used to make up each word.

1. ____________ **3.** ____________

2. ____________ **4.** ____________

B. Completion. Circle the words that create compound nouns. Then write the compound nouns.

1. class	(mate)	(room)	student	***classmate***	***classroom***
2. black	life	board	bird	________	________
3. out	side	one	doors	________	________
4. some	body	day	color	________	________
5. day	food	time	light	________	________
6. rain	wet	coat	water	________	________
7. sun	shine	set	yellow	________	________
8. up	hill	class	grade	________	________

Critical Thinking Discuss with a partner. Why do you think being an African American explorer in the 1900s was difficult? What qualities do you think Henson had that made him a good explorer?

Matthew Henson sits on his sled, dressed in warm furs.

Vocabulary Practice

A. Matching. Read the information below and match the correct form of each word in **red** with its definition.

When he was 13 years old, Jan Mela lost his left leg and right arm. Mela is the youngest person ever to go to both the North and South Poles.

Arctic Firsts

Following in the footsteps of Peary and Henson, many people have traveled to the North Pole. Here are some of their stories.

- 60 years after Peary's team, **well-known** British explorer Wally Herbert reached the North Pole. He completed the trip in 1969.
- Teenager Jan Mela became a **hero** to many when he **joined** Polish explorer Marek Kamiński and two others for 2004's "Together to the Pole" trip. They walked to both the North and South Poles in the same year.
- In 2007, a team from the TV show *Top Gear* became the first to **drive** a car to the North Pole. As part of the trip, the team raced against a dogsled. The car won, getting there **ahead** of the sled.

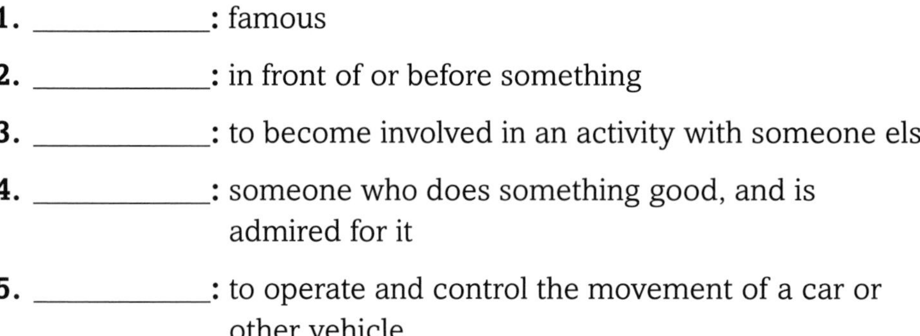

1. ___________: famous
2. ___________: in front of or before something
3. ___________: to become involved in an activity with someone else
4. ___________: someone who does something good, and is admired for it
5. ___________: to operate and control the movement of a car or other vehicle

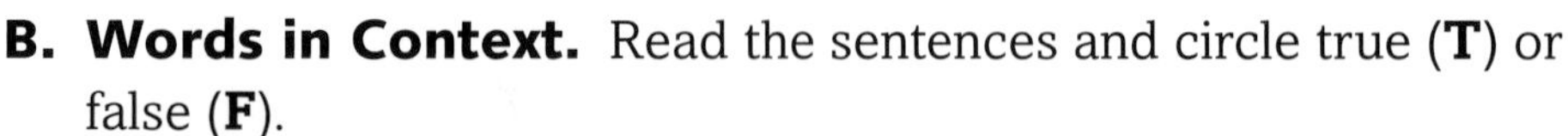

B. Words in Context. Read the sentences and circle true (**T**) or false (**F**).

1. People usually don't like their **heroes**. **T F**
2. A **trail** is a route or path, usually for walking. **T F**
3. If you make an **attempt** to do something, you try to do it. **T F**
4. When you are **ahead** of someone, they are behind you. **T F**
5. If you **follow** someone, you walk in front of the person. **T F**

Usage

You **drive** a car, bus, or truck. You **ride** a bicycle or motorcycle.

*I **drive** a car to work. My brother **rides** a bicycle to school.*

VIEWING Native Americans

Before You Watch

A. Warm Up. Look at the picture and read the caption. What do you know about Native Americans? Discuss with a partner.

When the first Europeans arrived in North America, they found a population[1] of one million Native Americans already living there. There were many tribes, each with its own culture and language. The new settlers[2] wanted the native peoples' land. There was a lot of fighting between the two groups. The Native American tribes lost their land. Today, many tribes are still trying to win back their land, while others work to rebuild parts of their culture and tribal identity.[3]

1 The **population** of a place is the number of people living there.
2 **Settlers** are people who travel to a new place and start to live there.
3 Your **identity** describes who you are.

B. Predict. What do you think happened to the Native Americans after Europeans came to settle in North America? Check (✓) your ideas below.

- ☐ Many of them got sick.
- ☐ They became a single tribe.
- ☐ Many left North America.
- ☐ They taught the settlers about their culture.
- ☐ Their population decreased.
- ☐ They had to leave their homes.
- ☐ They lived in bad conditions.
- ☐ Their culture grew stronger.

While You Watch

Checking. As you watch the video, check your answers in **Before You Watch B**. Were your ideas correct?

After You Watch

A. Sequencing. Read the events described below. Then complete the timeline.

☐ ☐ ☐ ☐ ☐ ☐

1. Humans first come to North America.
2. The first Europeans arrive in North America.
3. Many Native Americans die from new diseases.
4. Traditional art forms and ceremonies begin again.
5. The Native Americans become hundreds of different groups.
6. The government makes the Native Americans leave their land.

B. Completion. Look at the pictures below. Choose the correct word or phrase to complete each sentence.

1. People think the Native Americans came from (**Asia** / **Europe**).

2. This (**painting** / **totem pole**) is an example of Native American art.

3. Some tribes have held meetings with (**other tribes** / **the government**) to talk about getting their land back.

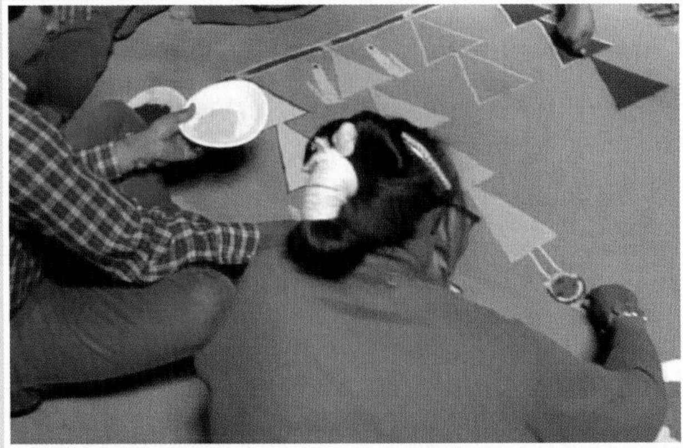

4. The patterns in this picture represent the (**cloud people** / **Europeans**).

C. Discuss. Discuss these questions with a partner. Who were the first people in your country? Can you still see their culture today?

7

An amazing 3-D drawing on the street plays tricks on our eyes and minds.

MIND'S EYE

Warm Up

Discuss these questions with a partner.

1. What is unusual about the picture above?
2. Do you usually remember your dreams? What is the last dream you remember?

Before You Read

Many people believe our dreams have meanings and can tell us more about our lives in the real world.

A. Matching. Many people have different ideas about what dreams might mean. Here are some interesting examples. What do you think it might mean if you dream about these things?

1. a snake •	• a. You're thinking about your mother.
2. a queen •	• b. You're thinking about a bad memory.
3. your teeth •	• c. You're afraid of something you can't see.
4. a bad smell •	• d. You have trouble sharing your thoughts.

B. Predict. Read the title and headings on the next page, and answer the questions below. Then read the passage to check your ideas.

1. How many kinds of dreams can you read about in the passage?

2. What do you think the passage will tell you about each type of dream?

The Meaning of Dreams

Did you have any interesting dreams last night?

Our dreams come from a part of the brain that contains our thoughts and memories. A person can have up to six dreams a night, and each dream usually **lasts** from 10 to 40 minutes. Everyone dreams, but not everyone remembers their dreams. Most people dream in color, usually with sound. And we usually dream about ourselves and the people we know.

Why Do We Dream?

Alan Siegel is a scientist who studies dreams. "Dreams help us get in touch with our deeper feelings," he says. "They can tell us a lot about ourselves, and can help us figure out **problems**." Another scientist, Robert Stickgold, thinks dreams come from our memories. He believes we dream to remember, because memories are **useful** to the brain. Stickgold says the purpose of dreaming through these memories is to help us learn from the past.

Here are a few types of dreams and what people think they mean.

Dream 1: You Meet Someone While in Your Pajamas[1]

Sometimes people dream that they meet someone they know while wearing their underwear (or nothing at all!). This dream may be the **result** of an embarrassing[2] event in your life. Some people think we dream about embarrassing situations if our brains are trying to deal with[3] an event in our own lives.

Dream 2: You're Flying

If you dream about flying, you are probably quite happy. This is a good **period** in your life. You may feel that other people see you as a **leader**.

Dream 3: You Didn't Study for a Test

This probably means you are **worried** about an important event coming in your life. If you're not **prepared** for the event, your dream may be telling you, "It's time to get to work!"

---

1 **Pajamas** are clothes that are specially made to sleep in.

2 If something is **embarrassing**, it makes you feel shy or ashamed.

3 If you **deal with** a problem, you try to do something about it.

Reading Comprehension

Multiple Choice. Choose the best answer for each question.

Main Idea

1. What is the main idea of the reading?
   a. Dreams come from only one part of the brain.
   b. Everyone has dreams, but not everyone remembers them.
   c. Dreams can help us to understand our feelings and problems.

Detail

2. Which of these sentences about dreams is NOT true?
   a. They usually have color and sound.
   b. Each dream usually lasts for 10 to 40 minutes.
   c. Most people have about ten dreams a night.

Detail

3. Robert Stickgold believes that dreams ________.
   a. can tell us about ourselves
   b. help us figure out problems
   c. are made from our memories

Vocabulary

4. In lines 9–10, another way to say *get in touch with* would be __________.
   a. talk to
   b. dream about
   c. find out and understand

Detail

5. According to the passage, which of these sentences is true?
   a. If you dream you're wearing no clothes, something embarrassing probably happened to you.
   b. If you dream you're flying, this is probably a difficult time in your life.
   c. If you dream you didn't study for a test, you're probably not getting enough sleep at night.

Inference

6. If someone says, "The concert is tomorrow, and I haven't had time to practice!" which dream from the passage might they have?
   a. Dream 1: You Meet Someone While in Your Pajamas
   b. Dream 2: You're Flying
   c. Dream 3: You Didn't Study for a Test

Did You Know?

Most people forget half of their dreams within five minutes of waking up. After ten minutes, 90 percent of their dreams are usually gone.

Creating a Concept Map

A concept map helps you organize information in a visual way. To create a concept map, start by writing the general topic or main idea of the text in a center box. Then write other key ideas related to this around the box, linking with lines to show relationships. After that, add and link additional details. Generally, ideas in a concept map move from general to specific as you move outward from the center.

A. Analyzing. Look back at the reading passage on page 93. What information is important to remember? Circle the main ideas and underline the key details.

B. Completion. Complete the concept map with words from the reading passage.

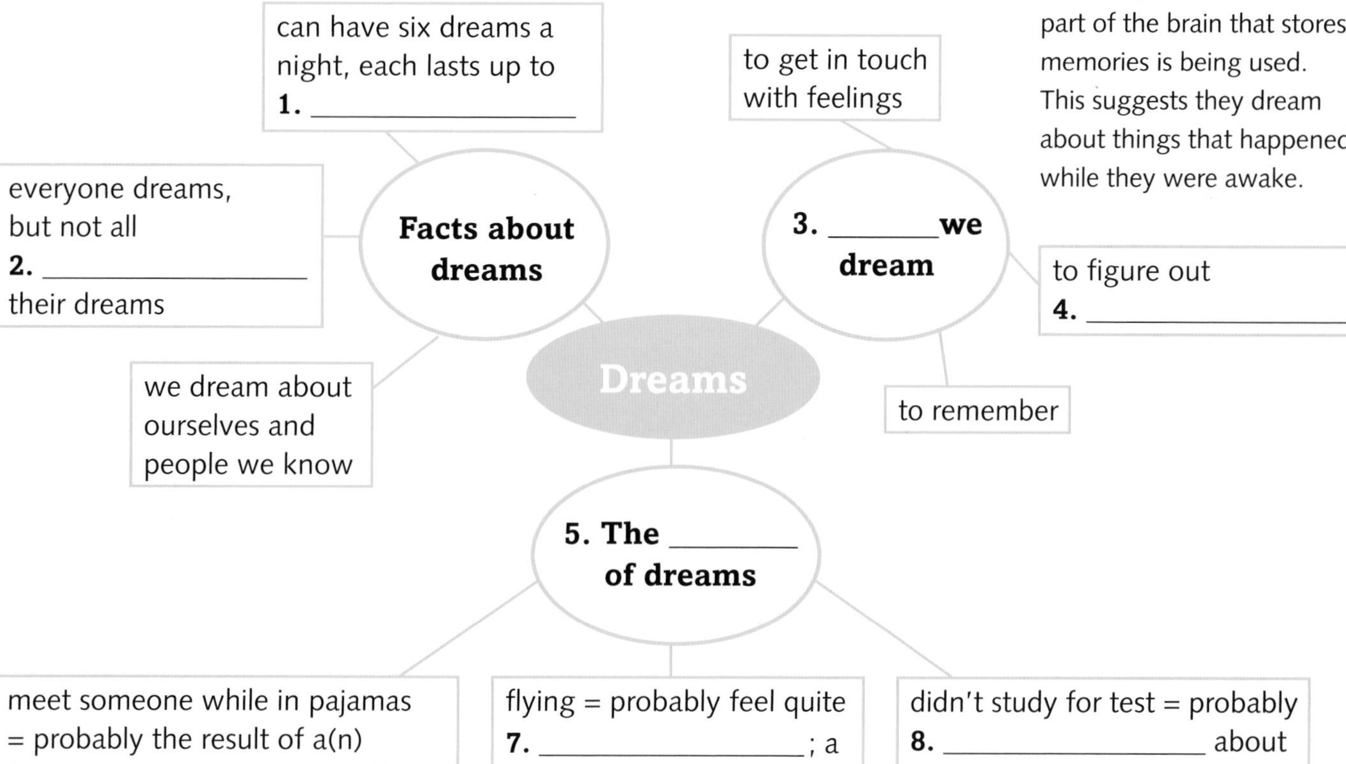

Scientists have found that animals have dreams, too. While they sleep, their brain waves show that they're dreaming, and that the part of the brain that stores memories is being used. This suggests they dream about things that happened while they were awake.

Critical Thinking Discuss with a partner. Which idea from the passage on page 93—Stickgold's or Siegel's—do you believe? Do you think dreams have meaning?

Vocabulary Practice

A. Definitions. Use the correct form of the words in the box to complete the definitions below.

last	**leader**	**period**	**prepare**	**problem**	**result**	**useful**	**worried**

1. A ____________ is something caused by something else.
2. If a class ____________ one hour, it's 60 minutes long.
3. If something is ____________, it's helpful in some way.
4. If you ____________ for something, you get ready for it.
5. Someone who fears something bad will happen is probably ____________.
6. ____________ are things that are difficult to deal with.
7. A ____________ of time is a length of time in which something happens.
8. A ____________ is someone who others follow.

B. Completion. Complete the information below with the correct form of the words from the box in **A**.

We spend about one-third of our lives sleeping. Children usually need a lot of sleep because they are still growing. Older people need to sleep for shorter **1.** __________ of time. In general, sleep that **2.** __________ seven or eight hours is enough for most people.

However, a lot of people don't get enough sleep. This causes **3.** __________ for the part of the brain that controls our emotions. For example, one of the **4.** __________ of not getting enough sleep is that we can become angry or **5.** __________ more easily.

If you have trouble sleeping, you can **6.** __________ for sleep by taking a warm bath or listening to slow music. Some people find it **7.** __________ to drink warm milk.

A glass of warm milk helps some people fall asleep. Milk contains melatonin, a chemical that causes us to feel sleepy.

Word Partnership

Use ***problem*** with: (*v.*) **cause** a problem, **solve** a problem, **fix** a problem; (*adj.*) **big** problem, **serious** problem, **major** problem, **common** problem.

7B

Seeing the IMPOSSIBLE

This photo was taken in the middle of Salar de Uyuni, the world's largest salt flat, in Bolivia. In the dry season, the area is completely flat and white, making photos like this one possible.

Before You Read

A. Discussion. Look at the picture above and read the caption. Then answer the questions below.

1. Can you explain what you see? How do you think this photo was taken?
2. Have you seen photos with illusions like this before?

B. Predict. Look at the title and the pictures on pages 97–99. What is unusual about each picture? Discuss each picture with a partner. Then read the passage to check your ideas.

Can you believe everything you see? Not always! Sometimes our minds and our eyes make **mistakes**. At other times, our eyes and minds can become confused.[1] This may be because we are looking at something called an *optical illusion.*

The word *optical* means "**related to** sight"—the way we see things with our eyes. An *illusion* is something that looks different from the way it really is. In short, an optical illusion is a kind of trick that our eyes play on us.

Look at these optical illusions and compare what you see with what your classmates see. The way we see things is often **personal**, so you may not see things the same way as someone else.

So can you **trust** your eyes? Perhaps the answer is "sometimes." Sometimes our eyes see something, and our minds understand it easily. At other times, we may need to look twice.

1 If you **confuse** two things, you get them mixed up.

Which red dot is larger?

Most people say it's the dot on the left. Now measure the dots. The red dot on the left may seem larger because of the small blue dots around it, but they're really the same **size**.

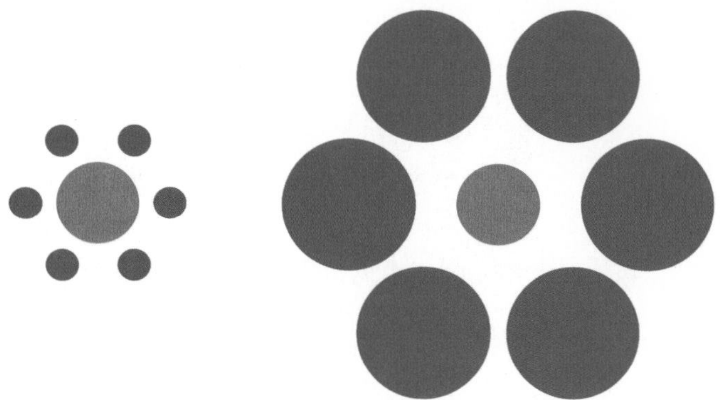

Look at this picture. What do you see?

Do you see a cup, or do you see two faces? Now look again! The illusion shows two different images at the same time. **Therefore**, our minds have to choose which image to look at. Scientists think this choice is difficult, because different parts of your brain are getting different information. One part "sees" the cup and another part "sees" the faces, so the image keeps changing.

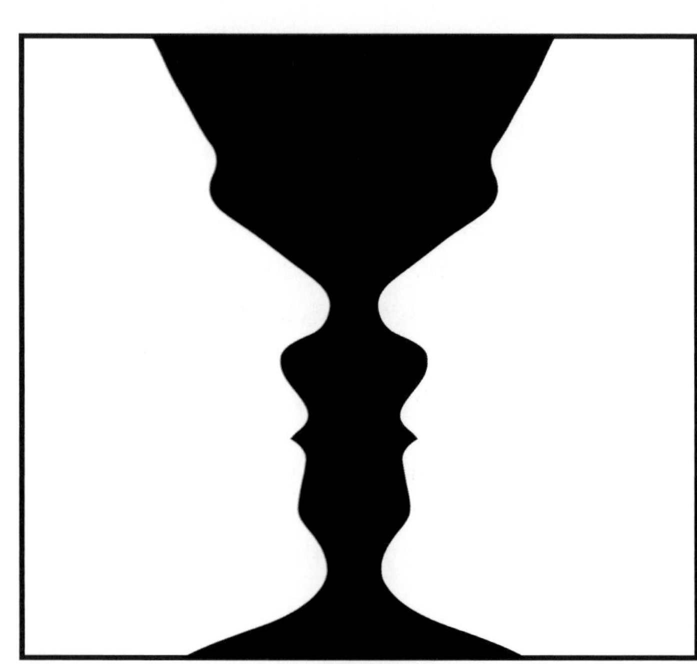

Are the circles moving?

When you **stare** at this picture, your mind may tell you that the circles are moving, but this is **impossible**! How can a picture move? Some people think the circles seem to move because, often, when we see circle-in-circle shapes, like in car wheels or snake bodies, they are usually moving. Our brains are used to seeing these shapes move. So when our eyes see this shape, our mind infers that the image is moving. Other scientists believe the illusion of movement is caused by the tiny movements of our eyes as we look at the different colors and patterns of the picture.

Reading Comprehension

Multiple Choice. Choose the best answer for each question.

Main Idea

1. What is the main idea of the first paragraph?
   a. Optical illusions can only be seen by a few people.
   b. Optical illusions are things that aren't real.
   c. Optical illusions make us think we see something that's not there.

Detail

2. What causes optical illusion 1 (from line 15)?
   a. The red dots aren't close to each other.
   b. We can see the blue dots clearly, but not the red dots.
   c. We compare each red dot with the blue dots around it.

Reference

3. The word *they're* (line 19) refers to the __________.
   a. red dots
   b. big blue dots
   c. small blue dots

Detail

4. What causes optical illusion 2 (from line 21)?
   a. Your left and right eyes see different things.
   b. Different parts of your brain get different information.
   c. Your brain thinks that it can see faces that aren't really there.

Vocabulary

5. In line 41, the word *tiny* can be replaced with _______.
   a. very fast
   b. very small
   c. very strange

Inference

6. Which of these is an optical illusion?
   a. hearing a voice in your head that isn't there
   b. seeing water on a road when it's not really there
   c. looking up at a strange cloud and noticing its shape

Did You Know?

3-D movies are a type of optical illusion.

Reading Skill

Understanding Compound Sentences

A compound sentence consists of two simple sentences joined by a comma and a conjunction. Conjunctions include *and* (to add information), *but* (to contrast information), *or* (to show a choice), and *so* (to show a result). Look at these examples.

I want to buy a new dictionary, ***and*** *I need some new notebooks.*
I want to buy a new dictionary, ***but*** *I don't have any money.*
I might just buy a new dictionary, ***or*** *I might just borrow my friend's.*
I want to buy a new dictionary, ***so*** *I'm going to go to the bookstore.*

This fountain in Ypres, Belgium, forms an optical illusion, that of a floating faucet.

A. Completion. Circle the correct conjunction to complete each sentence.

1. I like optical illusions. They're interesting to look at, (**and** / **or**) they can be a lot of fun.
2. You can find optical illusions in books, (**or** / **so**) you can look for them online.
3. Optical illusions play tricks on the mind, (**but** / **so**) they can make people very confused.
4. Optical illusions use color, light, and patterns, (**and** / **but**) they don't use sound.

B. Completion. Complete these sentences using words from the box. Then look back at the reading on pages 98–99 to check your answers.

or **so** **but** **and**

1. Sometimes our eyes see something, ______ our minds understand it easily. (lines 13–14)
2. The red dot on the left may seem larger because of the small blue dots around it, ______ they're really the same size. (lines 17–20)
3. Do you see a cup, ______ do you see two faces? (lines 23–24)
4. One part "sees" the cup and another part "sees" the faces, ______ the image keeps changing. (line 30–32)

Critical Thinking Discuss with a partner. Look back at the optical illusions on pages 98–99. Which of the illusions is most confusing to you? Why?

Vocabulary Practice

A. Completion. Choose the correct words to complete the information below.

Look at the photo. What do you see? Do you **1.** (**trust** / **stare**) your eyes? Maybe you shouldn't. Your eyes—and your mind—might be making a **2.** (**stare** / **mistake**).

If you see only dark camels crossing the desert, your eyes are playing tricks on you. The photographer took this photo toward the end of the day. **3.** (**Impossible** / **Therefore**), the sun was low in the sky and the camels had long shadows. The dark camel shapes you see in the photo are really just the camels' shadows. If you **4.** (**trust** / **stare**) at it closely, you can see that the real camels are the thin brown shapes below the darker camel shapes.

^ This photo of camels walking in the desert forms a kind of optical illusion. Sometimes optical illusions happen naturally.

B. Words in Context. Complete each sentence with the correct answer.

1. An idea that is **related to** something is ________ that thing.
a. linked with b. different from

2. It is **impossible** for an elephant to ___________.
a. carry a tree branch b. carry a large whale

3. The **size** of something is how ___________ it is.
a. heavy b. big

4. When you **stare** at something, you look at it for a __________ time.
a. short b. long

5. If you make a **mistake**, you do something that is ___________.
a. correct b. wrong

6. If something is **personal**, you _____________.
a. share it with everyone b. keep it to yourself

Word Partnership

Use ***mistake*** with: (*v.*) **make** a mistake, **correct** a mistake, **repeat** a mistake; (*adj.*) **terrible** mistake, **stupid** mistake, **common** mistake.

VIEWING Parasomnia

Before You Watch

A. Warm Up. Look at the picture and read the caption. Have you, or anyone you know, experienced parasomnia? Discuss with a partner.

Have you ever seen someone walking around while they're asleep? Their eyes may be open, but they don't seem to see anything. It may sound strange, but many people do get out of bed and move around without ever waking up. Sleepwalking is an example of a type of sleep problem called *parasomnia*. Other people who have parasomnia may move around in their sleep and seem to be having nightmares (bad dreams), or move their legs as if they are kicking something.

B. Predict. Answer the questions below. Discuss with a partner.

1. What causes people to experience parasomnia?

a. They have slept for too long.
b. A part of their brain is awake.
c. They're having a very scary dream.

2. Which of these is another example of parasomnia?

a. snoring very loudly
b. eating while sleeping
c. waking up many times in one night

While You Watch

A. Checking. As you watch the video, check your answers in **Before You Watch B**. Were your ideas correct?

B. Viewing. What other kinds of sleep activities does the video mention?

☐ fighting ☐ cooking ☐ dancing ☐ talking ☐ driving

After You Watch

A. Multiple Choice. Choose the correct answer for each question below.

1. The video says people who fight in their sleep may ______.

a. be angry with their partner

b. be worried about a problem

c. be dreaming about being attacked

2. When people with parasomnia wake up they ______.

a. think they're still in a dream

b. remember their dreams clearly

c. don't know what they have done

3. When people sleepwalk, their ______ is awake.

a. upper brain b. middle brain c. lower brain

B. Matching. Match the stages of NREM sleep with their descriptions.

Stage 1	Stage 2	Stages 3 and 4

1. Your body relaxes.

2. You're in deep sleep.

3. You sleep lightly.

4. Brain waves are small.

5. Heart beat and breathing get slower.

6. Brain waves are large and far apart.

7. Your brain shuts off sounds and movements from the outside world.

C. Discuss. Discuss these questions with a partner.

1. What do you think you should do if you see someone with parasomnia?

2. The video says parasomnia can be dangerous. In what ways do you think parasomnia can be dangerous?

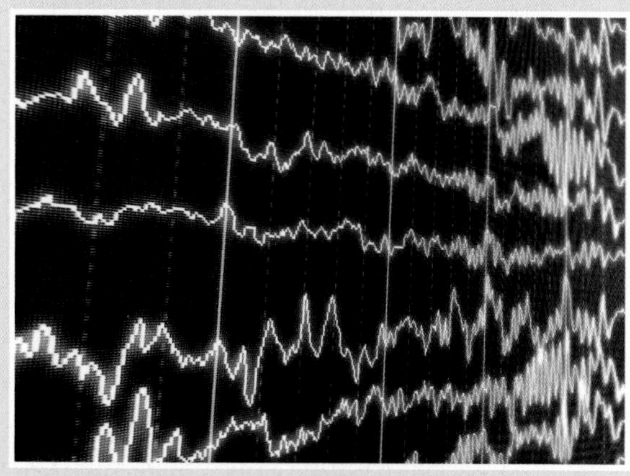

^ This pattern of lines shows a person's brain waves as he or she goes from R.E.M. sleep to waking up.

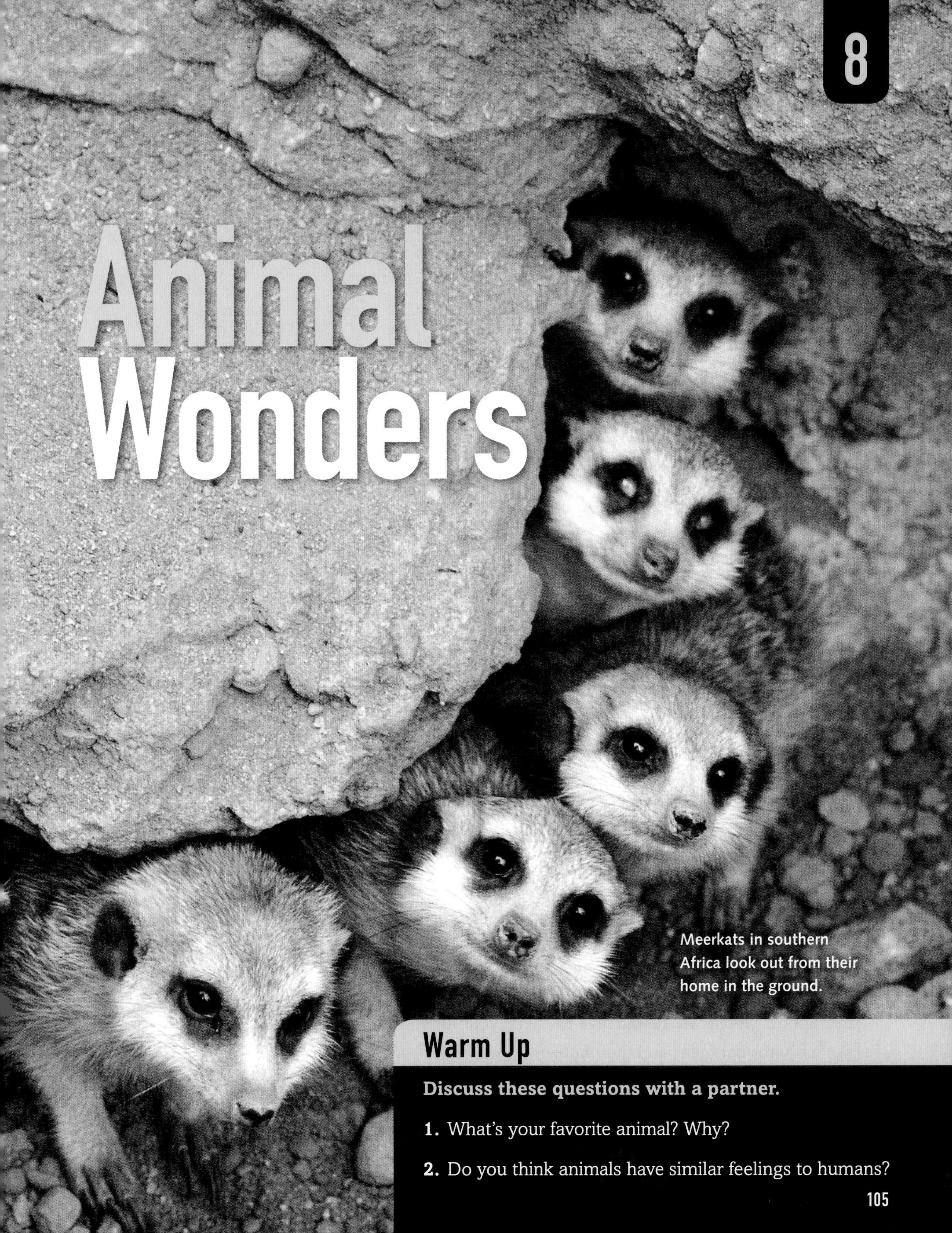

8

Animal Wonders

Meerkats in southern Africa look out from their home in the ground.

Warm Up

Discuss these questions with a partner.

1. What's your favorite animal? Why?
2. Do you think animals have similar feelings to humans?

Before You Read

^ In Antarctica, home of the emperor penguin, it can get as cold as -60°C (-75°F).

A. Quiz. What do you know about penguins? Mark each sentence below as true (**T**) or false (**F**).

1. Penguins can breathe underwater. **T** **F**
2. Wild penguins only live in Antarctica. **T** **F**
3. There are six different types of penguins. **T** **F**
4. Once a year, penguins lose all their feathers. **T** **F**
5. Penguins feed their babies food that they already ate. **T** **F**

B. Predict. Look quickly at the photos and headings on pages 107–108. Check (✓) the information you think you'll read about. Then read the passage to check your answers.

- ☐ emperor penguins and their babies
- ☐ young penguins getting older
- ☐ global warming and penguins

8A

A Penguin Family

Emperor penguins are the largest penguins on Earth. Each **adult** is over a meter tall, and can weigh[1] up to 40 kilograms.

For many months each year, emperors live near the sea in large groups called *colonies*. However, in May, the weather gets colder and ice covers large areas of ocean. Each colony moves many kilometers from the water. There, each mother penguin lays[2] just one egg. Then all the hungry mothers must walk back to the ocean to find food. The father penguins put their eggs on top of their feet, under a **special** piece of skin called the *brood pouch*.

Sharing the Work

For two months, the father penguins keep the eggs safe and warm. They do this through some of the coldest weather conditions on Earth. By July, it is winter in Antarctica. Most animals leave for warmer places, but the father penguins stay. In this time, without food, a father penguin can lose almost half of his body weight.

1 If something **weighs** 40 kilograms, that is how heavy it is.

2 When an animal **lays an egg**, it pushes it out from its body.

New Life

By August, the babies begin to hatch![3] The mother penguin returns just in time to see her baby come out of its egg. The chick[4] is then moved to her brood pouch. This can be difficult. If the chick falls, it can freeze[5] quickly, so the penguin **parents** must be very **careful**. Once this is done, the father penguin can go back to the ocean to find food.

Growing Up

Over the next few months, penguin parents **take turns** going to the ocean for food. They each make the trip **several** times, bringing back food for the chick. The chick grows quickly and is always hungry.

Into the Water

By December, winter is ending. The chick is five months old and can live **on its own**. Soon it **enters** the water for the first time. It will swim and eat until next April, and then return here. After a few more years, it, too, will start its own family.

---

3 If baby animals **hatch**, they come out of an egg.

4 A **chick** is a baby bird.

5 If a liquid **freezes**, it becomes solid like ice because of low temperatures.

A family of emperor penguins—mother, father, and baby—stands close together to keep warm.

Reading Comprehension

Multiple Choice. Choose the best answer for each question.

Gist

1. Another good title for this passage would be ______.
   a. A Study of Penguin Families
   b. Types of Penguins Around the World
   c. Emperor Penguins and Global Warming

Sequence

2. Which of the following things happens first?
   a. The adult penguins walk away from the ocean.
   b. The mother penguin walks to the ocean to find food.
   c. The father penguin loses half of his body weight.

Detail

3. When does the father penguin care for the egg without the mother penguin?
   a. from May to August
   b. from August to October
   c. from October to December

Vocabulary

4. The word *almost* (line 16) means ______.
   a. nearly
   b. exactly
   c. more than

Inference

5. What will probably happen if the chick falls onto the ice?
   a. Another penguin will take the chick.
   b. The chick will die because of the cold.
   c. The father penguin cannot go find food.

Reference

6. The word *here* (line 31) refers to ______.
   a. the water
   b. where it grew up
   c. where it learned to swim

Did You Know?

As young penguins grow, the adults leave them in groups of chicks called *crèches*. Some adults stay behind to care for the chicks.

Reading Skill

Paraphrasing

A paraphrased sentence has the same meaning as the original sentence, but uses different words and (sometimes) different grammar. Paraphrasing can make a passage more interesting. Look at this example.

Original: Emperor penguins are the largest penguins on Earth.

Paraphrased: There are no penguins on Earth larger than emperor penguins.

A. Multiple Choice. Which sentence correctly paraphrases the first? Circle **a** or **b**.

1. Penguins cannot fly.

a. Penguins are not able to fly.
b. Penguins swim but don't fly.

2. Penguins get all their food from the sea.

a. Penguins get some food on land.
b. Penguins only find food in the sea.

3. Penguins prefer to be around other penguins.

a. Penguins are never alone.
b. Penguins like to be in groups.

B. Completion. Look back at the passage on pages 107–108. Find and underline sentences from the passage that match what these paraphrased sentences mean.

1. The father penguin takes care of the egg for two months.
2. The mother penguin comes back from the ocean before the egg hatches.
3. It's not easy to do this.
4. The baby is getting bigger fast and needs a lot of food.
5. The baby is older and is living without its parents.

Critical Thinking Discuss with a partner. Which do you think is the more important penguin parent—the mother or the father? Why?

Vocabulary Practice

A. Matching. Read the information below and match each word in **red** with its definition.

- Siberian tigers are the largest tigers in the world. An **adult** male's body can grow to three meters (ten feet).
- Each tiger has a **special** pattern of black and orange marks on its fur. These make them difficult to see among the trees.
- Tigers generally like to live **on their own**. They leave their **parents** when they are still young.
- Most other cats do not like to **enter** water, but tigers love to swim.
- There are about 500 Siberian tigers in Asia, but few live in the wild. Most live in zoos today.

Today, wild Siberian tigers are found only in an area called Primorsky Krai, in Russia. It is very cold there, but the tigers' thick fur keeps them warm.

1. __________: father and mother
2. __________: not a child; fully grown
3. __________: alone, not with anyone else
4. __________: unusual; not like other kinds
5. __________: to go into (something)

B. Words in Context. Complete each sentence with the correct answer.

1. If you have **several** pets, you have ______ pets.
   a. one or two b. more than two
2. If you and a friend **take turns** riding a bike, you ride it ______.
   a. one after the other b. at the same time
3. You need to be **careful** when you are _______.
   a. carrying a glass statue b. trying to fall asleep
4. When you **enter** someone's house, you go ______.
   a. outside b. inside

Word Partnership
Use ***enter*** with: (*n.*) enter a **room**, enter **school**, enter **college**, enter a **contest**.

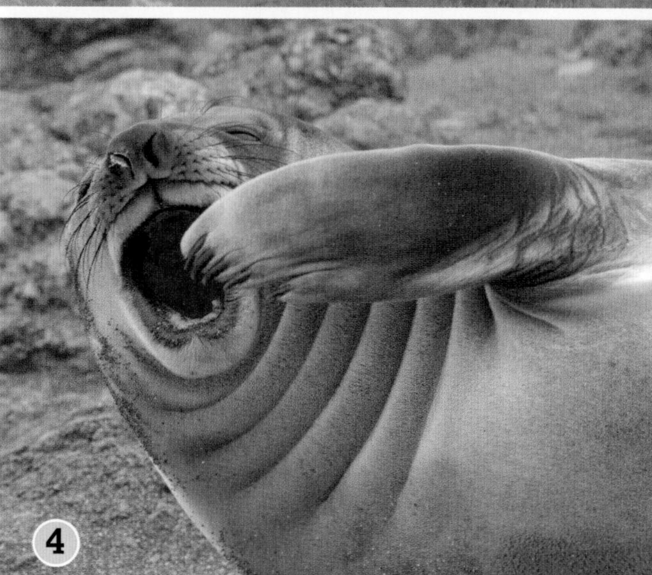

Through their faces and body language, animals often seem to show very humanlike emotions.

Before You Read

A. Discussion. Look at the photos above. Which word(s) in the box could describe each animal? Do you think animals really have these feelings?

anger	**boredom**	**happiness**	**surprise**

B. Scan. Quickly scan the passage on the next page. Underline the names you find. How many are there? Which are pets, and which are humans? Read the passage to check your answers.

Do Animals LAUGH?

We know animals have **emotions**. They can feel fear. We also think they feel love, since they have strong **relationships** with each other. So are animal emotions all **similar** to our own? And do animals have a sense of humor?[1]

A Parrot Named Bongo Marie

Sally Blanchard's parrot Bongo Marie didn't **get along** with her other parrot, Paco. In fact, Bongo Marie clearly didn't like Paco at all! One day, Blanchard cooked a chicken for dinner. She started to cut the chicken with a knife. "Oh, no! Paco!" Bongo Marie said loudly and **laughed**. Blanchard laughed, too, and said, "That's not Paco." "Oh . . . no," said Bongo Marie. This time, she sounded disappointed.[2] Then the parrot laughed at her own joke.[3]

Yoga Dog

Jean Donaldson enjoys doing yoga—and so does her dog Buffy. While Jean Donaldson does yoga, Buffy carefully places her **toys** on Donaldson's body. If a toy falls, Buffy runs to put it back. Does this **behavior** have any real purpose? "She thinks it's hilarious!"[4] says Donaldson.

Animal Laughter

Can dogs "laugh"? Recent research shows that dogs can tell each other when they want to play. They make a special sound—a kind of "laugh." Psychologist Patricia Simonet recorded the sound. Then she played it back to dogs to **assess** their behavior. "All the dogs seemed to like the laugh," says Simonet. So do animals have a sense of humor? If laughter is a clue, then perhaps the answer is "yes!"

Do dogs really laugh?

1 Someone's **sense of humor** is their ability to know what is funny.

2 If someone is **disappointed**, they are sad they didn't get what they wanted.

3 A **joke** is something that makes you laugh.

4 If something is **hilarious**, it is very funny.

Reading Comprehension

Multiple Choice. Choose the best answer for each question.

Gist

1. What does the author want to know?
a. Do animals have emotions?
b. Do animals have a sense of humor?
c. Do animals laugh in the same way as humans?

Detail

2. Which of the following sentences is NOT true?
a. Paco and Bongo Marie are both parrots.
b. Paco and Bongo Marie are good friends.
c. Sally Blanchard thinks Bongo Marie is funny.

Reference

3. The word *she* (line 12) refers to ______.
a. Paco
b. Bongo Marie
c. Sally Blanchard

Detail

4. Which of the following sentences is true?
a. Buffy feels sad when Jean Donaldson does yoga.
b. Jean Donaldson thinks Buffy has a sense of humor.
c. Buffy laughs at Jean Donaldson when she does yoga.

Vocabulary

5. In line 24, the phrase *played it back* is closest in meaning to ______.
a. recorded it again
b. played with the dogs
c. let the dogs hear the recording

Main Idea

6. What is the main idea of the last paragraph?
a. A scientist showed that dogs talk to each other, so they seem to be funnier than most animals.
b. A scientist showed that dogs make a laughing sound, so animals might really have a sense of humor.
c. A scientist recorded dogs making a laughing sound, but doesn't believe they have a sense of humor.

Did You Know?

Most African Grey Parrots, like Bongo Marie, are able to learn a few words, but some have a vocabulary of over 500 words and phrases.

Identifying Supporting Details

It's important to identify the main idea of a passage. But it's also important to identify details that support that idea. These might include reasons, examples, facts, or descriptions. As you read, ask yourself how well the author supports the main idea of the passage.

A. Analyzing. Circle the letters of the statements that support the idea "Elephants are very smart animals."

a. Elephants can live for 60 to 80 years in the wild.
b. Elephants know themselves when they look in a mirror.
c. Elephants can paint pictures and play music.
d. Elephants pull off tree branches and use them to keep flies away.
e. Elephants live in both Africa and Asia.
f. Elephants usually have a good sense of humor.
g. People often kill elephants for their tusks.

A picture of some flowers painted by an elephant

B. Completion. In the passage on page 113, the author asks, "Do animals have a sense of humor?" Complete the information below with words from the passage.

Sally Blanchard owns two parrots named Bongo Marie and Paco. One day, Bongo Marie told a **1.** ___________ and then she **2.** ___________.

Jean Donaldson's dog Buffy likes to put **3.** ___________ on Jean's body while she does yoga. If one falls, Buffy puts it back. Jean says that Buffy thinks this is **4.** ___________.

Psychologist Patricia Simonet thinks that dogs make a sound that is similar to a human **5.** ___________. The sound lets other dogs know when they want to **6.** ___________.

Critical Thinking Discuss with a partner. Do you think the supporting details in **B** helped you answer the question, "Do animals have a sense of humor?" Have you ever seen animals show emotions? Describe the situations.

Vocabulary Practice

A. Completion. Complete the sentences with the correct words from the box. One word is extra.

assess	behavior	laughter	relationship	similar

Chimpanzees are **1.** ____________ to humans in many ways. For example, the **2.** ____________ between chimps is often very close. This was clear when researchers studied a pair of brother and sister chimps, Kanzi and Panbanisha.

The researchers wanted to **3.** ____________ how well the chimps had learned to make stone knives. So they gave each chimp a box with a banana in it. They also gave the chimps the items they needed to make knives, to cut open the boxes.

Kanzi made a good knife, but his sister could not. When he saw that she was sad, Kanzi tried to give his knife to her. When no one was looking, he put his knife where his sister could find it, and she finally got her banana. Kanzi's **4.** ____________ showed the researchers that he cared for his sister.

Kanzi the bonobo can make knives from stone, play music, and understand more than 500 English words.

B. Words in Context. Read the sentences below. Then mark each sentence as true (**T**) or false (**F**).

1. If you **get along** with someone, you often fight with them. **T** **F**
2. If you **assess** something, you test or measure it. **T** **F**
3. A **toy** is something you can play with. **T** **F**
4. Two things that are **similar** are the same in some way. **T** **F**
5. **Emotions** are different from thoughts. **T** **F**
6. The sound of **laughter** is usually a happy sound. **T** **F**

Word Partnership
Use ***similar*** with: **be + similar + to**, e.g., *Animals are* ***similar*** *to humans in some ways.*

VIEWING Penguins in Trouble

Before You Watch

A. Warm Up. Look at the picture and read the caption. How do you think a leopard seal catches a penguin? Discuss with a partner.

^ Because their food comes from the sea, penguins spend as much as half their lives swimming. In the water, penguins can reach speeds of up to 27 kilometers per hour (17 miles per hour). However, this speed can't always save them from predators like the leopard seal. Leopard seals may seem too big to move quickly, but they can often move quickly enough to catch penguins. And penguins are one of their favorite meals.

B. Quiz. What do you know about leopard seals? Answer the questions below. Then check your answers at the bottom of page 118.

1. Adult (**female / male**) leopard seals are larger.
2. Leopard seals usually live (**on their own / in groups**).
3. A baby leopard seal is called a (**cub / pup**).
4. Leopard seals eat penguins, birds, and (**small whales / other seals**).

While You Watch

True or False. As you watch the video, mark each sentence below as true (**T**) or false (**F**).

In the video . . .

1. There is only one leopard seal but many penguins.	**T**	**F**
2. The penguins jump onto land, but the seal does not.	**T**	**F**
3. The seal catches two penguins.	**T**	**F**
4. The seal goes away hungry.	**T**	**F**

After You Watch

A. Cause and Effect. Match the causes with their effects.

Causes	so	Effects
1. the baby penguins are hungry	• •	a. they turn around fast
2. a leopard seal waits nearby	• •	b. they cannot move very fast
3. more penguins arrive, but they sense the leopard seal	• •	c. the penguins are in danger
4. the penguin that is caught relaxes its body	• •	d. the penguin parents have to fish
5. the penguins and seal are out of their usual environment, the water	• •	e. it can escape when the seal drops it

B. Paraphrasing. Use the information above to help you describe the events of the video in your own words to a partner.

C. Discuss. Discuss these questions with a partner.

1. The video says, "In Antarctica, every day is a fight for survival." What do you think this means?

2. How did you feel when the leopard seal caught the penguin or when the penguin got away? Why?

A leopard seal swims away with its lunch. >

1. female; **2.** on their own; **3.** pup; **4.** other seals

9

INCREDIBLE DOMES

High above Red Square in Moscow, Russia, the great domes of Saint Basil's Cathedral stand as reminders of Russia's colorful past.

Warm Up

Discuss these questions with a partner.

1. What do you think is the most interesting thing about this building?
2. What is the most famous building in your country? Why?

The Taj Mahal was built by the emperor Shah Jahan for the love of his life, Arjumand Banu Begum. The empress is more famously known as Mumtaz Mahal—*Chosen One of the Palace*.

Before You Read

A. Matching. Look at the picture and read the information below. Match the words in **bold** with their definitions.

The Taj Mahal in Agra, India, is one of the most famous **monuments** in the world. The **emperor** Shah Jahan built the Taj Mahal from white **marble**. The large **dome** at its center is one of the most famous parts of the building.

1. ____________: the male ruler of an empire
2. ____________: a rounded roof
3. ____________: a type of stone often used in buildings
4. ____________: large structures built to remind people of a famous event or person

B. Predict. Look at the title, photos, and captions on this page and the next. Why do you think Shah Jahan built the Taj Mahal? Read the passage to check your ideas.

A Love Poem in Stone

A painted picture of Shah Jahan and Mumtaz Mahal

Often called "a love poem[1] in stone," the Taj Mahal is well-known for being one of the most beautiful buildings ever created. It is also perhaps the most beautiful **expression** of love in the world.

The emperor Shah Jahan built the Taj Mahal for his empress, Mumtaz Mahal. The **couple** lived happily together for 18 years. Then Mumtaz died during the **birth** of their fourteenth child. Before she died, the emperor made her a **promise**. To remember her, he would build the most beautiful monument in the world.

The emperor poured his passion and wealth into building the Taj Mahal. It is said that it took more than 20,000 people and 1,000 elephants to build. They worked for over 20 years to build the monument and its central dome, which stands over 73 meters above the ground.

Soon after the building was **finished**, Shah Jahan's son became emperor. He put Shah Jahan in prison.[2] Shah Jahan lived there until his death in 1666, when his body was put in the Taj Mahal with the woman he loved.

There are many **legends** about the Taj Mahal. In one story, when the building was complete, Shah Jahan had the builders' hands cut off, **supposedly** so they could never build anything as beautiful as the Taj Mahal. Another says he also wanted to build a black Taj Mahal. These are interesting stories, but they are most likely not true.

The love story between Shah Jahan and his wife ended sadly. But the monument to their love still stands today. It is visited by millions of **tourists**, who come to see the marble change color in the light of the rising sun or a full moon.

---

1 A **poem** is a piece of writing that usually has rhythm; something beautiful.

2 A **prison** is a place where people who break the law are kept, where they cannot get out.

Reading Comprehension

Multiple Choice. Choose the best answer for each question.

Gist

1. What could be another title for this reading?
   a. The Emperor and Empress's Home
   b. How an Emperor Showed His Love
   c. The Beautiful Writings of Shah Jahan

Sequence

2. When was the Taj Mahal built?
   a. after the death of Mumtaz Mahal
   b. when Shah Jahan's son became emperor
   c. while Shah Jahan was in prison

Paraphrase

3. What is another way of saying *It is said that* (line 13)?
   a. It is true that
   b. We said that
   c. Some people believe that

Reference

4. Who does the word *He* refer to in line 17?
   a. Shah Jahan
   b. Shah Jahan's son
   c. Shah Jahan's father

Detail

5. Which of these statements about the Taj Mahal is true?
   a. It took 20 years to build.
   b. Shah Jahan died inside it in 1666.
   c. Its central dome was never completed.

Main Idea

6. What is the main idea of the fifth paragraph (from line 20)?
   a. The Taj Mahal has a very dark and sad history.
   b. Shah Jahan was known to be a terrible person.
   c. There are many stories about the Taj Mahal, many untrue.

Did You Know?

Shah Jahan used 28 different kinds of gems and stones to make the inside of the Taj Mahal beautiful. These gems and stones came from many places, including China, Afghanistan, Sri Lanka, and Arabia.

Reading Skill

Understanding Complex Sentences

Compound sentences consist of two independent clauses (see Unit 7). *Complex* sentences, on the other hand, consist of an **independent clause** and a **dependent clause** connected by a **conjunction**. Conjunctions include *before, after, when, while* (to show time), *if* (to show condition), *because* (to show a reason), and *but* or *although* (to show a contrast). In these examples, the dependent clause is underlined.

I plan to go on a trip after I save enough money.
If I save enough, I want to visit Florence.
I want to go there because I'm very interested in art.
Although I speak Italian, I'm going to take a phrase book with me.

A. Scan. Look back at the passage on page 121. Complete each sentence with a conjunction.

1. ________ Mumtaz Mahal died, the emperor made her a promise. (lines 8–9)
2. ________ the Taj Mahal was finished, Shah Jahan's son became emperor. (lines 16–17)
3. In one story, ________ the building was complete, Shah Jahan had the builders' hands cut off. (lines 20–21)
4. There are many interesting stories about the Taj Mahal, ________ they are most likely not true. (lines 23–24)

B. Completion. Choose the correct conjunctions to complete the information.

Tips for Visiting the Taj Mahal

1. Enter through the south gates (**because / although**) there are usually long lines at the east and west gates.
2. (**When / Because**) you visit, keep the areas inside and outside clean.
3. Take off your shoes (**although / before**) you enter.
4. You can also wear shoe covers (**while / before**) you are inside.
5. Do not bring video cameras (**while / because**) they are not allowed inside.
6. (**If / Although**) it is not required, consider hiring a guide.
7. (**Before / If**) you hire a guide, hire only the ones with official I.D. cards.
8. Do not touch the walls (**when / because**) this can harm the monument.

Critical Thinking Discuss with a partner. Do you know of any other famous or interesting ways that people have expressed their love?

Vocabulary Practice

A. Definitions. Read the information below. Then match each word in **red** with its definition.

The **legend** of the black Taj Mahal has been around for a long time. According to the story, Shah Jahan wanted a monument for himself. His monument would be similar to the Taj Mahal, but would use black marble. Some believe the monument was never **finished**. Others don't think the story is true.

Shah Jahan **supposedly** wanted to build his monument in a garden across the river from the Taj Mahal. Archeologists searched this area, and some thought they found pieces of black stone. However, these were just white stones that had turned black. They weren't black marble at all.

The archeologists also rebuilt part of a pool that was in the garden, which **couples** like to visit in the evening. When the couples look at the Taj Mahal in the reflection of the pool's water, it sometimes looks black. Perhaps this is where the story came from.

The reflection of the Taj Mahal at sunset may have started the story of the black Taj Mahal.

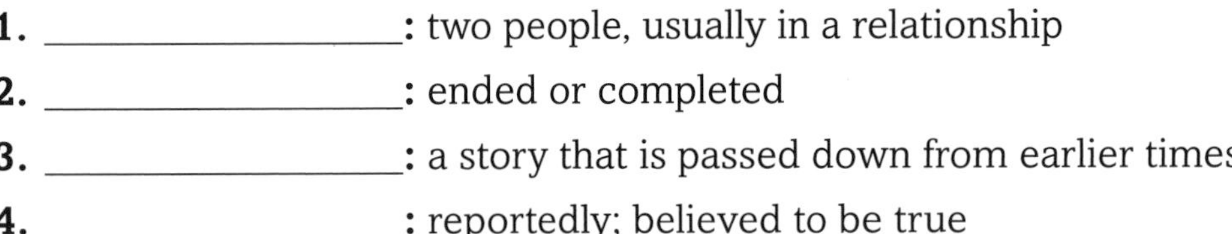

1. ________________: two people, usually in a relationship
2. ________________: ended or completed
3. ________________: a story that is passed down from earlier times
4. ________________: reportedly; believed to be true

B. Words in Context. Complete each sentence with the correct answer.

1. People often _________ to **express** love.
   a. give flowers b. hide their emotions
2. When you make a **promise**, you tell someone that you _____ something.
   a. can do b. will do
3. A **tourist** is someone who _______.
   a. travels for fun b. works in a different country
4. The **birth** of a person describes the time he or she _______.
   a. is born b. gets married

Word Partnership
Use ***promise*** with: (*v.*) **make** a promise, **keep** a promise, **break** a promise; (*adj.*) **broken** promise, **empty** promise, **false** promise.

The Great Dome of Florence

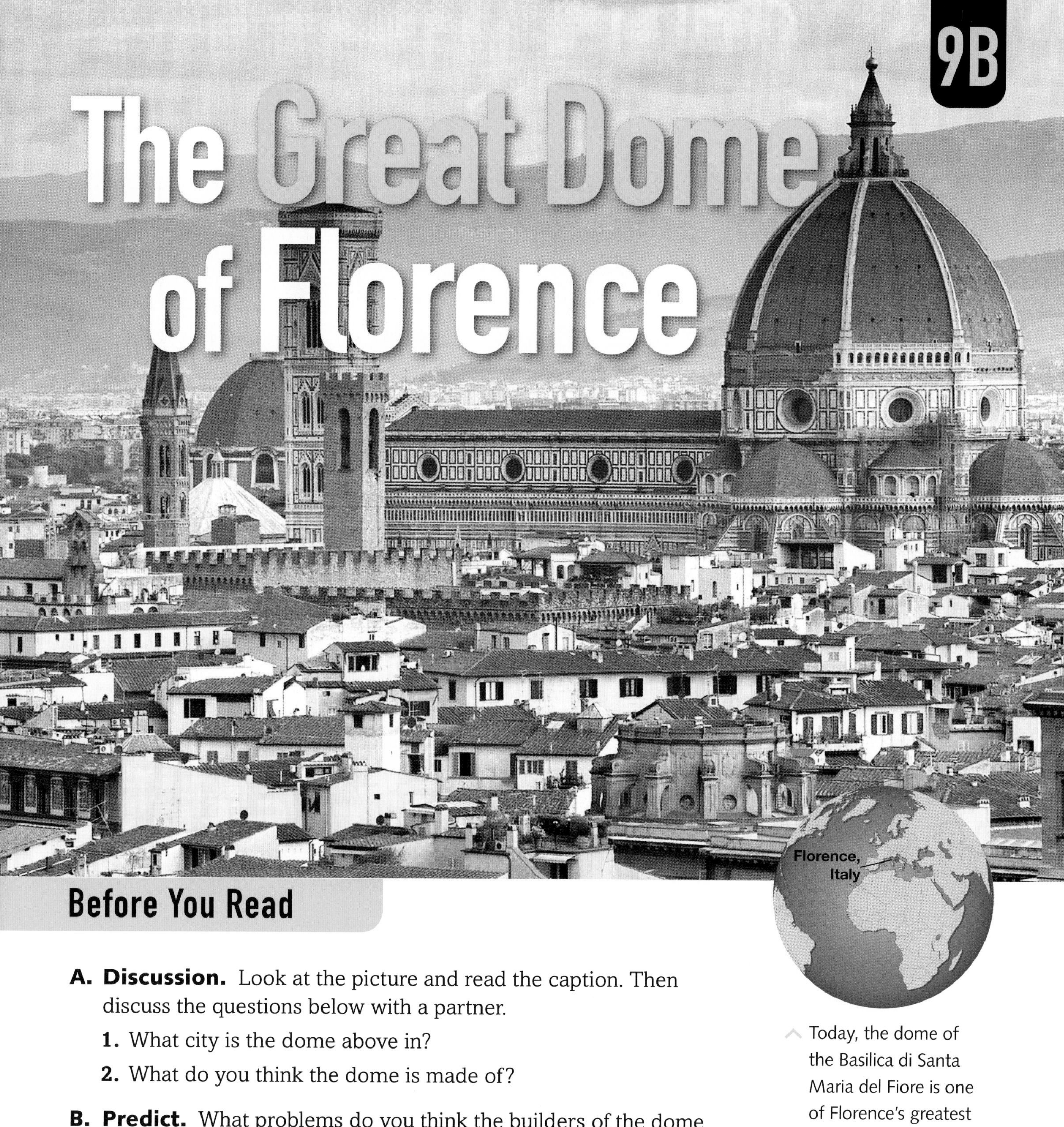

Today, the dome of the Basilica di Santa Maria del Fiore is one of Florence's greatest sights. But for over 100 years, the Basilica was unfinished because builders of the time couldn't build the dome.

Before You Read

A. Discussion. Look at the picture and read the caption. Then discuss the questions below with a partner.

1. What city is the dome above in?
2. What do you think the dome is made of?

B. Predict. What problems do you think the builders of the dome had? Check (✓) your ideas below. Then read the passage on pages 126–127 to check your answers.

The builders couldn't build the dome because they didn't know . . .

- ☐ what materials to use
- ☐ how to support the dome
- ☐ how to raise money
- ☐ how to lift things high up

Among the world's most amazing domes, the dome in Florence is second in size only to St. Peter's Basilica in Vatican City.

Brunelleschi and the Dome

In 1419, at the beginning of the Renaissance[1] in Italy, a clockmaker named Filippo Brunelleschi started work on a very difficult **project**. He was building the dome of Florence's main cathedral,[2] the Basilica di Santa Maria del Fiore. At 55 meters (180 feet) above ground, it would be the largest dome built since the Pantheon in Rome was finished 1,500 years before.

After most of the cathedral was built in 1296, many builders tried to complete the dome. But none could do it. No one knew what **material** to use. Many builders knew how to build concrete[3] domes. However, the dome in Florence needed to be wider than any dome ever built. Also, tall buildings of the time **relied** on structures that **supported** the heavy stone from the outside. The cathedral didn't have these structures, so a concrete dome was too heavy. It would easily fall. So, the cathedral's roof was left unfinished for over a hundred years.

Filippo Brunelleschi promised to **solve** all these problems. He said he would build *two* domes, an inner dome made of stone, and an outer one made of light bricks.[4] He would use lighter materials as he worked upwards, and would hold it all together with strong rings made of stone, wood, and iron.

Brunelleschi also had to find a way to **lift** the materials high into the air. What did he do? He **invented** a new machine to do the job.

Building the dome took 16 years. The crown at the top took another ten. Brunelleschi died a few years later, in 1446. He had done something no one else could. However, he left no pictures of his **design**. So—even today—experts don't fully understand how this amazing structure was built.

1 The **Renaissance**, meaning "rebirth," was a time of great thinkers, builders, and inventors.

2 A **cathedral** is a kind of church building, usually quite big and beautiful.

3 **Concrete** is a hard construction material similar to stone.

4 **Bricks** are pieces of baked clay used for building.

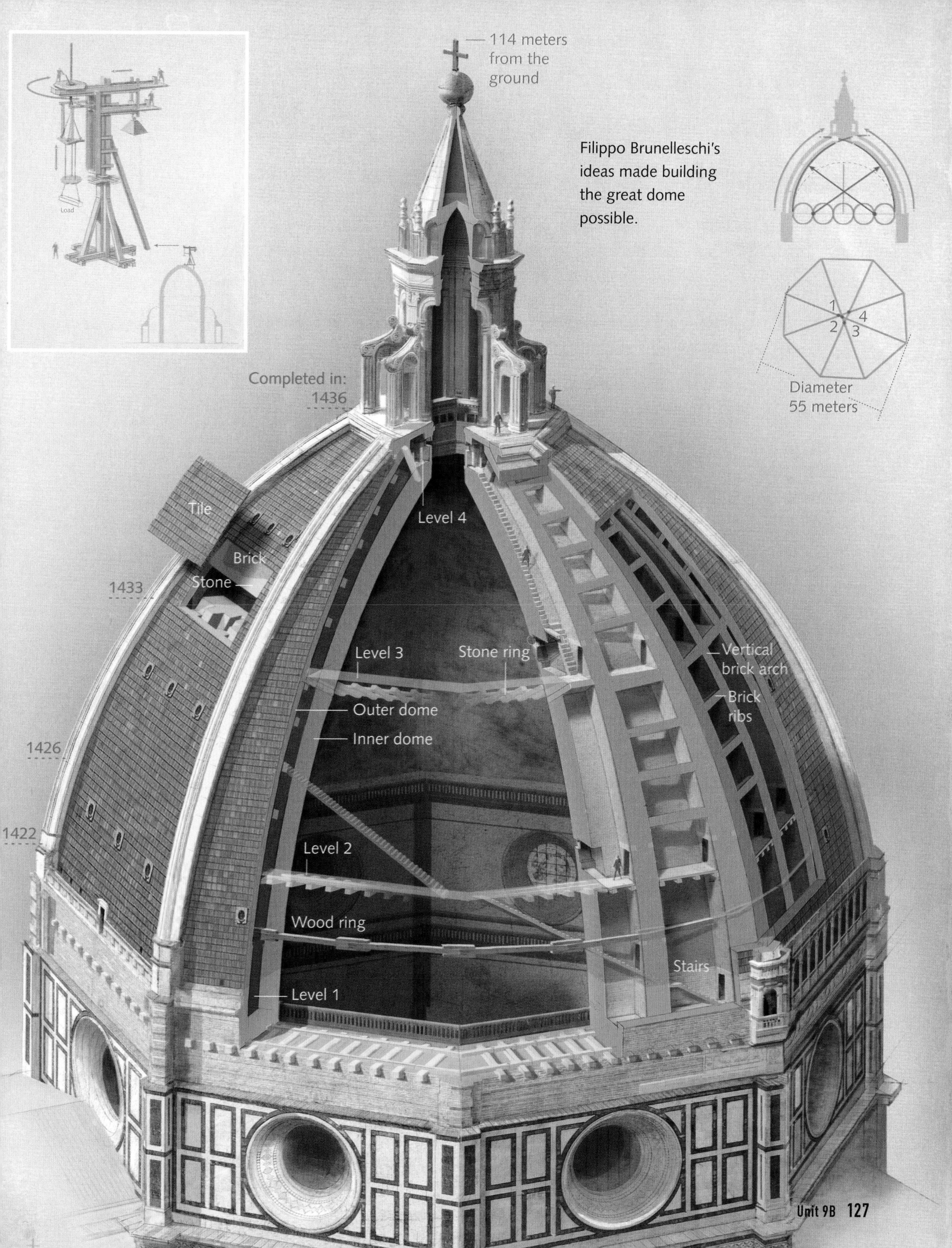
Load
114 meters
from the
ground
Filippo Brunelleschi's
ideas made building
the great dome
possible.
1
2
3
4
Diameter
55 meters
Completed in:
1436
Level 4
Tile
Brick
Stone
1433
Level 3
Stone ring
Vertical
brick arch
Brick
ribs
Outer dome
Inner dome
1426
1422
Level 2
Wood ring
Stairs
Level 1

Reading Comprehension

Multiple Choice. Choose the best answer for each question.

Detail

1. Which of the following is NOT given as a reason the dome was difficult to build?
   a. No one had ever built a dome from concrete before.
   b. No one had built such a wide dome before.
   c. The cathedral didn't have structures that could support a dome from the outside.

Purpose

2. What is the purpose of the third paragraph (from line 17)?
   a. to argue another side of an issue
   b. to explain a solution to a problem
   c. to provide background information

Sequence

3. Which of these things happened last?
   a. The Renaissance began.
   b. The cathedral was built.
   c. The dome was completed.

Detail

4. What is true about Filippo Brunelleschi?
   a. He built three domes for the cathedral.
   b. He died before seeing the dome completed.
   c. He invented a machine that lifted things into the air.

Cohesion

5. The following sentence would best be placed at the end of which paragraph? *As a result, there was a large hole in the cathedral's roof.*
   a. paragraph 1
   b. paragraph 2
   c. paragraph 3

Detail

6. Why don't we fully understand how the dome was built?
   a. Brunelleschi didn't leave any pictures of his design.
   b. Some structures are completely covered in concrete.
   c. The dome has been rebuilt many times over the years.

Did You Know?

Inside Florence's cathedral is a 700-year-old clock that places the end of each day—or the 24th hour—at sunset instead of midnight.

Reading Skill

Recognizing Prepositions

There are different types of prepositions, including those that indicate time (*on Monday*, *for a day*), place (*in India*, *at school*), movement (*to the library*, *into the water*), and possession (*a friend of mine*, *the boy with black hair*). Here are a few examples of English prepositions.

above	**at**	**behind**	**below**	**by**	**during**	**for**	**from**
in	**inside**	**near**	**of**	**on**	**to**	**under**	**with**

A. Recognizing. Read the information below. Find and underline all the prepositions.

Tips for Visiting the Great Dome in Florence

- Any visitor to Florence should climb to the top of the cathedral. It's an easy walk up the stairs to the dome area.
- The dome is covered with lovely paintings. Look closely at the walls for graffiti that was made by other tourists. Much of it is over a hundred years old. It gives you an idea of the many people who came before you.
- From the top, you get a great 360-degree view of Florence. You can see many of the famous places in the city from there.

The inside of the great dome of Florence

B. Completion. Complete the sentences with the correct prepositions from the box. You can use each preposition more than once. Then look back at the reading to check your answers.

for	**from**	**in**	**into**	**of**	**with**

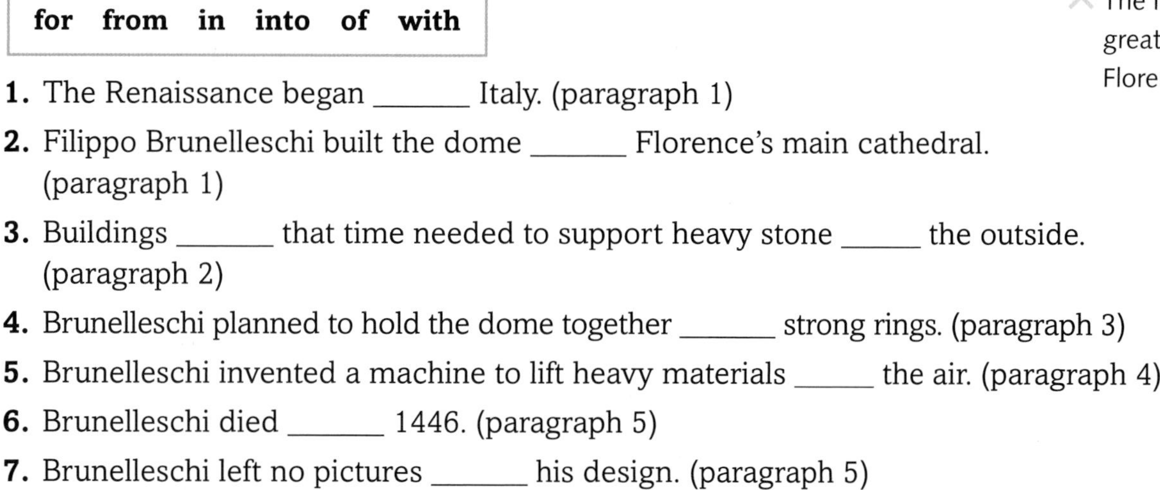

1. The Renaissance began ______ Italy. (paragraph 1)
2. Filippo Brunelleschi built the dome ______ Florence's main cathedral. (paragraph 1)
3. Buildings ______ that time needed to support heavy stone ______ the outside. (paragraph 2)
4. Brunelleschi planned to hold the dome together ______ strong rings. (paragraph 3)
5. Brunelleschi invented a machine to lift heavy materials ______ the air. (paragraph 4)
6. Brunelleschi died ______ 1446. (paragraph 5)
7. Brunelleschi left no pictures ______ his design. (paragraph 5)

Critical Thinking Discuss with a partner. Which do you think was more difficult to build—the Taj Mahal or the dome of Florence's cathedral? Why?

Vocabulary Practice

A. Completion. Complete the information below with the correct words in the box. One word is extra.

design	material	project	rely	supported

Some love it. Others hate it. But it looks like London's Millennium Dome is here to stay. The dome itself is made of a very strong **1.** __________ that is only a millimeter thick. This makes the dome very light. The air inside the dome is heavier than the roof itself. This material is **2.** __________ by twelve towers, one for every hour of the clock. This makes the whole dome look like a big clock from above.

When the dome opened in 2000, many were pleased with the interesting **3.** __________. But some were unhappy because—for such an expensive **4.** __________—it had not brought in as many visitors as the builders predicted. Today, the Millennium Dome is better known as the O2 Arena, and is a stadium for music and sporting events.

Designed by architect Richard Rogers, the Millennium Dome is 52 meters tall, each meter representing one week of the year.

B. Words in Context. Complete each sentence with the correct answer.

1. If you **invent** something, you ________ it for the first time.
   a. make   b. use
2. When you **lift** something, you move it to a _______ place.
   a. lower   b. higher
3. Someone who has **solved** a problem has found a way to _______.
   a. make it bigger   b. end it
4. If you **rely** on someone, you ________ them.
   a. don't believe   b. trust

Thesaurus
material Also look up: (*n.*) *cloth, fabric, textile, matter, substance, stuff, medium*

VIEWING Brunelleschi's Dome

Before You Watch

A. Warm Up. Look at the picture and read the caption. Pay attention to the words in **bold**. You will hear them in the video. Match the words with their definitions below.

In 1418, a contest was held to solve the problem of the great dome of Florence. Part of the problem was that the cathedral didn't have **arches** to support the dome. Also, the dome's **base** was an **octagon**, so it was not possible to build the usual **semicircle** dome. Filippo Brunelleschi, a master goldsmith,[1] had never trained as an **architect**, but he won the contest and built the dome, using a design that few understand, even today.

1 A **master goldsmith** is someone who is very good at working with gold.

1. architect •	• a. a shape that is half of a circle
2. arches •	• b. a shape with eight sides of the same length
3. base •	• c. curved structures that support a wall
4. octagon •	• d. someone who designs buildings
5. semicircle •	• e. the lowest part; the part on which something rests

B. Quiz. What do you know about Florence and its great dome? Answer the questions below. Then check your answers at the bottom of page 132.

1. There are (**163 / 463**) stone steps inside the dome.
2. Around (**400 thousand / four million**) bricks were used to build the dome.
3. When Brunelleschi died, his body was put (**in the dome / under the cathedral**).
4. (**Michelangelo's David / The Venus de Milo**) is a famous statue kept in Florence.

While You Watch

Checking. As you watch the video, check your answers in **Before You Watch B**. Were your ideas correct?

After You Watch

A. Completion. Choose the correct word or phrase to complete each sentence below.

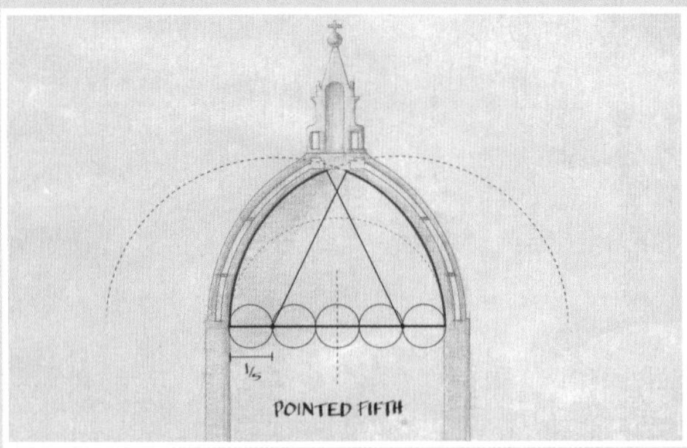

1. The dome needed to be (**eight-** / **sixteen-**)sided.

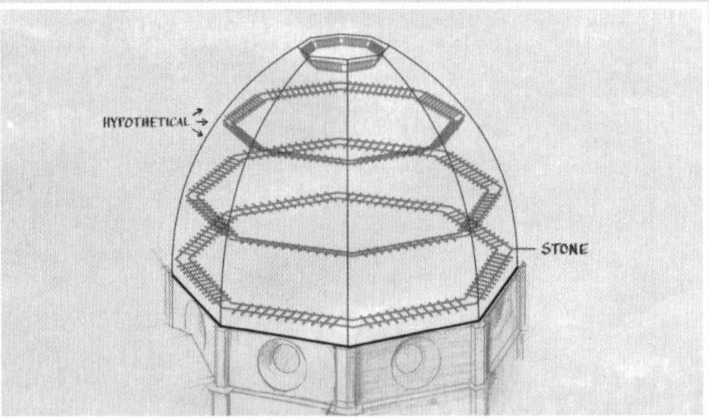

2. The rings in Brunelleschi's design would stop the (**dome from changing shape** / **arches from falling off**).

3. According to the video, Brunelleschi's machines were (**hard to use** / **ahead of their time**).

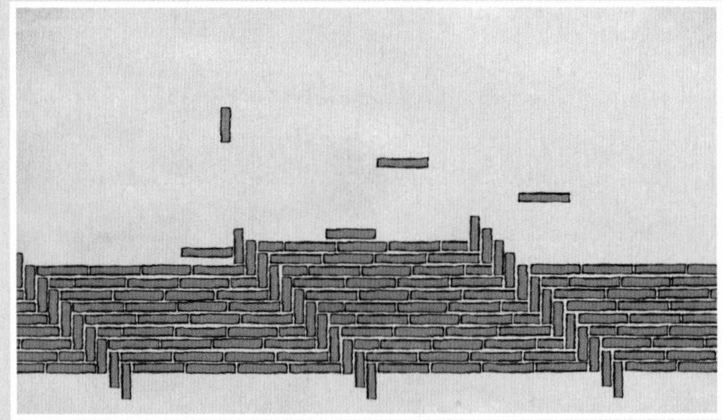

4. The special (**pattern** / **material**) of the dome's bricks helps hold them together.

B. Discuss. Discuss these questions with a partner.

1. Are there any interesting buildings in your city? Do you know why they were built that way?
2. Brunelleschi wasn't trained as an architect, but he was a master goldsmith and clockmaker. Do you think these skills helped him design and build the dome? How?

1. 463; **2.** four million; **3.** under the cathedral; **4.** Michelangelo's David

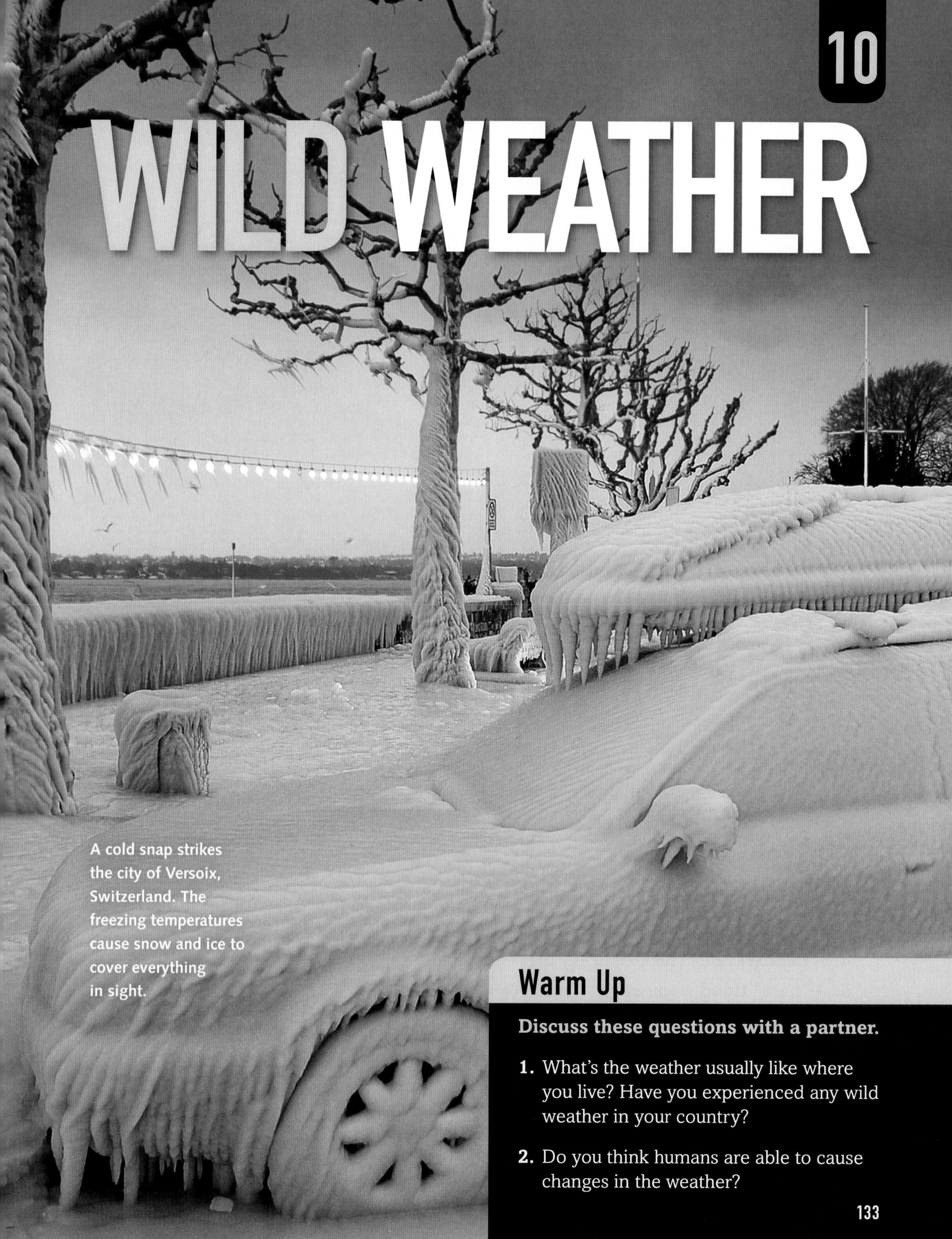

10

WILD WEATHER

A cold snap strikes the city of Versoix, Switzerland. The freezing temperatures cause snow and ice to cover everything in sight.

Warm Up

Discuss these questions with a partner.

1. What's the weather usually like where you live? Have you experienced any wild weather in your country?
2. Do you think humans are able to cause changes in the weather?

Before You Read

A. True or False. What do you know about wild weather events? Read the sentences below. Then mark each sentence as true (**T**) or false (**F**).

1.	The center of a **hurricane** is called its "head."	**T**	**F**
2.	A **drought** can happen when there's no rain.	**T**	**F**
3.	The country with the most **tornadoes** is Australia.	**T**	**F**
4.	A **heat wave** can happen in any part of the world.	**T**	**F**
5.	A "flash" **flood** is sometimes caused by snow melting.	**T**	**F**

B. Skim for the Main Idea. On this page and the next, skim the title, headings, photos, and captions. What is the passage mainly about? Circle **a**, **b**, or **c**. Then read the passage to check your answer.

a. why the U.S. is getting more dangerous storms

b. what scientists are doing to change the weather

c. how the weather is changing around the world

A Warming WORLD

Hurricanes, droughts, tornadoes, and floods are examples of wild weather events. This picture shows the result of a drought, leaving a pond in China completely dried out.

One weekend in May 2010, the weather **forecast** for Nashville, Tennessee, U.S.A., predicted 10 centimeters (4 inches) of rain. By Sunday, over 33 centimeters (13 inches) had fallen. Soon the city was flooded. On the roads, cars were covered by the rising water. "We've got buildings running into cars," the news reported as a small building **floated** by. There were 11 deaths that weekend.

Changing Weather

The weather is changing. Over the last few years, heavy rains have caused floods in Brazil, Pakistan, and Thailand. Droughts have struck Russia and Australia. Heat waves have killed thousands in Europe, and all over the world, hurricanes and tornadoes strike more **frequently** and with greater **force** than ever before. In 2011 alone, **losses** caused by the weather cost the world 150 billion dollars.

Warmer and Wetter

As more wild weather events happen, a worried world is beginning to ask questions like: *What is going on with the weather? And why?* Many also want to know: *Is this natural, or are we to* ***blame****?*

The answer seems to be: *a little of both*. Wild weather is natural. But most scientists agree human activity has made the Earth warmer. This global warming makes heat waves more likely to **occur**. The higher **temperatures** also cause more water to enter the air. This causes heavier and more frequent rain. Some scientists also believe global warming makes hurricanes and other storms stronger.

This means we're likely to see more wild weather. "[But] we don't have to just stand there and take it," says scientist Michael Oppenheimer. He and other experts say we need to stop the Earth from getting warmer. We also need to be prepared, to do things that will help save lives.

In May 2010, heavy rains caused floods in Nashville, U.S.A. The flood waters covered whole areas of the city, like this parking lot.

Reading Comprehension

Multiple Choice. Choose the best answer for each question.

Main Idea

1. What is the main idea of the reading passage?
a. There was a deadly flood in Nashville, Tennessee, U.S.A.
b. Global warming is causing wilder weather events.
c. Wild weather events are making people very worried.

Purpose

2. What is the purpose of the second paragraph (from line 8)?
a. to give examples of recent wild weather events
b. to describe the weather events that occurred in 2011
c. to predict how the weather will change in a few years

Paraphrase

3. Which of the following is closest in meaning to *What is going on with the weather?* (line 18)?
a. What will the weather do next?
b. What was the weather like before?
c. Why are we having such strange weather?

Reference

4. What does *this* refer to in line 19?
a. a worried world
b. the increase in wild weather
c. deaths caused by wild weather

Vocabulary

5. In line 28, the word *take* could be replaced by ______.
a. feel good about
b. do nothing about
c. find out more about

Inference

6. Which of the following statements would Oppenheimer probably agree with?
a. It is too late to stop global warming.
b. Stop global warming, and the weather will get better.
c. The most important thing, in preparing for wild weather, is to find ways to keep our things safe.

Did You Know?

Lightning is very hot—a flash can heat the air around it to temperatures five times hotter than the surface of the sun.

Reading Skill

Identifying Text Types

Each time you encounter a new reading passage, try to determine what type of text it is. Knowing the text type allows you to predict what kind of information the text may contain and how it is organized. This will help you follow it more easily. Here are four of the most common text types.

Narrative texts entertain the reader by telling a story.
Expository texts inform the reader by providing facts and general information.
Technical texts provide information that helps the reader perform a task.
Persuasive texts try to convince the reader to agree with an opinion.

A. Multiple Choice. Look back at the passage on pages 135–136. What kind of text is it? Circle **a**, **b**, **c**, or **d**.

a. narrative	**b. expository**	**c. technical**	**d. persuasive**

B. Matching. Read the four paragraphs below. Then match each one to the correct text type.

a. narrative	**b. expository**	**c. technical**	**d. persuasive**

1. ________ . . . since floods occur more often than tornadoes or earthquakes. There is a strong chance that you will experience a flood in your lifetime. This is why it's important to protect your home. Everyone should . . .
2. ________ . . . may just save your life. First, go to the safest place possible. This is usually in the basement of your building, if you have one. Next, go to the center of the room and keep away from windows. Stay there until you are sure the tornado ...
3. ________ . . . and just as we got to the top of the mountain, it started to rain. There was lightning all around, so we knew we had to find a safe place right away. I wanted to run under a tree, but my friends . . .
4. ________ . . . a cyclone is a collection of thunderstorms. In general, both typhoons and hurricanes are tropical storms, but they occur in different places. Cyclones in the Pacific are called typhoons, and those in the Atlantic are called hurricanes . . .

Critical Thinking Discuss with a partner. How prepared are you for "wild weather"? What are some ways you can be better prepared?

Vocabulary Practice

A. Completion. Choose the correct words to complete the information.

In early 2012, "once-a-century" floods in Ireland left large areas of land underwater. In June, very high **1.** (**losses** / **temperatures**) caused wildfires in Russia. Months later, Hurricane Sandy killed hundreds in North America with **2.** (**losses** / **forecasts**) that cost the country about $150 billion.

Each of these events was dangerous enough on its own. However, in 2013, *all* of these types of weather events **3.** (**blamed** / **occurred**) one after another in Australia. In fact, the country has experienced a huge increase in wild weather events in the past few years, including more **4.** (**frequent** / **floating**) droughts, tornadoes, and heat waves.

Because there is so much wild weather in Australia, more and more scientists are studying its weather patterns to see if they can help make better weather **5.** (**forecasts** / **temperatures**).

B. Words in Context. Complete each sentence with the correct answer.

1. An example of something that **floats** is ______.

a. a rock b. a piece of wood

2. The **force** of a tornado refers to its ______.

a. shape b. strength

3. If you **blame** someone, you say they ______.

a. caused something bad to happen b. stopped something bad from happening

4. Something that happens **frequently** happens ______.

a. often b. rarely

Word Partnership
Use ***temperature*** with:
(*adj.*) **high** temperature, **low** temperature, **average** temperature, **daytime** temperature.

A man carries a child through floodwaters in Jakarta, Indonesia

FREAKY FORCES of Nature

A giant cloud of dust, called a *haboob,* quickly covers the city of Phoenix, Arizona, U.S.A. The wall of dust is 1,500 meters (5,000 feet) tall and 160 kilometers (100 miles) long. It is just one of many strange weather events seen on Earth.

Before You Read

A. Discussion. Look at the picture above and read the caption. Then discuss these questions with a partner.

1. What other strange weather events have you heard of? Can you explain why they happen?
2. Do you know any interesting stories about strange weather?

B. Skim. Quickly skim the reading passage on page 141. Match the headings below to the correct paragraphs in the passage. One heading is extra.

a. Tornadoes of Fire b. Floods Rising!
c. Great Balls of Ice! d. Strange Rain!

When Weird Weather Strikes

10B

Most of us know about fires, hurricanes, droughts, and floods. But from time to time, Mother Nature[1] surprises us, and **delivers** a weather event that is really **weird**. Here are some examples of truly weird weather.

1. ____________________: One day in 2005, residents[2] of a small town in Serbia looked out their windows and saw an unusual sight. It was raining frogs! Without any **warning**, they found their streets filling with the little jumping creatures. "There were thousands of them," one resident told a **local** newspaper. "I thought perhaps a plane carrying frogs had exploded,"[3] said another. Scientists think a tornado passed over a lake. It sucked up animals that lived there. The frogs were carried into the air. Then they were **dropped** in the Serbian town, far away.

2. ____________________: As if tornadoes aren't dangerous enough, some of them can **actually** be made of fire. When a wildfire reaches very high temperatures, it causes the air to become hot and to rise. Cooler air **rushes** in to replace the hot air. This creates strong winds. These winds suck up burning plants and even the fire itself. When this happens, like it did on March 14, 2014, in Denver, Colorado, U.S.A., a tornado of fire is produced. This tornado can become 15 meters (50 feet) wide and grow as tall as a 40-story building.

3. ____________________: In 1942, hundreds of thousand-year-old skeletons were found under the ice of Lake Roopkund in the Himalayas. Many had holes in their skulls. But they weren't hurt in any other way. Scientists thought the people must have been hit from above. But for years, the cause of their deaths was a mystery.
Today, scientists think these people were killed by giant hailstones—balls of ice. Hailstones form when raindrops high in the sky turn into pieces of ice. The ice pieces **increase** in size until the wind cannot hold them up. This results in hailstones falling to the ground, often at speeds of over 160 kilometers (100 miles) an hour. For the unlucky people at Lake Roopkund, there was nowhere to run. They were all killed by the hailstones.

A tornado of fire is formed by strong winds in a forest fire.

---

1 **Mother Nature** is a term used to describe nature as if it were a woman.

2 A **resident** is a person who lives in a certain place.

3 If something **explodes** (e.g., a bomb), it suddenly breaks apart with parts flying outward.

Reading Comprehension

Multiple Choice. Choose the best answer for each question.

Gist

1. Another title for this reading could be ______.
   a. Unusual Tornadoes
   b. Humans vs. Nature
   c. Strange Weather

Vocabulary

2. The words *sucked up* in line 13 could be replaced with ______.
   a. lifted
   b. used
   c. blew

Detail

3. What is probably true about the frogs that rained down in Serbia?
   a. They fell out of an airplane that exploded.
   b. A tornado took them from a lake and dropped them over the town.
   c. They were carried away as babies, grew in the clouds, and then fell down to Earth.

Reference

4. The word *this* in line 22 refers to the moment when ______.
   a. a wildfire grows really big
   b. rushing winds suck up the fire
   c. the tornado of fire becomes 15 meters wide

Cohesion

5. The following sentence would best be placed at the end of which paragraph? *This makes them very dangerous.*
   a. paragraph 1 (from line 1)
   b. paragraph 2 (from line 6)
   c. paragraph 3 (from line 16)

Detail

6. What happens when little pieces of ice move around in the wind?
   a. They become bigger.
   b. They become raindrops.
   c. They fall to the ground as snow.

Did You Know?

In November 2007, residents in Changsha, China, were surprised when they found a street filled with "fish rain." They later found out it never really rained fish. The fish probably fell off a truck.

Identifying Cause and Effect

Identifying causes and effects in a passage can help you see how events change other events. To identify causes and effects, you can often look out for words like *cause, result, create,* and *produce*.

Sometimes causes and effects are described without using these words. When two events in a passage seem to be connected, ask yourself: *Which event occurred first? Did it change the event that follows?*

A. Scan. Look back at the reading on page 141. Find examples of causes and effects in the passage. Underline the causes and circle the effects.

B. Matching. Look at the chart below. Match the causes on the left with the effects on the right.

Causes			Effects
1. a tornado passes over a lake	•	•	a. hundreds of people died
2. a wildfire reaches high temperatures	•	•	b. hail falls to the ground
3. cool air rushes into a wildfire	•	•	c. strong winds are created
4. wildfire winds suck up the fire itself	•	•	d. the air becomes hot and rises
5. pieces of ice in the air grow too big	•	•	e. frogs are lifted into the air
6. hailstones fell from the sky	•	•	f. a tornado of fire is produced

Critical Thinking Discuss with a partner. What would you do if you were caught in a hailstorm? Saw a tornado of fire? Got rained on by frogs?

A fire tornado comes dangerously close to people's homes in California, in the U.S.

Vocabulary Practice

A. Completion. Complete the information with the words from the box. One word is extra.

actually	increase	local	rushing	warning	weird

Mystery Waves

Imagine this: You are out at sea, relaxing on a boat. It's a beautiful day. No rain is falling, and the winds are calm. All at once, something very **1.** ________ happens. Out of nowhere, you see a wall of water ten stories tall **2.** ________ toward you.

This is known as a *rogue wave*, also called a *freak wave*. Some people mistake them for tsunamis, but they are **3.** ________ very different. Tsunamis start out very small in the open ocean, and only **4.** ________ in speed and height as they get close to the coast. When a tsunami is coming, the water will often seem to be sucked back into the ocean. There is usually no **5.** ________ before a rogue wave strikes. This kind of wave can appear even in the best of weather.

Scientists aren't sure what causes these waves. In fact, as recently as 15 years ago, people thought these waves didn't really exist. But scientists now know they are very real—and very dangerous—even to the largest ships.

B. Words in Context. Complete each sentence with the correct answer.

1. If something **drops**, it ______.
a. falls to the ground b. moves up into the air

2. You are a **local** in the city, you ______.
a. grew up in b. just moved to

3. If you describe a movie as **weird**, you think it is ______.
a. funny b. strange

4. When you **deliver** a letter, you usually ______ someone.
a. bring it to b. get it from

Usage

Drop **vs.** ***fall***

Both *fall* and *drop* mean "to move downward quickly". However, we use *drop* when someone or something holds an object and lets it go, e.g., *I* ***fell*** *down the stairs.* vs. *I* ***dropped*** *my phone on the street.*

VIEWING Storm of the Century

Before You Watch

Warm Up. Look at the picture and read the caption. Then answer the questions below. Discuss your ideas with a partner.

^ Often, tropical storms with heavy rain and strong winds start in the Atlantic Ocean. When a tropical storm reaches wind speeds of 63 kilometers per hour (39 miles per hour), it is given a name, like Sandy, Dolly, or Hugo. When it gains wind speeds of 119 kilometers per hour (74 miles per hour), it is no longer a tropical storm; it is now called a *hurricane*.

The worst hurricane in U.S. history was the Great Galveston Hurricane of 1900, which killed between 8,000 and 12,000 people. That day, floodwaters came up to almost five meters. Since then, there hadn't been a storm as bad, until the arrival of what many are now calling "the storm of the century."

1. Does your country experience big storms? When was the last big weather event in your country?
2. The video is about Hurricane Katrina, which hit New Orleans in the U.S., in 2005. Have you heard of this hurricane? If so, what do you know about it?

While You Watch

A. Checking. Are your ideas from **Before You Watch** talked about in the video?

B. Multiple Choice. As you watch the video, choose the correct answer for each question below.

1. The video says that in recent years there were ______ as many strong storms.

   a. twice b. three times c. four times

2. Scientists use images that show ___________ to see the power of the storm.

   a. heat b. waves c. losses

3. Mayfield thinks that after people see what the storm did, they should _______.

   a. want to help stop global warming
   b. find a new place to live, away from the sea
   c. buy better weather-prediction machines

After You Watch

A. Completion. Complete the sentences below using the numbers in the box.

1	1	2	2	3

1. Katrina's winds reached about _________ hundred eighty kilometers per hour.
2. Over a few days, _________ million people lost their homes to the floods.
3. Katrina took almost _________ thousand lives.
4. Water levels in Mayfield's neighborhood rose to almost _________ meters.
5. The losses caused by Katrina cost the U.S. about _________ hundred billion dollars.

B. Discuss. Discuss these questions with a partner.

1. The video says that after Katrina, "for many, things will never be the same." What do you think this means?
2. Why do you think some tropical storms are given names? Do you think it's a good idea?

Rescue workers in a boat help a woman leave her flooded home.

Giants of the Past

Millions of years ago, super-sized creatures like the dinosaurs walked the Earth and swam the seas. But they are all gone now.

Warm Up

Discuss these questions with a partner.

1. Do you know of any animals that don't exist anymore?
2. What do you think caused these animals to die out?

The MAMMOTH'S Tale

Before You Read

Lyuba is the best-preserved mammoth mummy in the world.

A. Matching. Tens of thousands of years ago, woolly mammoths walked the Earth. These creatures were related to today's elephants. Read the information below. Then match the words in **bold** to their definitions.

MAMMOTH

- Long, thick hair
- Long, curved **tusks**
- Lived during the **Ice Age** in Siberia and North America
- Became **extinct** 4,000 years ago

ELEPHANT

- Thick skin but very little hair
- Short, straight tusks
- 470,000 elephants living today, mainly in hot places like India and Africa

1. ____________: no longer existing or living
2. ____________: a time when ice covered much of the Earth
3. ____________: long, pointed teeth used to fight or to find food

B. Predict. Look at the pictures and captions on this page and the next. What do you think happened to the mammoth after it was found? Discuss with a partner. Then read the passage to check your ideas.

__Imagine__ finding a body that had been lost for 40,000 years . . .

The strange animal in the ice looked like it was sleeping. Ten-year-old Kostia Khudi and his brother had never seen anything like it before. But they had heard stories of the *mamont*. It was an imaginary animal that lived in the ice-filled blackness of the Siberian underworld.[1] Their father, a reindeer herder[2] named Yuri Khudi, went to ask a friend for advice.[3] But when he returned, the body had **vanished**.

Yuri soon found the animal's body **leaning against** a store in a nearby town. While he was away, his cousin had sold it to the store owner. Dogs had eaten part of the tail and ear, but it was still in "as close to **perfect** condition as you can imagine," says scientist Daniel Fisher. The police came to help. The body was taken by helicopter to a museum.[4] The animal was a baby mammoth from the Ice Age. It was female, so the scientists named it after Yuri's wife.

From Siberia, the mammoth was sent to the Netherlands and Japan. Scientists there studied it more closely. **Detailed** studies of her teeth and tusks showed she was just one month old when she died. **Ongoing** research has also shown us the **sequence** of events that led to her death. Lyuba fell and died near a muddy river. The mud helped keep her body frozen until she was found, 40,000 years later. Scientists hope that **further** studies will help explain how mammoths, like Lyuba lived. They also want to know why mammoths became extinct.

Lyuba died when she fell into wet mud near a river.

The ground froze. It kept Lyuba's body whole.

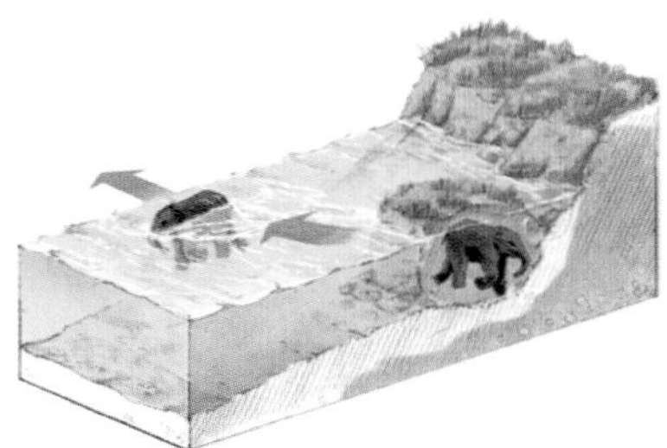

In 2006, melting caused Lyuba's body to wash free.

---

1 The **underworld** is an underground world, where some people believe the dead go.

2 A **herder** looks after a large group of animals.

3 If you ask someone for **advice**, you ask them what they think you should do in a particular situation.

4 A **museum** is a place where old things are kept on display.

Reading Comprehension

Multiple Choice. Choose the best answer for each question.

Gist

1. The passage is mainly about __________.
   a. animals that are now extinct
   b. an important discovery
   c. what life was like for a mammoth named Lyuba

Sequence

2. Which of the following happened first?
   a. Yuri's cousin sold the mammoth to a store owner.
   b. Lyuba's body was taken to a museum.
   c. The police arrived to take Lyuba's body away.

Purpose

3. What is the purpose of the second paragraph (from line 9)?
   a. to describe the condition of Lyuba when she was found
   b. to describe the difficulties of studying a mammoth's body
   c. to describe how Lyuba was found again and taken to a safe place

Reference

4. The word *it* (line 11) refers to the mammoth's __________.
   a. ear
   b. tail
   c. body

Inference

5. Which of the following can be inferred from the passage?
   a. Yuri's wife's name was Lyuba.
   b. The mammoth died when the Ice Age ended.
   c. Yuri's cousin didn't know what the mammoth was when he sold it.

Detail

6. How did Lyuba die?
   a. Dogs killed her.
   b. Hunters killed her.
   c. She died when she fell.

Did You Know?

Some scientists think mammoths died out because the Earth became too warm and they couldn't find enough food. Others think humans hunted them to extinction.

Recognizing Active and Passive Sentences

Reading passages often include a mix of active and passive sentences. In active sentences, *the subject* is the **doer** of the action (the verb). In passive sentences, *the subject* is the **receiver** of the action. Look at these examples and notice how passive sentences are formed.

Active	**Passive (*be* + past participle)**
The boys found a mammoth.	*A mammoth* was found (by the boys).
The man's cousin had sold it.	*It* had been sold (by the man's cousin).
Scientists will study it.	*It* will be studied (by scientists).

A. Analyzing. Read the sentences below. Circle the subject of each sentence. Then mark each as active (**A**) or passive (**P**).

Example: (People) found 158 paintings in a cave in France. (**A**) **P**

1. These pictures were painted by early humans. **A** **P**
2. The paintings show early man and mammoths. **A** **P**
3. Mammoth tusks were used to make tools. **A** **P**
4. These tools were used by early man to hunt. **A** **P**
5. People today search for more mammoth tusks. **A** **P**

B. Completion. Are these sentences active or passive? Choose the correct word or phrase to complete each sentence. Then check your answers on page 149.

1. Dogs (**had eaten / had been eaten**) part of the tail.
2. The body (**took / was taken**) by helicopter to a museum.
3. The mammoth (**sent / was sent**) to the Netherlands.
4. Further studies (**will explain / will be explained**) how mammoths lived and died.

Critical Thinking Discuss with a partner. Some scientists want to bring extinct animals, like mammoths, back to life. Do you think they should? Why or why not?

The tusk of a full-grown mammoth could grow as long as 5.2 meters (17 feet).

Vocabulary Practice

A. Completion. Complete the information below using the correct word or phrase.

Close your eyes. Can you **1.** (**lean against** / **imagine**) a crocodile so big that it eats dinosaurs? Scientists say such a crocodile really did live 110 million years ago in Africa, but it **2.** (**vanished** / **imagined**) from Earth even before the dinosaurs became extinct. They call it "SuperCroc."

In 2000, Paul Sereno and his team found some SuperCroc bones in the Sahara Desert. After some **3.** (**perfect** / **further**) searching, they had enough bones to make up 50 percent of SuperCroc's skeleton.

From their work, the scientists learned many **4.** (**sequences** / **details**) about SuperCroc's life. For example, they now know it grew to about 8,000 kilograms (17,600 pounds) and that its strong jaws and strong teeth were **5.** (**ongoing** / **perfect**) for catching and holding prey. The bones are now in museums, so people can learn about this amazing animal.

Paleontologist Paul Sereno studies dinosaurs and other creatures of the past. The SuperCroc fossils he discovered belong to a crocodile skeleton measuring 12 meters (40 feet) in length.

B. Words in Context. Complete each sentence with the correct answer.

1. If something is **ongoing**, it is ______.
   a. finished b. not finished
2. When you **lean against** a wall, you bend your body ______ it.
   a. toward b. away from
3. If something is **perfect**, you probably want to ______.
   a. keep it the way it is b. change it
4. A **sequence** of events refers to a number of events that come ______.
   a. one after another b. at the same time

Usage

The word **further** means "more" or "additional." The word **farther**, however, usually refers to a greater distance.

A *Tylosaurus* reaches for a shark with its great jaws.

Before You Read

A. Labeling. Read the information below. Then label the picture above with the numbers in **bold**. Write **1–5** in the circles.

At 14 meters (45 feet) long, *Tylosaurus* was one of the biggest sea monsters[1] of all time. By looking at fossils,[2] scientists know that *Tylosaurus* had great **1. jaws** and big **2. teeth**. Studies of its **3. stomach** contents show it ate fish, seabirds, and even sharks. It used its long **4. tail** to push itself through the water and its two shorter **5. fins** to change direction. *Tylosaurus* was not related to the dinosaurs, but it lived and became extinct around the same time.

1 The word ***monster*** usually refers to a large, frightening creature.

2 **Fossils** are the hard remains of animals or plants that lived millions of years ago.

B. Predict. Look quickly at the headings, pictures, and captions on pages 154–155. Answer the questions below. Then read the passage to check your answers.

1. How many "giants of the sea" does the passage mention?
2. What do you think was unusual about each creature?

Monsters of the Deep

Sea monsters are not just imaginary creatures. Millions of years ago, real monsters did actually live on Earth.

Today, scientists use fossils to help them **figure out** what these monsters were like. The fossils can help us understand some of the animals' unusual **characteristics**. After studying the fossils, the scientists can make very detailed pictures of these animals. So now, we can all see what they looked like.

Eyes in the Dark

Temnodontosaurus was **definitely** an unusual animal. Its name means "cutting-tooth lizard," and with good reason—it had very big teeth. It also had some of the largest eyes in nature. They were over 25 centimeters (10 inches) across! With such big eyes, *Temnodontosaurus* could easily find its food in the dark water.

Terror of the Deep

Kronosaurus—the "Kronos lizard"—lived in the seas that covered Australia. But it probably used its fins to climb out of the water and lay its eggs on land. Its head was two meters (seven feet) long. Its teeth were as big as bananas! The main **function** of strong jaws and teeth like these was to catch smaller animals. In fact, *Kronosaurus* was one of the most dangerous **predators** of all time.

The Stalker[1]

Known as the "lord of the seas," *Thalassomedon* was a large sea monster with a very long neck. It also had a special **means** of catching fish: It carried stones in its stomach! These helped keep the largest part of its body and tail down in the dark water. Meanwhile, its long neck slowly **rose** up toward the fish. The fish didn't have a **chance** to get away from *Thalassomedon*. They didn't see the sea monster until it was too late!

1 To **stalk** someone or something is to follow slowly and quietly.

Thalassomedon

Reading Comprehension

Multiple Choice. Choose the best answer for each question.

Purpose

1. What is the purpose of the reading passage?
   a. to describe the three most dangerous predators of all time
   b. to describe how the fossils of three sea animals were found
   c. to describe three sea animals from the past with unusual characteristics

Vocabulary

2. The phrase *with good reason* (lines 12–13) could be replaced with __________.
   a. and it was smart
   b. as will be explained
   c. this was useful because

Detail

3. Which of these sentences about *Kronosaurus* is NOT true?
   a. Its teeth were very large.
   b. It stayed in the water all the time.
   c. It was a very dangerous predator.

Reference

4. The word *these* in line 29 refers to __________.
   a. fish
   b. stones
   c. ways to catch fish

Detail

5. What is unusual about *Thalassomedon*?
   a. It laid its eggs on land.
   b. It had very large eyes.
   c. It had a very long neck.

Inference

6. Why did the fish not have a chance to get away from *Thalassomedon*?
   a. The fish were very slow swimmers.
   b. The fish thought *Thalassomedon* was friendly.
   c. The fish didn't see *Thalassomedon* as it came near.

Did You Know?

Kronosaurus was the largest sea reptile that ever lived.

Organizing Information in a Chart

One useful way to organize information is to write out important details in a chart. A chart can be a good way to "see" the information we want to compare or remember.

A. Completion. What do you know about these animals? How are they the same or different? Complete the chart with the animal names from the box.

crocodile **elephant** ***Kronosaurus*** **mammoth** **shark** ***Temnodontosaurus*** **whale**

	lives on land	lives in water
Living now		
Extinct		

B. Completion. Complete the chart below using information from the passage on page 154. Write one word in each space.

	Temnodontosaurus	*Kronosaurus*	*Thalassomedon*
Meaning of name	"cutting-__________ lizard"	"Kronos __________"	"lord of the __________"
Unusual characteristics	had very large __________ and __________	had teeth the size of __________	had a very long __________ and __________ in its stomach
Special abilities	could easily see its __________ in the dark water	could __________ smaller animals with its strong __________	was able to get close to __________ without being seen

Critical Thinking Discuss with a partner. In what ways are the three creatures in **B** the same? How are they different?

Vocabulary Practice

A. Completion. Complete the information using the correct form of words from the box. One word is extra.

chance	characteristic	definitely	figure out	function	means	predator	rise

For hundreds of years, people have heard reports of monsters that **1.** ___________ out of the sea to attack ships. Many people now think these "monsters" were probably giant squid.

Giant squid share many of the same **2.** ___________ as other squid. But they are much larger—up to 13 meters (43 feet) in length. They also have the largest eyes of any animal in the world. This helps them catch deep-sea fish.

Their only **3.** ___________ are some kinds of whales. When it is attacked, the giant squid has a very clever **4.** ___________ of getting away. It shoots dark ink into the water. The whale can't see, so the squid has a **5.** ___________ to swim away.

For years, scientists were unable to catch a giant squid on film. But they did find squid body parts in the stomachs of whales. The scientists were able to use these to **6.** ___________ how big the squid was. The first photos of a live giant squid were taken in 2004. It is **7.** ______________ as monstrous as people believed!

Squid have ten long sticky arms that they use to catch food.

B. Definitions. Use words from the box in **A** to complete the definitions below.

1. Features that are usual for someone or something are called ______________.
2. Your ______________ of doing something are your ways of doing it.
3. If there is a ______________ of something, there is a possibility it will happen.
4. The _________ of an object is how it is meant to be used.

Usage
Use **probably** to say something is likely. Use **definitely** if you are sure about something, and **possibly** if there is just a chance something is true or will happen.

VIEWING Days of the Dinosaurs

Before You Watch

Discuss. Look at the picture and read the caption. Can you name any other dinosaurs? What do you know about them? Discuss the questions below with a partner.

The word *dinosaur* means "great lizard"—it was once believed that all dinosaurs were simply giant lizards. Scientists have since found that many dinosaurs also had characteristics similar to those of other animals.

For example, *sauropods* (the long-necked creatures pictured here) walked on four legs but were able to stand on two, like elephants. They also traveled in family groups just like elephants. They had claws[1] and hollow[2] bones like birds.

1 **Claws** are sharp, curved structures at the end of animals' toes.

2 If something is **hollow**, it is empty inside.

1. What did dinosaurs look like? Describe some dinosaurs.
2. What do you think *sauropods* ate? What did other dinosaurs eat?
3. Did dinosaurs lay eggs?
4. What modern animal do you think dinosaurs are like?
5. How did the dinosaurs die out?
6. How do you think scientists today learn about dinosaurs?

While You Watch

A. Checking. As you watch the video, check your answers in **Before You Watch**. Were your ideas correct?

B. Completion. As you watch, choose the correct word or phrase from the video to complete each sentence.

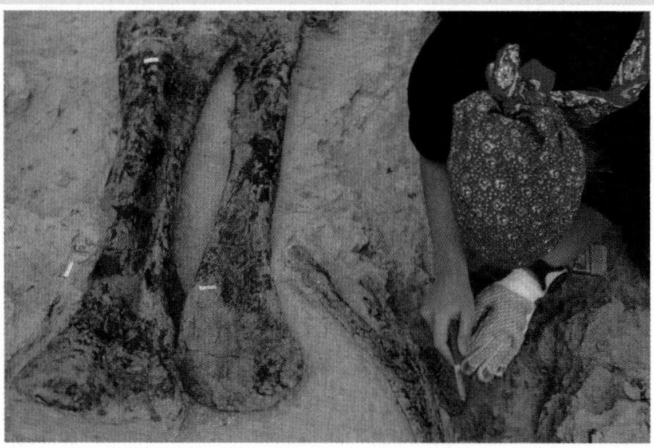

1. The scientists dig for (**fossilized bones** / **dinosaur eggs**).

2. The smallest dinosaur was less than (**one meter long** / **one kilogram**).

3. Dinosaurs likely died out because the planet was too (**hot and wet** / **cold and dark**).

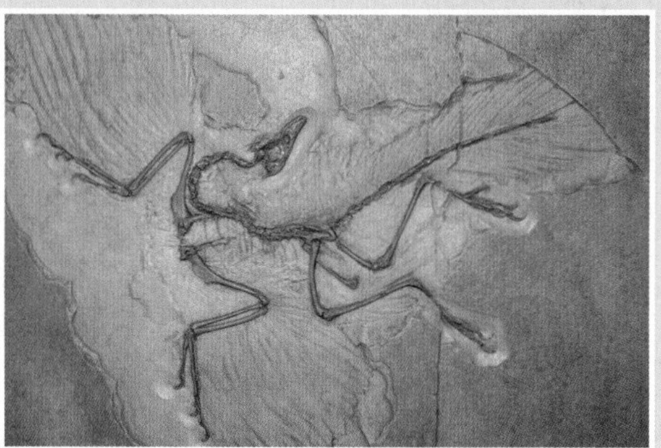

4. Scientists believe dinosaurs may be related to the (**birds** / **snakes**) living today.

After You Watch

A. True or False. Read the sentences below. Then mark each sentence as true (**T**) or false (**F**).

1. *Jobaria* ate meat.	**T**	**F**
2. *Jobaria* was longer than a city bus.	**T**	**F**
3. Most dinosaurs laid eggs.	**T**	**F**
4. Some dinosaurs lived in groups.	**T**	**F**
5. Scientists now know why dinosaurs went extinct.	**T**	**F**

B. Discuss. Discuss these questions with a partner.

1. In the video, the narrator compares the time since the moment dinosaurs first appeared to a single day. What is he trying to say?
2. Why do you think people like to watch movies and read stories about creatures from the past, like dinosaurs and mammoths?

TECHNOLOGY

As we mix more technology into our everyday activities, many believe that robots like this one will become part of our daily lives.

Warm Up

Discuss these questions with a partner.

1. What kinds of technology do you often use?
2. What kind of things do you think people will do differently 100 years from now?

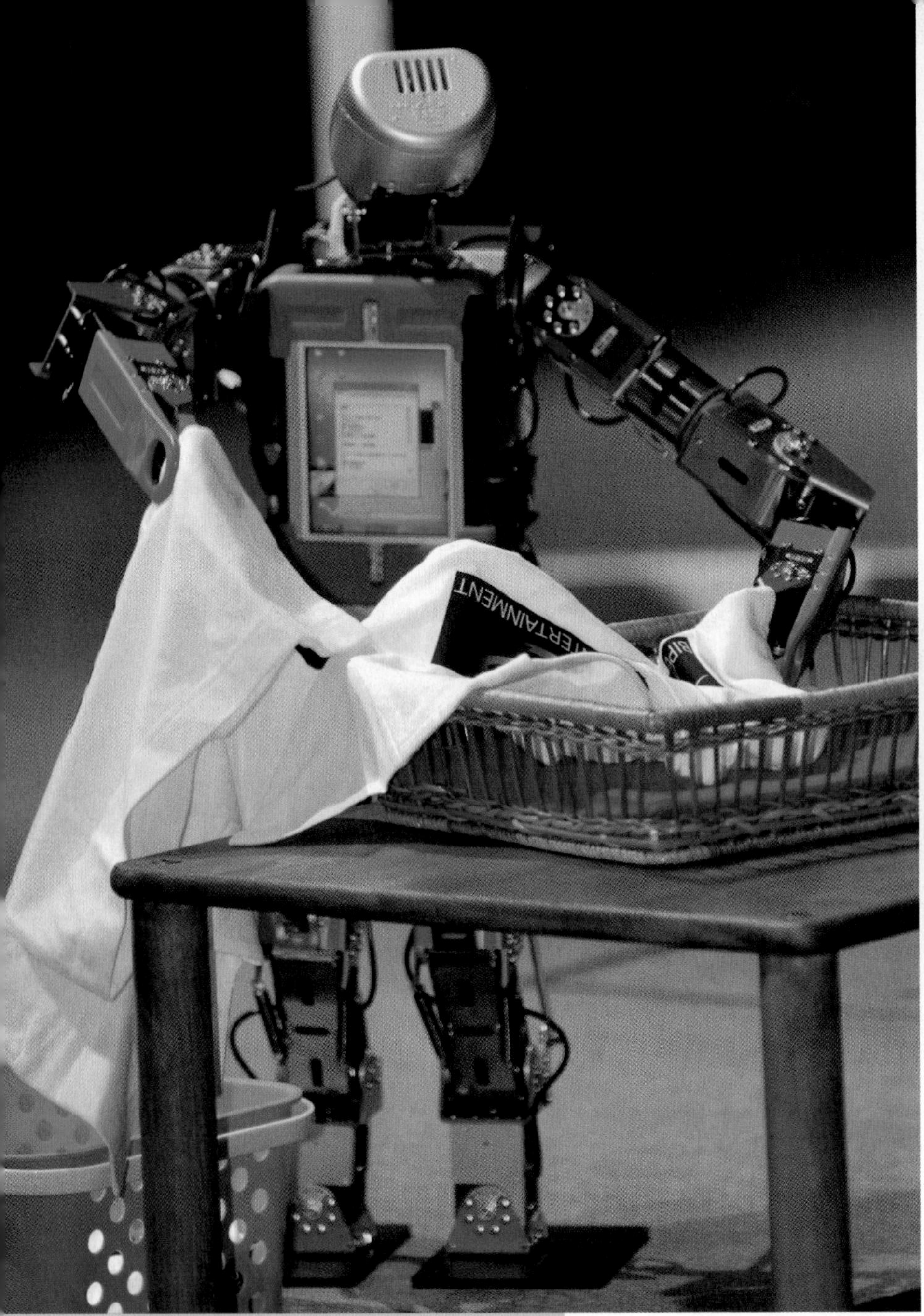

Robot helpers for the home and mini-soccer players are just some examples of the robots being built today.

Before You Read

A. Discuss. What can robots do that humans can't? What can humans do that robots can't? Use the words and phrases from the box, and add your own ideas.

climb stairs	feel emotions	fight fires
jump	play soccer	run
take care of people	drive cars	walk on water
walk up walls	work in space	write poems

B. Scan. Look quickly at the reading. Which of the things above are mentioned in the reading? Do you think today's robots can do them? Read the passage to check your ideas.

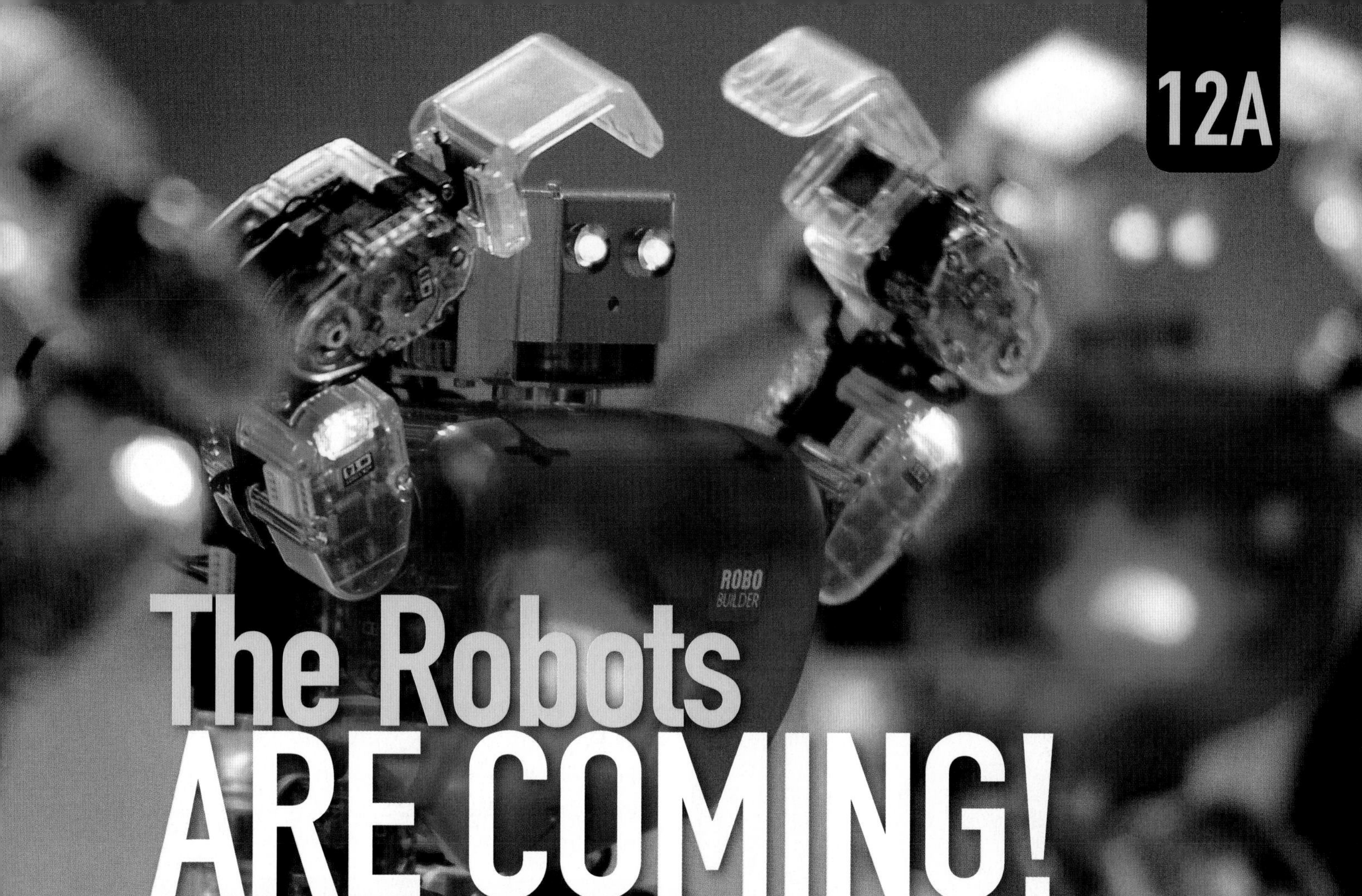

The Robots ARE COMING!

The year is 2045. A goal is scored at the soccer World Cup. Not by a human player, but by a robot. *A robot? Is that possible?* Many scientists believe it is. In fact, there are already robots that can play soccer. Of course, today's robots don't just play **sports**. Today's scientists are working on robots with various skills. For example, it is very possible that robots will soon help take care of children or the elderly,[1] or do dangerous jobs such as fighting fires.

When people started making robots, they were made to do just **simple** things, mainly in **factories**. Since then, however, robots have changed a lot. Early robots were **operated** by humans. Today's robots function on their own. Some can only move around a little, like robot vacuum cleaners,[2] but others, such as Honda's ASIMO, can do much more. He can run, climb stairs, dance, and yes, even play soccer.

Then there are robots designed to be like humans. These robots have faces and can show emotions. Such robots can learn new things, and show us how they "feel." Actroid-DER—a social robot—looks so human, she sometimes makes people feel **uncomfortable**.

---

1 Someone who is **elderly** is old.

2 A **vacuum cleaner** is a machine that cleans the floor by sucking up dirt.

Animal-bots

Scientists aren't just building humanlike robots. They are also making robots that look and act like animals.

At NASA, scientists are making a robot snake. They think it's a good **alternative** to vehicles with wheels. These snake-bots can enter holes and move over **rough** ground. They might one day help scientists look for **signs** of life on Mars. Other animal robots include the frog-bot, which can jump over objects, and the sticky-bot, which can walk up walls. There's even a robot called Water Runner that can walk on water.

But can a robot soccer team ever operate all on their own, or play as well as a human team? Many robot scientists definitely think so. Anything is possible. One day, they may even be world champions!

Among the robots of today are Honda's ASIMO (top left), the NASA snake-bot (bottom left), and Actroid-DER—the social robot (right).

Reading Comprehension

Multiple Choice. Choose the best answer for each question.

Gist

1. The passage is mainly about __________.
   a. things robots can do
   b. why people need robots
   c. how to make your own robot

Purpose

2. What is the purpose of the second paragraph (from line 8)?
   a. to describe how the earliest robots were used in factories
   b. to explain how today's robots are different from early robots
   c. to explain why early robots could not do things by themselves

Detail

3. Which robot is able to show its feelings?
   a. ASIMO
   b. Actroid-DER
   c. Water Runner

Reference

4. The word *they* (line 23) refers to __________.
   a. vehicles
   b. wheels
   c. snake-bots

Detail

5. Which of the following robots would best be able to move over a large rock in its path?
   a. A frog-bot
   b. Actroid-DER
   c. Water Runner

Inference

6. Which statement would the author probably agree with?
   a. A frog-bot can do more things than a sticky-bot.
   b. Robots should not have to do difficult jobs for humans.
   c. There could be robot soccer players that think for themselves in the World Cup by 2045.

Did You Know?

Leonardo da Vinci drew up plans for a humanlike machine in 1495. In 2009, artists made this model of Leonardo's design.

Reading Skill

Supporting Ideas with Examples

Writers often use examples to support their ideas or help explain difficult concepts. Words that show where examples are in a text include *for instance, for example, like,* and *such as.*

A. Completion. Look back at paragraphs 1 and 2 of the passage on pages 163–164. Find and write the example of each thing below. (Look out for words that show where the examples are.)

1. a sport that robots can play ________________
2. a skill other than a sport ________________
3. a dangerous job ________________
4. a type of robot that moves around a little ________________
5. a robot that does more than move around ________________

B. Completion. Choose examples from the box to complete the information below.

a. he could be seen at the Henry Ford Museum
b. "I am Elektro" and "My brain is bigger than yours."
c. sitting, barking, and begging for food
d. he could walk, talk, and move his arms and legs

One of the first humanlike robots was Elektro. Built between 1937 and 1939, he could do many basic human actions. For example, **1.** ________. He was first seen at the New York World's Fair in 1939, with Sparko, a robot dog that could do tricks, such as **2.** ________. In 1992, a dance band recorded a song that used some things Elektro once said, like, **3.** ________. Elektro's usual home is at the Mansfield Memorial Museum in Ohio, U.S.A, but he often travels to other museums. For instance, in 2013, **4.** ________.

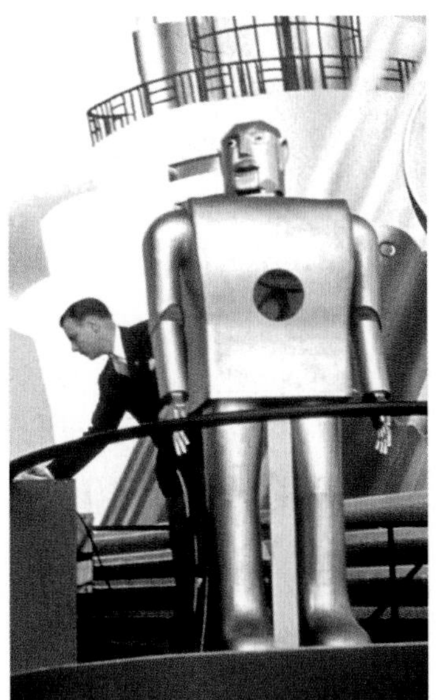

Elektro is 2.1 meters (7 feet) tall and weighs 120 kilograms (265 pounds).

Critical Thinking Discuss with a partner. Some people fear that one day robots will completely replace other human beings in our lives. Do you think this could happen? What jobs do you think robots could do better than humans? Are there things only humans can do?

Vocabulary Practice

A. Completion. Complete the information using words from the box. One word is extra.

alternative	operate	rough	simple	uncomfortable

Some robots today are learning to walk. Putting one foot in front of the other is usually so **1.** __________ that a child can do it. But walking is difficult for robots, and nearly impossible over **2.** __________ ground. Researchers are working to help robots walk better by giving them machine parts that act like human bones and muscles.

A robot pet provides a(n) **3.** __________ to keeping a real animal. It moves, cries, senses your movements, and can even learn basic words. But some people are **4.** __________ with robot pets. They worry that robot pets could replace contact with real animals or even other humans.

A robot seal named Paro helps elderly people feel better. Paro can play with people and even learn from them.

B. Words in Context. Complete each sentence with the correct answer.

1. __________ are examples of **sports**.
   a. Basketball and tennis b. Balls and nets
2. A **factory** is a place where products are __________.
   a. made b. sold
3. A **sign** of something __________.
   a. is a picture in your mind b. shows that it exists
4. If you **operate** a machine, you __________ it.
   a. use b. fix

Word Partnership
Use ***operate*** with: (*n.*) operate a **machine**, operate a **business**, operate a **company**.

An artist's idea of what a home in the future might look like

Before You Read

A. Predict. Look at the pictures on this page and the next, and read the captions. Then answer the questions below.

1. What do you think the passage will say about the future?
2. What other things do you think will be different in the future?

B. Skim. Skim the passage on page 169. Check (✓) the topics the author makes predictions about. Then read the whole passage to check your answers. Were your ideas in **A** correct?

☐ health	☐ entertainment	☐ clothing
☐ food	☐ transportation	☐ work

How Will We Live in 2035?

Welcome to life in the **future**!

You get up in the morning and look into the **mirror**. You've just had an anti-aging **treatment**, so your face looks youthful. In 2035, many people your age could live to be 150, so at 60, you're not old at all.

Science has also found amazing ways to keep people healthy. There are nanotechnology[1] treatments for many illnesses, including cancer. And if any part of your body is not healthy, you can "grow" a new one in a **laboratory**.

As you get dressed, you say to your shirt, "Turn red." It becomes red. In 2035, "smart clothes" contain nanoparticles that carry **electricity**. So you can **program** clothes to change colors or patterns.

On the way to the kitchen, you want to call a friend. Your cell phone is by the window because the material it's made of takes in energy from the sun. But you don't need to pick up the phone. You can just touch your jacket sleeve[2] to make the call.

These are just some examples of nanotechnology all around you. "Your whole body and **surroundings** [will] become part of the same network,"[3] says scientist Ampy Buchholz.

It's breakfast time. You reach for the milk, but a voice says, "Don't drink that!" Your fridge is reading a computer chip[4] on the milk. Every item from the **grocery** has a chip. Your fridge knows the milk is old, and tells the store you need new milk.

Finally, it's time to go to work. In 2035, cars drive themselves. Just tell your "smart car" where to go, and soon you will be there.

So, will all these predictions come true? Perhaps the future is much closer than we think.

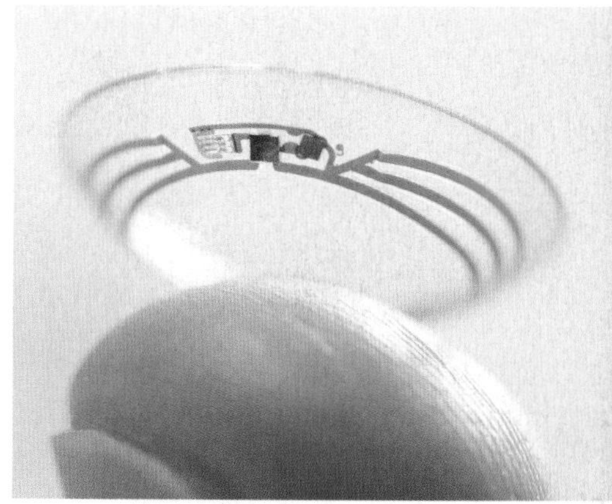

With pieces of wearable technology like Google's smart contact lens on the way to becoming part of people's daily lives, perhaps the future is not so far away.

1 **Nanotechnology** is the science of very small things that are measured in nanometers (one billionth of a meter).

2 The **sleeves** of a shirt or jacket are the parts that cover your arms.

3 A **network** is a set of computers that send information to each other.

4 A **computer chip** is a very small piece of electronic equipment.

Reading Comprehension

Multiple Choice. Choose the best answer for each question.

Gist

1. The passage is mainly about __________.
   a. medical treatments of the future
   b. how future technology may affect our lives
   c. how people will work and have fun in the future

Detail

2. What does the writer say about aging in the future?
   a. Age 60 will not be thought of as old.
   b. People who are 150 will look like they are 60.
   c. People who are 60 can expect to live 150 more years.

Vocabulary

3. In line 11, the word *smart* means ________.
   a. nice-looking
   b. good at learning
   c. with a computer

Reference

4. The word *it's* (line 15) refers to __________.
   a. the window
   b. the cell phone
   c. the sun

Detail

5. Which of the following predictions is NOT mentioned in the passage?
   a. You will be able to grow new body parts.
   b. Clothes will be able to change their patterns.
   c. There will be no more cell phones.

Inference

6. Which statement would Ampy Buchholz probably agree with?
   a. Nanotechnology will become very common in the future.
   b. Nano-sized particles may be dangerous to people's health.
   c. Life will be less interesting because everyone will look the same.

Did You Know?

A human hair is about 100,000 nanometers wide.

Reading Skill

Understanding Prefixes and Suffixes

Prefixes (e.g., *un-*, *dis-*, *mis-*) are found at the beginning of words, and suffixes (e.g., *-al*, *-ly*, *-istic*) at the end of words. Knowing the meaning of prefixes and suffixes can help you understand new words and help build your vocabulary.

A. Completion. Look at the prefixes, meanings, and examples. Write a new word for each prefix using words from the box.

act	paid	national

	Prefix	Meanings	Examples	Your ideas:
1.	re-	again/back to	return	________
2.	inter-	between/among	Internet	________
3.	pre-	before	predict	________

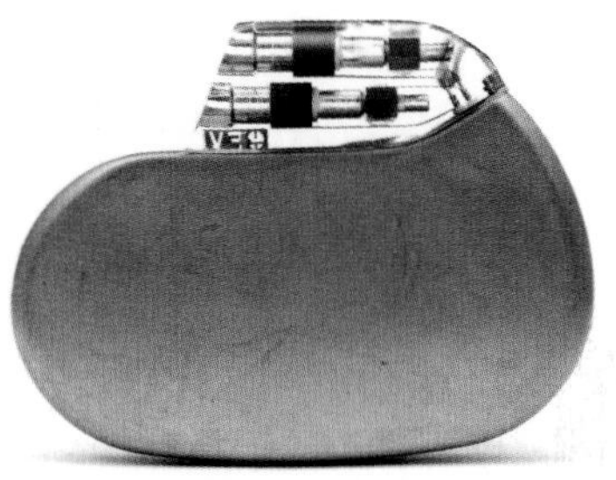

This pacemaker, a little machine that is put in a person's chest to help control their heart rhythms, is another example of how technology has changed our lives.

B. Completion. Look at the suffixes, meanings, and examples. Write a new word for each suffix using words from the box.

pain	assess	invent

	Suffix	Meanings	Examples	Your ideas:
1.	-ful	full of	careful	________
2.	-ment	act or manner	enjoyment	________
3.	-ion	act or process	action	________

C. Definitions. Find words in the first two paragraphs of the passage on page 169 containing these words. Write the word with its prefix or suffix. Then write a definition.

	Word	Word + prefix or suffix	Definition
1.	aging	________	________
2.	treat	________	________
3.	youth	________	________

Critical Thinking Discuss with a partner. Which of the predictions in the reading do you think will happen? Make a prediction about future technology. Does your partner agree?

Vocabulary Practice

A. Definitions. Use the words in the box to complete the definitions.

electricity	**future**	**grocery**	**laboratory**
mirror	**program**	**surroundings**	**treatment**

1. If you look into a(n) ____________, you see yourself.
2. A(n) ____________ store sells different kinds of food.
3. Your ____________ are the places, conditions, and things around you.
4. A(n) ____________ is a room full of equipment where scientists work.
5. After you receive ____________ for an illness, you usually look or feel better.
6. You ____________ a machine by giving it instructions so it performs an action.
7. The ____________ is the period of time that will happen after the present time.
8. ____________ is energy that travels through wires and is used to operate machines.

B. Completion. Complete the information using words from the box in **A**.

Science fiction writers have long dreamed of cyborgs—people who have machines as body parts. Now that dream is a reality. Scientists have discovered ways to **1.** ____________ machines to pick up signals from the brain, so people can operate them just by thinking.

After she lost her arm in a car accident, it was difficult for Amanda Kitts to do the **2.** ____________ shopping and other everyday activities. Now Amanda has a robotic arm.

This technology is still very new. Though it has been tested many times in a **3.** ____________, it needs to be tested with real people. It may not work for everyone. However, many believe it won't be too far into the **4.** ____________ before scientists succeed in fully joining humans and machines.

Amanda Kitts with her robotic arm

Word Partnership

Use ***future*** with: (*adj.*) **near** future, **distant** future, **bright** future; (*v.*) **predict** the future, **shape** the future, **face** the future.

VIEWING Deep-sea Robot

Before You Watch

Predict. Look at the picture and read the caption.
Then check (✓) the things below that you think ROPOS can do.

The ocean covers more than 70 percent of the Earth's surface, but only about 5 percent of the world's oceans have been explored, and we know even less about the creatures that live in its depths.[1]
In 2010, scientists from more than 80 countries started a project called the Census[2] of Marine[3] Life. They want to find out more about life in the ocean. It's a difficult project, but the scientists have help from a very special robot called ROPOS.

1 The **depths** of something refers to its deep places.
2 During a **census**, someone counts the number of people or animals in a place and gets information about them.
3 The term **marine** refers to anything to do with the ocean.

- ☐ record videos
- ☐ walk on land
- ☐ measure things
- ☐ cut things
- ☐ record sound
- ☐ take photos
- ☐ identify species
- ☐ help divers breathe
- ☐ pick up small animals
- ☐ suck up things
- ☐ think for itself
- ☐ dig in the ocean floor

While You Watch

Checking. As you watch the video, check your answers in **Before You Watch**. Were your ideas correct?

After You Watch

A. Multiple Choice. Choose the correct answer for each question below.

1. Why do the scientists use ROPOS to help them study deep-sea life?

a. It is too dark in the deep water for humans to see.
b. There are places too deep in the sea for humans to breathe.
c. Sea animals are scared of people but not of ROPOS.

2. ROPOS can go __________ meters down into the ocean.

a. 260 b. 2,600 c. 26,000

3. The video says ROPOS is the scientists' __________.

a. eyes and ears b. arms and legs c. hands and feet

4. What does ROPOS stand for?

a. Research Organism for Placement Of Sea Life
b. Robotic Ocean Performance for Optical Study
c. Remotely Operated Platform for Ocean Science

B. Matching. Match each of the following ideas from the video with their supporting details.

1. ____ We don't know much about our oceans.
2. ____ Scientists want to know more.
3. ____ A scientist says he can do things with ROPOS that he couldn't do before.
4. ____ ROPOS is a very well-equipped robot.
5. ____ ROPOS helps us understand more about deep-ocean life.

a. Many marine species are not known.
b. ROPOS has tools to cut, suck up, and dig.
c. Researchers have started the Census of Marine Life.
d. ROPOS helps the scientists see animals in their natural homes.
e. He can study animals in deep water as he could if they were found on land.

C. Discuss. Discuss these questions with a partner.

1. Do you think it's possible for humans to explore the whole ocean? Why or why not?

2. Do you think it's more important for humans to know about plants and animals in the ocean or on land?

Subarctic sunflower stars

A yeti crab

These sunflower stars and the yeti crab are some examples of species discovered by the Marine Census.

Photo Credits

1 Frans Lanting/NGC, **3** Joel Sartore/NGC, **4–5** Mikadun/Shutterstock.com, **7** Magrath/Folsom/Science Photo Library/Getty Images, **8–9** Aaron Foster/Photographer's Choice/Getty Images, **10** Tino Soriano/NGC, **11–13** (t) English Heritage/Heritage Images/Hulton Archive/Getty Images, **11** (bl) andrea crisante/Shutterstock.com, **12** (bl) Hulton Collection/Hulton Archive/Getty Images, **13** (cr) Robert Harding Picture Library Ltd/Alamy, **14**, **15**, **16–18** (t) Mondolithic Studios, **16** (cr) DEA/G. Dagli Orti/Getty Images, **17** (cr) Takaji Ochi/VWPICS/Visual&Written SL/Alamy, **18** (tr) Mike Matthews Photography/Flickr/Getty Images, **19**, **20** (tr) Keystone/Hulton Archive/Getty Images, **20** (tl), (cl), (cr), **47–48**, **62**, **76** (tl), (tr), (cl), (cr), **90**, **132** National Geographic, **20** (bl), (br) Daily Mail/Rex/Alamy, **21** Giuglio Gil/hemis.fr/Getty Images, **22** The Oven, from Saint-Romain-en-Gal (mosaic), Roman, (3rd century AD)/Musee des Antiquites Nationales, St. Germain-en-Laye, France/Giraudon/The Bridgeman Art Library, **23** AP Images/National Football League/John Minchillo, **24** (tr) Vitaly Korovin/Shutterstock.com, **24** (bl) Tino Soriano/NGC, **25** (t) Joe Gough/Shutterstock.com, **25** (bc) AP Images/Rex Features, **26–27** (t) Lauri Patterson/Vetta/Getty Images, **27** (cr) Dan Peretz/Shutterstock.com, **28** (tr) AP Images/Jeffrey Collins, **28** (tl) Fabrizio Troiani/Alamy, **28** (tc) Julian Eales/Alamy, **28** (cr) Andrew Wood/Alamy, **28** (c) Foodfolio/Food and Drink/SuperStock, **28** (bl), **31** (cr) FoodCollection/StockFood America, **29** (cr) Strdel/AFP/Getty Images, **30–32** (t) Greg Elms/Lonely Planet Images/Getty Images, **30** (bl) Igor Marx/Shutterstock.com, **32** (cr) Keith Dannemiller/Alamy, **33** Richard Ellis/Getty Images, **34** Richard Ellis/Alamy, **35** Paul Nicklen/NGC, **36** Joel Sartore/NGC, **37** (tl), (tr) Russell Chadwick, **38–40** (t), **38** (br) Darren Bennett/Animals Animals/AGE Fotostock, **39** (br) AP Images/Douglas C. Pizac, **40** (cr) AFP/Getty Images, **41**, **42** (t), **43**, **44–46** (t), **46** (tl), (tr) Joel Sartore/NGC, **42** (br) Jerod Harris/Getty Images, **44** (br) SSPL/Getty Images, **49** Michael Poliza/NGC, **50–51**, **53–55** (t) Raymond Wong/NGC, **52** (tr) Priit Vesilind/NGC, **52** (b) Emory Kristof/NGC, **53** (bc) General Photographic Agency/Hulton Archive/Getty Images, **55** (tr) Topical Press Agenc/Hulton Archive/Getty Images, **56**, **58–60** (t) Jon Foster/NGC, **57** (t) Amy Toensing/NGC, **58** (b) Martin Harvey/Gallo Images/Getty Images, **59** (cr) Enno Kleinert/dieKleinert/Alamy, **60** (tr) AP Images/Odyssey Marine Inc, **61** NOAA Office of Marine and Aircraft Operations, **63** Monty Rakusen/Cultura Creative/Alamy, **64** (tl) Exactostock/SuperStock, **64** (cl), (c) Lagowski/Custom Medical Stock, **64** (cr) Mikael Karlsson/Alamy, **65** Monty Rakusen/Cultura Creative (RF)/Alamy, **66** (tl) Pablo Paul/Alamy, **66** (tr) Sean Clarkson /Alamy, **66** (cr) deadgooddesigns/Alamy, **67–69** (t) Bildagentur Zoonar GmbH/Shutterstock.com, **67** (b) Prof. Maciej Henneberg/Natural Science, **68** (cr) bikeriderlondon/Shutterstock.com, **69** (tr) Florea Paul/Alamy, **70** R Parulan Jr./Flickr/Getty Images, **71** Joshua Roberts/Bloomberg/Getty Images, **72–74** (t) Kallista Images/Getty Images, **72** (br) Custom Medical Stock Photo/Newscom, **73** (br) nata-lunata/Shutterstock.com, **74** (tr) tobkatrina/Shutterstock.com, **75** Rebecca Hale/NGC, **76** (br) Sebastian Kaulitzki/Shutterstock.com, **77** Archive Holdings Inc./Archive Photos/Getty Images, **78** Lewis & Clark on the Lower Columbia River, 1905 (oil on canvas), Russell, Charles Marion (1865–1926)/Private Collection/Peter Newark American Pictures/The Bridgeman Art Library, **79** (tr) Lyn Alweis/The Denver Post/Getty Images, **80–82** (t), **80** (cr) North Wind Picture Archives/Alamy, **81** (br) David Grove/NGC, **82** (tr) Popperfoto/Getty Images, **83** NGC, **84** (bl) Robert E Peary/NGC, **84** (cr) NY Daily News Archive/Getty Images, **85** Everett Collection Historical/Alamy, **86–88** (t) Borge Ousland/NGC, **86** (cr) FPG/Hulton Archive/Getty Images, **87** (br) Everett Collection Historical/Alamy, **88** (tr) AP Images/Czarek Sokolowski, **89** Ira Block/NGC, **91** AP Images/Reebok CrossFit/Gary Prior, **92**, **94–96** (t) Kladyk Petro/Shutterstock.com, **93** Tim Robberts/Stone/Getty Images, **94** (br) Jose Luis Pelaez/Blend Images/Getty Images, **95** (tr) Hal Beral VWPics/SuperStock, **96** (br) coka/Shutterstock.com, **97** Mike Theiss/NGC, **98** (cr) Science Photo Library, **98** (br) ajith achuthan/Alamy, **99**, **100–102** (t) viphotos/Shutterstock.com, **100** (br) Petr Malyshev/Shutterstock.com, **101** (tr) Alistair Scott/Shutterstock.com, **102** (tr) Chris Johns/NGC, **103** Cultura RM/Ian Spanier/Getty Images, **104** Deco/Alamy, **105** irawansubingarphotography/Flickr/Getty Images, **106–107** Bill Curtsinger/NGC, **108** (bl), **109–111** (t), **109** (bl) Paul Nicklen/NGC, **111** Dr. Maurice G. Hornocker/NGC, **112** (tl) Dave Stamboulis Travel Photography/Flickr/Getty Images, **112** (tr) Wild Horizon/Universal Images Group/Getty Images, **112** (cl) Image Source/Getty Images, **112** (cr) Cultura RM/Brett Phibbs/Collection Mix: Subjects/Getty Images, **113** arturasker/Shutterstock.com, **114** (tl) Dave Hamman/Gallo Images/Getty Images, **114** (tc) Tatiana Gass/Shutterstock.com, **114** (tr) Muhammad Rais Sanusi/Flickr/Getty Images, **114** (cr) Joel Sartore/NGC, **115** (tl) Martin Harvey/Getty Images, **115** (tc) Pai-Shih Lee/Flickr/Getty Images, **115** (tr) Gary Vestal/Photographer's Choice/Getty Images, **115** (cr) Stuart Dee/Photographer's Choice/Getty Images, **116** (tl) Karl Schatz/Aurora Photos/Alamy, **116** (tc) Ralph Lee Hopkins/NGC, **116** (tr) Roger Eritja/Oxford Scientific/Getty Images, **116** (cr) AP Images/Great Ape Trust of Iowa, **117** Rosemary Calvert/Getty Images, **118** Paul Nicklen/NGC, **119** AJ Brustein/Flickr/Getty Images, **120**, **122–124** (t) RuthChoi/Shutterstock.com, **121** akg-images, **122** J. Palys/Shutterstock.com, **124** daewoosao/Shutterstock.com, **125**, **128–130** (t) Mikadun/Shutterstock.com, **126**, **127** Fernando G. Baptista/NGC, **128** (bc) wjarek/Getty Images, **129** (cr) dennisvdw/Getty Images, **130** Michael Dunning/Getty Images, **131** Rabatti-Domingie/akg-images, **133** Fabrice Coffrini/AFP/Getty Images, **134–135**, **137–139** (t) ChinaFotoPress/Getty Images, **136** Rusty Russell/Getty Images, **137** (br) Jhaz Photography/Shutterstock.com, **139** (br) Veri Sanovri/Xinhua/Photoshot/Newscom, **140**, **142–144** (t) Daniel J Bryant/Getty Images, **141** Nancy G Fire Photography, Nancy Greifenhagen/Alamy, **142** (br) CN1/WENN/Newscom, **143** (br) David McNew/Getty Images, **144** (r) Epic Stock/Shutterstock.com, **145** AP Photo, **146** Marko Georgiev/Getty Images, **147** Raul Martin/NGC, **148** (t) Laurent Fievet/AFP/Getty Images, **148** (bc) Kazuhiko Sano/NGC, **149** (t) Field Museum Library/Premium Archive/Getty Images, **149** (br) Kazuhiko Sano/NGC, **150–152** (t) elnavegante/Shutterstock.com, **150** (br) Charles R. Knight/NGC, **151** (cr) Dave King/Getty Images, **152** (tr) AP Images/Rick Bowmer, **153**, **154–155** (bkgd), **155** (cl), **155** (bl), **156–158** (t) Matte Fx, Matte Fx Inc./NGC, **156** (bl) Sergey Krasovskiy/Stocktrek Images/Getty Images, **158** (tr) 548901005677/Moment/Getty Images, **159** Mark Hallett/NGC, **160** (tl) Lynn Johnson/NGC, **160** (tr) Linda Bucklin/Shutterstock.com, **160** (cl) Mark Garlick/Getty Images, **160** (cr) Jason Edwards/NGC, **160** (br) Linda Bucklin/Shutterstock.com, **161** Matt Cardy/Getty Images News/Getty Images, **162** (tl) Yoshikazu Tsuno/Getty Images, **162–163**, **165–167** (t) Gerard Julien/AFP/Getty Images, **164** (cl) Bloomberg/Getty Images, **164** (br) Yoshikazu Tsuno/AFP/Getty Images, **164** (bl) NASA, **165** (bc) William West/AFP/Getty Images, **166** (cr) Sherman Oaks Antique Mall/Archive Photos/Getty Images, **167** (tr) The Washington Post/Getty Images, **168** Mondolithic Studios, **169–172** (t) YadvigaGr/Shutterstock.com, **169** (cr) AP Images/Rex Features, **170** (br) CMSP/Getty Images, **171** (tr) Fodor90/Shutterstock.com, **172** (br) Mark Thiessen/NGC, **173** Pacific Ring of Fire 2004 Expedition, NOAA Office of Ocean Exploration; Dr. Bob Embley, NOAA PMEL, Chief Scientist, **174** (bl) AFP/Getty Images/Newscom, **174** (bc) AP Images/Ifremer, A. Fifis

NGC = National Geographic Creative

Illustration Credits

29 (tr), **33** (c), **37** (cr), **57** (cr), **107** (cr), **125** (cr) National Geographic, **79** (br) National Geographic Maps

Text Credits

9 Adapted from "UFO Mystery," by Elisabeth Deffner: NGK, Mar 2008, **15** Adapted from "Unsolved Mystery: Atlantis," by Michael N. Smith and Debora L. Smith: NGK, Mar 2005, **23** Adapted from "A Slice of History," by Susan E. Goodman: NGE, 2005, **29** Adapted from "Hot Pod," by Catherine L. Barker: NGM, May 2007, **37** Adapted from "Grin and Bear it," by Russell Chadwick: NG World, Feb 2001, **42** Adapted from "An interview with Joel Sartore," by Joel Sartore: adapted from interviews from www.joelsartore.com, **51** Adapted from "Why is the *Titanic* Vanishing?," by Robert D. Ballard: NGM, Dec 2004, **57** Adapted from "Diamond Shipwreck," by Roff Smith: NGM, Nov 2009, **65** Adapted from "On the Case," by Dana Jensen and Natasha Metzler: NGE, Oct 2008, **71** Adapted from "Disease Detective," by Marylou Tousignant: NGE, Mar 2010, **79** Adapted from "Who was Sacagawea?," by Dana Jensen: NGE, Mar 2007, and "Searching for Sacagawea," by Margaret Talbot: NGM, Feb 2003, **84** Adapted from "Arctic Adventurer," by Dolores Johnson: NG Extreme Explorer, Jan-Feb 2010, **93** Adapted from "How to Decode Your Dreams," by Sarah Wassner: NGK, Aug 2005, **98** Adapted from "Optical Illusions: NGE, Apr 2005, **107** Adapted from "Destination Antarctica: Emperor Penguins," by Crispin Boyer: NGK, Apr 2009, "Emperor Penguin: NG Website (http://animals.nationalgeographic.com/animals/birds/emperor-penguin/), "Penguins March On," by Jennifer Peters: NGE, Nov-Dec 2005, "Trapped by Ice," by Ruth Musgrave: NGK, Jan-Feb 2003, and "Happy Feet," by Deborah Underwood: NGK, Nov 2006, **113** Adapted from "What's So Funny?," by Aline Alexander Newman: NGK, Apr 2006, **121** Adapted from "Taj Mahal: NG Website (http://travel.nationalgeographic.com/travel/world-heritage/taj-mahal/), **126** Adapted from "Brunelleschi's Dome," by Tom Mueller: NGM, Feb 2014; **135** Adapted from "Weather Gone Wild," by Peter Miller: NGM, Sep 2012, **141** Adapted from "Ten Freaky Forces of Nature," by Douglas E. Richards: NGK, Sep 2008, **149** Adapted from "Mystery of the Frozen Mammoth," by Kristin Baird Rattini: NGK, May 2009; and "Ice Baby," by Tom Mueller: NGM, May 2009, **154** Adapted from "Sea Monster: NGE, Mar 2006, and "When Monsters Ruled the Deep," by Virginia Morell: NGM, Dec 2005, **163** Adapted from "Robot Revolution," by Douglas E. Richards: NGK, Feb 2008, "Robot World," by Sean Price: NGK, Jan-Feb 2003, and "Robots," by Chris Carroll: NGM, Aug 2011, **169** Adapted from "It's 2035," by Ruth Musgrave: NGK, Sep 2005, "Nanotechnology: Nano's Big Future," by Jennifer Kahn: NGM, June 2006, and "The Big Idea: Organ Regeneration," by Josie Glausiusz: NGM, Mar 2011

NGM = National Geographic Magazine, NGK = National Geographic Kids Magazine, NGE = National Geographic Explorer Magazine

Acknowledgments

The Authors and Publisher would like to thank the following teaching professionals for their valuable feedback during the development of this series:

Ahmed Mohamed Motala, University of Sharjah; **Ana Laura Gandini**, Richard Anderson School; **Andrew T. Om**, YBM PINE R&D; **Dr. Asmaa Awad**, University of Sharjah; **Atsuko Takase**, Kinki University, Osaka; **Bogdan Pavliy**, Toyama University of International Studies; **Brigitte Maronde**, Harold Washington College, Chicago; **Bunleap Heap**, American Intercon Institute; **Carey Bray**, Columbus State University; **Carmella Lieske**, Shimane University; **Chanmakara Hok**, American Intercon Institute; **Choppie Tsann Tsang Yang**, National Taipei University; **Cynthia Ross**, State College of Florida; **David Schneer**, ACS International, Singapore; **Dawn Shimura**, St. Norbert College; **David Barrett**, Goldenwest College, CA; **Dax Thomas**, Keio University; **Deborah E. Wilson**, American University of Sharjah; **Elizabeth Rodacker**, Bakersfield College; **Emma Tamaianu-Morita**, Akita University; **Fu-Dong Chiou**, National Taiwan University; **Gavin Young**, Iwate University; **George Galamba**, Woodland Community College; **Gigi Santos**, American Intercon Institute; **Gursharan Kandola**, Language and Culture Center, University of Houston, TX; **Heidi Bundschoks**, ITESM, Sinaloa Mexico; **Helen E. Roland**, ESL/FL Miami-Dade College-Kendall Campus; **Hiroyo Yoshida**, Toyo University; **Hisayo Murase**, Doshisha Women's College of Liberal Arts; **Ikuko Kashiwabara**, Osaka Electro-Communication University; **J. Lorne Spry**, Contracting University Lecturer; **Jamie Ahn**, English Coach, Seoul; **Jane Bergmann**, The University of Texas at San Antonio; **Jennie Farnell**, University of Connecticut; **José Olavo de Amorim**, Colegio Bandeirantes, Sao Paulo; **Kyoungnam Shon**, Avalon English; **Luningning C. Landingin**, American Intercon Institute; **Mae-Ran Park**, Pukyong National University, Busan; **Mai Minh Tiên**, Vietnam Australia International School; **Marina Gonzalez**, Instituto Universitario de Lenguas Modernas Pte., Buenos Aires; **Mark Rau**, American River College, Sacramento CA; **Max Heineck**, Academic Coordinator/Lecturer, King Fahd University of Petroleum & Minerals; **Dr. Melanie Gobert**, Higher Colleges of Technology; **Michael C. Cheng**, National Chengchi University; **Michael Johnson**, Muroran Institute of Technology; **Michael McGuire**, Kansai Gaidai University; **Muriel Fujii**, University of Hawaii; **Patrick Kiernan**, Meiji University; **Philip Suthons**, Aichi Shukutoku University; **Renata Bobakova**, English Programs for Internationals, Columbia, SC; **Rhonda Tolhurst**, Kanazawa University; **Rodney Johnson**, Kansai Gaidai University; **Rosa Enilda Vásquez Fernandez**, John F. Kennedy Institute of Languages, Inc.; **Sandra Kern**, New Teacher Coach, School District of Philadelphia; **Shaofang Wu**, National Cheng Kung University; **Sovathey Tim**, American Intercon Institute; **Stephen Shrader**, Notre Dame Seishin Women's University; **Sudeepa Gulati**, Long Beach City College; **Susan Orias**, Broward College; **Thays Ladosky**, Colegio Damas, Recife; **Thea Chan**, American Intercon Institute; **Tom Justice**, North Shore Community College; **Tony J.C. Carnerie**, UCSD English Language Institute; **Tsung-Yuan Hsiao**, National Taiwan Ocean University, Keelung; **Virginia Christopher**, University of Calgary-Qatar; **Vuthy Lorn**, American Intercon Institute; **Wm Troy Tucker**, Edison State College; **Yohei Murayama**, Kagoshima University; **Yoko Sakurai**, Aichi University; **Yoko Sato**, Tokyo University of Agriculture and Technology